Strategic
Marketing
Management

Strategic Marketing Management

Meeting the Global Marketing Challenge

Carol H. Anderson
Rollins College, Crummer Graduate School of Business

Julian W. Vincze
Rollins College, Crummer Graduate School of Business

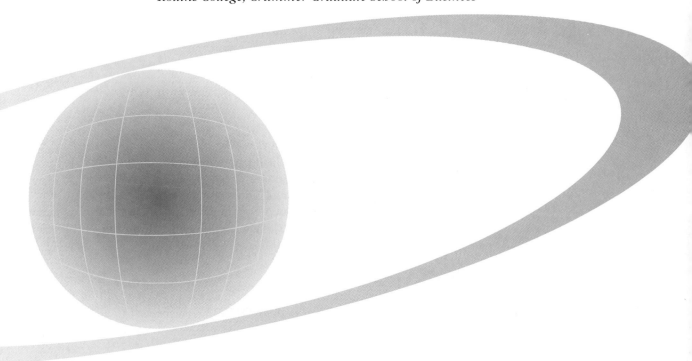

Houghton Mifflin Company   Boston   New York

Sponsoring Editor: Kathy Hunter
Associate Sponsoring Editor: Joanne Dauksewicz
Senior Project Editor: Margaret Kearney
Senior Production/Design Coordinator: Sarah L. Ambrose
Senior Manufacturing Coordinator: Marie Barnes
Marketing Manager: Melissa Russell

Printed in the U.S.A.

Library of Congress Catalog Card Number: 99-72026

ISBN: 0-395-87050-X

123456789-VH-03 02 01 00 99

Brief Contents

PART ONE An Introduction to Strategic Marketing Management 1

Chapter 1 The Changing Role of Marketing 2
Chapter 2 The Forces of Change and Their Impact 29

PART TWO Achieving Competitive Advantage 59

Chapter 3 Strategic Market Planning 60
Chapter 4 Marketing Intelligence and Creative Problem Solving 91
Chapter 5 Understanding Consumer Buying Behavior 125
Chapter 6 Business Markets and Buying Behavior 161
Chapter 7 Market Segmentation, Target Marketing, and Positioning 186

PART THREE Implementing Marketing-Mix Strategies 217

Chapter 8 Product Strategy 218
Chapter 9 Services Marketing Strategy 247
Chapter 10 Distribution Strategy 279
Chapter 11 Integrated Marketing Communications Strategy 314
Chapter 12 Integrated Marketing Communications Tools 333
Chapter 13 Direct Marketing 363
Chapter 14 Pricing Strategy 388

PART FOUR Managing Marketing Efforts 413

Chapter 15 Control and Measurement of Marketing Performance 414
Chapter 16 The Marketing-Oriented Organization 448

Contents

Preface   xvii

About the Authors   xxiv

PART ONE   An Introduction to Strategic Marketing Management   1

Chapter 1   The Changing Role of Marketing   2

VIGNETTE: Hewlett-Packard Faces Off Against the World   2

Marketing and Marketing Management Defined   4

Marketing in a Multilayered Environment   5   •   Marketing as Value Exchange   9

Evolution of the Marketing Concept   10

The Marketing Mix   11

Product (Good or Service)   11   •   Price (Value)   12   •   Place (Distribution)   13   •   Promotion (Integrated Marketing Communications)   13

Marketing Management in the Twenty-First Century   13

*The Importance of Marketing Relationships   14   •   Changes in Organizational Structure   15   •   **Innovate or Evaporate**: Starbucks: Coffee Making as a Brand of Cooking   16   •   Marketing and Entrepreneurship   18   •   Marketing in Nonprofit Organizations   18   •   **Marketing and Entrepreneurship**: Female Entrepreneurship Sets the Pace for a Fast-Growing Niche   19   •   The International Scope of Marketing   20*

Focusing on Customer Satisfaction   20

Customer-Oriented Strategies   20

Building Markets for the Long Term   24

Relationship Marketing versus Transaction Marketing   24   •   Networking   25   •   Building and Maintaining Strategic Alliances   26

Summary   26   •   Questions   27   •   Exercises   27

Chapter 2   The Forces of Change and Their Impact   29

VIGNETTE: Transforming a Motor Car Giant into an Integrated High-Technology Juggernaut: Daimler-Benz   29

The Marketing Ecocycle   31

The Natural Ecocycle   32   •   The Marketing Organization Ecocycle   33   •   Creative Destruction and Innovation   36

Four Business Revolutions   36

   *The First Revolution: Globalization   36   •   Trends in the U.S.
   Market   39   •   Marketing in the Global Village: Global Bicycle
   Peddler: David Montague   40   •   The Second Revolution: New and
   Emerging Technologies   43   •   The Third Revolution: The Information
   Age Economy   46   •   The Fourth Revolution: Changing Management
   Structure   47*

Impact of Change on Strategic and Tactical Marketing Decisions   50

   *Building Internal Relationships   51   •   Building External
   Relationships   51   •   Identifying Opportunities in a Time of
   Change   53   •   Managing Change   54   •   Innovate or Evaporate:
   The Chocolate Meltdown   55*

Summary 56   •   Questions 57   •   Exercises 57

PART TWO: Achieving Competitive Advantage   59

Chapter 3   Strategic Market Planning   60

   **VIGNETTE: High-Flying Strategy in the Friendly Skies: Airline Industry
   in Transition   60**

Marketing Management Decisions and Strategic Planning   62

   Strategy   62   •   Tactics   63

Strategic Market Planning: A Multilevel Process   64

The Strategic Planning Process   65

   *Mission-Driven Strategic Planning   65   •   Marketing in the Global
   Village: Russian Scientists Pursue a New Venture   68   •   Performance
   Objectives   68   •   Environmental Analysis (External)   68   •
   Organizational Analysis (Internal)   73   •   Strategic Objectives and
   Strategy Definition   75   •   Implementation and Tactics   75   •
   Execution   76   •   Evaluation and Control   76*

Planning for the Long Term   76

   *Sustainable Competitive Advantage: Basic Strategies   76   •   Strategic
   versus Tactical Marketing Decisions   78*

Strategic Planning and the Challenge of Change   78

   *Changes in Approaches to Strategy Development   79   •   Complexity and
   Uncertainty   81   •   Poverty of Time   82   •   The Importance of
   Flexibility and Adaptation   82   •   Innovate or Evaporate: High-Tech
   College Bookstore   83   •   Stakeholder Involvement   83   •
   Integrating Ethics and Social Responsibility   83*

Strategic Planning and a Customer Orientation   84

   Customer Satisfaction   85   •   Value Creation   86

Summary 88   •   Questions 88   •   Exercises 89

Chapter 4   **Marketing Intelligence and Creative Problem Solving   91**

VIGNETTE: **Listen to the Marketplace—or the Roar of a Harley   91**

Marketing Management Decisions and Creative Problem Solving   93

Need for Marketing Intelligence in a Changing World   94   •   Responsibility of Marketing Decisions   95   •   How Marketing Decisions Are Made   96   •   Creative Problem Solving (CPS)   97   •   Innovate or Evaporate: Hot Products from Hot Tubs and Other Approaches to Innovation   100

The Marketing Research Process   102

Step 1: Recognize the Need for Research   102   •   Step 2: Define the Research Problem and Objectives (Purpose)   103   •   Step 3: Specify Information and Data Requirements   103   •   Step 4: Develop the Research Plan   103   •   Step 5: Design the Method for Collecting Data   103   •   Step 6: Perform the Research   104   •   Step 7: Analyze the Data and Interpret the Results   104   •   Step 8: Communicate Findings   104

Key Information for Marketing Decisions   104

External Opportunities and Threats   105   •   Internal Strengths and Weaknesses   106

Sources of Information   107

Databases   108   •   Database Design and Creation   111   •   Database Management   112   •   Market Measurement and Forecasting Demand   113

Issues in Marketing Information Acquisition and Use   113

In-house or Outsource Research Task   113   •   Extent/Scope of Research   113   •   Organizational Resources   114   •   Research Quality/Quality of Information   115   •   International Marketing Research   115   •   Legal and Ethical Issues   116   •   It's Legal but Is It Ethical? Are You Being Investigated?   117

Summary   118   •   Questions   119   •   Exercises   119   •   Appendix: Dimensions of a Marketing Audit   121

Chapter 5   **Understanding Consumer Buying Behavior   125**

VIGNETTE: **Changing Values in American Society   125**

The Consumer Buying Process   127

Recognition of a Need   128   •   Search for Information   131   •   Evaluation of Alternatives   133   •   Choice/Purchase   135   •   Postpurchase Evaluation   135

Social and Cultural Influences on Buying Behavior   137

Cultural and Social Status   137   •   Marketing in the Information Age: Marketer: Know Thy Customer!   138   •   Group Influences   143

Individual Influences on Buying Behavior   146

Personal Influences   146   •   Psychological Influences   149

Consumers and Products   152

Consumers and Situations   153

Relationship Marketing   155

> *Buyer-Seller Relationships   155   •   **It's Legal but Is It Ethical?**
> Relationship Marketing and Privacy Issues   155   •   Quality,
> Satisfaction, and Long-Term Relationships   156   •   Relationship
> Marketing and the New Marketing Concept   156   •   Delivering
> Customer Value Through Market-Driven Management   157*

Summary   158   •   Questions   159   •   Exercises   160

Chapter 6   **Business Markets and Buying Behavior   161**

VIGNETTE: The U.S. Automotive Industry: World-Class Buyers and Sellers   161

Scope of Business Markets   163

> *Types of Customers   163   •   **Marketing and Entrepreneurship:** The
> Home-Office Worker   165   •   Changes in Market Size and Trends   167*

Differences Between Organizational and Consumer Buying Behavior   167

> ***Innovate or Evaporate:** The Light Goes on at GE's Lighting
> Division   168*

The Business-to-Business Buying Process   169

> *Steps in the Buying Process   169   •   Organizational Differences   170*

Organizational Structure and Buyer Characteristics   172

> *Organizational Structure   173   •   Key Players in the Buying
> Center   174*

Types of Business Purchase Decisions   175

> *Straight Rebuy   175   •   Modified Rebuy   175   •   New Task
> Purchases   176   •   Extended Taxonomy of Purchase Decisions   176*

Major Influences on Purchase Decisions   176

> *External Environmental Influences   176   •   Internal Organizational
> Influences   180   •   Personal Influences   181   •   Product
> Influences   181*

Relationship Marketing   181

> *Buyer-Seller Relationships   182   •   Quality, Satisfaction, and Long-Term
> Relationships   182   •   Relationship Marketing and the New Marketing
> Concept   182*

Summary   183   •   Questions   184   •   Exercises   184

Chapter 7   **Market Segmentation, Target Marketing, and Positioning   186**

**VIGNETTE: Hip! Hop! Shop Til You Drop! A Growing Middle Class Is Fueling the
Global Economy   186**

The Basics of Market Segmentation   188

> *Mass Marketing   188   •   Market Segmentation   188   •
> Why Subdivide Markets?   188   •   Customer Value and Target
> Marketing   189*

Target Marketing Strategies   189

A Multisegment Marketing Strategy   189   •   A Single-Segment Marketing Strategy   190

The Market-Segmentation Process   191

1. Define and Analyze the Market   192   •   2. Identify and Describe Potential Segments   192   •   3. Select the Segment(s) to Be Served   193   •   4. Determine the Product Positioning Strategy   193   •   5. Design and Implement the Marketing Program   193   •   Criteria for Effective Segmentation   193

Selection of Market Segments   195

*Bases for Segmenting Consumer Markets   196   •   **Marketing in the Global Village: A Multiracial Marketplace—in the United States   198   •** Bases for Segmenting Business-to-Business Markets   201   •   **Managing Change: Generation X: An X-citing Challenge to Marketers   202   •** Combining Variables to Identify Segments   205   •   International Implications of Market Segmentation   205   •   Technology and Marketing Intelligence as Segmentation Tools   206   •   Management Tools   206*

Ethical Issues in Market Segmentation   208

Positioning Strategies   208

Positioning versus Differentiation   209   •   The Positioning Process   209   •   Customer Value and Positioning   210   •   Key Variables for Positioning   211

Summary   213   •   Questions   214   •   Exercises   214

PART THREE: Implementing Marketing-Mix Strategies   217

Chapter 8   Product Strategy   218

VIGNETTE: Creating Customer Satisfaction: USAA Responds to Change with a New Product   218

What Is a Product?   219

Classification of Goods   220

Consumer Goods: Convenience, Shopping, and Specialty Goods   220   •   Organizational Goods   220

Product Strategy Issues   224

*Determining the Product Line   224   •   Determining the Width and Depth of a Product Line   225   •   When to Introduce or Delete Products   228   •   Packaging   230   •   **It's Legal but Is It Ethical? Wearable but Not Smokable: Hemp-Based Products   229   •** Product Safety   230   •   Product Liability   230   •   Warranty—Post-Sale Services   231*

The Product Life Cycle   232

Are Product Life Cycles Real?   232   •   Implications of the Product Life Cycle for Marketing Managers   233   •   Why Do Life Cycles Occur?   234

Test Marketing   236

Advantages of Test Marketing   236   •   Disadvantages of Test Marketing   237

Launching New Products   238

***Marketing in the Global Village:** Will the Swatchmobile Sweep Europe?   239*

Brand Strategies   239

Brand Equity Explained   240   •   Private Labels or Store Brands   242

Summary   243   •   Questions   243   •   Exercises   244

Chapter 9   Services Marketing Strategy   247

VIGNETTE: Busy Signal at AOL: A Services Marketing Mix Gone Awry   247

Services: A Major Force in the U.S. Economy   249

***Managing Change:** High-Quality Service at Everyday Low Prices   249*

Characteristics of Services Versus Goods   250

Services Are Intangible   252   •   Services Are Variable   252   •   Service and Consumption Are Inseparable   252   •   Services Are Perishable   253

Levels of Service   253

Primary Services   253   •   Ancillary Services   254

Service As Value   255

*The Importance of Strategic Planning   255   •   Benefits of Exceptional Customer Service   256   •   **Marketing in the Information Age:** USAA Leverages Processes for Strategic Advantage   258*

Service Marketing Issues   259

Market Segmentation   259   •   Perceived Risk   260   •   Evaluation of Service Attributes   261   •   Brand and Service Provider Loyalty   262   •   Adoption Process for Innovations   262

The Service Design Process   263

Determining Customer Targets   264   •   Determining the Nature of the Service   264   •   Determining Pricing Strategy   265   •   Addressing Complexity or Uncertainty   266   •   Assessing the Marketer's Resources   266   •   Determining the Number of Services   267   •   Determining the Level of Service   267

Setting Standards for Service Quality   267

Benchmarking   268   •   Planning Service Tasks and Activities   269

Service Delivery and Implementation   270

Organization Structure and Culture   270   •   Personnel Issues   273

Summary   276   •   Questions   276   •   Exercises   277

Chapter 10   **Distribution Strategy   279**

VIGNETTE: **Replacing Inventory with Information Technology: Compaq's Distribution Strategy for Long-Term Survival   279**

Distribution Channels: An Overview   281

Relationship to Organizational and Marketing Strategies   282   •   Need for Channel Intermediaries   283   •   Functions Performed by Distribution Systems   285

Channel Structures and Marketing Systems   286

Consumer Marketing Channels   286   •   Organizational Marketing Channels   287   •   Multiple Channels   289   •   International Channels   289

Channel Members   291

*Wholesalers   291   •   Retailers   293   •   **Managing Change:** Vendor-Managed Inventory and Integrated Supply   294   •   Other Channel Intermediaries and Facilitators   302*

Channel Selection and Design   302

*Channel Objectives   303   •   Channel Length and Number of Intermediaries   303   •   Selection Criteria for Channel Members   304   •   Evaluation of Channel Efficiency and Effectiveness   306   •   **Innovate or Evaporate:** Alternative Distribution Channels for Alternative Music   307*

Channel Management   308

Power and Relationships   308   •   Vertical Marketing Systems   309   •   Legal and Ethical Issues   309   •   Emerging Channels: Distribution in the Twenty-First Century   310

Summary   311   •   Questions   311   •   Exercises   312

Chapter 11   **Integrated Marketing Communications Strategy   314**

Vignette: **Streamline Delivers the Goods   314**

Integrated Marketing Communications   315

*Communications Theory   316   •   The Communications Mix   319   •   IMC Objectives   320   •   **It's Legal but Is It Ethical?** Company Struggles to Get Message Out   321*

Pull Versus Push IMC Strategies   323

*Pull-Through Communications   323   •   **Innovate or Evaporate:** Video Is Logical for Business-to-Business IMC   325   •   Push-Through Communications   325   •   IMC and Product Life Cycle Stages   326*

Financial Aspects of IMC   326

Calculating the Customer Response Index (CRI)   326   •   Calculating Communications Elasticity   327   •   Calculating Communication Carryover   327   •   Budgeting IMC   327

Summary   330   •   Questions   331   •   Exercises   331

| **Chapter 12** | **Integrated Marketing Communications Tools   333** |

VIGNETTE: Justice Department Applies Brakes to Hell-for-Leather Pace of Consolidation in Radio Industry   333

Managing Sales Force Activity   334

Defining the Sales Task   335   •   Investigating the Relationship Between Sales Activity and Productivity   337   •   Determining Salesforce Structure   340   •   Configuring Sales Territories   340   •   Determining Salesforce Size   342   •   Staffing and Measuring Performance   343   •   Developing a Compensation Plan   344   •   Directing and Motivating the Salesforce   345

Managing the Advertising Program   347

Determining Advertising Opportunities   347   •   Managing Change: Ricoh Changes Its Image   348   •   Identifying the Appropriate Audience(s)   349   •   Selecting the IMC Message   350   •   Determining the IMC Media   350   •   Marketing in the Information Age: U.K. Catalog Distributor Changes Customers' Perceptions   352

Publicity, Direct Marketing, and Sales Promotion   356

Publicity and Public Relations   356   •   Direct Marketing   357   •   Sales Promotion   357

Summary   359   •   Questions   359   •   Exercises   360

| **Chapter 13** | **Direct Marketing   363** |

VIGNETTE: Cutting Out the Middleman: Direct from Dell to You   363

Direct Marketing Defined   365

Integrated Marketing Communications Perspective   365   •   Distribution Channel Perspective   366

Factors Leading to the Growth of Direct Marketing   367

Innovate or Evaporate: E-Commerce and Direct Distribution in the Insurance Industry   368

Direct Marketing Tools   369

Direct Selling   369   •   Direct-Action Advertising   372   •   Electronic Media   373

Objectives of Direct Marketing   376

Build Customer Relationships   376   •   Direct Response or Transaction   376

Integrated Direct Marketing Communications   377

Integration Across Direct Marketing Tools   377   •   Integration with Other Communications Mix and Marketing-Mix Elements   377

The Direct Marketing Process   379

Customer Databases   379   •   Marketing and Entrepreneurship: High Impact from Low-Tech Direct Marketing   380   •   Interactive Marketing System   381   •   Measuring Results   381

Issues in Direct Marketing   383

    Customer-Related Issues   383 • *Organization-Related Issues   383* •
    Legal, Ethical, and Social Issues   384

Trends in Direct Marketing   384

Summary   385 • Questions   386 • Exercises   386

Chapter 14	**Pricing Strategy 388**

VIGNETTE: Toyota Camry Pricing   388

The Role of Price in Strategic Marketing   389

    Buyer's versus Seller's Point of View   389 • *An Example of Pricing
    Complexity   390* • *Actual Price   391* • *Pricing Conflicts   391* •
    Pricing Strategy as a Competitive Edge   392*

Product Life Cycle Pricing   393

    Introductory Stage   393 • **Innovate or Evaporate:** *CompuServe
    Pitches Upscale Niche   394* • *Growth Stage   395* • *Maturity
    Stage   395* • *Decline Stage   396*

Psychological Pricing   396

Odd Pricing   396

    It's Legal but Is It Ethical? *Fingerhut's Credit Pricing for Low-Income
    Customers   397* • *Prestige Pricing   398* • *Psychological
    Discounting   398* • *Impact on Manufacturer   398*

Strategic Pricing Models   399

    The Market-Based Pricing Model   399 • *The Cost-Plus Pricing
    Model   399* • *The Value-Based Pricing Model   400*

Pricing Strategy and Break-Even Analysis   404

    Break-Even Volume   404 • *Break-Even Market Share and Risk   405*

Pricing Strategy Decisions: Issues, Problems, and Legal Concerns   404

    Product-Line Pricing   406 • *Structuring Discounts   407*

Pricing Strategy and IMC   409

Summary   410 • Questions   410 • Exercises   411

PART FOUR   Managing Marketing Efforts **413**

Chapter 15	**Control and Measurement of Marketing Performance 414**

**Vignette: Measuring Performance in the Toy Business: Noodle Kidoodle Takes on
Barbie and the Power Rangers   414**

Controlling Marketing Efforts   418

    The Managerial Process   418 • **Marketing in the Global Village:**
    Turnaround at Volkswagen   419 • *Profitability and
    Productivity   420* • *The Control Process and Strategic Planning   420*

Levels of Analysis   424

Corporate Level Analysis   425   •   Business Level Analysis   426   •   Functional (Operating) Level Analysis   426

Measuring Performance   431

Factors to Analyze   431   •   Key Performance Criteria   432   •   Key Ratios and Their Implications   432   •   Strategic Profit Model: Framework for Analysis   438   •   Data Sources and Quality   439   •   Marketing in the Information Age: Measuring Internet Traffic   441

Summary 444 • Questions 445 • Exercises 446

Chapter 16 **The Marketing-Oriented Organization   448**

Vignette: A Virtual Organization in Operation   448

The Marketing Organization's Structure   449

The Role of Top Management   449   •   The Role of Divisional Management   450   •   The Role of Functional Management   451   •   The Flow of Authority   451   •   The Flow of Information   454

The Evolving Marketing Organization   454

Marketing in the Information Age: Who Owns Ideas?   455   •   The Marketing Organization Circa 1946   456   •   The Marketing Organization Circa 1960   457   •   The Marketing Organization Circa 1980   458   •   Marketing Organizations in the 1990s   460

Integrated Management Systems   462

Key Elements of the Integrated Management System   462   •   The IMS Organization   465

Recent Trends in Management Practice   465

Total Quality Management   465   •   Managing Change: Companies Are Creating Programs to Help Employees Learn Leadership   467   •   Managing Change   469

The Virtual Organization   470

Summary 472 • Questions 472 • Exercises 473

Index   I-I

Preface

All over the world, marketing activities touch and influence people's lives, as individuals and businesses attempt to sell, buy, or exchange goods and services. Thus, marketing is one of the most dynamic and exciting aspects of business, and one that each of us can relate to easily. As we enter the new millennium, the dynamic nature of marketing has become even more evident. Emerging technologies, the Internet and World Wide Web, increased globalization, and changing management structures have dramatically influenced the way we do business. These changes will continue to have a significant impact on the marketing process in the years to come. And there always will be new challenges and new frontiers for marketers to conquer.

In *Strategic Marketing Management,* marketing is viewed as a dynamic *process* designed to achieve distinctive strategic competence and global advantage. This is accomplished through value-added marketing activities and operations that are designed to create and sustain long-term relationships. Our goal is to help future marketing managers achieve success by taking the best from traditional marketing theory and practice and combining it with contemporary, innovative approaches to meeting challenges in a fast-paced, often uncertain environment.

KEY FEATURES

The key features of this text can be organized around its thematic emphasis on change and innovation, coverage of cutting-edge topics, integrated approach, and chapter pedagogy.

Emphasis on Change and Innovation.   In addition to providing current and comprehensive coverage of marketing management concepts, the text focuses on change and innovation as we enter the twenty-first century. We emphasize the need for marketing managers to recognize, embrace, and manage change in today's global business environment, which is buffeted by many forces: globalization of markets; increased computerization and emerging technologies; the information superhighway and an information age economy; and changing managerial hierarchies and organizations.

Changes in the marketing environment and the changing role of marketing in society pose serious challenges for the marketing managers of today and tomorrow. Successful marketing strategies require innovative solutions and proactive decisions to deal with the forces of risk, uncertainty, and change. The marketing planning process must include the building of longer-term strategic alliances and closer relationships with all constituencies. Customer satisfaction (including internal customers) will be increasingly focused on quality and value. Integration among the various marketing functions and among marketing and other business functions is a necessity.

Two unique chapters highlight the key theme and emphasis of this text: Chapter 2, "Forces of Change and Their Impact," and Chapter 15, "Control and Measurement of Marketing Performance."

Coverage of Cutting-Edge Topics.   Two other special chapters have been included because of their critical importance to successful marketing management today: Chapter 9, "Services Marketing Strategy," and Chapter 13, "Direct Marketing."

We also focus on many key and current topics in marketing management practice, including change management, total quality management, continuous process improvement, reengineering, cross-functional work teams, information technology advances, decision support systems, electronic communications revolution (electronic commerce and electronic marketing), virtual offices and virtual organization design, relationship marketing (customers, employees, suppliers, and all other stakeholders), ethical and social issues, changing role of marketing in society, and creative problem solving. Both qualitative and quantitative aspects of marketing decisions are presented throughout the book.

Integrated Approach.   Because we view marketing management as an integral part of an organization and its environment, we have provided a conceptual environmental model that represents the integration of marketing management elements and functions within a global marketplace. This model will help students to grasp the complexities and interconnectedness of today's business world and to recognize the role of marketing management within a global economy. Within this environmental context, an additional model portrays the "ecocycle" that is generally followed by marketing organizations.

Chapter Pedagogy.   The text includes a wide variety of elements to enhance understanding, facilitate analysis, and illustrate relevance.

- *Opening scenarios* for each chapter focus on actual companies and illustrate the relevance of chapter content.

- *Margin definitions* provide a convenient glossary of key terms for quick reference.

- *Boxed inserts* provide additional examples to make chapter concepts more relevant. Highlighted inserts are entitled:

   "Innovate or Evaporate"—focusing on innovative approaches taken by marketers

   "Marketing and Entrepreneurship"—focusing on successful marketing strategies for small businesses

   "Managing Change"—focusing on marketing decisions made by organizations in a time of change and uncertainty

   "Marketing in the Global Village"—focusing on decisions made from a global marketing management perspective

   "It's Legal but Is It Ethical?"—focusing on marketing management decisions made within the parameters of ethical and socially responsible behavior

   "Marketing in the Information Age"—focusing on the use of databases, communications technology, and electronic commerce in marketing

- A chapter *summary* presents an overview of the major concepts discussed in the chapter, providing an excellent "advance organizer" before reading the chapter and a review after reading the chapter.

- End-of-chapter study *questions* are thought provoking, facilitate deeper understanding of chapter content, and provide a good basis for enlightened class discussion.

- End-of-chapter experiential *exercises* offer "hands-on" learning opportunities to apply concepts discussed in the chapter to real-life situations.

- Clear and abundant *figures and tables* emphasize key points and provide further explanation of text discussion to facilitate comprehension and learning.

TEXT ORGANIZATION

Part One is an introduction to strategic marketing management. The changing role of marketing in contemporary organizations is discussed in Chapter 1. Chapter 2 emphasizes the forces of change that operate in the marketing environment and their impact on marketing management decisions.

Part Two presents the challenges that face marketers in their attempts to achieve and sustain competitive advantage. Discussion includes strategic market planning (Chapter 3), marketing intelligence and creative problem solving (Chapter 4), and developing an understanding of customer characteristics and buying behaviors (Chapters 5, 6, and 7).

Part Three focuses on marketing mix strategies and their implementation. Chapters 8 and 9 provide a basis for managing goods and services through product management and service strategies, respectively. The importance of efficient and effective distribution channels and supply chain management is emphasized in Chapter 10. Integrated marketing communications strategies and tools are discussed in depth in Chapters 11 and 12, followed by the increasingly important direct marketing approach (Chapter 13) that may be considered as both distribution and integrated marketing communications strategies. The factors that must be considered in the development of pricing strategies are presented in Chapter 14.

In Part Four, discussion returns to the broader view taken in Part One and addresses the issues of controlling and measuring the results of marketing activities (Chapter 15), and establishing organizational structures that will facilitate successful marketing ventures (Chapter 16).

A COMPREHENSIVE INSTRUCTIONAL RESOURCE PACKAGE

Strategic Marketing Management is supported by an excellent package of teaching and learning aids, including the following:

Casebook. *Cases in Strategic Marketing Management* (Vincze and Anderson) is designed to be used as an instructional companion to *Strategic Marketing Management*. The case collection is current, with all situations taking place in the

1990s. Cases cover a wide range of industries and organizational sizes, as well as for-profit, nonprofit, product, service, consumer, and business-to-business marketing environments. Some cases contain important social responsibility issues, and most are decision-centered rather than descriptive. All have been classroom tested and have proven to be interesting and challenging to students.

Instructor's Resource Manual (to accompany STRATEGIC MARKETING MANAGEMENT). Many useful features are provided in the Instructor's Resource Manual to enhance the quality of instruction: chapter summary, chapter learning objectives, annotated chapter outlines, answers to end-of-chapter questions that provide a basis for stimulating classroom discussion, and suggestions for completion of the applied end-of-chapter experiential exercises.

In addition to these basic features, additional experiential exercises are included for use in applying chapter concepts in class. A selected bibliography of suggested articles and books is also provided for additional insights. Each chapter contains a complete listing of the available PowerPoint Slides and Transparencies. There is also a list of appropriate cases from Vincze and Anderson, *Cases in Strategic Marketing Management,* which correspond to the topics covered. In addition, we have also provided a list of Harvard Business School cases that can be coordinated with each chapter.

Instructor's Resource Manual (to accompany CASES IN STRATEGIC MARKETING MANAGEMENT). A separate Instructor's Resource Manual has been developed to accompany the casebook. It includes general teaching guidelines as well as suggestions for using the cases. It also includes a comprehensive matrix indicating where each case can be used with textbook topics. For each case, an extensive teaching note is provided. Teaching notes most often include summaries, background company information, answers to discussion questions, and additional references and resources.

Test Bank. An extensive test bank is available to assist the instructor in assessing student performance. There are approximately 1,600 items created in the form of true/false, multiple choice, matching, and short-answer essay questions. Answers are provided for all questions as well as text page references. In addition, all multiple-choice questions have been labeled as testing either knowledge, comprehension, or application of the concepts presented in the text.

Electronic Test Bank. An Electronic Test Bank version allows instructors to generate and change tests easily on the computer.

PowerPoint Slides. A package of approximately 350 professionally developed PowerPoint slides is available for use by adopters of this textbook. Slides include chapter figures as well as additional exhibits that highlight chapter concepts. Instructors who have access to PowerPoint can edit slides to customize them for their classrooms. A viewer is also included for instructors who do not have the program. Slides can also be printed for lecture notes and class distribution.

Color Transparencies. In addition to the PowerPoint slides, a package of color transparencies accompanies the book. These are replicas of many of the Power-Point slides, which include art and tables from the textbook as well as additional exhibits.

Videos. A selection of videos is available to adopters. Videos are selected to correspond with the concepts and topics highlighted in each chapter. A video guide is included to facilitate selection of the video for a particular instructional unit.

STUDENT AND INSTRUCTOR WEB SITES

Specially designed web pages enhance the book content and provide additional information, guidance, and activities.

The student site includes Internet exercises with hyperlinks related to key concepts; additional study aids, such as questions related to chapter concepts and suggested applications of course content (e.g., applied projects, research papers, etc.); and recommended Internet sites for research on many marketing management topics as well as company information.

The instructor site provides lecture notes, PowerPoint slides, comments on the Internet exercises, as well as additional cases, caselets, scenarios, and/or critical incidents that can be used for testing purposes or to provide additional examples of course concepts.

YOUR COMMENTS AND SUGGESTIONS ARE VALUABLE TO US

We consider ourselves fortunate to be members of a discipline where so many exciting things are happening and where so many individuals have been willing to share their knowledge and expertise with us. We have attempted to write a book that will convey both the theory and the "nuts and bolts" applications of strategic marketing management to students of marketing. Your feedback would be most welcome, and we look forward to your valued comments, suggestions, and criticisms, because our challenge is to continue to create better teaching materials for our students.

ACKNOWLEDGMENTS

It is said there is nothing new under the sun, and perhaps this book is another testimony to that statement. Leading researchers and thinkers in marketing and other disciplines have inspired much of the content of this text. They have made available a plethora of marketing thought through publications, seminars, conferences, and personal conversations. We have attempted to distill many of these notable contributions to marketing and other disciplines and to combine them with current business practices and an understanding of pedagogy, to deliver a book that is interesting, is easy to read, and at the same time stimulates deeper levels of introspection and understanding. Many individuals have contributed to this book in a variety of ways, including our students, colleagues, publisher, reviewers, school, and families. We apologize in advance for any names that may be inadvertently omitted.

Students. We are inspired by our students who hold us accountable for excellence in education. Learning in our classrooms is a two-way street where we learn a great deal from our students while we teach them about marketing. Many of our students at the Crummer Graduate School are practicing managers who bring a wealth of experience and insights to classroom discussions. *Strategic Marketing Management* is greatly influenced by many years of teaching in public and private business schools, where we have learned from past successes and failures in an attempt to find the best teaching methods and materials to maximize student learning. We believe that this relationship with our students provides the type of feedback that has made it possible for this book to fill a gap in marketing education.

Crummer Graduate School of Business at Rollins College and Other Colleagues.   We owe a debt of gratitude to many professional and personal influences that have helped us form our views of the marketing discipline over the years. In particular, we appreciate the encouragement of our colleagues at the Crummer Graduate School, and the support of our Dean, Ed Moses, along with prior Deans Marty Schatz and Sam Certo, who have created a professional and technical environment that encourages and supports textbook writing. Colleagues such as Jim Higgins, and many others, have provided valuable input. We also appreciate the contributions of our talented secretarial staff and graduate assistants at the Crummer School.

Houghton Mifflin Editors.   We believe we have worked with the best folks in the industry over these past months, starting with Sponsoring Editors Jennifer Speer and Kathy Hunter. We owe a special debt of gratitude to Joanne Dauksewicz, our Associate Sponsoring Editor, who helped everyone maintain their sanity and stay on course—and enjoy themselves in the process. To her goes much of the credit for the professionalism of the final product. Maggie Kearney, Senior Project Editor, was a major contributor to the professional appearance and readability of the book. We'd also like to thank Monica Hincken, Editorial Assistant, for her help with the art program and with the casebook.

Other Important People.   We'd also like to especially thank Professor Charlie Cook of the University of West Alabama for developing an extremely attractive PowerPoint program, as well as Professor Brahm Canzer of John Abbott College for creating an excellent and comprehensive Test Bank.

Reviewers.   We appreciate the time and effort spent by reviewers on our manuscripts throughout the developmental process. Their willingness to share a wealth of marketing knowledge and insights enhanced the quality of the book. Our thanks to the following reviewers:

Mark Alpert
University of Texas at Austin

Craig Andrews
Marquette University

James Camerius
Northern Michigan University

James Gaius Ibe
Morris College

Constantine Katsikeas
University of Wales, Cardiff

Craig Kelley
California State University, Sacramento

Peter LaPlaca
University of Connecticut

James H. Underwood III
University of Southern Louisiana

Thomas Marpe
Saint Mary's University of Minnesota

Brian Van der Westhuizen
California State University

Anil Mathur
Hofstra University

Family. Our families deserve a huge "thank you" for their support during this project. Their love and encouragement have been invaluable. In particular, we want to express our appreciation to our spouses, Alexander ("Lex") Wood and Linda Vincze, for their patience and understanding.

To all those named above, and to all those unnamed contributors to this book, we express our deep appreciation for the many ways in which you helped to bring this project to reality.

Carol Anderson (Wood)
Julian W. Vincze

About the Authors

CAROL H. ANDERSON

Dr. Carol H. Anderson holds a Ph.D. and MBA from Texas A & M University, an M.Ed. from the University of Houston, and a B.S. from Cornell University. Prior to joining the Crummer faculty at Rollins College, Dr. Anderson was a member of the faculty at Southern Illinois University at Carbondale. At SIUC, Dr. Anderson received numerous awards for outstanding teaching, including the university-wide Outstanding Undergraduate Teacher Award. At the Crummer Graduate School of Business, students and colleagues have also recognized Dr. Anderson as an excellent faculty member, honoring her with the Welsh Award.

Dr. Anderson's teaching philosophy is student-oriented with a focus on practical applications of marketing theory, including comprehensive strategic marketing plans and research projects conducted by students for area companies and organizations such as Tupperware, Hewlett Packard, Coalition for the Homeless of Central Florida, and Walt Disney World, among others.

Research and publication efforts have focused primarily on strategic marketing management issues, marketing education, retailing, and entrepreneurship, with articles published in the *Journal of Retailing,* the *American Journal of Small Business,* and the *Journal of Marketing Education,* as well as presentations at numerous professional meetings.

Dr. Anderson is active in a number of professional associations, such as the American Marketing Association, the American Collegiate Retailing Association, Midwest Marketing Association, Midwest Business Administrative Association, and the American Business Hall of Fame.

JULIAN W. VINCZE

Dr. Julian W. Vincze holds a Ph.D. from the University of Bradford in the United Kingdom; an MBA from the University of Western Ontario in London, Canada; and an undergraduate degree from the University of Montana. He has industrial experience in the United States, Canada, and the European Community and has held academic positions in the United States, Canada, The Netherlands, the United Kingdom, and Australia. Dr. Vincze's extensive practical and graduate teaching experiences have enabled him to be a leader in internationalizing the curriculum at the Crummer Graduate School of Business at Rollins College. In 1992, he received the Charles A. Welsh Award for outstanding faculty performance.

Dr. Vincze has been a member of the faculty at Rollins College since 1977, and he has been active in several professional associations. He has held various leadership positions, such as National Program Chairman and member of the Board of Governors for the Academy of Marketing Science (AMS) and Vice-President of the Case Clearing Center for the North American Case Research Association (NACRA). Dr. Vincze remains active in several associations, including the World Association for Case Research and Applications (WACRA).

Dr. Vincze has extensive international experience and has been a consultant to a wide variety of businesses. He specializes in domestic and global strategic planning and marketing strategy.

Strategic
Marketing
Management

PART ONE

An Introduction to Strategic Marketing Management

1. The Changing Role of Marketing
2. Forces of Change and Their Impact

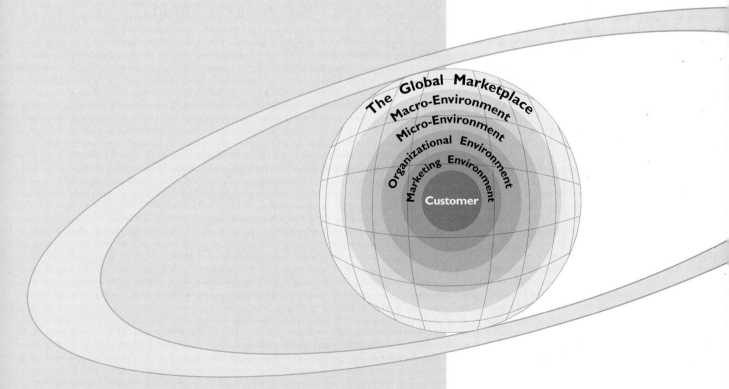

The Global Marketplace
Macro-Environment
Micro-Environment
Organizational Environment
Marketing Environment
Customer

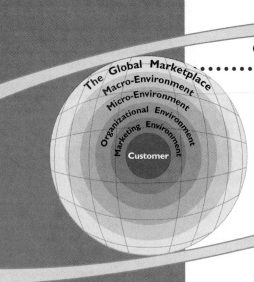

The Global Marketplace
Macro-Environment
Micro-Environment
Organizational Environment
Marketing Environment
Customer

CHAPTER I

The Changing Role of Marketing

Marketing and Marketing Management Defined

Evolution of the Marketing Concept

The Marketing Mix

Marketing Management in the Twenty-first Century

Focusing on Customer Satisfaction

Building Markets for the Long Term

There are marketers that make things happen. There are marketers that watch things happen. And then there are marketers that ask, "What happened?"

Hewlett-Packard Faces Off Against the World

It was 1993, and Hewlett-Packard Co. faced a major challenge from NEC Corp. The Japanese electronics giant had planned to attack H-P's market share in the burgeoning computer printer market. In time-honored Japanese fashion, NEC's strategy was to build market share by undercutting prices with new, better-designed models. This same tactic had allowed other Japanese companies, a decade earlier, to grab the lead from H-P in a business it had pioneered—hand-held calculators.

However, months before NEC could introduce its inexpensive monochrome inkjet printer, H-P launched an improved color version and, over a 6-month period, slashed prices on its best-selling black-and-white model by 40 percent. This move forced NEC to withdraw its now overpriced and noncompetitive offerings after about 4 months on the market. "We were too late," said John McIntyre, a marketing director for NEC. "We just didn't have the economies of scale [to compete with H-P]."

In the early 1990s, U.S. companies dreaded Japan's unbeatable speed to market and economies of scale in many industries, and computer printers were a prime example: Four out of five computer printers bought in the United States in 1985 were made in Japan. But today many U.S. firms, like H-P, are continuing to turn the tables on the Japanese. In September 1994, an annual global survey showed that for the first time since 1985, the United States had replaced Japan as the world's most competitive economy.

H-P's market dominance has continued throughout the 1990s. In 1996, H-P ranked number one worldwide in laser, inkjet, color, and large-format inkjet printers. In that year, nearly 82 percent of the $38,889 million in product and service orders were for computer products, service, and support (including printers, plotters, and scanners). Overseas customers accounted for 37.8 percent of the total, maintaining H-P's market leadership.

Sources: Stephen K. Yoder, "How H-P Used Tactics of the Japanese to Beat Them at Their Game," *Wall Street Journal* (September 8, 1994), p. A1, A9; Hewlett Packard Company Corporate Facts, Microsoft Internet Explorer (1997).

Excitement . . . challenge . . . opportunities for creativity . . . meaningful contributions to society. Marketing management offers all of these—and more—as for-profit and nonprofit organizations plan for the twenty-first century. Marketing activities occur at the *cutting edge,* that is, between an organization and its customers, suppliers, and other constituencies. Thus the high visibility of marketing management decisions lays them open to constant external and internal scrutiny. Opportunities abound for alert and innovative managers to develop and maintain successful enterprises. However, these opportunities are not without risk, as firms find themselves operating at an accelerated pace in an increasingly complex and uncertain global marketplace.

The marketing function is undergoing significant changes due to a variety of simultaneous and rapidly occurring environmental pressures. Some of the most noteworthy catalysts for change include

- increased globalization of markets on both the supply and demand sides,

- implications of new technology, advances in telecommunications, and the World Wide Web,

- computer applications and extensive databases, and

- redesigned organizational structures.[1]

Global competition has intensified because of mergers, acquisitions, joint ventures, and other alliances formed by major marketing firms in industries such as automobiles, appliances, and food products. Worldwide telecommunications are at the forefront of the global business revolution, with partnerships being formed among telephone and cable companies and a wide spectrum of publishing and entertainment enterprises. The Internet and the World Wide Web bring markets and suppliers much closer together. The growth of computing power has a major impact on low-tech as well as high-tech businesses. Computer power levels the playing field between large and small businesses by generating mutual advantages in creating new product designs, higher efficiency in production, shorter order lead times, innovative marketing programs, closer long-term buyer-seller relationships, and other widely used applications. Organizations are leaner, with fewer layers. A smaller number of workers can accomplish more work in less time with more flexibility as they communicate across departments, companies, and nations by computer, fax, Internet, and other information technology. These revolutions—and others yet to come—will continue to provide both opportunities and threats for marketing managers entering the twenty-first century.

MARKETING AND MARKETING MANAGEMENT DEFINED

The definition of *marketing* is shifting rapidly from the traditional, transaction-based view of microeconomics and production efficiency to marketing as a mutually beneficial exchange process built on long-term relationships between buyers and sellers. While both customers and products have a major influence on marketing decisions, companies are devoting more attention than ever before to customers' wants and needs. Likewise, marketing efforts are more focused on attracting, retaining, and developing profitable relationships with employees, suppliers, customers, and others.

How is *marketing* defined? The term can be defined as narrowly or as broadly as you like. The simplest definition of marketing is: Find a need and fill it! Many people equate marketing with personal selling and advertising, but marketing encompasses much more than this. The American Marketing Association's (AMA's) definition has evolved over the years to reflect the realities of the marketplace. Early definitions focused on selling goods that had already been produced, with little recognition of customers' wants and needs or the use of marketing in nonprofit organizations. In 1960, the AMA defined *marketing* as

> the performance of business activities that direct the flow of goods and services from product to consumer to user.[2]

In 1985, the AMA definition was broadened to view marketing as a system and marketing activity as a process that can be performed by nonprofit organizations as well as by businesses selling goods and services for profit:

> Marketing is the process of planning and executing the conception, pricing, promotion, and distribution of ideas, goods, and services to create exchanges that satisfy individual and organizational objectives.[3]

Based on the daily decisions and activities of contemporary marketing managers, we believe that the definitions of marketing and marketing management have extended further to encompass more aspects of the organization and its environment. Borrowing heavily from Frederick E. Webster, we believe that

Marketing
Management function responsible for developing and maintaining customer relationships through superior value.

> **Marketing** is the management function responsible for assuring that every aspect of the organization focuses on customer relationships by delivering superior value, recognizing that the organization's ongoing relationships with customers are its most important asset.[4]

Marketing management
Continuous process at all organizational levels and across business functions from formulation to implementation of marketing strategy.

Marketing management is a continuous process that occurs at all levels of an organization and across all business functions. At the total organizational level, marketing management involves creating and maintaining the organization's culture—a set of values and beliefs about the necessity of satisfying customers' needs. These values and beliefs dictate that long-term cooperative relationships should be built and maintained through an analysis of market structure, customer behavior, and positioning within the value-adding process. At the strategic business unit (SBU) or divisional level, marketing management involves strategy—defining how the organization is to compete within the market and focusing on market segmentation and targeting, positioning of goods/services, and deciding when and how to partner. At the operating level, marketing management develops tactics—specifics about the marketing mix (product offerings, place/distribution policies, pricing, promotion/communication)—and manages customer and reseller relationships. Each level of marketing management and activities must be developed in continuity with the preceding level as the organization moves from formulation to implementation of marketing strategy. This includes the integration of marketing with other business functions at both the strategic and tactical levels.

Marketing in a Multilayered Environment

The environment in which marketing occurs likewise can be viewed from a number of levels, starting with an individual customer and expanding to a broader view of the entire global marketplace, as shown in Figure 1.1.

The Customer at the Core.   At the heart of the marketing environment is the customer or primary purchasing unit, the reason for an organization's existence. A customer may be an individual consumer or a single company, nonprofit organization, or government agency that is the buyer or receiver of goods and services produced for its benefit. When aggregated into markets, the number and types of these

FIGURE 1.1

A Model of the Marketing Environment

customers, their locations, buying habits, and wants and needs are of particular interest to marketers who are interested not only in their present characteristics but also in the direction that these will take in the future.

The Internal Marketing Environment.   Various aspects of the marketing function create a unique environment within an organization. The marketing function is closest to customers and consists of all the influences and actions taken by the marketer to satisfy customer needs. The firm's mission and marketing strategy provide a basis for designing the **marketing mix**—the combination of products (goods and services), prices, promotion (communications), and place (distribution) decisions that make up a particular marketing program design.

Marketing mix
The "4 P's" of product, price, place (distribution), and promotion (communications).

The Internal Organizational Environment.   Marketing and other functional activities are performed within an integrated organizational environment. Business functions other than marketing include accounting, finance, human resources, operations, information systems, and other areas required for operating an efficient and effective marketing organization. These functions may be extended to encompass other areas such as research and development (R&D), manufacturing, purchasing, and other functions with the potential to have a positive or negative impact on marketing strategy outcomes.

The External Micro-Environment.   The external micro-environment consists of relationships among customer markets, competitors, suppliers, marketing intermediaries and distribution channels, and any other public or private entity that may have a direct influence on a firm's ability to market its products.

Customer markets are diverse in their characteristics and in their demand for goods and services, making it necessary for marketing managers to monitor them constantly. For example, consumers of all types exhibited a growing preference for sports utility vehicles (SUVs) and mini-vans over the more traditional passenger cars in the 1990s. Thus the markets for SUVs experienced significant growth during this time.

Marketers may be faced with both direct and indirect *competition*. The Ford Explorer sports utility vehicle competes directly with domestic models such as the Jeep Cherokee and Chevy Blazer, among others. Ford also faces global competition in this category from the Nissan Pathfinder, Honda Passport, Mercedes M-Class, and other foreign SUVs. Indirect competition may come from all other types of vehicles and modes of transportation.

A vast array of *suppliers* provides the goods and services that are needed for the manufacture, production, and sale of finished goods, as well as the general operation of a business. For example, the manufacturer of a truck needs to buy electrical power, telecommunications and computer services, raw materials such as steel and petroleum products, component parts such as ignition switches and tires, and office equipment and cleaning supplies, to name but a few of the purchases necessary to run a business.

Marketing intermediaries include wholesalers and retailers (middlemen) that form channels of distribution to move products from producers to final customers (see Chapter 10). Other intermediaries transport goods and services to and from the business via trucks, planes, trains, or ships—or perhaps via telephone lines, cable, or satellite. Intermediaries also may provide financing, credit, risk insurance, a wide range of business services, and other critical resources that can have a direct effect on the success of the business. Sales of the Ford Explorer are facilitated by local dealerships and trucking lines that transport the SUVs from the factory to the retailer. Lending institutions provide the necessary financing for inventories held by manufacturers, wholesalers, and retailers. Consumer loan companies provide financing for auto purchases, and automotive insurance companies cover potential losses that the customer may incur. Facilitating services also may include media advertising, market research, outside sales representatives, and many others.

There are many *public and private entities* within a firm's micro-environment that can have an impact on marketing efforts. Examples include political activist groups such as political action committees (PACs), the Sierra Club, antiabortionists or pro-choice groups, the tobacco lobby, the American Association of Retired Persons (AARP), the Better Business Bureau, and a variety of others. Many organizations have experienced market success or failure as a result of the efforts of such groups. Manufacturers of SUVs, for example, must monitor and respond to a number of issues that go beyond the law but are reflected in public opinion in terms of ethical and socially responsible behavior. Public and private entities pose a number of issues for SUV manufacturers, including safety features, deceptive advertising, credit terms, and other issues that go beyond present legal requirements.

The External Macro-Environment. Forces in the macro-environment can have a major impact on marketing outcomes and management decisions, but they are largely beyond the control of the firm. These forces include the demographics of the marketplace, economic factors, physical or natural conditions, technological advances, legal and political constraints, and social or cultural issues.

Marketers must constantly monitor and respond to the *demographics of the marketplace*. Shifting populations throughout the world create new opportunities and problems as the number of potential customers increases or decreases in a particular area. Demographics are analyzed in terms of changes and trends in age distribution; population size, growth rates, and mobility; household structure (including gender roles, working members, etc.); immigration and emigration patterns; ethnic markets; level of education; the nature of various market segments; and other factors of interest to the marketer.

Some *economic factors* that can affect marketing strategy and buyer responses to marketing efforts include income levels and social class distribution, demand for various goods and services, interest rates, savings and debt levels, inflation, taxes, employment, and international currency exchange rates. For example, the financial crisis in Asia during the late 1990s demonstrated that a severe financial crisis in one part of the world can have a significant impact on business conditions throughout the rest of the world.

The *physical environment and natural conditions* will continue to have a major impact on marketing decisions into the twenty-first century. Natural events such as hurricanes, tornadoes, earthquakes, and floods that occur in all areas of the world affect the availability of resources to create and buy goods and services. (The impact of *el Niño* was felt throughout many nations in the late 1990s with its devastating weather patterns and disruption of normal daily lifestyles for a multinational marketplace.) Environmentalists demonstrate concerns over the condition of our planet in terms of renewable and nonrenewable resources (e.g., alternative energy sources, availability of raw materials, and air and water pollution), resulting in more government regulation throughout the world. Each of these factors can have an effect on marketers and their customers.

Technological advances and the rate of change associated with technological innovations represent one of the most dynamic environmental influences on marketing management decisions and the daily lives of a worldwide marketplace. Issues faced by marketers in the technological environment include R&D expenditures, rapidly changing lifestyles and business operations, changing market boundaries, new forms of communication and data transmission, automation, and so forth. Each technological breakthrough has the potential to affect the marketing mix directly or indirectly, including areas such as product design (e.g., computer-assisted design) and production (e.g., robotics), communications media (e.g., the Internet), distribution (e.g., catalogs, direct marketing, and the Internet again), and pricing (e.g., higher technology generally results in increased efficiency, decreased costs, and lower customer prices). New and emerging technologies also can enhance service performance by shortening the response time needed to handle customer complaints, tracking merchandise shipments to provide customers with immediate order status information, and generally enabling the firm to be more customer-oriented.

The *legal and political environment* both protects and frustrates marketers and their customers. Protection is provided for customers in terms of product safety, fair pricing practices, truth in advertising, the right to redress when treated unfairly, and other actions that might be harmful to the buyer. Protection also is provided for one business against another regarding unfair restraint of trade, contractual relationships, and so forth. Frustrations occur in the amount of "red tape" or details required to produce and sell goods and services in the United States and throughout the world. Fiscal policies, tariffs, foreign trade agreements and market entry requirements, import/export restrictions, government type (e.g., democratic versus totalitarian), growth of public interest groups (e.g., PACs), and many other legal and political environmental factors affect marketing decisions.

Social/cultural issues comprise another macro-environmental force that is of particular interest to marketers. The norms, beliefs, behaviors, values, and attitudes of individuals and organizations are beyond the direct control of marketers. Although these may shift over time for a given segment of the population, changes occur rather slowly and must be monitored and understood by marketers. The cultural revolution in China and other developing countries has major implications for marketers from all over the world who plan to do business there. Within the social/cultural environment, marketers are interested in present and emerging gender roles, social and household roles, ethnic and nationalistic allegiances, environmental concerns, consumer attitudes toward business (and vice versa), attitudes toward materialism and self, and many other factors related to culture, subculture, and social behavior. Knowledge of these environmental factors can be used to determine what products to market and how to market them to a desired target market.

Each of the internal and external environmental forces just described is discussed in more detail with relevant topics later in the book. Chapter 2 discusses the role played by various environmental factors in bringing about or responding to the challenges of a changing world. As you read about change, keep in mind the "ripple effect" that a major change in one aspect of the dynamic global marketing environment shown in Figure 1.1 can have on other environmental factors at every level.

Marketing as Value Exchange

Marketing is the process of *value exchange*—the exchange of tangible goods, services, ideas, time, and other intangibles that represent value—between two or more parties. The key to a successful exchange is that each party has something of value desired by the other. For an exchange or transaction to occur, relationships must be established at some level between buyer and seller. This, in turn, requires that the parties communicate and deliver value. Of course, each party must be free to accept or reject the offer and must believe that dealing with the other is both acceptable and desirable. Marketers are increasingly aware of the fundamental need to stress mutual benefits to facilitate an exchange. When all parties involved experience a sense of fulfillment, a transaction can be considered successful.

Many types of "buyers" and "sellers" may be involved in marketing transactions. Examples include manufacturer and retailer, retailer and consumer, dentist and patient, hair stylist and client, teacher and student, voters and elected officials, congregation and clergy, worker and employer, community residents and police, and donors and the needy.

The level of satisfaction experienced by each partner in an exchange directly correlates with the ability of each to identify and satisfy the needs of the other. If both sides do not define *need* similarly, dissatisfaction may result. It is the role and responsibility of each buyer and seller to ensure satisfaction and to deal with dissatisfaction appropriately when it occurs. This may result in a series of multiple exchanges over time and ideally lead to a positive long-term relationship between buyer and seller.

The quality of exchange relationships underlies the profitability of many small businesses. Whereas customers often feel "unimportant" or as if they are just a "number" to a large business, many small businesses are more inclined to cater to individual customer needs. People in small businesses may call customers by name and provide extra personal services that increase the value of the transaction to the buyer. This, in turn, generates repeat business and referrals through word-of-mouth. Of course, many large businesses are able to develop more personal customer relationships with computer-assisted sales support (e.g., American Airlines' AAdvantage frequent flyer numbers allow American Airlines personnel to call customers by name and have more personal information about a vast array of customers).

While the focus of this text is primarily on organizations that engage in marketing for profit, the nonprofit sector has become more attuned to the need for marketing strategies to achieve a variety of objectives such as fund-raising, volunteer involvement, and acceptance by target audiences. Successful marketing efforts by nonprofits such as the American Red Cross, food banks, and homeless shelters also must stress mutual benefits that will result in an exchange or transaction in which all concerned find an acceptable level of satisfaction. Nonprofit institutions are particularly concerned with competing with other organizations for needed funds. Professional fund-raisers understand that successful fund-raising requires the customization of proposals, a dynamic marketing orientation, and emphasis on mutual benefits to stimulate an exchange.[5]

EVOLUTION OF THE MARKETING CONCEPT

"Build it and they will come" represents the mentality of the earlier views of marketing, with an emphasis on production and selling. Historically, marketing's role has been to sell all the goods and services a firm could produce, often using aggressive tactics or a "hard sell" to do so, with little regard for the customer's perspective. Within this context, the marketing function was narrowly defined and generally performed from either a mass-marketing perspective ("one size fits all") or a sales and advertising perspective in order to create a market. This approach tended to limit the scope of marketing activities and to isolate marketing management from other management aspects of the business.

Marketing concept
Organizations must be customer-focused, market-driven, global in scope, and flexible in delivering superior value.

More recently, the **marketing concept** generally has come to reflect the belief that organizational goals are best achieved by determining the needs and wants of target markets and delivering these benefits and satisfactions more effectively than competitors. Historically, companies have used five different approaches in marketing their products or services. A sixth approach follows a redefined marketing concept. The choice of marketing approach represents the philosophy that drives the organization's marketing activities, as follows:

1. *Production concept.* Firms following the production concept in conducting their activities will strive for high production efficiency, wide distribution, and low-cost operations, based on the premise that customers will opt for products that are widely available and low in cost.

2. *Product concept.* Firms using the product concept focus on producing good products and continuously improving them, in the belief that customers will buy the "best" products, that is, products that offer the most quality or performance.

3. *Selling concept.* Based on the belief that customers will not buy enough of the firm's products if left to their own devices, the selling concept focuses on selling and promoting the company's product aggressively rather than making what will sell.

4. *Marketing concept.* When a company follows the marketing concept, it must deliver what the market needs and wants and do so more efficiently, effectively, and with more value added than its competitors. Both internal and external marketing efforts are necessary. This philosophy is based on

   - a market focus (the firm cannot be everything to everyone);

   - customer orientation (this means taking customers' points of view to attract, retain, and satisfy them—including a global perspective);

   - coordinated marketing (this involves coordinating among marketing functions and between marketing and other company units); and

   - profitability (how else can organizations achieve their goals?).

5. *Societal marketing concept.* Organizations following the societal philosophy recognize the need to focus on the long-term consequences of their marketing activities. An expansion of the marketing concept, it includes consideration of the well-being of customers and society as a whole. The organization's respon-

sibility is to determine the needs, wants, and interests of target markets and to deliver the desired satisfactions more effectively and efficiently than competitors. This should result in preservation or enhancement of the well-being of consumers and society.[6]

6. *The "new" marketing concept.* The evolving and expanded role of marketing is driven by a redefined marketing concept. As we enter the twenty-first century, organizations that adopt the "new" marketing concept for long-term profitability and survival must be customer-focused, market-driven, global in scope, and flexible in their ability to deliver superior value to customers. At the same time, customers' preferences and expectations may change continuously as customers are exposed to new product offerings and communications. Further, this concept holds that

   - value is defined in the marketplace—not in the factory;

   - customer knowledge and customer and employee loyalty go hand-in-hand in building long-term relationships;

   - innovation and continuous improvement apply more to processes than to products (although products are often a by-product); and

   - the age of mass production has yielded to the era of mass customization.

   In short, customer value must be the central element of all business strategy. "In the end, the survivors will be organizations that have the ability to reinvent themselves as market conditions change and make a full commitment to the new marketing concept."[7]

THE MARKETING MIX

The marketing mix includes the basic tools used by marketing managers to sell goods and services to target customers (Figure 1.2). Elements of the marketing mix include the organization's *product* (good or service), *price* (value), *place* (distribution channel, location), and *promotion* (integrated marketing communications)—sometimes referred to as the "4 P's." Marketing managers must design and coordinate these elements to achieve synergy in the marketplace.

Product (Good or Service)

The good or service offered by an organization represents more than manufacturing or production specifications. It is a bundle of benefits that is being delivered to meet the needs of the organization's customers. In the past, superior product design or performance was thought to be sufficient to attract large numbers of customers at the expense of competitors. Today, however, customers and suppliers are becoming involved in product development and management. They are being brought into the design process by many manufacturers to maximize market acceptance and purchase. Product positioning strategies have become more finely tuned to customer needs and perceived benefits, frequently from a value-added perspective.

FIGURE 1.2
· ·
The Marketing Mix

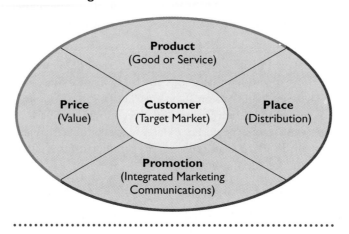

Services may be the major offering (i.e., a service product) of marketing organizations such as airlines and banks, the telephone company, or your favorite dry cleaner. On the other hand, services may be viewed as ancillary to the sale of tangible products such as automobiles, televisions, and appliances. In either case, there is an increased effort to deliver higher-quality services and to make them tangible with clues that the consumer can recognize as a way to differentiate one firm's product or service from that of another. Services also can be considered a major marketing tool within the marketing mix. Additional services offered with the sale of goods or other services have become an important asset in building customer loyalty and gaining long-term competitive advantage.

Product proliferation in both goods and services has made it more difficult for marketers to maintain brand identity and for consumers to decide among options that are available to them. The computer industry is an excellent example of this trend with the increasingly shorter time to market of new hardware and software and related peripheral products. The Windows 95 launch and the more recent MMX Pentium microprocessor chip with its superior technology are two such product introductions. These, too, will be surpassed shortly by newer, more powerful innovations.

Price (Value)
· · · · · · · · · · · · · · · · · · · ·

Price is basically the amount a customer is willing to give up to obtain a desired good or service. Traditional pricing approaches tended to be cost-based and adjusted according to demand and price elasticity, indicators of what the customer was willing to pay. Today, the focus is on pricing strategies such as everyday low prices, price-quality-value, and value-added. These are but a few of the "buzz words" that characterize the current and evolving approach to pricing. Consumers and organizational customers want real value for their money. However, value is determined by the relationship between quality and price; the better the quality for the price charged, the higher is the perceived value of the purchase.

Place (Distribution)

The place or distribution element of the marketing mix refers to the channels and/or locations that sellers use to reach their buyers. For example, direct sales from manufacturer to final customer represent the shortest channel. Longer channels may involve manufacturer, one or more wholesalers or agents, retailers, and final consumers.

As buyers and sellers strive to decrease the time to market for their products, distribution channels have become shorter. One result is a trend toward more discount operations, such as Sam's Warehouse Clubs and Best Buy. Specialty superstores handle large volumes of merchandise and thousands of customers. Barnes & Noble superstores, for example, represent one of the fastest-growing trends in book retailing, with stores that range from 20,000 to 40,000 square feet and 100,000 titles that are sold at a 10 to 20 percent discount. They also feature food and entertainment.[8]

The growth of direct marketing represents another major change in distribution strategies, where the middleman is eliminated wherever possible—generally resulting in a cost reduction. Information technology, efficient management of customer databases, and a "poverty of time" on the part of many customers have fueled this trend, which is expected to escalate. Database marketing allows firms to respond to market needs for goods and services and to build closer relationships with their customers.

Promotion (Integrated Marketing Communications)

The promotional or communications mix consists of all the tools that an organization uses to communicate with its customers: advertising, personal selling, sales promotion, direct marketing, and publicity/public relations. All organizations involved in moving a product through the channels of distribution are involved in communications strategies as they sell to buyers at the next level. However, today, many of the traditional communications methods are being challenged.

With the advent of sophisticated multimedia opportunities, marketers have expanded their ability to communicate with their target customers. In addition to the traditional print and electronic media (i.e., newspapers, magazines, direct mail, radio, television), today's marketing messages can be transmitted by interactive television, home shopping networks, direct-mail video catalogues, computer services, and other electronic avenues. The globalization of markets challenges marketing managers to design and execute effective communications programs for foreign audiences at home and abroad.

MARKETING MANAGEMENT IN THE TWENTY-FIRST CENTURY

Managers of a broad range of contemporary organizations have come to recognize the importance of marketing. Involvement of marketing managers throughout the entire strategic planning process (described in Chapter 3) and effective implementation of tactical marketing decisions are critical for short-run survival and long-run sustainable competitive advantage. Marketing also contributes to an organization's survival during severe economic downturns and a subsequent decrease in financial resources, increased numbers and types of competitors, a more highly diversified customer base, and other dynamic environmental factors.

The Importance of Marketing Relationships

Relationship marketing
Activities focused on building long-term relationships with customers.

Contemporary marketing management can be viewed as a value-adding process directed toward **relationship marketing.** If marketing management is to achieve distinctive strategic competence and global advantage, it requires designing marketing operations that will create and sustain long-term relationships well into the twenty-first century. The model in Figure 1.3 represents a critical set of relationships whose combined efforts carry out this dynamic process.

This process involves all the activities that marketers perform to ensure that mutually beneficial relationships endure in the constantly evolving global business environment. As you can see, relationships are the key: relationships with customers, suppliers, producers, employees, distributors, and marketing facilitators. Marketers need to be innovative, flexible, creative, and both proactive and reactive in their marketing decisions if these relationships are to be mutually beneficial and add value. R&D is one area where such relationships have proved effective. Close collaboration among internal business units and external sources of expertise has proved effective in decreasing time to market and increasing customer satisfaction. For example, General Electric Co. has instituted a "one-coffeepot" product-development team that unites GE researchers, manufacturers, and marketers in a single location to work on everything from a new light bulb to a locomotive as they drink coffee. Rockwell International Corp. has worked with Tupelov, Russia's supersonic jet manufacturer, on how to smooth the airflow over a future American supersonic passenger plane. Rockwell has more than 200 formal relationships with universities, government laboratories, and others. Many of

FIGURE 1.3

The Marketing Global Superhighway

Rockwell's ideas have come from China and Russia, as well as from other business partners.[9]

The importance of relationships in the marketing process becomes even more compelling in view of the highly volatile and uncertain global business environment. The nature and strength of these relationships, as well as the overall management of the marketing process, are affected significantly by such changes as the technology explosion characterized by the enhanced information-transfer capabilities of the Internet and the World Wide Web.

The activities performed by marketing managers, although also constantly evolving, generally may be categorized as researching, planning, formulating strategy, developing marketing programs and budgets, and implementing, controlling, and evaluating the programs and results. While each of the relationships shown in the model is important, the unity (or integration) of the total marketing process is equally important to businesses. General Motors, Macy's, Sears, and other power marketers suffered financial reverses in recent years not only because of forces beyond their control (e.g., the economy) but also because of their lack of focus on core businesses and key customers. Although these firms subsequently have turned their businesses around, opportunities were missed as a result of a lack of understanding of the market and an inability to deliver what the market needed. When a firm loses touch with its customers or fails to remember its core business, the buyer-seller relationship is in jeopardy.

It is within this "marketing global superhighway" that specific marketing activities are performed and managed. These activities are both external and internal, domestic and international. They vary from those noted earlier to a broader definition of marketing that includes networking, building and maintaining strategic alliances, continuous process improvement, R&D, and involvement in product design, as illustrated in preceding examples. In addition, throughout the marketing management process, marketers must be continuously sensitive to social responsibility issues and the expectation of highly ethical behavior.

Changes in Organizational Structure
....

The problems of recession, restructuring, downsizing/rightsizing, and privatizing have led to a new marketing environment where organizations are flatter and time horizons are shorter. Many companies have removed one or more layers of middle management, so managers tend to be younger and to have a new sense of time horizon that is almost exclusively short term. Such managers tend to belong to several teams and are expected to perform as **cross-functional team** players who are involved in a variety of business areas such as cost reduction and logistics. At the same time, they must maintain a clear sense of goals, product positioning, and business positioning. Marketing imagination must be applied to areas that go far beyond the traditional demand stimulation and order-getting.[10]

Historically, most marketing transactions have been market-based and carried on within the constraints of traditional bureaucratic hierarchical organizations. Today, a new breed of marketing organization has emerged in the form of strategic partnerships and networks. The transformation that is taking place includes a shift from a microeconomic model that emphasizes transactions and profit maximization to the management of strategic partnerships. In order to deliver superior value to customers, firms are positioning themselves between vendors and customers in the

Cross-functional teams
Project management teams made up of members from many functional areas (marketing, accounting, engineering, production, etc.) who work together to achieve a common goal.

Starbucks: Coffee Making as a Brand of Cooking

Starbucks coffee can be found in cafés from Seattle to Japan. The company has transformed a formerly routine, often mundane coffee-drinking habit into an upscale, gourmet experience. Coffee is certainly not a new product, nor are cafés where coffee is sold. Starbucks has proven itself to be a successful innovator in a market where coffee consumption has declined since the 1960s. However, 50 percent of the adult population drinks one or more cups every day.

Specialty coffee retailers like Starbucks, Barnie's, and the Coffee Beanery have ambitious plans underway to expand distribution through retail storefronts, brand extension, and joint ventures with other business partners. Starbucks, which does not franchise, opened a new store every business day in 1996 to reach a total of 1000, with another 325 planned for 1997.

How has innovative marketing management paid off for Starbucks?

- Product: High-quality product, upscale atmosphere and pricing; coffee drinking transformed into a gourmet experience

- Distribution: Cafés and retail storefronts, bookstores (Barnes & Noble), cafeterias, airlines (United), ice cream (Dreyer's), and others.

- Brand extension: Coffee beans in a wide range of gourmet flavors; frozen coffee drinks (e.g., Frappucino, also bottled for sale in supermarkets), plunger pots, Brita filters.

- Internal marketing: Over 20,000 highly trained employees (referred to as *partners* or *baristas*), higher-than-average pay, generous benefits;

extensive employee training program with an emphasis on quality performance and customer service in sessions named "Brewing the Perfect Cup at Home," "Coffee Knowledge," "Customer Service," and "Star Skills." It pays particular attention to the needs of and issues of importance to its predominantly Generation X work force.

As Starbuck's employee training manual states:

As Americans, we have grown up thinking of coffee primarily as a hot, tan liquid dispensed from fairly automatic appliances, then "doctored" as needed to make it drinkable.

We open the three-pound "value" can, shovel the grounds into a paper filter, push a button, then go about our business.

The opposite of this approach is to treat coffee making as a brand of cooking. You start with the best beans you can buy, making sure they are fresh. You use your favorite recipe. You grind the beans to the right consistency and add delicious, fresh-tasting water. To keep the coffee warm, you put it into a Thermos.

If coffee seems like small business, remember that a person who consumes a latté and scone every day has a $1,400-a-year habit.

*The box title is attributed to James M. Higgins, *Innovate or Evaporate* (Winter Park, FL: New Management Publishing Company, 1995).

Source: Jennifer Reese, "Starbucks: Inside the Coffee Cult," *Fortune* (December 9, 1996), pp. 190–200.

Value-adding process
All actions and organizations involved in transferring goods and services, as well as satisfaction, from suppliers to end-customers.

value-adding process. Relationships with customers are becoming the key strategic resource of the business.[11]

Changes in the Marketing Function.   Changes in organizational structures, market demand, and technology not only have redefined the marketing function but also have altered the way in which marketing decisions are made and executed. For example, marketing decisions may be made within the framework of a matrix or cross-functional organization where marketing is integrated with other functional areas, or marketing tasks may be assigned to outside experts due to the cost-effectiveness and popularity of project teams and outsourcing.

Decisions within each aspect of marketing management are associated with some element of risk. As a result, the role of marketing research has been reoriented in many firms to meet the challenges of decreased financial resources, a more diverse customer base, intense competition, shorter product life cycles, and other concerns. For example, market researchers have become recognized partners in making marketing decisions in the pharmaceutical industry, taking on the role of expert predictive consultants who share risk and accountability as they try to understand their customers and define outcomes research.[12]

Changes in the Relationship Between Marketing and Other Business Functions. The distinct traditional functional boundaries of the past are becoming blurred as organizations develop more flexible structures to deal with the rapid changes in their operating environments. As Webster notes,

> ... the intellectual core of marketing management needs to be expanded ... to address more fully the set of organizational and strategic issues inherent in relationships and alliances. ... We are now considering phenomena that have traditionally been the subject of study by psychologists, organizational behaviorists, political economists, and sociologists. The focus shifts from products and firms as units of analysis to people, organizations, and the social processes that bind actors together in ongoing relationships.[13]

This statement recognizes the changes that are taking place—or should be taking place—at each level of an organization: corporate, strategic business unit (SBU), and operating levels. Although the three key dimensions of marketing—culture (basic set of customer-oriented values and beliefs), strategy, and tactics—can be found at all organizational levels, they are emphasized at the corporate, SBU, and operating levels, respectively.

In this new role, marketing managers are integral members of cross-functional networks of specialists formed as a partnership rather than a hierarchy. Marketing managers cannot work in a vacuum; marketing decisions have an impact on, and are impacted by, decisions made by financial, accounting, operations, human resources, and other functional managers. Thus a synergy can be realized from an internal confederation of managers who work together to achieve a common goal—for both external and internal (employee) customers and partners.

The relationship between marketing and other business functions includes an expanded role for the organization's customers. Whereas customer surveys and other research were used primarily to determine marketing strategies in the past, customers are now providing important input into decisions in other functional areas. For example, a growing number of manufacturers are bringing their customers into the design process for new products and services at an early stage. This trend is consistent with a customer orientation and the desire to reduce risk associated with the development and introduction of new products.

Conversely, some manufacturers who are becoming frustrated with the dual role demands of being both product innovator and customer nurturer may deemphasize marketing to do what they feel they do best—manufacturing. However, marketing-savvy manufacturers who rely on consultative selling and extensive support services for evolving technologies that customers consider critical will be prime candidates for change in the struggle for balance between manufacturing and marketing.[14]

Marketing and Entrepreneurship

While many start-up and small firms have benefited from planned marketing programs, others have ignored the need for marketing until it was too late. However, more small business owners and entrepreneurs are recognizing the need to coordinate marketing with manufacturing, distribution, operations, financial, and other decisions. As Hisrich points out, the relationship between marketing and entrepreneurship is important because the entrepreneur must use marketing appropriately to launch and develop new ventures successfully, many entrepreneurs have a limited understanding of marketing, and entrepreneurs are often poor planners and managers.[15]

On the other hand, successful entrepreneurs have learned to use marketing to their advantage. America's fastest-growing companies include entrepreneurial firms such as Blockbuster, Boston Market, Outback Steakhouse, Gymboree, and Office Depot, which share a number of common characteristics.[16] They make "ever-whirling change the driver of super growth." They are not wedded to any one product or idea, but keep experimenting. They not only expect failure in the entrepreneurial process—they almost require it. They identify what is sacred to competitors and then take advantage of it. Most prefer antihierarchical organizations where ideas flow freely and believe that would-be entrepreneurs who sit around waiting for a great idea to strike them are destined to fail. These characteristics represent the kindred spirit shared by marketing and entrepreneurship.

Marketing in Nonprofit Organizations

Numerous nonprofit organizations, such as the American Red Cross, churches, art museums, foundations, hospitals, and schools, have used marketing tools to reach their respective audiences for some time—but on a more ad hoc, informal basis. As managers of these nonprofit organizations encounter new, more complex problems in their respective marketplaces, there is an increasing trend to formalize the marketing function with assigned responsibility and specified position within the organizational structure. These managers are recognizing the need to analyze their markets, resources, and mission as a basis for marketing strategy decisions. For example, market analysis is focused on identification of markets and their needs, customer behavior and satisfaction, and attitude/awareness. Resource analysis includes recognition of internal strengths and weaknesses relative to external opportunities and threats. Mission analysis focuses on defining the organization's business mission, customers/needs served, competitors, and market positioning.[17]

Volunteers make up one of the most important market segments for nonprofit organizations, but they are becoming more difficult to recruit because many would-be volunteers are faced with time and money constraints.[18] The emerging type of volunteer is eager to help but is also "careerist and project-oriented." This creates

MARKETING AND ENTREPRENEURSHIP

Female Entrepreneurship Sets the Pace for a Fast-Growing Niche

Many entrepreneurial success stories are due to oversights made by large industry leaders. Ellen Wessel was somewhat of a renegade in 1977 when she launched her women's running apparel company, Moving Comfort, Inc. Two decades later, sales have reached $12.5 million, and other female entrepreneurs have entered the market. Missy Park's Title Nine Sports, a $10-million-a-year catalog business, grew out of the former Yale athlete's difficulty with poorly fitting men's sports gear.

These female entrepreneurs and others are leaders in the $21 billion growth market for women's sports equipment and apparel. They focus on customer wants and needs, hire women athletes as advisors, and design products that are appropriate for the female physiology. In response to the growing popularity of women's professional sports and a maturing men's market, Nike has hired more women to carry out plans to double its sales of women's athletic gear to $2 billion by 2002.

Meanwhile, entrepreneurs like Park and Wessel are keeping a keen eye on competition. Park's Title Nine catalog business grew out of her interest in the civil rights law that mandated equality for women in school athletics, along with her own memories of having to wear ill-fitting men's athletic uniforms and shoes. To achieve her goal of becoming the "women's Nike," Park is focusing on her catalog business (including a new toll-free telephone number) and has opened a retail store in Berkeley, California. In addition to her own products, Park's catalog features items from other serious female athletes who have become leading sports entrepreneurs for their gender.

Wessel's Moving Comfort has gained a competitive edge through exceptional customer service and attention to details. Her products benefit from the expertise of female employees, including many athletes who test the products. Moving Comfort is expanding to appeal to non-runners (in competition with Nike and others), increasing retail distribution through larger, all-purpose sports chains such as Sports Authority.

Wessel, Parks, and other female sports entrepreneurs have developed a strong lead in their niche markets. The challenge will be to maintain their competitive edge against Nike and other large, aggressive sports marketing companies.

Source: Brad Wolverton, "Our Sports Gear, Ourselves," *Business Week* (September 1, 1997), p. 12.

---

the need for a different type of marketing approach, where meeting the needs of volunteers and tapping the resources of corporate America have become major keys in marketing programs. Organizations such as Boy Scouts of America, Ronald McDonald House, and Big Brothers/Big Sisters of America have had to scramble to attract and keep their volunteers. New York City's Boy Scouts council has started paying college students $8 an hour to lead troops, in response to the tripling of its ratio of scouts to adult volunteers in five years. Many nonprofit organizations are using marketing tactics to recruit minorities, retirees, and teens as volunteers while extending their agencies' operating hours to evenings and weekends, designing low-commitment, flexible service opportunities, and developing new relationships with corporations. As one nonprofit director said, "People want to do something that's going to make them feel good quickly," which sounds very much like a direct application of the marketing concept.

The International Scope of Marketing

As domestic firms face heightened competition from developed and developing countries, their need to use marketing becomes evident. Developing markets for American products and emerging foreign competition from Japan, China, South America, Asia, and other parts of the world have brought about changes in marketing. For example, product and packaging designs have been adjusted, international distribution channels have been expanded or realigned, promotional methods have been adapted to local audiences, and organizational structures have been redrawn.

Hewlett-Packard's marketing strategy for its inkjet printers, described in the opening scenario for this chapter, is a vivid illustration of how large U.S. companies can compete successfully under effective leadership in the global marketplace. They can exploit their creativity while investing heavily in R&D to grow or maintain market share. This involves cutting costs, sustaining frequent new product introductions (or variations of products), cutting prices, and targeting customer groups that can be satisfied in a manner superior to competitors' efforts. H-P lost the calculator business because most top executives of that time had preached high profits from high-cost products aimed at niche markets. "If you're going to leverage American culture but compete globally, you need a balance of entrepreneurship and central leverage," said Richard Hackman, a retired H-P executive, now a director. Takashi Saito, head of Canon, Inc.'s inkjet printer business said, "H-P understood computers better, it understood American customers better, it got good products to market faster." Japanese makers' culture hindered the kind of quick decision making needed, he said, and as a result, "The market is H-P's garden."[19]

FOCUSING ON CUSTOMER SATISFACTION

Customers experience feelings of either satisfaction or dissatisfaction with each purchase of a good or service. While these feelings may extend from a mere shrug of the shoulders to legal action, it is important to understand the marketing implications of either state. Satisfied customers are repeat customers. They are a good source of new business through word-of-mouth communication. On the other hand, dissatisfied customers tend to buy elsewhere and to share their "bad" experiences with even more potential customers, thus having a negative impact on a company's marketing efforts. **Customer satisfaction** is not easy to define or measure, but in simplest terms, most customers are satisfied when their purchase experiences meet or exceed their expectations.

Customer satisfaction
Difference between expectations and perceived benefits received.

Customer-Oriented Strategies

Customer-oriented strategies are developed with customer satisfaction and company profitability as the primary motivators. Therefore, it is necessary to know precisely who the customers are, why they buy, and what it takes to satisfy them. At both the organizational and consumer levels, many changes have taken place in buying motives and purchase behavior—as well as the customer's role in marketing management decisions. Table 1.1 provides a summary of several recent customer-oriented strategies initiated by various organizations.

Customer-oriented strategies
Customer-satisfaction focal point for all long-term plans.

TABLE 1.1
....
Recent Examples of Customer-Oriented Strategies

- British Airways learned that ground services such as showers, dressing rooms, and pressed clothes are important to its arriving first-class passengers. The company also has provided the option of having dinner on the ground, because some passengers want less service in the air and more in the terminal.

- Baxter International, the $9 billion health care and services company, has shared business risk with some customers by jointly setting targets and sharing the savings or extra expenses as part of its buyer-seller relationships. Baxter has found that 80 percent of its incremental sales are from large customers with which it has already developed a relationship.

- BancOne (Columbus, Ohio) watches customers' checking account balances closely. In an effort to increase its "depth of relationship" with its retail customers, as soon as it notices a bulging balance, the bank calls the customer and tries to sell him or her a certificate of deposit or other product.

- At Weyerhaeuser, hourly employees visit customers' plants on a regular basis so they can better understand their customers' needs.

- Ford Motor Co. identified about 90 items that customers want on the sales and service spectrum, including a ride to their next stop after dropping their cars off for service and appointments within one day of a desired date. One of the most important sales standards that customers wanted was "a pleasant, nonpressured purchase experience," a company standard that Ford has been working on with its dealers.

- For many firms and their customers, the value equation includes the addition of interactive technology to their marketing effort. For example, an independent pizza restaurant in Lomboc, California, created an award program called the "Supper Club." The value equation includes not only extra benefits (e.g., meals, merchandise) for the customer and repeat business for the restaurant but also the extra benefit of interactive technology. The owner installed a PC-based system in a kiosk, with a magnetic card reader linked to his point-of-sale order-taking equipment. Supper Club members present their cards at checkout to get their points, and they can interact directly with the kiosk any time they want to check out their account or claim rewards. Companies of all sizes and types are adding value through "smart cards" and other interactive technology.

Source: Rahul Jacob, "Why Some Customers Are More Equal Than Others," *Fortune* (September 19, 1994), pp. 215–224; Richard Cross and Janet Smith, "The New Value Equation," *American Demographics* (June 1996), p. 20.

Changes in Markets and Their Buying Behavior.   Shifting demographics, changing family roles, economic concerns, advances in technology—all these factors and many more have contributed to changes in the role of marketing to final consumers. For example, as more women enter the work force, more men and teenagers take on the responsibility of shopping for the family. A 1990 Opinion Research Corp. report found that almost 40 percent of supermarket shoppers were male.[20] Such trends are growing and have implications for marketing communications, distribution, and other aspects of the marketing mix.

Economic influences have contributed to the growing popularity of shopping at superstores like Barnes & Noble for books, Best Buy for computers, Circuit City for appliances, Home Depot for building supplies, or Toys 'R' Us for games and toys. The significant growth in Hispanic, Asian, and other ethnic markets has prompted manufacturers and retailers to adapt products and marketing communications strategies to meet the needs of these important segments. Further, as marketers distribute their goods and services across international borders, they must implement new marketing strategies that are consistent with local realities.

Organizational buying practices have been affected significantly by world economic conditions. Bottom-line profitability, total quality management, and service before, during, and after the sale have become the basis for buying decisions within the context of the optimal price-value-quality relationship and avoidance of risk. In addition, the purchasing process has been streamlined in many instances through telemarketing, computerized ordering systems and inventory control, satellite links, and other advances in technology.

Changes in markets and their buying behavior should be monitored continuously. In order to understand and act on these changes, marketers must first be able to identify the factors that are most important to customers and then be able to measure those factors accurately. The general assumption is that certain changes in the marketing mix or the purchase process will deliver greater satisfaction to customers. However, before making major changes in the marketing program, businesses should use market research to determine the customer satisfaction/behavior relationship by analyzing how a specific change in customer satisfaction is related to a specific change in buying behavior. Marketers use panels, focus groups, and test markets to explore the need for change and how to approach it successfully.[21]

Involving the Customer Earlier in the Marketing Process. Customer wants and needs are being considered more seriously than ever before in the design and delivery of both goods and services, as noted earlier. Innovative marketers are accomplishing this in a number of ways, but one of the most important approaches concerns the use of point-of-sale scanning technology to capture, store, retrieve, and use customer-based information.

Involvement of the customer in the design and delivery process is not limited to tangible goods. Services marketers also have found it advisable to include customers in their marketing decisions. For example, the savings and loan industry is implementing marketing technology to understand each customer's needs and wants. This industry, along with many others, is focusing on the customer rather than the institution and its traditional offerings because of increased competition, deregulation, expanded product and service offerings, and growth in the financial sophistication of consumers.[22]

At the industrial level, changing markets and market conditions require shorter response times by manufacturers. Therefore, industrial designers are becoming deeply involved earlier in the engineering and manufacturing process to meet more sophisticated marketing demands.[23]

Value-Added Marketing Strategies. *Value-added marketing*—the right combination of quality, service, and value—is the key to market success. Customers generally perceive value as high quality at a reasonable price, but not necessarily the lowest price. Quality includes both product features and the quality of service that is delivered before, during, and after the sale. Manufacturers are increasingly concerned with preventing quality glitches before a product reaches the customer. Several examples were evident in the automotive industry at the time of delayed production and distribution of GM's Saturn and Chrysler's Cirrus models. Vexed by needed quality improvements in new models, Chrysler Chairman Robert Eaton launched a major campaign to put more focus on improving the quality of Chrysler cars.[24] Quality defects found by customers after the sale could drive demanding customers away forever in their quest for quality, service, and value.

In the past, the factors that established "value" were determined at the top of an organization. Today, the ability to deliver added value requires local market input in terms of knowledge, decision making, and procedures. If a company is to deliver value to its customers successfully, it must make a total commitment to making the necessary changes. This may involve the adoption of new attitudes and philosophies, implementation of new approaches to the marketing process, and redesign of the organizational structure. In particular, certain marketing decisions should be decentralized to place them closer to the customer but coordinated through the organization's centralized information system.

Advances in technology have added value to goods and services for overall quality improvement. For example, Collins & Aikman (C&A) received top quality awards from many of the auto makers the company supplies.[25] C&A is a textile manufacturer that operates the world's largest carpet molding facility and uses computer-aided design (CAD) systems to design intricate molds for auto carpets. Use of the CAD system has resulted in fewer mistakes and an improved relationship with auto makers. It also has made it possible for the plant to operate on virtually nonexistent between-process inventories and to reduce materials handling significantly.

Quality and value often are defined in terms of service quality. Poor service quality results in customer dissatisfaction and the likelihood that the customer will change suppliers and brands. In a study of bank customers, it was found (not too surprisingly!) that poor service causes customers to change banks and that perceptions of quality service are likely to change throughout the product life cycle.[26] As noted previously, service evaluation depends on those factors which the customer values as important and may differ by customer segment.

Internal Marketing Strategies.   Organizations are beginning to recognize that one of their most valuable customer segments is their own employees. Comprehensive **internal marketing** programs that motivate employees to focus on the external customer should be directed toward employees at all levels—because service is everybody's business. In the new American economy ". . . service—bold, fast, unexpected, innovative, and customized—is the ultimate strategic imperative, a business challenge that has profound implications for the way we manage companies, hire employees, develop careers, and craft policies."[27] In the early 1990s, Toyota created a new standard for pleasing customers in the automotive industry with its Lexus luxury car, supported by regular national and regional training courses for all Lexus employees. Taco Bell, a fast-food chain that delivers food to college campus kiosks or wherever people want to munch, has implemented self-directed work teams rather than managers at many outlets. ServiceMaster's TruGreen-Chemlawn and other subsidiaries, as well as Johnson Controls' manufactured products and facilities management services, are doing work that people no longer want to do for themselves. Their success has come largely from internal marketing and empowering employees at all levels to do more for their customers while keeping costs down.

Internal marketing can lead to high employee retention, which generally means that a company has a work force that understands its customers' needs and can be highly productive. In other words, to retain valued customers, it is necessary to retain valued employees. Internal marketing includes, but is not limited to, higher pay. Employees are motivated when management listens to and acts on their suggestions

Internal marketing
Motivating, training, and empowering employees as the organization's internal customers.

for serving internal and external customers more effectively. For example, the chief operating officer at AT&T Universal has quarterly meetings with employees and acts on their input. Ritz-Carlton Hotel Co. empowers its employees to spend up to $2,000 to redress a guest grievance. Customers who have problems resolved are more loyal than customers who did not have a problem at all, according to those who are experts on the subject.[28]

Although we no longer seem to be in an era of guaranteed job security and deeply held company-employee loyalty, many companies have recognized the need to market themselves as desirable places to work. The "new deal" being crafted by many companies requires employees to continuously look for ways to add value to the organization, making them more responsible for their own work and careers—while giving them the freedom and resources to perform well.[29]

Employers are more aware of the need to make work meaningful, even for the lowest-level employees who must perform mundane tasks. A number of companies have implemented programs to help employees realize their values and find more personal meaning on the job, that is, opportunities for self-actualization. For example, Silicon Graphics, Inc., gives annual "spirit" awards that include Hawaiian vacations and sitting on a management advisory board for a year. Lotus Development Corp. formed a "soul" committee to study ways to improve employee morale, resulting in more flexible work hours and inclusion of subordinates' views in performance evaluations of some senior managers. These and the hundreds of other programs in existence often provide an additional benefit by helping employees achieve a better balance between their personal and work lives.[30]

BUILDING MARKETS FOR THE LONG TERM

Marketing managers must build long-term relationships with customers, suppliers, employees, and other important constituents. The traditional transactional approach to marketing is insufficient in most cases today. Instead, it is necessary to build and maintain strategic alliances and functional networks.

Relationship Marketing versus Transaction Marketing

Relationships with customers have become a primary concern of marketers, as described below. The more traditional model of marketing considered a marketer actively involved in managing a marketing mix to match the needs of passive customers in a fragmented market. The focus was on products and transactions. Today's marketers (particularly those in industrial markets) are converting these unrelated market fragments into niches, with more focus on relationships and interactions, because they now have a better understanding of the long-term interactive relationships that are formed between buyers and sellers.

Companies are moving away from the mass-marketing strategies of the past to the practice of *relationship marketing*. Relationship marketing involves treating each customer as a unique segment to maximize customer share. New technologies make it possible to begin outside the company by knowing more about the wants and needs of key customers and then working backward to develop strategies for the marketing organization and brand.

Relationship (or database) marketing, as it is perceived by packaged-goods marketers and retailers, has resulted in a number of changes in the marketing process.

Databases contain coded and specified information that makes it possible to tailor marketing decisions to specific customer traits and buying behavior, thus enhancing the opportunity for a long-term relationship between buyer and seller. Customer databases are used frequently as an important tool for direct-marketing programs. Direct marketing can be done without an extensive customer database, but merely contacting customers directly is insufficient to build relationships.

Networking

Network organization
Flexible coalition or confederation guided from a central hub to develop and manage resources, alliances, and other factors that encompass the network.

A number of marketing organizations, such as IBM and Corning Inc., have reinvented themselves as "network" organizations. A **network organization** is a flexible coalition or confederation guided from a hub where key functions include development and management of strategic alliances, financial resource and technology coordination, core competence and strategy definition and management, developing customer relationships, and managing information resources that encompass the network (Figure 1.4). Marketing is the function responsible for keeping all partners in the network focused on the customer and informed about competitor product offerings and changing customer needs and expectations.[31]

IBM used the network approach in designing the personal computer. An IBM management task force gathered informally at a Florida retreat. Actual manufacturing depended on a network of hardware and software suppliers for all components. IBM contributed design work, an assembly plant, and testing time and later brought back some manufacturing activities. The IBM experience represents a new type of organization, where the traditional approach to the purpose and organization of the marketing function is reexamined. In a network organization, marketing activities are focused on long-term relationships with customers, partnerships, and strategic alliances.[32] Such efforts may involve cross-functional teams that work directly with external customers to design and execute total-quality-management principles.

FIGURE 1.4

Network Organization

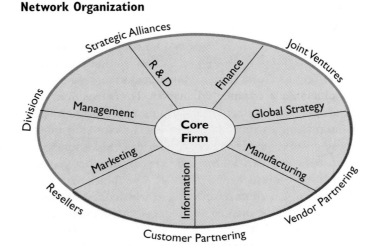

Source: Federick E. Webster, Jr., "The Changing Role of Marketing in the Corporation," *Journal of Marketing,* Vol. 56 (October 1992), p. 9. Reprinted by permission of the American Marketing Association.

FIGURE 1.5

....

The Range of Marketing Relationships

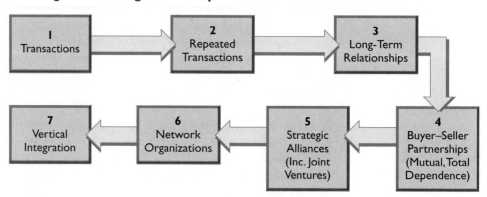

Source: Federick E. Webster, Jr., "The Changing Role of Marketing in the Corporation," *Journal of Marketing,* Vol. 56 (October 1992), p. 5. Reprinted by permission of the American Marketing Association.

....

Building and Maintaining Strategic Alliances

....

Strategic alliance
Formal or informal relationship that in essence creates a new venture within the context of an organization's long-term strategic plan.

The range of marketing relationships extends from a single transaction to vertical integration, as shown in Figure 1.5. A true **strategic alliance** takes the form of an entirely new venture, such as the partnership between a supplier and its customer. Such an alliance should be formed and achieve goals within the context of a company's long-term strategic plan. Because such strategic alliances are focused on improving a firm's competitive position, they can be viewed as an important marketing phenomenon. Marketing is involved in the formation and management of strategic alliances because of their involvement with customers, resellers, or competitors for the development of new technology, new products, and new markets.[33]

Summary

....

New opportunities and challenges arise from the rapidly changing environment in which today's marketers operate. Marketing management decisions are affected by both internal and external forces—from a single buyer to a world marketplace. Increased globalization and computerization, new technology, the Internet and the World Wide Web, and redesigned organizational structures have both positively and negatively affected the marketing management process.

The definition and role of marketing in the organization have shifted from a traditional transaction-based view to one that perceives marketing as a mutually beneficial exchange process built on long-term relationships between buyers and sellers.

Marketing management occurs at three distinct levels: organizational (culture), strategic business unit (strategy), and operating level (tactics). Marketing is the process of exchanging tangible goods, services, ideas, time, and other intangibles that represent value between two or more parties.

The future role of marketing is driven by a newly defined, expanded marketing concept that is customer-focused, market-driven, global in scope, and flexible in its ability to deliver superior value to continuously changing markets.

The marketing mix consists of an organization's products, price, place, and promotion. Each of these strategic elements also has had to respond to environmental changes.

Changes in organizational structures, market demand, and technology not only have redefined the marketing function but also have altered the way in which marketing decisions are made and executed. The relationship between marketing and other business functions is characterized by increased interdependence as cross-functional teams work together. Entrepreneurships and nonprofit organizations that use marketing tools are achieving greater success in reaching their objectives.

Customer satisfaction is critical in building long-term relationships. Thus marketers must continuously monitor changes in markets and buying behavior and involve the customer earlier in the marketing process.

Value-added marketing strategies center on the right combination of quality, service, and value from the customer's perspective. Customer satisfaction also relies on effective internal marketing to employees who must be trained and empowered to meet customer needs. Internal marketing is a major factor in employee satisfaction and productivity, which translates into higher levels of customer satisfaction and profitability.

Relationship marketing, strategic alliances, and networking are important ways to build long-term relationships with customers, suppliers, and other partners. These relationships are key factors in the new role of marketing in organizations.

Questions

1. List the major forces that make up (a) the internal marketing environment and (b) the external marketing environment. Name internal and external crises that have brought about change in a marketing organization. Evaluate the response of marketing managers to these situations. How would you have responded?

2. Describe the four major environmental changes that have an impact on marketing decisions. Identify and analyze a current marketing situation that illustrates a response to each of these environmental pressures.

3. Discuss the evolution of marketing approaches used by organizations to sell their goods and

services. Give examples of each concept, explaining why elements of each may continue to exist in today's markets.

4. Create your own definition of *marketing*. How is this similar/dissimilar to the definition given in the text, and why?

5. What does *marketing as value exchange* mean? Describe the "value" you received in a recent purchase of (a) clothing, (b) a restaurant meal, (c) educational services, (d) household products, and (e) a gift for a family member or friend.

6. Discuss the changes that have taken place in organizational structures and the impact of these changes on performance of the marketing function for (a) a new automobile, (b) a new movie release, (c) an existing brand of detergent, and (d) computer software targeted at a manufacturing firm.

7. Define *customer satisfaction*. Based on recent purchases, discuss specific factors that led to your satisfaction and/or dissatisfaction with this experience. What role, if any, does the customer play in ensuring satisfaction?

8. Explain the relationship between internal marketing, customer satisfaction, and profitability.

9. Discuss and give examples of (a) relationship marketing, (b) networking, and (c) strategic alliances.

Exercises

1. Outline a possible marketing mix (product, place, price, promotion/communications) for (a) a new car, (b) a new movie, (c) an existing brand of detergent, and (d) computer software targeted at a manufacturing firm.

2. Contact a nonprofit organization in your community and determine whether and how marketing tools are currently used to achieve its objectives. Include marketing's place in the organizational structure, assignment of responsibility for marketing tasks, and an evaluation of current marketing activities. What are your recommendations for changing or expanding this

nonprofit organization's marketing program? Justify your answer.

3. Interview a small business owner or manager regarding the effect of the environmental forces described in the text (globalization, computerization and databases, the Internet and the World Wide Web, and organizational restructuring) on his or her business from a marketing perspective.

Endnotes

1. Thomas A. Stewart, "Welcome to the Revolution," *Fortune* (December 13, 1993), pp. 66–68, 70, 72, 76, 80.

2. Ralph S. Alexander (chairman), *Marketing Definitions: A Glossary of Terms* (Chicago: American Marketing Association, 1960), p. 15. Reprinted by permission of the American Marketing Association.

3. "AMA Board Approves New Definition," *Marketing News* (March 1, 1985), p. 1. Reprinted by permission of the American Marketing Association.

4. Frederick E. Webster, Jr., "The Changing Role of Marketing in the Corporation," *Journal of Marketing* 56 (October 1992), pp. 1–17.

5. G. Worth George, "What Part of No Don't You Understand?" *Fund Raising Management* 23(6) (August 1992), pp. 38–41.

6. Philip Kotler, *Marketing Management: Analysis, Planning, Implementation, and Control,* 8th ed. (Englewood Cliffs, NJ: Prentice-Hall, 1994), p. 29.

7. Frederick E. Webster, Jr., "Defining the New Marketing Concept," *Marketing Management* 2(4) (1994), pp. 23–31.

8. Sunita Wadekar Bhargava, "Espresso, Sandwiches, and a Sea of Books," *Business Week* (July 26, 1993), p. 81.

9. Peter Coy, Joy Billups, and Lars Hansen, "Blue-Sky Research Comes Down to Earth," *Business Week* (July 3, 1995), pp. 78–80.

10. Kenneth G. Hardy, "Tough New Marketing Realities," *Business Quarterly* 57(3) (Spring 1993), pp. 77–82.

11. Webster (1992), *op. cit.*

12. Larry Belford, "The Changing Role of Market Research," *Medical Marketing and Media* 29(1) (January 1994), pp. 50–54.

13. Webster (1992), *op. cit.,* p. 10.

14. Bob Donath, "Solving the Manufacturing vs. Marketing Contradiction," *Marketing News* 26(24) (November 1992), p. 21.

15. Robert D. Hisrich, "The Need for Marketing in Entrepreneurship," *Journal of Consumer Marketing* 9(3) (Summer 1992), pp. 43–47.

16. Andrew E. Serwer, "Lessons from America's Fastest Growing Companies," *Fortune* (August 8, 1994), pp. 42–62; "Your Child Gets More Out of Childhood at Gymboree" (1997), Gymboree Home Page: *http://www.service.com/Gymboree/home.html.*

17. Philip Kotler, "Strategies for Introducing Marketing into Nonprofit Organizations," *Journal of Marketing* 43 (January 1979), pp. 37–44.

18. Keith H. Hammonds and Sandra Jones, "Good Help Is Hard to Find," *Business Week* (April 4, 1994), pp. 100–101.

19. Stephen Kreider Yoder, "How H-P Used Tactics of the Japanese to Beat Them at Their Game," *Wall Street Journal* (September 8, 1994), pp. A1, A9.

20. Dennis Rodkin, "Marketing to Men—A Manly Sport: Building Loyalty," *Advertising Age* 62(16) (April 15, 1991), pp. S1, S12.

21. Richard Kitaeff, "Customer Satisfaction: An Integrative Approach," *Marketing Research: A Magazine of Management & Applications* 5(2) (Spring 1993), p. 4.

22. William E. Storts, "Using Technology to Shape S&L Marketing Strategies," *Bottomline (BTL)* 7(3) (March 1990), pp. 11–16.

23. Walter B. Herbst, "The Changing Role of the American Designer," *Appliance Manufacturer* 39(9) (September 1991), pp. 23–24.

24. David Woodruff, "Bug Control at Chrysler," *Business Week* (August 22, 1994), p. 26.

25. "Automotive: C&A's Largest Market, By Far," *Textile World* 143 (June 1993), pp. 56–60.

26. R. Eric Reidenbach and Ann P. Minton, "Customer Service Segments: Strategic Implications for the Commercial Banking Industry," *Journal of Professional Services Marketing* 6(2) (1992), pp. 129–142.

27. Ronald Henkoff, "Service Is Everybody's Business," *Fortune* (June 27, 1994), pp. 48–60.

28. Rahul Jacob, "Why Some Customers Are More Equal Than Others," *Fortune* (September 19, 1994), pp. 215-224.

29. Brian O'Reilly, "The New Deal: What Companies and Employees Owe One Another," *Fortune* (June 1994), pp. 44–47, 50, 52.

30. G. Pascal Zachary, "The New Search for Meaning in 'Meaningless' Work," *Wall Street Journal* (January 9, 1997), B1, B2.

31. Webster (1992), *op. cit.*

32. Webster (1992), *op. cit.*

33. Webster (1992), *op. cit.*

CHAPTER 2

Forces of Change and Their Impact

The Marketing Ecocycle

Four Business Revolutions

Impact of Change on Strategic and Tactical Marketing Decisions

---

Did the dinosaurs hold management training seminars when their world started changing? "No longer are we guaranteed good weather, plentiful food and big mud holes to wallow in," said the facilitator, a tyranno-saurus. "We have to take responsibility for our own survival. If we don't adapt, we're history." To which a weary brontosaurus, from his perspective in the middle of the food chain, replied, "We've always done things this way. Why change? Besides, you guys are always coming up with these hot survival fads and they never stick. Remember values-based evolution?"[1]

Transforming a Motor Car Giant into an Integrated High-Technology Juggernaut: Daimler-Benz

The three-pointed star has been recognized throughout the world as the trademark of Mercedes vehicles. For many years, the company clung to the belief that consumers would continue to pay dearly to drive the best vehicle in the world and did not feel the need to expand its product lines.

In the late 1980s, Edzard Reuter, then chairman of Mercedes-Benz and the *Kapitan* of German industry, correctly forecasted that the era of glob-alization had arrived and that Mercedes-Benz needed to enter new mar-kets and develop new products to balance the cyclic sweep of the automotive industry. Today, Mercedes-Benz is an integrated technology company that is still widely known throughout the world for its luxury automobiles, as well as trucks, aircraft, space systems, microelectronics, trains, satellites, and engines.

Reuter is the visionary and driving force that revitalized Daimler-Benz's once-stodgy corporate culture and gave the company a global presence. How do you transform a $67 billion behemoth with 330,600 employees on six continents into a market-oriented company that can anticipate market trends and respond quickly? Reuter did this by eliminat-ing jobs, cutting costs, tapping global financial markets, opening factories throughout the world, and diversifying from the company's vehicle-making base.

What were the results of Daimler-Benz's transformation? In 1995, the formerly parochial German company was listed on 17 stock exchanges

29

throughout the world. It built cars in South Africa, southern Alabama, and South Korea; it built minivans in China and railroads in Shanghai and other exotic places; and it was a major competitor in microelectronics and aerospace. Mercedes-Benz's global sales revenues have increased, largely due to the popularity of the C-class car introduced in 1994, which revitalized the popularity and perceived value of German-made luxury automobiles. Likewise, bottom-line profitability has improved as a result of restructuring and cost-cutting measures.

Reuter has been modest about his accomplishments, saying he did what was necessary to "compel a company that had grown unwieldy to be more responsive to economic realities." He cautions that success can make a company inattentive to change and that companies like Daimler-Benz must have an existing, technology-oriented global vision. His corporate vision was expressed in the words of Antoine de Saint-Exupery at a stockholders' meeting in the late 1980s: "If you want to build a ship, then don't drum up men to gather wood, give orders, and divide the work. Rather, teach them to yearn for the far and endless sea." This vision is carried out in a more open, communicative corporate culture, with mutual respect for the opinions of others. Reuter compares an organization to a dinosaur that faces extinction if it doesn't pay attention and adapt to changes. Thanks to his efforts, Daimler-Benz will not share the fate of the dinosaur; instead, it has been transformed into an elephant that can dance. The size of the elephant and its global impact are evident in its change from being only an automobile manufacturer to becoming an integrated technological group. Daimler-Benz AG, the parent company, has overall management control of operations and oversees four "pillars" or groups of diverse products and services.

Subsidiaries are reviewed constantly for their ability to contribute to the company's profitability, resulting in strategic acquisitions, divestitures, or mergers to enhance their businesses. Jürgen Schrempp replaced Reuter as chief executive in 1995. At that time, profits were sliding due to the rising German mark (and high labor costs), management disputes, and losses from Reuter's diversification strategy. Schrempp's approach has been to focus on the core automotive and truck business, which generates most of the group's profits, and to close or slim down operations in the Daimler-Benz Industrie and DASA Daimler-Benz Aerospace units.

These business units include

- Mercedes-Benz, which builds passenger cars and commercial vehicles. (The company merged with the American auto manufacturer Chrysler Corporation in 1998 to form Daimler-Chrysler, expanding global opportunities for both the Mercedes and Chrysler brands. Freightliner Corp. purchased Ford Motor Co.'s heavy-duty trucks unit in 1997.)
- AEG Daimler-Benz Industrie, which is involved with rail systems, microelectronics, diesel engines, automation, and energy-systems technology (with emphasis on transportation).
- Daimler-Benz Aerospace, which constructs aircraft (Airbus Dornier), space systems, defense and civil systems, and propulsion systems and has interests in other business fields.
- Daimler-Benz InterServices, which trades in high-quality services (e.g., financial services, insurance brokerage, trading, mobile communications, marketing, and real estate management).

Daimler-Benz clearly has evolved within the constraints of its environment into an energetic elephant that is nimble enough to dance its way around the world.

Sources: Mike Sheridan, "Making Daimler-Benz Dance," *SKY* (May 1995), pp. 58-74; Silvia Ascarelli, "Daimler-Benz Swings to a First-Half Net after Shedding Money-Losing Units," *Wall Street Journal* (August 30, 1996), p. A6; "Daimler Halts Funds to Ailing Fokker," *Wall Street Journal* (January 23, 1996), p. A10; Nichole M. Christian and Matt Marshall, "Ford to Sell Its Producer of Big Trucks," *Wall Street Journal* (February 20, 1997), p. A3; Oscar Suris, "Now, BMW and Mercedes Seem Sensible," *Wall Street Journal* (November 6, 1996), pp. B1, B8; John Templeman and David Woodruff, "How Mercedes Trumped Chrysler in China," *Business Week* (July 31, 1995), pp. 50-52; John Templeman, "The Shocks for Daimler's New Driver," *Business Week* (August 21, 1995), pp. 38-40.

Change is inevitable, as the saying goes, and nowhere does it seem to be more evident than in the marketing environment. The impact of change is felt throughout the world as marketing managers make far-reaching strategic and tactical decisions to avoid the fate of the dinosaurs. Successful marketers concentrate on building solid internal and external relationships as a foundation for dealing with the opportunities and risks inherent in coping with change. In order to compete in a rapidly changing global environment, the marketing process relies on managing information effectively and capitalizes on the use of cross-functional teams, integrative and interactive marketing, and strategic partnerships such as the Daimler-Chrysler alliance.

THE MARKETING ECOCYCLE

Complex natural systems experience a continuous process of change from birth to maturation and throughout their continued development, ultimately facing a crisis of some sort. Crisis may lead to extinction (like the dinosaurs), or it can be viewed as "creative destruction" that leads to the renewal or rebirth of the system. Survival depends on the ability of the system to renew (or reinvent) itself and once again emerge as a living, vibrant system. This process of change and renewal is referred to as an *ecocycle,* which can be pictured in the form of an infinity loop (as shown in Figure 2.1, where it is applied to a marketing organization).

David Hurst adapted the theory of natural systems to explain the process of crisis and renewal experienced by most organizations as they evolve.[2] The general

FIGURE 2.1

Marketing Organization Ecocycle

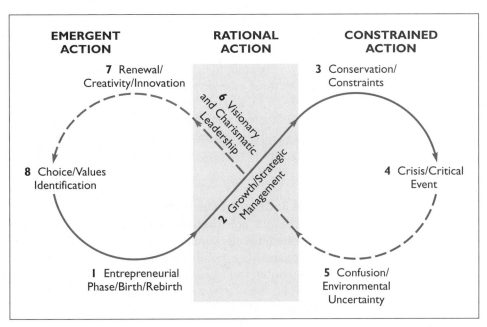

management literature tends to focus on the rationality of managers and the stability of organizations. However, when unexpected random events do occur, it is helpful to view organizational change as an ongoing process—one that should be expected and welcomed for the creative opportunities it provides. This means "that a manager's influence is often occasional, indirect, and delayed rather than constant, direct, and immediate. It recognizes that managers may often be constrained in their ability to act and confused as to what to do."[3] This approach enables marketing managers to view the process of crisis and renewal as a way to maintain continuity during periods of change. Natural ecocycles show us that patterns tend to form "rhythms of life" as they repeat themselves. The key for marketers is to be able to recognize that these patterns will recur.

The Natural Ecocycle

. . . .

Natural ecocycle
Continuous loop of birth, conservation, creative destruction, and renewal followed by natural organisms.

A **natural ecocycle** has four basic phases: birth, conservation, creative destruction, and renewal. These phases are continuous, with some part of the system in every phase at any one time. Hurst uses the forest ecosystem to illustrate the phases in the natural ecocycle.[4] Although the continuous loop has no absolute beginning or end, this chapter will provide a simple description of the complex process by starting with the birth phase of the conventional forest life cycle. (Later an extended ecocycle model will be applied to managing change in marketing organizations.)

Phase 1: Birth.   Ecologists call this the *stage of exploitation,* where a number of processes occur simultaneously, leading to rapid colonization of the forest. Resources are plentiful and readily available, and little investment is required to harvest them (e.g., fallen trees). Eventually, this space also becomes crowded with natural growth.

Phase 2: Conservation.   As the forest space becomes more crowded, competition intensifies, and there is a need for more efficiency. A greater investment is needed for survival, and resources are used to defend territories. The entire system is becoming more tightly connected, and resources are more constrained. Hierarchical structures emerge that dominate the system and control the niches beneath them (e.g., a very large tree). The ecosystem is more homogeneous and specialized, making it more vulnerable to catastrophe (e.g., forests containing only limited species of trees that are susceptible to disease and insects). This reduced flexibility, variety, and resilience of the forest can result in catastrophe if there is a disaster (e.g., a forest fire).

Phase 3: Creative Destruction.   Continuing with the example of the forest fire, the system is only partially destroyed in order to be renewed. The existing highly developed, tightly connected hierarchical structure is shattered. Those that will survive are those mobile enough to escape (e.g., forest animals), those prepared for the situation, and those that are lucky. The forest ecosystem is out of equilibrium, and even small events occurring in the system can create large changes in outcomes.[5]

Phase 4: Renewal.   This phase represents the reconception of the system. The dynamics are difficult to observe because the large, conservative hierarchical systems that dominated the ecosystem in phase 2 have now been reduced to small-scale, widely scattered structures. Resources become loosely connected to one another, forming a large-scale network. Once again, conditions favor fast growth because resources are more accessible and little investment is required to harvest them. The ecospace now can be recolonized by a large variety of small-scale organisms in this far-from-equilibrium system within the natural constraints of the overall environment.

The Marketing Organization Ecocycle

Marketing organization ecocycle
An adaptation of the natural ecocycle with the addition of the human ability to take conscious, rational action.

The difference between a natural system, such as a forest, and a marketing organization is the ability of humans to take conscious, rational action. Thus Hurst adds rational action to the emergent and constrained action components of the natural ecocycle.[6] The **marketing organization ecocycle** illustrated in Figure 2.1 and discussed below extends the model and applies it to managing change in the marketing environment. The rational action component is expanded to incorporate the problem-solving process under proactive and reactive conditions.

Like complex natural ecosystems, the marketing management process can be viewed as a continuous system of change and renewal following the natural rhythms of an organization's existence. Note that Figure 2.1 is comprised of two half-loops. The solid-line portion of the loop is similar to a traditional S-shaped life-cycle curve. This is generally a period of growth and planning where outcomes are somewhat predictable. Outcomes are less predictable in the dotted-line portion of the loop, which represents crisis and renewal in response to change in the organization's environment.[7] Both loops represent a learning curve under different conditions and with different motivations.

Phases of the marketing organization ecocycle are discussed briefly below and are illustrated with familiar marketing examples. However, the processes of integration and disintegration that characterize the system make it difficult to follow the progress of any one organization through the entire ecocycle. The phases are numbered for discussion, but in reality, the marketing management process is a continuous loop without a clearly defined beginning or end.

Phase 1: Entrepreneurial Phase.   In the formative start-up (or a later regenerative stage), the organizational culture promotes spontaneous behavior and learning. The entrepreneurial organization prospers and grows in a seemingly unplanned way, eventually becoming larger and more structured. Planning tends to be short term and involves tactical decisions (often in the absence of a long-term strategy to provide direction).

For example, in Nike's start-up phase, entrepreneurs Phil Knight and Bill Bowerman had the vision and energy to market a high-performance running shoe that soon replaced the ordinary sneaker and created major changes in the athletic shoe industry. Their vision was to gain a competitive advantage over popular German imports by applying high-technology, mass manufacturing, and sophisticated marketing techniques to shoes made at low cost in factories in the Far East. In this early stage, there were no clear guidelines for running the business and no clear boundaries between Nike and its environment. Those who were involved in designing, manufacturing, selling, and wearing the shoes were evolving together through loosely connected relationships and an informal communications network. The entrepreneurs and their employees had a shared vision and enthusiasm for working together to solve problems and to get the job done.[8]

Phase 2: Strategic Growth.   As the organization increases in size and complexity, managers lose the control of the operation that they once enjoyed. More emphasis is placed on formal strategic planning and proactive problem solving. Companies formalize those things which work well into a strategy that can be repeated in different situations. Nike's growth during the 1970s was based on extending the strategy that gained it a leading position in high-performance track and field shoes to products for other sports. A flexible organization and a little investment in production facilities enabled Nike to move from basketball to tennis, football, soccer, and other activities. There were few precedents for Nike to follow in developing the aggressive marketing strategy that was working so well for it. Nike was among the first to capitalize on the endorsements of professional athletes and coaches and to sponsor the Olympic Games and other events. Learning by trial and error led to repeatable strategies in a largely untapped sports shoe market. However, with this success came increased competition and a more sophisticated consumer. Specialization increased, and new materials and production methods required more efficiency.

Phase 3: Conservation/Constraints.   Behavior of the marketing organization becomes constrained in the face of increased competition (and possible lack of competitive edge), scarcity of resources, and environmental threats (e.g., recession, new legislation, entry of formidable competitors). Some would argue that constraints keep the business from straying from its mission. Conversely, constraints may inhibit innovative processes and the ability to adapt to change. For example, for Daimler-Benz in 1995, the rising German mark, high labor costs, management disputes, and losses from the company's diversification strategy placed significant financial constraints on the company's ability to be profitable.

Phase 4: Crisis/Critical Event.   The organization now finds itself vulnerable. Any crisis can threaten its survival. On the positive side, a crisis can shatter the constraints that hampered the organization in phase 3. Unwieldy hierarchies are flattened, formal policy manuals are discarded, unions and employees may join forces with management to save the firm, and new channels of information are opened. The typical result is a renewed focus on the core business and a downsizing of the operation. (Note that critical events may occur during all phases of the ecocycle in a learning organization. Further, marketing managers may create their own preemptive crises by restructuring the business, bringing in a new style of management, or other means for the purpose of using innovative processes to renew the organization.)

For example, a number of years ago, the U.S. automotive industry experienced a serious dilemma on several fronts: the 1973 worldwide oil crisis, Lee Iacocca's move from Ford to Chrysler in 1978 just before the fall of the shah of Iran, and extremely high interest rates (over 20 percent) in the United States that significantly slowed auto sales.[9] All the major U.S. auto manufacturers were affected by these critical events and subsequently entered the next phase of the ecocycle—confusion and uncertainty over their collective future.

Phase 5: Confusion/Environmental Uncertainty.   In this phase, the organization moves from what appears to be the end of its life cycle into the early stages of the renewal curve of the ecocycle. (This process is similar to the evolution of social and political systems that have arisen from oppression or other crises.) Confusion and uncertainty prevail as managers attempt to adapt to change so as to salvage the operation. In response to the crisis, additional constraints may be generated internally or externally through changes in the corporate culture, mergers and acquisitions, shortage of resources, and other factors. The challenge is to use creative problem solving to find a more innovative way to do business.

The plight of the U.S. auto manufacturers discussed earlier, along with financing concerns, threatened their survival. The industry infrastructure changed drastically as many costs were shifted from manufacturers to suppliers, and new relationships were formed. Large, vertically integrated firms found it difficult to adopt more competitive and cost-effective ways of doing business. Through this process the "Big Three" became more accepting of Japanese automakers' production methods and entered into cooperative arrangements with them. The learning process seemed slow, but new methods were developed to facilitate the renewal process as the companies responded to changes in their environment.[10]

Phase 6: Visionary and Charismatic Leadership.   Many organizations have been able to turn devastating crises into memorable successes through the efforts of charismatic leaders. Management experts maintain that organizations survive during this period because of leadership and shared values.

For example, Jack Welch has been known as a charismatic leader at General Electric Co. for the past two decades. Welch reorganized GE to focus on its core business and encouraged managers to be creative and to take leadership roles at all levels in the newly decentralized organization. Open communication and the sharing of ideas were encouraged through cross-functional teams and personal relationships to facilitate the renewal process.[11]

Phases 7 and 8: Renewal/Creativity/Innovation and Choice/Values Identification.   The close relationships and interdependence of these learning-curve phases and the entrepreneurial/rebirth phase described earlier make it difficult to separate them for discussion. The renewal phase is characterized by a creative problem-solving process in which alternatives are explored and evaluated. Choices are made among the alternatives, generally consistent with the values of the organization. The examples of the charismatic leadership of General Electric's Jack Welch, Nike's Phil Knight, and Microsoft's Bill Gates illustrate the need to create an environment that encourages creativity and innovation. Each of these organizations has recognized the need to maintain maximum flexibility and personal initiative in order to develop the new ideas needed for success. For example, during its renewal phase, Nike has shown an ability to "break down the fences" in its now much larger, more formal organization. Novelty continues to be introduced to the enterprise through methods such as the "Launch Group" that successfully took the Air Jordan shoe to market, intentionally disrupting the formal system to retain an entrepreneurial spirit.

Most start-up organizations have clearly defined values that drive their organizational and marketing decisions. Unfortunately, some lose their sense of core values during the growth cycle, making it difficult to maintain their identity during times of crisis. In the renewal phase, the organization has a new opportunity to define (or redefine) the values that drive the business. This may mean new products, new markets, and more creative use of the marketing mix.

Creative Destruction and Innovation

Constant change in the environment ultimately affects the life of a marketing organization, just as it does in any natural or human ecocycle. We have seen that it is sometimes beneficial to create a crisis to ensure the ongoing viability of a company. Many innovative marketing opportunities have emerged from internal and external environmental threats. Wars have led to new technology and communications devices. Weather-related disasters have created ideas for new housing materials, and automobile and airplane accidents have created ideas for safer cars and planes. Bankruptcies have enabled companies to reorganize and reinvent themselves. AT&T's divestiture of the "Baby Bell" subsidiaries in the 1980s created smaller, more flexible organizations that can adapt to a changing environment more easily and can capitalize on the changes with new marketing innovations.

Remember that changes are inevitable and that crises will occur. Whether these events will result in creative destruction—or just total destruction—is up to the ability of marketing managers to exploit positive events and to create marketing opportunities out of negative crises.

FOUR BUSINESS REVOLUTIONS

Four simultaneous revolutions are at the forefront of a vast spectrum of change: *globalization of markets, growth of information technology and computer networks, changing management hierarchies,* and *the information age economy* that is a product of these revolutionary forces.[12] (These "winds of change" are illustrated in Figure 2.2.) As shown in Table 2.1, if marketers are to survive and prosper in the twenty-first century, they must continue to reorient themselves to anticipate change, capitalize on marketing opportunities, and minimize the negative consequences of unwelcome surprises that occur within the context of the environmental forces described earlier.

The First Revolution: Globalization

Globalization
A world view of a global marketplace implying world standards and common customer needs across nations.

Today's marketers operate in a global economy. Whether a company restricts itself to domestic markets, several international markets, or markets to the entire world, the effect of **globalization** cannot be avoided. It may appear in the origin of finished goods or component parts, product design, distribution strategies, new foreign competition, products to satisfy multicultural ethnic markets, or other forms. Thus the globalization of markets requires an understanding of both customers and

FIGURE 2.2

Business Revolutions and Change

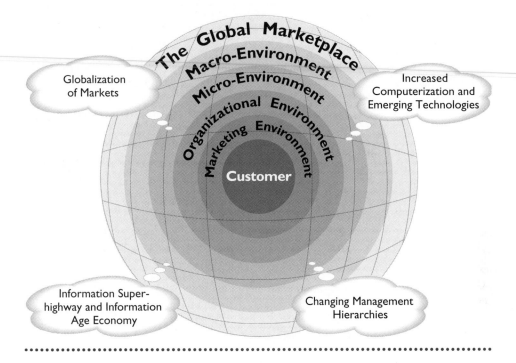

products and the need for a good fit between the two. McDonald's, Coca-Cola, and AT&T have successfully entered many diverse markets with a basic corporate mission and set of core values that translate across national boundaries, cultures, and stages of economic development. (See Figure 2.3.) On a much smaller scale, a locally owned Mexican restaurant or jewelry importer also exhibits the effects of globalization.

The North American Free Trade Agreement (NAFTA) created an economic partnership to expand trade across the U.S., Mexican, and Canadian borders. Canada, one of the most important customers of the United States, is buying even more from American producers—from heavy machinery to baby carriages, as well as large increases in telecommunications equipment, music tapes, and CDs, for example. Mexican companies have bought more made-in-the-U.S.A. products from manufacturers such as Caterpillar, which had a 77 percent increase in exports to Mexico in the first 6 months of 1994.[13] The emergence of the European Common Market and other trade agreements, such as the General Agreement on Tariffs and Trade (GATT), make international trade easier and more desirable as new markets open to companies throughout the world.

Today, consumers and organizational buyers judge suppliers by world standards. When a company can enter almost any market, success is judged by who is the best in the world. The key is to determine the world standard and benchmark against world champions in every facet of the business (e.g., product design, manufacturing, distribution, and customer satisfaction). It is also important to watch for trends

TABLE 2.1
··············
Convergence of Business Revolutions and Environmental Factors

| Environmental Factors | Business Revolutions | | | |
	Globalization of Markets	Growth of Information Technology and Computer Networks	Changing Management Hierarchies	Information Age Economy
Customer (Buying Unit)	Increasingly diverse national and ethnic mix of customers	Internet shopping; purchase of high-tech products	Customer may be included in marketing management decisions	Increased opportunities for direct marketing
Marketing Function ("4 P's")	McDonald's restaurant location decisions; Coca-Cola's ad campaigns	Shorter product life cycles and new product development time; marketing research	Networks and cross-functional teams	DSS; two-way communication; better information for management decisions
Organizational Environment (All Business Functions)	Integration of business functions to produce global products (such as "world car")	DSS; internal communication (LANs)	Flatter organizational structures; more use of project teams (e.g., Chrysler)	Quick access to business data for planning (e.g., sales, accounting, financial)
Micro-environment (Direct influence on marketing functions; Marketer can exert some control)	NAFTA trade agreement; new marketing intermediaries and distribution channels	Cellular phones and wireless communication	Increased outsourcing to suppliers and marketing intermediaries	More current and accurate competitive information
Macro-environment (Marketer cannot directly control these forces)	AT&T's Network Systems Group's joint venture in China and other countries	Alliances among technical companies	Flatter organizations due to increased computerization; increased importance of organizational culture	Information superhighway market information regarding market and demographic trends; timely capture of economic data, etc.

or events that may change these standards and then set goals that stretch performance. At one time, German automobiles were considered top quality in the world; then the Japanese entered overseas markets with models that offered superior customer value—high quality for the price. Detroit's Big Three auto makers believe that today they are positioned to deliver a world standard of quality at the best price in the world. The winners are determined in the constantly changing global

FIGURE 2.3
··
McDonald's Establishments Throughout the World

1948	The world's first limited-menu, self-service, drive-in was opened in San Bernardino, California by Richard and Maurice McDonald.
1954	Ray Kroc was granted exclusive U.S. franchising rights by the McDonald brothers.
1955	Ray Kroc opened his first McDonald's in Des Plaines, Illinois, and founded the company that evolved into McDonald's Corporation.
1996	Year end systemwide sales were $31.812 billion. • Over 59 percent of the operating income comes from McDonald's restaurants outside the U.S.
1997	More than 23,000 restaurants in over 100 countries. • Nearly 12,400 U.S. outlets own 42 percent of the nation's fast-food hamburger business. • Opening five new overseas outlets each day, focusing on the Asia/Pacific region and Central Europe.
1998	Acquired minority interest in Chipolte Mexican Grill, a small Mexican food restaurant chain.
1999	Acquired London coffee chain Aroma, and Donato pizza chain opened 25,000th restaurant.

Source: McDonald's System: http://www.mcdonalds.com/a system; http://www.hoovers.com/premium/profiles.
··

marketplace, where more alliances of auto makers are expected to follow the 1998 megamerger of Daimler-Benz (Germany) and Chrysler (United States), and others such as the sale of Volvo Cars to Ford Motor Company in 1999.

Opportunities to trade in goods and services in the global economy are not restricted to large corporations. Opportunities abound for smaller entrepreneurial firms as well, as shown by the worldwide market success of David Montague's folding mountain bikes, which is described in the box on the next page.

Trends in the U.S. Market
··

A discussion of global markets would not be complete without acknowledging some significant trends in domestic U.S. markets. This subject will be discussed further with buying behavior issues in Chapters 5 and 6. However, within the context of global market changes, the U.S. market is a leading consumer of the world's goods and services—and changes in the U.S. market affect production and distribution decisions made by businesses throughout the world.

The U.S. marketplace emerged as an increasingly complex, multidimensional, multicultural customer base in the 1990s, and the trend is expected to continue into the twenty-first century. The "typical American" no longer exists, and a new middle-class profile is evolving. Four major trends are discussed within the categories of demographic, geographic, income distribution, and lifestyle changes based primarily on comprehensive U.S. Census data.[14]

MARKETING IN THE GLOBAL VILLAGE

Global Bicycle Peddler: David Montague

The information age and advances in technology have leveled the playing field between large and small firms for entrepreneurial firms like Montague Corp., a manufacturer of unique folding mountain bikes. Co-owner David Montague claims that he was weaned on a fax machine, an important tool for sometimes daily transmitting of design changes back and forth between three continents. The bicycle company designs its bikes in Cambridge, Massachusetts, makes them in Taiwan, and sells most of them in Europe. The information technology that underlies the new global economy makes it possible for small businesses like Montague Corp. to compete globally.

In 1984 when the first Montague prototype was built, the design was praised by *Bicycling* magazine as being the best for a full-size, high-performance bicycle that folds. In 1992, Montague Corp. entered a joint venture with BMW, manufacturer of German cars. BMW sold 10,000 bicycles in Germany alone in one year, and the program is now operating in other countries, including the United States. BMW was the official mountain bike sponsor for the 1996 Olympic Games in Atlanta. As part of its promotional effort, BMW provided 1,500 specially designed Official Olympic Games mountain bikes to the Atlanta Committee of the Olympic Games. Other car and bicycle manufacturers have since formed partnerships to link high-performance cars and bicycles as a relationship marketing tool.

Sources: Alan Farnham, "Global—or Just Globaloney?" *Fortune* (June 27, 1994), pp. 97–100; Christen Kinsler, "(Two-)Wheeling and Dealing," *Ward's Auto World* (September 1996), p. 112; Montague home page: bicycle@montagueco.com.

Demographic Changes.   American families, like corporations, are reinventing themselves and changing the traditional household structure, as shown in Table 2.2 and Figure 2.4. This, in turn, has a significant impact on the nation's economy and the ways that marketers respond to these changes. Although married couples still dominate the affluent market, there are fewer married couples with children than in the past. The numbers of single-person, single-parent, and nontraditional, middle-aged, and elderly households have increased, while there are fewer households in the under-35 age group. Marketing implications range from a need for smaller apartments to convenient food packaging and automobile preferences related to household size and age.

Americans are better educated, more technically skilled, and more likely to be employed in service occupations than previously. There also are more Americans, primarily due to a reversal in the declining birth rate of the 1980s, and the influx of 4.6 million immigrants moving to the United States from 1990 to 1995. During this same period, 20.4 million babies were born, and longer life expectancies were reported for the elderly, who are living healthier, more active lifestyles.

Increased consumer diversity presents both opportunities and problems for marketers. One out of every four Americans can be classified as some type of minority, with Hispanics and Asians making up the fastest-growing minority segments. The minority population growth tends to be concentrated among children. Among

TABLE 2.2
·············
Households to 2010

	1995		2000		2010		Percent Change, 1995–2010
	Number	Percent	Number	Percent	Number	Percent	
All Households	98,733	100.0%	103,775	100.0%	114,699	100.0%	16.4%
Under 25	5,156	5.2	4,957	4.8	5,670	4.9	10.0
25 to 34	19,229	19.5	17,229	16.6	16,669	14.5	−13.3
35 to 44	22,963	23.3	24,211	23.3	20,986	18.3	−7.8
45 to 54	17,394	17.6	20,788	20.0	25,298	22.1	45.4
55 to 64	12,327	12.5	13,745	13.2	20,017	17.5	62.4
65 and older	21,664	21.9	22,844	22.0	26,059	22.7	20.2

Note: Numbers in thousands, percent distribution of households by age of householder, and percent change, 1995 to 2010. Numbers may not add to totals due to rounding. Between 1995 and 2010, growth will concentrate in middle-aged households.
Source: Berna Miller, "Household Futures," *American Demographics* (March 1995), p. 4. Reprinted by permission of the author.

all groups, the growth in the youth market is shifting to teenagers, who are more sophisticated consumers than their counterparts of the past.

These population shifts have many implications for marketing. For example, there is a growing need for more goods and services targeted to an older population and more factual, youth-oriented advertising messages for a younger population that is turned off by outrageous claims and "hype." Baby-boomers and the youth market are computer- and technology-literate, increasing the demand for a wide range of products for the home and office. As more people are employed in the service and entertainment industries, businesses will need to adapt their business hours to accommodate those who work in other than 9-to-5 jobs. Clearly, there is a growing market for ethnic foods, literature, entertainment, and other goods and services. Many of these are narrowly targeted and create opportunities for entrepreneurial niche marketers.

Geographic Changes.   Over half of all U.S. residents live in the ten most populous states, led by California, Texas, and New York, with many coming from the Northeast, where the greatest net losses in population have occurred. The South and West have experienced rapid growth, but this growth is increasingly international. Most of the immigrants to the United States between 1990 and 1995 settled in California, Texas, or Florida, accounting for 37 percent of all U.S. growth during that period despite the heavy out-migration from California to other states. These demographic shifts demonstrate the importance of focusing on ethnic, as well as regional, market differences. Geographic shifts, combined with population trends, influence marketing decisions for leisure-time activities, product assortments, retail expansion, and other customer-focused strategies.

Changes in Income Distribution.   Marketers are faced with changes in the distribution of income and how these changes affect spending patterns among various

FIGURE 2.4

....

Demographic Changes in Households

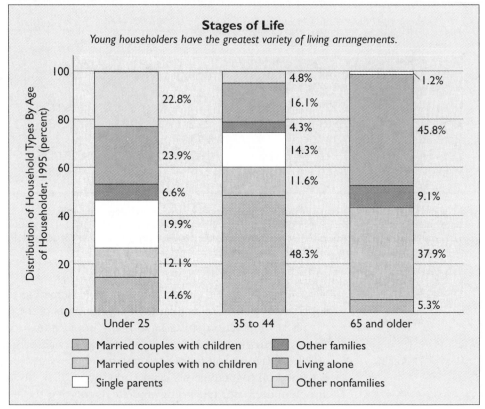

Source: Berna Miller, "Household Futures," *American Demographics* (March 1995), p. 6. Reprinted by permission of the author.

....

market segments. Middle-aged wage earners make up the top-earning households. Although many household incomes have dropped in real terms as a result of corporate downsizing and recessions, households headed by 45- to 54-year-olds have median incomes 48 percent higher than the national average. Despite an increase in average annual income in the United States, median annual income has declined. As income continues to increase in higher-income households, everyone else's income is losing ground. This trend indicates that the middle class is shrinking in terms of average household income and purchasing power. In fact, all household age groups find that they have less to spend, with the youngest experiencing the sharpest declines. The problem of declining disposable income is magnified by rising prices for consumer goods and services, including escalating health and education costs.

These trends in personal income and buying power indicate the importance of value pricing strategies at all income levels, offering best quality at a fair price. Consumers are keeping durable products such as cars and appliances for a longer time, creating a greater need for maintenance services and parts businesses. Homes are claiming more of the consumer dollar for home repairs, remodeling, furnishings, and landscaping, spurring growth in the do-it-yourself (D-I-Y) market and fueling the expansion of D-I-Y power retailers such as Home Depot.

Lifestyle Changes.   From the "land of plenty" mentality of the 1980s when conspicuous spending was the norm, consumers of the mid-1990s showed a tendency to be more practical and value conscious. Consumer researchers describe present American workers, parents, and single adults as "stressed out" due in large part to the uncertainties of corporate downsizing, job insecurity, and longer working hours. The result is a search for healthy ways to relax. Opportunities abound for both for-profit and nonprofit organizations that can respond to the contemporary American mindset. Marketers of personal care services (e.g., spa vacations, physical fitness, yoga) and outdoor activities have capitalized on this trend. Many leisure activities are targeted to families and couples by for-profit companies like Club Med and hotel chains and nonprofit organizations like Little League, churches, scouting, and the YMCA. Stressed consumers find relief in a simple cup of gourmet tea or by visiting one of the increasingly popular coffeehouses that provide a contemporary answer to the happy hour of the 1980s. The rapid expansion of Starbucks and other coffeehouses into malls, bookstores, and other locations illustrates a successful response to changing consumer lifestyles.

Along with less conspicuous consumption, today's value-oriented buyers seek honest bargains but not necessarily "cheap" prices. They want value at a fair price and a quality product that will last. Mass merchandisers and off-price retailers responded quickly to this mood by positioning themselves successfully on the dimensions of price, value, and quality. This strategy appeals to both aging baby-boomers (who buy for themselves and their Generation Y children), and to marketing-averse Generation Xers.

As men and women take on more of each other's life roles and responsibilities, the changing dynamics between the sexes shape consumer attitudes, making it necessary for marketers to use different approaches to sell their products. For example, traditional advertising that is gender-specific is shifting to reflect changing male-female roles.

In summary, most of the changes in the U.S. marketplace have occurred because of population shifts in the distribution of age, ethnic groups, income levels, and consumer lifestyles. These trends have an impact on consumer, industrial, governmental, and nonprofit organizations as they attempt to design the most effective marketing mixes. Using the impact of an aging population as an example, retailers and manufacturers must adjust product assortments to the needs of the elderly. This affects not only retail distribution strategies (e.g., location, delivery, and hours) but also the need for safer, more convenient packaging, lighter-weight materials, and labels that are easy to read. Health care and insurance providers are experiencing a significant upswing in demand for their services by middle-aged baby-boomers and their parents.

The Second Revolution: New and Emerging Technologies

Rapidly emerging technologies redefine our economy as companies develop new goods and services and find new ways to conduct business. Creative use of technology is essential to successful marketing as we enter the twenty-first century. The impact of computers and advances in telecommunications extend from the workplace to the home and leisure activities and permeate our educational system. Customer databases, computer networks, and other technological advances overcome the constraints of geography and time and provide a competitive edge to their users.

Microprocessors, innovative software, and laser optics have taken marketers of tangible goods and intangible services into the information age. Work can be performed literally anywhere with a computer and communications software as management structures flatten, networks and team efforts become the norm, and strategic alliances extend the capabilities of the traditional marketing organization.

Technology and the External Environment.   Outside the firm, many environmental forces have an impact on, and are affected by, technology. Whole industries have been created, re-created, or obliterated by advances in computer power and telecommunications. Cellular telephones and wireless communications, interactive video games, location-based entertainment, more powerful and smaller computers, and computer software are but a few examples of fast-growing, technology-based industries. Product life cycles are shortening as new technology makes the old obsolete, making the new product development process a critical marketing function for those who compete in this fast-paced, high-tech market.

The entertainment industry is redefining and re-creating itself as strategic alliances are formed among cable and telephone companies, television station owners, computer firms, movie producers, and a host of other support organizations as they develop home-based and location-based entertainment venues to appeal to various population segments. Advances in technology also make it convenient for customers to shop or conduct business from their homes or offices, thus changing the distribution system for many goods and services. On-line shopping is becoming increasingly efficient, convenient, and user-friendly. Emerging technology includes standardized software for Web shopping, standard protocol for credit card purchases on the Web (secure electronic transaction, or SET), new merchant-ware for both consumers and business customers, digital IDs, and other technology to make shopping on the Web safer and easier.

The growth in on-line shopping has created lucrative opportunities for companies such as Yahoo!, an Internet search service. Yahoo! scuttled a year-old contract with VISA to develop its own shopping site on the Web, enabling Yahoo! to focus on claiming the lead in the $5 billion that Internet advertising is expected to reach by 2000.[15] Yahoo! has incorporated links to advertising partners (such as Datek, Sabre, and Amicon.com) in its own pages. For this, Yahoo! receives a flat fee and a commission on sales generated by the link.[16]

Emerging information and communications technologies have brought together partners from many diverse organizations. Although many of the technology alliances are occurring among larger companies, a number of entrepreneurs have found exciting opportunities as well. Bill Gross owns a small educational software company called Knowledge Adventure, started in 1991, where his 8-year-old son has served as a new-product tester. Knowledge Adventure creates CD-ROMs that use animation and video clips to explain subjects such as American history, dinosaurs, space, and the human body. At the end of 1994, the company had over 300,000 registered users and over $35 million in annual sales.

Many suitors have attempted to buy Gross's electronic games company or take it public, but Gross was not interested until film producer and director Steven Spielberg came along. Spielberg creates memorable characters to enhance Knowledge Adventure's products, such as replacing a graphic of a human skeleton with an animated character that literally steps into his skin. The Gross-Spielberg combination of interactive software, innovative programming, compelling characters, and special effects has added excitement to educational software.[17]

Transportation methods have benefited from innovative technologies as well. For example, computers are used extensively in designing automobiles and are responsible for many of the features we take for granted in our cars. Aircraft navigation and communications are made easier and safer with high-tech know-how. Innovative applications of existing technology result in new marketing opportunities and a redefined competitive environment. For example, the Eurotunnel that was built as a joint venture between Great Britain and France enables passengers to go from London to Paris by train through a tunnel under the English Channel in about the same time as going by plane, including taxi and airport waits. The 3-hour trip makes it easy for a Parisian to shop at Harrods and a Londoner to visit the Louvre for the day. This not only presents new market opportunities but also creates a new competitive environment within the transportation industry as airlines and railways seek new ways to market their services in a changing world.

Technology and the Internal Environment.   The introduction of new technology may serve as creative destruction, that is, the crisis phase of the marketing organization ecocycle. Leading firms such as Bank of America and American Airlines gained competitive advantage by introducing information technology to their operations. As early as 1950, Bank of America management recognized the need to use technology for a more efficient business operation when a rapid increase in check usage was straining the bank's ability to keep up with demand. The check-clearing process was done manually, going through at least two banks, perhaps requiring the efforts of seven or more employees over more than two days. The implementation and continuous upgrading of an information technology system continue to improve the bank's performance and have facilitated a marketing orientation.

In a similar scenario, American Airlines was having problems about the same time with its manual system of matching passenger lists with seat inventory and obtaining timely flight information, as demand for airline services escalated. American's technological solution was in the development of the computerized SABRE system that handles telephone calls, makes passenger reservations on American and other airlines, and handles other services. The technology adopted by these industry leaders significantly changed the basis of competition within the banking and airline industries, as their information technology applications continued to evolve and competitors emulated their successes with their own applications.[18] Today, the ability to obtain and use timely, accurate information is essential for maintaining a marketing orientation.

Technology and Today's Marketing Orientation: Building Relationships.   As markets change, new products proliferate, competition accelerates, and the pressure on profit margins intensifies, marketing managers must keep up with all aspects of their internal and external environments. The increased capacity of computers and the ability to manage huge databases have made marketing research easier and have facilitated providing timely environmental information for decision support systems. The focus should be on building relationships with customers, suppliers, and other stakeholders by using information effectively in all aspects of the business, such as

TABLE 2.3

Technology and the Marketing Mix

Marketing Mix Element	Technology/Application
Product (Goods and Services)	Computer-assisted product design, automobile design
	Inventory management, retail, manufacturing
Promotion (Communications)	Personal selling, video conferencing
	Advertising, Internet
	Sales promotion, electronic "virtual" displays
	Reseller support, automatic on-line ordering
Place (Distribution)	To customers, Internet
	Warehouses, automated package moving equipment
	Transportation, package tracking
Pricing (Value)	Demand forecasting, computerized models
	Cost accounting under different scenarios, computerized models

creating innovative products to satisfy customer needs, managing inventory, evaluating suppliers, and monitoring market trends and competitors' actions.

All elements of the marketing mix (product, promotion or communications, place or distribution, and price) have been affected by emerging technologies, as shown by the examples in Table 2.3. Some of the most obvious changes have occurred in promotional and distribution methods, largely due to the capabilities of interactive electronic media.

Staples, a discount office-supply retail chain, has applied technology successfully in its efforts to maintain a small-company spirit while experiencing impressive growth for over a decade. Staples maintains a massive customer database drawing on information obtained from customers using its membership discount card. Interestingly, through use of this membership card, the company learned that it did well with lawyers and dentists but not with school principals. Staples has since used this information to make decisions about new store locations, choosing sites that are convenient for law office customers, for example.[19]

The Third Revolution: The Information Age Economy

Tremendous changes will continue to take place in the ways that workers, customers, suppliers, and others communicate with one another. Internet, World Wide Web, WAN and LAN networks, e-mail, e-commerce, cyberspace, telecommuting, and mobile computing are but a few of the terms that may crop up in a discussion of the **information superhighway.** The convergence of telephones, televisions, and computers introduced a new information age that affects the way people work, interact with one another, make purchases, and pursue leisure activities. Many of the former constraints of time and distance have all but disappeared.

Information superhighway
Convergence of telephones, computers, television, cable, and other electronic technologies to provide instantaneous interactive communication.

How does the information superhighway affect marketing activities? It has brought about changes in markets and in the marketing mix in a "chicken and egg" relationship, since changes in one tend to bring about changes in the other. For example, consumers are purchasing more personal computers and other high-tech equipment for their homes, and more organizations are realizing the advantage of conducting business from networked facilities or virtual offices. As on-line business activities, purchasing, and entertainment venues increase, the need to reduce fraud has spawned growth in the security industry. Recognition technology has gained acceptance in response to this need, using technologies such as biometrics to identify people through various bodily characteristics, which enables a company to lower costs through an increase in automated services.[20]

The information superhighway not only makes change possible but also makes change necessary in all elements of the marketing mix. Advanced information technology will continue to affect decisions about product design (or redesign), development, and overall product management; communication tools and media; place or location and distribution channels; and pricing strategies. This emerging technology has proliferated a vast array of new products and services on the market. Each new product, in turn, opens up other marketing opportunities and challenges in business-to-business as well as consumer markets.

Many new media forms are available for marketers to use to reach their customers with advertising messages. New information technology (e.g., Web sites, the Internet) can be used by a company to support its salesforce's interaction with customers and the company. Likewise, marketing efforts play a major role in promoting the benefits of the new high-tech products, increasing demand and widening distribution.

The information superhighway is a major distribution channel for many products because customers make purchases via on-line computer and home-shopping networks. It also has made possible more effective worldwide electronic tracking of shipments. Major package-delivery companies use computerized tracking to locate a package anywhere in their worldwide system at any time and provide customers with software to make shipping preparation more efficient. Electronic kiosks have become popular in malls, where customers can bank on-line, review real estate, or download new software and charge it to their accounts on the spot. In addition to customer convenience, this type of distribution system lowers costs by selling direct, thus keeping consumer prices down. (See Figure 2.5.)

The Fourth Revolution: Changing Management Structure

Extensive computerization and advances in information technology have changed the way that work is organized in marketing and other business functions. In the past, most companies of any size were managed through a complex hierarchy with narrowly defined lines of reporting and decision making. Marketing departments tended to work as a staff function with little or no meaningful interaction with other functional divisions. Today's organizations are considerably flatter and less hierarchical as technological capabilities allow marketers to make quick, well-informed responses to their markets. As a result, the traditional role of middle managers has been eliminated or redefined as organizations become downsized or rightsized.

Concurrent with the flattening of the middle-management level of the organizational hierarchy, firms are placing greater reliance on computers to gather and analyze information. There is a greater focus on sticking to core competencies internally and outsourcing noncore work. Product management is a popular approach to

FIGURE 2.5

....

Electronic Shopping on the Internet. Many grocery shoppers are finding their need for speed and convenience met by on-line shopping. Many traditional food stores have expanded their distribution to the Internet; others operate strictly from a warehouse or direct to other suppliers—without a physical storefront. An example of the latter is Peapod, one of the largest on-line grocery shopping services in the United States. As of August 1998, Peapod had grown from a membership base of 400 in 1990, its first year of operation, to over 98,000 members in eight metropolitan markets in the United States—making it the leading Internet supermarket. In 1998, Peapod entered a multi-year marketing alliance with Excite, Inc., giving Peapod dominant placement on many of the most important Web sites and access to over 35 percent of all Internet users.

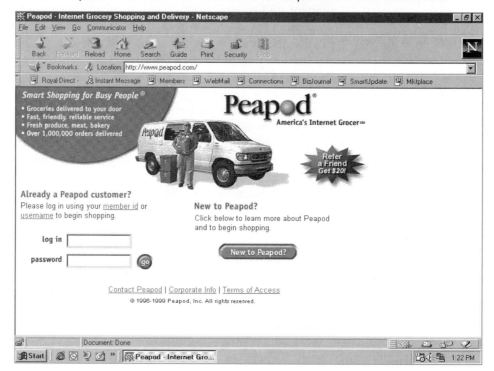

Source: http://www.peapod.com.

....

executing organizational tasks and may be performed by internal project teams or outside experts. While there is a trend toward using outside consultants in marketing and other areas, the career path to the top of many organizations includes managing an important project.

Project-based (versus position-based) work is not new, having been used for decades in such industries as construction, the movie industry, and many professional services. Coca-Cola hired an experienced outside project leader to help reorganize its New York area distribution. Chrysler designed and produced new cars by deploying cross-functional "platform teams" rather than using the traditional method of passing work through the corporate hierarchy. Project-based work also increases the sales of supporting products, such as Microsoft Project. This is a software program targeted first toward construction and aerospace and then quickly adapted by banking, telecommunications, retailing, and general manufacturing. Project management allows mass customization of a basic product, such as computer software, to solve the problems of a particular customer.[21]

Many leading companies believe that the ability to reconfigure their organizational designs when and how needed is critical to success in the information age. Those who have revolutionized their organizational processes successfully include General Electric, Allied Signal, Ameritech, and Tenneco.[22] As General Electric's CEO, John F. Welch, says,

> You've got to be on the cutting edge of change. You can't simply maintain the status quo, because somebody's always coming from another country with another product, or consumer tastes change, or the cost structure does, or there's a technology breakthrough. If you're not fast and adaptable, you're vulnerable. This is true for every segment of every business in every country in the world.

And this is particularly true in the consumer appliance industry, where GE has been a long-time market leader.

Firms that choose to operate in highly flexible structures where information can be obtained readily from an office computer rather than going up, over, and down the organization should meet the following requirements that are consistent in organizations where change is managed successfully:

- First, everyone from the top executive to the entry-level hourly worker should share the same vision and company values so that they can all work toward achieving the same objectives.

- Second, managers and employees must view change as an ongoing process of adaptation to market needs and company capabilities—rather than a one-time occurrence.

- Third, a customer orientation must drive the business—determining what products should be produced, when, where, and how they should be sold so as to deliver the greatest value and satisfaction to customers.

- Fourth, flexibility infers the need for "all-purpose" managers who can function as team members in multiple areas. In some cases, work may be performed in a matrix organization where marketing and other functions are integrated throughout the company. The focus tends to be on skill and ability rather than on position in the company.

How have radical changes in organizational structures affected the marketing function? Marketers have been able to decrease time to market for new products, improve production efficiency, and monitor changes in their markets or company as a result of smaller, more flexible organizations and because of easier access to timely information.

As marketing firms develop more customer-oriented processes, it becomes necessary to break down the walls that traditionally separate marketing from production, engineering, research and development, finance, and other functional groups in order to implement marketing strategies successfully. As discussed earlier, cross-functional project or work teams have gained popularity as part of an overall customer-oriented process, where the reward system emphasizes teamwork over individual contributions to the success of a project. Marketing professionals play an important role on the project team, often bringing in the customers themselves to participate in the process.

Project teams
Cross-functional work groups organized and empowered to carry out a particular project.

Chrysler has experienced success with **project teams,** as mentioned earlier. When the company wants to create a new car or revamp an old one, it forms a team of about 700 people from engineering, design, manufacturing, marketing, finance, and a broad range of specialists. A vice president serves as "godfather" to the group, but the actual work is directed by leaders below that rank, and the group decides how it wants to be organized to get the work done. Management works out a contract with the team and then sets it loose. The team has the power to create the car without interruption and work out disputes among themselves, as well as the responsibility for meeting the budget. As a result, Chrysler has a reputation for having the newest products and an enviable cost structure. This type of teamwork makes the marketing process more effective because marketing personnel are able to provide input about customers' needs, with the result being a car that has a high probability of success in the marketplace.[23]

When Thermos, famous for Thermos bottles, lunch boxes, cookout grills, and other products, replaced its bureaucratic organization with flexible interdisciplinary teams, innovation and new product creation flourished. The original bureaucratic system organized by functions (e.g., marketing, manufacturing, engineering) was replaced with flexible product-development teams whose members were drawn from diverse disciplines. The charge was to focus on the marketplace—that is, on the customer rather than the product. The first product of this approach was the new Thermos Thermal Electric Grill, a cookout stove that quickly became a hot item in retail stores. Its success was largely due to Thermos's realization that most new product failures are due to not understanding the needs of the market, emphasizing the need for management support and research funding for a successful project.[24]

IMPACT OF CHANGE ON STRATEGIC AND TACTICAL MARKETING DECISIONS

The preceding discussion indicates that changes in the marketing environment bring about changes in long-range organizational strategies and day-to-day tactics as marketers position themselves to remain competitive. In some cases marketers are the primary catalysts for change, although they may be responding to perceived opportunities in the environment. New product development and distribution technology illustrate the creation of goods and services that revolutionize what and how customers buy. When new products such as cellular telephones, CD-ROMs, fiberoptics, and microwave ovens were first introduced, they contributed to major lifestyle changes and spawned many new product lines that continue to evolve. In other cases, marketers respond to change with strategies such as mass merchandising and value pricing for cost-conscious consumers, convenience products for hectic lifestyles, automobiles to meet the specific needs of families and single individuals, or travel and hospitality services for busy executives.

Strategies
Long-term plans associated primarily with building external relationships consistent with organizational mission.

While both strategies and tactics affect relationships inside and outside the firm, **strategies** are associated primarily with building external relationships because of

Tactics
Shorter-term plan associated with building internal relationships and motivating employees to carry out strategic intent.

their long-term implications. **Tactics** tend to be associated more with building internal relationships in order to encourage creativity and motivate employees to execute the tactical decisions successfully. (Strategies and tactics are discussed further in the next chapter.)

Building Internal Relationships

The process of changing organizational structures to meet the needs of a changing marketplace requires the implementation of effective internal marketing programs to promote the company's vision and goals to its internal customers. Part of the internal marketing effort is focused on cross-functional teams that have a major impact on marketing personnel as they become involved in all customer-related aspects of the organization. Such marketing personnel may work on several projects at one time, sharing their expertise in identifying the match between the company's products and its markets. Working on a project from beginning to end gives marketing professionals better insights into corporate strengths and weaknesses and a better understanding of the goals to be achieved by the marketing mix. The internal marketing effort should be focused on gaining loyalty to the project and company, as well as to the employee.

Marketing research, consumer studies, and the salesforce provide invaluable feedback for managing new and existing products. Honda makes changes in its automobile designs in response to information obtained from focus groups and customer surveys to satisfy its markets. USAA, an insurance and financial services company that markets primarily to military officers and their families, surveys one-half million customers a year to determine their present satisfaction and their future insurance and financial needs as a basis for product and service development. Many companies keep track of customer complaints and telephone requests in order to know their customers better and take action when needed. Restaurants, hotels, and other service firms ask customers to complete questionnaires at the point of sale to indicate their level of satisfaction with the service experience.

Although the primary objective of marketing research may be to build relationships with external customers and sell products, another important objective should be to use the results in internal marketing programs in order to improve service quality and responsiveness to customer needs as part of the overall marketing mix. Internal marketing research also should be used to assess employee satisfaction, to identify human resource needs (e.g., training, flexible scheduling, child or elder care, etc.), and to obtain employees' suggestions for improvement in all facets of the business.

Building External Relationships

Establishing long-term external relationships is particularly important in times of significant environmental changes. Many formal and informal corporate relationships have emerged as a result of the converging business revolutions described earlier. A marketing company cannot be global without foreign partners, whether it is in manufacturing, distribution, or other areas. The fast-paced advances in information technology and computerization have created alliances among firms in the

- The company must know its product and the benefits that it provides for customers.

- Perhaps most important of all, marketers must listen to customers and understand their wants and needs.

Managing Change

Leading marketers such as Southwest Airlines, Home Depot, Microsoft Corp., Hewlett-Packard Co., and Levi Strauss & Co. have prospered in recent years by making ongoing adjustments and managing change effectively. A rapidly changing world market has provided Microsoft with tremendous multinational opportunities for its software business in developing economies such as China, Latin America, Eastern Europe, and Africa, as well as developed economies such as Europe and Japan. Microsoft's sales offices and wholly owned subsidiaries can be found in nearly 60 countries. A highly successful strategy is achieved by fostering independent local software developers and distributors in countries with vast growth potential such as India and China.[25,26]

Many large firms such as Sears, General Motors, and IBM experienced setbacks before becoming successful in their attempts to make much needed changes. The hot-growth companies tend to act small while thinking big. Home Depot carved out a unique market niche for itself, and revenues climbed by 36 percent and profits by 44 percent a year during the 5 years ending in 1994, as other retailers' sales suffered. Software developer Microsoft's 5-year record includes annual increases of 47 and 53 percent, respectively. On the other hand, Standard and Poor's reported that run-of-the-mill large companies in the $2 billion plus league increased sales by only 7 percent while net earnings dropped slightly each year.

Hewlett-Packard operates in an industry with an extremely short product life cycle where constant change is a necessity. H-P constantly innovates with new products in new markets. In March 1994, the company introduced the world's best-selling computer printer, a black and white inkjet model. The following October H-P introduced a newer model that offered an optional color printing kit at just $49 more than the older monochrome model. As H-P's chief executive says, "We've developed a philosophy of killing off our own products with new technology. Better that we do it than somebody else." H-P revamped its product development to shorten the time to bring a new product to market from 6 years to less than 9 months. To accomplish this takes a sincere commitment to change.[26,27]

The success stories of companies that have prospered in dynamic, changing environments suggest that they possess a number of common characteristics.[27,28] Lessons to be learned about managing change in a marketing organization include the following:

- Focus on your customers and understand your markets; this should drive internal organizational changes.

- Listen to customers to learn how they define customer value and satisfaction and how they perceive your company versus its competitors.

- Welcome change and be prepared to review and update goals and procedures continuously.

INNOVATE OR EVAPORATE*

The Chocolate Meltdown

Mars is a family-owned global marketer that spends millions of dollars to keep the names of its popular candy brands before customers. M&M's (the world's number 1 chocolate candy), Snickers, Milky Way, and other Mars candies are part of American culture, eaten "straight" as candy or added to other food concoctions. While Mars is an industry leader in confectionery, pet food, and other food-related businesses, in the mid-1990s it faced problems in developing successful new products and disdained sharing ideas or forming alliances to improve its competitive position.

Mars continued to emphasize quality control and manufacturing efficiency, but growth was inhibited by a process technology that resulted in a serious lack of new hit products. Mars focused on global expansion, continually seeking converts to its brands in one country after another but not worrying about losing brand loyalty in existing markets. Hershey and other competitors took market share from Mars through aggressive marketing and acquisitions. Hershey increased both market share and profits in a flat market and also bought Cadbury's U.S. confectionery operation and two other brands to gain even more market dominance—while Mars stood pat. Although it attempted to adjust to change, Mars did not develop and manage its supply chain relationships successfully. In particular, the company did not react well to innovations in the retail and wholesale distribution chain, where consolidation had shifted buying power to large supermarket chains and mega-wholesalers that demand lower costs from suppliers. Mars enraged some segments of the trade by making abrupt policy changes that reduced retailers' profits by not supplying enough product to fill the orders they took, focusing on production rather than sales, eliminating some promotional deals, and taking an imperialist approach to management that stifled innovation and growth.

By 1998, Mars had revitalized its position as the number 2 candy maker in the $21 billion U.S. candy industry, second only to Hershey. Mars was rated by the *Forbes Private 500* as the sixth-largest U.S. company. Mars regained momentum by launching creative new advertising campaigns and introducing successful extensions of its leading candy brands. New promotions included the 1997 Super Bowl campaign and promoting M&Ms as the "official candy of the millennium" (MM is the Roman numeral for 2000). Another new product extension, M&M's Crispy Chocolate Candies, was developed for introduction during the 1999 Super Bowl—supported by a $70 million advertising and promotional campaign. The tag line for the launch: "The Feeding Frenzy Has Begun."

*The box title is attributed to James M. Higgins, *Innovate or Evaporate* (Winter Park, FL: New Management Publishing Company, 1995).

Sources: Bill Saporito, "The Eclipse of Mars," *Fortune* (November 28, 1994), pp. 82–92; www.hoovers.com/premium/profiles; Laura Liebeck, "Novelty Hasn't Worn Off for Candy Manufacturers," *Discount Store News* (July 13, 1998), pp. 8, 110; Anya Sacharow, "Mars' Stars," *Brandweek* (May 25, 1998), pp. I-28-I-30.

- Inform everyone in the company why change is necessary, communicate the vision for the future, and provide all necessary information to remove the fear and uncertainty that accompany change.

- Decentralize authority for quicker decision making, and place high value on teamwork versus individualism.

- Recruit, hire, train, and reward skilled people at all levels who are versatile and responsive.

- Empower your people to make decisions related to their areas of responsibility, and make clear what results are expected.

- If you lack the expertise to take advantage of opportunities that fit your corporate goals, obtain it by outsourcing, acquisition, or strategic alliances.

- Remove all walls between functional areas in the company, and develop cross-functional or project teams.

- Involve suppliers and other important stakeholders in providing input for dealing with change, and create alliances and include them in project teams.

- Don't lose sight of the company's core values in the process of making changes; successful companies realize that some things should never change.

Summary

As shown in this chapter, the marketing environment is changing faster than ever. Organizations that continuously monitor change are in a better position to capitalize on new opportunities and minimize risk. Those which remain passive and do not adapt to change face possible extinction. Many environmental forces can have an impact on marketing decisions. The process of change and renewal in marketing organizations can be compared with the phases of an ecocycle of complex natural systems where survival depends on the ability of the system to emerge from crisis as a living, vibrant system.

The challenges faced by marketers today are fueled primarily by four concurrent business revolutions: (1) the globalization of markets, (2) the growth of information technology and computer networks, (3) changing management hierarchies, and (4) the information age economy. The globalization of markets requires an understanding of customers, products, and the fit between the two, whether the marketer is dealing across continents or across town.

American consumers buy a significant amount of the world's goods and services. Thus it is impor-
tant to look at changes in the U.S. market, where the "average American" no longer exists due primarily to population shifts in the distribution of age, ethnic groups, income levels, and consumer lifestyles.

New technology is a catalyst for change in the types of goods and services that are produced and the ways they are marketed. Technological advances in computerization and telecommunications have affected organizations in the way that work is performed, buying and selling activities take place, and relationships are built. Rapid advances in technology have brought about many strategic alliances in entertainment, telecommunications, computers and software, and other industries. Technological progress has opened the information superhighway, where telephones, television, and computers converge to communicate instantaneously around the world, creating a new distribution channel for goods and services.

Changing management structures are evolving to enable organizations to deal effectively with environmental change. Today's organizations are flatter, less hierarchical, and more likely to use integrated cross-functional teams to manage projects. Computers and their ability to handle large databases efficiently have lessened the need for traditional middle managers by using more project managers and task-oriented work groups. The focus is on flexibility so that changes can be made quickly in response to the marketplace.

Changes in the environment affect both marketing strategies and tactics. Internal marketing programs are necessary to motivate internal customers (employees) to execute external programs successfully and build long-term relationships with customers. Shortened product life cycles, particularly for high-tech or fashion products, require a constant long-term strategic vision and the ability to adapt short-run tactics as needed.

There are many approaches to identifying opportunities in a constantly changing environment, including formal and informal scanning techniques, databases, and a variety of primary and secondary research methods. Identification of opportunities is only the first step. It is also necessary to manage the change that accompanies taking advantage of new opportunities. Hot-growth companies tend to act small while thinking big. They have a vision for the future but do not neglect customers, suppliers, and other important stakeholders in the present.

Questions

1. Explain the concept of a marketing organization ecocycle. Using a familiar company or nonprofit organization, describe the phases that make up the continuous process represented by the ecocycle.

2. Discuss the four business revolutions that have led to major changes in marketing, as described in this chapter. Are there others that should be included? Explain and justify your answer.

3. Describe a recent international event that has influenced the marketing process for a familiar company or product category and has created a need to adapt the marketing mix to this new situation in order to be competitive in a global marketplace.

4. Discuss the major trends that marketers need to monitor in a wide range of technological developments and information processing.

Explain how each can influence a specific marketing decision (e.g., product specifications, distribution methods, promotional media, pricing strategy, and others).

5. Illustrate how the building of internal and external relationships between marketers and their internal and external constituents can contribute to successful marketing management in a time of change.

Exercises

1. Interview a marketing professional from a local company about possible crises or environmental changes that have made it necessary for him or her to change some aspect of his or her marketing organization and/or marketing mix.

2. Sketch the marketing organization ecocycle, and using the experience of actual companies, describe (a) the best-case scenario and (b) the worst-case scenario for how these companies managed change in their internal or external environments.

3. Describe the ways that marketing managers can identify opportunities in a time of change as they are discussed in the chapter. Create your own innovative method for identifying potential crises and opportunities, and explain how you would implement this method to manage change in your own organization.

Endnotes

1. Hal Lancaster, "Managing Your Career: The Right Training Helps Even Dinosaurs Adapt to Change," *Wall Street Journal* (March 28, 1995), p. B1.

2. David K. Hurst, *Crisis and Renewal: Meeting the Challenge of Organizational Change* (Boston: Harvard Business School Press, 1995). Much of this section of the chapter is based on Hurst's organizational ecocycle model and examples.

3. *Ibid.,* p. 2.

4. *Ibid.,* pp. 97–103 and Fig. 5-1, p. 97.

5. Further explanation of the far-reaching impact of natural events can be found in the chaos theory

(e.g., the flapping of a butterfly's wings in South America can cause strong wind currents in Europe) or the Japanese concept of *tsunami.* The latter term refers to a huge sea wave in the ocean caused by a submarine disturbance such as an earthquake or a volcanic eruption.

6. See Hurst, *op. cit.,* Organizational Ecocycle, Fig. 5-2; organizational ecocycle model illustrated (p. 103) and model components described (pp. 103–115). The eight phases in Hurst's model are (1) strategic management, (2) conservation, (3) crisis, (4) confusion, (5) charismatic leadership, (6) creative network, (7) choice, and (8) entrepreneurial action.

7. See Hurst, *op. cit.,* Model of Organizational Change, Fig. 3-3 (p. 72), discussion (pp. 71–73), and Fig. 5-2 (p. 103) and discussion of types of rational action (pp. 105–113). Hurst maintains that these two half-loops represent two different types of rationality: instrumental means-end rationality in the life-cycle phase (1. strategic management) and values-based rationality in the renewal phase (2. charismatic leadership).

8. Source of Nike examples used with discussion of ecocycle model: Hurst, *op. cit.,* pp. 35–49, 105–106, 114–115, 165–166, and others.

9. Hurst, *op. cit.,* p. 128.

10. Hurst, *op. cit.,* pp. 129–130.

11. Hurst, *op. cit.,* pp. 112–113.

12. Thomas A. Stewart, "Planning a Career in a World without Managers," *Fortune* (March 20, 1995), pp. 72–80.

13. Vivian Brownstein, "The U.S. Is Set to Be the Winner from Worldwide Expansion," *Business Week* (November 28, 1994), pp. 22–23.

14. Peter Francese, "America at Mid-Decade," *American Demographics* (February 1995), pp. 23–31.

15. J. D. Mosley-Matchett, "Show Me the (Cyber) Money!" *Marketing News* 31(12) (June 9, 1997), p. 18.

16. Edward W. Desmond, "Yahoo: Still Defying Gravity on the Web," *Fortune* (September 8, 1997); David Stipp, "The Birth of Digital Commerce," *Fortune* (December 9, 1996), pp. 159–164; and J. D. Mosley-Matchett, "Show Me the (Cyber) Money!" *Marketing News* 31(12) (June 9, 1997), p. 18.

17. Alan Deutschman, "Putting Zip in Educational Software," *Business Week* (November 28, 1994), p. 200.

18. James L. McKenney, *Waves of Change: Business Evolution through Information Technology* (Boston: Harvard Business School, 1995).

19. Rahul Jacob, "How One Hot Retailer Wins Customer Loyalty," *Fortune* (July 10, 1995), pp. 72–79.

20. Saul Hansell, "Use of Recognition Technology Grows in Everyday Transactions," *New York Times* (August 20, 1997), p. 1.

21. Stewart, *op. cit.*

22. Stratford Sherman, "A Master Class in Radical Change," *Fortune* (December 13, 1995), pp. 82–90.

23. Marshall Loeb, "Empowerment that Pays Off," *Fortune* (March 20, 1995), pp. 145–146.

24. Brian Dumain, "Payoff from the New Management," *Fortune* (December 13, 1993), pp. 103–110

25. Brent Schlender, "Microsoft: First America, Now the World," *Fortune* (August 18, 1997), pp. 214–217.

26. Wendy Zellner, Robert D. Hof, Richard Brandt, Stephen Baker, and David Greising "Go-Go Goliaths," *Business Week* (February 13, 1995), pp. 64–70.

27. Noel M. Tichy, "Revolutionize Your Company," *Fortune* (December 13, 1993), pp. 114–118.

28. Zellner et al., *op. cit.*

PART TWO

Achieving Competitive Advantage

3. **Strategic Market Planning**
4. **Marketing Intelligence and Creative Problem Solving**
5. **Understanding Consumer Buying Behavior**
6. **Business Markets and Buying Behavior**
7. **Market Segmentation, Target Marketing, and Positioning**

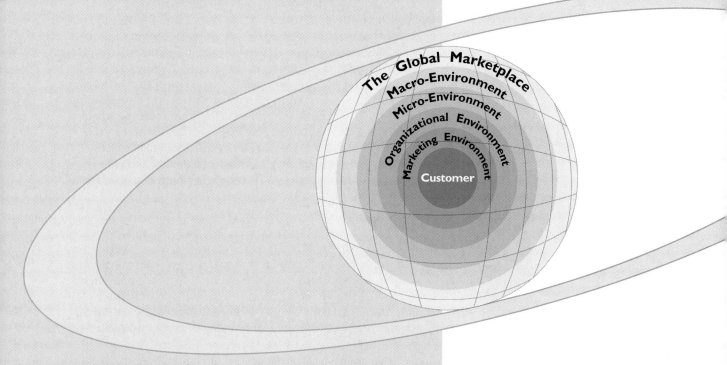

The Global Marketplace
Macro-Environment
Micro-Environment
Organizational Environment
Marketing Environment
Customer

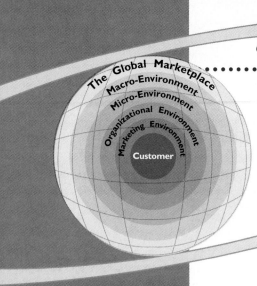

The Global Marketplace
Macro-Environment
Micro-Environment
Organizational Environment
Marketing Environment
Customer

CHAPTER 3

Strategic Market Planning

Marketing Management Decisions and Strategic Planning

Strategic Market Planning: A Multilevel Process

The Strategic Planning Process

Planning for the Long Term

Strategic Planning and the Challenge of Change

Strategic Planning and a Customer Orientation

High-Flying Strategy in the Friendly Skies: Airline Industry in Transition

Victorious warriors win first and then go to war, while defeated warriors go to war first and then seek to win.[1]

Few industries have experienced more volatility than the U.S. airline industry over the past several decades. The invention of the jet engine in the early 1960s and the deregulation of the U.S. airline industry in 1978 led the phenomenal growth of commercial airlines. Jet engines allowed commercial aircraft to travel at greater speeds with greater fuel efficiency and safety, thus lowering the cost of passenger air travel and encouraging more passengers to fly. Other contributors to growth include the acquisition of more aircraft and the operating efficiencies of larger planes that can carry more passengers over greater distances. A generally healthy economy throughout the world, global business expansion, and increased leisure travel also have contributed significantly to growth in commercial airline travel.

Competitive Environment

According to the U.S. Department of Transportation, there are twelve major airlines within the U.S. airline industry that earn annual revenues of $1 billion from airline transportation services. Ten of these are passenger airlines, and two are freight carriers (FedEx and United Parcel Service). The status of each of the major passenger airlines is ranked according to the number of passengers carried, revenue passenger miles, and passenger revenues. In terms of number of passengers carried, the top ten passenger airlines rank as follows: Delta, American, United, USAir, Southwest, Northwest, Continental, Trans World, America West, and Alaska. These domestic carriers face stiff competition from smaller domestic carriers, as well as increasingly aggressive foreign competition.

Industry Stability and Volatility

The U.S. government's deregulation of the airline industry turned pricing and routing control over to the airlines to create a more competitive environment. Since that time, airlines have been competing aggressively for passengers—often at the expense of profits. Price-cutting strategies and costly sales promotions have caused the demise of some airlines and have driven others to declare bankruptcy while they attempt to restructure. Further, the airline industry is affected by economic conditions, with business suffering during recessionary times and booming during periods of significant growth. Airline travel is seasonal and cyclical, with demand fluctuations during certain periods, such as time of year, day of the week, or hour of the day.

Trends

While business and leisure travelers are flying more than ever, the airlines continue their struggle to be profitable. In addition to the price wars and marketing promotions noted earlier, escalating operating costs erode profits. Increases have occurred in the price of fuel, labor costs (due to union contracts), and a variety of required taxes and fees.

What strategies are the airlines using to maximize their opportunities for growth and prof-

itability and to minimize threats to profitability and survival in this volatile environment? Several trends include industry consolidation, "hubbing," increased use of technology, strategic alliances, and international expansion.

Southwest Airlines

Southwest Airlines has enjoyed success as somewhat of a renegade in the volatile airline industry for more than a quarter of a century. At the time of its founding in 1971, Southwest had three Boeing 737 aircraft that served three Texas cities (Dallas, Houston, and San Antonio). By the end of 1997, the company was flying 275 Boeing 737s and provided passenger service to 53 airports in 52 cities throughout 26 states in the United States. Southwest had more than 25,875 employees, averaged 2350 flights a day, carried 50.4 million passengers in 1997, and had $3.8 billion in operating revenue and $317.7 million in net income.

In the 26 years of its operation, Southwest has become the fifth largest U.S. airline in terms of domestic passengers carried. The secret to its success seems to be its strategic positioning as the country's only major short-haul, high-frequency point-to-point carrier. Southwest's key success factors include innovation, customer satisfaction, motivated employees, "young" aircraft, a good safety record, and a focus on its core competencies. The airline continues to seek expansion routes into selected markets within its current business philosophy of being *the* low-cost airline by achieving operating efficiencies—without sacrificing customer satisfaction.

Sources: Airline Quarterly Financial Review (second quarter), Department of Transportation, Office of Aviation Analysis, Economic and Financial Analysis Division, Washington, D.C., 1997, p. 4; Southwest Airlines, *1996 Annual Report;* Southwest Airlines, *1997 Annual Report; Standard & Poor's Industry Surveys,* A–L, Airlines, March 27, 1997; *The Airline Handbook* (Washington, D.C.: Air Transport Association of America, 1995), Chap. 3, p. 1.

S trategic market planning is about having a vision for the future and a winning plan in place before battling competitors in the marketplace. The strategic planning process is critical to achieving long-term success in meeting the challenges of a rapidly changing and uncertain environment.

MARKETING MANAGEMENT DECISIONS AND STRATEGIC PLANNING

The strategic planning process and the marketing process are closely related, since marketing management decisions must be consistent with a firm's overall business strategy. Although strategic market planning can occur throughout the marketing organization ecocycle, it is most noticeable in the growth phase,[2] where conscious, rational decisions are made to guide the direction of the company. (See Figure 2.1 on page 31.)

Strategic decisions are related to an understanding of customers' needs, competitors' activities, and the financial implications of each decision. In turn, tactical marketing plans are based on a clear vision of the firm's overall business strategy and an understanding of its marketing strategies. Both strategic and tactical planning must be responsive to changes in the marketplace. For example, PowerCerv, a client-server application company (creating database and end-user software for industry use), enjoyed rapid growth from 1992 to 1993. In 1993, PowerCerv launched one of its own software applications, PowerTOOL, as a separate product for sale only to its current customers. By the end of 1994, the rapid growth of client-server technology and the initial success of PowerTOOL caused the company to reconsider its original strategic vision, and PowerCerv repositioned itself with a differentiation strategy that focused on services built around its own software products.

There are many definitions of *strategy,* depending on one's point of view. As can be seen in the preceding example, further confusion arises because there often is a fine line between the point where "strategy" ends and "tactics" begin. Since business-level strategy is the focus of this book, the following definitions of *strategy* and *tactics* provide a basis for discussion.

Strategy

Strategy

Explicit statement that provides direction for coordinated business decisions, a longer-term vision for the future.

The term *strategy* is used interchangeably with *competitive strategy* or *business strategy.* **Strategy** embodies a firm's objectives and reasons for being in business. It includes corporate policies, resource allocations, customer markets, and the competitive environment in which it chooses to operate. A firm's strategy is its vision of its future. It is an explicit statement that provides direction for coordinated business decisions in marketing and other functional areas.

Strategy can be defined by four basic dimensions that apply to all businesses and by two additional dimensions that apply to multiple businesses. The typical business strategy includes a specification of the following:[3]

1. *The product market in which the business will compete.* For example, Southwest Airlines has chosen to compete in the domestic, short-haul passenger transportation market.

2. *The level of investment in a strategic unit.* For firms such as Southwest, a strategic unit may be determined on the basis of geography; for example, how many flights and how many planes should be committed to the Dallas-Orlando route?

3. *Functional area strategies required for competing in the chosen product market.* Southwest must design an effective marketing mix, consisting of strategies for promotion, pricing, distribution, and airline services.

4. *Underlying strategic assets and skills that give the firm a sustainable competitive advantage.* As discussed in the opening scenario of this chapter, Southwest has a low-cost, efficient operation and motivated employees and has received many accolades for its service and safety performance.

Two other dimensions must be determined for firms having multiple business units:

1. *How the firm's resources will be allocated across business units.* For example, Delta Airlines must allocate financial resources and personnel across Delta Airlines, Delta Express (its shuttle service), and other business units in which it has an interest (e.g., Worldspan computer reservation service and code-sharing alliances with non-U.S. carriers).

2. *How to create synergies across the businesses (i.e., creation of value by complementary business units).* Delta Express short-haul shuttle service passengers find it convenient to connect with Delta Airlines flights to more distant destinations. Delta benefits from shared facilities, maintenance, ticketing, and so forth.

Tactics

Tactics
Plan for the shorter-term, day-to-day operating decisions, what to do.

Whereas *strategy* refers to the longer-term, broader statement of direction for an organization, **tactics** refers to the shorter-term, day-to-day operating decisions. In other words, *strategy* refers to a broadly stated plan of action, that is, "what to do," that enables a firm to compete successfully in its environment. *Tactics* refers to "how the strategy will be carried out." Military strategy analogies often are used to explain the difference between these two concepts.

A frequently quoted Chinese strategist, Sun Tzu, laid the foundation for Eastern military strategy with his *Art of War*, written in 500 B.C. Sun Tzu's premise is that winning requires good strategy and that those who are well skilled in battle can overcome their enemy's army without fighting. "The ultimate strategy is to subdue the enemy's army without engaging it. To take cities without laying siege to them. To overthrow his forces without bloodying swords." This represents the strategic perspective—*doing the right thing* (marketing *strategy*).

On the other hand, the German general Carl von Clausewitz provides a foundation for Western military strategy in his book, *On War*, written in the eighteenth century. His premise is that winning is based on fighting the big battle, that is, *doing things right* (action-oriented marketing *tactics*).[4]

This chapter provides an overview of the strategic planning process, the challenge of changing strategic planning, and the integration of a customer orientation into the strategic planning process. Marketing management decisions are made within the context of a firm's strategic plan and are designed to carry out its strategic intent and achieve its strategic objectives.

STRATEGIC MARKET PLANNING: A MULTILEVEL PROCESS

Regardless of the size or scope of an organization, strategic planning generally occurs at several levels: corporate, division or strategic business unit, and functional or operating level. (See Table 3.1.) Managers at these levels are responsible for making a group of interdependent decisions that vary somewhat at each level. At the corporate level, managers have primary responsibility for satisfying customers and for the financial performance of the entire company over the long term. They also are responsible for the relationships among divisions of the company and the organization's culture and values in the greater society. Corporate-level tactics become the strategy that drives decisions at the next lower level, the division or strategic business unit (SBU).

Divisional managers are most concerned with strategies for their separate business unit(s) or profit centers that are operated within the larger corporation. Each division has its own mission and objectives within the parameters of the corporate strategic plan, but its focus may be on a different set of customers and competitors than the other divisions of the company. Each division typically has responsibility for the implementation and control of its strategic plan. Divisional tactics formulate the strategy for the next lower level, the functional or operational level.

Functional-level managers take a shorter-term view of strategy than managers do at higher levels in the business, although the day-to-day decisions must be made within the requirements of the corporate and divisional strategies. Functional managers are responsible for determining the tactical marketing plan for achieving the functional-level strategy (which is the same as the divisional-level tactical plan). The

TABLE 3.1
. . . .
Marketing, Strategic Planning, and Organizational Levels

Level in Organization	Marketing Input	Marketing Task Description
Corporate	Customer viewpoint and competitive analysis for corporate-level strategy	Corporate marketing decisions for entire company (longer-term planning)
Division/SBU	Each division focuses on its own set of customers and competitors for its own business unit(s)	Strategic marketing for each business unit or profit center; drives tactical plan at operating level
Operating/Functional	Design of marketing mix and implementation of tactical marketing plans	Marketing management—shorter-term implementation of strategy

Source: From *Marketing Planning and Strategy,* 3rd edition, by Subhash Jain, ©1990. Reprinted with permission of South-Western College Publishing, a division of International Thomson Publishing. Fax 800 730-2215.

tactical plan includes identification of the market segment(s) to be pursued and the appropriate marketing mix (i.e., product, pricing, promotion, and distribution) to reach the desired market(s). In some organizations, the strategic process continues on to lower-level department or group managers who have accountability for carrying out the functional-level strategy.

The primary focus of this book is on the business unit level, where marketing strategy is developed and executed. At this level, there are three major forces that must be taken into consideration: the company, its customers, and its competitors—the *strategic 3C's*.[5] Marketing strategies address the questions of how the firm can most effectively differentiate its offerings from those of competitors and match the firm's resources and strengths to the needs of the marketplace. The ability to accomplish this allows a company to deliver the greatest value and satisfaction to its customers within a defined marketing environment.

THE STRATEGIC PLANNING PROCESS

The strategic planning process involves a number of fundamental steps, although managers may differ somewhat as to the exact nature or order of each step. In fact, strategic planning generally follows an iterative process, rather than following a specified sequence, as new information is made available that may affect decisions made in a preceding step.

The process starts with a clear understanding of the firm's mission and philosophy, because long- and short-range plans must be consistent with the firm's reason for being in business. Both an external environmental analysis (i.e., customers, competitors, and market) and an internal self-analysis must be performed to make informed strategic decisions. Based on the firm's corporate mission and performance objectives and the results of the environmental analyses, the next step is to determine strategic objectives and define the broad strategy to achieve those objectives. This step is followed by a plan for implementation and tactics (marketing mix strategy), execution of the plan, and evaluation and control measures. (See Figure 3.1.)

Mission-Driven Strategic Planning

Mission statement
Defines the reasons for the business's existence in the present and in the future.

The **mission statement** clearly defines (and in some cases redefines) the reason for a business's existence in the present and in the future. Thus the mission statement provides guidelines for strategic planning. Strategic marketing decisions will be based on answers to these questions:

1. What business are we in? (What is the customer orientation? Who and where are our customers? Which ones will we serve and how will we serve them?)

2. What business will we be in? (What is our response to the environment? What are the customer needs to be served? How will these needs be satisfied?)

3. What business should we be in? (What are the product/market opportunities for new or existing customers? What is the product/market "fit" with present customers?)

FIGURE 3.1
....
Strategic Planning Process

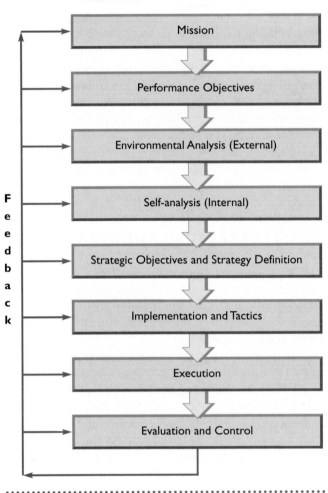

The business mission, then, is a general statement about the strategy of a business, as illustrated in Figure 3.2. It addresses the scope of the business (product markets in which it does and does not want to compete), direction for future growth, general idea of the functional area strategies, and the strengths (key assets and skills) that form the basis of the business.[6]

Strategic Readiness. Classic marketing concepts such as "strategic windows"[7] and "marketing myopia"[8] demonstrate that the advantage of developing a strategic plan is twofold. A "strategic window" represents a short period of time when there is an optimal "fit" between the organization's capabilities and a new opportunity to satisfy the needs of the market. *Marketing myopia* refers to missed op-

FIGURE 3.2

....

Mission Statement

> Southwest Airlines is dedicated to the highest quality of Customer Service delivered with a sense of warmth, friendliness, individual pride, and Company Spirit.
>
> We are committed to provide our Employees a stable work environment with equal opportunity for learning and personal growth. Creativity and innovation are encouraged for improving the effectiveness of Southwest Airlines. Above all, Employees will be provided the same concern, respect, and caring attitude within the Organization that they are expected to share externally with every Southwest Customer.

Source: Reprinted with permission of Southwest Airlines.

....

Strategic readiness
Ability to take advantage of unexpected market opportunities by having a long-term strategic plan and vision in place.

portunities caused by focusing on the product at the expense of paying attention to the customer and the needs of a changing marketplace. The plan provides a blueprint for long- and short-term decisions that allow marketing managers to maximize opportunities and minimize threats. Since it is not possible to foresee all possible opportunities and threats, a formal strategic plan provides a basis for making better decisions in unexpected circumstances, that is, for being in a state of **strategic readiness.**

Strategic Vision versus Strategic Opportunism.[9] The strategic process is influenced greatly by an organization's structure, systems, and culture, and by the personnel who are responsible for planning and implementation. **Strategic vision** takes a longer-term, futuristic perspective and requires considerable patience and determination to adhere to the planned strategy. In contrast, **strategic opportunism** focuses on the present and positions the firm in a dynamic, uncertain environment where the future is relatively unpredictable. Each has its advantages and disadvantages: Strategic vision provides managers and employees with a sense of purpose and direction, whereas strategic opportunism emphasizes flexibility and responsiveness as new opportunities arise. Skillful managers can benefit from a combination of these approaches by being ready to seize opportunities that are consistent with the firm's long-range vision.

Strategic vision
Longer-term, futuristic perspective; requires patience and determination.

Strategic opportunism
Focus on present, and seizing market opportunities in a dynamic, uncertain environment.

Henry Ford can be counted among the earliest U.S. strategic visionaries with the advent of his "horseless carriage." Since that time, the auto industry has experienced many examples of both strategic vision and strategic opportunism as the leaders vie for market share. Ford and General Motors have jockeyed for the market leader position for decades, but the last time Ford outsold GM was during 1930. GM enjoyed as much as a 2 to 1 advantage over Ford during the 1950s and 1960s, but Ford is expected to take the lead at the turn of the century. What strategic moves have brought about this turnaround? Four major challenges have confronted the auto industry over the past quarter century: fuel economy, quality, shift in buyer tastes, and more intense competition. Ford's strategic vision has been customer-oriented, with an understanding of shifting customer tastes and market needs and the market's demand for quality. The company's strategic response included the production of

MARKETING IN THE GLOBAL VILLAGE

Russian Scientists Pursue a New Venture

 Numerous examples of strategic opportunism can be found in emerging economies and in rapidly evolving industries where new ventures arise to fill the needs of the marketplace. One such example can be found in the former Soviet Union, where scientists in the defense industry had little or no job security at the end of the cold war. A strategic opportunity was seized by Viktor Bannikov, who led a group of scientists formerly employed by an aviation plant into a new venture that currently designs and produces titanium golf clubs.

The company, Metal Park, was a pioneer in making titanium club heads for golfers in the United States in 1994. However, the company lost its early advantage to larger, domestic rivals when the market exploded in 1995 and 1996. The scientists used their core competencies to develop an innovative product and enter a new market; however, their strategic opportunism in this and other ventures apparently did not include an understanding of developing and maintaining a competitive advantage in a growth market.[10]

smaller vehicles for more efficient fuel use and a focus on quality improvement embodied in the philosophy "Quality is job one." In addition, Ford made a strategic decision to diversify its product line to include new truck models and utility vehicles and implemented a growth strategy to build market share through brand loyalty with quality products and service.[11]

Performance Objectives

Once the mission statement has been determined, the next step is to establish the goals and objectives that the strategic plan is expected to accomplish. Performance objectives generally are stated in measurable terms, such as return on investment or other profitability or productivity measures that are to be accomplished within a specified period of time. Strategic objectives can be determined for separate divisions, departments, or other organizational units. Objectives established for one level or business unit should support and be compatible with those of other levels or units of the business.

Environmental Analysis (External)

One of the purposes of strategic market planning is to be able to anticipate and respond to environmental changes that may affect the firm. Managers need a clear understanding of the firm's external and internal environments in order to plan and carry out strategies successfully. A marketing information system or management decision support system provides needed information throughout the entire strategic planning process, as discussed in Chapter 4. It is particularly useful for conducting an ongoing environmental analysis.

Macro-environment
External forces over which a company has little or no control.

The external environment consists of a **macro-environment** (i.e., economic, legal/political, sociocultural, demographic, physical, and technological—factors over

FIGURE 3.3

· ·

Dynamic Global Marketing Environment and External Marketing Environment

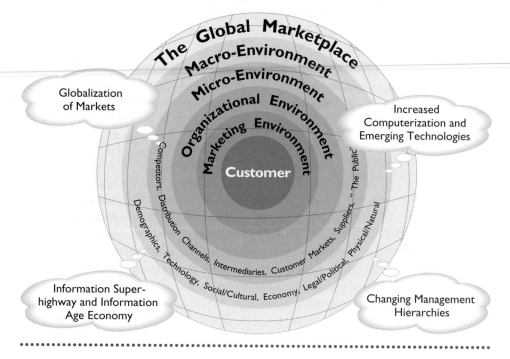

· ·

Micro-environment
Operating or task environment (competitors, markets, suppliers, and intermediaries).

which the company has little or no control) and a **micro-environment** (i.e., competitors, markets, suppliers, and intermediaries—sometimes referred to as the *operating or task environment),* as shown in Figure 3.3. In this chapter, our focus is on the major external environmental factors that influence the strategic planning process: the firm's customers, its competitors, the market, and an organized procedure for environmental scanning and forecasting.

Customers.   Successful marketing strategies in both consumer and business-to-business marketing focus on ways to satisfy customer needs and how to do this better than competitors. In order to achieve its strategic intent, a firm first must know *who* makes up its customer base, where they are located, and how to reach them. Questions that should be answered about present and prospective customers include the following:

- Which customers are the best prospects today, and which will be the most profitable over the long term? What shifts are likely to occur in the present customer mix?

- Do the identified customers fall into segments that can be differentiated from one another on similar traits (e.g., geographic, demographic, product use, buying patterns, brand loyalty, etc.)?

- What are the key buying motives for each customer segment? What do they perceive as "value"? Are perceptions of value changing?

- What are the major causes of customer satisfaction and dissatisfaction from the present company and its competitors?

- What customer needs are not being satisfied at present? Given the level of demand and intensity of competition, is it feasible to pursue products or markets to fulfill these unmet needs?

Companies that market upscale pet foods and other products make up a growing industry that has profited from customer analysis. Adjectives such as *gourmet, low-fat,* and *specialized* describe products for pampered pets, particularly cats and dogs. A survey conducted by the American Animal Hospital Association (AAHA) found that 70 percent of consumers put pets on an equal par with children, with the number of pets growing by 7 percent a year in the United States.[12] Experts describe several factors that motivate consumers to buy upscale, pricey products for their pets. In many households, pets are a substitute for children (or are given equal status with children). Pet owners have the desire and willingness to pay premium prices for quality similar to that bought for human children (value perceptions), and there is a spillover to pets from the healthy-living trend among humans (satisfaction/dissatisfaction with present products). This consumer information has been incorporated into marketing strategy in terms of targeted market segments, performance goals based on market forecasts, distribution strategies to reach desirable segments, and other customer-focused management decisions.

Manufacturers of trucks, vans, and sport utility vehicles (SUVs) experienced sales increases of nearly 10 percent from 1991 to 1996 as consumers traded in their traditional passenger cars for more rugged vehicles. Some industry observers consider this phenomenon a cultural shift. That is, families with small children need small minivans; families with older children may prefer a more powerful, more stylish SUV. When the children have grown up and leave home, they may drive off in their own pickup or smaller SUV, and the parents are ready for a luxury car. Consistent with this pattern, sales of trucks and vans slowed during 1997, but SUVs gained sales. In response to this shift in consumer preferences, auto manufacturers developed more luxurious SUVs that combine sporty styling with luxury, such as the Ford Expedition, Lincoln Navigator, Mercedes M-class, and others.[13] Shifting consumer preferences such as this have strategic implications for product/market expansion, competitive positioning, performance objectives, and other strategic planning decisions.

Competitors.   Marketers seek to achieve a sustainable competitive advantage in the markets in which they operate. Therefore, it is necessary to know the identity of key competitors, to understand their strategies, and to anticipate their tactics. While attention typically is focused on direct competitors, it is also wise to monitor indirect competitors who have enlarged their own customer base or have found new ways to satisfy unmet customer needs. Competitors may be selling the same or similar (substitute) products. They may be selling these products through the same distribution channels or reaching customers in an entirely different and innovative way. It is important to recognize all primary sources of competition that can affect a firm's position in the marketplace and to determine the competitive assets and skills that each possesses.

Answers to questions such as the following about competitors should be determined in strategic market planning:

FIGURE 3.4

Five-Factor Model of Profitability

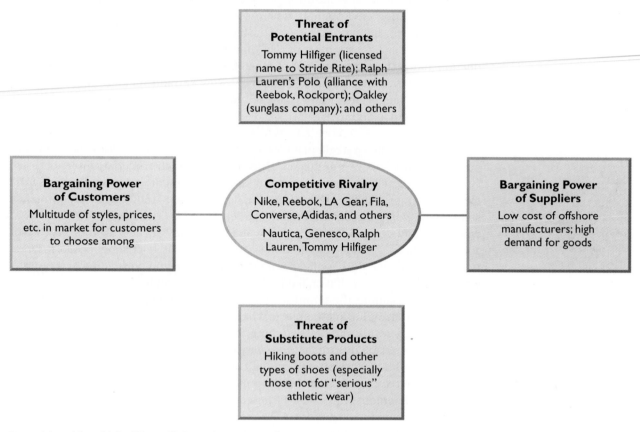

Source: Adapted from Michael Porter, "Industry Structure and Competitive Strategy: Keys to Profitability," *Financial Analysis Journal* (July–August 1980), p. 33.

- Who are the present competitors? How do they rank in order of threat to our market position? What strategies are they pursuing? What are their key success factors?

- Who are the potential competitors? What are their strategies and objectives? What barriers to entry exist to protect our position?

- What new products or technologies are gaining a competitive edge?

If the firm is considering entry into a new industry or product line, similar questions must be answered within the new competitive set.

The **five-factor model of profitability** is a popular framework for assessing the strength of competition.[14] (See Figure 3.4.) At the core of the model is the competition among existing firms within a given industry. The intensity of competition depends on the number and relative size of competitors, degree of similarity of their products and strategies, high versus low fixed-cost structure, level of commitment to the business, and entry and exit barriers. The five-forces model also directs

Five-factor model of profitability
Framework for assessing strength of present and potential competition.

marketing managers' attention to the threat of potential entrants, the threat of substitute products, and the bargaining power of both customers and suppliers.

The U.S. athletic shoe industry provides an excellent example of a highly competitive marketing environment, where 1996 sales totaled over $11 billion, an increase from $3 billion in 1984. Industry leaders, such as Nike and Reebok, dominated the market for most of that time. However, because of the low-cost production and high-profit potential of athletic shoes, many other firms have entered the market, with others planning to follow.[15] New entrants include clothing companies such as Nautica and Tommy Hilfiger and sunglass manufacturers such as Oakley, as illustrated in Figure 3.4.

The Market.   The strategic planning process must take into consideration the primary characteristics of the market segment(s) in which the company chooses to compete. In particular, it is necessary to know the present and potential size of the market, the rate and direction of growth, and relevant trends that may influence strategy development and execution. Market analysis is combined with analysis of customers and competitors in order to determine key success factors, cost bases and perceptions of value, distribution systems, and relative channel position. Questions involving each of these factors must be answered and considered in the strategic planning process, as illustrated in the following example.

Procter & Gamble, the dominant player in the $4.3 billion detergent market, is faced with a changing marketplace where consumer preferences for powdered laundry detergent are rapidly switching to liquid detergent. Technological breakthroughs have enabled manufacturers to extract most of the water from liquid detergents to produce an ultraconcentrated laundry soap and to package it in newly designed, compact bottles that keep the liquid from running down the outside. In 1997, liquid detergent enjoyed an 11 percent increase, compared with a 0.9 percent increase for powdered detergents. As a result, Procter & Gamble must assess its strategy for maintaining a lead in the liquid detergent category, where sales of its Liquid Tide have grown nearly 16 percent compared with sales increases of over 30 percent for Arm and Hammer and 20 percent for Surf brands. Thus the detergent market not only is growing, but it is growing in the direction of liquid detergents. In addition, premium consumer prices and higher profit margins attract numerous competitors.[16]

Environmental Scanning and Forecasting.   In addition to being informed about the micro- or operating-environment factors discussed earlier, marketing managers also must be informed about the macro-environment—forces such as economic conditions, legal and political influences, sociocultural trends, and technological developments. These forces are beyond the direct control of the firm but can shape the development of strategy and its results.

Environmental scanning and forecasting can take a number of forms. The basic requirements include the management of a relevant database and the continuous gathering and interpretation of meaningful data. Computerized decision models are used to facilitate this process.

Detergent manufacturers, for example, should monitor the impact of the economy on consumer spending patterns and the cost of supplies and equipment for manufacturing. The legal and political environment must be monitored to deter-

Environmental scanning and forecasting
Continuous gathering and interpretation of meaningful information about the environment.

mine the effect of present and pending legislation regarding detergent ingredients, environmental protection, trade practices, and so forth. Further, sociocultural trends may lead to use of different types of fabrics or dry cleaning versus home laundering. Technological developments, such as the breakthroughs for ultraconcentrated detergent and improved packaging, also must be analyzed as part of the strategic marketing planning process.

Organizational Analysis (Internal)

In order to determine the best strategic fit between a firm and its environment, it is necessary to conduct a self-assessment of the firm's resource strengths and competitive weaknesses. Each firm has a set of resources that determine its strategic position versus competitors in its industry: financial, physical, human, technological, and organizational resources. The firm's self-assessment can be accomplished by analyzing internal databases (i.e., sales records, customer and competitive data, research and development reports, financial performance for each product category, and so forth) to determine its key success factors and areas that need improvement.

Financial Resources.   A firm's current financial position may determine the level of commitment that can be made for a particular strategic option—or it may place constraints on funds for desirable strategic options. Financial analysis includes a review not only of the present financial assets but also of the sources and uses of those assets, as reported in the firm's financial statements. Sources include sales, interest, dividends, investments, and borrowed funds. Uses may include inventories, promotion and other marketing expenses, interest, taxes, dividends, and other types of financial outlay.

Many companies cut back on expenses, particularly for marketing programs, when faced with declining sales or profits. Spending for advertising and sales force activities may be cut by companies faced with decreased earnings or slow growth. However, this often is done at the expense of attracting much needed business, making it difficult to carry out the firm's strategic intent over the long run.

Physical Resources.   Analysis of physical resources includes an understanding of those required for successful implementation of marketing strategy. This involves an assessment of resources presently available versus those needed in the short and long term, including property, plant (buildings, etc.), and equipment, as well as inventory. For example, the airlines discussed in the opening scenario count among their physical resources their fleet of airplanes, terminal locations and equipment, maintenance facilities, and related equipment. Physical resources related to an airline's corporate headquarters also may be included.

Human Resources.   The talents and abilities of its managers and all other personnel are an indicator of a firm's ability to carry out its strategic intent successfully. A broad definition of a firm's human resources may be extended to include outside specialists, key suppliers or customers, or others who are involved in some way in strategic planning and implementation.

Business Week's top twenty-five managers of 1997 were chosen for their ability to "break away from the pack and clearly outperform" in a year of global upheaval and near-constant change. They were a diverse group from a variety of countries, industries, and businesses. Their talents and management approaches are different, but all these managers "have won the ultimate kudos: respect, and sometimes fear, from their peers. Many have also inspired near-fanatical employee loyalty. Each has put his or her personal imprint on operations. And all have moved quickly when necessary, seizing opportunity before rivals have had the chance to react."[17] An example of their strategies includes American Express's counterattack against Visa and MasterCard with its market-expansion strategy of linking its credit cards to airline frequent-flier programs and building its financial advisory business on its base of credit card holders.

The chief executive of Adidas, the sport shoe maker, implemented a low-cost production strategy and used the savings to market the brand's retro appeal to young adults. Other notable strategies implemented by these outstanding managers include

- Sun Microsystems' high-risk strategy of positioning its Java programming language as the most serious challenger to Microsoft's software dominance;

- Gap's differentiation strategy for the Banana Republic stores with upscale clothes for young professionals and a new line of home furnishings; and

- SAP's (German software firm said to be Europe's answer to Microsoft) strategic alliance with Intel in an Internet commerce venture.[18]

Technological Resources.   Technological resources may be related to both products and processes. Technology may be the product in a high-tech company that markets products such as computer hardware and software, telecommunications, or laser applications. On the other hand, technology may be a strategic strength or weakness on the production line in a manufacturing firm or used to manage large databases in an accounting firm or marketing research service, for example. In these companies, technology can include patents and processes, as well as general know-how.

Many firms achieve a competitive advantage through strategic use of technology. For example, Compaq Computer Corp. developed an efficient computer system to handle orders for its core desktop computers. This innovation was needed in response to a production and order-processing problem caused by producing on the basis of customer orders rather than on the basis of forecasts. The result is a revamped factory that can turn out a custom-built PC in 3 to 4 hours due to a special technique for loading software in 6 minutes. Thanks to this technology, Compaq expected to be able to produce all 8.5 million of its annual business PCs based on actual orders in 1998.[19]

Organizational Resources.   The strategic planning process includes an analysis of a company's structure, systems, and procedures. Structure includes the various business units or divisions that make up the company and the degree of centralization for decision making. The organizational structure should be conducive to development of a strategic marketing plan, and it also should support implementation of that plan.

Strategic Objectives and Strategy Definition
••

Once management has a clear understanding of its external and internal environments, the next step is to establish realistic objectives to be achieved by the strategic plan. These are generally stated in terms of marketing objectives and financial objectives. Financial objectives generally are stated in terms of profitability, performance, or productivity (e.g., 18 percent return on investment). Marketing objectives generally are stated in such terms as sales, market share, customer satisfaction, or communications objectives (e.g., 25 percent market share, 30 percent increase in brand awareness). After the strategic objectives are established, the strategy that will be used to accomplish these objectives must be defined. This is a broad statement for the longer term and is used to drive the details of the specific short- and long-range plans.

Implementation and Tactics
••••••••••••••••••••••••••••••••••••••

The implementation phase of the strategic planning process is concerned with the allocation of resources needed to carry out the tactical, day-to-day strategic intent. Tactics are the short-range plans that are designed to carry out the goals of the broader strategic plan. Elements of the marketing mix—product, price, communication, and distribution—form the basis for tactical plans targeted at selected market segments.

Resource Allocation.   Implementation involves top management commitment to make available the tools that are necessary to carry out the strategic plan. This refers to the level of financial, human, physical, and other resources that will be used for the planned marketing activities during the execution phase. Budget details are determined, decisions are made about internal versus external sources of funds to support the budget, and a timeline is established for obtaining and using these funds. *Human resources* involve all levels of personnel that hold some responsibility for execution of the strategy—from top management accountability to entry-level employee specifications. *Physical resources* refer to the property (e.g., land, buildings, etc.), equipment, or other tangible capital goods that are instrumental in executing the strategy.

Target market(s)
Homogeneous group(s) of customers that a company chooses to serve.

Target Market and Marketing Mix.   A critical aspect of the strategic planning process is identification of the **target market(s)** that the company will serve. There must be a strategic fit between the customers who are selected and the design of the marketing mix to reach each segment. The tactical plan is based on decisions regarding the design of the marketing mix. The product, communication, pricing, and distribution strategies must provide a consistent, synergistic approach to carrying out the strategic intent during the execution stage. For example, Southwest Airlines' no-frills short-haul flights, low prices, selected routes and destinations, and promotional messages are consistent and effective in achieving the company's objectives.

Execution

For many, the execution phase is the make-or-break stage for the strategic plan. Execution involves the physical performance of the tasks and activities identified in the implementation stage. Successful execution of the plan should achieve the strategic objectives specified previously. It is important to note that the best of strategies can fail if implemented poorly. Likewise, a poor strategy may lead to success if executed well.

In 1997, analysts believed that Novell, once the leader in networking software, had lost its focus and sense of direction while yielding market share to Microsoft and SAP despite its attempt to develop a strategy for a sustainable competitive advantage. Although the company is known for its technical know-how and innovative products, the execution of its strategy for the Jefferson Project for sharing and managing documents over the Internet met with problems. Novell lost its early-mover advantage and uniqueness by being delayed more than 6 months after its much-touted delivery date, making it necessary to face stiff competition from Netscape and Microsoft.[20]

Evaluation and Control

In this phase of the strategic planning process, actual results are compared with the planned marketing and financial objectives established in an earlier stage. Results of the plan can be monitored during and after execution. If measured during execution, midcourse corrections may be made. It is not enough to know *whether* the objectives were achieved; it is perhaps more important to know *why* the objectives were or were not achieved. Control mechanisms should be in place before the plan is executed, and all involved parties should be accountable for their part in making the plan work. Continuing the preceding example, Novell may gain insights from evaluating its new product-development process, marketing strategies, and other factors involved in shortening the time to market for its new products.

PLANNING FOR THE LONG TERM

Over the long term, strategic marketing planners must focus on two major considerations: developing basic strategies to maintain a sustainable competitive advantage and making a distinction between strategic and tactical decisions. Most marketing management decisions have long-term consequences and so must be consistent with a firm's overall strategic intent.

Sustainable Competitive Advantage: Basic Strategies

Sustainable competitive advantage
Long-term success based on unique assets and skills that determine strategic thrust.

The most common routes to **sustainable competitive advantage** involve one or more of the following basic strategies: differentiation, low cost, focus, preemptive move, and synergy. Each of these is described in the following sections and illustrated in Table 3.2.

TABLE 3.2
....
Basic Strategies for Sustainable Competitive Advantage

Basic Strategy	*Description*	*Example*
Differentiation	Strategy for distinguishing one company's product from its competitors' on the basis of greater perceived benefits and/or more value	Oral-B added a patented blue dye to the center of its toothbrushes to indicate when they should be discarded and replaced with a new toothbrush.
Low Cost	Marketer achieves cost advantage by controlling costs of production, product components, marketing programs, etc.	Best Buy Co. and other discount retailers control operating costs with no-frills store environments, self-service, and volume buying, permitting higher profits and lower consumer prices.
Focus	Concentration of the business on specific market segment(s) and/or product group(s)	Intel concentrates its product mix on microprocessor chips; sales are primarily to business-to-business customers.
Preemptive Move	First-mover advantage from being first to enter market with a new product, innovation, etc.; creates barriers to entry for competitors	Microsoft gained a first-mover advantage by preempting competitors through alliances with computer manufacturers to install its software on new PCs.
Synergy	Combining the assets and skills of two or more business units by sharing business functions, customers, marketing personnel, etc.	1998 merger of Daimler-Benz and Chrysler created synergy by extending each company's customer base, distribution, and manufacturing expertise.

Differentiation
Strategy based on distinguishing a company's offering from that of competitors based on value-added benefits.

Differentiation.   With **differentiation,** one company's product (goods and/or services) is distinguished from that of its competitors by giving customers more value and greater perceived benefits than they could obtain elsewhere. Differentiation can be on the basis of both objective (e.g., measurable performance, added design features) and subjective (e.g., prestige, style) dimensions. When these differentiating factors clearly give a significant advantage over competitors, they can be used effectively in the firm's product positioning statements. A differentiation strategy based on dimensions that are important to customers offers an effective way to create value.

Low-cost strategy
Strategy based on ability to add value to the product and/or processes that results in lower prices and/or higher operating margins.

Low Cost.   A **low-cost strategy** should not be confused with the idea of being inexpensive. Today, the ability to gain a cost advantage by controlling costs of production, delivery, product components, and other expenses has become crucial for competitive superiority. Customers demand more value for their money, causing marketers to examine creative ways to deliver value to their customers. While value does not necessarily mean that the customer will pay less for a good or service, it does generally imply value added at some point in the process of manufacturing and/or delivering the good or service to the customer.

Focus strategy
Strategy that concentrates on specific market segment(s) and/or product group(s).

Focus.   A **focus strategy** involves concentration of the business on specific market segment(s) and/or product group(s). Focus can be combined with other strategic marketing techniques, such as differentiation or low cost, to achieve sustainable competitive advantage.

Preemptive move strategy
First-mover advantage, first to enter the market.

Preemptive Move.   A **preemptive move strategy** involves gaining strategic advantage by being the first to enter the market with a new product, a new use for an existing product, a new distribution method, or other innovation. This strategy can create barriers to entry for companies that attempt to follow the first mover into the market.

Synergy
Two or more business units combining assets and skills to achieve strategic advantage.

Synergy.   Firms that are comprised of two or more business units often can obtain **synergy** by combining the assets and skills of these units to achieve strategic advantages. This may involve sharing certain business functions, such as centralized accounting, production, and so forth. They also may be able to offer multiple products or services to the same customer, that is, one-stop shopping, by using the same salesforce to cross-sell each company's offerings.

Strategic versus Tactical Marketing Decisions

At this point in the chapter, it seems appropriate to re-emphasize the differences between strategic and tactical marketing decisions. It is also important to recognize the interdependent relationship between these two concepts. Japanese companies, such as Sharp and Fuji, are using preemptive moves to change from being a market follower to being a market leader. Their strategy is to use technology to bring new products to market that will amaze their consumers. At the tactical level, organizational leadership must provide a climate that will encourage this type of commitment to meeting customer needs with high-quality high-tech products. Sharp has concept-design centers where management is involved in the process and personnel are motivated to develop the innovative products desired by the market and the company.[21] Beyond the tactical marketing decisions related to product design, Sharp must determine the best methods for distributing and selling its products, the most appropriate pricing strategy, and the level of service to provide.

STRATEGIC PLANNING AND THE CHALLENGE OF CHANGE

Forces of change and their impact on the marketing management process were discussed in the preceding chapter. In this chapter we look at the impact of change on strategy development. In the past, strategic plans could be developed with some level of confidence for perhaps 5 to 10 years. Today, however, the rate of change in most industries is such that the strategic planning horizon is more likely to be 3 to 5 years maximum, with periodic reassessment during this time to determine the need for strategic realignment. In dealing with change, an organization needs to consider several factors:

- What changes are occurring in the ways that firms are approaching strategy development?

- What roles do flexibility and adaptability play in long-range planning?

- Who are the firm's stakeholders, and what levels of involvement do they have or should they have in determining strategic direction for the long term?

- With ethics and social responsibility issues permeating the business environment, how should these concepts be integrated into practice through the strategic planning process?

- What is the role of marketing information systems in strategic market planning, and what criteria should be considered in determining the types of data to include?

Changes in Approaches to Strategy Development

The complexity and uncertainty that face most business organizations today in their rapidly changing operating environments have had a major impact on the strategic planning process. As a result, managers experience the frustration of not being able to predict the future with a desirable degree of accuracy and not having sufficient time to engage in necessary long-range planning activities.

Strategic inflection point
The point at which the threats of a changing environment can be converted into opportunities by following certain actions.

Dr. Andrew Grove, chief executive and president of Intel, suggests a methodology for distinguishing a **strategic inflection point** (turning point) from the "normal hurly-burly of corporate life."[22] The threats of change can be converted into opportunities by following a generic series of actions. The *five forces model* that is used to analyze the competitive environment was presented in Figure 3.4. These forces include suppliers, buyers, potential entrants, and substitutes, with the fifth comprised of the force of rivalry and competition within the industry. A more recent update of this model has added a sixth force—*complementors*. (See Figure 3.5.) This force is described as both subtle and significant. It is the dependence developed in a business on other companies whose products work in conjunction with its own, creating a synergistic effect.

An example is found in the relationship between Microsoft (software) and Intel (microprocessors) in the personal computer industry. Neither company would be as effective without the other. Where these forces are more or less in equilibrium with one another, the industry environment remains relatively favorable. However, when one of these forces becomes significantly larger or more powerful than another force, the environment is less favorable. For example, a substitute may be introduced to the market with a force that is many times greater than existing forces, distorting the usual way of doing business. (See Figure 3.5a.) The result is generally a change in the framework in which the business operates, eventually leading to a different type of framework where the business operates under a different set of influences. Essentially, the business is reinvented and becomes a completely different structure. Grove refers to the period of time during the transition as the *strategic inflection point*. (See Figure 3.5b.) "During a Strategic Inflection Point, the way a business operates, the very structure and concept of the business, undergoes a change. But the irony is that at this point itself nothing much happens. That is the nature of an Inflection Point: it is a kind of a gentle curve. Yet at a point where nothing else

FIGURE 3.5
· ·
Strategic Inflection Point: A Six Forces Adaptation of the Five Forces Model

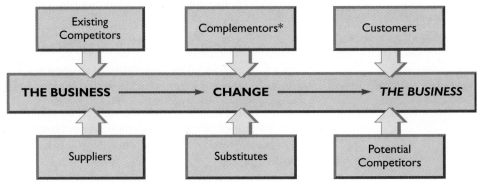

*Significance: Complementors counteract substitution.

(a) Imbalance of Environmental Forces (Substitutes)

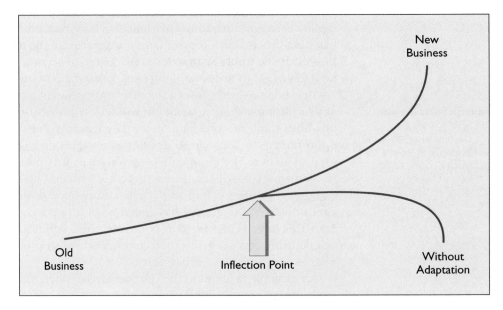

(b) Strategic Inflection Point

Source: Adapted from Andrew S. Grove, "Navigating Strategic Inflection Points," *Business Strategy Review* (Autumn 1997), pp. 11–18. Copyright London Business School. Reprinted by permission of Blackwell Publishers.
· ·

happens, you must determine whether the future trajectory of that curve is going to head up or down."[23]

When a firm is at a strategic inflection point, the effect is so subtle that the change may be missed. There are many examples. Many small-town retailers have underestimated the changes that can come about when a new Wal-Mart comes to town. The 1984 decision of AT&T executives to go along with the breakup of the AT&T U.S.-wide monopoly in long-distance and regional local access providers rather than fight the U.S. Justice Department's antitrust suit provides another example of an action taken at a strategic inflection point.

Although he does not guarantee a precise formula, Grove identifies some warning signs that indicate a strategic inflection point in a time of change:

- *Try the "silver bullet test."* If you anticipate a change in your key competitor, imagine that you have a silver bullet that you can use to shoot one competitor. If you have only one choice, which one will it be? You must decide. When this answer changes to another competitor, this is a good indication that you are passing through a strategic inflection point. One of the signs that you are facing a different business scenario is when the people who threaten you change.

- *Do you have that feeling that the people around you have "lost it"?* If so, apply the "silver bullet test" to complementors—those on whom you are most dependent to make your product work best. Listen for people to use phrases that represent a whole new vogue; if these words sounds like gibberish to you, there may be cross-currents going on in your organization that need to be analyzed. When you or someone else doesn't "get it," maybe the "it" is no longer what you used to talk about—a warning sign that something is changing.

- *Listen to the bearers of bad news (i.e., what people think is going wrong) in your organization.* Those who are closest to a problem (e.g., technology, sales or customer situation) generally see the first signs of a strategic inflection point. Sales organizations are particularly good at this.

- *Use debate as an important measuring tool for sorting through the "is it" or "is it not" questions.* This process helps to remove the inconsistencies and identify important events and changes.

Identification of strategic inflection points is one of a number of methods used to identify "turning points that can make or break even the strongest of businesses." The important lesson is that marketing managers need to take actions to "convert the threats of change into opportunities." Each of the forces in the traditional five forces model must be monitored, along with the sixth force—complementors—in order to develop a winning strategy.

Complexity and Uncertainty

The complexity and uncertainty that characterize most industries today—particularly in high-technology areas such as telecommunications and computer hardware and software and others such as managed health care—have caused many firms to reassess their long-term strategies. In these industries, the legal/political ramifications are evolving and uncertain, and competitive actions and reactions are not always predictable.

Complexity refers to the intricacies and interrelationships of a company and the industry in which it operates, making it difficult to analyze, understand, or solve complicated problems. Strategic marketing management requires the ability to separate elaborately intertwined environmental forces to simplify their analysis to the extent possible.

Uncertainty refers to vagueness and doubt about a company's industry and general operating environment—not being sure what is happening now or what is going to happen in the future. Several scenarios generally are possible, ranging from worst case to most optimistic. The question is, Which is most likely to occur, and how soon?

Industries with a high level of complexity and uncertainty include those related to telecommunications, computers, and software. Government regulations, strategic alliances among competitors, rapid advances in technology, and other factors present both threats and opportunities. Intel, whose position as the leading high-tech computer chip manufacturer seems to make it invincible, has addressed the issues of complexity and uncertainty with strategic alliances. As noted earlier, one of these alliances is with Microsoft. Another is with Compaq, a personal computer manufacturer, to create a number of networking innovations and provide a competitive edge to the product lines of both companies in order to preempt rival market entries. This action was taken, in part, to remove the uncertainty of a possible threat from the industry consortium of AIM (Apple, IBM, and Motorola).[24] Strategic alliances are also considered by some to be an effective way to diversify a firm's industry position so as to ward off antitrust allegations.

Poverty of Time
. . . .

Traditionally, small business managers have less time available for strategic planning than do managers in large businesses. In larger firms, the strategic planning process tends to be more formal, often with individuals or departments charged with this responsibility. Further, stockholders, lenders, and other interested parties demand evidence of accountability that may be found in a firm's strategic marketing plan. The rate of change and resulting volatility in business environments increase the need to anticipate the future in order to maximize opportunities and minimize threats. Many firms have turned to outside analysts who are knowledgeable about their industry and experts in strategic planning to facilitate this process. Many of the major consulting firms and former "Big Six" accounting firms have expanded their services to fill this need. Regardless of the size of the business, time must be made available for reflection and planning for the future.

The Importance of Flexibility and Adaptation
. . . .

The strategic planning process establishes clear guidelines for future marketing decisions, but at times this formal process may result in establishing directives and constraints that make it difficult for a firm to adapt to changing circumstances. Therefore, a realistic strategic plan should allow for needed flexibility and provide parameters for adapting to new situations. This requires easily understood guidelines that cover a relatively broad range of decisions—particularly focused on the firm's mission and objectives to maintain consistency and take advantage of the company's core competencies.

The rapid growth of Internet commerce has tested the flexibility of many organizations and their ability to adapt to an entirely new way of doing business. One major challenge is that the Internet is a global marketplace, introducing new competition and new markets to firms throughout the world. Small local marketers no longer must worry only about local competition. They suddenly are thrust into the world of international commerce, requiring a new approach to strategic market

INNOVATE OR EVAPORATE*

High-Tech College Bookstore

Follett Corp. developed a new college bookstore concept that illustrates an innovative way to adapt to change. The company opened a 20,000 square foot, freestanding three-level concept store at the University of Illinois at Champaign-Urbana. The store, called Folle^{2}tt [energy squared], offers all the traditional textbooks with various 1990s amenities, including a two-story "cyberwall," an in-store café, computer stations with Internet connections, publishing and copy services, music, and software. The store uses a curriculum-centered merchandising strategy, grouping all items related to an academic discipline in one of nine subject-related locations or "worlds." Follett has responded to environmental changes to meet the needs and lifestyles of college students, most of whom are of the MTV generation.

*The box title is attributed to James M. Higgins.

Source: Cyndee Miller, "Marketing Textbooks to the MTV Generation," *Marketing News* 31(21) (October 13, 1997), pp. 1, 12.

planning. Foreign companies have discovered the lucrative American market, and U.S. companies that adapt to doing business on the Internet can benefit from new markets, less regulation, and expanded business relationships.

Stakeholder Involvement

Stakeholders
All external and internal parties involved in the life of an organization.

Many firms bring their important stakeholders into the strategic planning process. These valued **stakeholders** may include customers, suppliers, employees at various levels in the organization, consultants, and others. Their contributions may be in the nature of market feedback; projections about product supply and demand; and information about competitors, technological breakthroughs, legal and political activities, and other environmental issues. A firm's overall marketing effort should include the development of strategic relationships with key stakeholders that can provide useful insights throughout the strategic planning process. Information gained from each of these sources can be included in the marketing decision support system (MDSS), discussed in Chapter 4.

Integrating Ethics and Social Responsibility

If a direction for ethics and social responsibility is not integrated into the strategic market planning process from the very beginning, the organizational culture may not provide the needed direction for ethical and socially responsible marketing programs.[25] In the drive for profits, productivity, and efficiency—all values that are necessary for success—the process illustrated in Figure 3.6 introduces other core values that help to define acceptable limits for strategic and tactical decisions.

Ethical behavior is fundamental to building trust and long-term relationships between a company and its employees. Companies need to develop and enforce a

FIGURE 3.6

• •

Integration of Ethical and Socially Responsible Plans into Strategic Decision Making

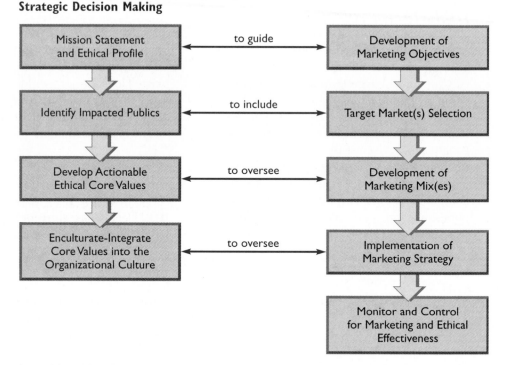

Source: Adapted from Robin, Donald and R. Eric Reidenbach (1987), "Social Responsibility, Ethics, and Marketing Strategy: Closing the Gap Between Concept and Application," *Journal of Marketing* 51(1) (January 1987), pp. 44–58. Reprinted by permission.

• •

code of ethics that will guide decisions in marketing and other business areas. A code of ethics sets standards and provides guidelines for acceptable behavior. The American Marketing Association's Code of Ethics is shown in Figure 3.7.

STRATEGIC PLANNING AND A CUSTOMER ORIENTATION

• •

It has become increasingly evident that a successful strategic plan must start with the customer. Marketing opportunities are based on an identification of market wants and needs, an understanding of how customers make buying decisions, how they use the goods and services they buy, and their level of commitment to current brands. The strategic planning process should incorporate the following:

• Outstanding approaches to delivering customer satisfaction

• A plan for value creation from the customers' perspective

• Plans for continuous quality improvement in products and processes

• The ability and willingness to re-engineer and/or redesign as indicated by the marketing environment or internal conditions.

FIGURE 3.7

American Marketing Association Code of Ethics

Members of the American Marketing Association (AMA) are committed to ethical professional conduct. They have joined together in subscribing to this Code of Ethics embracing the following topics.

Responsibilities of the Marketer

Marketers must accept responsibility for the consequences of their activities and make every effort to ensure that their decisions, recommendations, and actions function to identify, serve, and satisfy all relevant publics: consumers, organizations, and society. Marketers' professional conduct must be guided by:

1. The basic rule of professional ethics: not knowingly to do harm;
2. The adherence to all applicable laws and regulations;
3. The accurate representation of their education, training, and experience; and
4. The active support, practice, and promotion of this Code of Ethics.

Honesty and Fairness

Marketers shall uphold and advance the integrity, honor, and dignity of the marketing profession by:

1. Being honest in serving consumers, clients, employees, suppliers, distributors, and the public;
2. Not knowingly participating in conflict of interest without prior notice to all parties involved; and

3. Establishing equitable fee schedules including the payment or receipt of usual, customary, and/or legal compensation for marketing exchanges.

Rights and Duties of Parties

Participants in the marketing exchange process should be able to expect that:

1. Products and services offered are safe and fit for their intended uses;
2. Communications about offered products and services are not deceptive;
3. All parties intend to discharge their obligations, financial and otherwise, in good faith; and
4. Appropriate internal methods exist for equitable adjustment and/or redress of grievances concerning purchases.

It is understood that the above would include, but is not limited to, the following responsibilities of the marketer:

In the area of product development management:

- Disclosure of all substantial risks associated with product or service usage
- Identification of any product component substitution that might materially change the product or impact on the buyer's purchase decision
- Identification of extra-cost added features

(continues on next page)

Customer Satisfaction

The ultimate success of a strategic marketing plan lies in the amount of customer satisfaction and profitability that it can generate. A strategy that results in high levels of customer satisfaction gives a firm one of the greatest long-term assets it can have: loyal customers who return time and again for repeat purchases. However, the ability to deliver customer satisfaction must start with a customer focus, and this business philosophy must start with top management. This requires giving attention to the quality not only of the goods and services offered by the business but also of the processes involved before, during, and after a sale, as indicated in Chapter 1 and throughout this book.

FIGURE 3.7 *(continued)*
....

American Marketing Association Code of Ethics

In the area of promotions:

- Avoidance of false and misleading advertising
- Rejection of high pressure manipulations, or misleading sales tactics
- Avoidance of sales promotions that use deception or manipulation

In the area of distribution:

- Not manipulating the availability of a product for purpose of exploitation
- Not using coercion in the marketing channel
- Not exerting undue influence over the resellers' choice to handle a product

In the area of pricing:

- Not engaging in price fixing
- Not practicing predatory pricing
- Disclosing the full price associated with any purchase

In the area of marketing research:

- Prohibiting selling or fund raising under the guise of conducting research
- Maintaining research integrity by avoiding misrepresentation and omission of pertinent research data
- Treating outside clients and suppliers fairly

Organizational Relationships

Marketers should be aware of how their behavior may influence or impact on the behavior of others in organizational relationships. They should not encourage or apply coercion to obtain unethical behavior in their relationships with others, such as employers, suppliers, or customers.

1. Apply confidentiality and anonymity in professional relationships with regard to privileged information.
2. Meet their obligations and responsibilities in contracts and mutual agreements in a timely manner.
3. Avoid taking the work of others, in whole, or in part, and represent this work as their own or directly benefit from it without compensation or consent of the orginator or owner.
4. Avoid manipulation to take advantage of situations to maximize personal welfare in a way that unfairly deprives or damages the organization or others.

Any AMA members found to be in violation of any provision of this Code of Ethics may have their Association membership suspended or revoked.

Source: Reprinted by permission of the American Marketing Association.

....

Value Creation
....

Value is "in the eye of the beholder." It is important to consider the perspective of the final consumer or business customer when deciding how to add value to a company's goods and services. The value added to a sale differentiates one company's offering from that of a competitor. It provides the basis for a positioning strategy that can be used in product design (or redesign) and marketing communications. While many firms pursue a low-cost strategy and many purchase decisions are made on the basis of price, the most successful approaches include a competitive advantage obtained through a value-added strategy. Customer value may be created in a variety of ways, such as exceptional customer service, product assortments, unusual product design features, unique packaging, creative distribution methods, and higher-quality component parts and materials.

FIGURE 3.8

....

The Value Chain

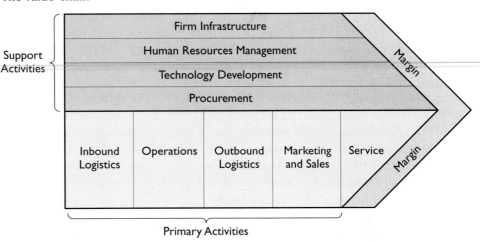

Source: Reprinted with the permission of the Free Press, a Division of Simon & Schuster, Inc. from *Competitive Advantage: Creating and Sustaining Superior Performance* by Michael E. Porter. Copyright ©1985 by Michael E. Porter.

....

Value chain
Set of primary and secondary activities concerned with creating and delivering value for customers.

Porter's **value chain**[26] includes both primary and secondary activities that create value for customers. (See Figure 3.8.) The value chain reveals ways to obtain competitive advantage through differences in primary and secondary value-creating activities. Primary value activities include inbound and outbound logistics, operations, marketing and sales, and service. Secondary value activities include procurement, technology development, human resource management, and the firm infrastructure. Each of these activities may be a strength or weakness when compared with competitors.

One way to add value is through more convenient, lower-cost distribution methods. In the United States and throughout the world, shopping centers and malls have responded to customers' demands for one-stop shopping and discount centers. In Japan, there are six supermalls (compared with nearly 700 in the United States), with more on the way. The Japanese make up only 2 percent of the world's population but purchase two-thirds of the world's branded products. Known for their demand for quality, Japanese consumers now are also demanding lower prices. Japan's economic difficulties of the 1990s created customer resistance to the higher prices they once paid without question during the affluent 1980s. Japanese consumers have turned to discount outlets and shopping in stores overseas or ordering from foreign catalogs to obtain value. It is estimated that Japanese shoppers spend over $40 billion overseas each year. One response to this trend is the development of supermalls in Japan. These supermalls offer a variety of retail shops, dining, and leisure activities, with emphasis on lower prices and more value for the money. Economies of scale are obtained through increased efficiency in inbound and outbound logistics (e.g., highway access, containerized shipping), spreading fixed costs over a larger operation, and other value-added activities.[27]

Summary

The strategic planning process and marketing management are closely related, since marketing management decisions must be consistent with a firm's overall business strategy. A formal strategic plan provides a basis for making better decisions in all circumstances because strategic decisions are based on an understanding of customers' needs, competitors' activities, and the financial implications of each decision. The firm's overall business strategy and an understanding of its marketing strategies drive tactical marketing plans. Both strategic and tactical decisions must be responsive to changes in the marketplace.

Strategic plans are developed at several levels of an organization: corporate, division or strategic business unit, and functional or operating level. The focus of this book is on the business unit level. Stages in the strategic planning process include determination of the firm's mission and corporate performance objectives, analysis of external and internal environments, marketing objectives and strategy, implementation and tactics, execution of the plan, and evaluation and control measures.

The major external environmental factors to be analyzed in the strategic planning process are the firm's customers, competitors, and market where it will compete. Marketing managers must continuously scan the external environment to identify opportunities and threats and to be able to identify market trends and forecast demand. The major internal factors that should be included in a firm's self-analysis are competitive strengths and weaknesses related to its financial, physical, human, technological, and organizational resources.

Marketing planners must design strategies that will give them a sustainable competitive advantage over the long term. The most common routes taken to achieve strategic advantage involve one or more of the following basic strategies: differentiation, low cost, focus, preemptive move, and synergy.

The forces of change discussed in the preceding chapter and the rate at which these changes occur have a significant impact on the strategic market planning process. The approach to strategy development has changed due to the rate of change, environmental complexity and uncertainty, inability to accurately predict the future, and time constraints faced by managers for planning activities. Because of this, many marketing managers have had to settle for shorter planning horizons and allow for flexibility needed to adapt to new circumstances.

Many firms gain insights and support from customers, suppliers, employees, and other important stakeholders throughout the strategic planning process. Firms also are finding it expedient to integrate ethics and social responsibility into their strategic market planning and include core values to help define acceptable limits for strategic and tactical decisions. Because a successful strategic plan must start with the customer, the strategic planning process should include outstanding approaches to delivering customer satisfaction, a customer-oriented plan for value creation, and the ability and willingness to change with market conditions.

Questions

1. Explain the relationship between the strategic market planning process, the marketing management process, and the success of an organization. Use an existing nonprofit or for-profit organization to illustrate your answer.

2. Discuss the purpose of a formal strategic plan for a high-tech telecommunications company that is faced with the challenge of managing change in a volatile, uncertain marketing environment. Would your answer be different for a manufacturer of a low-tech, staple product such as paper goods for an office? Why?

3. Describe each of the stages in the strategic planning process. Explain how aspects of this process might be different for a cellular telephone company versus the American Red Cross.

4. Give an example of each internal and external environmental force that can affect the success of a marketing program, and state why it is important to analyze each of these. Which of these forces can be controlled (at least to some extent) by the organization, and what are some ways that this can be accomplished?

5. Identify a recent macro- or micro-environmental change that has had an impact on marketing decisions. Explain how this has affected product design or availability and pricing, promotion, or distribution strategies. (Be sure to differentiate between strategy and tactics and between organizational levels in your answer.)

6. Describe the major strategic approaches that marketers can use to achieve sustainable competitive advantage over the long term. Give a specific example of how each has been used by a marketer of goods or services and why you think it has been successful (or unsuccessful).

7. Record the details of a recent purchase experience, and analyze your perceptions of whether the organization's marketing strategy is based on a customer orientation. Why and how should the customer be considered in developing a strategic marketing plan?

8. Explain the role that core values and ethics should play in developing a strategic marketing plan. How can these concepts be integrated into the strategic plan and effectively implemented on a day-to-day basis?

Exercises

1. Obtain annual reports or other company literature from a variety of companies (e.g., auto manufacturers, packaged food products, tobacco, telecommunications, banks, etc.). Identify their mission and/or vision statement, objectives, and long-term strategies, and evaluate their effectiveness.

2. Determine the mission statement, objectives, and long-term strategies for a nonprofit organi-

zation such as the American Cancer Society, a church, or the Girl or Boy Scouts of America. Discuss the differences, if any, in the purposes of strategic planning for the types of organizations discussed in this exercise and Exercise 1.

3. Select an industry that is experiencing a rapidly changing environment (e.g., telecommunications, personal computers, software, insurance, etc.). For this industry, analyze the following:

    a. Major competitors in the industry and their relative position in terms of market share and profitability.

    b. Industry growth rates (size and direction) and emerging trends that will affect future strategic decisions (either positively or negatively).

    c. Key success factors to ensure profitability over the long term.

    d. Comparative strengths and weaknesses of each of the industry competitors described in part a and your opinion of whether their relative positions are subject to change.

4. Visit the Web sites of the companies discussed above. Analyze the content of these Web sites to determine how they support the company's strategy and how use of this medium offers them a competitive advantage with their customers.

5. Develop a strategic marketing plan for an entrepreneurial venture in which you are interested (or for an organization to which you belong). What advice would you give to someone else about pitfalls and challenges that were encountered in this planning process?

Endnotes

1. Quote taken from *Bartlett's Book of Business Quotations*, compiled by Barbara Ann Kipher (Boston: Little, Brown and Company, 1994), p. 265.

2. The *growth phase* as used here refers to the early stages of the firm when it is emerging from its start-

up phase or to any point in the organizational cycle where strategic marketing decisions are made. This may apply to strategic growth plans, new product development policies, and so on.

3. David A. Aaker, *Strategic Market Management,* 4th ed. (New York: Wiley, 1998), pp. 4–6.

4. Gerald A. Michaelson, "Winning the Marketing War," in Jeffrey Heilbrunn (ed.), *Marketing Encyclopedia: Issues and Trends Shaping the Future* (Chicago: American Marketing Association, 1995), pp. 170–172.

5. Subhash C. Jain, *Marketing Planning and Strategy,* 3d ed. (Cincinnati: South-Western Publishing, 1990), pp. 24–27.

6. For further discussion, see Aaker, *op. cit.,* pp. 27–29; and Carol H. Anderson, *Retailing: Concepts, Strategy, and Information* (Minneapolis/St. Paul: West Publishing, 1993), Chap. 2.

7. Derek F. Abell, "Strategic Windows," *Journal of Marketing* (July 1978), pp. 21–26. (A strategic window represents a short period of time when there is an optimal "fit" between the organization's capabilities and a new opportunity to satisfy the needs of the market.)

8. Theodore Levitt, "Marketing Myopia," *Harvard Business Review* (July–August 1960), pp. 45–56. *Marketing myopia* refers to missed opportunities caused by focusing on the product at the expense of paying attention to the customer and the needs of a changing marketplace.

9. Aaker, *op. cit.,* pp. 149–156.

10. Patricia Kranz, "How Do You Say 'Fore' in Russian?—Cold War Rocket Scientists Blast into the Titanium Clubs Business," *Business Week* (October 6, 1997), p. 162.

11. John Schnapp, "Ford Is Right on GM's Tailpipe," *Fortune* (October 27, 1997), pp. 54, 58.

12. Ian P. Murphy, "A Dog's Life," *Marketing News* 31(16) (August 4, 1997), pp. 1–2.

13. Corey Takahashi, "Midlife Crisis? Trucks, Vans Start to Lose Their Luster," *Wall Street Journal* (August 4, 1997), p. B1.

14. Michael E. Porter, "Industry Structure and Competitive Strategy: Keys to Profitability," *Financial Analysis Journal* (July–August 1980), p. 33.

15. Kelly Barron, "Jostling Nike," *Forbes* (October 20, 1997), p. 159.

16. Tara Parker-Pope, "Boom in Liquid Detergents Has P&G Scrambling," *Wall Street Journal* (September 25, 1997), pp. B1, B3.

17. "The Top 25 Managers of the Year," *Business Week* (January 12, 1998), pp. 54–68.

18. *Ibid.*

19. Evan Ramstad, "Compaq CEO Takes Tricky Curves Fast," *Wall Street Journal* (January 5, 1998), p. B4.

20. John Fontana, "Breaking Down Group Wise—Novell Says New Strategy Helps Developers Write Collaborative Apps," *Internet Week* (September 2, 1997), Issue 682, Section: News and Analysis.

21. Motokazu Orihata, "Steering a New Course for Japanese Management," *Strategy & Business* (Second Quarter 1997), pp. 50–56.

22. Andrew S. Grove, "Navigating Strategic Inflection Points," *Business Strategy Review* (Autumn 1997), pp. 11–18.

23. *Ibid.*

24. Tom Davey, "Intel Steps Up," *Information Week* (September 29, 1997), Issue 649, pp. 16–17.

25. Donald Robin and R. Eric Reidenbach, "Social Responsibility, Ethics, and Marketing Strategy: Closing the Gap Between Concept and Application," *Journal of Marketing* 51(1) (January 1987), pp. 44–58.

26. Michael E. Porter, *Competitive Advantage: Creating and Sustaining Superior Performance* (New York: Free Press, 1985), Chap. 2.

27. Virginia Kouyoumdjian, "Supermalls Build on New Shopping Strategy," *Wall Street Journal* (September 29, 1997), p. B12.

The Global Marketplace
Macro-Environment
Micro-Environment
Organizational Environment
Marketing Environment
Customer

CHAPTER 4

Marketing Intelligence and Creative Problem Solving

Marketing Management Decisions and Creative Problem Solving

The Marketing Research Process

Key Information for Marketing Decisions

Sources of Information

Issues in Marketing Information Acquisition and Use

Listen to the Marketplace—or the Roar of a Harley

We are living in a second industrial revolution, one propelled by information instead of steam.[1]

As motorcycle manufacturer Harley-Davidson, Inc., entered the 1990s, the company found itself in a familiar quandary—whether to expand and risk a market downturn or to stay the course and continue to enjoy its good position in the industry. During the late 1970s and early 1980s, Harley experienced serious losses, primarily due to lack of quality from too-rapid expansion. In the late 1970s, AMF, the sporting goods conglomerate that was Harley's parent company, had invested to expand its manufacturing capacity and capitalize on the Harley name, but the result was a drop in the quality of the bikes and a drop in sales.

Following the largest leveraged buyout up to that time, Harley-Davidson became an independent company in 1981. During the 6 months that followed the buyout, the company lost $20 million and more than a third of its employees, and it nearly went bankrupt over the next 2 years. Its reputation was "soiled like the pavement underneath a leaky crankcase." Loyal Harley fans had a favorite joke then: "Harleys don't leak oil, they just mark their spot."

Harley's outlook changed as it began to regain its quality reputation. By 1989, the company had introduced a new engine design, Softtail suspension, and other product improvements. The company also added customer-service innovations such as test-ride programs (a first in the industry) and guaranteed trade-in allowances. In 1985, Harley shipped 30,000 motorcycles and had a market share of 27 percent in the heavyweight bike category. By 1989, the company shipped 44,000 bikes, and its market share rose to 57 percent with a profit of $53 million.

Although Harley had recaptured its earlier success, the company was unwilling to be caught in another downturn. Harley's scanning of the environment indicated that the market for heavyweight bikes was shrinking, and it needed to know whether Harley-Davidson's growth could continue. One option was to try to reverse the industry's downward trend and become an industry leader, but the company also noticed that a new kind of customer seemed to be fueling market growth. In the middle 1980s, white-collar motorcycle enthusiasts (nicknamed "Rubbies," for rich urban bikers) contributed to increased sales and added to the company's success and image. Harley was concerned, however, about whether "Rubbies" would continue to be reliable long-term customers.

Harley-Davidson management had several research questions that needed to be addressed: Are the newer white-collar customers going to stay with Harley or move on when the next fad comes along? Should its products be marketed differently to different audiences (without alienating its core clientele of traditional bikers who had remained faithful to Harley during its leanest years)? Was there a universal appeal to owning a Harley (i.e., what is the customer mindset)?

To answer these questions, Harley-Davidson began to gather market intelligence. The company first invited focus groups comprised of current owners, would-be owners, and owners of other brands to participate in an exercise where they created cut-and-paste collages to express their feelings about Harley-Davidsons. Common themes emerged from the artwork produced by this diverse group: enjoyment, the great outdoors, and freedom. Next, the company mailed 16,000 surveys that contained a battery of psychological, sociologic, and demographic questions typical of similar studies and received a 30 percent response rate. Seven core customer types were identified from the responses: the "Adventure-Loving Traditionalist, the Sensitive Pragmatist, the Stylish Status-Seeker, the Laid-Back Camper, the Classy Capitalist, the Cool-Headed Loner, and the Cocky Misfit." The universal appeals of "independence, freedom, and power" were appreciated by all the groups, with tremendous loyalty across the board, which meant the company could increase production and sales of its motorcycles without having to overextend itself.

Source: Ian P. Murphy, "Aided by Research, Harley Goes Whole Hog," *Marketing News* 30(25) (December 2, 1996), pp. 16–17.

Successful organizations know how to create and satisfy customers better than their competitors. Whether organizations are large or small, for-profit or non-profit, or represent any of a vast number of industries or social causes throughout the world, their long-term profitability and survival depend on a thorough understanding of the environment in which they operate. This includes customers, competitors, suppliers, employees, and all the other external and internal stakeholders and environmental forces described in preceding chapters. Because customers and their needs and wants keep changing, critical marketing intelligence must be

FIGURE 4.1

Problem Solving, Research, Information, and Decisions

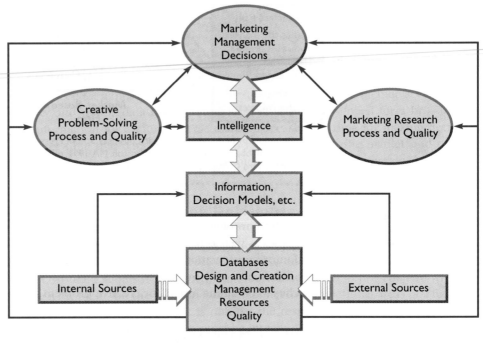

gathered continuously through ongoing data collection and research activities to provide insights for marketing management decisions.

This chapter focuses on the important role of timely and accurate market information in marketing management decisions and creative problem solving that will deliver value to satisfied customers. The relationships between the creative problem-solving process, the marketing research process, and marketing intelligence are discussed, as well as the sources, types, and uses of marketing information and issues that should be considered in the acquisition and use of marketing information. (See Figure 4.1.) Market intelligence should focus not only on "what is"—the existing solutions to customers' problems—but also on "what isn't"—those new ideas, products, processes, and methods which provide innovative breakthroughs to satisfy needs that the market may not even recognize until a solution becomes available. As illustrated in Figure 4.2, what the market needs and is willing to pay for must be reconciled with what the firm has the ability and willingness to provide.[2]

MARKETING MANAGEMENT DECISIONS AND CREATIVE PROBLEM SOLVING

Marketing managers are challenged with the need to make many diverse decisions, many of which require an understanding of new products, new applications, new markets, new competitors, or new methods of doing business. In order to remain competitive and arrive at innovative solutions, it is necessary to take a creative

TABLE 4.1
....
Organizational Level and Information for Marketing Decisions

	Examples	
Level	*Decision Areas*	*Information Needs*
Corporate Level	Satisfying customers and achieving financial objectives; long-term financial performance	Market intelligence for strategic growth plans; performance data for SBUs; market forecasts
Division or SBU Level	Strategies for separate SBUs or profit centers (may focus on different set of customers and competitors than other divisions of the company)	Market demand; competitive intelligence; site-selection/location analysis; operating level performance data
Functional/ Operating Level	Tactical marketing plan to achieve the functional-level strategy; market segments to pursue; appropriate marketing mix; details on product performance	Return on advertising expenditures; customer satisfaction research; front-line employee productivity (sales, etc.); detailed data on product performance

Unless all functional areas are convinced by their collective research that a plan should be implemented, it will be doomed to failure. For example, General Motors and Ford conceptualized the minivan long before its introduction by Chrysler. However, the interpretation of market data by some of the more influential GM and Ford managers of the time indicated that the market would not support the minivan and that it was not financially feasible. The rest of the story of wide acceptance of the minivan by consumers is history.

How Marketing Decisions Are Made
....

There are probably as many ways to make a decision as there are decision makers. As markets become more global and competition becomes more intense, marketing managers have fewer strategic and tactical options available to them than previously. Unfortunately, it is not always possible to make decisions with the confidence provided by "perfect" information. In the ideal world, some assumptions about the ability to support marketing management decisions with high-quality market intelligence might include the following:[7]

- There is adequate time for accurate research conducted at a reasonable price.

- Existing information relevant to the problem is brought to the manager's attention early enough to determine other information needed for the decision.

- The need for a research effort can be communicated early enough for a quality research project.

- The managers responsible for making a decision and the researchers who are responsible for gathering the marketing intelligence each have a good understanding of what is needed and the processes followed by each party.

- Research results are unambiguous and clearly support a particular decision.

- The most desirable decision is also feasible to implement and can be implemented with a clear understanding of the degree of uncertainty and/or risk involved.

What managers appear to be searching for in their quest for high-quality marketing intelligence is a set of assumptions and decision rules that will provide some reasonable degree of assurance for their decisions. For those managers who make a series of similar decisions, these assumptions and decision rules can be applied to multiple situations when proven to work successfully. Decision-making and research needs are determined to a large extent by the degree of complexity and uncertainty involved and the time available for making an informed decision.

Routine versus Complex Decisions. Routine decisions often are "programmed"; that is, they are guided by policies and predetermined guidelines. They usually are made by fewer decision makers to cover a shorter time period. Routine decisions also typically are made in recurring or similar situations where market conditions and company factors are quite predictable.

Complex decisions tend to involve new situations where there is little or no previous experience in making similar decisions. These situations may involve a high degree of risk, require a high level of investment, or be subject to a rapid rate of change such as that brought about by accelerated technological changes. When one or more of these conditions are present, it is considerably more difficult to make a well-informed decision, and there is a greater need for marketing intelligence.

Time Factor. Complex decisions obviously require more time for information gathering and analysis and more time for planning whenever possible. One of the greatest challenges to marketers in the twenty-first century will continue to be the drive to get new products to market faster and more successfully than competitors. Shortened product life cycles and time frames for making decisions require high-quality information and an efficient decision support system to expedite the decision process and reduce risk.

Creative Problem Solving (CPS)
. . . .

Creative problem solving
"Stepping outside the box" to find creative solutions to business problems and opportunities.

Most marketing textbook chapters that address marketing research and decision making tend to do so from a quantitative perspective. While quantitative inputs may be essential for a complete understanding of the situation, managers also must use qualitative inputs that cannot be measured with a high degree of accuracy. Often these inputs are referred to as a manager's judgment or intuition that may require **creative problem solving**—"stepping outside the box" to find creative solutions to business problems and opportunities. The usefulness of marketing intelligence is only as valuable as the decision maker's ability to look at the data in new ways and to consider new possibilities, that is, "color outside the lines," to come up with innovative solutions.

A nationwide study found that 89 percent of the advertising, marketing, and marketing research professionals who responded to a survey frequently use intuition to

FIGURE 4.3

· ·

Stages in the Creative Problem-Solving (CPS) Process

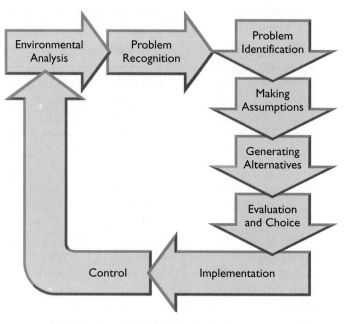

Source: James M. Higgins, *101 Creative Problem Solving Techniques: The Handbook of New Ideas for Business.* Winter Park, FL: New Management Publishing Company, Inc., Figure 2-1, p. 18, 1994. Reprinted by permission.

· ·

guide some part of their decision making. One explanation is that marketing professionals do not have the time to gather data to support every decision in today's fast-paced, downsized, and urgent business environment.[8]

Higgins[9] states: "Problem solving is an integral part of organizational life. Every time a manager or leader directs people in producing a product or service, problems are being solved, decisions made. Every time any member of an organization thinks of a new way to reduce costs, invents a new product or service, or determines how to help the organization function better in some way, problem solving is taking place. But, whether the problem solving occurring in these situations is truly creative is another question. . . . [T]he development of creative problem-solving skills is a necessity, not a luxury. . . . The most innovative individuals and organizations are the ones most likely to prosper." The emphasis here is on taking a *creative* approach to solving problems using an eight-stage process, as illustrated in Figure 4.3. A brief description and an example of the analytical and creative process of each of the eight stages[10] are provided below.

Stage 1: Analyzing the Environment.   Both the external and internal environments must be monitored constantly to identify problems and opportunities. The information gathered from the environmental analysis enables managers to respond quickly to change and new business opportunities and to resolve problems successfully. In a customer-oriented organization, everyone should assume responsibility for being informed about what is happening—or what is about to happen—around him or her. For example, Harley-Davidson became aware that a new type of customer—the white-collar urban professional—was buying its bikes in the mid-1980s, and it felt the need to know more about the buying motives of its present and potential customers.

Stage 2: Recognizing a Problem.   Before a problem or opportunity can be solved or identified, the decision maker must be made aware of it. The awareness may come from formal or informal environmental scanning or from a vague, intuitive feeling that something is "wrong" or that an exciting opportunity is "around the corner." Sometimes problem recognition occurs with a sudden flash of insight, but more often a period of time is required for subconscious processing of environmental information, followed by conscious analysis of the qualitative and quantitative indicators. Harley-Davidson recognized that the traditional biker customer might be alienated by the image that was being created by the newer type of customer.

Stage 3: Identifying the Problem.   In this stage of the creative problem-solving process, the symptoms are separated from the real problem. In this way, the problem-solving process can focus on establishing objectives and determining decision criteria to use in evaluating the available options. Problem identification is primarily a rational process, but intuitive thinking also is involved. Questions should be answered about the past and present status and what is anticipated for the future. In this stage of the CPS process, managers should have a clear idea of the real problem by gaining insights about what has happened, who was affected, where it happened and where it had an impact, how and why it occurred, and what could be done to be more successful. Harley-Davidson focused on finding out whether there was a universal appeal to owning a Harley bike across its diverse customer base.

Stage 4: Making Assumptions.   Before generating alternatives, assumptions must be made about future conditions that are related to the problem situation. Assumptions need to be made about internal resources (e.g., financial, human, physical, etc.) required to solve the problem or take advantage of the opportunity or the anticipated support of managers and others. Assumptions also need to be made about the external macro- and micro-environments regarding economic conditions, market demand, competitive reaction, and other factors. In the case of Harley-Davidson, the company assumed that conditions for growth would remain positive and that brand equity would fuel expansion.

Stage 5: Generating Alternatives.   The generation of alternatives involves both rational and intuitive thinking. Those alternatives which are already known can be listed and contemplated through rational thought processes. Managers who limit possible alternatives to those which are already known miss a chance to come up with innovative solutions through creative problem-solving processes. The quantity of new alternatives is more important in this stage, the point at which people tend to be most creative. Rather than worry about the quality of each idea that is being generated, this stage gives people a chance to brainstorm and to come up with unique alternatives.

Stage 6: Choosing Among Alternatives.

The process of choosing among available alternatives involves systematic evaluation of each available option to determine whether it meets the criteria established in the problem identification stage. Considerable attention should be given to the outcomes that would be expected with each alternative, its chances of success, and the resources needed for implementation. Although rational thinking plays a major role in evaluating and choosing among acceptable alternatives, intuition and judgment (often based on years of experience) also enter into the choice process—particularly where the decision is very complex and insufficient information is available to make a rational decision.

Stage 7: Implementing the Chosen Solution.

Stages 1 through 6 provide a sound basis for carrying out the chosen solution to the problem. At this point, the problem has been clearly identified, and a well-thought-out plan should be in place for action. The establishment of objectives to be achieved by the plan and a time line for accomplishing them provide much-needed direction. In addition, specific individuals should be made accountable for their areas of responsibility for executing the planned solution and be given the support of key individuals in the organization. Successful implementation requires constant attention to details and awareness of potential obstacles that may hinder the success of the plan. Continuing with the Harley-Davidson example, the company will need to ensure that every detail of the chosen solution is carried out as planned—from product design and production to distributors and sales personnel to customer service and so on.

Stage 8: Control.

When we think about "creative" problem solving, we sometimes ignore the need for control and evaluation of the plan once it is under way. A clear idea was formed during the preceding stages of the CPS process about the nature of the problem and the most likely solution. The control stage offers an opportunity to know whether the actions taken actually solved the problem and whether

INNOVATE OR EVAPORATE*

Hot Products from Hot Tubs and Other Approaches to Innovation

Successful innovations in products, communication, distribution, and pricing generally come about because of someone's creative problem-solving skills. Hirotaka Takeuchi, an esteemed Japanese professor, has argued that "an organization's ability to sustain innovation—and thus revenue growth—depends on creating and spreading knowledge among middle managers." He further stated that neither training nor individual genius is sufficient to create the knowledge necessary for systematic and continuous innovation.

In his quest to determine where knowledge comes from, Takeuchi started with the premise that companies in Japan and in the West follow different innovation processes. He concluded that "knowledge creation has nothing to do with Japanese management—it's universal" and that cultural differences are important because they allow us to learn from one another. The strength of Western companies is that one individual can

*The box title is attributed to James M. Higgins.

take a big innovation to market quickly (e.g., Bill Gates and Microsoft), but the question is where the next great ideas will come from. In contrast, Japanese companies rely on groups of ordinary people to come up with innovations. Although the process is time consuming, middle managers are expected to push all team members to a higher level of shared understanding, where the knowledge base of the group can create a major competitive advantage.

According to Takeuchi, the real excitement comes when the Japanese and Western approaches are combined. For example, a hydraulic shovel was developed jointly by Caterpillar and Mitsubishi. Mitsubishi learned "how good the Caterpillar guys are at putting everything they knew into a manual." The Caterpillar people thought the 10-minute staff meeting (*chorei*) that started every day was "for the birds," but they gradually realized that the process of getting people together every morning is a major strength of this system.

Knowledge creation relies on two different types of knowledge—explicit and tacit—and each culture is most comfortable with only one of these in the knowledge-creation process. Americans are most comfortable with explicit knowledge, made up of information "that can be verbalized, written down in documents, put into computers, and readily communicated." However, the Japanese are more comfortable with using tacit knowledge, "which comes from personal experience and is usually difficult to express. It's not purely rational because it's connected to emotions and beliefs." Tacit knowledge is "what you feel in your gut when you have a hunch or an inspiration. . . . [I]t's more a bodily knowledge than something in the mind. Americans are not as comfortable with that."

Some measures taken by Japanese companies to benefit from employees' tacit knowledge (note that these approaches may not be as acceptable in the United States) include:

- Work hard to create a feeling of unity. "The influence of Zen makes us believe that the best state of intellectual ability comes when the body and mind become one." No explicit verbal communication is needed in the ideal form of communication, the "breath of *ah-un*." (One approach is a night out with the boss. Everyone gets drunk and says what he or she thinks—a "ritual that clears the air and promotes understanding without any penalties.")

- Have an off-site meeting (a *gasshuku*, or "camp-in") at a hotel and exchange ideas to remove barriers and share ideas. (One suggestion is to take people to an off-site mountain resort with a hot spring, where everyone can soak together with their clothes off. "That's how we communicate. The experience we share is symbolic of our unity. We're all naked in the same pool together. That leads to a deeper understanding, a feeling of trust.")

Unlike the United States, where middle managers often are considered nonessential, Japanese middle managers play a key role in many companies. Top management is driven by ideals, but front-line people must put those ideals into practice. When top and middle management share information freely, knowledge spirals up and down the organization. Most of the successful product development observed by Takeuchi and Nonaka was due to the efforts of project teams using a process they have labeled "the rugby approach," where "everyone is on the field from day one—engineers, production, quality control, sales. Whenever a problem comes up, they all pile in together. That's very different from the relay approach, in which one functional team passes the baton to the next."

The key point in this scenario is that innovation requires knowledge creation, which in turn requires a convergence of tacit and explicit knowledge.

Source: Reprinted from the April 29, 1996 issue of *Fortune* by special permission; copyright 1996, Time Inc.

the plan was executed appropriately. Creative problem solving in this stage consists of recognizing those things which work and—building on this knowledge—making them work even better. CPS also involves recognizing deficiencies in the solution and creatively adapting new thinking to improve the success of the plan.

THE MARKETING RESEARCH PROCESS

The CPS process and the marketing research process are closely related, and both processes influence the quality of the management decision process. It is important to have a clear understanding of the purpose of the research and the nature of the decision in the beginning of the process. High-quality marketing intelligence and a poor-quality decision process, and vice versa, do not lend themselves to successful creative problem solving. Each stage of the research process must be approached creatively.

Marketing research specialists tend to follow a sequence of steps in designing and executing a research project. The exact order or description of each step may vary by researcher and project, but the research process generally includes the activities described below and illustrated in Figure 4.4.

Step 1: Recognize the Need for Research

The first step in any marketing research effort is to be aware that unresolved problems or opportunities exist and that available information cannot provide satisfactory answers. Sometimes this recognition is brought about by a crisis, or it may be a by-product of other research or just a vague sense that there are issues that need to be addressed. For example, the company may be concerned about sales declines in

FIGURE 4.4

Steps in the Marketing Research Process

a particular market and realize that it really does not understand the buying habits of its key customers or why they are buying less of the company's product.

Step 2: Define the Research Problem and Objectives (Purpose)

As James Thurber said, "It is better to know some of the questions than all of the answers."[11] What is it that managers really need to know? What are the specific managerial decisions that require the insights provided by the research results? The vaguely stated issue in step 1 above can be restated as: Sales of our brand of canned vegetables declined by 40 percent in Minnesota for the month of February, and we need to know what consumer characteristics or market forces are driving this decline. (See stages 2 and 3 in the CPS process.)

Step 3: Specify Information and Data Requirements

The type of information needed for an informed decision must be determined before going any further in the research process. This information should be focused directly on the research problem identified earlier and not a "shotgun approach" to gathering any and all data available. The quality of the research and the quality of the management decision will be much higher if the focus is on meaningful data inputs. Continuing with the example of a sales decline in canned vegetables, examples of useful information include buying habits, brand loyalty, and brand switching in Minnesota. The necessary information may be obtained from **primary data** (e.g., survey questionnaires, personal interviews). Other information might include an assessment of distribution effectiveness and competitive activity that could be obtained from **secondary data** (e.g., company records, industry reports). Steps 2 and 3 are where the most errors are apt to occur, because the value of the research is seriously threatened if the basic research problem and the information needed (research questions) are not identified correctly.

Primary data
Information gathered specifically for a current marketing management decision.

Secondary data
Information from published or other sources that was gathered for another purpose.

Step 4: Develop the Research Plan

In this stage the preliminary data-collection method is determined, such as whether it will be obtained by primary research or from secondary sources. A schedule for performing the research activities and a budget are developed. (This happens throughout the CPS process.)

Step 5: Design the Method for Collecting Data

This step involves designing the method for collecting needed information, including data sources, questionnaire or data-collection instruments, sampling design, and sample size. Primary data may be collected by mail, telephone, or personal interviews, whereas secondary data may be obtained from internal or external information sources. The questionnaire or other type of data-collection instrument is developed consistent with the research method to be used. The proper sample of respondents is identified in this stage, a critical decision due to the need for those who provide the data to be representative of the population that the company is interested in knowing more about. The number of respondents also is determined at this point, with the number large enough to ensure useful data but small enough to meet time and budget constraints. (This is necessary throughout the CPS process.)

Step 6: Perform the Research

At this stage in the research process the researcher is responsible for the actual work involved in data collection. The research plan must be followed as planned to maintain consistency of the data, and research quality must be monitored and controlled. The questionnaires or other data-collection instruments must be administered according to plan, and precautions must be taken in their handling to avoid potential errors and bias. The key here is to *listen to* (or *see*) the respondent's viewpoint. (This occurs throughout the CPS process.)

Step 7: Analyze the Data and Interpret the Results

The researcher is responsible in this stage of the research process for reviewing the data-collection instruments and culling out any that are not usable. The data are coded and prepared for analysis (i.e., the data usually are input into a computer program for statistical analysis). The data are then tabulated, analyzed, and organized in a format for interpretation. The results generally formulate a pattern that provides insights about the issue being investigated. At this stage precautions must be taken to remain objective and avoid misinterpretations of the data. (See steps 1 through 6 in the CPS process.)

Step 8: Communicate Findings

In the final stage of the research process the researcher prepares a final report and presents the findings to those who will use the information for decision making. This usually involves both a formal written report and a presentation. The focus of this report should be on the agreed-on information that addresses the research problem and objectives. The interpretation of the results also includes the researcher's recommendations for action. (See steps 7, 8, and beyond in the CPS process.)

KEY INFORMATION FOR MARKETING DECISIONS

Marketing decisions involve one or more of the internal and external environmental factors described in preceding chapters. (See Figure 4.5.) The driving forces of change discussed earlier (i.e., globalization, computerization, information age and technology, and management hierarchies) have created a situation where high-quality marketing intelligence is essential for long- and short-term decisions. Further, merely having the information is insufficient if it is not used *creatively*. Rapid changes in the marketing environment have created the need for shorter planning horizons and less certainty about the "right" decision. These conditions require finely tuned creative and conceptual skills, as well as the ability to process information and make informed judgments. The question is, Of all the information that is available to managers, what information do they really need? The basic types of information needed are related primarily to external opportunities and threats and internal strengths and weaknesses, as discussed next.

FIGURE 4.5
....
Global Marketing Environment and Marketing Intelligence

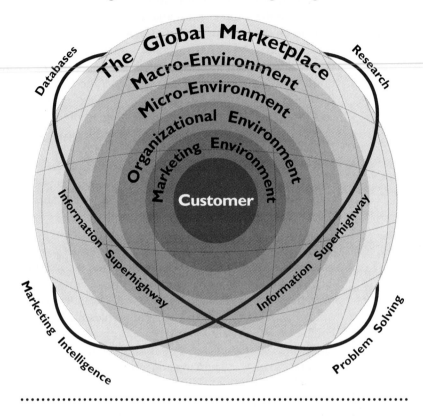

External Opportunities and Threats
....

External information needed by marketing managers falls into two general categories: opportunities and threats. The key external factors that must be analyzed include the market, its customers, and the firm's competitors. Some types of external information needed by managers are described below, followed by a discussion of possible sources of information in the next section.

Market demand
Present customer needs to be fulfilled by a product category based on ability and willingness to buy.

Market potential
Maximum sales and profit that can be reasonably expected under given conditions.

Market and Buyer Analysis.   An organization must be fully informed about current trends in its market(s) and anticipate changes that may occur. The first research task is to define the market for the firm's goods or services, followed by determining the **market demand** and **market potential**—the present and projected rates and directions of growth for the identified market. The next task is to determine the characteristics and buying habits of consumers (e.g., needs and wants, buying preferences, lifestyles, etc.) and organizational customers (e.g., industry, size, location, etc.) in the segment(s) of interest. Once the firm has a solid understanding of the dimensions and characteristics of its market and the buying behavior of its present and potential customers, it is ready to develop marketing programs to satisfy market demand.

Competitive Analysis.   Elements of competitive analysis were described in Chapter 3 within the context of Porter's "five forces" model. Marketing intelligence must include information about both *direct* and *indirect* competitors. **Direct competitors** serve the same target market(s) and satisfy the same basic needs. Competition may be on the basis of preferred brands or distribution channels, selective product characteristics, or various product forms that satisfy a generic need. For example, consider the need for transportation. For the buyer of an automobile, direct competition on the basis of brands might include Honda, Ford, and Toyota purchased through competing distribution channels (e.g., manufacturer dealership, CarMax, or an independent auto-buying club). Competition in the auto industry is particularly intense on the basis of product characteristics (e.g., engine type, fuel economy, safety features) and forms (e.g., sports utility vehicle, minivan, truck, four-door passenger). Automobile manufacturers and their advertising agencies rely on information about prior and forecasted sales, demographic and psychographic market characteristics, and other data in their decisions about how to design and market their diverse range of products.

Direct competitors
Serve the same target market and satisfy the same customer needs.

Indirect competitors may be from the same or other industries and appeal to customers with substitute products or ways of doing business. For example, not only do auto manufacturers and dealers face competition from each other; they also face competition from other modes of transportation. Many urban dwellers rely on mass transit buses or trains or choose to carpool with neighbors. Travel by air or rail offers a competing solution to automobiles for long-distance travel. Other indirect competitors to the auto industry are the auto repair shops and mechanics that keep older cars running longer, diminishing the owner's need for a new car. Researchers must be creative in knowing and anticipating the sources of indirect competition.

Indirect competitors
May be from same or other industries and appeal to customers with substitute products or business methods.

Internal Strengths and Weaknesses

An analysis of an organization's internal strengths and weaknesses relative to competitors provides an understanding of its ability to compete successfully for customers and build market-share profitably. The internal information most commonly used for marketing decisions includes an analysis of the firm's major resources, such as financial, human, and technological resources, as well as the effectiveness of its marketing activities.

Financial Resources.   The firm's internal databases include a record of its assets and liabilities. Assets are most often in the form of physical properties and equipment, investments, inventories, cash, accounts receivable, and so forth. Liabilities consist of debt in the form of loans, taxes, and other financial obligations. Financial ratios can be calculated from the accounting statements and financial records and compared with industry ratios for determination of the firm's financial position relative to competitors.

An analysis of financial resources also should include an analysis of the level of risk faced by the firm and/or its industry. In a rapidly changing business environment, volatility and uncertainty make it difficult to assess risk, but all available information should be used to make decisions that will have an impact on the firm's bottom line.

Human Resources. Information is needed about the firm's personnel requirements for carrying out its mission and the ability of present managers and employees to satisfy customers and deliver a profit to the company. Personnel records and management reviews can provide much of the information for this type of analysis. The basic question to be answered is, Can our people provide a competitive advantage with our customers? If so, how are they doing it? And what can they do better?

Technological Resources. As you will recall from Chapter 2, the major environmental forces driving change in all types of businesses are increased computerization, emerging technologies, the information superhighway, and the information age economy. The marketer who falls behind in these areas has little chance of survival and profitability over the long term. In a customer-oriented organization, information technology can be used advantageously to monitor the market, gather customer data, and create a marketing information system. Marketing intelligence in this area should focus on what technological applications are available, what they can do to enhance performance of the firm, and whether they will provide a competitive advantage.

Marketing audit
Thorough systematic evaluation of an organization's environment, objectives, and strategy.

Marketing Effectiveness. An important task of marketing research is to track the effectiveness of current (and planned) marketing programs. One analytical method that is used for this purpose is to conduct a **marketing audit**,[12] which is a thorough, systematic, objective evaluation of an organization's marketing environment, objectives, and strategies. The purpose is to identify potential problems and opportunities so that the company's marketing performance can be improved.

A marketing audit may examine any or all aspects of an organization's marketing situation. This includes factors within the marketing environment (macro- and micro-environments), marketing strategy, marketing organization, marketing systems, marketing productivity, and marketing function. (See this chapter's Appendix for a comprehensive list of questions that may be asked in each area.) One of the most compelling questions for any marketing manager is whether or not marketing programs are working. The marketing audit is an excellent way to determine answers to this question, since it can be used to assess the effectiveness of all elements of the marketing mix (i.e., products, price, distribution, and promotional tools). An audit should be conducted periodically and used to track important outcomes such as brand equity, customer satisfaction, and other items of ongoing interest.

SOURCES OF INFORMATION

Marketing intelligence is obtained from a wide spectrum of sources through both formal and informal methods. In its basic form, it consists of data and facts (or items assumed to be factual) about the realities of the marketplace. Data are analyzed and converted into information that is useful for management decisions. However, a number of factors can intervene in the process of moving through an information hierarchy that evolves from a mass of data to a wise managerial decision. One of the most compelling factors is the potential difference between the orientations of the information user and the information provider, referred to by Barabba and Zaltman

FIGURE 4.6

The Information Pyramid and the "Law of the Lens"

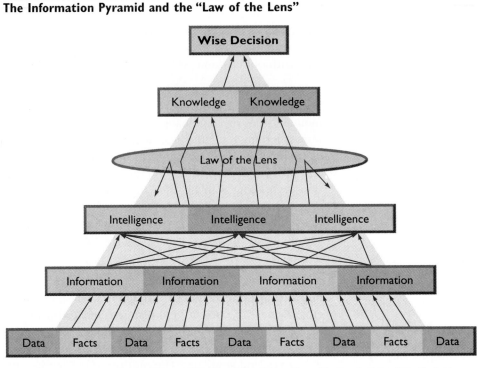

as the "law of the lens."[13] These differences may consist of interpretations of the marketing situation or research expectations, conflicts of interest regarding the purpose or outcomes of the research, internal versus external perspectives on the problem, or other differences that may be relevant to the gathering or use of the data. The transition from data to decisions and the difference between the domains of making decisions and producing information are illustrated in Figure 4.6. Note that data that in some way represent the realities of the marketplace can be gathered in any form and entered into an organization's information system, but the data may not be meaningful, accurate, or believable. When the data are interpreted in a meaningful way, they can be classified as information. When the information is believed to be true, it becomes intelligence that is easily understood, timely, reliable, and valid for use in management decisions.

Databases

Successful marketing organizations generally create and maintain databases that can manage the wide range of information that comprises their marketing intelligence systems. The two primary types of databases used by marketing managers are the marketing information system (MIS) and the marketing decision support system (MDSS). Data inputs may range from complex mathematical forecasting models to rumors and intuitive interpretations. They may be focused on one product in a narrowly defined geographic market segment, or they may cover multiple products throughout a global marketplace. The difficulty is in knowing what is a true reflection of reality. As Will Rogers once said, "It's not what we don't know that gives us trouble. It's what we know that ain't so."[14]

MIS—marketing information system
Formal complex of people, equipment, and procedures designed to provide timely, accurate, and useful information to marketing decision makers.

Marketing Information System (MIS). The **MIS** is a formal complex of people, equipment, and procedures designed to gather, organize, structure, analyze, evaluate, and distribute timely, accurate, and meaningful information to marketing decision makers. The data inputs may originate from inside or outside the company and involve a planned, continuous, orderly collection, analysis, and organization of relevant data for both short- and long-term decisions. We usually associate the use of a computer with an MIS, but reference libraries and even well-organized file cabinets can constitute important information for management decisions.

MDSS—marketing decision support system
A coordinated system of data and tools by which internal and external information is turned into a basis for marketing action.

Marketing Decision Support System (MDSS). The **MDSS** is a coordinated collection of data, systems, models, analytic tools, and computing power by which an organization gathers information from the internal and external environment and turns it into a basis for marketing action.[15] An MDSS is differentiated from an MIS and other technologically based systems by its humanistic focus on extending the problem-solving capabilities of marketing managers. An MDSS is essential in highly competitive markets where decisions must be made more quickly, more frequently, and with less tolerance for error. An MDSS is computer-based (for speed and data manipulation), interactive (on-line systems), flexible (for data access and integration from multiple sources), and discovery-oriented (looking for trends, identifying potential problems, and searching for answers to new questions based on the information provided), and is relatively easy to use. The three essential components of a MDSS are databases, a user interface, and a library of analytical and modeling tools.

Decision models are available from commercial sources or are developed inhouse to address issues such as the allocation of organizational resources (e.g., retail site selection, new production equipment, or other investments). Models also are used to determine the efficiency and effectiveness of promotional activities, including advertising (e.g., media placement and expenditures, measures of audience size and characteristics), salesforce allocation, and productivity, warehousing operations, and many other applications.

Point-of-sale (POS) system
Scanner system used to collect data at retail checkouts.

Types and Uses of Databases. There are many types of databases that serve the decision-making needs of managers. In a marketing-oriented company, databases are focused directly or indirectly on satisfying the customer. Some of the more widely used databases and their applications are presented in Table 4.2. For many organizations, data gathered internally for one purpose might provide an additional source of revenue when sold to outside users, such as the scanner data gathered through a **point-of-sale (POS) system** in retail stores and American Airlines' Sabre computerized airline reservation system.

TABLE 4.2
....
Types and Uses of Databases

Types of Databases	Uses/Applications
Internal Data and Information	
Sales records	Employee scheduling, sales events
Credit records	Direct marketing, consumer research
Inventory records	Sales histories, vendor and SKU analysis
POS scanner data	Inventory control, reordering, merchandising
Reservation system	Employee scheduling, purchasing
External Data and Information	
Standard Industrial Classification Manual (SIC codes and NAICS codes)	Coding system facilitates search for industry information; standards for comparison
Directories	Trade and professional association listings, company information, etc.
Various business information sources	Listings of company and industry data sources
Indexes to business literature and publications	Guide to periodical literature, business journals, and other media
Government databases	U.S. Census Bureau population statistics, Commerce Department trade data, FTC regulations, etc.
Commercial databases (e.g., Arbitron, Nexis/Lexis, etc.)	Specialized by company and market information, audience statistics, etc.

The users of databases are as diverse as the databases themselves, with each user having unique needs that must be met with marketing intelligence. A user may be a manufacturer, retailer, advertising agency, marketing research firm, or other marketing-oriented organization. Within a marketing organization, databases may be used to forecast market demand for a given product within a specified time frame, determine design features and production schedules to meet demand, develop pricing models for new and existing products, assess the effectiveness of promotional campaigns, and determine the efficiency and effectiveness of distribution channels.

Our emphasis here is on information systems used by managers and executives, but another important type of information system is gaining acceptance by customer-oriented firms. Customer-contact personnel tend to occupy the lowest tier in a hierarchical organization, yet their impact on customer satisfaction often is greater than that of any other group. Companies that invest in cutting-edge **front-line information systems (FIS)** achieve significant gains in service quality and reliability and subsequently high levels of customer satisfaction. FedEx, Frito-Lay, and Hertz are examples of companies that equip their front-line personnel with tech-

Front-line information system (FIS)
Data provided to customer-contact personnel to improve customer service.

nologies that improve their performance, and they also tend to have high levels of employee satisfaction. The data gathered at the FIS level can provide inputs for the upper management levels.[16]

Database Design and Creation

Database
Organized collection of a wide range of information used for decision making.

Perhaps the most important aspect of a **database** is its initial design and creation. At this point, the managers who will use the information must be able to communicate effectively with those responsible for providing the information so that the resulting database will be informative and useful. The design and creation of the database should be user-oriented and focused on helping the organization achieve its mission while satisfying its target market(s). The design should include both internal records and external marketing intelligence and meet the requirements of the information user and provider for making both strategic and tactical decisions.

Internal Records. A large quantity of internal data is generated in the course of doing business. Examples of data include routine departmental and functional area records such as marketing, accounting, finance, production, personnel, and so forth. Data may also include order processing records, sales figures, inventory status, customer accounts (receivables), supplier invoices (payables), and other data that will be useful for management decisions. Internal records can be used to compile sales and cost data, to calculate productivity measures and scheduling of activities and employees, and to determine budgets and future courses of action in a number of areas.

External Marketing Intelligence. Marketing intelligence can be obtained from either primary or secondary sources. Primary data provide answers to a specific marketing management problem. For example, a utility company may send a questionnaire to its customers to determine their level of satisfaction with the utility's services, or a market study may be conducted to determine the positioning of a company's product relative to its competitors. Strategic tracking studies are another form of primary data that are used to monitor consumer awareness, perceptions, and behavior through rapid changes in marketing technology, media, and distribution channels. They also can be used to track the effects of marketing programs as they are introduced, the evolution of brand awareness and brand image over time and how it is affected by competitors, advertising recognition and recall, characteristics of the optimal target market, and other useful information.[17] Data generally are collected by telephone or mail, with the quality of the research determined by its design and execution. As with other research methods, tracking studies can be good or bad depending on the sampling plan, questionnaire design, interviewing procedures, and data processing, but their real value is their ability to provide longitudinal data.

Often it is possible to obtain the needed marketing information from secondary data that have been compiled previously for some purpose other than the present management decision without conducting primary research. Secondary information is readily available from a variety of on-line and easily accessible databases such as library and on-line data sources, commercial or syndicated sources, government agencies, and others.

Information Requirements.   As shown in Figure 4.6, the "law of the lens" serves as a filter between the perspectives of the information user and the information provider. It is difficult under the best of conditions to design useful databases, develop an effective research methodology, and interpret the results in a way that will be a true representation of marketplace reality. Precautions should be taken to ensure that a database's underlying data and information are as accurate and unbiased as possible so that they can be integrated into the decision process with some degree of confidence.

The marketing manager must specify the types of decisions to be made and the specific types of information needed to make those decisions. This must be communicated clearly to the information provider (e.g., researcher, information systems personnel, etc.) to be used as a basis for system design and data-collection methods. Likewise, the two parties should have a common understanding about the type of information needed, how it will be used, how it will be obtained, and the format that will provide the most useful information. The process of determining information requirements is complicated by personal biases that may introduce subjectivity into the research process. Further, the manager of a database must consider whether the user is internal to the organization or one or more external parties with a variety of needs. A database may consist of proprietary internal and external data that are intended only for use in-house, or it may contain commercial data or information that is intended for sale to outside parties. In the first case, the user and the support system can be narrowly defined, but in the commercial sector the users and their applications may be more diverse and require more fine-tuning and technical support tailored specifically to different organizations and industries. The key is to recognize the actual customer of the research and to provide satisfaction through the research process and results.

Database Management

It is important to recognize that databases and the technology that makes possible the efficient management of large databases are merely tools to be used by managers. ". . . [M]odern database management abetted by technology should be more than 'list maintenance.' Systems should constantly analyze and highlight strategic opportunities the firm can exploit. Surviving in the fast-action markets of the future will demand it."[18]

Some potential pitfalls in database management include information overload and "analysis paralysis," unhelpful data, inward focus, and lack of commitment. Databases can become extremely large and unwieldy, containing data and information that are not relevant to the decisions they are meant to support. A periodic review of the database relative to management requirements can expose unhelpful data that should be eliminated and missing data that should be added in the appropriate format. The key to successful database management is to remember that data and information are tools to be used by managers. They are not solutions in themselves and should be designed and controlled from a marketing perspective supported by efficient and effective information technology.

Market Measurement and Forecasting Demand

Marketing managers must be able to estimate the results of their strategic or tactical decisions, often under different competing scenarios. Databases such as the MDSS can provide essential information for estimating market demand, market potential, and actual market size, as well as the company's present and desired market-share position for a given product or product category. Databases also are useful tools in forecasting future sales and profit figures for a given product or business unit within a specified time period and with a given level of marketing effort.

Forecast
What a firm expects to achieve under given conditions.

Market potential is the maximum that can be reasonably expected (usually stated in dollar or unit sales) under given conditions. A **forecast** is what the firm expects to achieve under given conditions and may provide target performance standards for the company, its business units, and individual personnel.[19] Potentials and forecasts can be calculated at several levels: industry and/or market, company, and product. Market potential estimates are used for decisions such as market entry or exit, location of a business facility, and as inputs for sales forecasts. Forecasts are used primarily to answer "What if" questions, set budgets, and establish a basis for monitoring deviations from forecasted sales. Data used to estimate market potential may come from government sources, trade associations, private companies, financial analysts, surveys, and other sources.[20]

ISSUES IN MARKETING INFORMATION ACQUISITION AND USE

The issues involved in acquiring and using marketing information are too numerous to discuss in this chapter, but some of the primary challenges include the decision as to whether to conduct marketing research with internal personnel or to use outside information providers. In addition, decisions must be made regarding the scope or extent of the research and the nature of organizational resources that will be involved. Other major issues include the quality of research methodology and results and the legal and ethical implications of all marketing intelligence activities.

In-house or Outsource Research Task

Marketing managers must assess the advantages and disadvantages of obtaining information from internal or external information providers. Criteria for making this decision include cost, time, objectivity, and expertise.

Extent/Scope of Research

The amount of information that is needed for a particular decision will vary, but the decision process is expedited when measures are taken to ensure that available information is relevant to the problem under consideration. Creative problem solving and the steps in the research process can be applied to this decision, starting with a clear problem definition and an understanding of the most useful data sources. Where existing information provides sufficient input for a quality decision, further data collection may not be necessary. Available secondary information also can help identify specific primary research needs within a more limited scope.

Organizational Resources

Within the context of organizational resources, there are a number of issues that can create constraints on the acquisition and use of marketing information. It is important to assess the expertise of in-house personnel; the quality of existing MDSS, MIS, or other databases that are used as management tools; the financial resources available for gathering and managing information; the amount of time that is available for gathering information in order to make a timely decision; and the ability and objectivity of management to use and act on the information.

In-house Expertise.   The research task should be clearly defined in order to guide the responsibilities of personnel who are assigned to obtaining marketing information. Likewise, criteria must be established for personnel hiring and performance for those people and departments which are involved in information gathering and research activities. Efforts should not be confined to marketing but should be integrated across all relevant functional areas, such as accounting, finance, operations, human resources, information systems, or others that may be involved in providing or using data for marketing decisions.

MDSS/MIS Availability (and Appropriateness/Quality).   The marketing decision support system and the marketing information system become an issue when the quality of the data and information is in question. All personnel who are involved in this process must have a mutual understanding of the importance of integrating qualitative and quantitative information into a useful format for analysis and decision making. Technology and the information system that it supports are useful tools but not an end in themselves in ensuring that their outputs will be appropriate or of high quality.

Financial Resources.   The gathering of information and the maintenance of a useful database require considerable financial resources. Costs can include the purchase of more sophisticated computer hardware or a specialized database from an outside source, the hiring of a consultant to gather and analyze needed information, or the support of an internal department or individual who is responsible for designing and maintaining the database. The quality of management information is related in large part to the organizational commitment to allocating funds to decision support systems and their maintenance.

Time Available to Make Decision.   Deadlines for making decisions become an issue when the marketing manager has insufficient information to make an intelligent decision. Managers are making more decisions than ever and have a shorter time in which to make them. This requires a readily available information system that is timely, accurate, and useful. Depending on the time available, more research can be conducted and more information added to provide additional insights into the problem. Often, the optimal decision cannot be made with the time and resources that are available. When the time that is available for decisive action is limited, insufficient financial resources and other constraints become a larger issue.

Managerial Objectivity and Ability to Use/Act on Information.   Assuming that all the preceding issues have been resolved, there is still the issue of whether managers who are responsible for interpreting information and making strategic or tactical decisions can remain objective throughout the process. Each decision maker has his or her personal set of experiences, biases, and motives that may enter into the decision (consciously or subconsciously). Some major marketing mistakes have been made because of the inability to remain objective about the fate of a particular product or company unit.

Research Quality/Quality of Information

Quality issues related to marketing intelligence can be broken down into three major types: quality of the research process, quality of the data and information obtained, and quality of the management decision process. Marketers are concerned with the quality of the goods and services they sell and the quality of production and other organizational processes. The same level of concern must be applied to the quality of marketing research and information used by managers to make marketing-related decisions, as well as to the quality of the overall decision-making process. "A quality decision can only be meaningfully defined as a decision which is irrevocably tied to allocations of resources, including capital and operating budgets, personnel, time, and so forth."[21] Implicit in this definition is the close relationship between the management decision and the allocation of resources to support that decision. For example, if the decision is to increase market share for a line of computers, the decision is not complete unless it also includes a plan for implementation and the resources necessary to carry out the plan. Quality of the research also should reflect a balanced view of the information from the perspective of the customer and the company and the information user and provider.

International Marketing Research

While the fundamental principles of obtaining and using marketing intelligence for management decisions apply to both domestic and international research, the process is more complex in international markets. Some issues that are more problematic in international research include the difficulty of making cross-cultural comparisons, social and language differences, and the availability and accuracy of secondary data. Costs tend to be higher because of the need for specialized research designs to accommodate country differences, training, acquiring population data, and so forth. Despite the challenges of international marketing research, however, it does offer considerable insight into potential opportunities and problems in overseas markets.

Legal and Ethical Issues
....

Legal and ethical issues abound in the acquisition and use of marketing intelligence. Government regulations and legal guidelines provide both protection and constraints for a company and its customers. As communication and database technologies become more sophisticated and widely used, privacy issues become a greater concern. Ethical and bias issues are present throughout the entire marketing research and decision-making process.

Regulatory Issues.   Government regulations, industry standards, and legal guidelines present many challenges for marketing intelligence users and providers. The major federal government regulations emanate from the Federal Trade Commission (FTC) and the Federal Communications Commission (FCC). The FTC Act, Section 5, declares unfair or deceptive acts to be unlawful. Such deception includes the use of research as a sales ploy or as a "foot in the door" technique. Other regulation may come from federal, state, and local governments or private property (e.g., shopping malls) where research may be conducted.

Industry standards for conducting marketing research provide objective criteria for evaluating the behavior of the profession and establish guidelines for companies that may not have their own code for conducting research. Industry standards also provide guidance for a researcher who is being influenced inappropriately by the information user.[22]

Privacy Issues.   Privacy is a concern that is embodied in both regulatory and ethical issues. The problem is present in the gathering and manipulating of marketing intelligence related to both consumers and business-to-business marketing. One of the most frequent abuses of privacy by marketing researchers is the promise of anonymity while gathering data and then identifying the respondent in a way that is harmful or inappropriate. For example, an unsuspecting respondent may be placed on a sales list with personal data, and perhaps that list also would be sold to another party.

Ethical Issues.   The term *ethics* often is used interchangeably with *moral values* and bears a strong relationship to the way one person treats the rights of another. Research ethics include honesty throughout the research process, not manipulating methodology or data to achieve desired results, and basically respecting the rights of respondents and all involved in the process to avoid deception and fraudulent practices. Marketing information can be used and abused in consumer and business-to-business markets, but marketing managers and researchers also are faced with an ever-increasing need to know more about their competitors. The question becomes how to obtain useful customer and competitive information and how to do so legally and ethically.

Bias Issues.   All sources of potential bias related to the researcher and the research process should be avoided in order to ensure high-quality marketing intelligence and decisions. Those who handle data and information have many opportunities to introduce bias into every stage of the CPS process and the marketing research process. Unbiased research relies on carefully listening to respondents and objectively processing the data and making inferences from it. Research bias

IT'S LEGAL BUT IS IT ETHICAL?

Are You Being Investigated?

What people can find out about you—quite legally—will scare you. Christine Varney, former Federal Trade Commissioner and currently an attorney specializing in Internet and data-collection issues, says, "Privacy is the key consumer protection issue of the Information Age." Databases can contain practically everything someone wants to know about you and is not "afraid to ask, exchange, trade, buy, sell or otherwise compile." Personal data have been stored in corporate and government files for many years, but the general public could not access them easily. The technical capabilities of the World Wide Web have made much of that same information accessible to anyone with a personal computer and Internet access. Sometimes there is a fee for the information, but more often it is free.

On the positive side, target marketers are building massive databases to gain a better understanding of their customers' demographics, lifestyles, and buying habits. *Relationship marketing* is a key term in target marketing and in providing customer satisfaction. However, many people are concerned about the amount of private information that is available to marketers—and to anyone. Many stories have been told in the media, including a cover story in *Time* magazine, about the violations of privacy. These include corporate Web sites that amass detailed mailing lists of children through on-screen questionnaires and a major error by the U.S. Social Security Administration, which failed to "secure" on-line data intended only for the person involved. Access to the site was too easy, and a few data checkpoints were all that stood between sensitive financial data and snoopy lawyers or relatives—name, Social Security number, date and place of birth, and mother's maiden name. (The site was shut down.) Sophisticated users know where to find this information—legally and quickly.

Here is the story of a reporter, John, who decided to find out for himself just how easy it is. He called a computer consultant who is an industry watchdog and an expert in corporate data-handling practices. John gave the consultant his full name and date of birth. With this information, the consultant learned the name of John's wife, his current address and three prior addresses dating back to the late 1970s, his Social Security number (key to a vast array of personal data), and several credit bureau reports (legal under the 1993 amendment to the FTC's Fair Credit Reporting Act). He also identified John's credit cards and their limit and bank line of credit (all obtained legally from Equifax, a major credit reporting bureau—with reports released only to those with "a legitimate business need"). He also learned the amount of his home mortgage and its balance and could deduce the make of his computer. Basically, the consultant had all the information he needed to impersonate John.

Other information that can be obtained by a knowledgeable Web surfer includes toll telephone call information (date and number dialed) for a 30-day period (if given the caller's telephone number) and account name and address. There is a gray area between ethics and legality here because the request to the service provider is not illegal if there is a legitimate reason for obtaining the information. However, AT&T and other phone companies do not authorize the release of proprietary customer information without a court order or warrant, and even then federal law requires the customer's permission. The assumption is that an Internet information broker has obtained these records illegally. The information provider offered to supply a bank account search that covers 85 to 90 percent of the banks in a specified intrastate region, including account type, account number, balance, and bank addresses.

There are many stories of invasion of privacy in the use of databases. There are also many legitimate uses of databases by for-profit and non-profit organizations. The challenge to marketers is to consider the ethical and moral implications involved in how they obtain and use private customer information. As one individual said, "Information in the computer age is the equivalent of hazardous materials. It can leak out without you knowing about it, and it can harm you 20 years later."

Source: John Grossman, "Everything Databases Wanted to Know about John Grossman," *SKY* (March 1998), pp. 74–80.

also can be controlled by presenting all relevant information to the information user (i.e., reporting exactly what the respondents said) and being truthful with the handling and analysis of the data (no data left out of the analysis or misinterpreted). It is virtually impossible to completely eliminate all sources of bias in a research project or database, but a wholehearted attempt should be made to remove every source of bias that is possible. This is essential for providing data that are reliable and valid for management decisions.

Summary

Timely, accurate, high-quality marketing intelligence has become a necessity in a rapidly changing world and increasingly complex marketing environment. Marketing decisions are made throughout all levels of an organization, from long-range strategic plans at the top management level to a front-line customer-contact employee's on-the-spot decision.

The quality of information available for management decisions is enhanced by integrating creative problem-solving techniques with the marketing research process. Whereas quantitative inputs may be essential for a complete understanding of a problem or situation, managers also must use qualitative inputs that cannot be measured with a high degree of accuracy. This involves creative problem solving—"stepping outside the box" to find creative solutions to business problems and opportunities.

The marketing research process is closely related to the creative problem-solving process. It involves eight steps: (1) recognizing the need for research, (2) defining the research problem/objective, (3) specifying the information required, (4) developing the research plan, (5) designing the method for collecting information, (6) performing the research, (7) analyzing the data, and (8) communicating the findings.

Marketing decisions require both external and internal information. External information focuses on environmental opportunities and threats, with an emphasis on analyzing the market and buyers and competitors. Internal information focuses on the company's strengths and weaknesses versus those of competitors. Areas of inquiry generally include financial, human, and technological resources and the effectiveness of marketing programs.

Marketing intelligence is gathered from a variety of sources through formal and informal methods.

In its most basic form, it consists of data and facts about the marketplace. When the data are analyzed and interpreted in a meaningful way, they become information. Information that is believed to be true becomes intelligence that is easily understood, reliable, and valid for use in management decisions. Data and information are aggregated into databases such as a marketing information system (MIS) or marketing decision support system (MDSS) that are capable of supporting decision models for a variety of purposes.

Issues involved in the acquisition and use of marketing information include whether to conduct the research in-house or through an outside provider, the extent and scope of the research, availability and quality of organizational resources, quality of information and the research process, challenges of international research, and legal, ethical, and bias concerns.

Questions

1. Explain the importance of timely and relevant information inputs for marketing management decisions. Give an example to support your answer.

2. Describe the basic problem-solving process, and give a detailed example of how this might be used in making a decision about how to introduce a new product to the market. (Select a specific product and target market.) At what stage(s) do you believe it is most important to be creative?

3. Describe the complete marketing research process, and give a detailed example of how this might be used by a regional fast-food restaurant that is considering expanding its locations to other regions of the United States. How would this process differ if the restaurant were planning to open new locations in Europe?

4. Discuss the uses and sources of information about the external environment that might be included in a marketing intelligence system for a personal computer manufacturer. Select one specific type of information and show how the PC manufacturer would use this in making a decision about new product features.

5. Describe internal environmental information that might be used by the PC manufacturer in conjunction with the external information described in Question 4, and show why this would be useful.

6. Give an example of a database that is used by marketing managers, and list several specific applications of the data that it contains. How is the data converted to information, the information to intelligence, the intelligence to knowledge, and the knowledge to wise management decisions?

7. Debate the advantages, constraints, and issues involved in the acquisition and use of information gained through marketing intelligence.

Exercises

1. Choose one article in current business media that illustrates the use of marketing information in a decision related to a product, distribution channel, promotional campaign, or pricing strategy. Critique the research or data-gathering approach taken by management in terms of its appropriateness for this marketing decision. What additional information, if any, should the company have obtained? Defend your answer.

2. Industrial buyers face considerable uncertainty in their selection of goods and services, and the problem is greater in international trade due to differences in culture, language, and distance. National product standards have been imposed to create artificial barriers that restrict trade among countries. The International Standards Organization (ISO) was created by 89 member nations to develop product and service standards (ISO 9000) that would be acceptable to all members. The result was that any product or service that meets the ISO 9000 standards could be distributed in all the member nations without being subjected to other national requirements. Locate a complete description of the ISO 9000 standards,

and determine the relationship between these standards and the specific type(s) of marketing intelligence that might be related to fulfilling the requirements for a multinational manufacturer of tennis shoes.

3. Develop a five-item survey to determine consumer preferences for soft drinks (following the marketing research process described in this chapter). Administer the survey to ten of your friends, and tabulate and analyze your results. What inferences can be made from this ministudy? What measures can be taken to ensure a better-quality research project?

Endnotes

1. Robin M. Hogarth, *Judgement and Choice*, 2d ed. (New York: Wiley, 1987), p. 3.

2. *Ibid.*, pp. 51–52; and Vincent P. Barabba, *Meeting of the Minds: Creating the Market-Based Enterprise* (Boston: Harvard Business School Press, 1995), pp. 61–67.

3. *Webster's New World College Dictionary,* 3d ed. (New York: Macmillan, 1996), p. 1072.

4. Alexander Hiam and Charles D. Schewe, *The Portable MBA in Marketing* (New York: Wiley, 1992), p. 126.

5. Vincent P. Barabba, *op. cit.,* pp. 138–141.

6. Vincent P. Barabba and Gerald Zaltman, *Hearing the Voice of the Market: Competitive Advantage Through Creative Use of Market Information* (Boston: Harvard Business School Press, 1991), pp. 23–24.

7. *Ibid.,* pp. 33–34.

8. Thomas R. Keen, "What's Your Intuitive Decision-Maker Quotient?" *Marketing News* 30(22) (1996), p. 6.

9. James M. Higgins, *101 Creative Problem Solving Techniques: The Handbook of New Ideas for Business* (Winter Park, FL: New Management Publishing Company, 1994), Chap. 2, pp. 17–33 (quote, p. 17).

10. For further discussion, see *ibid.,* pp. 20–28.

11. James Thurber, quoted in *Bartlett's Book of Business Quotations,* compiled by Barbara Ann Kipfer (Boston: Little, Brown, 1994), p. 92.

12. Philip Kotler, William Gregor, and William Rodgers, "The Marketing Audit Comes of Age," *Sloan Management Review* (Winter 1977), pp. 25–43. [In Philip Kotler, *Marketing Management: Analysis, Planning, Implementation, and Control,* 8th ed. (Englewood Cliffs, NJ: Prentice-Hall, 1994), pp. 758–761.]

13. Barabba and Zaltman, *op. cit.,* pp. 41–45.

14. Quoted in Barabba and Zaltman, *op. cit.,* p. 137.

15. For further discussion of MDSS, see William R. Dillon, Thomas J. Madden, and Neil H. Firtle, *Marketing Research in a Marketing Environment,* 3d ed. (Homewood, IL: Irwin, 1994), Chap. 22, pp. 645–664, which is the source of much of the information in this section; also see John D. C. Little, "Decision Support Systems for Marketing Managers," *Journal of Marketing* 43(3) (Summer 1979), p. 9–26.

16. Jagdish N. Sheth and Rajendra S. Sisodia, "Improving Marketing Productivity," in Jeffrey Heilbrunn (ed.), *Marketing Encyclopedia: Issues and Trends Shaping the Future* (Chicago: American Marketing Association, and Lincolnwood, IL: NTC Business Books, 1995), p. 234.

17. Jerry W. Thomas, "Strategic Marketing Tracking Shows How Efforts Pay Off," *Marketing News* 29(34) (August 28, 1995), pp. 34ff.

18. Bob Donath, "Business Marketing 2000: The Marketing Millenium Flowers," in Heilbrunn, *op. cit.,* p. 157.

19. For further discussion, see Donald R. Lehmann and Russell S. Winer, *Analysis for Marketing Planning,* 3d ed. (Burr Ridge, IL: Irwin, 1994), Chap. 6, pp. 112; and Kotler, *op. cit.,* Chap. 10, pp. 244–262.

20. For further discussion, see Donald R. Lehmann and Russell S. Winer, *Analysis for Marketing Decisions,* 3d ed. (Homewood, IL: Irwin, 1994), Chap. 6, pp. 116ff.

21. Barabba and Zaltman, *op. cit.,* p. 5.

22. See Dillon, Madden, and Firtle, *op. cit.,* pp. 711–712.

APPENDIX: DIMENSIONS OF A MARKETING AUDIT

Part I. The Marketing Environment Audit

Macro-environment

A. Economic-demographic
   1. What does the company expect in the way of inflation, material shortages, unemployment, and credit availability in the short run, intermediate run, and long run?
   2. What effect will forecasted trends in the size, age distribution, and regional distribution of population have on the business?

B. Technological
   1. What major changes are occurring in product technology? In process technology?
   2. What are the major generic substitutes that might replace this product?

C. Political-legal
   1. What laws are being proposed that may affect marketing strategy and tactics?
   2. What federal, state, and local agency actions should be watched? What is happening with pollution control, equal employment opportunity, product safety, advertising, price control, etc., that is relevant to marketing planning?

D. Cultural
   1. What attitude is the public taking toward business and the types of products produced by the company?
   2. What changes in consumer lifestyles and values have a bearing on the company's target markets and marketing methods?

E. Ecological
   1. Will the cost and availability of natural resources directly affect the company?
   2. Are there public concerns about the company's role in pollution and conservation? If so, what is the company's reaction?

Task Environment

A. Markets
   1. What is happening to market size, growth, geographical distribution, and profits?
   2. What are the major market segments and their expected rates of growth? Which are high-opportunity and low-opportunity segments?

B. Customers
   1. How do current customers and prospects rate the company and its competitors on reputation, product quality, service, sales force, and price?
   2. How do different classes of customers make their buying decisions?
   3. What evolving needs do the buyers in this market have, and what satisfactions are they seeking?

C. Competitors
   1. Who are the major competitors? What are the objectives and strategy of each major competitor? What are their strengths and weaknesses? What are the sizes and trends in market shares?
   2. What trends can be foreseen in future competition and substitutes for this product?

D. Distribution and dealers
   1. What are the main trade channels bringing products to customers?
   2. What are the efficiency levels and growth potentials of the different trade channels?

C. Distribution
1. What are the distribution objectives and strategies?
2. Is there adequate market coverage and service?
3. How effective are the following channel members: distributors, manufacturers' reps, brokers, agents, etc.?
4. Should the company consider changing its distribution channels?

D. Advertising, sales promotion, and publicity
1. What are the organization's advertising objectives? Are they sound?
2. Is the right amount being spent on advertising? How is the budget determined?
3. Are the ad themes and copy effective? What do customers and the public think about the advertising?
4. Are the advertising media well chosen?
5. Is the internal advertising staff adequate?
6. Is the sales promotion budget adequate? Is there effective and sufficient use of sales promotion tools, such as samples, coupons, displays, and sales contests?
7. Is the publicity budget adequate? Is the public relations staff competent and creative?

E. Sales force
1. What are the organization's sales force objectives?
2. Is the sales force large enough to accomplish the company's objectives?
3. Is the sales force organized along the proper principle(s) of specialization (territory, market, product)? Are there enough (or too many) sales managers to guide the field sales reps?
4. Does the sales compensation level and structure provide adequate incentive and reward?
5. Does the sales force show high morale, ability, and effort?
6. Are the procedures adequate for setting quotas and evaluating performance?
7. How does the company's sales force compare with the sales forces of competitors?

Source: Principles of Marketing, 6/e by Kotler/Armstrong, ©1996. Reprinted by permission of Prentice-Hall, Inc.

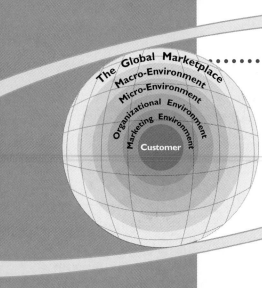

The Global Marketplace
Macro-Environment
Micro-Environment
Organizational Environment
Marketing Environment
Customer

CHAPTER 5

Understanding Consumer Buying Behavior

The Consumer Buying Process

Social and Cultural Influences on Buying Behavior

Individual Influences on Buying Behavior

Consumers and Products

Consumers and Situations

Relationship Marketing

Southwest Airlines insists on capitalizing the word customers *wherever it is used—in ads, brochures, even the annual report. The practice may seem picayune, but what better way to flag employees and the public that the Customer matters?[1]*

Changing Values in American Society

In the 1940s and 1950s, it was quite acceptable to hand out free cigarettes to GIs serving their country during World War II and to students on college campuses. Parents gave written permission for their high school-aged children to smoke on public and private school campuses. A large segment of the population "lit up" frequently for a variety of reasons. Few nonsmokers complained, many feeling they were in an unpopular minority if they did not smoke.

Today, the winds of change are borne on a collective puff of smoke, as social activists, health care advocates, politicians, and others join in the fight to stamp out smoking. Tobacco companies have lost major court battles regarding cigarette promotion and distribution, as well as reimbursement to state governments for health benefits paid out for smoking-related illnesses.

Considerable focus has been on promotion, with restrictions on cigarette advertising in all forms of media. Joe Camel, the smoker's icon—with more recognition among children than Barney, the friendly dinosaur—was the beast that bore much of the burden of the antismoking rhetoric and subsequent legislation.

Stringent restrictions have been placed on smoking in the workplace, public facilities, and modes of transportation. One man even sued his wife in court to make their home an enforceable no-smoking zone.

The antismoking movement in America reflects values that are consistent with greater health consciousness and general physical fitness. These values are captured in common descriptors such as *fat-free, sugar-free, cholesterol-free, high-fiber, aerobic, nicotine-free,* and *smoke-free.* Natural foods, alternative medicine, and other means to a healthy body and mind also are indicative of changing values in the United States.

Successful marketers recognize the importance of putting the customer first—always. Leading marketing and management gurus have maintained for many years that the primary objective of a business is to create customer satisfaction—with profit as a reward rather than an objective. In other words, when the customer is satisfied, everyone benefits—the company and its stockholders, suppliers, employees, and others. A satisfied customer finds value in a firm's goods and services and is willing to pay a reasonable price for them.[2] Thus marketers need to have a thorough understanding of their customers' needs, wants, and buying behavior, as well as how they define *value* in a rapidly changing marketplace.

Consumer behavior
Study of buying units and exchange processes involved in acquiring, consuming, and disposing of goods, services, experiences, and ideas.

Discussion in preceding chapters has paved the way for developing an understanding of **consumer behavior,** defined as "the study of the buying units and the exchange processes involved in acquiring, consuming, and disposing of goods, services, experiences, and ideas."[3] Note that this definition includes acquisition, consumption, and disposition in the exchange process for both tangible and intangible items. Likewise, this definition applies to both for-profit and nonprofit consumers. Consumer researchers are interested not only in how, why, where, and when customers buy but also in how they use the goods and services after purchase (perhaps for new uses or in different ways than originally intended) and how they dispose of goods once they no longer have a use for them (e.g., recycle, resale, etc.).

Previous chapters have stressed the importance of monitoring changes in the marketing environment to assess the potential for new market opportunities or threats to the organization. Timely and accurate environmental information is a critical element in market forecasting and developing strategic and tactical plans. Throughout this book, marketing is discussed from the perspective of customer-oriented value exchange, where long-term relationships benefit all parties involved in the exchange process as each party receives something of value from the other. The relationship between the study of consumer behavior and the strategic planning process is illustrated in Figure 5.1.

Customer value
All the benefits derived from a total product and all the costs of acquiring those benefits.

If value is the key to satisfying exchange relationships, then who defines *value*? In the past, the seller defined value—generally in terms of product features, low price, distribution method, and other company-oriented criteria. Today, however, value is defined in the marketplace by the customer. **Customer value** can be defined as "all the benefits derived from a total product and all the costs of acquiring those benefits."[4] This definition is in keeping with the new marketing concept that creates customer value throughout the entire marketing process by combining a customer orientation with total quality management principles. The result is a higher level of satisfaction among customers, employees, suppliers, and others, as well as higher profits for the company and its shareholders.

FIGURE 5.1

....

Consumers and Strategic Planning

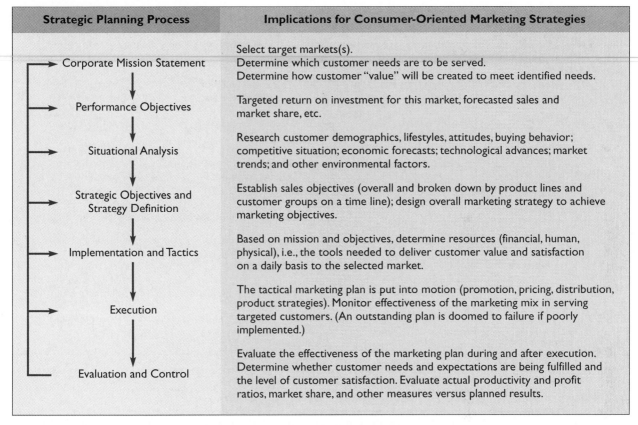

Strategic Planning Process	Implications for Consumer-Oriented Marketing Strategies
Corporate Mission Statement	Select target markets(s). Determine which customer needs are to be served. Determine how customer "value" will be created to meet identified needs.
Performance Objectives	Targeted return on investment for this market, forecasted sales and market share, etc.
Situational Analysis	Research customer demographics, lifestyles, attitudes, buying behavior; competitive situation; economic forecasts; technological advances; market trends; and other environmental factors.
Strategic Objectives and Strategy Definition	Establish sales objectives (overall and broken down by product lines and customer groups on a time line); design overall marketing strategy to achieve marketing objectives.
Implementation and Tactics	Based on mission and objectives, determine resources (financial, human, physical), i.e., the tools needed to deliver customer value and satisfaction on a daily basis to the selected market.
Execution	The tactical marketing plan is put into motion (promotion, pricing, distribution, product strategies). Monitor effectiveness of the marketing mix in serving targeted customers. (An outstanding plan is doomed to failure if poorly implemented.)
Evaluation and Control	Evaluate the effectiveness of the marketing plan during and after execution. Determine whether customer needs and expectations are being fulfilled and the level of customer satisfaction. Evaluate actual productivity and profit ratios, market share, and other measures versus planned results.

Source: Adapted from Anderson, Carol H. (1993), *Retailing: Concepts, Strategy and Information,* St. Paul, MN: West Publishing Company, Exhibit 6-1, pp. 225, 227.

....

In the following sections of this chapter we will discuss the consumer buying process, buying influences and motivations, and relationship marketing as it applies to final consumers. Successful marketing programs rely on a clear understanding of consumer needs and preferences relative to all aspects of the marketing mix—starting with the product offer and extending to an understanding of consumer responses to various pricing, distribution, and promotional strategies.

THE CONSUMER BUYING PROCESS

....

Consumer buying process
Five stages in consumer purchase decisions: need recognition, information search, evaluation of alternatives, purchase decision, and postpurchase evaluation.

The **consumer buying process** generally consists of five stages of related activities: (1) recognition of a need, (2) search for information, (3) evaluation of alternatives, (4) choice/purchase, and (5) postpurchase evaluation. (See Figure 5.2.) Consumers may expend a great deal of effort when making a purchase decision, or they simply may treat the purchase as a routine problem-solving situation where minimal effort is required. The level of complexity of consumer decision making is directly related to the consumer's level of involvement[5] with the purchase situation

FIGURE 5.2

••

Consumer Buying Process and Level of Involvement

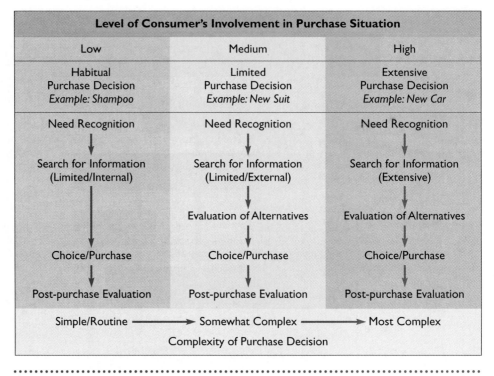

(rather than involvement with the product or product class). Consumer decision making is categorized as habitual, limited, or extended. The more involved the customer is in the purchase situation, the more complex is the decision process. Likewise, lower involvement results in routine or limited effort in arriving at a decision, as shown in Figure 5.2.

While we tend to think of this process in terms of specific products or brands, it also applies to the consumer's choice of specifically where and how to shop (e.g., retail store, home shopping network, etc.). In fact, many purchases start with the selection of a shopping center or store rather than with a particular product or product category. In Figure 5.3, a hypothetical automobile purchase is used to illustrate the various stages of the consumer buying process as they are described in the following sections.

Recognition of a Need

••••••••••••••••••••••••••••••

The purchase decision process starts with the recognition of a deficiency or felt need. This may be a specific need for a specific product (e.g., a required textbook for school) or an ill-defined sense of wanting or needing something (e.g., need for recreation to relieve stress from work or intense study or desire to munch on snack food). Social, physical, or psychological stimuli in the consumer's environment can

FIGURE 5.3

••

Consumer Buying Process for an Automobile

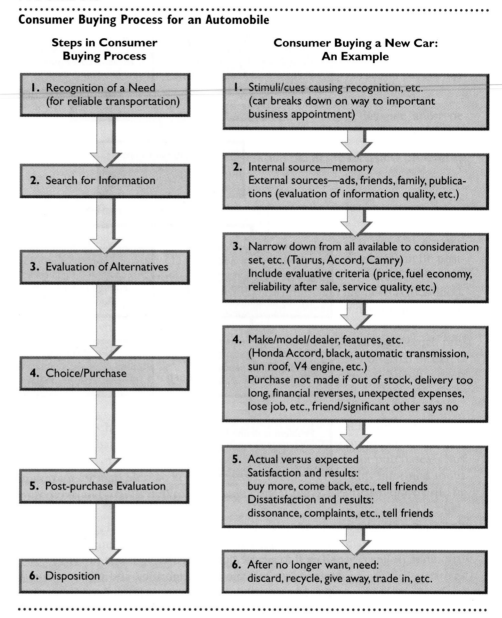

Steps in Consumer Buying Process

1. Recognition of a Need (for reliable transportation)
2. Search for Information
3. Evaluation of Alternatives
4. Choice/Purchase
5. Post-purchase Evaluation
6. Disposition

Consumer Buying a New Car: An Example

1. Stimuli/cues causing recognition, etc. (car breaks down on way to important business appointment)
2. Internal source—memory
   External sources—ads, friends, family, publications (evaluation of information quality, etc.)
3. Narrow down from all available to consideration set, etc. (Taurus, Accord, Camry)
   Include evaluative criteria (price, fuel economy, reliability after sale, service quality, etc.)
4. Make/model/dealer, features, etc. (Honda Accord, black, automatic transmission, sun roof, V4 engine, etc.)
   Purchase not made if out of stock, delivery too long, financial reverses, unexpected expenses, lose job, etc., friend/significant other says no
5. Actual versus expected
   Satisfaction and results: buy more, come back, etc., tell friends
   Dissatisfaction and results: dissonance, complaints, etc., tell friends
6. After no longer want, need: discard, recycle, give away, trade in, etc.

••

create a sense of imbalance that is likely to awaken a consumer need—thus starting the consumer buying process, as illustrated by the automobile purchase example in Figure 5.3.

When a consumer perceives that a significant difference exists between the actual and desired situation relative to a potential purchase, he or she is motivated to solve the purchase problem. However, this difference must be sufficiently large and important enough to cause the consumer to take action. (See Figure 5.4.)

The desired state is influenced by a number of factors, with the consumer's reference groups being one of the most important influences. Consumer choices are

FIGURE 5.5

Consumer Information Search

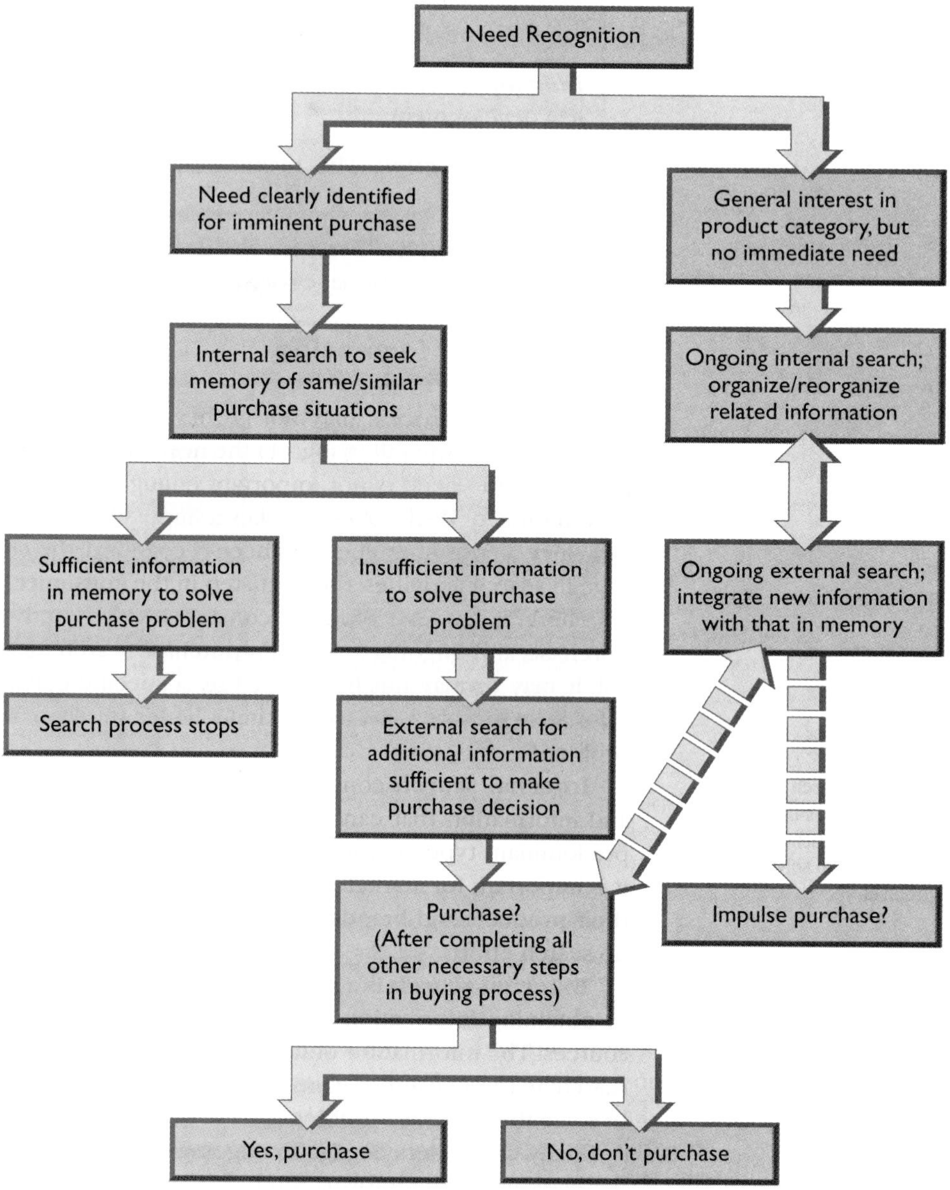

obtain the necessary information to make an informed decision. Much of this information is provided in advance of the recognized need—and in fact may trigger the felt need through advertising, sales presentations, advance publicity, trial, and other methods. Providing information early in the consumer buying process is an important element of internal search, to keep a company's products and brands at the top of the consumer's mind and thus have an impact on the final purchase decision.

Most consumer search efforts consist of searching one's memory for similar buying experiences and stored information that is relevant to the present situation. When information stored in memory is insufficient or unreliable, the consumer will consult external sources.

Information sources for external search include personal or group sources, marketing sources, public or independent sources, and personal experience. One of the most effective methods of promoting an organization's products and services is through word of mouth among family, friends, acquaintances, and other reference group members with whom the customer comes in contact. Although personal sources tend to have the highest level of credibility with consumers, they are the most difficult for marketers to manage effectively.

Marketing sources include advertising, salespeople, catalogs, on-line computer services, packages, displays, and so forth. Information from marketing sources is generally targeted toward prospective customers through the most appropriate media, stores, and other means of communication. McDonald's advertising can be found on television and radio stations, in newspapers and magazines, direct mailings, heavy couponing, point-of-sale materials, and sales promotion activities. The fast-food chain supports many local events and benefits from positive word-of-mouth promotion among its customers. McDonald's also communicates with PC users through McFamily, a site established in 1995 on America Online.[7] McFamily's features include information about parenting and family life, as well as a "Helping Others" section with information on the Ronald McDonald House, an on-line art gallery for children, contests, and "chat rooms" where individuals can share family-related success stories. Visitors to McFamily can order licensed merchandise and get advance information on future Happy Meal prizes—while building McDonald's customer database.

Public sources of information are made available to consumers through publications such as *Consumer Reports* and information disseminated by government agencies, newspaper articles, and publicity. Consumers tend to view this information as the most objective and reliable, since it is made available by an independent source and is not paid for by the marketer.

The amount of effort that the consumer is willing to expend in information search is determined by factors such as the amount of experience in making similar purchases; the search cost in terms of time and money; the amount of financial, social, physical, emotional, or other risks involved in making the "wrong" decision; and the degree of difference among the various purchase options.

Evaluation of Alternatives

Once the consumer has gathered the necessary information from internal and/or external sources to determine the alternatives available to satisfy a recognized consumer need, the next step is to weigh the identified alternatives according to a set of important criteria. (See Figure 5.6.) Both objective and subjective criteria may be used in evaluating purchase alternatives.

Objective criteria may include specific product features, such as price, design characteristics, warranty, performance measures, or other factors that can be compared easily across products, brands, and companies. In selecting a new home, a young family with children may focus on the price of the home, required down

FIGURE 5.6
· ·
Evaluation of Alternatives

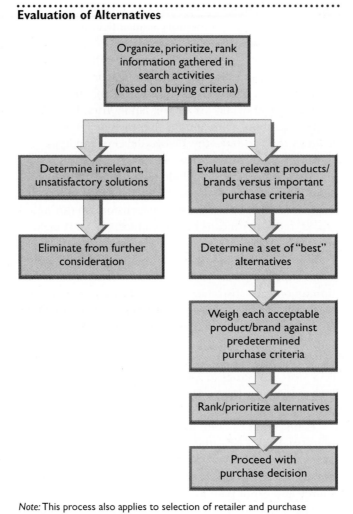

Note: This process also applies to selection of retailer and purchase method.

· ·

payment, mortgage terms, property taxes, distance to schools, quality of schools, and so forth.

Subjective criteria are more elusive, since they tend to focus on symbolic aspects of the product, style, and perceived benefits that the consumer expects to obtain from the purchase, such as status or pleasure. For the family purchasing a home, subjective criteria might include an element of nostalgia (past memories of a similar childhood home), feelings of safety or status, aesthetic responses to architectural features and landscaping, odors detected in the house, and a reaction to neighbors they happen to meet.

Quality and value, perhaps the most important purchase criteria considered by consumers, may be viewed as either objective or subjective components of a value-added strategy. These are discussed later in this chapter within the context of building relationships with customers.

Although consumers may consider a wide range of criteria in the process of evaluating purchase alternatives, the importance of each of these criteria may be weighted quite differently. In most buying situations, only a few salient criteria are used by the consumer in making the final purchase decision. Evaluative criteria apply not only to the goods and services being considered for purchase but also to entire product classes, brands, companies, countries of origin, and retail outlets.

Choice/Purchase

After the consumer has gathered information during the search process and ranked the various alternatives based on important purchase criteria, he or she is prepared to make a purchase decision. All potential brands and products can be placed into two major categories: an awareness set (products and brands known to the consumer) and an unawareness set (products and brands unknown to the consumer). The awareness set can be broken down further into three subcategories: *consideration set* (also called the *evoked set,* products and brands that the consumer actually would consider buying), *inert set* (products and brands that the consumer is indifferent toward, holding neither a strongly positive nor strongly negative attitude toward them), and *inept set* (products and brands that are known but are totally unacceptable to the consumer).

The extra baggy grunge look and hip-hop fashion became the consideration set for apparel worn by young consumers, characterized as Generation X. Conservative clothing could be classified as the inept set—totally unacceptable to this market. As youth fashions evolved into the mid-1990s, grunge and hip-hop fashions gave way to styles inspired by 1950s, 1960s, and 1970s films and memorabilia—a sort of "retro" look (e.g., Converse high-top sneakers) or "thrift shop" image. This, too, shall pass from the consideration set into the inert or inept categories. Because fashion cycles are relatively short, new designs must be created constantly to satisfy customers and maintain brand loyalty.

Within this discussion, it is assumed that a choice is made and a purchase is completed at this point in the consumer buying process. However, a consumer may make a choice but not actually purchase for several reasons. Some of these include: the retailer is out of stock on the item, the customer may find a better (previously unknown) alternative at point of purchase, the customer has insufficient funds or credit is not available, someone else (e.g., friend, salesperson) makes negative comments about the customer's choice, and other factors.

Postpurchase Evaluation

The consumer buying process does not stop with the purchase act. In creating customer value, marketers find that follow-up after the sale is an essential element in delivering customer satisfaction and building long-term relationships. The level of customer satisfaction is determined by the difference between expectations and performance. When the marketer delivers more than the customer expects, the result is a higher level of satisfaction. Likewise, when the actual performance of a product or sales experience does not meet customer expectations, dissatisfaction results, as shown in Figure 5.7.

FIGURE 5.7

....

Postpurchase Evaluation

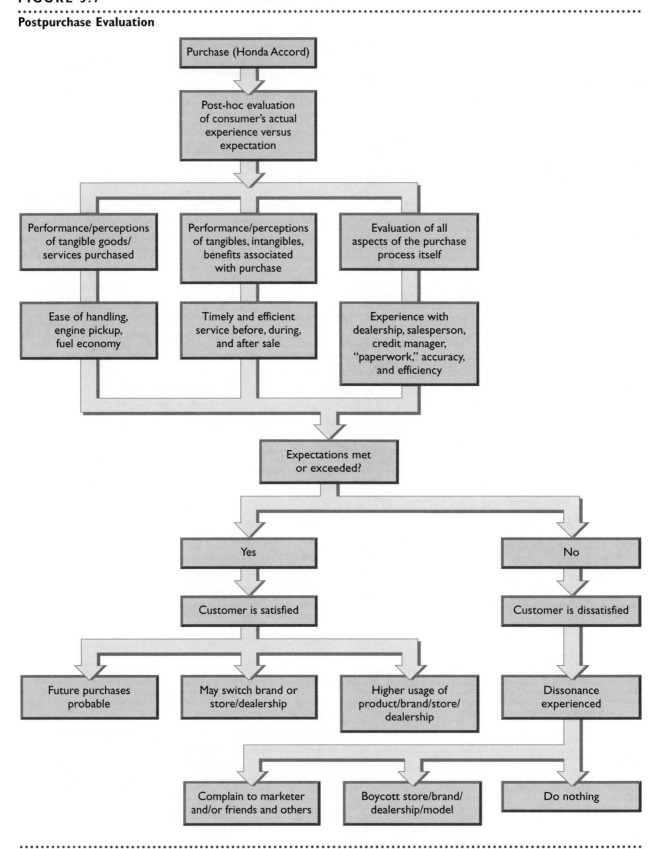

Successful marketers measure customer satisfaction in a number of ways. For example, hotels make customer response surveys readily available in guest rooms, and restaurants provide them on tables or with the check. Investment companies, banks, and a vast array of consumer product companies invite customers to provide feedback on their products and purchase experiences. The availability of 800 numbers, knowledgeable and well-trained customer service representatives, salespeople, and managers provides customers with ways to communicate both positively and negatively with the company. Satisfied customers are repeat customers. It is much less expensive to convert dissatisfied customers into satisfied customers than it is to attract new customers. Thus marketers need to know how they are evaluated after the sale.

SOCIAL AND CULTURAL INFLUENCES ON BUYING BEHAVIOR

Consumers function not only as individuals but also as members of a complex society that has a significant impact on purchase decisions. Therefore, the buying process is influenced by factors in the consumer's external environment as well as factors internal to the individual. Although many of these influences are beyond the direct control of the marketer, they must be considered carefully in designing effective marketing programs.

Consumer socialization
Process whereby people acquire the knowledge, skills, and attitudes necessary to perform as consumers.

Human behavior, including consumer behavior, is learned through a socialization process starting at a very young age and continuing throughout one's life. **Consumer socialization** is the process that enables people to acquire the knowledge, skills, and attitudes necessary to perform as consumers. Cultural values and norms are transmitted to the individual through direct or indirect interaction with other members of society, referred to as *socialization agents.* Direct socialization may occur through contact with friends, family, peers, or other "up-close" relationships. Indirect socialization may occur through the media, business efforts, the government, or other sources that do not have direct contact with the person being socialized. Marketers who know and understand their customers can be major agents in the consumer socialization process as they develop long-term relationships consistent with cultural norms.

Cultural and Social Status

An individual's culture, subculture, and social class are considered the most important societal influences on buying behavior. A person's needs, wants, behaviors, and values are shaped by the society in which he or she lives.

Culture
The complex of learned values and behaviors shared by a society.

Culture. A **culture** is defined as "the complex of learned values and behaviors that are shared by a society and are designed to increase the probability of the society's survival."[8] Culture supplies the individual with enduring core values and boundaries for behavior. Since culture is learned behavior, its influence is subject to change with new knowledge and experience; however, this process is very slow and complex.

Marketer: Know Thy Customer!

Marketers have discovered *the customer*—finally. Everywhere you look, there is advice on how to build relationships with customers. Customer orientation, creating value for customers, and total quality management are hot topics for marketing managers.

How well do we know our customers? One source claims that 81 percent of CEOs admit that they have a poor understanding of their customer base. Technology provides the means to capture and process huge databases, but 55 percent of the CEOs say that technology has not helped. Information may be in nonusable or inconvenient formats, or it may not be accessible to those who need it for daily decisions. To overcome this problem, companies such as AT&T's Global Information Systems combine communications and computer technology to provide clients with necessary customer-focused information. For example, AT&T's "Get IT, Move IT, Use IT" program helped a major retailer identify 70 percent of its inventory that was nonproductive. By knowing the customer better, the retailer was able to make each store location into a customer-driven neighborhood store. In addition, vendors now have inventory information in less than a week—shortened from 75 days.

Managers who previously believed that their company's success came directly from their product portfolio have come to realize that it is their customer portfolio that is their true source of success and most valuable asset. All types and sizes of organizations can analyze, cultivate, and manage their customer portfolios by following these four steps:

1. *Identify your customers, and determine what they contribute to profitability.* BancOne of Columbus, Ohio, found that all its profits came from the top 20 percent of its customers; the remaining 80 percent cost the bank money. In the cellular phone industry, the "best" customer segments are more than 10 times more profitable than the "worst" segments. Additionally, 20 to 25 percent of cellular customers provide 60 to 80 percent of industry revenues. In order to know how to serve these customer groups, it is important to know who they are and to understand their buying behavior.

2. *Benchmark your competition.* Find out everything you can about your competitors. What customer segments do they serve? How do they acquire and keep customers? Should you adopt any of their "best practices"? A health care company found that its low profit performance was due to a low-margin customer base. After benchmarking against others in the industry, the health care provider found that it had missed two particularly high-margin customer segments, which it subsequently pursued—and profits increased.

3. *Target selected customer segments.* Determine the customer segments to be targeted and customer needs that your firm can serve better than competitors. (Do not try to be all things to all customers.) ScrubaDub, a small family-owned car wash chain in the Boston area, has grown to be among the top 20 car wash operations in the United States. In 1990, ScrubaDub conducted market research to learn more about its customers, their critical needs, and how to differentiate its car washes from those of competitors. The company determined that its target customer was upscale with an annual household income of more than $75,000, lived within 3 miles of a ScrubaDub location, and owned cars that were 3 years old or less. The company's growth is due to understanding its customers and offering the value they want: personalized service, guarantees, and an attractive environment.

4. *Build long-term relationships.* Repeat business normally results in lower sales costs and higher profits. Disney, for example, is a master at building long-term relationships with its customers. Disney classic animated films are re-released every 5 to 7 years in theaters and on home video, creating a new generation of loyal Disney fans. Families take their children to Disney parks. Those children grow up and return with their own families, and on and on. Since an estimated two-thirds of Walt Disney World guests are repeat visitors to Disney parks, these long-term customer relationships provide long-term profits.

Continuously building and managing your customer portfolio has proven to be profitable, as shown in the preceding examples. The key lies in understanding your customers and delivering value that satisfies their wants and needs.

Sources: Duncan McDougall, "Know Thy Customer," *Wall Street Journal* (August 7, 1995), p. A12; Advertisement: AT&T Global Information Systems, *Wall Street Journal* (February 13, 1995), p. B12.

Cultural values are disseminated primarily through three basic institutions: the family, educational institutions, and religious organizations. With the decline of the traditional American family and the values associated with it and the movement of many young people away from religious organizations, schools have become an important force in the transmission of cultural values.

Consumer behavior is affected by three broad categories of values that vary across cultures:[9] self-oriented, environment-oriented, and other-oriented values. These categories can be broken down as follows:

- *Self-oriented values.* Self-oriented values are objectives and approaches to life that are desirable to individual members of society. They can be classified as active/passive, material/nonmaterial, hard work/leisure, postponed/immediate gratification, sensual gratification/abstinence, and humorous/serious.

- *Environment-oriented values.* Environment-oriented values prescribe a society's relationship with its economic, technical, and physical environments. They can be expressed as maximum/minimum cleanliness, performance/status, tradition/change, risk-taking/security, problem-solving/fatalistic, and admire/overcome nature.

- *Other-oriented values.* Other-oriented values are a society's view of appropriate relationships between individuals and groups within that society, such as individual/collective, limited/extended family, adult/child, competition/cooperation, youth/age, and masculine/feminine.

Subculture
Identifiable subgroup within a culture that shares values and patterns of behavior that are distinguishable from the overall culture.

Subculture. Diverse populations can be categorized into subcultures. A **subculture** is an identifiable group "within a culture that shares distinguishing values and patterns of behavior that differ from the overall culture."[10] The more heterogeneous a population, the more subcultures that can be identified within it. Each subculture determines its own set of values and acceptable behaviors, which are followed to varying degrees by its members. Subcultures may be identified on the basis of race, nationality, religion, age, geographic location, and other dimensions. Because buying motives and behaviors tend to be relatively consistent among the more narrowly defined subcultures, they are attractive target markets for marketing

TABLE 5.1
• • • • • • • • • • • • • •
Subculture Comparisons Across Age-Cohort Groups

Characteristic	Cohort Group		
	Depression Cohort (GI Generation)	**World War II Cohort (Depression Generation)**	**Postwar Cohort (Silent Generation)**
Years born	1912–1921	1922–1927	1928–1945
Age in 1995	74–83	68–73	50–67
Percent of adult population	7% (13 million)	6% (11 million)	21% (41 million)
Attitude toward money	Positive toward saving; negative toward debt; carry financial scars	Keep spending down and savings up; self-denial	Balance between saving and spending
Attitude toward sex	Intolerant	Ambivalent	Repressive
Music preferences	Big Band Era	Swing	Frank Sinatra (youngest segment was the "cool generation," first to dig folk, rock)
Other	First to be strongly influenced by contemporary media (radio, movies)	Shared experience of common enemy and common goal; intensely romantic	"War babies"; long period of economic growth and social stability; global unrest and nuclear threat

efforts. See Table 5.1 for a comprehensive subculture comparison of age-cohort groups.

Social class
An individual's status in society generally based primarily on occupation, education, and income.

Social Class.   Social status or **social class** represents another important societal influence on buying behavior. While social class structure is less evident in the United States than in many other countries, marketers and social scientists find it useful to determine a person's social status based on occupation, education, income, and other relevant dimensions. Although several acceptable systems are used to measure social class, they generally result in three broad class designations (upper, middle, and lower class) that can be subdivided further as shown in Table 5.2.

Consumption behavior is influenced significantly by the amount of prestige or esteem associated with a particular social class. Those within a certain social class tend to be similar in their purchase behaviors for goods and services—particularly visible items such as clothing, houses, cars, and recreational activities (e.g., restaurants, sports, travel, and other leisure activities). Although two consumers in different social classes may have the same amount of money to spend, they can be expected to spend it differently. For example, two teenage girls—one upper class and one lower middle class—may be shopping for gifts for family members. The

TABLE 5.1 *(continued)*
....
Subculture Comparisons Across Age-Cohort Groups

	Cohort Group			
Characteristic	*Baby-Boomers I Cohort (Woodstock Generation)*	*Baby-Boomers II Cohort (Zoomers)*	*Generation X Cohort* (Baby-Busters)*	*Generation Y Cohort ("Youthquake")*
Years born	1946–1954	1955–1965	1966–1976	Population burst from ±1980 to present
Age in 1995	41–49	30–40	19–29	Under 15 years / 4–8 years
Percent of adult population	17% (33 million)	25% (49 million)	21% (41 million)	N/A% (57 million in 1997) / N/A% (20 million in 1997)
Attitude toward money	"Spend, borrow, spend"	"Spend, borrow, spend"; debt acceptable to maintain lifestyle	"Spend? Save? What?"	Both groups indulged by parents
Attitude toward sex	Permissive	Permissive	Confused	Indications are they will be similar to baby-boomer parents
Music preferences	Rock and roll	Rock and roll	Grunge, rap, retro	Varied??
Other	Vietnam divides leading-edge and trailing-edge baby-boomers; Kennedy and King assassinations had major impact; economic good times and optimism for early baby-boomers	Youthful idealism disappeared with Watergate; later baby-boomers exhibited narcissistic preoccupation with self; age of downward mobility	Slacker set, cynicism and pessimism; latchkey kids of day care and divorce; political conservatism; "What's in it for me?"	Technologically adept; education a priority; environmentally conscious; achievement oriented; tolerant of diversity; socially "in-the-know"; greater gap between the "haves" and "have-nots"

*Birth years vary for Generation Xers; some experts designate the years from 1961–1981.
Sources: Adapted from Faye Rice, "Making Generational Marketing Come of Age," *Fortune* (June 26, 1995), pp. 110–114; Melinda Beck, "Next Population Bulge Shows Its Might," *Wall Street Journal* (February 3, 1997), pp. B1, B5; Jonathan Kaufman, "At Age 5, Reading, Writing, and Rushing," *Wall Street Journal* (February 4, 1997), pp. B1, B2; Ellen Graham, "When Terrible Twos Become Terrible Teens," *Wall Street Journal* (February 5, 1997), pp. B1, B8.

TABLE 5.2
....
Social Class Hierarchy

Upper Americans (about 14 percent of population)

Upper-uppers (less than 1 percent)
Inherited wealth (i.e., old money), old family names, charitable giving, multiple homes, prestigious schools, fine jewelry, luxury vacations, investments, imitated by other classes

Lower-uppers (about 2 percent)
High income or wealth earned through business or professions (i.e., new money), most moved up from middle class, active in social and civic affairs, achievement oriented, purchases represent status

Upper-middles (about 12.5 percent)
Well educated, intellectual elite, and professionals; lifestyle involves private clubs ("joiners"), causes, arts; quality homes (in "right" neighborhood); quality clothes, furniture, appliances

Middle class (32 percent)
Both average-pay white- and blue-collar workers; live on "better side of town" and try to "do the proper things" (respectability); focus on family; most have completed high school and may have some college; aim children toward college

Working class (38 percent)
Average-pay blue-collar workers and/or those who lead a "working-class lifestyle"—regardless of income, education, or employment; tend to stay close to home and parents and relatives, and to live in older parts of town; comprise mass market for consumer goods

Lower Americans

Upper-lower (9 percent)
"Working poor"; living standard just above poverty level; unskilled and poorly paid but striving to move up to higher class; behavior may be judged "crude" or "trashy"

Lower-lower (7 percent)
On welfare (public aid or charity), visibly poverty stricken; out of work or working "dirtiest jobs"; includes indigents, criminals; some are prone to every form of instant gratification if money is available; others struggle to achieve what they believe will be their heavenly reward for resisting earthly temptations

Sources: Adapted from Richard P. Coleman, "The Continuing Significance of Social Class in Marketing," *Journal of Consumer Research* 10 (December 1983), pp. 265–280; and John C. Mowen, *Consumer Behavior,* 4th ed. (Englewood Cliffs, NJ: Prentice-Hall, 1995), p. 761.

lower-class teenager may have more money to spend because her family expects her to work after school to earn money for many of her own consumer needs (as well as do well in school), whereas the upper-class teenager may have only money from allowances or occasional jobs because more of her time is focused on academic achievement, personal development, and social activities.

Many children's clothes and toys are targeted at different social segments. For example, the ever popular Winnie-the-Pooh merchandise can be found at a variety of retailers. The older, original characters' merchandise is found at exclusive, higher-priced stores such as FAO Schwartz and Tiffany. The "newer" Winnie-the-Pooh and friends' merchandise can be bought at lower-priced stores such as Kmart, Wal-Mart, and Target.

Group Influences

Consumers belong to a variety of groups—each with its own way of influencing purchasing behavior. Since it is difficult, if not impossible, for a consumer to act in complete isolation from others, it is important for marketers to understand the role of group influence in the consumption process. Individuals look to group members to define what is acceptable and unacceptable according to the group's norms, values, and beliefs. The groups that have the greatest impact on the formation of attitudes and behavior are *reference groups* and *family*. However, the influence of either of these groups is strengthened or weakened by the individual's *role* (real or perceived) and relative *position* within each group.

Reference groups
Groups that become a point of reference for an individual's behavior, beliefs, and attitudes.

Reference Groups.   People generally have a number of **reference groups** (or individual reference persons) that they use as a point of reference for their own behavior, beliefs, and attitudes. Consumers adopt and imitate the values of these groups but may look to different reference groups at different times based on proximity, purchase situation, and product class.

The proximity of reference groups can be described as either primary or secondary. **Primary reference groups** may be formal or informal and include individuals the customer interacts with most frequently on a face-to-face basis, such as family, friends, and co-workers. (Family influences on purchase decisions are discussed later in this section.) Reference group influence is most noticeable in the purchase of highly visible goods and services that are intended to show conformance to the norms of a particular group.

Primary reference groups
Influential individuals that the customer interacts face-to-face with most frequently.

Secondary reference groups may or may not involve formal membership and generally are those with whom the consumer has little or no interpersonal contact. Membership groups include those of which an individual is automatically a member (such as gender, age, marital status, social status) or may be those which a person joins and "belongs to." Groups that an individual belongs to may be primarily personal (e.g., social club, church, work group, college class) or nonpersonal (e.g., American Automobile Association, frequent fliers program, political party).

Secondary reference groups
Groups that influence consumer decisions despite the fact that there is little or no interpersonal contact with the consumer.

Reference Groups Can Be Positive or Negative.   A *positive reference group* represents desirable values and beliefs and is one to which a person aspires to belong, that is, an aspiration group. For example, people tend to dress like others they admire in their work group, particularly those with higher status. Cosmetic manufacturers are benefiting from a worldwide trend among young women to emulate American women in using makeup.[11] Avon is selling lipsticks and other beauty aids in "back road" areas of eastern Europe, veiled Muslim women in Kurachi and ex-Communists in Prague are buying American beauty brands with reformulated products and colors that appeal to local preferences, and Max Factor sells Vidal Sassoon hair products in the Far East (adding a pine aroma to some shampoos). These and other examples of American-type cosmetics sold overseas illustrate the concept of *mass customization,* adapting one basic product with minor modifications to satisfy the needs of a target market—in this case markets that see attractive American women as a reference group.

In contrast, a *negative reference group* is one that a person dissociates with as having totally unacceptable norms, beliefs, and behaviors, that is, a dissociative group—or a negative point of reference. For example, motorcycle manufacturers have been faced with the problem of dissociating their brands from Hells Angels or other bikers with a negative image. One of Honda's early commercials to overcome this problem promised that you would meet the nicest people on a Honda. Negative reference groups occur in every strata of society—even small children influence purchases based on reference group perceptions, as experienced by OshKosh B'Gosh, Inc., a manufacturer of work clothes. In the 1980s, well-dressed babies wore tiny bib overalls and work clothes from OshKosh. However, the company's image became closely associated with children's clothes, making it difficult for OshKosh to sell clothes to anyone else. A line of older children's clothes failed because 8-year-olds refused to wear baby clothes. The negative image also caused line extensions in adult apparel to fail.[12] (Conversely, Gap, Inc., managed to keep a positive image across generations with similar products.)

Family Influence.   Consumer decisions are influenced by two types of family: family of orientation and family of procreation. The **family of orientation** is the one that an individual is born to or adopted into and that shapes attitudes and behavior that tend to endure from childhood throughout one's lifetime. Parents give their children their first lessons in consumer behavior—the best kinds of food to eat, brands to buy, movies to see, television to watch, stores to shop in, and generally what is acceptable and unacceptable consumer behavior. A large percentage of a family's shopping is done by teenage children of working parents. This early influence carries on when the child is grown and no longer has to shop to please his or her parents.

The **family of procreation** is formed when the individual starts his or her own family and has a spouse and children. Consumer needs, wants, and buying roles change as new families are formed. Changes in today's lifestyles have a major impact on traditional consumer roles of the past. It is important for marketers to know and understand the various consumer roles played by family members and how these affect purchase behavior.

Family purchase decisions are influenced by size of the family and stage in the family life cycle, as illustrated in Table 5.3. Census data and marketing research indicate that it is more appropriate today to extend the family life cycle concept to the broader concept of a household life cycle. Households are the basic unit of consumption in the United States, making it essential to understand their composition. As noted in Chapter 2, the number of single-person households has increased significantly, along with an increase in nontraditional households (single parent with children, same-sex couples, cohabiting singles, and so forth). This trend must be monitored by marketers to determine consumer preferences for brands and goods and services, packaging specifications, distribution methods, and other marketing mix decisions.

Life Roles and Status in Groups.   Each person plays many roles throughout his or her lifetime. Some of these endure over a long period of time (e.g., son, daughter, mother, father), whereas others exist for a relatively brief time (e.g., president of a professional association, work supervisor). Each of the roles that a person performs—often simultaneously—has a set of expectations (and consumer needs) associated with it that have a major influence on buying behavior.

Individuals with the highest status in a group tend to set and enforce the group norms for most aspects of personal behavior. Those with lower status are most

---

Family of orientation
Family an individual is born into; shapes long-term attitudes and behavior.

Family of procreation
Family that an individual starts with his or her own spouse and children.

TABLE 5.3
··············
Family/Household Life Cycle and Buying Behavior

Stage in Household Life Cycle	Buying Behavior
Younger (under 35)	
Single/unmarried	May live at home, alone, or share residence; active social life; spends money on recreation, clothing, basic furniture.
Young married (or cohabitating) couple (< 35)	Highest purchase rate of durables (cars, appliances, electronics, etc.) and vacations; financially more secure than they can expect in future.
Full nest I (female < 35, children < 6)	Low liquid financial assets; home-buyers, child-related products, health care, etc.
Single parent (children < 6)	Low liquid assets; child-oriented purchases; convenience goods and affordable services.
Middle-aged (35–65)	
Single/unmarried	Many types: may be divorced, widowed, or never married; differing lifestyles which may or may not involve expenses for previous family, dating, and individual indulgences (expensive cars, luxury vacations, etc.).
Delayed full nest (female > 35, children < 6)	Better liquid asset position; heavy purchases of children's clothing, educational products, preventative health care, and family vacations.
Full nest II and III (couple with children > 6 at home)	Generally better off financially; active lifestyle; purchase "large size" packages, larger quantities of food, cleaning materials; buy sporting goods, larger vehicles, lessons, etc.
Single parent II (children > 6 at home)	May have less disposable income; active lifestyle for children and parent; may be juggling work, family, and social life; spending patterns will depend on financial status, but primarily children/family-oriented.
Middle-aged couple (< 65, no children at home, empty nest I)	Generally better off financially; may both be working; buy more expensive cars, home furnishings, vacations, and leisure activities; may be in new marriage and establishing new household.
Older (over 65)	
Single/unmarried (no children at home)	Includes never married bachelor, divorced, widowed; consumer characteristics determined by status of health and wealth; expenditures for medical care, wellness programs, entertainment (and dating), or just for mere subsistence.

(continues)

TABLE 5.3 *(continued)*
....
Family Household Lifecycle and Buying Behavior

Stage in Household Lifecycle	Buying Behavior
Older (over 65)	
Older couple (no children at home, empty nest II)	Similar to middle-aged couple in many respects; may be retired (with fixed income); more expenses for health care, leisure activities, vacations; may be helping to support children, grandchildren.
Other	Note that households are the primary consumption unit in society and that there is a great deal of diversity in the makeup of traditional and nontraditional households. Marketers must consider these factors, along with lifestyle, income, and other indicators when planning marketing programs.

Sources: Adapted from John C. Mowen, *Consumer Behavior,* 4th ed. (Englewood Cliffs, NJ: Prentice-Hall, 1995), pp. 660–664; Mary C. Gillis and Ben M. Enis, "Recycling the Family Lifecycle: A Proposal for Redefinition," in A. Mitchell (ed.), *Advances in Consumer Research,* Vol. 9. (Ann Arbor, MI: Association for Consumer Research, 1982), pp. 271–276; Del I. Hawkins, Roger J. Best, and Kenneth A. Coney, *Consumer Behavior: Implications for Marketing Strategy,* 6th ed. (Chicago: Richard D. Irwin, 1995), p. 191; and other sources.

likely to adopt the values and behaviors of the group leader. Parents set the expectations for children in a family—what they will eat or wear and what is acceptable behavior at home and away from home. The status of religious leaders, politicians, sports heroes, musicians, actors/actresses, and other prominent individuals provides a reference point for their followers, thus influencing the purchase (or avoidance) of many goods and services. Consumers are most likely to make purchases that communicate their status (real or perceived) to others, that is, status symbols. As marketers build relationships with their customers, it is important to know and understand their life roles and the status associated with these roles in order to create customer value consistent with these roles.

INDIVIDUAL INFLUENCES ON BUYING BEHAVIOR
....

Most of the influences just described are external in nature, although some have internal influence implications through interaction with one another. When we consider consumers as individuals, the primary influences on buying behavior are related more to personal characteristics and psychological factors. These are internal to the individual and thus more resilient to persuasive marketing tactics that are intended to change consumer attitudes and behaviors.

Personal Influences
....

Personal characteristics include age and stage in life cycle (discussed with family influence), occupation, economic circumstances, lifestyle, personality, and self-concept.

Life cycle stage
Family or household status, along with age, related to consumer lifestyles and preferences.

Age and Life Cycle Stage.   A person's age and **life cycle stage** dictate to a large extent distinct needs and preferences for food, clothing, leisure activities, medical care, and other consumer goods and services. Young, active singles and families are good customers for fast-food restaurants and takeout and catered food—most likely healthy and gourmet. Singles are a good market for sports cars, and young families buy a large percentage of the minivans and sport utility vehicles sold in the United States. Middle-aged consumers may opt for sit-down restaurants or gourmet food prepared at home from "scratch." Many prefer comfortable four-door luxury cars with safety features. Age also is related to a predisposition toward spending and saving. The oldest U.S. consumers grew up in the Depression era and tend to save their money and postpone gratification obtained through purchases. In contrast, baby-boomers have demonstrated a preoccupation with themselves and have incurred a high level of debt. Generation X, aged 19 to 29, among the youngest members of the population, are cynical consumers. Many have money to spend (because a large number are still living with parents), but research indicates that they have a deep distrust of business and a strong dislike of marketing "hype." Their younger brothers and sisters, Generation Y (under age 18), are computer savvy and more sophisticated than many of their predecessors (see Table 5.1).

Likewise, each stage in the life cycle has its own set of related consumer wants and needs. As a person changes status from a young, unmarried single to marital or cohabitation status, personal and household needs change, and new product categories are sought in the marketplace. When babies and children are added to the family or household, more new consumer decisions must be made, and so on throughout the life cycle as the children grow up and leave home and the adults are left with an "empty nest." Eventually, the life cycle ends with a single household member once again—only at this time the person is most likely elderly and seeks an entirely different array of consumer goods and services, depending on his or her health, economic situation, and personal interests.

Occupation and Economic Status.   Consumers typically purchase clothes, automobiles, homes, and other products that are consistent with their work roles. For example, a sales manager for a major computer manufacturer would be likely to buy good-quality business suits and accessories (as well as name-brand sports clothes for informal sales meetings), an upscale automobile model, a home in a "good" neighborhood, personal computer(s) and accessories, software, membership in local organizations, and quality family vacations. The production-line worker who makes the computers is most likely a good customer for work clothes, leisure wear, outdoor sporting equipment, pickup trucks, sport utility vehicles, and do-it-yourself home improvement products.

The sales manager and the production worker in the preceding example may earn about the same income but will spend it differently. Occupation and income are closely related and are major determinants of a person's socioeconomic status and ability to spend money. They are primary indicators of household income, personal debt, savings, and general ability and willingness to spend money for a wide range of consumer goods and services.

Lifestyle.   In the past, marketers relied heavily on their knowledge of a market's demographic characteristics in designing marketing strategies. Today, demographics

Lifestyle
The manner or style in which people live, how they use their time and money, and how they think.

are considered only part of the picture; **lifestyles** have become an important variable in understanding consumer behavior. Lifestyles are simply the way people live—how they use their time and money and how they think. Lifestyles are related to a person's attitudes, interests, and opinions (AIOs), which transcend social class, income, demographics, and other familiar ways of categorizing consumers.

Individuals from diverse backgrounds can be aggregated into one market segment for various products. Examples abound in the markets for pickup trucks (driven by blue-collar workers, corporate CEOs, farmers, young women, and a broad cross section of consumers). Other product categories that appeal to consumer lifestyles include athletic shoes for active sports or casual nonathletic wear, SONY Walkman and other headsets, health clubs, and most beverages.

Personality. An individual's personality has a major influence on consumer choices but is difficult to measure or to use directly in marketing programs. However, it is known that a personality type tends to be consistent and goal directed to create similar responses to similar situations. Personality traits are formed at an early age and do not change easily.

There are a number of reliable methods of measuring personality traits and behaviors related to these traits. Traits can be described in bipolar adjectives, with an individual's personality described on a continuum between extremes, such as conservative/liberal, reserved/outgoing, tough-minded/tender-minded, or independent/dependent. Although it is not efficient to measure the personality type of each consumer in a market, his or her responses and behaviors can be predicted with a high degree of accuracy.

Marketers can apply an understanding of attitudes and behaviors that are associated with certain personality traits to designing products, promotional campaigns, packaging, and other aspects of the marketing mix. This is particularly evident in marketing personal care products and beverages. Brands and marketing communications for a popular beverage can be designed to appeal to an outgoing personality, for example, by stressing group activities and acceptance. In contrast, marketing communications for the same product targeted toward a more reserved personality would stress enjoyment of the beverage in a quiet, comfortable setting.

Self-concept
Self-image, attitude toward oneself.

Self-concept. An individual's **self-concept,** or self-image, plays a major role in consumer decisions. People make purchases based on attitudes toward themselves—who they think they are or would like to be or how they think others see them. Many purchases are made to move a consumer's actual self closer to the ideal self. Self-help goods and services (health, fitness, personal grooming, books, seminars, etc.) have experienced increased sales as consumers attempt to improve their self-concepts.

Brand images are built on self-concept to a large extent. For example, low-income consumers buy national brands of canned goods rather than generics to indicate a higher-status self-concept. High-visibility products are influenced most by self-concept. In our upwardly mobile society, people tend to consume at the next higher level. For example, a person who considers himself or herself to be an innovative consumer is a good prospect for high-fashion clothing and home accessories, unusual artwork and jewelry, exotic vacations, and gourmet food. The innovator will pay more and expend more effort in the consumer buying process to be the first to own a new product. (Recall the "mad rush" to be the first owners of the new Windows 95 software.)

People who view themselves as economical consumers will search for good deals that offer high quality at low prices. A resurgence in used-car sales and increased traffic at thrift shops are strong indicators of a frugal self-concept (as well as an economic necessity in many cases today).

Self-concept can influence decisions about what not to buy. Brand loyalty and self-concept are closely related, so any brand that is inconsistent with a person's self-image will not be acceptable. Likewise, if role models and celebrities used in advertising and personal selling are inconsistent with an individual's self-concept, the message will be "tuned out" or viewed negatively. Consumer preferences and reactions should be determined in advance of marketing campaigns.

Psychological Influences

Psychological influences include motivation, perception, learning and memory, and beliefs and attitudes. Each of these is discussed briefly in this section.

Motivation.   Recognition of a consumer need will not automatically lead to purchase. The consumer must be motivated to take action to remove the sense of imbalance caused by the actual and desired state of affairs. Motives are internal drive states that direct an individual's behavior toward satisfying his or her felt needs. As a result, marketers need to understand the motives that underlie consumer decisions.

Hierarchy of needs theory
An explanation of motivation whereby the individual moves from lower to higher levels of need, having the greatest motivation to satisfy the lowest-level needs first.

While there are a number of theories of motivation, many marketers find it useful to apply Abraham Maslow's **hierarchy of needs theory** to marketing decisions.[13] This theory explains motivation in terms of a hierarchy, moving from lower to higher levels of needs, as shown in Figure 5.8. Individuals generally will not be motivated to satisfy a higher-level need until they have satisfied the lower-level, or more basic, need below it.

It is possible to regress in this hierarchy. That is, if someone has reached the point of self-actualization but suddenly is affected by a natural disaster (i.e., hurricane, fire, earthquake), he or she will experience basic lower-level needs and concentrate on satisfying the need for shelter, safety, and so forth. Economic setbacks also can cause a consumer to revert to fulfilling lower-level needs. For example, baby-boomers were known for conspicuous consumption—the "Me generation"—during the 1980s. Corporate downsizing and layoffs, rising prices, and other uncertainties in the 1990s have resulted in a trend by the baby-boomers to seek value and practicality in their purchases. (However, luxury and uniqueness are still powerful motivators.)

Perception.   Perception and motivation work hand in hand to direct consumer actions. As stated earlier, problem recognition starts with an internal (hunger, cold, loneliness, happiness) or external environmental stimulus processed through one or more of the five senses: vision, (magazine advertisement), hearing (radio commercial, friend's suggestion), smell (bread baking), taste (food sample), and touch (fine fabric). The stimulus may or may not motivate the consumer to make a purchase decision, depending on how the stimulus is converted into information and perceived by the individual.

FIGURE 5.8

....

Maslow's Hierarchy of Needs: Their Role in Consumer Buying Behavior

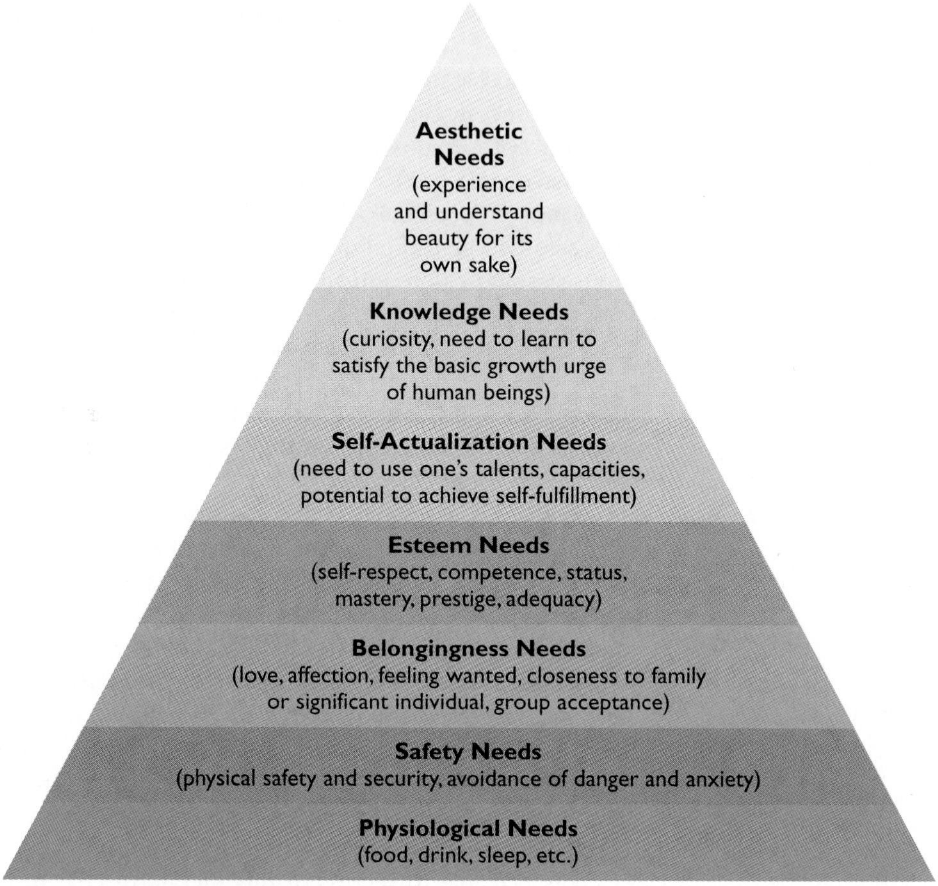

Aesthetic Needs
(experience and understand beauty for its own sake)

Knowledge Needs
(curiosity, need to learn to satisfy the basic growth urge of human beings)

Self-Actualization Needs
(need to use one's talents, capacities, potential to achieve self-fulfillment)

Esteem Needs
(self-respect, competence, status, mastery, prestige, adequacy)

Belongingness Needs
(love, affection, feeling wanted, closeness to family or significant individual, group acceptance)

Safety Needs
(physical safety and security, avoidance of danger and anxiety)

Physiological Needs
(food, drink, sleep, etc.)

Note: Aesthetic Needs and Knowledge Needs are difficult for most individuals to achieve and are not included in many representations of Maslow's hierarchy of needs.

....

Perception
The way people are exposed to information, pay attention to it, and make sense of it.

Perception is the way that people are exposed to information, pay attention to it, and make sense of it in order to understand and function in the world around them. Because effective communication is critical in executing successful marketing strategies, marketers are challenged to understand how consumers receive, interpret, and remember information about their products and brands. It is tempting to aggregate individual perceptions into one overall brand image, for example. However, in reality, each individual may hold a different perception of the same object due to three perceptual processes: selective attention, selective interpretation, and selective retention.

Selective attention
The way people screen out and pay attention to only those stimuli that are relevant to them.

Selective attention allows people to screen out and pay attention to a small portion of the hundreds of thousands of stimuli that bombard them each day. The question is: Which stimuli or messages will a person notice? In general, people are most likely to notice those stimuli that are related to a current consumer need (advertisement for new mufflers to replace one that is defective on their car), those that are significantly different in intensity from the usual (lower price than antici-pated, brighter color in ad, contrasting sound of voice or music in commercial), and those that they have a predisposition to notice and are particularly interested in at the time (muffler ads will stand out among ad clutter on a page full of ads).

Selective interpretation allows individuals to interpret or distort information any way that they please. They may accept or discount information based on their own existing beliefs and attitudes. If the company advertising the mufflers, for ex-ample, is believed to be unethical in its service policies, the low price and other as-pects of the ad will be interpreted in a way that supports the prior belief. Marketing messages must be designed to make the point intended as simply as possible and should be tested in advance for possible misconceptions.

Selective retention refers to an individual's ability to choose what to remem-ber and what to forget from the masses of information encountered each day. People tend to remember best those bits of information that support their precon-ceptions and discount information that is contrary to what they already believe. Therefore, one of the most challenging marketing tasks is to reinforce positive per-ceptions and overcome negative perceptions through all forms of personal and nonpersonal communication.

Learning and Memory.   Consumer behavior, like all human behavior, is largely learned. However, individuals can learn only what they perceive and thus experi-ence. Perception, therefore, plays an important part in the learning process. Individ-uals learn values, attitudes, behaviors, preferences, meanings, and feelings from their culture and social class, reference groups (family, friends), institutions (school, church, government), commercial sources, and their own personal experiences. Learning results in changes in long-term memory and related changes in the individ-ual's behavior. When an individual is motivated to act on a recognized need, the buying process becomes a learning experience. Motivation is greater in high-involvement purchase situations, making learning more focused and memory more lasting.

There are many theories of learning that are useful in understanding buyer be-havior. One of these is *learning through association*, a method whereby individu-als are able to make connections between stimuli or generalize from one situation to another similar situation. An example is the extension of a positive brand image to new products and services sold under the same brand. Disney uses this strategy successfully by extending customer loyalty across a broad range of entertainment venues (theme parks, movies, videos), licensed products (apparel, toys, memora-bilia), resorts and time-share vacations, hotels, cable television, and other goods and services. Likewise, consumers learn to discriminate among stimuli (brands, similar products, etc.) in order to choose among alternatives and either associate with or dissociate from various objects. Comparative advertising is one method used to help consumers make distinctions between favorable and unfavorable aspects of competing products, although the advertiser's product is presented most favorably.

When learning takes place, the information is accumulated in either short- or long-term memory. Short-term memory may be referred to as a working memory, a dynamic thought process that interprets previously stored information and experi-ences to solve current problems. Long-term memory consists of numerous types of information that is stored indefinitely in a person's mind. Marketers want customers

Selective interpretation
How individuals interpret or distort information any way that they please.

Selective retention
The ability that allows individuals to choose what to remember from the masses of information they receive.

to hold positive perceptions of their products and brands in long-term memory to build brand loyalty and long-term relationships between buyer and seller. Along with understanding what and how consumers remember, marketers also are concerned with what and how consumers forget. For products that are purchased frequently and consumed rapidly, marketers must keep their brand at the top of the consumer's mind. Reminder advertising helps consumers learn through repetition and is a deterrent to brand switching.

Attitudes and Beliefs.   An individual's education and experiences combine to form attitudes, which may be either positive or negative. **Attitudes** are made up of three components: cognitive (beliefs), affective (feelings), and behavioral (actions). Consistency among all three components is essential if an attitude is to endure and cause the person to behave in a relatively consistent manner. For example, heavy smokers tend to believe that smoking is not harmful, feel relaxed when smoking, and therefore buy and smoke cigarettes. In order for an attitude change to take place, the smoker will need to be convinced that smoking will shorten his or her life and/or use some means to produce negative feelings about smoking (develop bad cough) and/or stop buying and smoking cigarettes. When one component is out of sync, the rest will adjust to form a new attitude. If the smoker learns that he or she must quit to prevent serious illness, then new beliefs and feelings will be formed to support the new, nonsmoking behavior.

Beliefs are closely related to perception, learning, and memory, discussed earlier. Individuals form beliefs based on their perceptions of information stored in memory, but these beliefs may not be consistent with reality. For example, the smoker just described may base his or her beliefs on isolated bits of information that support his or her belief that smoking is not harmful. Marketers are particularly interested in the beliefs that consumers hold about their products, brands, and companies (i.e., image)—because these beliefs have a major impact on the consumer's willingness to buy.

Attitudes
Made up of three components (beliefs, feelings, and actions) that must be consistent if they are to endure over a long time.

Beliefs
Deeply held knowledge and opinions that may or may not be consistent with reality.

CONSUMERS AND PRODUCTS

Products that are the object of a purchase decision have a significant influence on the buying process. The classification of a good or service affects the amount of time and effort expended by a consumer in reaching a purchase decision. (Recall the discussion of the extent of the purchase decision process earlier in the chapter.) The steps in the buying process that are most affected are the amount and depth of information search, evaluation and ranking of available alternatives, and postpurchase evaluation. If the product is complex, expensive, unfamiliar, has a high element of risk (e.g., financial, social, physical, psychological) associated with it, and/or has many viable alternatives available to the consumer, the purchase decision will be more extensive.

Conversely, a simple, uncomplicated, low- or no-risk product can be purchased with relatively little effort in a more habitual or routine manner. The purchase of Band-Aids would be a routine purchase compared with an extensive decision process for choosing a surgeon. Selecting a dinner wine for special dinner guests (who are wine connoisseurs) is a much higher involvement and more extensive buying process than purchasing a regular brand of diet soda for everyday personal consumption.

Purchases are influenced by the relationship between consumers' life roles and the products they need to fulfill their responsibilities in each role. For example, a 32-year-old married man may be a sales manager who covers a three-state area for his company. He also has two children, aged 6 and 4. In his professional role, important product groups (or role-related product clusters) may include business suits and accessories, briefcase, notebook computer, on-line data services, good-quality wristwatch, and a late model "upscale" automobile. As the father of two children, his role-related product clusters may include child-oriented entertainment, fast-food restaurants with playground facilities, children's furniture, medical insurance, and so forth.

CONSUMERS AND SITUATIONS

The purchase situation is another important influence on the consumer buying process. There are several ways of categorizing situations related to the overall consumption process. Three broad categories include: the communications situation, the purchase situation, and the usage situation.[14] While the present discussion focuses on the purchase situation, let us consider each of the others briefly. The communications situation determines whether and how consumers hear or listen to marketing communications. People respond differently to marketing communications based on their moods, physical states, whether they are alone or with someone, and how much "clutter" surrounds the message. To be most effective, communication should be received by a reader or listener who is a highly motivated potential buyer—and with no other competing messages or "noise" to distract the consumer. However, this is rarely possible.

The usage situation also affects buying behavior, because people may buy different brands and quality of products for different occasions. For example, a jumbo package of inexpensive paper napkins for everyday family use is a routine purchase compared with high-quality paper dinner napkins purchased for a special occasion. (However, if the special occasion was to honor local environmental agency directors, cloth napkins probably would be more politically correct.)

The most frequently used classifications of situational influences on consumer buying behavior are physical surroundings, social surroundings, time or temporal perspectives, task definitions, and antecedent states,[15] as shown in Table 5.4. *Physical surroundings* include location, interior and exterior appearance, lighting, color, sound, climate, equipment, and all objects present in the environment. These factors combine to give customers an impression of spacious versus crowded conditions, pleasing atmospherics, and so forth, which, in turn, affect the customer's willingness to buy.

Social surroundings include all persons present in the situation. People tend to buy better-quality and more prestigious brands when buying for special people or important occasions. Within the shopping environment, other shoppers, salespeople, and others affect purchases. Obnoxious behavior on the part of salespeople and other shoppers may cause the consumer to leave without purchasing. Shopping environments that include pleasant, helpful salespeople are conducive to buying.

TABLE 5.4
....
Situational Influences on Consumer Behavior

Consumer Situation	Characteristics	Influence on Buying Behavior
Physical surroundings	Present one-bedroom apartment is "cramped" when couple has new baby	Purchase new home with room for baby and child-related purchases
Social surroundings	Rude, noisy customers and salespeople in crowded retail clothing store	Leave without purchasing or purchase less than planned; may not return
Temporal perspectives	No time to shop for significant other's birthday gift	Call florist; shop on-line for special gift
Task definition	Need to take care of lawn (at that new home)	Purchase lawn mower, edger, fertilizer, weed killer, etc.
Antecedent states	Stressed out, overworked, fatigued, in a "bad mood"	Indulge self with special purchase to "feel better," or order takeout food and video and become a "couch potato" for the evening

Friends who accompany the shopper also can exert a positive or negative influence on purchases. Social surroundings are evident in the "pub" scene. To capitalize on the impact of atmosphere and image on social behavior, the Irish Pub Co. creates and sells a completely finished pub to customers throughout the world. By late 1996, the company had exported more than 1,000 new Irish pubs to 35 countries. Guinness PLC has strongly supported the Irish Pub Co.'s efforts to promote cheer and beer. Guinness assists with finding investors, site selection, and other forms of assistance—but does not have a financial interest in Irish Pub Co. The real payoff to Guinness is increased beer exports through expanded distribution channels—supported by a staff of 40 full-time people responsible for helping entrepreneurs open new Irish pubs.[16]

Temporal perspectives refer to the amount of time available for shopping and how soon the purchase must be made. An emergency medication or a flat tire on the highway require immediate attention—little search activity, few or no alternatives to evaluate, and a choice to be made as quickly as possible. On the other hand, shopping for replacement furniture or appliances that are presently usable is not as critical. The typical purchase process will involve extended search and careful evaluation of alternatives.

Task definitions refer to the reason for buying the good or service—generally viewed in terms of using different evaluative criteria and shopping behavior when buying for oneself versus buying for another person.

Antecedent states are temporary moods or conditions that affect the consumer and influence purchases. For example, unseasonably hot weather may cause a consumer to postpone the purchase of winter clothing. A consumer who is feeling happy and energetic may be more inclined to make impulse purchases, and so forth.

RELATIONSHIP MARKETING

Relationship marketing
Building long-term buyer-seller relationships by understanding and fulfilling customer needs better than competitors do.

Today's successful marketers focus on **relationship marketing,** that is, developing continuous buyer-seller relationships consistent with the intent of the new marketing concept and market-driven management.[17] Discussion in this section includes the role of quality and satisfaction in developing repeat business rather than attracting one-time transactions. Further, the practice of relationship marketing is considered relative to the final consumer, the subject of this chapter. Buyer-seller relationships in the organizational markets will be discussed in the next chapter.

Buyer-Seller Relationships

Marketing was described in Chapter 1 within the context of value exchange. Recall that marketing exchanges can occur between a wide variety of buyers and sellers. Sellers may be for-profit or nonprofit organizations, commercial businesses, government agencies, and others. They may sell tangible goods, intangible services, or both to final consumers.

Consumers typically purchase goods and services for their own personal or household use. Buyers (customers, clients) in consumer markets are numerous—posing special problems for the seller who must determine how to create a lasting basis for a relationship with each and every one. They tend to purchase in smaller

IT'S LEGAL BUT IS IT ETHICAL?

Relationship Marketing and Privacy Issues

Relationship marketing is all the rage—but the extensive customer databases used to develop these relationships have raised a number of concerns about invasion of privacy. Retailers have found themselves caught in the middle—between having sufficient customer data for developing differentiation strategies and safeguarding that data against potential abusers.

Loyalty programs, "smart" cards, and market-basket analysis allow retailers to know when their best customers show up and what they buy. In the future, this may be accomplished with chip-embedded radio frequency "smart" cards and overhead sensors that can alert retailers to a customer's presence in the store and in a given department.

Is this the era of Big Brother? Some ways for retailers to avoid privacy invasions include the following: Keep shopping and behavioral data on minors under age 16 out of the information network. Do not make available information that consumer marketers crave, such as favored products and TV viewing habits. Give customers the option of not having their personal data provided to a third party. (Sears, Roebuck and Co. and J.C. Penney Company, Inc. tell customers they buy, but do not sell, data. Third-party credit cards present a more complex issue, however.) Customers can be paid some amount for permission to be included in a database. Finally, support efforts to develop (and uphold) acceptable industry practices.

Source: Murray Forseter, "Privacy Debate Puts Retailers in Middle," *Chain Store Age* (July 1997).

quantities and more frequently than organizational buyers, necessitating a greater number of contacts and a more personal relationship between the parties.

Sellers must have a thorough understanding of their markets in order to create value and deliver satisfaction to consumers. This is particularly difficult in highly competitive, mature markets where differentiation is based on giving greater value and doing it better than competitors. Marketers who are helpful to their customers on an ongoing basis have loyal customers who come back repeatedly for related products. Helpfulness takes many forms: making adequate information available before and during the sale, answering customers' questions intelligently and honestly, dealing with problems and complaints promptly and fairly, following up after the sale to say "thank you," and offering continued service.

Although successful companies thrive on close relationships with their customers, relationship marketing can be costly in terms of time, money, and effort required to build close ties with customers. Therefore, it is important to determine the desirable levels of relating to customers. Five levels of relating to customers include basic, reactive, accountable, proactive, and partnership.[18] The *basic level* involves a one-time transaction—the sale is made, and no attempt is made to follow up, particularly if customers are numerous and profit margins are low. At the *reactive level,* customers are encouraged to contact the salesperson or company if they have any complaints or questions. *Accountability* defines the level of the relationship when the salesperson follows up after the sale for feedback on whether customer expectations were met and what improvements are needed. This is characteristic of high-margin sales and few customers. The fourth level is *proactive,* where the salesperson continues to contact the customer every so often with product information updates and news of new products. The closest buyer-seller relationship is a *partnership.* The company works with the customer on an ongoing basis to find ways to satisfy the customer's needs better.

Quality, Satisfaction, and Long-Term Relationships

Membership can provide the basis for long-term buyer-seller relationships. Programs for frequent fliers and frequent guests abound in the travel and hospitality industries. Club marketing programs are targeted toward video game buyers (Nintendo), decorative accessories for the home (Lladro, Precious Moments figurines), high spenders in department stores, major depositors in banks, and so on. Membership lists allow the marketer to maintain close two-way communication with customers, generally providing opportunities for feedback through an 800 telephone number, surveys, and personal phone calls. In an increasing number of cases, relationship marketing is occurring on the Internet and other interactive electronic telecommunications systems. As long as the marketer delivers quality, value, and satisfaction, customers will remain members. If their participation and recommendations are ignored, they will seek a marketer who will listen and act on their needs.

Relationship Marketing and the New Marketing Concept

The marketing concept is operationalized through implementing organization-wide total quality management and creating exceptional value for customers. A key element of the new marketing concept is delivering quality to the marketplace—but who defines quality? Many organizations define quality in terms of products, processes, or people—such as precise engineering specifications, productivity in the manufacturing process, or organizational excellence within the context of human resources. While all these aspects of quality are important, they are insufficient if the customer is not considered first.

The new marketing concept suggests that the "true definition of quality is meeting and exceeding customer expectations."[19] The problem, of course, is that customers continue to change and increase their expectations. Thus quality and value are defined in the marketplace—a dynamic process that requires constant monitoring. Consumers continue to have higher expectations because of their own needs and wants and the promises and present performance of companies and their competitors. This is where total quality management (TQM) and continuous innovation from the customer's perspective are essential to maintain a competitive edge. Within this context, quality applies to all aspects of the marketing mix: product design and production process, efficient and effective distribution channels, marketing communications and promotional strategies, value pricing, and level of service provided before, during, and after the sale. The net result should be the ability to deliver quality that equals or exceeds customer expectations.

Delivering Customer Value Through Market-Driven Management

Marketers can implement the new marketing concept and compete successfully for long-term relationships with customers in a global marketplace by following fifteen key ideas:[20]

1. *Create customer focus throughout the business.* Everyone in the organization puts the customer first—starting with top management.

2. *Listen to the customer.* Encourage and listen to individual consumer feedback to gain valuable information about the customer and the company.

3. *Define and nurture your distinctive competencies.* Maximize your competencies by fitting your company's capabilities to the needs of your target market.

4. *Define marketing as market intelligence.* Up-to-date, complete, and accurate customer and competitor information provides understanding for customer-oriented decisions.

5. *Target customers precisely.* Know which customers should be yours and which are better suited to competitors (and why).

6. *Manage for profitability, not sales volume.* Profit is an indicator of a company's ability to create and deliver value to the customer and to do so efficiently.

7. *Make customer value the guiding star.* Customer value should be incorporated in the company's mission statement; value should be defined based on market intelligence.

8. *Let the customer define quality.* Quality, defined as meeting customer expectations, must be translated into specific product performance characteristics.

9. *Measure and manage customer expectations.* Know what the customer expects, be sure the expectations are realistic, and avoid overpromising.

10. *Build customer relationships and loyalty.* Customers are a company's most important business asset. Long-term buyer-seller relationships require time and effort. (However, some customers prefer price-based transactions to long-term relationships.)

11. *Define the business as a service business.* Value goes beyond the product purchased to include a bundle of services that determine customer satisfaction/dissatisfaction.

12. *Commit to continuous improvement and innovation.* Customers' constantly changing definitions of value and a company's commitment to delivering superior customer value make it necessary to continuously create new products and add customer value.

13. *Manage culture along with strategy and structure.* Top management must instill the entire organization with a customer orientation that focuses the firm outward on consumers and competitors.

14. *Grow with partners and alliances* Customer-focused organizations deliver greater customer value by forming strategic partnerships to extend their core competencies.

15. *Destroy marketing bureaucracy.* Marketing and the customer should be the responsibility of everyone throughout the firm, not only that of a marketing department.

Summary

Every organization relies on its greatest asset—customers—for success. The market-driven organization delivers value to its customers, understanding that value is defined in the marketplace and not in the factory. Marketers who thoroughly understand their customers are able to design products and marketing programs that deliver value, quality, and satisfaction.

The study of consumer behavior includes the acquisition, consumption, and disposition of goods and services by final consumers, or buying units, that purchase for their own use. At the heart of this process is a customer-oriented value exchange. The consumer buying process consists of a series of related activities: recognition of a need, search for information, evaluation of alternatives, choice/purchase, and postpurchase evaluation. The extent of this decision-making process may be habitual (or routine), limited, or extended, based on the complexity of the decision, level of consumer involvement, perceived risk, and so forth. This process applies to brands, stores, and shopping formats, as well as to individual products.

Buying behavior is affected by a number of cultural, social, and group factors. A person's culture, subculture, and social class are considered the most important societal influences on consumer behavior. A person's needs, wants, behaviors, and values are shaped by the society in which he or she lives. Individuals look to their reference groups to define what is acceptable or unacceptable according to the group's norms, beliefs, and values. Reference groups may or may not involve membership or face-to-face contact, and their influences may be positive or negative.

Individual influences on buyer behavior include both personal characteristics and psychological influences. Personal factors are represented by a person's age and life cycle stage, occupation and economic status, lifestyle, personality, and self-concept. Psychological influences include motivation, perception, learning and memory, and attitudes and beliefs.

Purchase decisions also are affected by product characteristics and the nature of the purchase situation. Product influences include the type of good or service being purchased, extent of the buying process, level of perceived risk, and the relationship between the product and consumers' needs. The purchase situation affects consumer decisions on the basis of social influences and physical surroundings, time perspective, task objectives, and antecedent states.

An emphasis on relationship marketing is consistent with the new marketing concept and market-driven management and is an underlying theme in the study of consumer behavior presented in this chapter. The focus is on continuously delivering value to consumers who will return for repeat business rather than concentrating on one-time transactions. Relationship marketing relies on a thorough understanding of consumers and a two-way communication process. Quality, value, and satisfaction are the cornerstones of relationship marketing. Long-term buyer-seller relationships are built not only on having superior products and processes and high quality at fair prices but also on perceptions of ethics and level of trust between the two parties.

Questions

1. Describe the stages in the consumer buying process for a major purchase, such as an expensive automobile or a new home.

2. Compare the buying process just described with the buying process for (a) a new suit and (b) a six-pack of soda. Explain the differences.

3. For a recent purchase that you have made, identify the key information sources and influences that affected your decision to buy (or not to buy) the good or service.

4. Give examples of how marketing efforts made (or could have made) a difference in the purchase process and final outcome described in Question 3.

5. Explain the concept of customer value and describe its relationship to the new marketing concept.

6. Give a specific example of each of the seven factors that influence the actual or desired state to trigger recognition of a customer purchase problem. Describe marketing actions that can be directed toward helping consumers recognize and resolve each of these deficiencies or felt needs.

7. As a marketing manager for a brand of packaged foods, you are responsible for developing consumer-oriented marketing programs. Within this context, evaluate the following influences on consumer purchases.

   a. Culture and subculture

   b. Social class

   c. Reference groups

   d. Personal characteristics

   e. Psychological factors

   f. Product characteristics

   g. Purchase situation

8. Find examples of relationship marketing in the business media and evaluate their effectiveness in terms of developing long-term buyer-seller relationships and delivering customer value.

Exercises

1. Identify and analyze five advertisements for consumer products in current media in terms of the following:

   a. Stage in the consumer buying process that is targeted

   b. Social and cultural influences that are represented

   c. Group influences that are represented explicitly or implicitly

2. Interview three individuals who represent distinctly different ages and life cycle stages regarding factors that influence their choice of (a) snack foods, (b) vacation destinations, and (c) automobiles. Analyze the differences (and similarities) in terms of the implications for marketing strategy.

3. Identify two examples of relationship marketing, and evaluate each one as to whether you believe it will or will not succeed in developing long-term buyer-seller relations, the potential ethical issues, and the ability to deliver bona fide customer value.

Endnotes

1. Alan Deutschman (ed.), *Fortune Cookies: Management Wit and Wisdom from Fortune Magazine* (New York: Vintage Books, 1993), p. 15.

2. For additional discussion, see Frederick E. Webster, Jr., *Market-Driven Management: Using the New Marketing Concept to Create a Customer-Oriented Company* (New York: John Wiley & Sons, 1994), Chap. 1.

3. John C. Mowen, *Consumer Behavior*, 4th ed. (Englewood Cliffs, NJ: Prentice-Hall, 1995), p. 5.

4. Del I. Hawkins, Roger J. Best, and Kenneth A. Coney, *Consumer Behavior: Implications for Marketing Strategy*, 6th ed. (Chicago: Richard D. Irwin, 1995), p. 7.

5. *Purchase involvement* is defined as "the level of concern for, or interest in, the purchase process triggered by the need to consider a particular purchase." It is considered a temporary state

experienced by the buyer, based on the interaction of characteristics of the individual, product, and situation. See Hawkins et al., *ibid.* (p. 425), for further discussion.

6. Carol H. Anderson, *Retailing: Concepts, Strategy and Information* (St. Paul, MN: West Publishing Company, 1993), pp. 235–237; based on Gordon C. Bruner II and Richard J. Pomazal, "Problem Recognition: The Crucial First Stage of the Consumer Decision Process," *Journal of Consumer Marketing* 5(1) (Winter 1988), pp. 53–63.

7. Kevin Goldman, "McDonald's Joins America Online to Send Information to PC Users," *Wall Street Journal* (September 5, 1995), p. B7.

8. Peter D. Bennett (ed.), *Dictionary of Marketing Terms* (Chicago: American Marketing Association, 1988), p. 50.

9. Del I. Hawkins, Roger J. Best, and Kenneth A. Coney, *Consumer Behavior: Implications for Marketing Strategy*, 7th ed. (Chicago: Richard D. Irwin, 1998), pp. 44–53, 80–86.

10. Bennett, *op. cit.*, p. 196.

11. Paulette Thomas, "Cosmetics Makers Offer World's Women an All-American Look with Local Twists," *Wall Street Journal* (May 8, 1995), pp. B1, B6.

12. Susan Chandler, "'Kids' Wear Is Not Child's Play," *Business Week* (June 19, 1995), p. 118.

13. Abraham H. Maslow, *Motivation and Personality* (New York: Harper & Row, 1954).

14. Hawkins et al. (1998), *op. cit.*, pp. 405–417.

15. *Ibid*; Russel Belk, "Situational Variables and Consumer Behavior," *Journal of Consumer Research* 2 (December 1975), pp. 157–163; John C. Mowen, *op. cit.*, pp. 568–570.

16. Charles Goldsmith, "Prefab Irish Pub Sells Pints World-Wide," *Wall Street Journal* (October 25, 1996), pp. B1, B8.

17. See Frederick E. Webster, Jr., *op. cit.*, Chaps. 3, 5, and 9, for further discussion of concepts discussed in this section.

18. Philip Kotler, *Marketing Management: Analysis, Planning, Implementation, and Control* (Englewood Cliffs, NJ: Prentice-Hall, 1994), pp. 48–49.

19. Webster, *op. cit.*, p. 67.

20. *Ibid.*, Chap. 9.

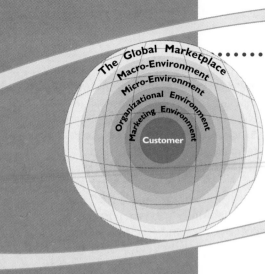

CHAPTER 6

Business Markets and Buying Behavior

Scope of Business Markets

Differences Between Organizational and Consumer Buying Behavior

The Business-to-Business Buying Process

Organizational Structure and Buyer Characteristics

Types of Business Purchase Decisions

Major Influences on Purchase Decisions

Relationship Marketing

The U.S. Automotive Industry: World-Class Buyers and Sellers

Purchasing is by far the largest single function at AT&T. Nothing we do is more important.[1]

What would life be like without cars and trucks and other vehicles? Imagine a world without cars, pickup trucks, minivans, or sport utility vehicles to transport a lone driver, a family of five, or a complete soccer team. Imagine a world without trucks to deliver mail, catalog orders, or a major piece of machinery that will keep the production line moving efficiently in the factory. The prospect of a nation at a standstill on its streets and highways dramatizes the importance of the automotive industry as a leading indicator of the health of the U.S. economy.

The consumer market for automobiles represents only the tip of the iceberg in the number and complexity of transactions related to the automotive industry. In order to satisfy the direct needs of the marketplace for transportation and its indirect needs for a variety of other goods and services, car and truck manufacturers throughout the world are involved in extensive buying and selling activities at all levels of distribution.

Organizational purchasing is driven by *derived demand*. That is, final consumers or other businesses "demand" vehicles for personal and commercial purposes from a manufacturer or dealer. In turn, the manufacturer must purchase the necessary goods and services to meet this demand. If customers cannot or will not buy a manufacturer's products, there is no need to make the purchases necessary to produce them.

Automobile manufacturers must purchase raw materials and component parts needed to produce a product for resale. This may include steel, plastics, rubber, leather, paint, tires, glass, and other items to complete a particular automotive design. Many suppliers of basic and custom goods depend on the business they derive from automobile makers. For example, a small company whose core business is sun visors may sell custom accessories for sport utility vehicles, light trucks, and vans. Major tire manufacturers such as Goodyear or Michelin derive their sales from new car sales and from the aftermarket. Each of these suppliers is influenced by events and trends in the macro- and micro-environments.

Manufacturers must understand the needs and wants of their customers in order to forecast demand levels and anticipate style preferences. For example, during the mid-1990s, trucks and sport utility vehicles gained popularity among "nontraditional" truck customers. Minivans, which had been in high demand for a number of years, began to take on the image of old station wagons. Demand for sports utility vehicles—including high-priced luxury models—escalated. At the same time, manufacturers experienced a decrease in demand for sports cars. (To overcome this trend, some manufacturers have capitalized on nostalgia by reincarnating a number of popular models from the past, such as the Corvette and the Volkswagen Beetle.)

Changes in the marketing environment have directly influenced the types of organizational purchasing decisions that need to be made. Globalization of the automotive industry has dramatically influenced organizational purchasing because of its effect on competition in this market. Final consumers can select a wide variety of makes and models from manufacturers throughout the world. Manufacturers can buy parts from the most profitable sources and assemble vehicles in overseas markets to meet the needs of their overseas customers. The effects of technology and computerization also influence organizational buying behavior. For example, consumers can now choose high-tech options such as an in-car satellite navigator, an infrared night-vision screen, collision-avoidance radar, radar-enhanced cruise control, and programmable traffic signs. Inventory-control issues involve having sufficient inventory on hand at the time it is needed and not having valuable financial resources (and space) tied up in inventory longer than necessary.

All these factors need to be addressed by organizational buyers in the automotive industry today. The ongoing challenge for marketing managers is to ensure that these organizational buyers will be strategically positioned to respond to changes as quickly as they happen.

Consumers and their buying behavior were discussed in the preceding chapter. Our attention now turns to buying behavior in business or organizational markets. Like the consumer market, the business market is made up of both buyers and sellers. However, rather than buying for personal consumption or household use, the organizational buyers who comprise the business market acquire goods and services to be used directly or indirectly in their own operations, which they in turn sell, rent, or provide to other organizations. Within this context, the buyer purchases on behalf of a business, government agency, institution (such as a school or church), or other type of organization (such as the Red Cross or other nonprofit organization).

Discussion in this chapter focuses on external buyers, but it should be noted that many organizations have suppliers who provide goods and services to internal customers who also have the option of purchasing from competing suppliers outside the organization. Although there are some unique dynamics involved in this type of purchase decision, traditional organizational buying concepts can be applied for a better understanding of the process.

SCOPE OF BUSINESS MARKETS

The business market can be described in terms of customer types, market size and trends, and the major industries that comprise the overall market. For example, retail buyers purchased goods and services from an array of producers and wholesalers in 1997 that resulted in $2,566.2 billion in retail sales to final consumers. Eating and drinking places alone accounted for $236.2 billion of the total in an innovative growth market. A few of the industries that serve this market include agriculture (e.g., meat, produce, dairy), beverages, baking, paper goods, plastics, kitchen equipment, computers, and other providers of goods and services.

Major industries comprising the business market include agricultural services, mining, construction, manufacturing, transportation, wholesale trade, retail trade, finance and insurance, and services. The magnitude of business purchases for each of these industries is reflected in their annual sales shown in Table 6.1.

Types of Customers

The organizations described in this section represent both buyers and sellers of a wide array of goods and services. However, we are most concerned here with purchase or acquisition. Business customers can be classified into four major groups (although these may overlap at times): business and commercial organizations, reseller organizations, government organizations, and institutional organizations.[2]

Business and Commercial Organizations. Lockheed-Martin Corp. may buy metals from a mining company, or an insurance company may buy computers from

TABLE 6.1

Major U.S. Industries*—Number of Establishments and Business Receipts, 1995†

Industry	Establishments (1,000)	Business Receipts (billion dollars)
Agriculture, forestry, fishing	108	133
Mining	27	137
Construction	634	782
Manufacturing	390	4,447
Transportation, public utilities	285	1,204
Wholesale trade	518	2,115
Retail trade	1,568	2,512
Finance, insurance, real estate	628	2,532
Services	2,386	1,757

*Corporations, partnerships, and nonfarm proprietorships.
†Excludes investment income except for partnerships and corporations in finance, insurance, and real estate.
Source: Statistical Abstract of the United States, 1998, Tables 856 and 867.

IBM for use by secretaries in its corporate office, or Birds-Eye may buy fruits and vegetables from a farmer to process in its frozen food business. In each case, the buyer is making a purchase in order to directly or indirectly produce another good or service—such as airplanes, insurance contracts, or food products. Most of these organizational customers can be classified as either **original equipment manufacturers (OEMs)** or user customers. Most organizational customers may be classified as both OEMs and users. For example, Birds-Eye not only buys produce from its suppliers but also needs equipment, products, and services to clean and maintain its manufacturing facilities.

Original equipment manufacturers (OEMs)
Buy component parts from a commercial supplier; these parts become part of a finished product sold to another organization or consumer.

An OEM buys component parts from a commercial supplier. These component parts then become part of the finished product that is sold to another organization or consumer. For example, as a buyer, Compaq Computer Corp. may buy microchips from a business-to-business supplier to use in the manufacture of its computers. The microchip would then become an integral part of Compaq's final product. OEMs also may be purchasers of services that become part of an "extended" product, such as Kitchen Aid purchasing General Electric's service capability to fulfill Kitchen Aid's appliance warranty obligations.

User customers purchase equipment, supplies, and services that are used directly or indirectly in the production of other goods and/or services that are sold to other organizations and/or to the consumer market. For example, a builder may purchase a power saw for carpenters to use in the construction of a building, or the builder may buy liability insurance to cover workers in case of an accident. Neither the saw nor the insurance policy becomes an actual part of the finished product, but both are necessary purchases for completion of the building that is being sold to another customer.

Intermediaries
Organizations such as retailers and wholesalers that buy from manufacturers and producers to resell at a profit to their customers.

Reseller Organizations.   Retailers and wholesalers are **intermediaries** in the distribution system, buying goods from manufacturers and producers to resell at a profit to their customers. They also purchase a variety of goods and services that are needed for their daily business operations. While resellers are closely related to the consumer market, they also represent a large share of the business customers that make up the total business marketing system. (Retailers and wholesalers will be discussed further in Chapter 10 within the context of distribution strategy.)

Retailers constitute an important group of customers in the business-to-business markets. As shown in Table 6.1, retailers purchased goods for resale to final consumers in 1995 that resulted in business receipts of $2,512 billion across 1,568 million retail establishments. In addition, these same retailers purchased a vast array of goods and services for their stores and retail systems, such as information systems, visual merchandising, fixtures, flooring, lighting, office supplies, and utilities. Retail buyers are customers of both manufacturers and wholesalers.

Middlemen
Wholesalers that buy from manufacturers or producers and resell at a profit to retailers.

Wholesalers serve as **middlemen** in the distribution channels, buying from manufacturers or producers and reselling at a profit to retailers. Wholesalers may carry many lines of merchandise and create assortments that are targeted to particular retail customers. Since wholesalers generally are involved in physical distribution activities, they are good customers for materials-handling equipment, trucks, warehousing supplies, and so forth. As noted in Table 6.1, 518 million wholesale establishments accounted for $2,115 billion in business receipts in 1995 in the United States.

MARKETING AND ENTREPRENEURSHIP

The Home-Office Worker

A New York research concern estimates that over 29 million Americans tele-commute or run home businesses, a 52 percent increase since 1991. Home-office workers represent a growing trend in the United States—people who choose to work in their own homes. Some are former executives who have been separated from their long-time employers and are using home offices as a base of operations for new careers as consultants, financial advisors, or brokers, for example. Others are still employed at major corporations such as AT&T, IBM, Holiday Inn, or The Travelers Corp., where the companies have developed programs that allow employees to work from home part of the time—and at the same time cut office overhead costs. While some that spend all or most of their time in home workplaces have come to miss the camaraderie of the traditional office scene, many others are enjoying the freedom that it provides. They can be at work in a matter of minutes, have more control over work schedules, and can spend more time with their families. For those who spend most of their days traveling, the home office allows more flexibility in the use of both professional and personal time.

The result of this working-at-home trend is that home-office workers are an important market for everything from computers and office furniture to staples and paper clips. These customers make many business-to-business purchase decisions for a wide variety of goods and services, even though their business operations do not mirror a corporate office. Estimates for setting up a home office can run from $3500 to $20,000 to provide basic furnishings, equipment, and other accoutrements of the information age. Companies like Office Depot and Staples have capitalized on this trend, offering competitive prices on everything the home-office worker might need. One home-office worker, who is constantly improving things, says:"You know how when some people get depressed, they drink or do drugs? ... Well, I go down to Office Depot or Staples, and I buy something. Even if it's just new batteries for my Sharp Wizard, it makes me feel better. My house is full of the stuff." As you can see, this type of customer tends to buy in smaller quantities and more frequently than the larger corporate account, presenting an opportunity for niche marketers and mass discounters to capitalize on their business.

Service businesses also have benefited from customers who work at home. Often, it is more cost-effective to outsource services such as printing and duplicating, secretarial, accounting, and a myriad of other services, enlarging the customer base for these businesses as well. In fact, a number of home-based entrepreneurs have found that home is the best place to have a power lunch with business associates. Letitia Baldridge declares:"Having lunch in someone's home is much more personal than going to an elegant private dining room or a great restaurant. ... It's very chic." Proponents enjoy the privacy and convenience that are particularly conducive to networking and deal making. Although home business lunches are not appropriate for every situation, there is sufficient interest to create business-to-business opportunities for those such as gourmet delicatessens and caterers.

Note: Statistics may vary depending on the type of home business arrangement; the same source reported in 1995 that about 43 million Americans were working at home full- or part-time, with the number increasing about 5 percent a year.

Sources: Michael J. Himowitz, "Setting Up Your Home Office," *Fortune* (July 10, 1995), pp. 124–136; Stephanie Mehta, "What's the Chic Spot for a Power Lunch?" *Wall Street Journal* (April 25, 1997), pp. B1, B2.

TABLE 6.2

....

State and Local Government Consumption Expenditures and Gross Investment (billions of dollars)

	1993	*1994*	*1995*	*1996*	*1997*
Consumption expenditures and gross investment	765	802.7	846	886.6	928.9
Consumption expenditures	631.6	663.8	698.6	730.9	762.9
Durable goods	13.2	13.9	14.7	15.3	15.8
Nondurable goods	64.3	67.8	73	78.2	80.6
Services	554.2	582.1	610.9	637.5	666.5
Gross investment	133.4	138.9	147.4	155.7	166
Structures	108.7	113.4	121	128.5	138.4
Equipment	24.7	25.6	26.4	27.3	27.6

Note: Gross government investment consists of general government and government enterprise expenditures for fixed assets; inventory investment is included in government consumption expenditures.
Sources: Statistical Abstract of the United States, 1998; U.S. Bureau of Economic Analysis, *National Income and Product Accounts of the United States, 1929–94,* Vol. 1; and *Survey of Current Business (August 1997).*

Government Organizations. According to the U.S. Census Bureau, in 1993 there were over 86,000 government organizations at the federal, state, and local levels.[3] Governmental customers vary widely in size, scope, and purchasing processes. However, they collectively form one of the largest markets in the world for goods and services, accounting for purchases in the trillions of dollars.[4] The magnitude of government purchases represents everything from stealth bombers for the U.S. Department of Defense to paper clips for the mayor's office in Cut-and-Shoot, Texas. State and local government consumption expenditures and gross investment alone accounted for $928.9 billion in 1997, as shown in Table 6.2.

Government consumption expenditures and gross investment at the federal level reached $458.0 billion in 1997. Federal government purchasing units may be classified as either civilian or military.[5] Government purchases for the civilian sector include goods and services for departments, administrations, agencies, boards, commissions, executive offices, and other independent establishments that serve the nonmilitary needs of the American population. Examples of nonmilitary governmental purchases include office supplies and furnishings, computers and telecommunications systems, vehicles, and research-oriented goods and services. Federal military customers include the U.S. Army, Navy, and Air Force, and the Defense Supply Agency that centralizes much of the buying for the armed services. These purchases include a wide range of products related to the military mission (e.g., armaments) and to military personnel (e.g., commissary assortments, housing, personal services).

America's fifty state governments are important customers for education, roads, institutions (e.g., hospitals, prisons), water, airports, and various types of maintenance and redevelopment projects. Local government customers may be classified further as counties, municipalities, townships, and special districts. Although metropolitan counties are greatly outnumbered by rural counties, their purchases represent most of the county-level governmental expenditures. Most of the purchases made by counties, municipalities, and townships tend to be related to building and maintaining streets and highways, providing police and fire protection, creating and maintaining parks and recreational facilities, solid-waste removal, and water supply and treatment. Counties also make purchases related to the preservation of natural resources. In addition, there are special districts formed to provide certain functions, such as water supply systems or fire protection. The district governmental unit must purchase the goods and services needed to perform these specialized functions successfully.[6]

Foreign governments are also a large market for U.S. manufacturing output and services. Industries such as defense, aircraft, and telecommunications, have prospered by selling to overseas customers. This trend is expected to continue. Buyers that represent overseas businesses, institutions, and governments may have a different set of buying criteria than domestic buyers. They may require product modifications to meet their government standards and local customer demands. The ordering process, payment method, and other aspects of the sales transaction also may need to be tailored to the buyers' needs.

Institutional Organizations.   All organizational customers that are not considered commercial businesses (OEMs, users) or government purchasers comprise the institutional market. While the classifications are not always clear-cut between private, government, and institutional organizations, institutional customers can be public or private, for-profit or nonprofit, large or small, domestic or international. Schools, churches, professional associations, little league teams, disaster-relief agencies, hospitals and health care facilities, and a diverse group of other institutions make up a large part of the organizational market. Thus it is necessary to consider their buying needs and behaviors.

Changes in Market Size and Trends

Total business receipts for U.S. firms in business and organizational markets reached $15,619 billion in 1995 (as shown by adding the figures in Table 6.1). Combined business receipts for U.S. retail establishments and wholesale businesses were $4,627 billion in 1995. Each of these markets has undergone significant changes that have affected buyers and sellers alike.

DIFFERENCES BETWEEN ORGANIZATIONAL AND CONSUMER BUYING BEHAVIOR

Derived demand
Goods demanded by consumers or organizational buyers creating a need for purchases by manufacturers or dealers to provide goods and services to satisfy this demand.

Businesses, governments, and institutions each have their own patterns of buying behavior. However, the broadly defined organizational buying process differs from the consumer buying process in a number of ways. In comparison with consumer purchases, the marketing challenges inherent in organizational purchases can be considered from both external and internal perspectives.[7] In general, an organization's external buyer-seller relationships are based on **derived demand,** a more complex buying and selling process, and a more concentrated customer base. In contrast, consumers and households buy for their own use, engage in a less complex process than organizations, and represent a diverse group of customers.

INNOVATE OR EVAPORATE*

The Light Goes on at GE's Lighting Division

General Electric's Lighting Division dramatically improved purchasing and logistics performance through creative use of the Internet. Innovative techniques and technologies include an Internet-based Trading Process Network (TPN) that provides the benefits of reduced cycle time, elimination of paper and mail processing, improved sharing of information with suppliers, improvement in quality, and reduction in costs.

The traditional time-consuming process for each individual purchase required a GE Lighting staff member to "request drawings from off-site storage, retrieve them, transport them to the buying office, photocopy them, fold them, attach them to requisition documents, stuff them into envelopes, and mail them to potential suppliers for price quotations." The process often took a week or more to send bid requests and another 3 weeks or more to select a supplier and place a requisition for parts—negatively affecting GE Lighting's flexibility, responsiveness, and ability to focus on more valuable strategic activities.

The Trading Process Network (TPN), instituted by General Electric Information Services (GEIS), now makes it possible for the buying office to send out a price quotation request in a matter of hours. The newer, more efficient process is described as follows: "Users access the requisition system on a desktop computer; create a new project file with the basic information on quantities, timing, and other factors; point and click to select the suppliers that should receive the request for quotation from an on-line supplier database; attach an electronic copy of blueprints and drawings that have been scanned and digitized into another central database; switch to their Internet browser; and instantaneously send out the bid package in an encrypted, secure format to anywhere in the world." Suppliers have approximately 1 week to respond to these requests through Internet-based bids. GE Lighting evaluates them on-line and is able to select a supplier and award the business virtually the next day. The entire requisition process can be completed in about 10 days.

In order to reap the benefits of TPN, GE Lighting had to address a number of critical factors: investment to enable scanning and digitizing of blueprints and drawings, creation of a comprehensive database of existing and potential qualified suppliers (along with their capabilities and qualifications), upgrades in desktop computing power, significant training among TPN users and suppliers, and commitment of senior management to making these changes.

*The box title is attributed to James M. Higgins.

Source: Richard Waugh and Scott Elliff, "Using the Internet to Achieve Purchasing Improvements at General Electric," *Hospital Materiel Management Quarterly* 20(2) (November 1998), pp. 81–83.

Internally, organizational buyers tend to place more emphasis than final consumers on technology and superior performance, customization to meet specific requirements, and the order-fulfillment process, which may include manufacturing to order rather than filling an order from an existing inventory of finished goods. These differences are due in large part to the nature of derived demand.

In contrast to final consumers, organizational buyers tend to buy more technical products, with less standardization, in larger quantities, and with more emphasis on services offered with the product. Organizational buyers have more opportunities to negotiate prices and to purchase direct from the manufacturer or through shorter distribution channels. Promotion to organizations tends to be concentrated on using the company's salesforce, trade media, and trade shows. In addition, organizational purchases generally are more complex, more direct, more structured and formal, involve more people in the process, and are based on longer-term relationships.[8]

In terms of characteristics, organizational buyers differ from consumers in that they generally

- are more specialized in the types of goods and services they purchase,

- function as a member of a team or buying center,

- purchase goods and services for use in providing goods and services for their own customers,

- are more professional and better trained,

- buy in larger quantities,

- purchase from fewer sellers,

- use shorter distribution channels,

- buy from manufacturers and distributors who are centrally located,

- negotiate prices and other terms of sale,

- form long-term relationships with key suppliers,

- require at least some level of customization in their purchases,

- emphasize specifications and performance,

- are more concerned with technology and rate of change, and

- require more services with their purchases.

THE BUSINESS-TO-BUSINESS BUYING PROCESS

While various types of organizations and buying situations tend to follow a similar series of steps in the purchasing process, there are differences in the approaches used by business, industrial, governmental, and institutional buyers. Organizational structure and buyer characteristics also affect the organizational buying process and decision making.

Steps in the Buying Process

Assuming that buying responsibility and authority are established within an organization, its buyers or purchasing agents tend to follow a similar sequence of decisions and actions. Within different types of organizations and buying situations, the purchase process varies in degree of formality, complexity, number of people

FIGURE 6.1
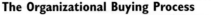

The Organizational Buying Process

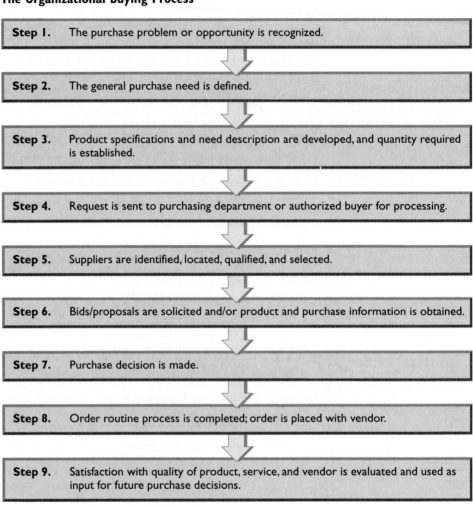

Step 1.	The purchase problem or opportunity is recognized.
Step 2.	The general purchase need is defined.
Step 3.	Product specifications and need description are developed, and quantity required is established.
Step 4.	Request is sent to purchasing department or authorized buyer for processing.
Step 5.	Suppliers are identified, located, qualified, and selected.
Step 6.	Bids/proposals are solicited and/or product and purchase information is obtained.
Step 7.	Purchase decision is made.
Step 8.	Order routine process is completed; order is placed with vendor.
Step 9.	Satisfaction with quality of product, service, and vendor is evaluated and used as input for future purchase decisions.

involved, and amount of effort required to make a good decision. Since there are certain basic activities that must be undertaken to complete a purchase, organizational buyers generally follow some or all of the steps shown in Figure 6.1 when making purchase decisions.

Organizational Differences

Although most organizational buying decisions can be described in terms similar to those illustrated in Figure 6.1, there are a number of differences in the approach to purchasing used by buyers in business and commercial organizations, reseller markets (retailers and wholesalers), government agencies, and institutions. A few of these differences are described in this section.

Business and Commercial Organizations.   Business and commercial organizations include OEMs, users, and a variety of industrial and producer customers, as discussed earlier. OEM, producer, and industrial purchasing agents make buying decisions that range from complex to routine. Purchases may include heavy and light equipment, computer systems, materials to use in production, consumable supplies for daily operations, and outside services. The more intricate nature of the buying decisions leads to more emphasis on customization, company-determined specifications, short lead times (so that production is not held up), many vendors (whose performance is carefully monitored), and a considerable amount of bidding and negotiation.

Users' purchases are focused on equipment, supplies, and services that are used to create other goods and services for resale. The nature of this buying process tends to be more routine and involve maintenance of a safety stock, automatic ordering, and other means of streamlining the purchasing process. Reordering may be facilitated by a direct satellite or computer link between buyer and seller for automatic order placement.

Reseller Markets.   The buying process followed by retailers and wholesalers in the reseller markets requires considerable negotiation and quantity buying. These buyers must be fully aware of events and trends throughout their distribution channels. Both retailers and wholesalers must be able to forecast demand accurately at the consumer level and be well informed about the goods and services that are available at the manufacturer or producer level that can satisfy the needs of the retail customers. Further, both parties must be able to determine the most effective and efficient buyer-seller relationships that will deliver the most value to the customer while yielding acceptable profit margins to the retailers and wholesalers. In many cases, this need has resulted in a retailer assuming the role of a wholesaler, and vice versa.

Government Agencies.   Purchases of goods and services for all levels of government agencies (and federal purchasing in particular) typically involve more layers of approval—first that the item is "needed" and then for the actual terms of the purchase itself. Government purchases frequently involve solicitation of numerous bids, with price being a major selection criterion; adherence to federal, state, or local legislation regarding the purchasing process; voluminous amounts of forms and paperwork, that is, bureaucratic "red tape"; and more attention to a vendor's ability to meet predetermined product specifications than to product superiority or marketing efforts. Finally, governmental purchases always are open to public scrutiny, creating a need for adherence to all legal and ethical rules of conduct.

Institutions.   The buying process followed by institutions is as diverse as the nature and number of institutions in the market. A small nonprofit agency, for example, may have an extremely informal, last-minute approach to purchasing. Conversely, a larger nonprofit organization such as the American Red Cross may have a more formal, standardized procedure. Some churches follow strict financial guidelines in purchasing goods and services that support their mission; others do not.

Most educational institutions have found it necessary to become more accountable and professional in carrying out the purchasing function. Decreased enrollments and increased operating costs in schools at all levels have focused attention on balancing institutional budgets. While tuition has increased at many schools, this alone cannot cover historic expense levels. Thus school purchasing agents are pressed to find the most value for their money, with cost and adherence to institutional policies providing the major buying criteria.

These problems have become magnified in today's health care systems. Hospitals, nursing homes, and other health care providers are faced with the need to provide adequate care for patients while keeping costs down in a relatively uncertain environment that is changing at a rapid pace. The need to benefit from economies of scale and keep costs down has led to mergers, acquisitions, and other horizontal and vertical alliances that have changed the purchasing process. Today's health care organizations place more restrictions on purchasing agents who must follow strict guidelines in their selection of goods and services, choice of vendors (often from preferred lists), specifications for order completion, shipping, and other details.

Some differences also exist between the buying process followed by for-profit and nonprofit organizations. For-profit institutions have bottom-line responsibility, and purchases must be made at a price that not only covers the cost of the good or service but also results in profitability for the firm. On the other hand, nonprofit organizations are more interested in breaking even—not spending more than they receive.

Nonprofit buying can be categorized in several ways, using a rather liberal interpretation of *buying*. First, there is the purchase of typical goods and services to fulfill the nonprofit's mission for its target market. Obviously, these purchases must be made under the most advantageous terms possible (low price, long payment period, etc.). Second, there is the solicitation of "free" goods and services from the community, the recruitment of volunteers, and the solicitation of donors. Third, nonprofits buy the goodwill of the community by "selling" the organization's services to its intended client base. Although little or no money is exchanged in the last two situations, there is a cost attached to "buying" the desired outcomes from each of these markets. Many of those who are recipients of the services provided by nonprofit organizations need to be convinced to participate. Those who populate the homeless shelters, for example, may not recognize—or accept—the need for job training and health care.

ORGANIZATIONAL STRUCTURE AND BUYER CHARACTERISTICS

Many business-to-business buying situations require close relationships between the buyer and seller. It is important to note here that marketers who desire to sell their goods and services to organizational customers must recognize not only the need to deliver value and quality but also the need to pay attention to the human aspect of the transaction. They also need to understand the implications of organizational structure for the organizational buyer as well as his or her role in the

TABLE 6.3

·············

The Changing Role of Organizational Buyers

Purchasing by businesses and other organizations has changed over the past decade. Some of these changes include:

More emphasis on profitability. The bottom line must be enhanced by each transaction.

Increased use of the computer. Forecasting and maintaining inventories to determine purchase needs; tracking market trends and supplier performance; computer may replace salesperson in many instances.

Improved technology. Shipping and receiving efficiencies; better warehouse facilities for purchases; rate of change and continuous need to upgrade in many product categories.

Consolidation, mergers, acquisitions. Business partners may change, long-term relationships may no longer be valid, and new strategic partnerships may need to be forged.

Distribution factors, relative channel power. Both buyers and sellers may cover larger territories; channel power shifting in many cases from sellers to buyers (e.g., large grocery and consumer goods manufacturers and supermarkets); shorter time to market.

Dynamic/changing global marketplace. Larger international base of customers, suppliers, and competitors; opportunities to cut purchase price through overseas purchasing; potential lack of reliability in dealing with overseas vendors; more regulations to contend with; global influence on product choices in consumer markets.

Organizational structure. Decentralization in many firms pushes purchasing decisions down to lower organizational levels; group decision making for major purchases (may include outside consultants, such as software providers and others with particular technical expertise); trend toward team emphasis and cross-functional project teams (that may become involved in purchase decisions).

In general, the world has become more complex for business-to-business buying and selling. The good news is that this complexity is made more manageable with the capabilities of the computer and other technological advances.

buying center. Table 6.3 outlines some of the changes taking place for organizational buyers.

Organizational Structure

····································

Just as consumers make most of their buying decisions within the structure of a household, the business-to-business buying process occurs within the boundaries of an organizational structure that may provide much or little latitude for the buyer. The structure determines who is involved in a purchase decision, who actually makes the decision of what to buy, and who is responsible for actually making the purchase. Further, the structure determines the specific procedures and the formality of the buying process.

One approach to understanding the composition of the purchasing organization is to view it as a *buying center,* discussed next. Keep in mind, however, that the size of an organization may determine the scope of a buyer's responsibilities and the degree of formality that is exhibited.

Key Players in the Buying Center

Buying center
All those who participate in the purchasing decision-making process and who share common goals and risks arising from the decisions.

The decision-making unit of an organization is generally referred to as the **buying center,** defined as "all those individuals and groups who participate in the purchasing decision-making process, who share some common goals and the risks arising from the decisions." The buying center is made up of individuals who are involved in six buying roles.[9] These roles include users or initiators, influencers, deciders, approvers, buyers, and gatekeepers, as described below using the purchase of a new computer local area network (LAN) system for a corporate headquarters.

Users or Initiators.   Generally, the person who will benefit most from the acquisition of a good or service will start the purchase process. However, the purchase also may be initiated by another individual who recognizes the same need and realizes the benefits of the acquisition. For example, a top executive discovers that individuals and departments cannot communicate critical information throughout the organization in a timely and efficient way and is somewhat aware that installation of a LAN system could fulfill this need.

Influencers.   As the name implies, influencers affect the buying decision. Typically, as the purchase becomes more complex and expensive and affects more people, more individuals are involved who have the potential for greater impact on the final decision. They may set specifications for the good or service and may be in a position to suggest viable alternatives for the purchasing agent to consider. This is particularly true for highly technical purchases that may be influenced by anyone from a production-line worker to a top manager. In the case of a LAN system purchase, influencers can include anyone with computer and systems expertise, users who have specific requirements for the system, and the financial officer who must consider this acquisition (and its administration and maintenance) within budgetary constraints.

Deciders.   Deciders are individuals who can approve or disapprove of the proposed purchase—including requirements for product specifications and terms of sale, selection of preferred suppliers, and making the final determination of whether or not to buy. Note that despite their significant role in the purchasing process, deciders generally do not sign the purchase order. For the LAN system, a decider may be a high-producing sales manager who needs to maintain better contact with the company's salesforce and production manager to provide up-to-date sales and inventory information. Because of the sales manager's ability to generate high revenues and perhaps some evidence that a poor communication system is causing the company to lose sales, his or her opinions will weigh heavily in the purchase decision.

Approvers.   Approvers are individuals who make a "go" or "no go" decision about proceeding with the purchase process and who decide whether activities are conducted appropriately. If the LAN system purchase is being influenced by the need of the sales department (see "Deciders" above), an approver might be the vice-president for sales or another top-ranking executive.

Buyers.   Buyers (or purchasers) may be one or more individuals, a buying center, or a purchasing department. Buyers have the responsibility and authority to select suppliers, negotiate terms of sale, and otherwise complete the details of the purchase according to specifications. For the LAN system purchase, a purchasing agent may choose between Microsoft and Novell to supply the specified network and may negotiate the final terms with their sales representatives after obtaining their offers or bids.

Gatekeepers.   Certain individuals in an organization are in a position to control information flows to those involved in purchase decisions. They have the ability to screen information about suppliers, products, or other aspects of a purchase and can determine whether or not to keep the "gate" open or shut for information. Further, they can decide what, if any, information to share with others involved in the buying decision. For example, a receptionist or secretary may decide for some reason to block a Microsoft sales representative's attempts to communicate with the buying center or may fail to deliver requested product information to the purchasing agent. Thus the buyer may interpret the absence of information as Microsoft's lack of interest in the sale—when the gatekeeper actually has controlled the critical information.

TYPES OF BUSINESS PURCHASE DECISIONS

Like final consumers, the amount of effort expended in the purchasing process can extend from a routine purchase that requires only a few simple decisions to an extremely complex buying situation that involves more decisions and more effort. In business-to-business markets, buying situations can be classified into three major groups or buy classes: straight rebuy, modified rebuy, and new task.[10]

Straight Rebuy

Straight rebuy
Routine ordering process, simplest organizational purchase.

The **straight rebuy** is the simplest type of purchase made by organizational customers. It generally involves a routine ordering process, often with the most commonly used goods and services ordered automatically by computer or satellite link. In many instances, regular suppliers on a preferred list may be authorized to replenish inventory on frequently consumed items that meet predetermined specifications and to place the order based on prior approval. This type of purchasing situation implies that the buyer has had considerable experience with the product and supplier, as well as the prescribed buying routine. It requires close relationships with trusted suppliers who can deliver quality products on time (just-in-time delivery) to keep inventories at a minimal level while preventing stockouts and work slowdowns.

Modified Rebuy

Modified rebuy
Routine buying procedures altered in some way, requiring consideration of other alternatives.

The **modified rebuy** occurs when the routine buying procedures are altered in some way, requiring the purchasing agent to consider a number of alternatives. A number of changes can occur: The vendor may be out of stock or discontinue the original routinely purchased item, features or specifications included in the original item need to be changed in some way, or the purchasing process itself may be changed. The result is that additional alternatives must be considered before a final purchase decision is made, often involving limited search efforts and the input of several internal and external parties.

New Task Purchases

New task purchase
Unfamiliar or infrequent purchase situation, most extensive and complex.

As the name suggests, a **new task purchase** involves buying a good or service that is relatively unfamiliar—one that has never been purchased before or one that is purchased very rarely. The purchase process tends to be extensive, generally starting with an internally recognized need and ending with an evaluation of either the good or service purchased and the supplier from whom it was purchased. A new task purchase is characterized by the expenditure of more time and search effort and the involvement of more individuals at all stages of the decision. Of course, the most expensive, complex, and/or risk-prone decisions require the most time, effort, and involvement. These buying decisions follow the most formal procedures, such as those illustrated previously in Figure 6.1.

Extended Taxonomy of Purchase Decisions

Bunn (1993) extended the three Webster and Wind (1972) classifications of business-to-business purchase decisions to six categories: casual, routine low priority, simple modified rebuy, judgmental new task, complex modified rebuy, and strategic new task.[11] The categories are distinguished from one another by a set of situational characteristics and buying activities. Situational characteristics include purchase importance, task uncertainty, extensiveness of choice set, and buyer power. Key buying activities include search for information, use of analysis techniques, proactive focus, and procedural control.

The extended taxonomy of buying decisions provides a useful basis for market segmentation strategies and a mechanism for developing adaptive selling approaches based on more narrowly defined buying situations and buying decision approaches. Descriptions of these approaches are provided in Figure 6.2.

MAJOR INFLUENCES ON PURCHASE DECISIONS

Business-to-business buying decisions are not only more complex than consumer decisions, but they also are subject to numerous internal and external influences. Many of the personal, interpersonal, organizational, and environmental factors that affect organizational purchases are beyond the direct control of the purchasing agent but must be factored into the final buying decision.

External Environmental Influences

Today's business-to-business marketers frequently operate in constantly changing, highly volatile, and uncertain environments, where risk involved in the purchasing function takes on more significance than ever. Market demand, competitive strategies, technological advances, economic conditions, and the regulatory environment

FIGURE 6.2

Taxonomy of Business-to-Business Buying Decisions

Descriptions of Buying Decision Approaches						
Variables	**1** **Casual**	**2** **Routine** **Low Priority**	**3** **Simple** **Modified** **Rebuy**	**4** **Judgmental** **New Task**	**5** **Complex** **Modified** **Rebuy**	**6** **Strategic** **New Task**
Situational Characteristics						
Purchase Importance	Of minor importance	Somewhat important	Quite important	Quite important	Quite important	Extremely important
Task Uncertainty	Little uncertainty	Moderately uncertain	Little uncertainty	Great amount of uncertainty	Little uncertainty	Moderately uncertain
Extensiveness of Choice Set	Much choice	Much choice	Narrow set of choices	Narrow set of choices	Much choice	Narrow set of choices
Buyer Power	Little or no power	Moderate power	Moderate power	Moderate power	Strong power position	Strong power position
Buying Activities						
Search for Information	No search made	Little effort at searching	Moderate amount of search	Moderate amount of search	High level of search	High level of search
Use of Analysis Techniques	No analysis performed	Moderate level of analysis	Moderate level of analysis	Moderate level of analysis	Great deal of analysis	Great deal of analysis
Proactive Focus	No attention to proactive issues	Superficial consideration of proactive focus	High level of proactive focus	Moderate proactive focus	High level of proactive focus	Proactive issues dominate purchase
Procedural Control	Simply transmit the order	Follow standard procedures	Follow standard procedures	Little reliance on established procedures	Follow standard procedures	Little reliance on established procedures

Source: Bunn, Michele (1993), "Taxonomy of Buying Decision Approaches," *Journal of Marketing,* Vol. 57 (January), p. 47. Reprinted by permission of the American Marketing Association.

each have a major impact on buying decisions made by professional purchasing agents.

The United Parcel Service, Inc. (UPS) workers' strike in August 1997 is a vivid reminder of the havoc that unexpected events can play with otherwise healthy business operations. The strike caused a ripple effect throughout the world and affected all types of for-profit and nonprofit businesses and customers alike. UPS, a company respected for its reliability and performance, lost significant ground in its dominant market share—yielding coveted business to its competitors, including the United States Postal Service and Federal Express Corp., among others. Workers suffered lack of income (or for some, permanent severance from their UPS jobs) in the short run, while strikers held out for more full-time employment, higher wages, and other benefits in the long run. Businesses that depended on UPS for package delivery could not fill customers' orders as scheduled. Catalog companies were hit particularly hard by the strike. Nonprofit organizations also suffered; for example, hospitals were unable to maintain critical blood supplies for emergencies. And then there were the intended receivers of goods scheduled for shipment by UPS, including disappointed final consumers and businesses that depended on order fulfillment to continue their business operations. While the effects of this strike were most evident in the United States, the impact was felt throughout the world.

Market Demand.   Since business-to-business purchases are based on derived demand, the business and consumer markets essentially dictate what is produced and purchased by organizational customers. Buying goods and services to use for production or resale requires the ability to forecast accurately what the market wants and needs. Market demand and product influences (discussed later in this chapter) interact to influence the purchase process and buying decisions.

Competition.   Organizational markets tend to have fewer competitors than consumer markets, but these competitors are larger and more powerful. Thus the dynamics between buyers and sellers may be subject to the relative power position of each party within the competitive environment. Competition can be viewed from the perspectives of both the buyers and sellers within an industry. On the seller side, numerous competitors who offer similar goods or services offer the organizational buyer more opportunities to negotiate favorable terms of sale—basically capitalizing on the principle of supply and demand. With fewer sellers, of course, there is less room for negotiations and deals.

On the buying side, purchasing decisions are influenced by the nature of the firm's competitors, their location, and their present (and planned) actions. Organizational buyers must be knowledgeable about trends and events in their industries in order to develop sustainable competitive strategies. Within this context, purchases take on strategic importance in achieving organizational objectives. (FedEx's recognition of the needs of suppliers and purchasing agents is illustrated in Figure 6.3.) The entire purchasing process also is affected by the relative sizes of the parties involved. One of the greatest influences in this context is the growth of mass merchandisers and discount chains and their buying "clout" compared with small retailers and suppliers. A large retailer, for example, can make demands on manufacturers and other suppliers in terms of specifications, order terms, delivery, and exclusivity. Most suppliers cannot afford to lose their largest customers and will cater to their demands, generally making purchases more difficult and expensive for smaller customers.

Technology and the Rate of Change.   Organizations must continuously be on the cutting edge of technological change in determining which goods and services they will buy and sell. Purchasing agents must stay informed about the latest technological advances in everything from computer systems to order forms. Changing technologies result in the need to update present production equipment, computer systems, and other inputs needed by the organization to remain competitive—as well as components for higher-tech products demanded by the marketplace.

FIGURE 6.3

FedEx Responds to Customer Needs

Now the hardest thing about shipping is mastering the complexities of the double click.

Introducing FedEx Ship,™ the revolutionary new desktop shipping software from FedEx. Now with FedEx Ship, you can handle virtually any aspect of shipping a package with just a few clicks of your mouse.

Using your modem, the software connects your computer directly to FedEx. It creates shipping labels and prints them on your own laser printer. Maintains a data base of your customers. Schedules pickups, tracks and confirms delivery of your packages. All faster and easier than ever before. Without so much as picking up the phone. FedEx Ship. Once you get the double click down, it's a whole new way of shipping packages. For a free copy of FedEx Ship software for Windows™ or Macintosh,® just call 1-800-GO-FEDEX® or download at http://www.fedex.com.

FedEx
Federal Express
Our Most Important Package Is Yours.®

JUST POINT, CLICK AND SHIP.

©1995 Federal Express Corporation.   Windows is a trademark of Microsoft Corp.   Macintosh is a registered trademark of Apple Computer, Inc.   *TDD: 1-800-238-4461.

Source: © 1995 Federal Express Corporation. All Rights Reserved.

Computers and software are perhaps the most visible examples of the rate of short life span of many technological advances. For example, the switchover to the Pentium chip in the mid-1990s adversely affected sales of Intel's older microprocessors. Later, the MMX chip and Windows NT had a similar impact on sales of the Pentium technology. In addition to the increased capability of both software and hardware, the "trickling down" of computer technology to more unsophisticated home users has had an impact on hardware design, with computers and other equipment being produced with more "stylish" designs.

Economic and Financial Conditions.   Business-to-business markets have undergone drastic economic shifts and volatile financial conditions during the past two decades. This has affected buying decisions in several ways. First, in a serious economic downturn, purchasing budgets may be frozen and budgets reallocated so that funds for purchasing new goods and services are not available. Second, having the financial strength to make purchases does not remove the element of risk associated with making a "bad" buying decision—particularly with large-ticket capital investments. Third, purchases made in response to derived demand from the organization's customers and their customers may decline, diminishing the need for new purchases.

Regulatory and Political Influences.   In comparison with final consumers, organizational buyers must observe more rules and regulations while engaged in purchasing activities. Regulations include fair trade practices, competitive actions, price discrimination, affirmative action requirements, and other legislation. Political and ethical influences also affect business-to-business buying decisions. Although a practice may be legal, it may be contrary to the current political climate or ethically unacceptable to a firm's stakeholders. Purchasing in a global marketplace requires knowledge of each country's laws and politics and the ethical norms of that culture.

Internal Organizational Influences

Just as household factors influence consumers' buying decisions, organizational characteristics influence buying decisions made by business-to-business buyers. Purchasing decisions must be made within the context of a firm's mission and objectives, company policies and procedures, and formal and informal systems. The size and structure of an organization also affect purchases in terms of whether buying is centralized or decentralized or oriented toward a dominant organizational function. For example, a production orientation would suggest that those involved in this function would dominate purchase decisions.

As noted previously, organizational buying involves joint decision making. The buyer must reach consensus with a variety of individuals from other functional areas and levels of the organization. Implicit in this team approach to buying is recognizing who really makes the buying decisions—whether it is the person who is authorized to sign the order or someone else who makes the decision behind the scenes.

Organizational buying policies and preferences include a number of guidelines that must be followed by purchasing agents. In an age of just-in-time (JIT) delivery, increased attention to quality and value, and the building of long-term strategic relationships between buyers and sellers, this may include a requirement to purchase only from a list of preferred providers, with departure from this list requiring upper-level approval. Buyers evaluate their vendors on a number of dimensions such as reliability, price, performance, and convenience of transactions and buy from those that score the highest on important factors.

Profit goals affect the price that can be paid for goods and services, with an established profit-margin goal entering into the cost equation. (See Chapter 14 for further discussion of pricing concepts.) A tradeoff must be made between price and performance at times, with the deciding factor often being the ability to maintain quality standards and to satisfy key customers.

Personal Influences

Personal traits and interpersonal dynamics among the members of the buying center influence all individuals involved in organizational buying processes. Although organizational considerations dominate buying decisions, the effect of personal traits on the decision process and interactions among joint decision makers cannot be ignored.

Demographic, psychographic, and sociologic characteristics affect organizational buying decisions in many of the same ways that they affect consumer decisions. The buyer's experience, position in the company, age, education, personality type, cultural background, perceived competence, and attitudes toward risk affect his or her approach to purchasing. Personal motivation and perceptions of his or her role in the organization and other life roles also influence an organizational buyer's decisions.

In interactions with joint decision makers, organizational buyers are influenced by many interpersonal factors. Relative position or status within the organization, degree of responsibility and authority, ability to empathize with others, and ability to persuade internal and external parties in the decision-making process all play a key part in purchases.

Product Influences

As discussed earlier within the context of types of organizational purchases, the nature of the good or service being purchased affects the buying process. Commodities such as paper products or telephone services are purchased on a routine basis, requiring the input of fewer individuals and little extra effort once the initial product specifications and providers have been determined. While routine product purchases typically involve smaller items and lower unit values, they usually are purchased in large quantities, making it necessary to negotiate favorable prices, delivery, and other terms of sales.

The purchase of products that are more complex, expensive, or riskier involves more extensive decision making. More individuals participate in the decision, both from inside and outside the company. Buyers must expend more time and effort in gathering relevant information and evaluating potential suppliers. They also must negotiate for more favorable terms such as guarantees, service after the sale, or price breaks.

RELATIONSHIP MARKETING

Relationship marketing was discussed in Chapter 5 as it applies to consumer markets. Here we will consider buyer-seller relationships within the context of business-to-business markets. Although many of the buying and selling units represented in business markets may be viewed as large, faceless conglomerates, relationships are not built between buildings and production lines and systems. They are built between the people who inhabit those buildings and operate within those systems from a market-driven perspective. Relationship marketing transcends organizational size or age, industry, nationality, or other characteristics; the need to build long-term relationships between buyers and sellers is universal.

Buyer-Seller Relationships

The highest levels of customer satisfaction are obtained from a series of relationships between buyers and their suppliers throughout entire channels of distribution. The very nature of business-to-business transactions is adversarial, yet suppliers and their customers must view one another as partners if they are to be profitable over the long run. While the new marketing concept puts the customer first,[12] it is helpful to view both buyers and sellers as customers who function as partners in building a lasting and mutually advantageous exchange relationship.

According to Webster,[13] relationship marketing is essentially a question of attitude, where the customer is a business partner rather than an enemy. This view of relationship marketing puts the customer first—before the company, before the product, and perhaps at the expense of a sale. Positive long-term relationships with customers require a high level of trust, cooperation, interdependence, and focus on customer satisfaction. In professional services marketing, for example, relationships are based on a mutual set of expectations and a belief in the other's integrity, competence, and confidentiality, where appropriate. However, it should be noted that it is not feasible to build relationships with all customers or all suppliers—some are not viable candidates for long-term relationships.

Quality, Satisfaction, and Long-Term Relationships

Organizational buyers develop loyalty to suppliers who provide them with quality, value, and service that meet or exceed their expectations. This loyalty results in a long-term, ongoing relationship that is valuable to both parties. Loyal buyers are more willing to pay premium prices or to ask for special inducements to buy from a supplier they view as a partner. The revenue stream from this partnership extends to future purchases of the same good or service or to additional revenues and profit from other products sold by the company. Additionally, a satisfied customer will tell other potential customers, generating highly believable word of mouth that will encourage others to buy.

Relationship Marketing and the New Marketing Concept

Fifteen guidelines for implementing the new marketing concept were described in Chapter 5.[14] Each guideline applies to building buyer-seller relationships in organizational markets as well as in consumer markets. From the perspective of an organizational buyer, the seller's focus should be on creating customer value, targeting the most viable customers, sharing goals and competencies, obtaining input from buyers about their expectations and definitions of quality and value, and making a commitment to continuous improvement and innovation that benefits customers.

Some illustrations of business-to-business relationship marketing include joint ventures between buyers and their key suppliers to develop innovative products or processes, JIT delivery systems, more efficient distribution channels, and possible cost savings. Marketing tactics (e.g., personal selling, advertising, customer loyalty programs) are geared toward the extra effort required to develop long-term buyer-seller relationships rather than closing a single sale. The United States Postal Service (USPS) implemented a customer-oriented strategy in the 1990s in an attempt to overcome past "bureaucratic" images of its service. Both the number and quality of services have increased to supplement the traditional core business of letter and parcel delivery service of the past, creating a more customer-focused organization. Many of these services are in direct competition with those offered by full-service packing and shipping companies like Mail Boxes, Etc. and delivery services like FedEx and Airborne Express. The added services also provide another source of revenue, as the volume of first-class mail slows due to competition from faster communications devices such as fax machines and e-mail. In 1997, the USPS announced that it was in the business of processing bills for corporations, in direct competition with banks and other private companies that vie for bill-processing contracts.[15] The service was launched with American Express Company as the first customer. The USPS took over the customer bill payments for American Express at its Staten Island, New York, processing center, in anticipation of expanding this service to other customers. While competitors maintain that the USPS has an unfair advantage, the agency maintains that such services are an extension of the services it provides to its customers.

Summary

In contrast to consumers who purchase for their own use, organizational buyers purchase goods and services to be used directly or indirectly in their own operations. In turn, they sell, rent, or provide goods and services to other organizations. Organizational buyers purchase on behalf of a business or commercial enterprise, government agency, institution, nonprofit, or other type of organization.

Major industries comprising the business market include agriculture, forestry and fisheries, mining, construction, manufacturing, transportation and public utilities, wholesale and retail trade, finance, insurance, real estate, and services. Most organizational customers can be classified as both original equipment manufacturers (OEMs) or user customers. An OEM buys component parts from a commercial supplier to use in the OEM's finished products that are sold to another customer. User customers purchase equipment, supplies, and services that are used directly or indirectly in the production of other goods and services that are sold to other organizations and/or to the consumer market. Reseller organizations include retailers and wholesalers who are intermediaries in the distribution system. Governmental customers vary in size, scope, and purchasing processes but comprise one of the largest markets throughout the world. Institutions are made up of purchasers that are neither commercial nor governmental. They can be public or private, for-profit or nonprofit, large or small, domestic or international.

Organizational buying patterns differ from those of consumers in a number of ways. An organization's purchases are based on derived demand and involve a more formal and complex process, with more individuals involved in buying decisions. More attention is given to specifications, performance, the order-fulfillment process, and building long-term relationships. Customers tend to be concentrated by industry and geography, and purchases tend to be less standardized, more technical, and in larger quantities.

The organizational buying process follows a sequence of decisions and actions that are followed in varying degrees depending on the nature of the purchase and the type of organization. Buying decisions are made within the boundaries of an organizational structure that determines who has responsibility for purchasing and what procedures will be followed. A buying center approach, comprised of individuals who perform the roles of users or initiators, deciders, approvers, buyers, and gatekeepers, may be used for purchasing.

Organizational purchases can range from routine decisions that require little effort to extremely complex decisions that involve a great deal of effort. Buying situations can be classified as straight rebuy (routine, automatic), modified rebuy (changes to familiar purchase), or new task (relatively unfamiliar purchase). These basic decision types can be extended to a taxonomy of six types, based on situational characteristics (purchase importance, task uncertainty, extensiveness of choice set, and buyer power) and buying activities (search for information, use of analysis techniques, proactive focus, and procedural control).

Factors in both the external and internal environments have an effect on organizational purchase decisions. External factors include market demand, competition, technology and the rate of change, the economy, and the regulatory environment. Internal factors include the firm's mission and objectives, policies and procedures, formal and informal systems, size, and organizational structure. Other influences on buying decisions include personal characteristics and the nature of the good or service being purchased.

Buyer-seller relationships are an important aspect of organizational purchasing. Despite the adversarial nature of many business-to-business purchase situations, formal or informal partnerships are formed on the basis of customer satisfaction and high-quality goods and services. This type of relationship marketing is consistent with the marketing concept.

Questions

1. Discuss each of the stages in the buying process for organizational purchases. Illustrate with an actual or hypothetical company purchase of new office equipment.

2. For the purchase just described, identify (a) the key information sources that would most likely be consulted and (b) the primary influences that can affect this purchase decision.

3. Create a scenario to explain how a supplier may have to deal with a buyer's expectations (and vice versa) in an industrial, organizational, or governmental buying situation.

4. What impact, if any, does the type of purchase or product class have on purchase behavior in the scenario described in Question 3?

5. Compare and contrast the complete purchasing decision-making process for an individual versus a company for specific products such as (a) fax machine, (b) truck, (c) light bulbs, and (d) long-distance telephone service. (You may wish to present your answer in a comparative table or flowchart.)

6. Discuss the implications of situational characteristics and buying activities for marketing strategies or tactics within each of the buying decision approaches presented in Figure 6.2.

7. As the sales manager for a computer software company, explain how you would approach the key players in a target customer's buying center to convince them to buy your product.

8. Describe and give an example of the relationship between quality, satisfaction, and long-term relationships between buyers and sellers.

Exercises

1. Find business-to-business advertisements in trade publications or general business media. Critique the effectiveness of these on the basis of your perception of the following:

   a. Type of organization targeted

b. Influences used to encourage customer response

c. Type of purchase decision

2. Interview a retail buyer or industrial purchasing agent regarding the changes that are occurring in the buying process in his or her company and industry. Also determine how he or she is meeting the challenge posed by these changes.

3. Obtain a copy of an RFP (Request for Proposal) from a government agency or other organization that is seeking bids for specific goods and/or services. Determine how this process is different from the usual nonbidding purchase process and the decision maker(s).

Endnotes

1. S. Tully, "Purchasing's New Muscle," *Fortune* (February 20, 1995), p. 75. (A statement made by AT&T's executive vice-president for telephone products to indicate the importance of purchasing in the organizational hierarchy.)

2. Robert W. Haas, *Business Marketing Management: An Organizational Approach*, 5th ed. (Boston: PWS-Kent Publishing, 1992), Chap. 1.

3. *Statistical Abstract of the United States, 1997* (Washington: USGPO, 1998), Tables 834, 845; U.S. Department of Economic Analysis, *Survey of Current Business, July 1994*; U.S. Department of Commerce, *Federal Expenditures by State, Fiscal Years 1995-1997.*

4. U.S. Department of Commerce, *Federal Expenditures by State, Fiscal Years 1995-1997.*

5. Robert W. Haas, *Business Marketing Management: An Organizational Approach*, 5th ed. (Boston: PWS-Kent Publishing, 1992), p. 14.

6. For additional discussion, see Haas, *ibid.*, Chap. 1.

7. See V. Kasturi Kangan, Benson P. Shapiro, and Rowland T. Moriarty, Jr., *Business Marketing Strategy: Cases, Concepts, and Applications* (Chicago: Richard D. Irwin, 1995), Chap. 1; and John C. Mowen, *Consumer Behavior*, 4th ed. (Englewood Cliffs, NJ: Prentice-Hall, 1995), pp. 676-682.

8. Mowen, *ibid.*, p. 677.

9. Frederick E. Webster, Jr., and Yoram Wind, *Organizational Buying Behavior* (Englewood Cliffs, NJ: Prentice-Hall, 1972), pp. 10, 78-80.

10. For further discussion, see Patrick J. Robinson, Charles W. Faris, and Yoram Wind, *Industrial Buying and Creative Marketing* (Boston: Allyn & Bacon, 1967).

11. Michele D. Bunn, "Taxonomy of Buying Decision Approaches," *Journal of Marketing* 57 (January 1993), pp. 38-56.

12. For further discussion of relationship marketing and the new marketing concept, see Frederick E. Webster, Jr., *Market-Driven Management: Using the New Marketing Concept to Create a Customer-Oriented Company* (New York: John Wiley & Sons, 1994).

13. *Ibid.*, p. 142.

14. *Ibid.*, Chap. 9.

15. Staff Reporter, "Postal Service Seeks Business of Processing Bills for Corporations," *Wall Street Journal* (June 11, 1997), p. B15.

CHAPTER 7

Market Segmentation, Target Marketing, and Positioning

The Basics of Market Segmentation

Target Marketing Strategies

The Market-Segmentation Process

Selection of Market Segments

Ethical Issues in Market Segmentation

Positioning Strategies

HIP! HOT! SHOP 'TIL YOU DROP! A GROWING MIDDLE CLASS IS FUELING THE GLOBAL ECONOMY

A new population force is emerging in our society, increasingly demanding rapid response, easy access, and a sense of control. Already shaping our on-line environments, its members are drawing on their experiences in cyberspace to form their expectations for everyday life. It is the e-generation . . . defined not by common demographics but by a common set of experiences.[1]

Hip young professionals, white-collar workers, factory workers, and other members of central Europe's rising middle class are growing in sophistication as well as numbers as they enjoy higher incomes and increased confidence in their economy. Half of all Czechs consider themselves middle class, according to a recent poll, although their wages are but a fraction of their western European counterparts. Countries like Poland, Hungary, and the Czech Republic, the region's leading economies, have become a hot global market segment for all types of consumer goods— particularly those which enhance desirable lifestyles, such as appliances, automobiles, fashions, cosmetics, and financial services.

Some 17 million Czechs, Hungarians, and Poles—nearly one-third of the central European population from all walks of life—are less than 30 years old and eager to buy the latest in fashion, electronics, leisure activities, and other goods and services. Ad agency Young & Rubicam Inc. labels 11 percent of the Hungarian population as "aspirers," people who have dreams of the good life—and buying habits to go with their dreams. Companies are positioning a diverse array of products as ways to improve, or transform, the lives of central Europeans. After 50 years of communism and the more recent harsh realities of the transition to capitalism, pur-

186

chases that signal a better standard of living are a welcome change. Young professionals are building new houses on the outskirts of Warsaw, and others are renovating their Soviet-era apartments with new kitchens, built-in wooden cabinets, and expensive double-paned windows. Companies like Ikea Holdings (a Swedish furniture company) and Potten & Patten (a Czech marketer of high-end Western cookware and cutlery) are benefiting from this trend.

The shopping spree in central Europe also creates change in its distribution networks. Hypermarkets and shopping malls have replaced many of the traditional mom-and-pop retail stores in the major cities. Poland's largest shopping center was opened in Czeladz in the industrial heartland by Metro, a German retailing giant. Metro spent $56 million to build the center and will invest $555 million in Poland over the next 5 years. Lehman Brothers Inc., a U.S. investment bank, is spending $150 million to develop ten new malls in the Czech Republic, Hungary, and Poland. Consumer spending has a ripple effect throughout the distribution channels, causing service companies such as DHL International to expand their distribution networks to meet the growing transportation needs of both foreign importers and local manufacturers.

A global marketplace requires a broad understanding of the differences and similarities among the world's populations for the development of market segmentation, target marketing, and positioning strategies. Central Europe (Czech Republic, Hungary, and Poland) is but one example of the exciting hot markets around the globe. Other attractive foreign markets include the Chinese Economic Area (CEA, made up of China, Hong Kong, and Taiwan), South Africa, India, Turkey, and Argentina, along with other growing Asian and Latin American markets.

Sources: David Woodruff, James Drake, Christopher Condon, and Peggy Simpson, "Ready to Shop Until They Drop: Central Europe's Rising Middle Class Is on a Buying Binge," *Business Week* (June 22, 1998), pp. 104–114; Roberta Maynard, "Hot Markets Overseas," *Nation's Business* (June 1995), pp. 42–44; Rahul Jacob, "The Big Rise: Middle Classes Explode Around the Globe, Bringing New Markets and New Prosperity," *Fortune* (May 30, 1994), pp. 74–90; and others.

The rate of change in the twenty-first century is expected to outpace the magnitude and speed of change experienced by marketers in the late twentieth century. New product proliferation, shifting population demographics, and a promising but increasingly complex world marketplace challenge marketers to make informed decisions about the customers they will serve. Selection of a target market is a conscious choice, made on the basis of organizational goals and values and the attractiveness of each customer group. A mistake in this area could be extremely costly. As Frederick E. Webster has observed:

> The most important strategic choice any company makes is choosing the customers it wishes to do business with. It is a choice that defines the business. . . . Changing the definition of the served market changes the definition of the business. Customers shape the business, which is why customer choice is the critical strategic decision. If management has not defined a strategic vision of what it wants to be, and who is the desired customer, it has no control over the forces shaping its business. A business that tries to be all things to all customers is not a business at all, because it has failed to define its product/market scope.[2]

THE BASICS OF MARKET SEGMENTATION

An organization can approach its market in one of two primary ways. It may choose to sell to everyone in the market, aggregating all types of customers into one mass market. Or it can choose to segment a large market into smaller groups.

Mass Marketing

Mass marketing
Attempt to sell to everyone in the market assuming that demand is homogeneous; one marketing mix is used for all customers.

Mass marketing is appropriate when demand is homogeneous, or every potential customer has the same basic need that can be satisfied in the same basic way. In many ways, this resembles a "shotgun approach," where one marketing mix is used for all customers in hopes that everyone will buy. A mass-marketing strategy can be applied successfully where customers' wants and needs are similar across the market, goods and services can be standardized, and customers can be expected to respond in similar fashion to marketing programs. For example, the manufacturers of staple food items, such as sugar or salt, can be said to practice mass marketing by having their products packaged in only one size and color.

In today's marketplace, companies are more apt to use a market-segmentation strategy because not everyone in the market qualifies or is interested in buying the good or service offered, nor can the company satisfy the wants and needs of every customer. As a result, most organizations choose to target those segments of the market which they can serve most successfully.

Market Segmentation

Market segmentation
Process of dividing a large market into smaller groups or clusters of customers with similar characteristics.

Market segmentation is the process of dividing a large market into smaller groups or clusters of customers. The similarities within each segment make it possible for marketers to reach all members of a particular segment effectively with one basic marketing mix. That is, customers are expected to respond similarly to the same product features, promotional campaigns, distribution methods, and pricing strategies. Groups of customers may be located in the same geographic area or share similar buying habits, media preferences, or product usage, for example.

Why Subdivide Markets?

The business revolutions described earlier in this book contribute to an increased interest in subdividing the market into identifiable segments. Globalization has opened up world markets to more competitors, with a more diverse customer base in both consumer and organizational markets. Customers have more choices of goods and services to buy than ever before, and more companies are eager to fulfill their needs. Increased computerization, technological advances, and an information age economy make it possible to gather and manipulate enormous databases. These databases provide up-to-the-minute information about customer traits, their buying habits, and other data that can be linked to additional databases containing more personal information. Using these data, a marketer can reach a narrowly defined segment of customers with a marketing program tailored to their wants and needs.

A number of benefits are derived from following a market-segmentation strategy. The most obvious benefit is the ability to use a specially designed marketing

Target marketing
Using a specially designed marketing mix to target a smaller market with greater precision; permits closer buyer-seller relationships.

mix to target a smaller market with greater precision. Hence the term **target marketing.** Target marketing is more costly than mass marketing, but it is more precise and allows the marketer to deploy resources where they can be most effective—the traditional efficiency versus effectiveness argument. Segmentation permits closer relationships between buyer and seller and the ability to identify new marketing opportunities—perhaps a chance to satisfy a need that is not presently being fulfilled.

Customer Value and Target Marketing

Organizations must have a clear understanding of *value* as the customers in its target market define it. Customer satisfaction is related closely to perceptions of the value or benefits received from products, brands, stores, suppliers, and other sources. To ensure satisfaction, marketing managers must be able to identify and rank the factors that contribute to exceptional value as perceived by customers. A company not only must be able to deliver the value that its customers expect, but also must be able to do so better than the competition if its target marketing strategy is to be successful.

TARGET MARKETING STRATEGIES

Target marketing strategies are developed in accord with customer demand patterns relative to customers' wants and needs for particular goods or services. During the segmentation process, estimated market-demand figures are used to forecast expected sales and profitability for each segment. The nature of customer demand determines the type of marketing strategy to be pursued and whether to target the entire market (mass marketing, as discussed earlier) or one or more distinctly different segments of the market (multiple- or single-segment target marketing).

A Multisegment Marketing Strategy

Multiple segmentation
Focus on two or more distinguishable market segments; each segment is treated as a unique market, with its own unique marketing mix.

Marketers may choose to focus their target marketing strategy on two or more distinguishable market segments. This strategy is referred to as **multiple segmentation,** or a clustered or selective specialization strategy. Each segment is treated as a unique market, with its own unique marketing mix.

There may or may not be synergies among the different targeted segments, but each is selected for its own attractive opportunities relative to company objectives. For example, photography companies focus on multiple segments such as travelers, professional or hobby photographers, and active elderly people. Ford Motor Co. targets multiple customer groups based on lifestyles and demographics through product design, pricing approaches, positioning, and promotional strategies. The Ford Taurus appeals to a number of distinct market segments such as companies purchasing for business use, young families, singles, and older adults. Likewise, Ford targets different models such as the Mustang convertible, Explorer sports utility vehicle, Escort, and others to one or more customer groups based on the benefits desired by each segment.

A multisegment strategy is effective when there are two or more distinct segments. Extra costs are incurred because each segment requires a different target marketing approach. However, this strategy also increases the opportunity for marketers to maximize the return from each segment while spreading risk if any segment fails to perform as planned.

A Single-Segment Marketing Strategy

A concentrated target marketing strategy may be used for a single market segment with a distinct set of needs. Two approaches to a single-segment strategy are niche marketing and one-to-one marketing, as discussed next.

Niche marketing
Marketing effort highly focused on a single segment that seeks special benefits; seller must have distinct advantage over competitors and provide superior goods and services.

Niche Marketing.   **Niche marketing** is a strategy that is highly focused on a single segment that seeks special benefits. Customers in a niche market will go to considerable effort and pay higher prices to obtain the good or service they demand. An example of a niche market with special needs includes youthful wheelchair users, many of whom are victims of urban violence and do not want the prototypical chrome wheelchair of the past. ". . . [M]any want from their wheelchairs what young men everywhere want from cars, running shoes and bicycles: style, performance, and pizzazz." As a result, a number of wheelchair manufacturers have developed sporty, collapsible, lighter-weight models that are highly maneuverable and come in bright colors. Options sound more like a sports car: ". . . high performance, oversized tires; cambered, pop-off wheels designed for speed; Roller-blade-like casters that allow for reflex-quick maneuverability; and sleek, flashy spoke guards that are the equivalent of fancy hubcaps."[3]

There are numerous examples of niche marketing strategies. Ford Motor Company's Jaguar division targets upscale drivers who want a sporty, high-performance car. Loan companies and pawnshops (often unscrupulously) target low-income customers who have high debt levels. Health food stores such as Whole Foods Market (based in Austin, Texas) target upper-income, health-conscious consumers who want high-quality, unique food products. Think about the possible niche markets you might be a member of for business or personal purchases. What makes each niche unique?

Marketers who pursue a niche marketing strategy must have a distinct advantage over competitors and must be able to satisfy customers with superior products and services. Niche marketing can be a successful strategy for small firms that need to focus their marketing efforts because of limited resources and abilities. This strategy allows smaller firms to compete successfully with larger firms. Nevertheless, smaller firms may find it difficult to compete with larger competitors on a more extensive scale.

Micro-marketing
Precise segmentation strategy that capitalizes on databases and information technology to implement one-to-one marketing or mass customization.

One-to-One Marketing.   Over the past several decades, market-selection strategies have evolved from mass marketing to market segmentation to niche marketing. Fueled by comprehensive databases and communications technology, marketers have progressively become more informed about their individual customers and can narrow down markets more precisely. The result is the implementation of one-to-one marketing strategies, where mass customization and **micro-marketing** dominate. This strategy is an extension of multisegment or niche marketing where the needs of a single customer are given special consideration. Related concepts include relationship marketing, database marketing, and customer-satisfaction initiatives. The extreme case is one customer (or buying unit) and one customized product such as a house, wedding gown, or telecommunications system. More often, one-to-one marketing is practiced within existing segments to satisfy the needs of individual buyers.

Mary Naylor found success with one-to-one marketing in her company, Capitol Concierge, in Washington, D.C. The company sets up concierges in office-building lobbies to provide an array of personal and business services, everything from managing a catered lunch to doing errands. The key to Naylor's success is learning enough about her customers to be able to anticipate their needs—even before they are aware of them. In 1995, one-to-one marketing and great customer service brought in $5 million in revenues and earned Capitol Concierge a place on the Inc. 500 list.[4]

Examples of one-to-one marketing can be found in every industry where unique customer demands exist. Levi Strauss & Co., considered by many to be a mass marketer of blue jeans, uses laser technology to custom fit jeans for its customers.[5] Target, owned by Dayton-Hudson Corp., adopted a micro-marketing strategy in its discount chain of more than 620 retail stores throughout the United States. The retailer uses a "consumer-driven, technology-packed" strategy to tailor its merchandise selection to the preferences of each store's customers. Micro-marketing is used to cater to consumer preferences based on individual racial, ethnic, and lifestyle diversity.[6]

THE MARKET-SEGMENTATION PROCESS

The market-segmentation process starts with a commitment to provide satisfaction to one or more groups of customers. Decisions about the products to be offered and the customers to be served also must be consistent with the organization's operating policies, performance goals, and ability to provide the desired benefits. Effective market segmentation requires an understanding of the product (good or service) that is being marketed—in particular, the product's intended use for a given market and its distinctive characteristics or specifications.

Marketing managers also must consider environmental factors throughout all steps in the market-segmentation process. The selection of the most attractive and profitable segments to serve starts with a clear understanding of the organization's internal and external environments. This knowledge is needed to assess competitive strengths and weaknesses and external opportunities and threats in the customer segments that the organization pursues. It is assumed that the marketer has full knowledge of the current situation or will obtain the necessary information prior to, and during, the process of selecting one or more market segments to target.

The process of dividing markets into meaningful segments involves five major types of activities. (See Figure 7.1.) However, the sequence of these steps and their description may vary from one marketing situation to another. The important point is that all the tasks enumerated here must take place sometime during

FIGURE 7.1

....

The Market-Segmentation Process

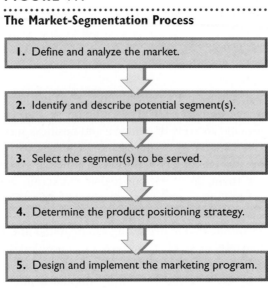

1. Define and analyze the market.

2. Identify and describe potential segment(s).

3. Select the segment(s) to be served.

4. Determine the product positioning strategy.

5. Design and implement the marketing program.

....

the segmentation process. Often this process is iterative; that is, new information is discovered that requires going back to a previous step in order to re-examine the process or the results.

1. Define and Analyze the Market

....

Before a market can be analyzed, its parameters must be determined within the organization's mission and business definition, as well as its strategic intent. Markets may be defined according to characteristics that can include or exclude customers from a group (e.g., types of customers, types of products, geography, channel position). Once the overall market boundaries have been delineated, the market size and growth rate, competitive environment, and other issues must be ascertained relative to the organization's objectives. The challenge in this step is to define the market narrowly enough to create a focused marketing strategy for the selected segment(s) and at the same time to define the market broadly enough to include attractive new opportunities.

2. Identify and Describe Potential Segments

....

The next step is to decide what dimensions or variables would be most useful for selecting members of potential market segments. Potential market segments are identified on the basis of the selected dimensions, and relevant data are collected and analyzed for each segment. To the extent possible, these variables are selected in advance, either *a priori* or based on preliminary marketing research results.

Next, final consumers or organizational customers are aggregated into homogeneous groups, and a profile of the characteristics of each group (segment) is developed. The attractiveness of each segment is evaluated, and segments are ranked according to their desirability. This process may require several research approaches, such as gathering secondary marketing intelligence, conducting a survey or focus groups, or analyzing databases.

3. Select the Segment(s) to Be Served

In this stage of the segmentation process, the final target market selection is made. Each segment is evaluated against predetermined criteria that reflect the organization's ability to serve the market profitably while providing customer satisfaction. Each segment is then ranked according to its performance on each criterion, and specific target market(s) are selected. Finally, the segmentation strategy is determined.

4. Determine the Product Positioning Strategy

Products and markets are closely intertwined, making it imperative to determine the best "fit" between the two. At this point, possible positioning concepts or alternative approaches for each target market are determined according to the features most desired by customers. From the possible alternatives, the most desirable positioning strategy is selected. This strategy must take into consideration factors such as competitors' positioning strategies, the market situation, and overall organizational goals.

5. Design and Implement the Marketing Program

In this stage, the tactical marketing plan is developed, and objectives are determined for the marketing program. The marketing-mix strategy is designed and developed to communicate the positioning concept to the target market. All elements of the marketing program design must be consistent with the selected positioning strategy. The final step in the segmentation process is to implement the marketing program for each target market and to control and evaluate its effectiveness in achieving the planned goals.

Criteria for Effective Segmentation

The development and implementation of a market segmentation strategy can incur greater costs (e.g., market research, separate promotional campaigns and distribution channels, etc.) than a mass-marketing strategy. Therefore, each segment must meet the following basic criteria.

1. The Organization Must Be Able to Identify and Measure Each Segment.
Some segmentation variables are relatively easy to identify. For example, it is relatively easy to count the number of consumers who are teenagers or under age 30 in Hungary (assuming the necessary population data are available). Obviously, it

must be possible to identify relevant dimensions before they can be measured objectively.

It is more difficult to identify and measure variables such as personality traits, brand loyalty, or cultural values. For example, it is more difficult to count the number of "aspirers" identified by ad agency Young & Rubicam Inc. in the opening scenario. The latter would require lifestyle research conducted with a representative sample of the identified segment. While this lifestyle characteristic can be used in promotion and product development, it is not possible to identify every "aspirer" for one-to-one marketing opportunities. Personal characteristics are most often inferred from other measures that may be more subjective and intuitive. However, both objective (quantitative) and subjective (qualitative) information must be considered in a description of a potential market segment.

2. The Market Must Be Substantial Enough.   Profitability is an important factor in selecting a market segment. Therefore, the segment must be sufficiently large, with substantial potential to generate desired revenue and profit levels. Multiple criteria are used to measure the size and profitability of an identified segment, including the present size and sales potential of the segment, its growth potential in revenues and number of customers, and the degree of fit with the present organizational product line and resources. In addition to the attractiveness of a given segment, the organization also must consider its ability to create customer value and long-term satisfying relationships with customers in the segment.

In many developing economies, personal consumption is outpacing rapid growth in the gross domestic product (GDP)—figures that can be calculated and estimated from available data. It is possible to measure the increase in the number of middle-class workers with purchasing power parity of $10,000 to $40,000 in the world's ten largest emerging markets (China, Indonesia, India, South Korea, Turkey, South Africa, Poland, Argentina, Brazil, and Mexico—named by the U.S. Department of Commerce). However, there is disparity in the definition of middle class. McKinsey & Co. estimates that in China middle-class household incomes are more than $1,000 per year. A former privatization minister in Poland estimates middle-class income there at $3,000 a year, and a market research firm in Indonesia defines middle class there as a family with more than $140 in shopping bills in a month. Data indicate that the developing countries are the fastest growing market for U.S. exports. Demographic data such as these can be obtained or estimated with some degree of accuracy, although people often underreport their income in surveys.[7]

3. The Organization Must Be Able to Reach Customers.   Some markets are very attractive and indicate significant potential for future growth but are not easily accessible to the company and its products. Accessibility includes the ability to reach the market segment through distribution channels, advertising media, personal selling, and other aspects of the marketing mix. Barriers between a company and potential customers in a given market segment also may include unfavorable laws and regulations, trade barriers, economic factors, or other factors.

The tobacco industry and producers of alcoholic beverages have a large potential market of underage smokers and drinkers that many would like to reach in order to establish brand preference at an early age. However, U.S. legal constraints provide a barrier to this market. The populations of China and Russia are enormous, and their buying power is increasing rapidly. However, marketers may not be able to reach their sales and profit objectives as quickly as they would like because of an inadequate infrastructure to support the business (e.g., transportation, media for advertising) or other reasons.

4. Customers in the Selected Segment Must Be Responsive.   The targeted customers must have the money and willingness to buy the good or service offered. In other words, if the company is to achieve success with its marketing programs, its plan must be realistic and actionable. Positive, negative, or indifferent market response may be due to a number of factors, such as the relative strengths and weaknesses of the company and its products versus those of competitors.

For many years, personal computers were priced too high for many consumers. In 1997, manufacturers marketed a large number of PCs for less than $1000. The market response was positive, and many first-time computer owners were born, thus opening up the market for related merchandise such as games, word-processing software, and Internet connections. The PC market is very competitive, and any company entering the market must have a unique selling point against its competitors.

5. Characteristics of the Segment Are Relatively Stable Over a Long Period. A segmentation decision is a long-term strategy, so it should be consistent with the organization's mission and longer-term strategic objectives. The degree of anticipated volatility and uncertainty in the market is directly related to the ability to forecast demand patterns and plan future actions. Many firms delay or abandon decisions to enter markets where conditions will have a negative impact on profits. Conditions such as closed manufacturing plants and high unemployment without any indication that the economy will improve or political upheaval and military action in war-torn countries like Serbia make it difficult to predict future purchase behavior and revenues. Segments with intensive competition for their business also may exhibit a lack of stability for the long term and therefore be less attractive.

SELECTION OF MARKET SEGMENTS

Following identification of the overall market to be pursued, the next step is to group customers within that market into more narrowly defined segments. Variables used to determine membership in a segment should be chosen for their usefulness in forecasting sales and predicting customer response to the company's offer.

A unique target marketing strategy is designed to appeal to each market segment based on the set of common characteristics shared by individuals in that segment. Although a single characteristic such as geographic location may be the predominant basis for selecting a given market segment, it is more likely that a combination of variables will be considered. For example, the number of people in a household (or business) and level of income may be considered in addition to geographic location.

Bases for Segmenting Consumer Markets

Target marketing decisions are based on attributes of the customers in a selected market. The problem is that there are many possible ways to divide a market, often making it difficult to know which are the most appropriate. Creative problem-solving techniques can be applied to gain competitive advantage through innovative segmentation, targeting, and positioning approaches.

A number of innovative approaches have been used to market a variety of products to the elderly. One of the best known is the Sony Walkman, targeted to energetic senior citizens (among other segments). Point-of-sale displays and media advertising depicted a happy older woman dressed like a "hip" teenager on roller skates, listening to her Walkman headset. Creative marketing and positioning strategies have been used to target fashion-conscious seniors with higher discretionary income and an active lifestyle for everything from exotic travel destinations to streamlined wheelchairs.

Marketers use demographic, socioeconomic, and geographic data extensively to describe their markets. This type of descriptive information is quantifiable and relatively easy to obtain and verify, but it provides only a general description of a customer group. For example, consider the diverse characteristics of all members of your age and income group in your city or community. Are they all prospective customers for the same goods and services that you own or plan to buy? Imagine all the possible segments that can be identified for a basic good or service such as a quart of milk or automotive repair.

To gain more insights into differences among customers within a broadly defined segment, marketers expand the quantitative market definition with relevant qualitative information such as behavioral, situational, psychographic (lifestyle), and psychological descriptors, as well as the benefits or satisfactions that are sought by customers. Classifications such as the "aspirer" identified by Young & Rubicam Inc. among Hungarian consumers desiring a "good life" may be determined by a combination of quantitative and qualitative data, perhaps using existing population data and a survey questionnaire to gather the data.

Demographic and Socioeconomic Descriptors. The most frequently used demographic variables include age, gender, marital status, household (or family) size, stage in the household life cycle, religion, race or ethnic group, and nationality. Variables that describe consumers' socioeconomic status include income, occupation, education, social class, and asset ownership. Both demographic and socioeconomic characteristics are preliminary indicators of how purchases are made and how they are used. Clearly, many of these categories are interrelated and must be considered simultaneously to provide a better understanding of buyer behavior. Multiple demographic and/or socioeconomic descriptors—such as age, income, household life cycle stage, and social class—may be used to describe a market segment. Although useful, these dimensions do not reveal important differences among consumers in terms of their attitudes or preferences that often transcend demographic categories.

Past and projected shifts in demographics based on U.S. Census Bureau race and ethnicity classifications, as well as the total population by age, are illustrated in Figure 7.2.

FIGURE 7.2
....
U.S. Population by Race and Age

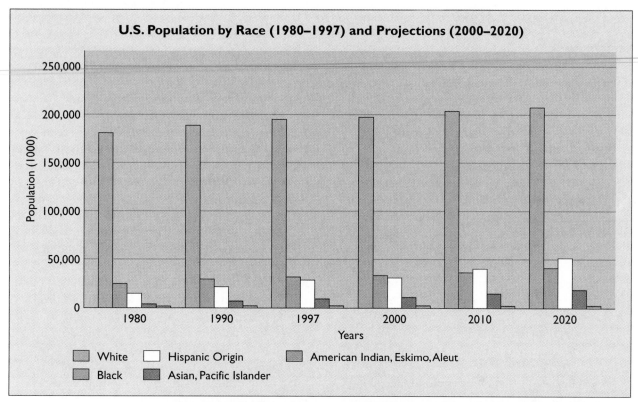

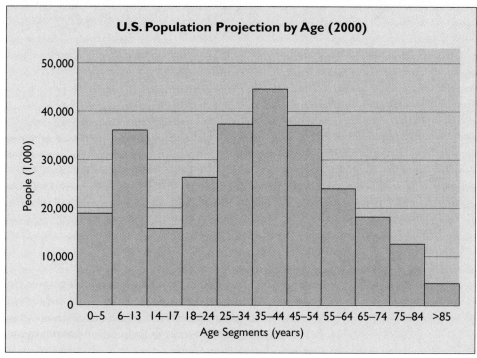

Source: Statistical Abstract of the United States, 1998.
....

MARKETING IN THE GLOBAL VILLAGE

A Multiracial Marketplace—in the United States

According to the 1996 Current Population Survey, there were 1.3 million married mixed-race couples and 1.5 million households where a Hispanic was married to a non-Hispanic in the United States. The growing number of minorities—led by Hispanics and Asians—and the growing number of mixed-race families, particularly those with school-aged children, led the fight to revise the existing standards for categorizing racial and ethnic data. The major arguments were that the data did not accurately represent the American population because respondents could not indicate more than one race and school-aged children had to identify themselves by the race of only one parent. In response to these concerns, and after much deliberation, the Office of Management and Budget (OMB) of the federal government revised the standards for the classification of federal data on race and ethnicity to take effect with the census of 2000. The new census will include five minimum categories for data on race (American Indian or Alaska Native, Asian, Black or African American, Native Hawaiian or Other Pacific Islander, and White), as well as two categories of data on ethnicity (Hispanic or Latino and Not Hispanic or Latino). The tabulation for the five basic categories of race data could result in 64 cells. When the breakdown includes Hispanics and non-Hispanics by race, the number of cells could reach 128. To illustrate one of the possible combined categories, Tiger Woods, the popular young professional golfer, will be classified by the census of 2000 as a multiracial "Cablinasian"—because of his mixed Caucasian, black, American Indian, and Asian ancestry. Previously, the response categories forced him into the single category of African American.

As American consumers become more racially and ethnically diverse, consumer goods marketers and service companies seek more information about the differences among these groups. While the new classifications will make it difficult to make historical comparisons of data or to forecast trends based on past data, the census of 2000 will provide a clearer picture of an increasingly multiracial population. Ethnic marketers say the results will dispel some of the previous myths and stereotypes used in advertising and other marketing efforts. The data will be used extensively in marketing research and marketing program design. As the director of research for an advertising agency in Chicago that specializes in the African American market says, "I think it reinforces the need to have diverse messages because we are not a monolithic society. . . . It recognizes and embraces the totality of this country and reinforces diversity."

Sources: Christy Fisher, "It's All in the Details," *American Demographics* 20(4) (April 1998), pp. 45–47; William O'Hare, "Managing Multiple-Race Data," *American Demographics* 20(4) (April 1998), pp. 42–44; Rochelle L. Stanfield, "Multiple Choice," *National Journal* 29(47) (November 22, 1997), pp. 2352–2355; Office of Management and Budget, "Revisions to the Standards for the Classification of Federal Data on Race and Ethnicity," Washington, United States Government, *http://www. whitehouse.gov/WH/EOP/OMB/html/fedreg.htm.*

Geographic Descriptors. Many market segments are selected because of their geographic location for several reasons. Customers for a company's goods and services tend to be concentrated in a particular geographic area. Products may be developed for use in a particular type of physical environment (e.g., snowboards are more popular in Denver than in Miami, and earthquake insurance is in greater demand in California than in Vermont). Decisions about the locations of retail stores and the distribution centers that serve them are made relative to concentrations of desirable retail customers. Other reasons for geographic segmentation include media availability (e.g., effective television or newspaper coverage to reach the targeted customers) and efficient uses of company resources (e.g., salesforce coverage, customer service).

Geographic variables apply to all degrees of magnitude, from the location of a small group of key customers to the entire world. In market-segmentation decisions, it is more meaningful to aggregate populations from smaller to larger geographic areas. Some levels of geographic segmentation include country (United States), region of the country (southwestern United States), state (Texas), county (Harris), metropolitan area (Houston), zip code, and neighborhood. The size and density of the population also are used to identify customer segments. For example, Wal-Mart's winning strategy for many years was to locate stores in small towns with populations under 20,000. Finally, climate and seasonal changes are related to many consumer needs and wants in different areas, such as the demand for four-wheel-drive vehicles in snow and rugged terrain and convertibles in sunny climates. Approaching geographic segmentation in this manner permits the marketer to identify variables that may have an impact on buying decisions differently within the larger geographic area.

Behavioral and Situational Descriptors. The ways consumers buy and use goods and services provide useful dimensions for breaking up a larger market into smaller segments. Purchase behavior variables include the consumer's status as a present, past, or future user or nonuser of the product class, brand, or supplier.

An emerging segment of the population, which is referred to as the "e-Generation," draws on experiences in cyberspace to form their expectations for everyday life. The e-Generation, representing a market segment that is prevalent across all age groups and Web site content, is defined by a set of common experiences, not by demographics.

More than half this group are professionals, over two-thirds have at least a college education, and nearly half have incomes over $75,000. Their most powerful behavioral characteristic is time sensitivity, in terms of convenience and efficiency. They are more interested in instant gratification and speedy completion of tasks than in being entertained. The e-Generation's on-line interactions in cyberspace ripple throughout other consumer contact channels, including telephone calls to follow up on something they saw on a Web site or searching the Web for information featured on television.[8]

Degree of loyalty to the brand, the product category, and the company also are useful variables for deciding which markets to target. Frequent fliers and frequent shoppers are rewarded with free goods and premiums to motivate them to buy more because large numbers of loyal, heavy users ensure long-term profitability.

Buyers may be segmented on the basis of situational factors such as the nature of the purchase occasion (e.g., a special event) or the consumer's readiness to make this purchase decision. Airlines combine geographic and demographic variables for target marketing decisions. Present and prospective airline passengers are segmented according to air travel routes, places of departure, and destinations. They also are segmented on the basis of demographics such as first class, business class, and coach and on passenger loyalty and frequent flier status. Each combination of variables (e.g., New York to Los Angeles business travelers who are members of the airline's frequent flier program versus a one-time pleasure traveler flying coach) may require a different marketing approach. For example, in 1998 TWA reversed its strategy of offering the industry's most spacious economy section by taking 2 inches (about 15 percent) of the legroom from each row in the back in order to nearly double the number of first-class seats. As a result, more first-class seats are available to business travelers who want to upgrade. Clearly, the focus is on satisfying business customers whose companies have been willing to spend more on travel in a booming economy.[9]

Psychological and Psychographic Descriptors.   These dimensions are useful for planning marketing activities but are difficult to measure directly. Among the more commonly used psychological variables are personality types, consumer motivations and needs, and attitudes. Marketers can determine typical profiles of their prospective customers within a market segment and use this information to determine product positioning, promotional messages, media, and distribution strategies, for example.

Consumer lifestyles (psychographics) have gained increased attention in recent years as an important predictor of buying behavior. Lifestyles tend to transcend age, gender, income, and other segmentation dimensions. The decade of the 1990s saw a major shift toward healthier living across all generations and income levels. The general population became more interested in a variety of sports, and professional sports gained in popularity among a diverse group of players. Fitness clubs and health-food stores grew significantly during this time, along with the producers of all health-related goods and services. Increasingly active lifestyles have opened up new marketing opportunities for diverse demographic groups and created a need for a better understanding of their needs and buying motives.

Benefits Sought.   Benefit segmentation is related to the previous two groups of segmentation variables but is considered separately because of its importance to customers. Any one customer might be seeking an endless list of benefits, but most are seeking quality, value, and service combined with other wanted benefits. Two major benefits that are demanded by consumers today are goods and services that provide convenience and self-improvement. In today's fast-paced society, consumers depend on many convenience goods and services. This trend has generated many new businesses and has changed the way many existing businesses operate to meet this demand. Banks have opened more branch offices, expanded the number of ATMs in remote locations, and provided service from mobile units and in churches. Many service businesses have extended their hours to accommodate workers who work other than from 9 to 5. Sales of prepared and partially prepared gourmet foods have grown in response to the needs of busy people who like to serve quality food.

Self-improvement benefits transcend all demographic, geographic, behavioral, psychological, and other categories and have proliferated to include many new products. Markets desiring educational improvement extend from preschool children to senior citizens. For-profit and nonprofit organizations alike are pursuing this market with a vast array of classes, programs, books, videos, and enlightening experiences. The same is true for physical fitness, spiritual growth, and a myriad of other benefits that various market segments are eager to buy.

Bases for Segmenting Business-to-Business Markets

Many of the general segmentation variables that are used in consumer markets also can be used to divide organizational markets. However, the specific variables within each dimension are selected for their predictability and marketing applications for business and organizational customers.

Standard Industrial Code (SIC)
Standardized method of classifying businesses to provide uniformity in business reporting and to facilitate aggregation of data for an entire industry; a useful basis for determining market segments to target.

Demographic Descriptors. The most widely used demographic variable for segmenting businesses is the industry classification. The **Standard Industrial Code (SIC)** is a standardized method of classifying businesses to provide uniformity in business reporting and to facilitate the aggregation of data for an entire industry. A company selling office equipment may sell similar supplies to a school, automobile manufacturer, hospital, and cheese processing firm but treat each segment as a different target market. Information about each group of customers can be tracked conveniently by using its industry classification. The SIC is represented by a two-, three-, or four-digit number, with the two-digit number being the broadest industry definition and the four-digit number being the narrowest. For example, SIC classifications for the cheese industry would be referenced as major group 20—food and kindred products; industry group 202—dairy products; industry number 2022—cheese. Some classifications can be extended up to seven digits, but for many businesses, data are available for only a two- or three-digit classification.

Market segments often are selected on the basis of the size of an organization. Size may be measured according to sales volume, number of employees, and number of locations. Age of an organization generally is related to its size, measured in terms of years in business. This helps to distinguish between start-up ventures and established businesses, for example.

The way a product will be used by the customer is another way to distinguish among market segments. In the business-to-business market, the primary end-uses are related to the type of customer: original equipment manufacturers (OEMs), aftermarket user (parts and repairs), wholesale trade (resale to another member of the distribution channel), and retail trade (resale to final consumers). Marketers who are targeting other businesses not only must develop products and marketing programs that will satisfy the needs of their immediate customers but also must be aware of the nature of derived demand from the final purchaser. For example, manufacturers of plumbing supplies need to monitor trends in the construction and remodeling of business and residential properties to determine patterns of future demand for kitchen and bathroom fixtures.

Geographic Descriptors. Location is an important variable for segmenting organizational markets. Many industries are concentrated in one geographic area, such as automobiles in Detroit, furniture in North Carolina, computer software in Silicon Valley, California, and fine-quality watches in Switzerland. A synergy can be obtained

Generation X: An X-citing Challenge to Marketers

 Age and lifestyle categories can be helpful in marketing segmentation decisions, but they also can be inaccurate and misleading without deeper understanding. Many broad—and often erroneous—assumptions have been made about Generation X, an age group that represents $125 billion in annual purchasing power for many consumer goods. Xers (also called baby-busters) include 45 million young adults, mostly twenty-something to mid-thirties born in the 1960s and 1970s, who have been the center of attention for marketers and the media (along with their predecessors, the baby-boomers) as experts try to describe their lifestyles and buying behaviors.

Earlier descriptions of Xers portray them as slackers, cynics, and drifters who show a lack of drive and ambition, mistrust of business, disrespect for authority, and "disconnectedness" from society. However, it has become evident that the predominant traits in this generation include tremendous ambition to make money, spend money, and save money. They just want to do it their own way. Although half the Xers still live at home, they are always looking for the better deal and looking for opportunities that are not as confining as the careers of their parents.

In 1997, Yankelovich Partners, a prominent polling firm, and TBWA Chiat/Day, a major advertising agency, collaborated in conducting a comprehensive survey. The research project, called The New American Dream Study, compared three generations, including Generation Xers, baby-boomers (born from 1946 to 1964), and matures (born from 1909 to 1945). The results? "The youngsters are ambitious get-aheads—even more so than their parents or grandparents. They are confident, savvy and . . . materialistic." The researchers found Generation Xers to be committed, connected, and craving success American-style. This "X-citing, X-igent, X-pansive"

generation that grew up with MTV, Beavis and Butthead, net surfing, and a fear of ending up in "McJobs" has challenged the earlier distorted views of forecasters, salespeople, and pundits—many of whom were middle-aged baby-boomer parents of perplexing Generation X offspring.

The matures grew up during the Depression and World War II, which shaped their values, economic behavior, and general outlook on life. Baby-boomers grew up in an affluent society—the "me generation." They took economic progress for granted, allowing them to focus on idealism and personal growth and to engage in conspicuous consumption to satisfy materialistic desires during their earlier years. In contrast, Xers endured the recession of the 1980s, the 1987 stock market crash, and the recession of 1990–1991—causing them to believe they could never assume success. Smith and Clurman, in their book *Rocking the Ages*, blame the Xers' woes on their baby-boomer parents: "Forget what the idealistic boomers intended, Xers say, and look instead at what they actually did: Divorce. Latchkey kids. Homelessness. Soaring national debt. Bankrupt Social Security. Holes in the ozone layer. Crack. Downsizing and layoffs. Urban deterioration. Gangs. Junk bonds. . . ." The climate of the 1980s and 1990s has left its mark on the members of this generation—economic, psychological, and concerned—but they are energetic and competitive. The Yankelovich poll results indicate that a vast majority likes to compete because it makes them perform better. Most of those polled like extreme sports and believe they have to take what they can get in this world because no one else is going to give it to them. They identify more with success than integrity, even if they sometimes have to compromise their principles.

How did the sneaker makers, brewers, car manufacturers, and other marketers misjudge the Generation X market? A managing partner at

TBWA Chiat/Day offers an explanation: "The baby-boomers of the media and marketing world were desperate to explain a generation they didn't understand, so they reduced Xers to a cartoon. . . . It may be the most expensive mistake in history." A Washington "think tank" conducted another survey that showed that nearly three-fourths of 18- to 24-year-olds believe their generation "has an important voice, but no one seems to hear it." Their perception of how older generations viewed them was "lazy," "confused," and "unfocused." In contrast, they viewed themselves as "ambitious," "determined," and "independent." How would you describe and reach this important market segment?

Source: Margot Hornblower, "Great X-pectations: Slackers? Hardly. The So-Called Generation X Turns Out to Be Full of Go-getters Who Are Just Doing It—But Their Way," *Time* (June 9, 1997), pp. 58–69.

through geographic segmentation where many similar customers are located in close proximity. It is more efficient and cost-effective to serve this type of market, particularly when a high level of service is required or when shipping high-volume or heavy goods that have a low unit value. Industry concentrations also provide opportunities for related businesses that locate in the same area to sell goods and services to the primary industry.

Overseas market segments can be analyzed according to geographic characteristics, usually considered with other variables such as economic conditions or population size. For example, manufacturers of bulldozers, dump trucks, and other construction equipment experienced strong sales gains during Europe's economic recovery in the mid-1990s. Sales growth in heavy construction equipment spurred investment in manufacturing plants, new product development, and other new business opportunities in Europe.[10]

Behavioral and Situational Descriptors.   Organizational customers for many products can be classified on the basis of technology, such as high-tech/low-tech, innovative, or conservative. The types of products desired and the ways they are marketed differ among these segments. For example, a telecommunications company that markets integrative systems will likely have more potential customers among high-tech, innovative firms that desire state-of-the-art connectivity with employees and customers.

It is useful to identify the heavy, medium, and light users, as well as the nonusers, of a product. The marketing effort then can be focused on selling additional goods and services to the heavy users (while rewarding them for their purchases), increasing sales to medium and light users, and converting nonusers to users. Related to users' demand level is usage rate and frequency and order size. Customers who use a product rapidly, purchase frequently, and buy in large quantities offer economies of scale and profitability.

Other behavioral and situational dimensions for business markets include variables related to the customer's organization. It is important to know how the buying process is carried out, starting with the structure of the buying organization and identification of the appropriate buying unit, such as a buying committee or a purchasing agent. The organization may be centralized or decentralized, which means the actual purchasing may be done in one central location or buying responsibility may be dispersed throughout a number of geographic locations. Further, the organization's purchasing policies may affect segmentation decisions, such as whether its purchasing is done through sealed bids, selections are made from a list of preferred providers, or there is an existing close relationship between the customer and supplier. In terms of targeting a particular buying unit, it may be useful to segment on the basis of who has the most influence on purchase decisions. These individuals may be production or marketing personnel, technical experts in the area, or others. They may or may not be the final decision maker, but they may be targeted because of their influence on the purchasing process.

The situation in which purchases are made, the type of purchase, and the customer's state of readiness to buy also can be used to select market segments. Buying situations include the nature of the purchase, that is, whether it is a routine stock refill or a complex purchase involving more extensive decision making, whether it is a new application or technology, and whether the product is customized for the buyer. In addition, segments may be selected on the basis of customers' readiness to buy the product, such as those who are fully informed and desire to buy the product immediately versus those who are unaware or poorly informed about its benefits. Homeowners in Florida who are concerned about an impending hurricane season are ready and anxious to buy disaster supplies such as plywood to cover windows, flashlights, and bottled water. Suppliers can target manufacturers, and manufacturers can target retailers that cater to these concerned homeowners with appropriate product assortments, timely deliveries, and sales efforts targeted toward specific customer buying situations.

Psychological and Psychographic Descriptors.   These variables may apply to the individual or group that makes the final buying decision or may reflect the characteristics or culture of the organization as a whole. Attitudes toward the product, brand, or seller can provide insights for segmentation, including attitudes toward risk, innovation, economic motives, and so forth. Knowledge of customer groups that exhibit similar attitudes makes it possible to design a marketing program tailored to each group. The degree of loyalty that customers exhibit toward a company also provides a useful segmentation dimension. For instance, segments may be identified according to whether they are loyal, repeat buyers or have negative or indifferent attitudes toward the company and its products.

Although more difficult to isolate as a segmentation variable, personal traits of the person(s) responsible for making a purchase are considered for organizational customers just as they are for consumers. Personal characteristics include factors such as decision-making style, experience related to the purchase, and knowledge of the product category and its application.

Benefits Sought.   Some of the benefits most frequently sought by organizational customers include value (defined as low price and high quality), service, and delivery. Customers can be segmented on the basis of economic motives and price sensitivity. An expensive, high-fashion apparel manufacturer would consider retailers such as Neiman Marcus to be a more desirable market segment than discounters such as Kmart. An important selling point for many suppliers is the ability to provide goods and services that can cut costs and enhance the bottom line. As products become more complex and businesses outsource more functions, the availability of service before, during, and after the sale becomes a key factor in making a purchase decision. This is particularly true in high-tech markets where customers may be grouped according to the need for a service representative or on-site consultant as part of the sales deal.

Logistics represent a major expense for many firms, making transportation costs and convenience another important benefit for customers. Segments can be identified according to delivery distances from distribution centers, order quantity or dollar value to qualify for delivery services, and so forth. Many companies open new factories or distribution centers to serve new markets. Others may expand their target market by using rapid-response commercial delivery services. FedEx, for example, warehouses repair parts for certain customers in its centrally located facility in Memphis, Tennessee.

Combining Variables to Identify Segments

From the many possible variables that can be used to segment a larger market into smaller groups, there is no one variable that is comprehensive enough to do this effectively. The segmentation process must start with the most important dimension(s) that will provide a starting point for further analysis of the market. The next step is to continue to refine the market definition with a series of predictive variables, until this is no longer useful. For example, a firm that develops computer software for production-line applications may start by gathering data for a specific industry, such as automotive manufacturing. The focus would become narrower based on variables that predict purchase, such as geographic location relative to the rest of the industry, company size, level of technology and acceptance of software innovations, specific types of software applications needed, and the software developer's ability to provide the desired benefits.

While individual segments are selected on the basis of unique dimensions that distinguish one group from another, the company must be able to manage multiple segments simultaneously. The software developer just described also may target auto parts manufacturers, computer hardware manufacturers, and farm equipment manufacturers. The basic software product may be customized to meet the needs of each target market, but the marketing efforts would need to be tailored to each group. Smaller segments can be combined into a larger segment where there are sufficient similarities, and synergies can be obtained for marketing activities such as similar promotional media, distribution channels, salesforce coverage, or manufacturing processes.

International Implications of Market Segmentation

The increased globalization of markets brings new approaches to international market segmentation. Rather than consider an individual country as a single segment with similar needs and wants, marketers find it more meaningful to identify similarities among consumers across multiple international markets. One segment that has attracted the attention of marketers is the teenagers of the world, who have a similar desire for products that symbolize an American Western lifestyle. From country-western bars in Berlin to rock music in Tokyo, teenagers are responding to global marketing appeals.

Vivendi, formerly Compagnie Ge'ne'rale des Eaux, is a world leader in environmental services and a major European communications and construction business with annual sales of $35 billion ($2 billion in the United States). Vivendi segments the global market on the basis of customers' needs for improvement in quality of life by offering its services to 90 countries in the areas of pure water, energy, transport systems, waste management, construction and property, communications, and telecommunications. Vivendi's customer segments share similar needs across national boundaries for each of these service lines.[11]

Technology and Marketing Intelligence as Segmentation Tools

Segmentation decisions require an in-depth knowledge of the market, gained from marketing research and the company's marketing intelligence (MIS) and decision support (MDSS) systems. We are entering the twenty-first century with more personal information about customers than ever before. Databases provide highly specialized details about all participants in the market, as discussed in Chapter 4. Information technology capabilities make it possible to process huge amounts of data and analyze them with complex statistical procedures quickly and efficiently. Target market selection depends on the ability to convert these data into information and information into knowledge that will enable wise decisions based on demand forecasts for each market segment.

Management Tools

A number of management tools provide inputs for segmentation decisions, including psychographic and geodemographic methods.

VALS. VALS™ (Values and Lifestyles), from SRI Consulting is a frequently used consumer lifestyle and psychographic classification system. VALS taps relatively enduring psychological characteristics and several key demographics to classify consumers into eight groups with distinctive mindsets. Two concepts are key to understanding the VALS scheme: self-orientation (principle-, status-, and action-oriented) and resources. The self-orientation describes the patterns of attitudes and activities that help people reinforce, sustain, or modify their social identities. Resources (age, education, income, health, self-confidence) reflect the individual's ability to express his or her self-orientation. The eight VALS consumer groups are depicted in Figure 7.3. Through a partnership with Simmons, NY, about 20,000 U.S. adults are surveyed to identify their product, service and media preferences and VALS-type. GeoVALS™ provides estimates of the percentages of the VALS groups by zip code and block group. JapanVALS™ is a system developed specifically for Japan.[12]

PRIZM and GLOBAL SCAN. Two popular systems of geolifestyle or geodemographic analysis are the PRIZM (Potential Rating Index by Zip Market) system from Claritas Inc. and GLOBAL SCAN system from Backer Spielvogel Bates Worldwide (BSBW). The rationale for using geodemographic analysis to segment markets is that people who share similar cultural backgrounds, socioeconomic status, and perspectives tend to gravitate to the same neighborhoods. Over time, these individuals tend to emulate their neighbors, adopting similar social values, preferences, expectations, and consumer buying behaviors.

The PRIZM system can profile every neighborhood in the United States in terms of 62 lifestyle clusters organized into 12 broad social groups, each having similar within-group lifestyles but with heterogeneity between groups. PRIZM does not measure values and attitudes.[13]

FIGURE 7.3

VALS Consumer Lifestyle Segments

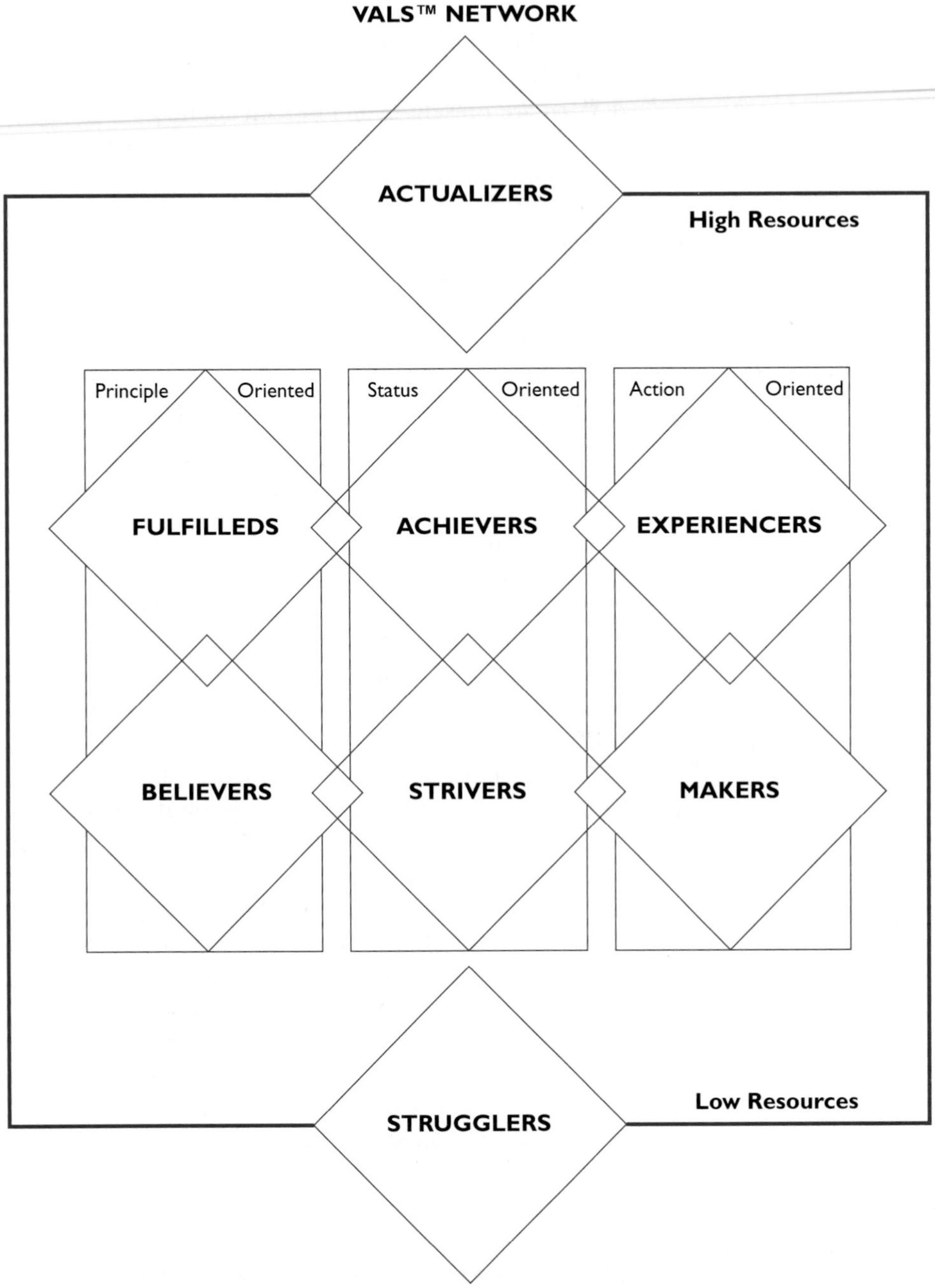
VALS™ NETWORK
ACTUALIZERS
High Resources
Principle
Oriented
Status
Oriented
Action
Oriented
FULFILLEDS
ACHIEVERS
EXPERIENCERS
BELIEVERS
STRIVERS
MAKERS
Low Resources
STRUGGLERS

Source: SRI Consulting. ©1999 SRI Consulting. All rights reserved. Unauthorized reproduction prohibited. VALS™ is a trademark of SRI International.

Although VALS and PRIZM are oriented toward the United States, BSBW's GLOBAL SCAN extends lifestyle analysis beyond the United States. Each year GLOBAL SCAN surveys 15,000 consumers in fourteen countries to measure over

250 value and attitude components, in addition to buying preferences, media usage, and demographics. GLOBAL SCAN is based on three critical factors: nationality, demographics, and values and their relative importance. Core values are intrinsic to a person's identity and inherent beliefs, go much deeper than behavior or attitude, and are more enduring over the long term. From the survey data, BSBW can identify five global lifestyle segments (strivers, achievers, pressured, adapters, and traditionals) that are present in all fourteen countries, although the proportion in each category may vary by individual country. Marketers can use lifestyle analysis to develop cross-cultural marketing strategies tailored to those lifestyle segments that cut across cultures. For example, the median age of GLOBAL SCAN's "strivers" is 31 years. They are young people living hectic lives; they work hard to achieve success, but they have difficulty meeting their goals. They are further characterized as materialistic, seeking pleasure and instant gratification, and seeking convenience in all aspects of their lives because they are short of time, money, and energy.[14]

ETHICAL ISSUES IN MARKET SEGMENTATION

The decision to focus marketing efforts on one or more groups of customers can raise a number of ethical and social responsibility issues. The nature of target marketing is that some customers are "in" and some are "out" of the group. This can present an ethical dilemma, as witnessed by the social pressures and long legal battles faced by the tobacco industry during the 1990s over the targeting of cigarette ads to children and minorities. The beer and alcohol industries have faced similar public censure for targeting underage drinkers, minorities, and "winos" with their promotional programs.

The R.J. Reynolds Tobacco Co. (RJR) planned to introduce Uptown cigarettes to the market in 1989, targeted toward black smokers. Although RJR's research supported this product introduction, RJR canceled plans for the cigarette because of a public outcry against Uptown and its planned advertising campaigns. Likewise, Heileman Brewing Co. targeted PowerMaster, an extrastrong malt liquor, toward its heavy users—blacks in low-income neighborhoods. An industry commentator said, "The category was developed for a consumer who wanted a fast buzz, so the advertising plays that up." When Heileman announced plans to introduce PowerMaster, it caused an uproar among antialcohol groups and black leaders. They expressed deep concerns about the targeting of this malt liquor toward communities that suffered disproportionately from alcohol and other drug problems. PowerMaster was withdrawn from the market. Although the underlying rationale for the Uptown and PowerMaster strategies was carefully thought out and executed by the firms, their target marketing practices were severely criticized by the public. Research conducted by Smith and Cooper-Martin[15] to determine ethical concerns related to target marketing found that consumers' criticisms are greatest when the targeted customers are particularly vulnerable and/or the product is particularly harmful.

Positioning
Customer perceptions of a product image or benefits that distinguish it from the competition; it's what you do to the mind of the prospect, not what you do to the product.

POSITIONING STRATEGIES

Just what is **positioning?** The concept of positioning was introduced and made popular by Ries and Trout, whose classic definition states, "Positioning starts with a product. A piece of merchandise, a service, a company, an institution, or even a person. Perhaps yourself. But positioning is not what you do to a product. Positioning is what you do to the mind of the prospect. That is, you position the product in the mind of the prospect. So it's incorrect to call the concept 'product positioning.' You're not really doing something to the product itself."[16]

Positioning versus Differentiation

Product positioning often is confused with segmentation and product differentiation. The concepts are related but not identical. Positioning refers to customer perceptions of a product image or benefits that distinguish it from the competition. A widely accepted view of **product differentiation** is that it refers to the product itself, where the product offer includes features that are different from the usual offerings of competitors. Differentiation may be on the basis of physical differences such as special product enhancements or additional services included with the product or other characteristics that give the company a competitive edge. Another view of differentiation is related to marketing communications, where advertising messages, packaging, and other marketing tactics are used to make the company's product appear superior to that of the competition. Others relate product differentiation to segmentation strategies, that is, offering different products to different market segments.

Product differentiation
Refers to enhancing the product itself with special features, additional services, or other characteristics.

The Positioning Process

The positioning process consists of a set of key elements that provide a foundation for designing the marketing mix consistent with the chosen market-segmentation strategy.

- Identify the target market(s) to be pursued.

- Determine the specific customer needs, wants, and benefits desired by each target market.

- Analyze the attributes and perceived images of each present and potential competitor in each target market.

- Compare your position and that of competitors on each important dimension desired by customers. (This may be done using a technique called *perceptual mapping,* as shown in Figure 7.4.)

- Identify a unique position that offers a combination of benefits that are desirable to the target market and that are not offered by competitors.

- Design a marketing program that will persuade customers that there are good reasons to buy from the communicating firm rather than from its competitors.

- Continue to assess and reassess present and potential target markets and competitors, as well as the marketing efforts to reach them.

- Continue to monitor the market for segments with unmet needs where there is an opportunity for your firm to introduce a better offering that will displace, or replace, present competitors.

FIGURE 7.4

Perceptual Mapping and Positioning Decisions

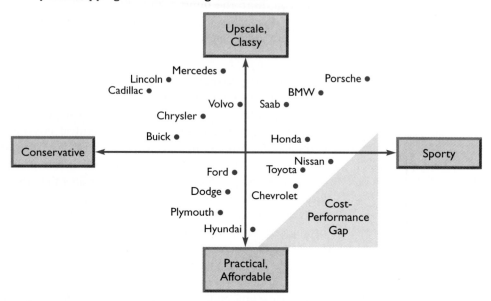

Source: Alexander Hiam and Charles D. Schewe, *The Portable MBA in Marketing* (New York: John Wiley & Sons, 1992), p. 227. Copyright ©1992 by John Wiley & Sons. Reprinted by permission of John Wiley & Sons, Inc.

Customer Value and Positioning

Value proposition
Part of the positioning strategy, how the organization plans to deliver superior value to its customers; the image that marketers want customers to have of their product, brand, or company.

Webster[17] extends the definition of positioning to include **value proposition,** or the way that the organization plans to deliver superior value to customers. The positioning statement—or value proposition—is the result of the strategic decision-making, analytical, conceptual, and creative processes that put into words the image that marketers want customers to have of their product, brand, or company. The positioning statement becomes the selling proposition to prospective customers, offering a reason to buy the company's product rather than that of competitors. The value-proposition concept focuses on creating customer value and goes beyond the classic definition that positioning is based solely on communication. The value statement also can be used internally to communicate to the entire organization the reason they are in business, thus focusing everyone's efforts on a common purpose of satisfying the targeted customers. Long-term, sustainable competitive advantage can be realized from the positioning statement if the organization's resources, knowledge, and skills support it. The value proposition or positioning statement addresses three questions:[18]

1. *Who is the target customer?* (Defined in the market-segmentation process.)

2. *Why should the customer buy?* (Benefits to customer, why company's product is superior to competitors.)

3. *What are we selling?* (Definition of the product from the viewpoint of the customer.)

Volkswagen used nostalgia symbols to position its new Volkswagen Beetle with the tag line "Less flower. More power" and a bud vase "perfect for a daisy plucked straight from the 1960s" built into the dashboard. The position is a combination of romance and reason—modern convenience in an old-style package. The original Beetle was the first car driven by many baby-boomers and an icon of the 1960s. Baby-boomers are again the primary target market, and the appeal of the Beetle is both emotional and economical. From the perspective of today's target market, the car is positioned as an inexpensive-to-own, fun-to-drive symbol of baby-boomer youth in the "Age of Aquarius"—an era of rebellion against conventions.

Creative problem-solving techniques can be applied to answering six questions posed by Trout and Ries[19] for those wanting to apply positioning thinking to a brand or company:

1. *What position, if any, do we already own in the prospect's mind?* (This should be determined from the marketplace. Spend the money for research, if needed.)

2. *What position do we want to own?* (Use creative problem solving and the best information available to determine the best position from a long-term point of view.)

3. *What companies must be outgunned if we are to establish this position?* (Try to select a position that no other company "owns" rather than going head-to-head against a market leader.)

4. *Do we have enough money to occupy and hold the position?* (Do not try to achieve the impossible without sufficient money to establish a position—and to hold it.)

5. *Do we have the guts to stick with one consistent positioning concept?* (Having few but strong marketing programs provides consistency for the positioning statement and makes more efficient use of the marketing budget.)

6. *Does our creative approach match our positioning strategy?* (The positioning strategy should drive the creative strategy, such as advertising, etc., not the other way around.)

Key Variables for Positioning

A number of approaches can be used to position a company's product in the minds of consumers. Each approach must take into consideration the nature of the customer, the product, and the unique selling proposition that will set the company's product apart from its competitors.[20] Some of the most common positioning strategies are based on attributes of the product or brand, price and quality, use or application, product user, product class, or competitor. Since positioning is customer-focused, another approach that is used successfully involves positioning by benefits, problem solutions, or basic needs.

Positioning on Product Attributes.   A frequently used positioning strategy is to associate a company's product or brand with an attribute or product feature. The simplest approach is to select one dimension that is most important to customers, such as toothpaste that fights cavities. However, some companies choose more than one dimension in order to attract more customers. In addition to being positioned as a cavity fighter, Crest's positioning strategy for its toothpaste includes the benefits of tartar control, cleaning power, and taste. Marketers are cautioned, however, that positioning on too many attributes can lead to a confused image of the product and can detract from a unique selling proposition.

Positioning on Price and Quality.   Price indicates quality for many consumers and relates to perceptions of value received. High quality at a fair (not necessarily the lowest) price indicates excellent value. Higher prices also can signal a higher level of service and performance when the customer finds it difficult to judge quality. Gasoline prices are consistent with octane levels or expected quality of performance. Theater seating is priced according to the desirability of seat locations. The Ferrari automobile is positioned as a luxury sports car. Higher prices of organically grown foods indicate higher-quality, more healthful produce.

Positioning on Use or Application.   Products can be positioned according to the way they are used by customers. Many products are positioned according to a special use, such as laundry detergents that contain bleach for extra cleaning power, Arm & Hammer baking soda as an odor-killer in refrigerators, or legal services that focus on international law. Successful positioning strategies focus on a unique selling proposition, but this may be extended to multiple uses. For instance, baking soda is used not only for cooking but also for relief from insect bites and as an ingredient in many industrial and consumer products to enhance their performance.

Positioning by Product User.   This strategy involves associating the product with a class of customers who use the product, perhaps by using a celebrity endorser who symbolizes the attributes of the product. Nike sells athletic shoes to multiple market segments using a desire to enhance athletic performance (or status for owning the shoes that are icons of this accomplishment) as a selling proposition.

Positioning on Product Class.   Product class associations are used to position a product with both direct and indirect competitors, such as healthy drinking "waters" like Evian, Perrier, and Clearly Canadian or sports utility vehicles like the Ford Explorer, Chevy Blazer, Jeep Cherokee, and Nissan Pathfinder.

Positioning Against Competitors.   Competitive positioning is considered in all positioning strategies, but explicit reference to a particular competitor can take advantage of an entrenched position. Avis, Inc., a car rental company, "tries harder" than first-place Hertz Corp. Amazon.com, the pioneer Internet bookseller, is positioned as a high-tech competitor against other book retailers like Barnes & Noble Inc. or Waldenbooks.

Positioning by Benefits, Problem Solutions, or Basic Needs.   The growth of ethnic diversity in the United States has brought with it the challenge of serving customers whose lifestyles, languages, and buying preferences may be very different from an organization's existing customer base. Banks, among other businesses, have extended their target markets to include the special needs of ethnic and minority populations. MetroBank, founded by Taiwanese Americans in 1987, is one of the fastest growing banks in Houston, Texas. MetroBank is positioned as a banker for a multicultural client base, in recognition of the mutual problems—and mutual opportunities—shared by newcomers to America. The bank has been able to capitalize on the swiftly changing demographics of the nation's fourth largest city by carving out a special niche with pent-up demand for banking services.[21]

Summary

One of the most important strategic choices any organization can make is choosing the customers it wants to serve. This decision defines the scope of the business and provides direction for marketing programs. An organization can use a mass-marketing approach to serve everyone in the market. This strategy is advisable where customers' needs and wants are similar across the market, goods and services can be standardized, and customers can be expected to respond in similar fashion to marketing programs. Alternatively, an organization can choose to serve one or more distinctively different segments of the market—a single- or multisegment approach. Each segment has its own distinctive needs and wants and requires a specialized marketing approach. Niche marketing and one-to-one marketing are two approaches to single-segment markets.

Steps in the market-segmentation process include market definition and analysis, segment identification and description, segment selection, product positioning strategy, and marketing program design and implementation. Criteria for effective segmentation include segments that are identifiable, measurable, and reachable. The segment also must be large enough to be profitable, customers must be responsive to the company's offer, and segment characteristics should be relatively stable over time. Commonly used quantitative bases for segmenting consumer markets include demographic, socioeconomic, and geographic data.

These data usually are combined with relevant qualitative information such as behavioral, situational, psychographic, and psychological descriptors, as well as the benefits or satisfactions sought by customers. Organizational markets are segmented on many of the same dimensions, but specific variables are selected for their predictability and marketing applications within a business-to-business context.

Segmentation can be viewed from a global perspective. Rather than consider each country as an individual segment, marketers look for similarities among customers across multiple international markets. Technological advances facilitate the segmentation process through databases and marketing intelligence capabilities. Likewise, customers' level of technology is itself an important segmentation variable. Ethical issues in target marketing focus primarily on the exploitation of vulnerable customers and the sale of harmful products.

Positioning strategies are used to differentiate a firm's offering from that of the competition. Positioning is not what you do to the product; it is your place in the mind of the customers. The process starts with the customer value proposition that addresses three key questions: Who is the target customer? Why should the customer buy? What are we selling? Variables that are used frequently for positioning include product attributes, price and quality, use or application, product user, product class, positioning against competitors, and positioning by benefits, problem solutions, or basic needs.

Questions

1. Describe the role of market segmentation in an overall marketing strategy. Illustrate with a specific example.

2. Discuss the different approaches to target marketing and the conditions where each approach is appropriate.

3. Explain the process that you would follow when determining a market-segmentation strategy for a new line of exercise equipment. Would the process be different for the services of a nonprofit disaster relief organization? Justify your answer.

4. What specific criteria were used to select the most attractive market segments discussed in Question 3? Explain the rationale for using these criteria.

5. Assume you are the marketing manager for a line of home entertainment equipment. Discuss the impact of the segmentation variables described in the text on your selection of the most attractive consumer and organizational markets to target, including:

   a. Changing demographics and buying behavior (e.g., gender influences, age groups, income, education).

   b. Changing geographic influences (e.g., population movement, population density, climate, international).

   c. Changing behavioral and situational influences (e.g., ways of shopping, value equation, time, awareness, brand loyalty).

   d. Changing psychographic and psychological factors (e.g., lifestyles, motivation, attitudes).

   e. Changing preferences for benefits (e.g., convenience, economy, self-improvement, relaxation, challenge).

Exercises

1. Find examples in the media that illustrate the relationship among market segmentation, target marketing, and positioning. This may be in the form of an article, television program, advertisement, packaging, or other format. Critique the way this relationship is represented in the source selected. What would you do differently? Why?

2. (a) Analyze population data in a representative source such as U.S. Census Bureau reports, the *Statistical Abstract of the United States*, or other government documents to determine major population shifts that are occurring in the United States. Interpret your findings relative to market projections for a specific good or service that might be useful in developing a target marketing strategy. (b) Analyze industry data to determine trends occurring in one or more organizational markets, using government or trade association data sources. Interpret your findings relative to market projections for a specific good or service that might be useful in developing a target marketing strategy.

3. Using personal or media sources, develop and conduct a survey to determine the role of the following in segmentation strategy decisions:

   a. Global economy

   b. Technology

   c. Changes in the marketplace related specifically to a company or its products

   d. Ethics and social responsibility

   e. Innovation

   f. Other contemporary issues

Endnotes

1. David Edelman, Carlos Bhola, and Andrew Feller, "Keeping Up With the 'e-Generation,'" *Marketing News* 31(18) (September 1, 1997), p. 2.

2. Frederick E. Webster, Jr., *Market-Driven Management: Using the New Marketing Concept to Create a Customer-Oriented Company* (New York: John Wiley & Sons, 1994), pp. 95–96.

3. Angelo B. Henderson, "The Wheelchair Turns Hip as New Generation of User Demands Style," *Wall Street Journal* (September 28, 1995), pp. A1, A11.

4. Susan Greco, "The Road to One-to-One Marketing," *Inc.* (October 1995), pp. 56–66; also see Don Peppers and Martha Rogers, *The One to One Future: Building Relationships One Customer at a Time* (New York: Currency Doubleday, 1993).

5. Greco, *ibid.,* p. 58; and elsewhere.

6. Gregory A. Patterson, "Target 'Micromarkets' Its Way to Success; No 2 Stores Are Alike," *Wall Street Journal* (May 31, 1995), pp. A1, A8.

7. Rahul Jacob, "The Big Rise: Middle Classes Explode Around the Globe, Bringing New Markets and New Prosperity," *Fortune* (May 30, 1994), pp. 74–90.

8. Edelman, Bhola, and Feller, *op. cit.*

9. David Leonhardt and Wendy Zellner, "Airlines Raise Their Class Consciousness," *Business Week* (February 23, 1998), p. 40.

10. Greg Steinmetz, "Europe Is Becoming Solid Ground for Earth Movers," *Wall Street Journal* (May 3, 1995), p. B3.

11. Vivendi Advertisement, *Business Week* (June 22, 1998), pp. 118–121.

12. For further discussion, see T. P. Novak and B. MacEvoy, "On Comparing Alternative Segmentation Schemes," *Journal of Consumer Research* (June 1990), pp. 105–109; M. F. Riche, "Psychographics for the 1990s," *American Demographics* (July 1989), pp. 25ff; Values and Lifestyles Program, *Descriptive Materials for the VALS2 Segmentation System* (Menlo Park, CA: SRI International, 1989); and Del I.

Hawkins, Roger J. Best, and Kenneth A. Coney, *Consumer Behavior: Building Marketing Strategy,* 7th ed. (New York: McGraw-Hill, 1998), pp. 438–445.

13. Hawkins, Best, and Coney, *ibid.,* pp. 445–446; and Tom Miller, "Global Segments from 'Strivers' to 'Creatives,'" *Marketing News* 32(15) (July 20, 1998), p. 11.

14. Hawkins, Best, and Coney, *op. cit.,* pp. 447–449.

15. Craig N. Smith and Elizabeth Cooper-Martin, "Ethics and Target Marketing: The Role of Product Harm and Consumer Vulnerability," *Journal of Marketing* 61(3) (July 1997), pp. 1–20.

16. Jack Trout and Al Ries, *Positioning: The Battle for Your Mind* (New York: Warner Books, 1986), p. 2.

17. Webster, *op. cit.,* pp. 106–108.

18. *Ibid.,* pp. 107–108.

19. Jack Trout and Al Ries, "The Future of Positioning," *AMA Marketing Encyclopedia: Issues and Trends Shaping the Future,* edited by Jeffrey Heilbrunn (Chicago: American Marketing Association, 1995), pp. 51–52.

20. See David A. Aaker and J. Gary Shansby, "Positioning Your Product," *Business Horizons* 24(3) (May–June 1981), pp. 56–62; and Alexander Hiam and Charles D. Schewe, *The Portable MBA in Marketing* (New York: John Wiley & Sons, 1992), pp. 223–226.

21. Rick Wartzman, "How Tiny MetroBank Wins Big by Catering to an Ethnic Market," *Wall Street Journal* (January 15, 1996), pp. A1, A7.

PART THREE

Implementing Marketing-Mix Strategies

8. **Product Strategy**
9. **Services Marketing Strategy**
10. **Distribution Strategy**
11. **Integrated Marketing Communications Strategy**
12. **Integrated Marketing Communications Tools**
13. **Direct Marketing**
14. **Pricing Strategy**

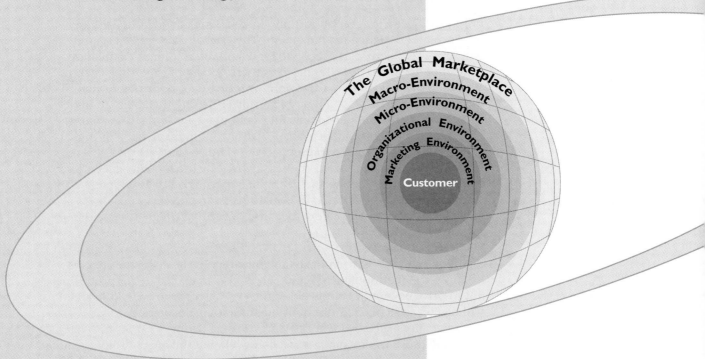

The Global Marketplace
Macro-Environment
Micro-Environment
Organizational Environment
Marketing Environment
Customer

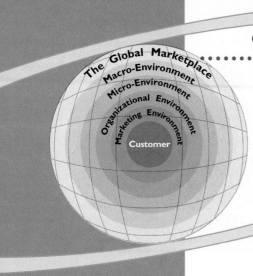

CHAPTER 8

Product Strategy

What Is a Product?

Classification of Goods

Product Strategy Issues

The Product Life Cycle

Test Marketing

Launching New Products

Brand Strategies

There is nothing more difficult to take in hand, more perilous to conduct, or more uncertain in its success, than to take the lead in the introduction of a new order of things.[1]

Creating Customer Satisfaction: USAA Responds to Change with a New Product

In July of 1998, USAA (a San Antonio insurer) introduced Choice Ride—a new product designed for the elderly. This "product" is really a service whereby the elderly can choose to be chauffeured to their destinations instead of having to drive themselves there. As people age, they eventually reach the stage where their sight or reflexes, or both, deteriorate to the point where they should no longer drive. Losing the ability to drive equates to losing independence and freedom for most elderly persons.

True, they can use public transportation, but in many parts of the country the public transportation system is not well developed, has restricted route coverage, and is not easily used by the mobility-challenged elderly—especially for short trips to the supermarket or convenience store or to out-of-the-ordinary destinations. Even taxi service is not viewed favorably by the elderly because of relatively high costs and frequent driver surliness.

Choice Ride customers pay $1,080 in advance every 3 months and in that time can take 30 round trips to anywhere in the coverage area, for example, the metropolitan Orlando area. Also, in exchange for promising not to drive except in emergencies, the customers who are still insurable will receive a 90 percent discount on automobile insurance.

Janice Marshall, president of USAA Alliance Services Co., a subsidiary that handles USAA's member services, developed the idea of Choice Ride because she dealt with seniors who had so many accidents and violations that the company could no longer insure them. And since no other company was likely to insure them, Ms. Marshall was essentially telling them they could no longer drive their own automobiles.

Ms. Marshall realized that USAA and the auto insurance industry in general did not offer any alternative services to the elderly and had not gone beyond offering discounts to seniors who take driver-improvement classes. Instead, most efforts had gone into more punitive measures, such as identifying high-risk drivers as they grow older. These initiatives may clear the road of some dangerous drivers, but they also sentence many seniors to a life of isolation. "It's a death penalty for a lot of them," says Susan Ferguson, vice-president of research at the Insurance Institute for Highway Safety in Arlington, Virginia. No place illustrates the need for mobility programs for the elderly more than Florida, which already has 1.6 million drivers over age 70. And Florida's sprawling suburban development and lack of mass transit make it virtually impossible to get around without a car.

"We clearly don't have adequate alternatives to driving, and as baby-boomers grow old, we are going to have an even bigger problem," says John Eberhard, senior research psychologist at the National Highway Traffic Safety Administration in Washington, D.C.

USAA's appeal is that Choice Ride costs less. It cites an AAA Auto Club estimate that says people spend $5,500 a year to operate their automobile.

Source: Adapted from Chad Thurhune, "Insurer Offers Seniors an Alternative to Driving," *Wall Street Journal,* (May 13, 1998), pp. A1, A3; and personal mail-out from USAA during May 1998.

As illustrated by the Choice Ride example, the product often is the principal means by which a company provides consumer satisfaction. Sometimes, the package in which a product is contained may satisfy a need for convenience or safety, such as a plastic container for shampoo. The brand identity of a product also can add meaning—perhaps assurance or social status. The seller of a product may include a service, such as delivery or financing. All these things enhance the consumers' satisfaction and are, by definition, part of the company's product strategy. At the corporate level, product strategy is the engine that drives the rest of the marketing strategy; without it, there is nothing to distribute, nothing to promote, nothing to price. At the divisional level, product strategy is equally important as the basis for divisional overall marketing strategy and marketing activities. From a tactical viewpoint, product offerings determine the remainder of the marketing-mix aspects of distribution, pricing, and communication plans and actions.

WHAT IS A PRODUCT?

Product
A physical commodity or an idea, cause, or other intangible that provides customer satisfaction.

The term **product** refers not only to a physical commodity but also to anything offered by an organization to provide customer satisfaction. A product can be a single commodity, a group of commodities, a product-service combination, or even a combination of several tangible goods and intangible services. Or a product can be an idea, a cause, or any other intangible factor that satisfies customers of nonprofit or for-profit organizations.

Theodore Levitt was one of the first to suggest a useful term to describe this concept of a product:[2] the *augmented product,* which is the aggregate of physical, psychological, and sociologic satisfactions that a buyer obtains. When an industrial marketer sells a major item of machinery, the product may be augmented in several ways. A small electric motor manufacturer may (1) provide financing, (2) ensure a constant supply of maintenance and replacement parts, (3) guarantee the performance of the motors for a specified period of time, (4) make technicians available to advise customers on the installation and use of the motors, and (5) train the customer personnel who actually will operate the motors. The customer does not simply buy an electric motor; the customer purchases a core product augmented by financial, warranty, service, and training benefits.

CLASSIFICATION OF GOODS

A tradition of classifying goods and services exists in marketing. The two most commonly used classification schemes are those adopted by the American Marketing Association's Committee on Definitions. The first classification scheme applies to consumer goods and is based on purchasing patterns (i.e., convenience goods, shopping goods, and specialty goods).[3] The second classification scheme applies to both consumer and organizational goods and is based on the rate of consumption and tangibility (i.e., nondurable goods, durable goods, and services). The next sections will describe the particular attributes of consumer and organizational goods.

Consumer Goods: Convenience, Shopping, and Specialty Goods

Convenience goods
Consumer items purchased with a minimum outlay of time and effort.

Shopping goods
Consumer items purchased after comparison with other available offerings.

Specialty goods
Consumer items purchased for specific attributes after considerable effort.

Consumer goods can be classified into three subtypes: convenience goods, shopping goods, and specialty goods. (See Table 8.1.) **Convenience goods** are goods that the shopper desires to buy with a minimum outlay of time and effort. Items stocked in convenience stores typically include confections, bread, milk, beer and soda, cigarettes, and magazines. **Shopping goods** are goods that consumers wish to compare with other available offerings before making a selection. Household furnishings, clothing, and recreation equipment are in this group. **Specialty goods** are goods that buyers are willing to go to considerable lengths to seek out and purchase. Such goods may be custom made, or they simply may be very successfully differentiated products such as a high-performance tennis racquet or high-fashion designer apparel.

Organizational Goods

Organizational goods
Goods purchased by businesses in order to produce other goods or for operations.

Organizational goods are goods, such as chemicals, component parts, office supplies, and so on, that are purchased by businesses in order to produce other goods or for operating a business. Organizational goods, including those purchased by governments and nonprofit organizations, represent marketing opportunities that are as important as those for consumer goods. The methods of organizational marketing

TABLE 8.1
....
Classes of Consumer Goods—Some Characteristics and Marketing Considerations

	Type of Product		
	Convenience	**Shopping**	**Specialty**
Time and effort devoted by consumer to shopping	Very little	Considerable	Cannot generalize; consumer may go to nearby store and buy with minimum effort or may have to go to distant store and spend much time and effort
Time spent planning the purchase	Very little	Considerable	Considerable
How soon want is satisfied after it arises	Immediately	Relatively long time	Relatively long time
Are price and quality compared?	No	Yes	No
Price	Usually low per unit	High	High
Frequency of purchase	Usually frequent	Infrequent	Infrequent
Importance	Unimportant	Often very important	Cannot generalize
	Marketing Considerations		
Length of distribution channel	Long	Short	Short to very short
Importance of retailer	Any single store is relatively unimportant	Important	Very important
Number of outlets	As many as possible	Few	Few, often only one in a market
Stock turnover	High	Lower	Few; often only one in a market
Gross margin	Low	High	High
Responsibility for advertising	Producer's	Retailer's	Joint responsibility
Importance of point-of-purchase display	Very important	Less important	Less important
Brand or store name importance	Brand name	Store name	Both
Importance of packaging	Very important (silent salesperson)	Less important	Less important

Source: Adapted from William J. Stanton, Michael J. Etzel, and Bruce J. Walker, *Fundamentals of Marketing,* 9th ed., ©1991, New York, McGraw-Hill, Inc., pp. 171, 174. Used with permission of The McGraw-Hill Companies.

are somewhat specialized, but in general, the concepts presented in this book are valid for the organizational marketer as well as for the consumer goods marketer.

Agricultural, Other Extractive Products, Raw Materials.   Farms, forests, mines, and quarries provide raw materials. Most agricultural products and all extractive products undergo some processing before consumption. Demands for extractive products are derived from the demands for the goods into which they are transformed.

Manufactured Organizational Products.   Manufactured products are those which have undergone some processing. There are a number of specific types of manufactured organizational goods. *Semimanufactured goods* are raw materials that have gone through some stages of manufacturing but require further processing before they can be used. *Parts or components* are manufactured items that are ready to be incorporated into other products. *Process machinery or installations* are major pieces of equipment used in the manufacture of other goods. *Accessory equipment* involves lesser items of a productive nature. *Operating supplies* are materials used in the course of business that are destroyed or consumed in the process.

Unique Characteristics of Organizational Goods.   Organizational goods are different from consumer goods, although the basic nature of their marketing is similar. First, many organizational goods are highly technical products. Even a commodity-type product such as copper tubing is the result of highly sophisticated metallurgical and process research. Many organizational products are extremely expensive or are purchased in such large quantities that very large sums of money are involved. Organizational products, other than rapidly changing high-technology products, tend to have longer life expectancies than consumer products. Introductions often are slower paced, growth is achieved over a long period of time, and mature organizational products flourish for years before going into decline. Relatively few organizational products are perishable, although some, such as chemicals, do lose their purity or potency over time. Some organizational products are toxic, flammable, or dangerous in some other way; hence they require extremely careful handling in transit, storage, and use. Organizational products, far more than consumer goods, create serious environmental problems in waste disposal.

The Demand for Organizational Goods.   The demand for organizational products is derived—that is, it stems from the existence of a demand for something else. The demand for a machine tool exists because there is a demand for the item that the tool can make. There is a demand for oil rig replacement parts because there is a demand for crude petroleum. Derived demand tends to be highly cyclic, because relatively modest changes in final demand can drastically affect the derived demand.

For example, an industrial company that sells plastic injection-molding machines has a large customer that regularly buys about $150,000 of equipment for expansion and replacement of old machines. If this customer experiences a 15 percent decline in demand, the organization may decide not to increase capacity or to replace older machines. Instead of buying $150,000 of new molding equipment, it may buy only $50,000 worth. This 15 percent decline for the plastics manufacturer turns out to be a 66.7 percent decrease for the machinery company. Of course, if the customer's business were to increase by 15 percent, the equipment manufacturer's sales would be proportionately higher. Derived-demand relationships may result in drastic swings in the sales of organizational products—swings that make both forecasting and marketing planning very difficult.

The Marketing Mix for Organizational Goods.   The marketing-mix concept is applicable to organizational marketing. However, the character of the organizational marketing mix may be quite different from the consumer product marketing mix. Because organizational products are often complex and technical in order to meet rigid specifications established by industrial buyers, there is much more customizing of organizational products than of consumer products. This results in very broad product lines that reflect thousands of relatively minor differences in customers' requirements.

While new product development is important in organizational marketing, it often tends to be more technically driven than market directed. True, organizational product managers and sales personnel work closely with key customers in the development of new products to meet customers' needs, but a substantial number of ideas for new products are generated within the seller's research and development (R&D) and engineering departments.

Capital goods
Items categorized as business assets and capitalized for accounting purposes.

Organizational products often require extensive after-sale service. This is especially true of **capital goods,** such as stamping machinery, printing presses, or mainframe computers. Organizational products are often augmented products that include technical consultation, maintenance and repair service, and purchase financing.

The distribution channels for organizational goods are very specialized. This means that industrial companies may lose direct control of their products once they are sold. Many companies that sell through distributors do not know what happens to their products once they have been shipped from the factory. In part to overcome this problem, some industrial firms have acquired their own distributors. Others have used franchising or other contractual arrangements to establish some vertical control over their channels of distribution.

Organizational marketers make extensive use of personal selling and comparatively little use of mass communication. This may be the single most obvious difference between the consumer product marketing mix and the organizational marketing mix. Industrial firms do advertise, but the use of mass communication is limited, and the amounts of money spent on it are considerably less than in consumer goods marketing.

The pricing of organizational products is extremely complex, largely because of the many variations in customer status and product lines that are involved. In the extreme, a price is established for each transaction. Price is always subject to negotiation, even if the seller wants to establish some uniformity in the pricing approach. Reliance on a limited number of large customers (whether users or resellers) gives the buyer a great deal of bargaining power.

These differences in product, distribution, communications, and pricing strategies for the organizational marketer are important because they lead to different overall strategies than those used in consumer goods marketing. But the planning process by which the organizational marketing strategy is developed and the concepts on which the organizational marketing program are based are not fundamentally different.

PRODUCT STRATEGY ISSUES

Developing a product strategy is not easy. A number of elements are involved, and many appear to be hopelessly entangled. With a systematic approach to strategy design, these entanglements can be straightened out. First, the various issues involved in developing product strategy must be isolated and broken down into their components. By concentrating separately on each of these important issues, it is discovered that each is related to some other issue. The elements of product strategy are not terribly complicated, once these relationships are recognized. Developing product strategy becomes a process of making decisions about the individual issues that are discussed next.

Determining the Product Line

The basic question of paramount importance in developing product strategy is: What products should we sell? But the fundamental marketing opportunity is not to sell things but rather to provide satisfactions. Thus the question probably should be rephrased to: What satisfactions or benefits should we provide? In most organizations, satisfactions are delivered via products, services, or product-service combinations.

The first step in deciding what to sell is identification of a product's potential ultimate consumers through analysis of the marketing situation. The marketing strategist should then select the target market segment. Having identified the consumer, the product planner's second step is to determine the use (satisfaction) specifications that the product will have to meet. Unfortunately, this important step often is omitted. Product planners may be tempted to jump immediately to the design of product characteristics, which could be a critical mistake. Product designers need to know exactly what the product is supposed to do, how the product will be used, how often, and with what efficiency it is supposed to operate. From a marketing viewpoint, it is not as important to know what a product is capable of doing as it is to understand what consumers expect it to do and to create a "fit" between the two.

However, it is not sufficient simply to satisfy ultimate consumers. A product must provide satisfactions for wholesalers and retailers as well. These are not consumption satisfactions but reseller satisfactions. For a product to fit into a retail assortment, it must match the reseller's expectations in terms of inventory requirements, stock turnover, margin, packaging, and so forth. If it fails to meet these needs, the product will not be stocked.

The final step in answering the question of what products a company should sell involves matching both the customers and the resellers with appropriate product quality characteristics. Generally, product quality design involves developing three important characteristics: performance, cost, and appearance. These characteristics may affect both the product and its package. The form of a product (its specifications) should match its function, and its function is to satisfy consumers and resellers. It must do so profitably. This is the product's principal function from the manufacturer's viewpoint. In addition, other objectives may dictate product functions. For example, it may have to be made in existing facilities, or it may have to be designed to fit into a line of products. Or the products may have to meet legal or other constraints.

Determining the Width and Depth of a Product Line

Product mix
The composite of products a company offers.

Product line
Those items in the mix that are closely related.

Product width
Refers to how many different products are offered.

Product depth
Refers to how many items of each type are sold.

Line extension
Process of building either the depth or the width of a product offering.

Determining the appropriate product line means making decisions concerning the number of different items in each product line and the number of different lines to be handled. See, for example, Table 8.2. The composite of products a company offers is called its **product mix.** Those items in the mix that are closely related are referred to as a **product line.** For example, Procter & Gamble has an extensive mix of products ranging from beauty care to food and beverage and paper products. Its line of products is extensive and well illustrates the concepts of width and depth. **Product width** refers to how many different products are offered, and **product depth** defines how many items of each type are sold. Procter & Gamble's product line has a fairly broad width, with five major categories and twenty subcategories. Product depth varies within each category. For example, as indicated in the Laundry/Cleaning Products category in Table 8.2, the Laundry Cleaners category includes ten product brands, the Hard Surface Cleaners category includes four, and the Bleach category has only one.

The process of building either the depth or width of a product offering is **line extension.** Why should a company offer so many products? Is such diversity necessary? A consumer generally buys only one product at a time unless the products are complementary in nature. However, because different customers have different requirements, it may be necessary to offer a number of products in order to satisfy several different market segments.[4] This is obviously necessary when opening or entering a new market; however, it is not as easy as it might seem. Both Post Cereals and Quaker Oats Co. have introduced new lines of breakfast cereals to bolster stagnant sales of their established products.

However, the addition of new products cannot go on endlessly or the company may find that it is in competition with itself (referred to as *cannibalization*).[5] This can be done purposely, as when a new product is introduced as a substitute for an older one. Or it may be done to dominate a category by marketing two brands or products rather than just one. Ultimately, the manufacturer must decide on an optimal width and depth of line that is most profitable in the long run. Theoretically, a company should continue to add products as long as incremental revenues generated by the new product are greater than the incremental costs of adding it. Occasionally, a product may be added even though its contribution to profit is negligible. Offering a full line to serve retailers or providing special products for the handicapped are examples.

A critical factor in establishing an effective product mix is consistency. The term *line* means the products must be meaningfully related. The Procter & Gamble product mix is a good example. Products may be related by using common manufacturing processes. Some of Procter & Gamble's products are manufactured by essentially the same methods. The products in a line may move through the same distribution channel. This is true of all the company's grocery products. Finally, the items in a line are consistent if they have similar end-use or consumption patterns. Attempting to market a diverse line of products can be confusing and wasteful if

TABLE 8.2
....
Procter & Gamble's North American Product Mix

Beauty Care Products

Cosmetics

Cover Girl	Oil of Olay
Max Factor	

Deodorants

Old Spice	Sure
Secret	

Fragrances

Giorgio Beverly Hills	Red
Hugo Boss	Venezia
Laura Biagiotti-Roma	Wings
Old Spice	

Hair Care

Head & Shoulders	Rejoy/Rejoice
Mediker	Pert Plus
Pantene Pro-V	Vidal Sassoon

Skin/Beauty Care

Camay	Noxzema
Ivory	Oil of Olay
Coast	Safeguard
Clearasil	Zest

Food and Beverage Products

Consumer Products Group

Crisco	FatFree Pringles
Folgers	Pringles
Jif	Sunny Delight
Millstone	Tender Leaf Tea
Olean	

Commercial Products Group

Coffee (Folgers)	Primex
Crisco Kitchen	Whirl
Frymax	Professional Crisco

Other Products Group

Amines	Glycerine
Fatty Acids	Methyl Esters
Fatty Alcohols	

Health Care Products

Gastrointestinal

Living Better	Pepto-Bismol
Metamucil	

Incontinence

Attends

TABLE 8.2 (*continued*)
....
Procter & Gamble's North American Product Mix

Oral Care	
Crest Toothbrush	Gleem
Crest Toothpaste	Scope
Fixodent	

Respiratory Care	
The Vicks Family of Cough/Cold Products	Sinex
Chloraseptic	VapoRub
Cough Drops	VapoSteam
DayQuil	Vicks 44
Inhaler	Vitamin C Drops
NyQuil	

Laundry/Cleaning Products

Bleach	
Biz	

Dish Care	
Cascade	Ivory Dish
Dawn	Joy

Fabric Conditioners	
Febreze	

Hard Surface Cleaners	
Comet	Spic and Span
Mr. Clean	Swiffer

Laundry Cleaners	
Bold	Era
Bounce	Gain
Cheer	Ivory Snow
Downy	Oxydol
Dreft	Tide

Paper Products

Baby Diapers	
Luvs	Pampers

Baby Wipes	
Pampers Baby Fresh	Luvs Ultra Thicks
Kids Fresh	

Feminine Protection	
Always	Tampax

Tissues/Towels	
Bounty	Puffs
Charmin	Royale

Source: Product information from http://www.pg.com.

not handled carefully. Successful firms have decentralized marketing responsibility and do not attempt to market disparate items such as smoke alarms and razors as part of a single line. Such decentralization is practiced by Gillette Co. with success.

When to Introduce or Delete Products

As highlighted earlier, many firms struggle with deciding when new products should be developed and introduced in today's highly competitive marketplace. There is little choice because rapid technological obsolescence forces every seller to consider the necessity of introducing new products in order to survive and grow. Even without technological obsolescence, declining competitive distinctiveness demands a planned program of new products to maintain market share. A benchmarking study of 161 business units uncovered the key drivers of new product performance. Two key performance dimensions—profitability and impact—defined the "performance map." Four key drivers of performance were identified, namely, a high-quality new product process, the new product strategy for the business unit, resource availability, and R&D spending levels.[6]

The issue of dropping unprofitable products was mentioned previously. However, candidates for deletion should be identified well in advance of when they are to be dropped. The deletion of "sick" products and the timing and method of their withdrawal from the company's line are all-important aspects of the problem. Abandonment, however, is not the only strategy available for the mature product.[7] It may be the last resort. Alternative approaches include product improvement, repackaging, private branding, and so on.

The timing of changes in the product line is always difficult. New products may not be available when the company would like to introduce them. Developing new products usually takes longer than anticipated, and sometimes a competitor actually beats the company to the punch. The timing of product deletions is also difficult because sales departments are reluctant to abandon products that are producing any sales. A product should be dropped when it ceases to contribute to overhead. In practice, this situation is hard to detect. If no replacement is available, it may be best to continue to sell unprofitable items rather than having a gap in the product line. New products should be developed while older ones are in their declining stages, and introduction of the replacement product should be timed to coincide with or lead removal of the old.

Packaging

Packaging is always important in developing product strategy.[8] Most consumer goods are packaged in one way or another, and many industrial products also are packaged—especially shelf items that are sold through warehouse distributors and **jobbers.** Creating an effective package is complicated. There are many factors to consider; only the most important can be touched on here.

Environmentalists have attacked packaging, especially of beverage containers. One-way (nonrecyclable) containers—cans and nonreturnable bottles—have been outlawed in some areas. Product-development engineers have designed remarkable package improvements in response to environmentalists' concerns. Reusable and re-

Jobbers
Specialized resellers who act as marketing agents for manufacturers.

IT'S LEGAL BUT IS IT ETHICAL?

Wearable but Not Smokable: Hemp-Based Products

Have you consumed, bathed with, or worn something made from hemp (the source of marijuana) recently? If not, you may be seriously out of the ecologic loop. Hemp—seeds, oil, and fiber—is now the Earth-friendly raw material of choice by the ecologically correct. Environmentally, hemp is appealing because it grows without insecticides, clears fields of weeds, and replenishes nutrients in the soil. Although growing hemp is illegal in the United States, hemp-based products are not.

Worldwide sales of hemp have exploded recently, growing from $5 million in 1993 to $75 million in 1997, and Hemp-tech in California expects sales of $600 million by 2001. Although related to the marijuana plant, this hemp is not the kind you smoke. Hemp products are appearing in everything from bath soaps and sunscreens to backpacks, bedding, and even beer. Mercedes-Benz is using hemp as soundproofing. Calvin Klein and Ralph Lauren included hemp fabric in their luxury home collections, and Adidas and Vans produce sneakers having hemp-fabric uppers.

Lexington Brewing Co., in Lexington, Kentucky, introduced a new brew called Kentucky Hemp beer and recently released a series of poster ads that use drug imagery to play up hemp's illicit image. Each of the ads has a psychedelic pattern in the background, and each features a chilled bottle with a marijuana leaf on the label. "Undetectable to police dogs" reads one poster. "Eliminates cotton mouth" reads another, referring to a symptom pot smokers may experience.

Hemp is a hot product because new product designers are tapping into its naughty appeal. But Marjorie McGinnis, president of Frederick Brewing Co. of Frederick, Maryland, and a competitor with its own hemp-spiked brands Hempen Ale and Hempen Gold, noted that it was a controversial product and suggested, "We need to be responsible with it." McGinnis positions her products as upscale microbrews, suitable for beer snobs' discriminating palates. Her ad copy brags about "award-winning taste." The Body Shop, a more recent advocate, introduced a line of hemp-oil products worldwide in 1998 using the slogan "Hemp Is Hope, Not Dope."

Sources: Anne M. Spitza, "Ecology, Industry Entwined," *The Orlando Sentinel* (July 15, 1998), pp. E1, E4; Sally Beatty, "This Hemp Beer Is Legal, but Its Ads Hint Otherwise," *Wall Street Journal* (July 15, 1998), pp. B1, B6

cyclable containers, self-disposing closures, and biodegradable package materials have been developed, often at considerable expense. A recent concern over packaging is safety, particularly for hazardous or toxic products.

Package design is closely related to product image and promotion. These relationships must be considered whenever self-service and mass merchandising are involved. For example, impulse buying is the result of delivering a sensory cue at the point of sale. Unique packaging may be the only technique available for attracting consumers to certain products. Various brands of detergents, dehydrated milk, salt, sugar, and other staples, which are almost identical in content, may be differentiated effectively by packaging. Major promotional programs for firms such as Coca-Cola and Pepsico also may be based on packaging.[9] In another example, recently many supermarket chains have realized that "store" brands with innovative packaging can be a vital component in effecting and maintaining store image.[10]

Manufacturers should never ignore the packaging requirements of resellers. From a retailer's point of view, good consumer packaging has display impact. It moves merchandise off the shelves. In addition, resellers' mechanical requirements must be met. Packages must be appropriately sized. They should shelve or stack conveniently and should be easy to price mark. Packages also should be strong enough to withstand routine handling by store personnel and shoppers.

Cost is the final important consideration in packaging. Very elaborate packaging is costly. For products such as aerosol insecticides and shaving cream, the cost of the container may be greater than that of the contents. The cost of packaging always must be considered in relation to its contribution to marketing strategy.

Product Safety

. . . .

When the use or misuse of a product harms a consumer, the courts have held that manufacturers (and recently, wholesalers and retailers) are liable for the injury or damage inflicted.[11] Claims for heavy damages and extremely liberal awards have caused drastic increases in premiums for product liability insurance and have made manufacturers more reluctant to introduce new, "untried" products.

In the 1980s, product safety problems were experienced by pharmaceutical and personal care product companies. Procter & Gamble Co. decided to take its tampon product Rely off the market. G. D. Searle also withdrew a pair of products attempting to curtail mounting litigation costs. Another drug maker, A. H. Robbins, filed for bankruptcy, as did Manville Corp. in a similar case involving asbestos.[12]

A discussion of product strategy would be incomplete without a reference to the tampering with drug and food products that occurred in the early to mid-1980s. In October 1982, the first cyanide-tainted capsules of Johnson & Johnson's Tylenol were discovered. For the next few years, similar situations arose with Johnson & Johnson's products as well as those of other companies. Eventually, most companies abandoned the capsule package and determined ways in which tampering could be stopped or at least detected.[13]

Product Liability

. . . .

Product liability is a major concern to marketing managers. Lawsuits and the high cost of insuring against them have forced managers to find ways of dealing with the liability issue. Various strategies have been employed. Some companies have withdrawn products; others have attempted to raise prices to finance the added cost. Where possible, changes in product and packaging have been made.[14] But not all claims for injury end up in the courts. Data dealing with the increase in product liability are hard to obtain, but it is a serious problem. The escalation in insurance premiums testifies to this. Fred Morgan indicated that in 1982, 96 percent of all claims were settled without a court verdict. Nevertheless, court decisions establish the boundaries within which out-of-court settlements are reached. After inspecting the case law dealing with product liability litigation, Morgan had a number of conclusions to offer. (See Table 8.3.)

TABLE 8.3
....
Pertinent Observations Concerning Product Liability

Fred Morgan offers the following conclusions reached after inspecting the case law that has accumulated on product liability litigation:

1. Companies can be held liable for damages under negligence and warranty pleadings resulting from marketing communications—statements by salespersons, advertised messages, and packaging and labeling.
2. Marketing communications can result in liability because of innocent misrepresentation of facts.
3. Because strict liability is based on a product defect, advertising and personal selling activities are generally irrelevant in a strict liability pleading.
4. Courts have interpreted defective labels, warnings, and packaging as defective products, thereby establishing strict liability actions.
5. Distributors—retailers and wholesalers—are generally not liable for the misrepresentations of manufacturers. Distributors' communications to customers can, however, misrepresent the product.
6. Distributors are less likely to be found liable for product-related damages than manufacturers because the former are often able to assign the defense to the latter.
7. Distributors who brand products as their own are treated as manufacturers, thereby exposing themselves to manufacturers' liability under all theories of liability.
8. One channel member's warranty generally does not bind another channel member unless the latter, either explicitly or through its actions, has adopted the warranty. The negligent acts of one channel member can result in other channel members being held liable if they should have anticipated the negligent act.
9. The negligent acts of one channel member can result in other channel members being held liable if they should have anticipated the negligent act.

Addendum

A decision (*Sindell* v. *Abbott Laboratories et al.*) established a new doctrine of causation in product liability. Under this doctrine, the manufacturers of a product, if found guilty of charges of negligence filed against them, would be assessed damages in proportion to their market share, even though the plaintiff could not identify which of those manufacturers produced the particular product that caused the injury.*

*See Mary Jane Sheffet, "Market Share Liability: A New Doctrine of Causation in Product Liability," *Journal of Marketing* (Winter 1983), p. 35.
Source: Fred W. Morgan, "Marketing and Product Liability: A Review and Update," *Journal of Marketing* (Summer 1982), p. 69. Reprinted by permission of the American Marketing Association.

Warranty—Post-Sale Services
....

Because a firm is in business to provide satisfaction, its marketing effort is not complete until satisfaction has been delivered. When satisfaction is not completely delivered at the time of purchase, post-sale servicing becomes necessary. When a product is intended to provide longer-term satisfaction, it is probable that an effective warranty and service policy also will be included in the marketing mix. Sears, Roebuck and Co. has found it effective to remind its customers, "We Service What We Sell"; General Motors Corp. emphasizes its Mr. Goodwrench program; and all car manufacturers promote warranties of their products.

Building post-sale services into the product strategy is a powerful marketing technique. However, some managers think of customer service and customer complaint handling as the same thing. This is not so. Active consumer satisfaction policies add to the effectiveness of marketing programs. Companies such as American Express, General Electric, Whirlpool, General Motors, IBM, and Procter & Gamble incorporate after-sale service programs as important elements in their marketing strategies, and many firms such as 3Com have revised their programs to become more solutions oriented rather than just service oriented.[15]

Marketing consumer durables and most industrial products involves post-sale servicing. For example, the marketing of equipment installations often requires that the seller supply technical service for setup, maintenance, and repair. This type of activity is important in keeping the customer "satisfied" and encourages repeat purchases. Its effect on longer-run marketing success makes post-sale servicing a vital part of the continuing marketing program.

THE PRODUCT LIFE CYCLE

Product life cycle (PLC)
Graphically portrays the sales history of a product into four stages: introduction, growth, maturity, and decline.

The **product life cycle (PLC)** is one of the most frequently encountered concepts in marketing management. Levitt popularized the concept; others have criticized or elaborated on it.[16] The PLC portrays graphically the sales history of a product from the time it is introduced to the market until the point when it is withdrawn. (See Figure 8.1.) There are four major stages to the PLC: introduction, growth, maturity, and decline.

- *Introduction* is the period when a new product is presented to the marketplace. Initial distribution is obtained, and promotion is initiated.

- *Growth* is the period when consumers and the trade accept the product. Initial distribution is expanded, promotion is increased, repeat orders from initial buyers are obtained, and word-of-mouth advertising leads to more and more sales.

- *Maturity* is the period when competition becomes intense. Toward the end of this period, competitors' products cut deeply into the company's market growth.

- *Decline* is the period when the product becomes obsolete, and its loss of competitive advantages results in sales decreases. Decline is accelerated by disintegration in product distinctiveness, evidenced by obsolescence. A final stage, called *dropout,* occurs when the product is deleted or abandoned.

Figure 8.1 shows the behavior of cost and profit over the PLC. During introduction, high development and market-entry costs result in losses. Profits swell during the growth stage, but in decline, squeezed profit margins due to severe price competition result in losses.

Are Product Life Cycles Real?

Both a theoretical life cycle model and a real-world PLC exist. Reality seldom conforms to theory.[17] Marketing executives believe in the PLC concept—but streetwise marketers point out that unusual circumstances may interfere with expected life cycle behavior. William Jensen, a marketing manager at *Time* magazine, expressed it well: "The life cycle of a product is dependent on the actions and decisions of people, both of buyers and sellers, not on a set of formulae independent of the fickle fingers of consumers."[18] Torelli and Burnett examined over 1,000 industrial businesses to determine the extent PLCs exist. They concluded that market growth rate is only one of the aspects determining the shape of the real-world sales curve. The shape

FIGURE 8.1

Product Life Cycle

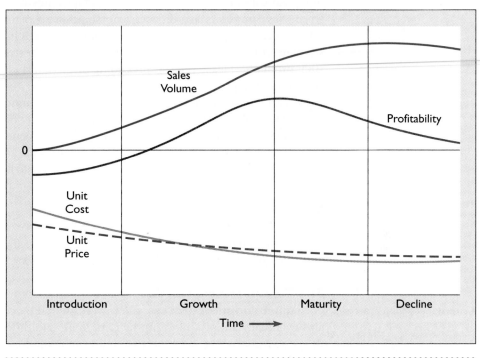

and duration of the life cycle also depend on such factors as market innovation, market concentration, competitive entry, and spending on R&D and marketing.[19]

Implications of the Product Life Cycle for Marketing Managers

The PLC's usefulness is its application as a guide to marketing strategy. Changes in the marketplace require marketing managers to adapt to these developments. Marketing managers recognize the usefulness of the PLC concept as a tool for planning and decision making. For example, retailers and manufacturers have identified the need for tracking capabilities of products throughout the supply chain. Full product life cycle management is cradle-to-grave management of a product as it progresses through the logistics pipeline.[20] Harrell and Taylor report that the concept has validity for predicting the sales volume of a product class. They also note that the PLC's greater significance is to highlight factors that influence the shape and amplitude of volume projections, in order to assess opportunities and risks realistically.[21]

Attempts to generalize about the appropriate strategy for each stage of the PLC have been made. Most are matrices showing the various stages of the PLC and the strategies typically associated with each. An example of this approach is shown in Figure 8.2.[22] The product is the firm's chief competitive weapon, so contending with the PLC is best accomplished by making changes in the product itself.

Product strategy is most critical in the first and last stages of the PLC. A new product is necessary for the PLC to begin. The competitive distinctiveness or technological superiority of a new product determines its success in the introductory stage. New products are the ultimate solution to maturity and decline problems when decisions must be made on abandoning a declining product. However, the strategies of marketing mature products are not restricted to the elimination of such products. (Please refer to preceding discussion.)

Although a product strategy matrix as shown in Figure 8.2 is useful, it is not a "roadmap" for market mixing.[23] For example, one cannot simply determine the life cycle stage, follow the column down to the product strategy row, and find the correct thing to do. The matrix merely displays what is generally done. Every marketing situation is unique, and the marketing manager must be alert to the many factors that influence strategy at any given time. And the stage in the PLC is only one factor.

Why Do Life Cycles Occur?

Two theories have attempted to explain the product life cycle. The first is the consumer adoption process; the second is adoption theory.

The Consumer Adoption Process.   An explanation of the PLC is found in the **consumer adoption process,** the process whereby consumers become aware of and eventually adopt a new product. As more and different people move through the adoption process, sales increase until the market is saturated. This process usually takes time. People become aware of new products only after they have been on the market for some time, and they accept such innovations gradually. Everett Rogers has identified the steps in this innovation adoption process as follows:

Consumer adoption process
The process by which consumers become aware of and adopt new products.

1. *Awareness.* The individual becomes aware of the innovation but lacks information about it.

2. *Interest.* The individual is stimulated to search for information about the innovation.

3. *Evaluation.* The individual considers whether to try the innovation.

4. *Trial.* The individual tries the innovation on a small scale to test its usefulness.

5. *Adoption.* The individual decides to make use of the innovation on a regular basis.[24]

Adoption Theory.   **Adoption theory** provides further insight into the PLC by its extension into the *diffusion process.* This refers to the spread of a new idea from its introduction to its final general acceptance. Such a spread would follow a normal pattern of communications, except some people are more prone than others to accept new products and ideas.[25] Rogers classifies the adopters of innovations using five categories:[26]

Adoption theory
Refers to the spread of a new idea from introduction to final general acceptance.

1. *Innovators* are the first people to accept a new product. There are relatively few of them. Only about 2.5 percent of all adopters fall into this category.

2. *Early adopters* constitute about 13.5 percent of innovation acceptors.

FIGURE 8.2

....

Product Life Cycle Strategies

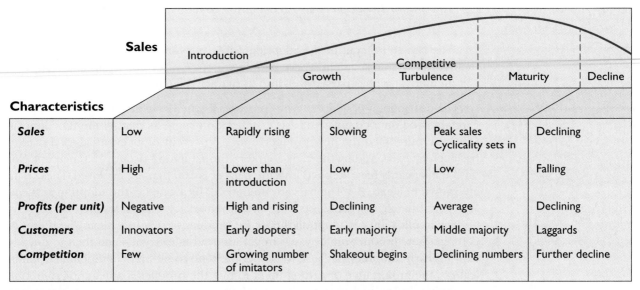

Characteristics

	Introduction	Growth	Competitive Turbulence	Maturity	Decline
Sales	Low	Rapidly rising	Slowing	Peak sales Cyclicality sets in	Declining
Prices	High	Lower than introduction	Low	Low	Falling
Profits (per unit)	Negative	High and rising	Declining	Average	Declining
Customers	Innovators	Early adopters	Early majority	Middle majority	Laggards
Competition	Few	Growing number of imitators	Shakeout begins	Declining numbers	Further decline

Strategies

	Introduction	Growth	Competitive Turbulence	Maturity	Decline
Overall	Create awareness and trial R&D and engineering are critical	Market share penetration	Protect and strengthen niche	Protect share— manage for earnings Emphasize com- petitive costs	Reduce expenditures and harvest
Product	Basic	Offer extensions, features, service	Tighten line, improve quality	Diversity of brands and models	Phase out weak items
Price	Cost plus	Market broadening	Match or beat competitors	Defensive	Maintain profit margins
Distribution	Selective	Build intensive coverage	Strong dealer support	Intensive and extensive	Selective
Communications	Create awareness	Stimulate wider trial	Maintain consumer franchise	Stress brand differences and benefits	Phase out maintenance only
Manufacturing	Subcontract Short runs Overcapacity	Centralize Shift to mass production Undercapacity	Long runs Some overcapacity Stability of manufacturing process	Many short runs Decentralize	Revert to subcontracting

Source: From *Analysis for Strategic Market Decisions,* 1st edition, by G. Day, © 1986. Reprinted with permission of South-Western College Publishing, a division of International Thomson Publishing. Fax 800-730-2215.

....

3. The *early majority adopters* are those who precede the other half of innovation acceptors. About 34 percent of adopters fall into this class.

4. *Late majority adopters* also account for about 34 percent of all innovation acceptors.

5. The last 16 percent of the adopting public, classified as *laggards,* constitute a more extreme segment. These people are often price conscious and wait until an innovation has passed well into its mature stage before adopting it.

The distribution of adopter types provides further insights into the PLC when it is retabulated on a cumulative basis. Retabulation suggests that by the time innovators have purchased the new product, only 2.5 percent of its eventual total market has been realized. Adding the early adopters, the saturation rises to 16.0 percent. Not until the laggards have stepped into the market is 100 percent achieved. These data are shown in Figure 8.3. The bars are "smoothed" by averaging the adoption percentages over the range, which gives a curve that remarkably resembles the PLC curve.

The implications of adoption theory for product strategy are clear. The secret of getting a new product underway is to get innovators to try it—and then to quickly capture early adopters. Because these people tend to be highly influential opinion leaders, the importance of getting them to buy the product is apparent. Promoting to opinion leaders and, through them, to the larger market is described as a two-step communication process. The next stage involves making the product readily available to the early and late majority. Laggards generally will come along by themselves. The diffusion process also helps explain the difficulties companies encounter in the decline period of the PLC. What happens is that many original customers begin experimenting with competitors' products.

TEST MARKETING

Test marketing
Investigates marketability of products and variables such as differing prices or communication themes or media mixes.

In the past, test marketing was used principally as a screening device. Products that were unsuccessful in a test market simply did not get the opportunity for national marketing. Marketing managers extrapolated the results of the test to the national market and made a final "go/no go" decision. Today however, **test marketing** is expected to investigate variables in the marketing plan other than just the product, such as differing prices or differing communications themes or media mixes.

Product modification might be recommended as a result of test marketing, but this is no longer the principal reason for test marketing. One company emphasized that test marketing is not a screening device by stating, "It should be undertaken with the prior knowledge that all the important odds for success are high."[27]

Advantages of Test Marketing

Rollout
A market-by-market introduction of a new product.

What specific questions can be answered by test marketing?[28] First, the overall workability of the marketing plan can be evaluated. A test market is like a shakedown cruise for a new ship. Grocery manufacturers actually use test marketing as the first step in a planned program of market entry. True, minor adjustments in subsequent markets of the **rollout** (market-by-market introduction) may occur, but the rollout is planned from the day the product is first introduced into the first test market.

FIGURE 8.3
••

Cumulative Distribution of Innovation Adopters

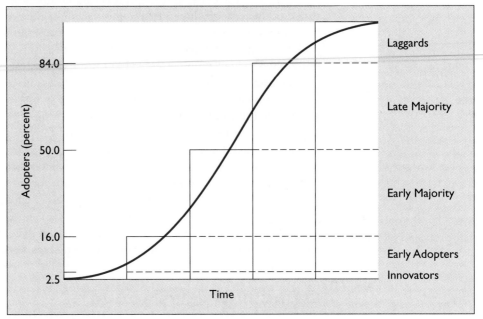

Source: Adapted with the permission of The Free Press, a Division of Simon & Schuster, Inc. from *Diffusion of Innovations,* Fourth Edition by Everett M. Rogers. Copyright © 1995 by Everett M. Rogers. Copyright © 1962, 1971, 1983 by The Free Press.

••

A second question that test marketing can answer involves evaluating alternative allocations of the budget. The level of spending can be varied in each of several test markets and differences in consumer response measured. Similarly, apportionment of the budget among various elements of the mix may be tested. In one market, the principal effort may be directed toward in-store promotions and merchandising deals. In another market area, the main thrust of the introduction may be consumer sampling and mass-media advertising. Different advertising media may be tested in the different markets. Radio and newspapers may be used in one area; television in the other. These experiments are always carried on under tightly controlled conditions. Store-audit data and warehouse-withdrawal information, brand-awareness studies, coupon redemptions, and other measures are used to judge the relative effectiveness of various approaches to market entry.

Disadvantages of Test Marketing
••

There are several reasons for deciding not to pursue test marketing.[29] First, test marketing is expensive. Therefore, many companies now use test marketing as the first phase of national distribution. Second, test marketing takes time to complete—the average duration appears to be about 6 months. This is more than enough time for dangerous developments to occur. For example, the distinctiveness of the innovation can decay drastically. It will no longer be a new product when it goes into the national market. Third, test marketing is criticized because it prematurely informs competitors of a company's plans. Test marketing is very visible, and a good marketing intelligence system will immediately report its existence to a competitor's management. The least that can happen is that competitors will be ready to meet the threat of the new product when it enters national marketing. Other competitive tactics, however, may be more disastrous. Some competitors "jam" a test market by purposely altering their marketing programs in tested areas. Competitor reactions are not limited to just jamming test market results, however. A small competitor actually may be able to beat a national marketer to full-scale distribution while the larger seller is still involved with testing.

Successful companies have been speeding up the new product introduction process—a process once believed to take up to 2 years to complete. Some companies are eliminating test marketing altogether. Others are compressing or dispensing with steps that provide information that is useful but not critical to the new product's marketing plan. Windows of opportunity for new products open and close swiftly. David Miller, a client services director at ad agency Ogilvy & Mather, points out that when multinationals such as Procter & Gamble, Unilever, and Kraft Jacob Suchard develop a new product, they plan to sell it in at least thirty to forty markets, so they are basically using countries as their test markets.[30]

LAUNCHING NEW PRODUCTS

As illustrated by the Swatchmobile example, one of the first major decisions in launching a new product is timing. We mentioned that the strategic window of opportunity for new products is open for a limited time. However, many new product opportunities remain viable long enough for a company to decide between an early or a late entry. Although it is possible to identify the advantages of both early and late entry, it is very difficult to predict accurately what will be the outcome of either strategy, because the market forces are so dynamic.[31] A recent examination of early entry by Szymanski and colleagues concluded that, on average, market order entry exerted a significant and positive direct impact on market share. However, they also stated that pioneer advantage was augmented by service quality, vertical integration, R&D expenditures, shared facilities, shared customers, market growth rate, and immediate customer purchase frequency.[32] This and other research suggests that entry timing is not always the critical factor.[33] A long-run leadership position is usually attained by the firm that develops the strongest competitive advantage.

Once the decision to enter has been made, there are several choices open to the marketer. Two of these are of primary importance. First, a decision must be made either to market to a selected segment or to approach the market as a whole. The second is between a rollout (market-by-market) introduction or an attempt to obtain immediate national or global distribution. This decision must be made on the basis of potential in the segments being considered and on the relative profitability of developing separate strategies for each segment. Test marketing might be used to resolve this issue. Careful analysis of all available data should indicate the approach to take. If true segments exist, and if the cost of preparing individualized programs can be justified, a segmented approach is desirable, since the appeal of the product and its promotion can be keyed more closely to specific consumer needs than they can in an undifferentiated marketing program.

MARKETING IN THE GLOBAL VILLAGE

Will the Swatchmobile Sweep Europe?

In October 1998, the Swatchmobile was introduced at 110 dealerships throughout the European Union at a selling price of approximately US$8,500. Sized just a little bigger than a go-cart, with a plastic exterior that never rusts or dents and that can be switched in color for about the price of an evening dress, the Swatchmobile is designed for city commuting. It is easy on fuel, produces minimal pollution, and turns on a dime. Alexis Mannes (a dealer in Brussels) decided: "Maybe that [Swatchmobile] was something that would change the car business." This is exactly what Daimler-Benz (now Daimler-Chrysler) had in mind in 1995 when it initiated the joint project with Société Suisse de Microélectronique et d'Horlogerie (maker of Swatch watches). To make the car dramatically smaller, Micro Compact Cars, the Daimler-SMH joint venture that manufactures Swatchmobile, redesigned the basic "three-box concept" of the traditional car with a hood, a cockpit, and a trunk by putting the engine in the back, like the original VW Beetle, and moving the rest of the car's mechanical aspects below the passenger cabin. Moreover, suppliers do not just supply parts; they supply "modules," like entire doors, front ends, or cockpits. The suppliers also install the modules, leaving Micro Compact as a coordinator in a factory where most of the employees are on someone else's payroll. The result is that the factory in Hambach, France, is capable of building 900 cars a day with virtually no parts inventory of its own. Moreover, because only 25 percent of the Swatchmobile value is added in final assembly, it takes just 4.5 hours to assemble, compared with 20 hours for the VW Polo.

Source: Brandon Mitchener, "Can Daimler's Tiny 'Swatchmobile' Sweep Europe?" *Wall Street Journal* (October 2, 1998), pp. B1, B4.

The choice between a rollout program and one of national marketing rests on a number of other factors. If new distribution is necessary, national marketing cannot be achieved quickly, but market potential may dictate a national effort. If the total amount of business to be had is spread very thinly, it may not be worth trying to cultivate any particular market intensely. Another factor that may influence the decision to go national is the threat of potential competition. A market-by-market introduction may take as long as 18 months to complete—plenty of time for competitors to enter the picture. Finally, if a marketing program is to rely heavily on national advertising media, the waste involved in going through a series of local markets may be substantial.

BRAND STRATEGIES

The primary focus of product strategy for some firms is to build brand equity (the set of assets or liabilities associated with a brand),[34] whereas others use branding strategies to strengthen product image. Bagozzi and colleagues suggest that firms that employ a brand strategy must decide on several factors such as whether to use individual brands for each product or a family of brands. For example, Kellogg Co. promotes Kellogg's Rice Krispies or Kellogg's Frosted Flakes (a family brand strategy), whereas General Foods Corporation, with its Jell-O, Maxwell House Coffee, or Log Cabin syrup brands, promotes individual brand names.

Companies that use *multiple brand names* for related products decide to allow their products to succeed or fail on their own merit. Some advantages of using multiple brand names are (1) a firm can separate in customers' minds each product it markets, (2) product(s) can be targeted at specific market segments, and (3) the impact of one failed product is minimized. Also, managers must decide on what brand names to use in order to achieve forceful symbolic impacts on customers. Additionally, managers must decide where to market, that is, what market segments to pursue at what locations. And finally, managers must decide on the appropriate marketing-mix elements—price, distribution, and communications.[35]

Other factors that increase brand image are (1) product quality—products that perform beyond customer expectations (e.g., Lime Away and Kleenex); (2) consistent advertising—communications that effectively highlight a brand's competitive advantages, both often and well (e.g., Tide and Lexus); (3) distribution effectiveness—customers are exposed to the brand when shopping (e.g., Dentyne chewing gum); and (4) brand personality—the brand represents a specific image (e.g., Levi's).[36] For example, the brand strength of Coca-Cola is widely attributed to its universal awareness, availability, and trademark—all of which resulted from strategic decisions made previously by Coca-Cola's corporate managers.

The brand name is the most important aspect of packaging, serving as a unique identifier. A **brand** can be a name, term, design, symbol, or other feature that identifies one firm's product or service as different from all other goods and services. The legal term for *brand* is **trademark.**[37] An effective brand name can evoke feelings of security, trust, and confidence, as well as other desirable characteristics.[38] Many firms use branding strategies to carry out market-development strategies such as line extensions that use a brand name to facilitate entry into new market segments (e.g., Ice Beer or Concentrated Tide). A similar strategy is *brand extension,* where a current brand is used to enter a completely different product class (e.g., Arm and Hammer Baking Soda Chewing Gum, a tooth cleaner sold only in the toothpaste aisle).

Brand Equity Explained

Many firms realized that brand names were valuable assets and that successful brand extensions could lead to additional loyalty and profits. However, ineffective brand extensions can damage brand association, since brand perceptions are transferred from one product to the other.[39] **Brand equity** is the set of assets (or liabilities) associated with a brand that add (or subtract) value.[40] The value of brand equity depends on the marketplace's relationship with the brand. Figure 8.4 lists the elements of brand equity that are determined by the consumers' assessment of the product, the company that manufactures and markets the product, and other factors that affect the product between manufacturing and consuming.

Aaker, a recognized authority on brand equity, notes that the assets and liabilities of brand equity differ from context to context. He suggests that they be grouped into the following four categories for active management: perceived quality, brand awareness, brand associations, and brand loyalty. *Perceived quality* affects return on in-

Brand
A name, term, design, symbol, or other feature that identifies and differentiates one firm's product or service from all others.

Trademark
The legal term for *brand*.

Brand equity
The set of assets (or liabilities) associated with a brand that add (or subtract) value.

FIGURE 8.4

Elements of Brand Equity

Source: Reprinted with the permission of The Free Press, a Division of Simon & Schuster, Inc. from *Managing Brand Equity: Capitalizing on the Value of a Brand Name* by David A. Aaker. Copyright © 1991 by David A. Aaker.

vestment directly because the cost of retaining customers is reduced, and perceived quality affects return on investment indirectly because it allows a higher price to be charged and enhances market share while not increasing costs.[41] Perceived quality also may drive stock return, a measure that reflects long-term performance.[42]

Brand awareness differentiates brands along a recall/familiarity dimension—people like the familiar. Second, brand awareness via name recognition may signal commitment and substance—both attributes valued by consumers. Third, the prominence of a brand will determine if it is recalled at key times in the purchasing process. An extreme example of this is brand dominance, where the brand is the only one recalled when the purchasing process is initiated. Brand awareness can be extremely durable and very difficult to dislodge. The name *Datsun* was as strong as *Nissan* 4 years after the name change occurred.[43]

Brand association is anything that is directly or indirectly linked in the consumers' memory to the brand. Product attributes and customer benefits are the associations with obvious value because they provide customers with reasons to buy and a basis for brand loyalty. However, strong brands go beyond product attributes to differentiate on associations such as organizational associations, brand personality, symbols, emotional benefits, and self-expressed benefits. Determining the brand's identity or vision—the associations that the brand aspires to represent (as opposed to the image or existing associations)—is key to creating and managing

39. David A. Aaker and Kevin Lane Keller, "Consumer Evaluation of Brand Extensions," *Journal of Marketing* (January 1990), pp. 27–41.

40. A detailed discussion of brand equity is given by David A. Aaker, *Managing Brand Equity* (New York: Free Press, 1991).

41. Robert Jackobson and David A. Aaker, "The Strategic Role of Product Quality," *Journal of Marketing* (October 1987), pp. 31–44.

42. David A. Aaker and Robert Jacobson, "The Financial Information Context of Perceived Quality," *Journal of Marketing Research* (May 1994), pp. 191–201.

43. Aaker, *op. cit.,* p. 57.

44. For a complete discussion of brand equity, the reader should examine David A. Aaker, *Strategic Market Management*, 5th ed. (New York: John Wiley & Sons, 1998), pp. 175–180.

45. A complete discussion of brand equity is available in Geoffrey L. Gordon, Roger J. Calantone, and C. A. di Benedetto, "Brand Equity in the Business-to-Business Sector: An Exploratory Study," *Journal of Product & Brand Management* Vol. 2(3) (1993), pp. 4–16.

46. Joe Berry, "National Brands on the Rebound but the War Is Far from Over," *Brandweek* (February 27, 1995), pp. 17–18.

47. A discussion of private label brands can be found in Hillary Miller, "Store Brands Are Looking Good," *Beverage Industry* (April 1995), pp. 60–61; or in Marcia Mogelonsky, "When Stores Become Brands," *American Demographics* (February 1995), pp. 32–36.

48. Gary Levin, "No Global Private Quake—Yet," *Advertising Age—International Supplement* (January 16, 1995), pp. 1–26.

49. Jeffery D. Zbar, "Industry Trends Hold Private Label Promise," *Advertising Age* (April 3, 1995), p. 31.

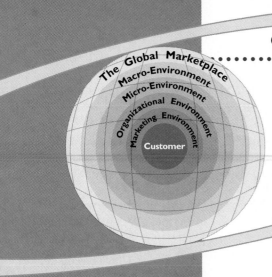

The Global Marketplace
Macro-Environment
Micro-Environment
Organizational Environment
Marketing Environment
Customer

Services Marketing Strategy

Services: A Major Force in the U.S. Economy

Characteristics of Services versus Goods

Levels of Service

Service as Value

Service Marketing Issues

The Service Design Process

Setting Standards for Service Quality

Service Delivery and Implementation

Delivering great service, one customer at a time, day after day, month after month, is difficult. Nothing . . . suggests that the excellent service journey is easy. It is not. But it is immensely rewarding, not just financially, but spiritually. Excellence nourishes the soul.[1]

Busy Signal at AOL: A Services Marketing Mix Gone Awry

December 1996 was a time to remember for many subscribers to America Online (AOL), America's largest on-line Internet service with over 8 million subscribers and $1 billion in revenue. In order to attract new subscribers, AOL promoted a flat-rate pricing strategy of $19.95 per month for unlimited use. Response was overwhelming—in fact, demand was so great that it created a customer service crisis during late 1996 and early 1997. Old and new customers, individuals and businesses alike, were frustrated by busy signals for hours as they tried unsuccessfully to go on-line. AOL did not have enough capacity to keep up with demand, despite its sophisticated technology, user-friendly service design, and position as a market leader in providing access to the World Wide Web.

Industry analysts and media experts following the service crisis offered a number of perspectives. Some considered that the problem was related primarily to technology and others to management issues. Still others felt that the issues were predominantly legal and ethical. While most of the problems caused by the added demand for AOL Internet services have been resolved, the situation does represent several critical issues that are of particular interest to services marketers. These include the following:

- *Achieving a balance between capacity and demand.* In AOL's drive to increase demand, it strained the capacity of its system to deliver promised services to loyal long-term customers as well as new subscribers. (AOL spent about $250 million in the first half of 1997 to expand the capacity of its network to meet the growth in demand.)

- *Maintaining market leadership in a rapidly changing, volatile environment.* AOL's competitive position was threatened by flat-rate pricing moves by AT&T's Worldnet and others in their attempt to take market share from AOL, as well as the need to maintain technological dominance in a highly competitive industry.
- *Interaction of all elements of the marketing mix.* The AOL debacle is an excellent example of the effect one element of the marketing mix can have on the others. In this case, a combination of a low price, aggressive advertising, product (software) improvements, local access opportunities, and a market that eagerly responded to the benefits implied in AOL's offer provided a synergy that escalated demand beyond AOL's ability to manage the resulting surge in use.
- *Impact on consumer and organizational buying decisions.* Many disgruntled AOL users canceled their subscriptions, and many would-be subscribers delayed or changed their decisions to buy based on perceived risk and inconvenience. Further, a general mistrust of Internet service providers has resulted in more careful assessment by buyers.
- *Service quality and customer satisfaction.* Time and convenience are major factors in determining level of customer satisfaction, but repeated attempts to get on-line during this crisis gave the impression of poor-quality service. AOL's inability to meet the demand of business customers extended to the ability of these businesses to service their own customers—thus poor service "rippled" throughout entire distribution systems.
- *Legal and ethical ramifications of marketing decisions.* Some customers felt that they had been swindled by the flat-rate pricing scheme. Long-time customers felt abandoned; newer customers felt cheated by advertising that promised a product that could not be reliably delivered. Attorneys general in 36 states filed class action suits against AOL by the end of January 1997 on behalf of disgruntled customers. As a result, AOL agreed to compensate frustrated subscribers with refunds and free access time.
- *Reaction by competitors.* Although AOL experienced tremendous success as a result of this marketing ploy, it served as a wake-up call for AOL and its competitors. Most Internet providers have reconsidered their pricing and promotional strategies to avoid a repeat of this situation. Many AOL competitors seized the opportunity to lure dissatisfied customers away from AOL. Perhaps one of the boldest marketing moves was by CompuServe, who took direct aim at AOL's customer traffic jam with a million-dollar ad during the 1997 Super Bowl. The 30-second commercial started with 15 seconds of a black screen accompanied by busy signals representing unsuccessful attempts to log on to an unnamed on-line service. This was followed by silence, CompuServe's logo, and a message printed across the screen that read: "Looking for dependable Internet access? CompuServe. Get on with it."

Sources: Amy Barrett, Paul Eng, and Kathy Rebello, "For $19.95 a Month, Unlimited Headaches for AOL," *Wall Street Journal* (January 27, 1997), p. 35; Walter S. Mossberg, "AOL Is Improving Its Service Package, but Problems Remain," *Wall Street Journal* (November 14, 1996), p. B1; Thomas Petzinger, Jr., "'Gunning for Growth,' AOL's Steve Case Shot Himself in the Foot," *Wall Street Journal* (January 14, 1997), p. B1; Jared Sandberg, "CompuServe Uses Super Bowl Ad to Rub in AOL's Growing Woes," *Wall Street Journal* (January 24, 1997), p. B16; Jared Sandberg, "AOL to Pay Refunds to Its Customers," *Wall Street Journal* (January 30, 1997), pp. A3, A6; Bob Wallace and Mitch Wagner, "AOL Debacle Raises Service Quality Fears," *Computer World* (February 3, 1997), pp. 1, 16.

Irst impressions are crucial for all types of marketing efforts, but services marketers are most vulnerable to customer perceptions that lead to satisfaction or dissatisfaction. A negative first impression may lead to a one-time transaction or none at all, whereas a positive impression generally leads to repeat business.

Although tangible goods and intangible services are both referred to as *products*, in this chapter we emphasize the marketing of services that comprise an organization's core business. However, considerable attention also is given to those additional services which have become increasingly important to the sale of all types of products in both business-to-business and consumer markets at all levels of distribution.

SERVICES: A MAJOR FORCE IN THE U.S. ECONOMY

The service sector contributed $1539.5 billion and 33.586 million jobs to the U.S. economy in 1996. This represents a 3.4 percent real growth rate since 1995, with the greatest percentage increase occurring in the motion pictures sector (9.6 percent). Sales and trend data for leading service categories are provided in Table 9.1.

An increasing number of services have evolved in response to a focus on productivity and profits by organizations and the poverty of time experienced by active, overly busy consumers. For example, many of the activities that consumers once performed for themselves are now included with the sale of goods and

---

MANAGING CHANGE

High-Quality Service at Everyday Low Prices

Today, not only the higher-priced marketers are expected to provide outstanding service; the cost-cutting manufacturers and distributors also must please customers with excellent service (and low prices). Staples, a fast-growing office supply superstore, has competed successfully with Office Depot and Office Max by pleasing customers with services that set Staples apart from the competition.

A small business owner walked into a Staples store to buy map pins, expecting the typical discount store lack of service. The store did not have the unusual variety of map pins that he needed—but he was surprised at the store's extra efforts to satisfy his needs. The sales associate immediately contacted the manufacturer of a similar pin and faxed information on the pins to the customer's office—all for an order of no more than $20. Several months later when the customer returned to the store, the sales associate impressed him by remembering his name. The business owner is now a regular Staples shopper and spends a couple of thousand dollars a year at the store.

How does Staples do this? The company focuses on developing a service culture that sets it apart from other office supply retailers. Its sales associates use a massive database (including data from a membership card) to know their customers well, as noted in Chapter 2 regarding the successful use of technology. The company creates customer-friendly stores, encourages managers to spend time with customers, gives incentives to employees for outstanding service, and treats its people as it would like them to treat Staples' customers.

Source: Rahul Jacob, "How One Red Hot Retailer Wins Customer Loyalty," *Fortune* (July 10, 1995), pp. 72–79.

TABLE 9.1
• • • • • • • • • • • • •
Expenditures for Services, 1990–1996
(billions of real 1992 dollars)

Services	1990	1994	1995	1996	Percent Change 1995–1996
Health services	356.9	369.7	371.6	376.6	1.35
Business services	216.5	247.1	271.3	295.7	8.99
Legal services	91.5	86.0	85.5	85.1	–0.47
Hotels and other lodging places	49.2	54.4	55.4	55.8	0.72
Auto repair services and garages	54.0	53.3	53.3	55.3	3.75
Amusement and recreation services	42.8	47.5	49.7	51.6	3.82
Educational services	44.3	48.9	49.6	50.7	2.22
Social services and membership organizations	32.5	41.6	43.7	44.9	2.75
Personal services	41.7	42.6	42.4	43.3	2.12
Motion pictures	22.1	21.8	23.9	26.2	9.62
Other services	160.4	175.4	184.6	192.9	4.50

Source: Statistical Abstract of the United States, 1998, GDP in Real (1992) Dollars by Industry (Table 716), based on information provided by U.S. Bureau of Economic Analysis, Survey of Current Business, Washington, DC, August 1997.

services or sold separately as a convenience to the customer. This includes services such as personal shopping, delicatessen meals, take-out food, pickup and return of cars for repair, lawn services, house cleaning, and grocery deliveries. Both marketers and customers are trying to find ways to make buying easier (while holding prices down at the same time!).

Growth in the service industry has taken many forms, affecting all categories of goods and services and all stages of the purchasing process. Service marketers have added or increased customer services such as shopping convenience through location or distribution strategies (e.g., ATMs, branch banks, branch warehouses, just-in-time delivery), longer business hours, one-stop shopping, better trained sales and service personnel, more liberal warranties or adjustment policies, improved customer service response systems (personal, telephone, on-line), and availability of information before, during, and after a sale.

Current trends are expected to continue and to escalate in the direction of more services at higher quality, performed to build long-term relationships with satisfied—perhaps even pampered—customers. Value beyond price and quality will continue to be defined and redefined in the minds of buyers and will drive the types of services that are offered. Table 9.2 provides a summary of some of the innovative service approaches we will likely see in the twenty-first century.

CHARACTERISTICS OF SERVICES VERSUS GOODS
• •

The unique characteristics of services, in contrast to physical products, present special challenges to marketing managers. Services are intangible, variable (or inconsistent), inseparable, and perishable.[2] Each trait affects the design and delivery of successful customer service programs, as shown in Figure 9.1.

TABLE 9.2
················
New Trend Expectations in Service Marketing

Examples of innovative approaches that are expected to escalate in the twenty-first century include:

• Internet shopping for all types of goods and services (e.g., Amazon.com for books, Land's End for clothing, CD-ROMs downloaded from a Web page, parts for production machinery, and others)

• More automation in the service process (e.g., banking and financial services, package delivery and tracking)

• Information on-line, books downloadable from the Internet to a small hand-held computer

• Integrated communications delivery (combining cable television, movies, telephone, computers, and other hardware, software, and media content)

• More business-to-business services as home offices and mobile workstations become more popular, that is, for all practical purposes, a "virtual office" without traditional walls, made possible by technology

• Increased database marketing and attention to long-term customer relationships

• A need for more well-trained service employees to produce services that involve high-tech equipment, computers, and other applications

FIGURE 9.1
···
Unique Service Characteristics: Marketing-Mix Implications

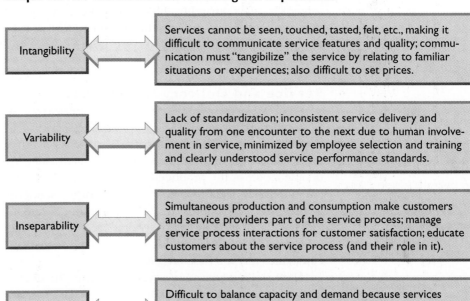

Intangibility	Services cannot be seen, touched, tasted, felt, etc., making it difficult to communicate service features and quality; communication must "tangibilize" the service by relating to familiar situations or experiences; also difficult to set prices.
Variability	Lack of standardization; inconsistent service delivery and quality from one encounter to the next due to human involvement in service, minimized by employee selection and training and clearly understood service performance standards.
Inseparability	Simultaneous production and consumption make customers and service providers part of the service process; manage service process interactions for customer satisfaction; educate customers about the service process (and their role in it).
Perishability	Difficult to balance capacity and demand because services cannot be inventoried; services cannot be returned for credit or exchange; need to manage demand in peak periods, utilize capacity in off-periods, and have good service recovery.

Services Are Intangible

Intangibility
Services cannot be seen, felt, tasted, heard, or smelled by customers before purchase, making them more difficult to evaluate than tangible goods.

Since services have **intangibility,** meaning they cannot be seen, felt, tasted, heard, or smelled before purchase, customers find them more difficult to evaluate than goods. For example, a customer cannot see, feel, or otherwise sense the extraction of a wisdom tooth by an oral surgeon before the procedure is completed, nor the value of dental insurance or regular dental checkups until they can be experienced. Similar experiences from the past, word-of-mouth from others, and an individual's imagination are major sources of prepurchase evaluation. The oral surgeon's facilities, employees, communications, equipment used to perform the service, symbols and logos, and even price can be used to give the service tangibility. For example, neatly dressed, professional personnel, a clean and comfortable waiting room and surgery area, accurately written instructions, and even the "age" of the magazines in the waiting room can provide physical evidence of service quality for this dental service.

Services Are Variable

Variability
Services are affected in some way by human beings, and therefore it is nearly impossible to achieve consistent service delivery from one customer and/or employee to the next.

Services are performed—or supported in some way—by human beings, making it nearly impossible for them to be delivered consistently from one customer and/or employee to the next. **Variability,** or inconsistencies, can be overcome by using quality control measures, increasing customer satisfaction by having effective service systems in place, monitoring customer satisfaction regularly, and managing the behavior of customers and employees in each service encounter.

One area where service quality varies is in handling customer complaints. At different times in the same business environment different employees may handle the same type of complaint differently with different customers. In one situation, the complaint-handling process may flow quickly and efficiently, increasing the customer's satisfaction and likelihood of making additional purchases. In another situation, the same customer may be treated rudely or even accused of trying to take advantage of the company's service policies—effectively showing that customer that he or she is not important.

Service and Delivery Are Inseparable

Inseparability
Services are consumed as they are performed, and customers are involved at some level in the service process, making the customer, the service provider, and the service itself inseparable.

Customers are involved at some level in the service delivery process, giving the services the quality of **inseparability.** Because services are consumed as they are performed, it is difficult to separate the service provider from the service itself, making people a part of the product. For example, a telephone company's truck or a company's physical facilities are seen as part of the service received by a customer; that is, they are inseparable. The service personnel become the business in the customer's eyes; therefore, poor service creates the image of an undesirable store or other business, as described in the following scenario, illustrating a service that accompanies the purchase of tangible goods.

Mary Smith is returning a wedding gift to the housewares department of a well-known department store, expecting to make another selection. The salesperson that she approaches does not want to deal with a return, so she rudely sends Mary to customer service in another part of the store—meanwhile approaching another customer who looks like a better prospect for a sale. When Mary arrives at customer service, two employees seem inconvenienced by Mary's request as they discuss their lunch plans. Neither they nor the salesperson asks Mary if she would like to make another selection. The irony is that the store's liberal return policy is tainted by the "don't care" attitude of employees who actually perform the service, and the retailer misses an opportunity to make an additional sale and build a long-term relationship with the new bride for future purchases.

Services Are Perishable

Services cannot be inventoried, except for the equipment and supplies necessary for their performance. They are time-dependent; if they are not used one day, they cannot be inventoried for the next. Service marketing managers must balance consumer demand for services with the availability of service employees and facilities. When demand is steady, **perishability** is not a problem because employee schedules can be adjusted to meet forecasted needs. However, service marketers do experience fluctuation in demand, making it difficult to schedule the necessary resources. For this reason, many service providers find it more profitable to maximize use of part-time employees and contract out some services, such as accounting or promotion.

Perishability
Services cannot be inventoried, except for the equipment and supplies needed for their performance; they are time-dependent.

LEVELS OF SERVICE

There are two basic levels of service: primary services and ancillary services. Managers must decide on whether and how the responsibility for service performance will be shared by the company and its customers. Often, pricing strategies are tied to the degree of full service or self-service performed across both primary and ancillary customer service offerings.

Primary Services

Core services
Major activity of a business or organization.

Primary services
Considered essential to completion of a transaction and necessary to make and keep a sale.

Core services refer to the major activity of a business (or nonprofit organization). **Primary services** are considered to be essential services that are the basis of a transaction and necessary to make and keep a sale.

Let us take two examples of relatively complex products. For customers purchasing intangible investment services, the use of a brokerage account to buy and sell stocks is a primary service. For those purchasing a complex tangible good, such as a computer for the first time, important primary services may include knowledgeable sales assistance, the availability of credit and extended warranties, and the ability to return defective merchandise.

For most consumers, the purchase of a car is a complex process requiring a high level of sales assistance. However, high-pressure sales tactics and the resulting consumer discomfort and mistrust created an opportunity for a new way to meet the need for essential services without the expected hassle of dealerships and used-car lots. Consumers have changed the rules for new and used-car retailers. Large retail chains, such as Circuit City, Price Costco, and Wal-Mart Stores, Inc., have taken the superstore concept to the car business. At the same time, these retailers recognize that today's automobile customers are better informed and demand a higher level of "essential" services to make a sale (without sacrificing low prices). For example, CarMax, Circuit City's chain of used-car superstores, offers a wide range of services: no-haggle sales assistance, computer kiosks on the showroom floor with complete information on automobiles wanted by the customer, detailed payment plans, and child care.[3]

Ancillary Services

. . . .

Ancillary services
Offered as an expected or optional supplement that adds perceived value to the primary purchase but may not be required as a necessary or usual part of the sale.

Ancillary services are offered as expected or optional supplements to the primary purchase. The customer generally expects them, although they are not required as a necessary or usual part of a sale. However, ancillary services do add perceived value for the customer and contribute to the marketer's image and competitive position.

Many services previously considered "extra" are now demanded by consumers as "essential" to a sale, increasing the number of extras required to differentiate one firm's offering from that of competitors. Examples of expected consumer services include carryout at most supermarkets, convenient free parking, credit, and alteration or assembly services provided by a retailer. Business-to-business customers expect prompt delivery, favorable credit terms, and responsive customer service, perhaps through a 24-hour 800 number "hotline."

Optional services are another form of ancillary service that customers may or may not pay for. For example, many retail consumers welcome a personal shopping service that is performed on a formal or informal basis. Personal notification of the arrival of special merchandise, gift registries, or a travel agency may be attractive to an important customer segment. Customer experiences in department stores, specialty shops, and shopping malls have raised awareness and perceptions of service across all types of retailers. Baby-sitting services have become popular among shoppers. Club Med, hotels, and shopping malls have expanded their services to include something for the entire family, in response to the active, time-poor lifestyles of their customers who want to maximize opportunities for family fun.

The cosmetics industry has long provided a high level of personal sales assistance (beauty consultants, cosmetologists) in department stores. However, a large percentage of cosmetic products are sold through drugstore chains and mass merchandisers, generally known for their self-service formats and lack of personal service. To differentiate in this highly competitive beauty market where the same products are sold in thousands of outlets, drugstore chains and mass merchants have recognized the need for a higher level of customer assistance. Some drugstores believe that a cosmetician may be just as influential in attracting and retaining customers as a pharmacist. Increased attention to retail services in this market has led to more training and better compensation and rewards for service personnel. It also has resulted in the use of point-of-sale data for employee scheduling at peak service times, better point-of-sale displays for customer assistance, and more emphasis on the services of beauty consultants and cosmeticians in drugstores and mass discount chains.[4]

Organizational customers are expecting and demanding an increasing number of optional services with primary product purchases. These may include on-site training or assistance with inventory management, marketing, and technical expertise. A number of business marketers have developed consulting services to satisfy many of these customer needs. In many cases, these ancillary services evolve into a new core business. For example, large accounting firms have added investment advising to their traditional accounting and financial services, with the permission of the Securities and Exchange Commission (SEC). For some accounting firms, investment advising has become a separate business—enabling the firm to provide "one-stop" service to its accounting clients.

SERVICE AS VALUE

What differentiates a desirable purchasing experience from an undesirable experience? Today's consumers and organizational buyers not only want the opportunity to buy quality products at the right price, but they also expect to buy from qualified personnel with maximum benefits and minimum effort. They demand *value*—an intangible concept that is frequently defined in terms of exceptional customer service that accompanies exceptional product quality and value-based prices.

At the consumer level, many competing marketers offer similar brands and merchandise selections to the same group of customers, giving them many shopping alternatives. Successful retailers, such as Nordstrom, Inc., differentiate themselves by competing on the basis of superior customer service to build long-term customer relationships. This is often the only dimension that distinguishes one marketer's offerings from those of a competitor.

The Importance of Strategic Planning

The strategic planning process followed by marketers of services and goods is similar. It starts with the business philosophy or mission, which provides the basis for the company's objectives and other elements of the strategic plan. For example, a luxury cruise line might follow this strategic planning process:

Strategic Planning Process	Strategic Marketing Example
1. Corporate mission statement	Cruise line; luxury travel to exotic locations
2. Performance objectives	$50 million in sales; 10% return-on-investment
3. Situational analysis	Increase in older, affluent population; globalization of business; availability of cruise ships, hospitality crew, port access; presently operating under capacity
4. Strategic objectives and strategy definition	Increase number of first-time passengers and build loyalty for repeat business; offer cruise plus land travel packages
5. Implementation and tactics	Budget and prepare promotion to travel agents; direct mail to professional group membership lists
6. Execution	Launch advertising campaign in select media; mail promotional literature to carefully screened mailing list; sell cruises to ship capacity
7. Evaluation and control	Assess increase in number of passengers, customer satisfaction and intent to repeat purchase, achievement of sales and return on investment targets

In developing its marketing strategy, a service organization must have a clear understanding of how it is (or should be) positioned relative to the competition and what competitive moves are taking place. The company also must decide whether it wants to be a service leader or follow the leader.

Competitive Positioning.   Since marketers do not operate in a vacuum, they must monitor their competitors constantly. Essentially, services should be positioned competitively in every aspect of the service product itself and in all methods the company uses to communicate the service's features and benefits to its target market. In other words, the **service image** (position) can be managed effectively by careful attention to the actual service design and performance and to everything that represents the service to customers (written and verbal communications, physical evidence, etc.). The customer should believe that the service he or she is receiving is superior on relevant dimensions to that provided by the competition.

Service image
Competitive positioning conveyed by everything that represents the company and its service products; dimensions used in positioning should be valued by customers.

Service Leadership versus Follow-the-Leader.   Marketers of services also must decide whether to position their company and service products as leaders in the industry or to wait for competitors to set the standards and follow their lead. Market-entry strategies are beyond the scope of this chapter, but the companies that are first to market are not always those which emerge as service leaders. For example, CompuServe was first to market with Internet on-line services but eventually was eclipsed by America Online and other service providers who set the parameters for quality service. Despite AOL's pricing debacle in early 1997, the company retained a competitive edge with its overall service quality. (In September 1997, it was announced that AOL would acquire CompuServe and its customer base.) There are a number of other well-known and not so well-known examples that demonstrate this type of service leadership. Among them are Southwest Airlines, a service leader among both discount- and regular-fare airlines, Nordstrom department stores, and smaller computer companies that have out-serviced industry giant IBM.

Benefits of Exceptional Customer Service
. . . .

Marketers of both goods and services have learned that one of the most effective ways to differentiate themselves from competitors is through exceptional customer service offered with each purchase. The "extras" provided by customer service add to the cost of doing business, but customer-oriented businesses have found that the benefits of offering a range of services desired by customers generally far outweigh the costs for the following reasons:

1. Services attract and keep customers.

2. Service is instrumental in recovering lost or about-to-be-lost sales.

3. There is a strong relationship between levels of service quality and levels of customer satisfaction.

4. Customer service activities generally lead to a profitable return on investment over the long term.

5. Services play a major role in the marketing mix.

Attracting and Keeping Customers.   Services such as availability of credit, convenient locations and hours, knowledgeable salespeople, no-hassle return privileges, responsive service personnel, and free delivery add value to purchases. The service relationship between buyers and sellers is ongoing, as illustrated in the following retail examples for an automotive repair business and an apparel retailer.

Before the sale, media advertisements, signage, and sales assistance provide both types of customers with the necessary purchase information. During the sales process, the apparel customer may be given assistance in selecting and trying on appropriate garments and having them fitted for alterations. The auto repair customer may be shown a diagram that explains the problem area in the car and the tradeoffs for different methods of repairing the problem and may be given a "loaner" car to drive during the repair process. Both customers may use a credit card for payment.

After the sale, the altered garment or the repaired auto may be delivered to the customer's home, and the salesperson may call to thank the customer for the business, offer future assistance, or tell the customer about an upcoming special sales event. In addition to these expected or essential services, other optional services may provide a sustainable competitive advantage in any type of business. For the apparel customer, extras might include baby-sitting, unusual merchandise assortments, or locating items in a competing retail store. For the auto repair customer, extras might include vacuuming the interior of the car and checking the oil and tire pressure.

Recovering Lost or About-to-be-Lost Sales.   Customers who are frustrated, upset, disappointed, or otherwise negatively affected by a buying experience usually want to know that someone cares about their problem, will listen to their dilemma, and will try their very best to do something about it. Customers have more economic power than ever before, patronizing the businesses that are best at problem resolution.

The Staples sales associate described earlier recovered the sale of map pins to the small business customer by going the "extra mile" in service—and not only saved the $20 sale but also developed a long-term relationship with a customer who now spends 100 times that amount every year.[5]

A Sears, Roebuck and Co. sales associate recovered the sale of a broken garage door opener by taking prompt action to correct the problem. Another Sears representative called 2 days later to see if the problem had been resolved and offered extended warranties on the garage door opener and other Sears items. The retailer admitted the mistake, fixed it quickly, and exceeded the customer's expectations, leaving a positive impression.[6]

Linking Customer Satisfaction to Service Quality.   Customer expectations about the types of services that should be offered and their criteria for performance of these services have a major impact on the level of satisfaction or dissatisfaction felt with the total purchase experience. This can be represented as

Customer satisfaction
Difference between customers' service expectations and perceptions of service actually received.

Customer satisfaction = (service expectations − perceived service performance)

If performance exceeds expectations, then satisfaction should be high. Conversely, if service expectations are not met (or are unrealistic), dissatisfaction will result. Loyal, satisfied customers give a marketer a long-term competitive advantage. Of course, expectations vary according to retail type; for example, less service is expected from an off-price retailer and more from a boutique.

MARKETING IN THE INFORMATION AGE

USAA Leverages Processes for Strategic Advantage

The re-engineering of many businesses has resulted in a shift from a purely functional organization to a structure that focuses on creating an efficient horizontal workflow. These processes often change the way work is performed. In a service organization, processes are the dominant factor in customer and employee satisfaction, because it is the processes that provide evidence of service quality.

United Services Automobile Association (USAA) is a major provider of insurance and financial services to active and retired military personnel and their families. Robert Herres, chairman and CEO, says, "At USAA, we have always had processes linking together our basic activities. There's an underwriting process, a rate-setting process, a loss-management process, a catastrophe-management process, as well as the usual collection of functional processes." Although these processes seem to work well, Herres says, "We found that if you really want to exploit new technology—and for us, that includes both communications and information systems—you have to analyze how the work in your organization actually gets done and decide which steps can be tailored to a machine and which are best left to people." He explains that this is accomplished by developing detailed process maps and getting the entire organization to think in terms of processes.

USAA started out as a direct writer of insurance in 1922, operating by mail and telephone from one centralized location in San Antonio, Texas. When the company began to think about how it could apply new technology, it discovered that many traditions had built up over the years in its administrative organization, creating a number of unnecessary steps. Paper was lost or hard to find—or not even missed. The existing processes had to be re-evaluated before they could be integrated with modern information systems.

Herres says, "Technology also forced us to think about how and where our processes intersect. Alignment across businesses is critical for us because our goal is to exploit the efficiencies of centralized information management while we decentralize service delivery." In order to leverage technology across the company, someone has to ensure that one area of the company (such as insurance) is not creating systems and processes that do not interface well with the corporate system. For example, most of USAA's customers move once every 3 years, and the company was confronted with a seemingly simple—but inefficient—system of changing addresses. It took a year and a half to set up the necessary systems and processes so that a customer could call any of USAA's lines of business and have an address change posted immediately in all business sectors. This process cuts across all parts of the organization.

USAA recognizes the growing importance of technical skills and the need for information technology people to communicate with businesspeople in key positions. The company provides ambitious programs to teach computer skills to employees who do not have the necessary background. Senior managers are more involved with processes today than in the past—management processes (e.g., how the CEO runs the company), business processes (e.g., service design, customer service), and work processes (e.g., how the work actually gets done).

"As technology improves and the pace of change accelerates, all three types of processes become faster moving and more interactive. Decision-making cycles tighten, feedback loops are shorter, and there's less room for error. The risks go up because you can get left behind a lot more quickly."

Source: David A. Garvin, "Leveraging Processes for Strategic Advantage," *Harvard Business Review* (September–October 1995), pp. 77–90.

Realizing a Profitable Return on Investment.   Most businesses achieve successful results when they invest in customer service activities. Just as services are designed to satisfy the needs of different customers, the costs of these services vary according to business type, service product assortment, and customer base. However, the cost to provide a service may not be proportionate to the perceived value placed on it by a customer.

Performing a Major Role in Marketing.   Because of their contribution to sales and profitability, services are an important component of the overall marketing mix. Having the right products in the right place at the right price and right time is critical for marketing success, along with the effective use of promotional tools. However, these factors are insufficient without the added value offered by integrating wanted customer services into the overall marketing-mix strategy.

SERVICE MARKETING ISSUES

The unique characteristics of intangible services often make it more difficult to target customer groups and to anticipate how they will respond to service offerings. Some approaches to marketing primary and ancillary services to defined market segments are described below. In addition, several other factors need to be considered relative to the purchase of services. Perceived risk, service attributes, brand and service provider loyalty, and the diffusion of innovations (adoption process) are discussed briefly.[7]

Market Segmentation

Successful services marketing starts with an understanding of customers' wants and needs. This includes identifying the customer group(s) to be served, their particular service needs, and how they make their buying decisions.

The general bases for market segmentation discussed earlier in this book can be applied to final consumers and business customers for both goods and services. The characteristics of these segments provide direction for the service marketing mix. Some useful bases for identifying customer segments for a variety of services include:

Demographic	*Consumer:* Income, age, family life cycle, etc. (e.g., child care and child-sized bathrooms for younger customers, wheel chairs and rest areas for senior citizens)
	Business: Company size, location, number of employees (e.g., assistance with inventory management or promotion for smaller customers)
Geographic	*Consumer:* Proximity to the store, type of neighborhood, etc. (e.g., delivery services and catalog or telephone shopping services for distant customers)
	Business: Concentration relative to an industry, sales territory characteristics, etc.
Psychographics/ lifestyle	*Consumer:* A combination of similar demographic and psychological characteristics (e.g., activities, interests, opinions); tendency to follow similar consumer

behavior patterns (e.g., personal shopping and delivery for time-poor dual-career couples with children, to satisfy their need for convenience)

Benefits sought
Customers: Expect certain benefits from the purchase of primary services and from the services that accompany the purchase of physical goods. Benefits may include convenience, avoidance of risk (e.g., warranties, money-back guarantees), or exceptional value for the price.
Consumers: May seek other benefits such as status or enhancement of personal image.
Businesses: May seek benefits such as improved productivity, efficiency, and increased profits.

Price sensitivity
Consumers: Demand for retail services, such as sales assistance, delivery, or warranties, is related to their sensitivity to charges for these services (e.g., "economic shoppers" prefer self-service and cash-and-carry transactions to keep the purchase price as low as possible).
Businesses: Seek value through added services, such as assistance with promotional events or inventory management.

Perceived Risk

Perceived risk
Higher levels of risk or uncertainty experienced by customers when buying services versus tangible goods due to factors such as lack of information, experience, and standardization.

Buyers tend to feel a higher level of **perceived risk** when buying services than when buying tangible goods for several reasons: lack of purchase information, customer involvement, inability to return or exchange, and lack of standardization.[8]

Lack of Purchase Information.   Service customers are hampered in their purchase decisions by a relative lack of evaluative criteria for judging the quality of a service and the benefits that it offers. They also typically suffer from a lack of purchase information. This inability to evaluate many service attributes before purchase, or even after purchase, can lead to a higher level of perceived risk by the buyer. Financial services are one area where customers may feel a sense of inadequacy in making a purchase decision. For example, many South Africans were introduced to banking services for the first time in 1996 in locations where people previously were considered too poor or illiterate to be valuable customers for a bank. The ability to open a bank account and to use an ATM were new experiences for this vast, underdeveloped market, where people needed an easy, safe way to stash and access cash. Bank employees helped customers with usage information as long as needed, with the goal of educating them to help themselves.[9]

Customer involvement
In the simultaneous production and consumption process for services, increases the level of customer anxiety and perceived risk.

Customer Involvement.   The personal nature of many services, requiring a high degree of **customer involvement** in the production process, can cause anxiety about potential risk (e.g., a complex medical procedure). The simultaneous production and consumption of many services lead to differences in purchase behavior, such as more attention given by customers to characteristics of service providers and other customers. These factors are inseparable components of the total service experience. For example, beauty salons cater to a wide range of customers with different hair and skin characteristics and different styling preferences. Customers often develop a personal relationship with a stylist and enjoy the social aspects of a visit to the salon.[10]

No Returns or Exchanges.   Since many services are consumed as they are produced (e.g., dental services, computer repair), a dissatisfied customer cannot return or exchange defective work in the same way he or she can return a shirt or copy machine. Guarantees and service warranties may be offered but may be difficult to implement satisfactorily. For example, customers of a beauty salon cannot return a bad permanent to get a new hairdo. Restitution can be made, but not without possible embarrassment and inconvenience. To overcome this type of perceived risk, many service marketers are pursuing a differentiation strategy that provides more warranties and guarantees for the quality of their work.

Lack of Standardization (Variability).   Because services tend to be more variable and less standardized than products, customers attach considerably more risk to their purchase. Service outputs usually are not as consistent as manufactured products. On the other hand, variability can be an advantage where a service can be customized to the needs of the individual buyer. While the hair stylists described earlier can customize their services for a wide variety of customers, they are expected to provide the same quality of service every time a customer visits their salon, regardless of the specific service provided.

Evaluation of Service Attributes

Purchase behavior is influenced by the degree to which services lend themselves to evaluation. Three attributes of services influence the evaluation process: search properties, experience properties, and credence properties.

Search properties
Attributes of a service that the customer can discern prior to purchase.

Search Properties.   Attributes of a service that a customer can discern prior to purchase, such as price or location, are referred to as **search properties.** For example, a medical patient facing the prospect of surgery may be limited to prehospitalization service attributes such as appearance of the physical facilities, hospital personnel, and "paperwork."

Experience properties
Attributes that can be discerned only during or after the service has been performed.

Experience Properties.   **Experience properties** are those attributes that can be discerned only during or after the service has been performed. For our surgery patient, this may be an evaluation of the physical comfort or discomfort that was experienced, the concern demonstrated by the surgeon and the hospital staff, and response to care-related questions.

Credence properties
Service attributes inferred from a subjective evaluation of the entire process.

Credence Properties.   Some service attributes cannot be determined with any accuracy, even after the service has been performed. For example, the surgery patient is generally not a medical expert who can determine the medical success of the procedure. Rather, **credence properties** must be inferred from a subjective evaluation of the entire process.

Brand and Service Provider Loyalty

Differences in the ways customers purchase goods and services are due to psychological involvement, personal interaction, and fewer impulse purchases. Loyal customers feel more confidence and less risk in repeat purchases from the same service provider.

Psychological Involvement.   The fact that most services require participation of the customer to some degree increases the personal level of psychological involvement in the service process. When combined with a relatively high level of perceived risk and inadequate information before the purchase, loyalty to a service provider is likely to occur. When purchasing services, such as those of a physician or long-distance telephone company, a customer may lack prepurchase information about possible substitute services and may be influenced not to change or consider other providers due to perceived costs of time and money.

Personal Interaction.   The inseparability, at some level, of the service provider and customer should lead to a relationship of mutual trust. As each party gains a better knowledge of the other's ability and needs through personal interaction, a higher level of loyalty evolves. Companies that maintain meaningful databases on their customers can have an advantage in building brand loyalty through personal relationships with their customers

Fewer Impulse Purchases.   Customers are more likely to make impulse purchases for physical goods than for intangible services because of the perceived risk factor. This is particularly true for first-time service purchases, which generally come about after a need has been recognized and a search for information about alternatives has occurred. Once a customer has had a good service experience, it becomes time-consuming to revisit the alternatives, and brand loyalty minimizes perceived risk associated with the service.

Adoption Process for Innovations

Rate of diffusion
Pace at which innovations are accepted by the target market.

Service innovations tend to be diffused into the market at a slower rate than goods innovations. It can be difficult to implement change due to customers' resistance to trying an unproven service or method of delivering the service. The **rate of diffusion** depends on the innovation's relative advantage, ability to communicate, complexity, compatibility, and ability to test or sample. Figure 9.2 provides a graphic example of the rate of acceptance and adoption of Internet shopping services.

Adoption process
Length of time for a segment of the market to accept and purchase new services.

The **adoption process** is shortened when customers perceive that an innovation offers greater benefits than existing alternatives. However, service innovations tend to be adopted more slowly than physical product innovations because it is more difficult to evaluate their relative advantages in advance. In part, this is due to the difficulty in communicating intangible benefits that cannot be displayed, seen, touched, or tested in advance. (The communication task is easier when the service can be explained relative to a tangible good.)

FIGURE 9.2

• •

Adoption Process for Service Innovations*

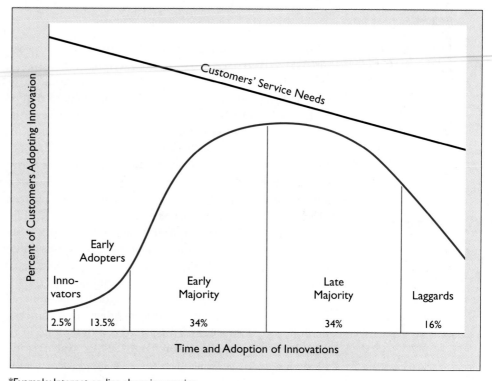

*Example: Internet on-line shopping service.

• •

The complexity of a service also slows down the adoption process. Innovative approaches to financial services (such as on-line banking and investing), for example, contain features that are complex and difficult to explain to a prospective customer. The length of time that it takes for customers to adopt a service innovation also depends on its compatibility with the customers' past experience and existing values relative to this purchase. Finally, the customers' ability to try out the service, risk-free, before purchase affects the time to adoption. It is difficult for a consumer to "sample" a new haircut or tooth extraction in advance or for a company to try out an entire local-area network (LAN) system on its own premises before commitment to the innovation. Therefore, marketers must "tangibilize" these benefits to the extent possible.

THE SERVICE DESIGN PROCESS

• •

The service design process starts with a determination of the right type(s) of services to offer, which in turn depends on customer segments to be served, nature of the service, pricing strategy, level of complexity or uncertainty of purchase (including perceived risk), and the firm's resources. Services marketing managers also must decide how many services to offer and at what level. Finally, managers must determine the details involved in actually delivering the service, that is, what is needed to carry out each task.

Determining Customer Targets

As discussed previously, the needs and wants of the target market should drive service marketing decisions. Different segments have different service needs, ability or willingness to pay, and profitability potential for the firm.

The travel and entertainment industries recognize the need to cater to shifts in their target markets. Intrawest, owner of a network of North American ski resorts from West Virginia to California, believes it has the formula for luring the most desirable skiers. These skiers typically like to take vacations at "destination" resorts such as Blackcomb Mountain located 90 miles north of Vancouver, Canada, and spend four times more than day-trippers on items other than lodging and lift tickets. Blackcomb provides multilingual ski instructors to serve destination skiers from places other than North America. Intrawest focuses on enhancing uniqueness while assuring guests of uniform excellence. The company's strategy is to create destinations—total mountain villages that extend beyond the usual ski resort concept.[11]

Wal-Mart Stores, Inc., and Bloomingdale's Inc. generally target two different customer segments, although a large number of customers (known as *cross-shoppers*) may shop in both stores. Thus there is a difference in retail services demanded by customers from a mass merchandiser like Wal-Mart and a department store like Bloomingdale's. At Wal-Mart, the self-service format emphasizes availability of merchandise assortments, easy unassisted shopping (information in shopping carts, convenient layout, wide aisles, easy-to-read signs), informed help from nonsales employees, a large number of checkout registers, and empowered employees to carry out the store's "customer is always right" philosophy. In contrast, Bloomingdale's has responded to the service needs of its clientele by replacing many part-timers with full-time salespeople, offering Godiva chocolates, and sending thank-you notes to preferred shoppers. Bloomingdale's also holds private shopping nights where the store gives "gifts of service" such as free alterations and free delivery of furniture.[12]

Determining the Nature of the Service

The type of service has an impact on service design in a number of ways. Primary (core) services related to medicine, investments, software design, and other relatively complex areas require considerable support services and qualified customer contact personnel. On the other hand, automated services, such as ATMs, require more design effort behind the scenes than at the point of customer contact. Restaurant services run the gamut from extensive personal service in a fine-dining sit-down establishment to the less personal, automated service at a fast-food drive-through restaurant.

The design of ancillary services follows the same logic as that for core services. If the support service is relatively complex and is instrumental in providing differentiation from competitors, it will require a more elaborate service design (people, equipment, processes). Large, heavy items such as furniture and appliances may require the design of delivery and repair services. Apparel retailers may need to incorporate alteration services, and a bicycle shop or toy store may need to assemble purchases. Each aspect of a primary or ancillary service must be designed to deliver customer satisfaction.

Determining Pricing Strategy

The ideal position for a service marketer is to achieve differentiation based on exceptional, high-quality service while maximizing profits and minimizing costs. The pricing strategy that will deliver these results is based on all elements of the service design (e.g., complexity, customization, resource requirements, etc.), along with the marketer's ability to contain costs without sacrificing quality. However, pricing strategy also depends on what the market is willing to pay, as well as competitors' pricing strategies.

Pricing decisions must be made for ancillary services that are performed to enhance the value of a core service or good. For example, upscale retailers are expected to offer a wide range of services at no additional charge to justify their higher pricing structure. Examples include free alterations, intensive effort to locate wanted merchandise if not available locally, personal shopping, and lenient merchandise return privileges. Upscale consumers also may expect the unexpected—optional services such as special store hours, refreshments while shopping, and a comfortable place to relax, with a phone or fax machine available. Pricing decisions for ancillary or supporting services present the dilemma of whether to charge a fee or not. Marketers at all levels of the channel react to customer demands for service, believing that these services will build sales and develop long-term relationships. However, additional sales may come at too high a price if the firm does not consider the cost of providing these services and the impact on profits. Table 9.3 illustrates the relationship between customer classifications, the cost to serve each segment, and the net realized price.

Pricing strategies can be determined according to customer segments, based on amount and frequency of purchases, types of services (or goods) purchased, new versus potential buyers, and so forth. Assuming that the services offered are considered necessary to make the sale, then other questions must be answered about the

TABLE 9.3
The Customer-Cost-Price Relationship

Customer Type	*Average Cost of Customer Service to Marketer*	*Price of Service to Customer*
New customer	High	Low to moderate
Frequent buyer/heavy user	Low	Varies
High-tech		
Informed/sophisticated	Low	Low
Naive/beginner	High	High to moderate

effect of service fees on buying, such as: Will a "heavy user" of a good or service stop buying if he or she has to pay for a particular service? And what is the company-wide impact on all purchases made by that customer? Should the fee be adjusted? Are there other services that are more important?

The cost of providing a service is directly related to the level of service provided. Some of these costs are wages for personnel (sales, service performance, credit, etc.), physical facilities (initial cost, maintenance, use of non-sales-producing space), necessary technology and equipment (computers, databases, production equipment, etc.), and cost of price adjustments or allowances. Both direct and indirect costs are associated with customer dissatisfaction caused by poor service or service that is not valued by the customer.[13]

Direct costs are associated with actual service performance, making customer adjustments in terms of repeating the service or refunding payment, honoring warranties and guarantees, and costs (mostly marketing) of attracting new customers on the basis of service. *Indirect costs* include customer turnover rate (dissatisfied customers buy less or stop buying) and word-of-mouth referrals (satisfied customers are the best form of advertising, negative word of mouth travels fast from dissatisfied customers).

A potential cost is related to the firm's lack of customer orientation. Managers must heed their customers' complaints and suggestions for customer service improvements and/or innovations. Otherwise, this oversight may result in lost business. Another indirect cost that often is overlooked and difficult to measure is loss of productivity as a result of the time and energy required by service managers and employees to "put out fires" for customers when no quality service plan is in place.

Addressing Complexity or Uncertainty

Complex services (home building, investments) and physical goods (automobiles, electronics, computers) frequently require extensive sales assistance, demonstrations, and service guarantees. Complexity is related to a feeling of uncertainty or risk when purchasing expensive or complex products. Thus the marketer needs to assure the customer that the company stands behind the purchase (e.g., after-sale assistance, help phone number, no-risk returns).

Health care needs often are related to high levels of complexity and uncertainty. Most patients find the details of medical problems difficult to understand, and treatments are not guaranteed to cure. As a result, medical practitioners need to provide patients with information that they can understand in order to remove as much anxiety as possible. They also should demonstrate a personal interest in follow-up procedures to reduce the uncertainty felt by the patient.

Assessing the Marketer's Resources

The ideal is not always achievable. Customers may want more services at a higher level than it is reasonable for the services marketer to provide. Services require human, financial, and physical resources (personnel, facilities, equipment) that may be needed elsewhere. A small service business, for example, may have to outsource ancillary customer services such as accounting, delivery, and credit (although there are advantages and disadvantages to contracting out services). Larger service businesses may allocate more resources to physical facilities and expansion in order to offer more services to more customers. The opening scenario for this chapter described the problems faced by America Online during its $19.95 flat-rate promotion. Clearly, AOL's capacity (resources) was inadequate to provide quality service to customers during early stages of the promotion.

Determining the Number of Services

It is not necessary to offer all possible services to customers. Customer services should be prioritized by their perceived value to customers, with these rankings weighed against the cost of providing each service. Concentration should be on offering those services that make a difference in the consumers' present and future purchase decisions. Note that customers may be willing to pay some or all of the cost of highly desirable services if the value is evident. For example, novice computer users usually need help setting up a new PC and loading software and perhaps basic instruction. Business customers may require the assistance of a consultant who has identified marketing problems in implementation of the recommended solution. Since the level of service required differs by the experience and/or sophistication of the customer, services can be bundled as a package with several different pricing structures.

Determining the Level of Service

The level of customer service offered by a service provider can extend from full service with maximum assistance before, during, and after the sale to a completely self-service operation where the customer shops relatively unassisted until the sale is finalized. Examples include an upscale restaurant versus a self-service cafeteria line or an automated car wash versus a full-detailing service to clean a car.

The service-level decision must be consistent with the types of services offered and their importance in making a sale and keeping a customer. We previously classified services as essential (primary or core) or expected and optional (ancillary). Recognize that while some services may be essential for one group of customers, they may be optional for another customer segment.

SETTING STANDARDS FOR SERVICE QUALITY

Most customers believe that they have relatively clear definitions of service quality and judge service experiences accordingly. However, when it comes to specifying and describing service design features, the marketer is faced with a much more formidable task. Each detail of the service, both seen (or experienced) and unseen by the customer, must focus on how to deliver quality.

Andersen Consulting suggests seven best practices to achieve better service:[14] (1) develop a situational service strategy (know where you are relative to your competition), (2) integrate customer service throughout every aspect of the business, (3) define all points of service, and communicate what is expected of employees, (4) hold everyone accountable for quality of customer service, (5) define, communicate, and execute an all-out recovery strategy, (6) give customer contact personnel the ability to solve customers' problems immediately, and (7) focus on continuous improvement in customer service.

One effective approach to designing and delivering quality service is to benchmark against superior service marketers. It is also essential to establish and communicate quality standards, identify actual and potential gaps in service quality, and have an effective service retention and recovery program in operation.

Benchmarking

Benchmark
Compare a company's service performance against the performance of competitors or other business leaders that are recognized for excellent practices.

Companies should **benchmark** their own service performance against the performance of competitors or other leaders in the business world. At the forefront of outstanding customer service are companies such as Nordstrom, Inc., Walt Disney World, Stew Leonard, Marriott International Inc., and many others. Each industry has a service leader that sets the standard for everyone else. Think about the service marketers that you deal with for personal or business services. Who does customer service right, and who fails miserably? What are the reasons for success or failure in delivering high-quality services?

Nordstrom, Inc., started out as a relatively obscure department store in the Pacific Northwest but has risen to national prominence, outstripping its would-be competitors on a well-deserved and highly publicized reputation for exceptional customer service. How has the company done this? Everyone—even the Nordstrom family—has to start on the selling floor. A decentralized organization pushes decisions as close to the customer as possible. Salespeople are encouraged to provide

TABLE 9.4

Dimensions of Service Quality

1. Tangibles	Appearance of the company's physical interior and exterior environment, equipment, personnel, and communications materials. (The customer contact and service areas for selling and performing the service, handling complaints, etc., should be convenient and attractive, with cheerful, positive, well-informed personnel.)
2. Reliability	The marketer's ability to perform the promised service dependably and accurately time after time after time. Do it right the first time and every time thereafter.
3. Responsiveness	The marketer's willingness to help customers and provide the needed service promptly. Resolve the problem quickly and answer the customers' questions intelligently and accurately. Honor promised schedules and follow up as needed.
4. Assurance	Service employees' knowledge and courtesy, their ability to convey a sense of trust and confidence to customers. They should know what they are talking about (or find out from someone who does) and treat the customer with respect.
5. Empathy	The ability of service personnel to convey to each customer that he or she is important and that the service provider and company care about the customer and his or her problem. (This is sometimes difficult when the customer is being unreasonable or obnoxious, but it does pay off in the long run.)

Source: Adapted from Valarie A. Zeithaml, A. Parasuraman, and Leonard L. Berry, *Delivering Quality Service: Balancing Customer Perceptions and Expectations* (New York: Free Press, 1990), pp. 15–33.

feedback to management, empowered to take returns, and always expected to do the unexpected for their customers.

Specific standards for service quality should be based on input from customers, employees, and managers who are responsible for carrying out the intent of the service design. Service quality standards must be stated clearly to ensure proper implementation by customer service personnel and to allow accurate measurement of their effectiveness in satisfying customers' service needs and achieving management's performance objectives.

Leading service marketers have identified the key dimensions of service quality. Based on extensive market research with thousands of respondents in different service industries, Zeithaml, Parasuraman, and Berry[15] have narrowed the key factors that influence customers' evaluations of service quality down to five basic dimensions, as shown in Table 9.4. In many studies, reliability has been identified as the number one factor used in assessing service quality. Thus, do what you say you are going to do—and do it better than anyone else—every time!

Planning Service Tasks and Activities

For each individual type of service, management must identify the specific tasks and activities needed to carry it out. An example of customer service activities involved in handling complaints and the resources needed to support them is shown in Table 9.5.

TABLE 9.5

Customer Service Tasks, Activities, and Resources: An Example for Complaint Handling*

Service Tasks, Activities	Resources to Carry Out Service Task
Initial customer contact, communication	Sales or service personnel, physical setting if in person, or telephone or mail response capability
Discuss problem; listen!	Service personnel training, empathy
Identify problem	Knowledge of service process, procedures, and options
Determine alternative solutions	Computer, database, policy manual; trained, empowered employees; availability of relevant information for decision
Choose "best" solution	Training and experience in matching customer needs and service solution
Act quickly to implement solution	Clear implementation guidelines; necessary systems, personnel, and resources available to carry out solution
Follow up contact with customer	System for record keeping, documentation of transaction

*Ideally, customer complaints should be recognized and corrected before the sale is completed. After the sale, remedies are more limited and more expensive.

Blueprinting.   Ideally, of course, problem areas should be recognized before they occur. **Blueprinting** or flowcharting techniques can be used to provide a visual representation of all the steps involved in delivering a particular service to a customer. This makes it possible to discover missing steps or redundancies in the process and to determine necessary remedies and resources.

Blueprinting
Similar to flowcharting, provides a visual representation of all steps involved in delivering a service to a customer; can be used to identify failure points in service quality.

The process of delivering a particular service to a customer usually involves many discrete activities and individuals. The customer assumes that all elements in this process are working together to solve his or her problem. Frustration mounts when the system breaks down because employees do not communicate with each other about the customer's problem and they do not comprehend the complete service process. To overcome this problem, the marketer can take the customer's perspective to learn where the customer gets "lost" in the system.[16] This can be done by flowcharting each step in the customer's experience to gain a better understanding of the process and by blueprinting (a more sophisticated extension of flowcharting) every activity needed to create and deliver the service. This process also requires identification of the critical linkages between activities. A blueprint of the customer service process for an express mail delivery service and a hotel is illustrated in Figure 9.3. Critical incidents can occur at each point in the process, resulting in customer satisfaction—or in service failure.

Identifying Gaps in Service Quality.   Service-quality problems tend to be related to expectations, perceptions, and communications problems. These problems can be classified into five service-quality gaps that have important implications for marketing managers at all levels of an organization:

Gap 1. Difference between consumer expectations and management perceptions of customer expectations.

Gap 2. Difference between management perceptions of customer expectations and service-quality specifications.

Gap 3. Difference between service-quality specifications and the service actually delivered.

Gap 4. Difference between service delivery and what is communicated about the service to customers.

Gap 5. Difference between consumer expectations about the service and perceptions of the service actually delivered (a summary of gaps 1 through 4).[17]

SERVICE DELIVERY AND IMPLEMENTATION

The process of delivering high-quality customer service must start with an organizational culture that nurtures a customer-oriented perspective. Marketers not only must identify those services most desired by their customers but also must determine the best ways to deliver high-quality service to achieve customer satisfaction and recognize the important role of customer contact personnel.

Organization Structure and Culture

The organization must encourage and facilitate a service philosophy—from the top managers to the lowest employee. Experience in successful service organizations suggests that if front-line employees are to perform high-quality service, then the

FIGURE 9.3

Blueprinting the Customer Service Process

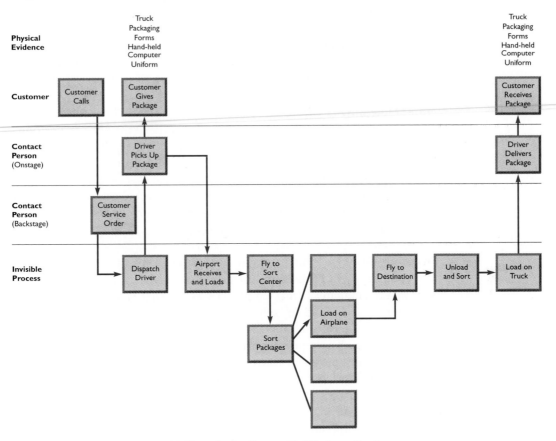

(a) Blueprint for Express Mail Delivery Service

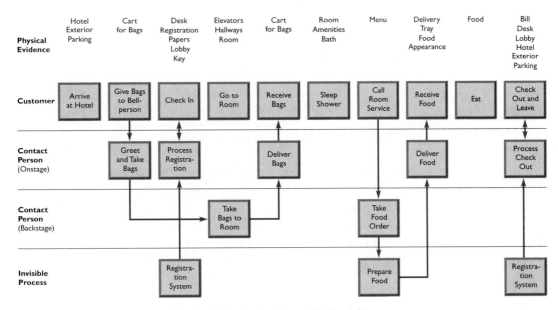

(b) Blueprint for Overnight Hotel Stay

Source: Reprinted from *The Service Quality Handbook,* by Eberhard E. Scheuing. Copyright © 1993 AMACOM, a Division of American Management Association International. Reprinted by permission of AMACOM, a division of American Management Association International, New York, NY. All rights reserved. http://www.amanet.org.

entire organizational structure must be designed with a customer-orientation focus. Some successful service organizations also boast an informal structure that makes customer service everyone's responsibility; every employee has ownership when it comes to serving the customers. Further, management must ensure that the necessary support exists for successful implementation of customer service activities.

Top-Management Commitment.   Senior executives have to believe in the benefits of allocating resources to providing exceptional services to customers. Otherwise, the lack of commitment to customers and their service needs will filter down through the entire company. The service commitment can be carried out at different levels, from lowest-level self-service, do-it-yourself, cash-and-carry, bag-it-yourself, no-returns operations to high-level sales assistance, credit availability, exclusive image packaging of purchased goods and services, lenient complaint resolution, and considerable pampering of customers.

Treating Employees as Internal Customers.   To infuse personnel throughout the company with enthusiasm for giving each and every customer top-notch service, many companies treat employees as internal customers. Internal marketing programs are designed to "sell" employees on their company and its products, as practiced by Warner Bros. Inc., Disney World, Stew Leonard, and Southwest Airlines. When employees have positive attitudes about their company and believe in what it represents, this attitude is conveyed to customers and the community. It has been said that if you can sell the employees on the company, they will sell the customers. In customer service activities this is particularly important because of the human element involved and the fact that many customer services exist to take care of negative customer problems.

Viewing Service as a Performance.   Service firms like Disney World and premium resort hotels refer to their customers as "guests" and to employees as "cast members." To these service-oriented companies, every service activity is a performance and is designed from a dramaturgical (or theatrical) point of view. Elements of a drama can be related to service design and delivery: the setting (servicescape, social and physical characteristics), scene (with script), performance (service delivery), cast of actors and actresses (service providers), and audience (customers). Viewing service as a performance should result in better management of a company's image and higher levels of customer satisfaction.

Ensuring Service Recovery.   An important aspect of the service design and delivery process is the retention of customers. Although retention achieved by providing high-quality service throughout the entire service process is the most desirable way to accomplish this, unanticipated problems can occur. Effective service-recovery procedures must be in place to overcome such problems, regardless of the type of business. A memorable headline, "Puh-leeze, won't somebody help me?"[18] expresses the frustration felt by exasperated service customers every day. A firm's ability to solve customers' problems, give needed assistance, fix disappointments, and give service beyond what is required or expected is instrumental in developing long-term relationships.

Certainly, some mistakes will occur in business transactions; for example, a repair may not be completed satisfactorily, the wrong product may be shipped or ar-

TABLE 9.6
. . . .
Suggested Actions for Successful Service Recovery

Service recovery can be successful when the following actions are taken:

- *Measure the costs of effective service recovery.* The costs of losing a customer include the loss of repeat purchases and negative image and word-of-mouth communications with other customers.

- *Break the silence.* Good service recovery starts with listening to the customer to identify the problem. Since most customers do not complain, marketers must be proactive in identifying the problems that customers may not communicate but that would make them purchase elsewhere.

- *Anticipate needs for recovery.* Managers must continuously review their organization to find potential failure points in marketing, operations, or other areas that affect the performance of high-quality customer service.

- *Act fast.* Customer service problems tend to escalate rapidly, so it is important to identify them quickly (preferably before the customer does) and prove a commitment to the customer by taking care of them immediately.

- *Train employees.* Train customer contact personnel and give them the skills they need to deal effectively with upset customers. Employees should understand the entire service delivery process—not just an isolated function that may seem to have a questionable purpose.

- *Empower the front line.* Customer contact personnel should be empowered and given the authority, responsibility, and incentives to recognize, be concerned about, and take care of customers' problems. (Limits to the monetary value of service recovery actions may be set.)

- *Close the loop.* The customer should be kept informed about corrective actions taken to resolve his or her problem or given an explanation of why the situation can't be "fixed." This can be done by telephone, letter, or asking for feedback or suggestions that have a chance of being implemented.

Source: Reprinted by permission of *Harvard Business Review.* From "The Profitable Art of Service Recovery" by Hart, Christopher, W. L., James L. Heskett and W. Earl Sasser, Jr., July/August 1990. Copyright © 1990 by the President and Fellows of Harvard College; all rights reserved.

rive late or defective, a salesperson may not call a customer back as promised, the wrong price may be charged, or a billing error may occur. No matter how diligently marketers try to avoid product or service errors, it is virtually impossible to achieve "zero defects." Whether a customer problem seems inconsequential or a complaint seems like whining over a petty issue, it must be resolved. Thus companies must have a plan for service recovery—to win back customers one at a time. Everyone in the organization must be trained and motivated to provide customer satisfaction and be given the ability to make decisions on the spot. Employee attitudes should never communicate an "I don't care" or "It's not my job" attitude. Suggested actions for successful service recovery are described in Table 9.6, and the high cost of losing just one customer is presented in Figure 9.4.

Personnel Issues
. . . .

Quality of customer service can be traced to a number of personnel issues: hiring the "right" people, training them properly in customer service techniques, empowering them to respond to customers' needs, and compensating them on customer satisfaction as well as on sales or profits.

FIGURE 9.4

• •

The Importance of Customer Retention

Cost of Losing One Customer

The ripple effect of one unresolved customer problem can be felt throughout an entire marketing organization. There are losses in sales, profits, and employee and customer goodwill when customers are convinced that managers and employees do not care. Psychological and emotional costs are not easy to quantify, but the impact for a hypothetical retailer of losing one customer and the dollars from a particular sale can be calculated as follows:

- One dissatisfied customer will tell 11 others.
- These 11 people will each tell 5 others (67 people told).

Assume that only 1 in 4 decides not to buy from this retailer and would spend an average $50/week:

- Result = 67 people told x 1/4 who won't buy
  = 17 x $50 per week x 52 weeks = $44,200 per year in lost sales

Customer service research suggests that it costs about six times as much in marketing and other costs to attract a new customer as it does to keep an existing customer. For example, one study determined relative costs:

- It costs $19 for a retailer to keep one customer happy
- It costs $118 to attract a new customer into the store
- Total impact: $118 x 17 customers = $2,006 to attract 17 customers.

Source: Adapted from Paul R. Timm, *50 Powerful Ideas You Can Use to Keep Your Customers* (Hawthorne, NJ: Career Press, 1992), pp. 9–12.

• •

Adequate Staffing.   Adequate staffing for performance of service activities requires the ability to manage demand and supply. Service marketers experience a frequent imbalance between service cost and productivity. It often seems that customer service needs and problems occur at times when the fewest personnel are available, they are the busiest with other customers, or they are fatigued. Poor service also may result from "slow" times when there are few demands on employees to perform, resulting in potential boredom and low productivity.

The Importance of Training.   Customers become frustrated and unhappy when employees are not prepared to perform expected customer services satisfactorily. Service businesses should be committed to providing the necessary training and courtesy skills for all employees who come in contact with customers in person, by telephone, by mail, or by any other means. This includes everyone from the CEO to the janitor—a customer orientation should prevail throughout the company. In addition to product knowledge, service personnel need to be kept informed about company policies and procedures, acceptable ways to deal with customers, and the status of actions taken on any customer preferences and problems with which they are involved.

Employee training can be directed toward overcoming the most common customer service mistakes.[19] Customers want to feel that someone is listening to them and understands and cares about their needs, that they are liked and respected, that their business is appreciated, and that their problems will be solved—but mostly that someone cares and will respond to their concerns.

Marriott International Inc., Walt Disney World, and other marketers known for their commitment to customer service emphasize the importance of finding, training, and keeping the best service workers. Front-line workers, the people who actually face your customers every day, can make or break your business—despite the plans and intentions of top management.[20]

Empowerment.   Once customer service knowledge and skills have been developed, service personnel should be empowered to serve and given adequate support to provide satisfying solutions for their customers. Within the context of quality-service design and delivery, Berry[21] says, "Empowerment is a state of mind." An empowered employee experiences feelings of (1) control over how to do the job, (2) awareness of how the work fits into the "big picture," (3) accountability for his or her own work output, (4) shared responsibility for performance of the work group or organization, and (5) equity in the way rewards are distributed based on individual and collective performance.

Some of the benefits of empowerment are that employees feel like part owners of the business; they feel knowledgeable, responsible, and accountable; and they feel good about their jobs and their flexibility in dealing with service problems. A word of caution, however: Empowerment is not for everyone. Training empowered employees costs money, and there is the risk of making the "wrong" customer service decisions. The secret to successful empowerment seems to lie in a commitment to quality service and a deep sense of trust between management and lower-level service personnel.

Compensation, Awards, and Recognition.   Many service businesses reward customer contact personnel mainly on the basis of sales figures. However, if a customer orientation is to prevail, then reward systems must go beyond commissions or wages based on sales to include measures of customer service and satisfaction. A combination of compensation based on sales or straight salary and additional awards and recognition for high levels of performance in customer service activities can motivate employees to "put the customer first."

A diverse group of service firms (e.g., fast-food restaurants, banks, hotels, and others) have revamped their pay practices, compensating service employees on the basis of how well they have served customers. They believe in a service ethic that focuses on customer retention: When the customer is happy, the employee is happy, and vice versa, reducing loss of customers and employees. Au Bon Pain, a fast-growing chain of sandwich shops in the Northeast, believes in paying higher wages to attract higher-quality workers and improve customer service. Store managers may earn from $50,000 to $165,000 a year, based on their contribution to sales and profits. Crew workers are paid up to $25,000 a year but must work at least 50 hours a week. The result has been high productivity, low absenteeism, lower training costs due to lower turnover, and a loyal clientele that keeps coming back for first-class service.

MasterCare auto service centers started linking pay to customer retention after a survey of 4000 car owners revealed that they despised MasterCare's hard sell and poor service and that honest, courteous service is twice as important to them as the price of a repair. The company now polls customers from each store regularly, asking them whether they received good service and plan to return to MasterCare. Employees receive bonuses of about 10 percent of their salaries for keeping customers loyal, and even the mechanics' pay depends on survey scores.[22]

Summary

The phenomenal growth of the service sector of the U.S. economy is expected to continue well into the twenty-first century in both consumer and organizational markets. However, marketers must consider the unique characteristics of services versus tangible products when making marketing management decisions. The four most prominent differences are intangibility (cannot touch, feel, see, or otherwise experience the service before purchase), variability (inconsistency in service delivery from one time to the next), inseparability (of the service provider, the service process, and the customer), and perishability (cannot inventory for future sale).

Services may be considered primary (necessary for completion of a sale) or ancillary (related to the good or service being sold but not essential for the sale; usually a source of competitive differentiation). Value perceptions of services start with strategic planning and competitive positioning. Exceptional customer service attracts and retains customers, helps in service recovery, and increases customer satisfaction and return on investment.

Services marketing issues include choice of market segments, reduction of customers' perceptions of risk, customers' evaluation of service attributes, brand and service provider loyalty, and the adoption process for service innovations.

The service-design process includes determination of customer targets, the nature of the service, and the pricing strategy. It also addresses the complexity or uncertainty that may be associated with the service and evaluates the resources available to

the marketer to deliver a high-quality service. In addition, the number of services and the level of service also must be determined.

Service quality is a major issue and requires well-defined standards and implementation. Service firms may use benchmarking to identify excellent business practices that may apply to their operations. Blueprinting (or flowcharting) of the entire service process can help to identify potential gaps in service quality and failure points that may require service recovery procedures. Service delivery and implementation are affected by the structure and culture of the organization and by personnel issues. Successful service organizations have the commitment of top management, treat employees as internal customers, and view service as a performance. Personnel issues include adequate staffing, training, empowerment of front-line employees, and compensation, awards, and recognition.

Questions

1. Describe the four main characteristics that differentiate the marketing of services from the marketing of tangible goods. Give an example of how each characteristic might affect management decisions regarding the marketing of an automobile versus the marketing of automobile insurance or repair services.

2. Flowchart a recent service experience, including the initial decision to use this service, all interactions that you had with the service provider, and the outcome (i.e., the service ac-

tually received). Identify and evaluate the positive and negative aspects of this encounter, as well as the primary and ancillary services that were involved.

3. Discuss the ways that marketers can benefit by providing exceptional customer service. From the customer's viewpoint, create a "hierarchy of horrors"—five of the worst things that an organization can do to its customers—and how these problems can be eliminated or minimized.

4. Explain the factors that contribute to a customer's perceptions of risk when purchasing services. What are some ways that a marketer can overcome these perceptions in purchase situations such as the following: (a) minor surgery performed by an unfamiliar physician, (b) a long-awaited cruise vacation, (c) a major automobile repair, and (d) drycleaning services for an expensive suit.

5. Analyze your purchase process for (a) financial services, (b) a haircut, and (c) home repair in relation to brand and service provider loyalty. Consider the level of psychological involvement, personal interaction, and the tendency to make impulse purchases.

6. Outline the service-design process that might be followed by managers of an upscale restaurant who must plan, create, and deliver excellent service to their customers—every time. Give an example of each step, and demonstrate the close linkage that exists between the service product and its delivery system.

7. Continuing with your answer to Question 6, consider a restaurant service encounter that you may have experienced. Develop a blueprint that depicts the "frontstage" and "backstage" elements of this service. Identify the potential failure points or gaps in service quality that may be present in this service design and/or its implementation.

8. Discuss the role of the following in the successful delivery of high-quality services to an organization's customers: (a) organizational structure and culture, (b) personnel issues, and (c) planning for service recovery.

Exercises

1. Obtain examples of ways that service firms reward their customers for frequent purchases (e.g., frequent-flier miles, buyer clubs, etc.). Evaluate the nature of each program's appeal and its ability to attract and retain loyal customers. Describe specific actions that have damaged your relationship with a service provider that you previously felt a loyalty toward and whether/how these actions could be avoided or corrected.

2. Review advertisements for service firms, and identify recent technological developments that are being used in the design and delivery of services. For each new or emerging technology, evaluate whether it offers useful enhancements to provide quality service or is simply a short-term gimmick to attract customers.

3. Compile a list of costs for five services that you might use one or more times over the course of a year, including all types of costs that you might incur in buying and using these services. Explain how your price perceptions affect the concept of "value" received compared with interpretations of "value" expressed by the service firm in its marketing communications. If there is a significant discrepancy in the definitions of value by the firm and its customers, how can this gap be overcome?

Endnotes

1. Leonard L. Berry, *On Great Service: A Framework for Action* (New York: Free Press, 1995), p. 3.

2. For further discussion of the differences between physical products and intangible services, see Philip Kotler, *Marketing Management: Analysis, Planning, Implementation, and Control,* 7th ed. (Englewood Cliffs, NJ: Prentice-Hall, 1996), pp. 466–468; Christopher H. Lovelock, *Services Marketing,* 3d ed. (Englewood Cliffs, NJ: Prentice-Hall, 1996), pp. 14–19.

3. Keith Naughton, with Kathleen Kerwin, Bill Vlasic, Lori Bongiorno, David Leonhardt, and bureau reports, "Revolution in the Showroom," *Business Week* (February 19, 1996), pp. 70–76.

4. Faye Brookman, "Chains: Service Is Key," *Women's Wear Daily* (April 1996), pp. 6, 26.

5. *Ibid.*

6. Susan Reda, "Seven Keys to Better Service," *Stores* (January 1996), pp. 32–34.

7. For further discussion, see Carol H. Anderson, *Retailing: Concepts, Strategy and Information* (St. Paul, MN: West Publishing Company, 1993), pp. 181–189.

8. Valarie A. Zeithaml, "How Consumer Evaluation Processes Differ Between Goods and Services," in James H. Donnelly and William R. George (eds), *Marketing of Services* (Chicago: American Marketing Association, 1981), pp. 186–190.

9. Ken Wells, "Its New ATMs in Place, A Bank Reaches Out to South Africa's Poor," *Wall Street Journal* (June 13, 1996), pp. A1, A10.

10. Calmetta Y. Coleman, "Style over Substance: Power of a Good Perm Brings Us Together," *Wall Street Journal* (September 27, 1995), pp. A1, A6.

11. William C. Symonds, "The Club Med of the Ski Slopes?" *Business Week* (March 18, 1996), pp. 64, 66.

12. Teri Agins, "Retailing: Stores Try to Boost Their Service—But Cheaply," *Wall Street Journal* (December 16, 1992), p. B1.

13. Earl Nauman, *Creating Customer Value: The Path to Sustainable Competitive Advantage* (Cincinnati: Thomson Executive Press, 1995), Chap. 6.

14. Reda, *op. cit.*

15. Valarie A. Zeithaml, A. Parasuraman, and Leonard L. Berry, *Delivering Quality Service: Balancing Customer Perceptions and Expectations* (New York: Free Press, 1990), pp. 15–33.

16. For further discussion of flowcharting and blueprinting, see Lovelock, *op. cit.,* pp. 60–62ff.

17. Valarie A. Zeithaml, Leonard L. Berry, and A. Parasuraman, "Communication and Control Processes in the Delivery of Service Quality," *Journal of Marketing* 52 (April 1988), pp. 35–48.

18. Stephen Koepp, "Puh-leeze, Won't Somebody Help Me?" *Time* (February 2, 1987), pp. 28–34.

19. Kristin Anderson and Ron Zemke, *Delivering Knock Your Socks Off Service* (New York: AMACOM, 1991), pp. 36–38.

20. Ronald Henkoff, "Finding, Training, and Keeping the Best Service Workers," *Fortune* (October 3, 1994), pp. 110–122.

21. Berry, *op. cit.,* pp. 208ff.

22. Patricia Sellers, "What Customers Really Want," *Fortune* (June 4, 1990), pp. 58–68.

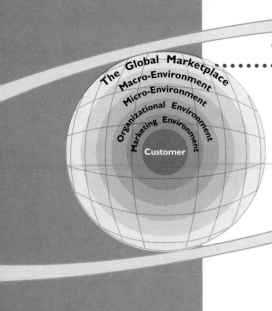

The Global Marketplace
Macro-Environment
Micro-Environment
Organizational Environment
Marketing Environment
Customer

Distribution Strategy

Distribution Channels: An Overview

Channel Structures and Marketing Systems

Channel Members

Channel Selection and Design

Channel Management

Replacing Inventory with Information Technology: Compaq's Distribution Strategy for Long-Term Survival

Can you sell a product on Tuesday and have it back on the shelf by Wednesday? If your answer is no, then you should be determining now how to make this type of replenishment part of your supply system; otherwise, you are not following the trends of the current leaders.[1]

Personal computer manufacturers operate in a highly volatile environment with short product life cycles, fierce competition, and fragmented distribution. Several years of strategic planning led Compaq Computer Corp. to implement a revolutionary business model. The Optimized Distribution Model (ODM) created customer value by enabling "the industry's most satisfying and complete product-ownership experience and the most efficient, cost-effective, and comprehensive order fulfillment process." A key component of ODM is a build-to-order (BTO) concept where information technology is, in effect, used to replace inventory.

In July 1997, news headlines announced that Compaq had cut prices on desktop computers, pricing three models below $1,000. While the lower prices were newsworthy, the real news centered on an innovative corporate initiative focused on the more significant issues of customer satisfaction, product quality, reliability, and stockholder value, made possible by implementation of the ODM. Eckhard Pfeiffer, Compaq's president, said, "With the launch of ODM, we are sending a shock wave through the industry. ODM sees our entire business from the customer's point of view. The new model will shape the way all Compaq products are designed, built, configured, distributed, ordered, purchased, serviced, and upgraded, as well as the way Compaq engages customers and works with its reseller partners. . . . This is our way of enhancing relationships with our customers while increasing shareholder value."

In launching its ODM strategy, Compaq first implemented its BTO model, a set of integrated business processes that extend the full length of the supply chain from suppliers to end-customers. A former Compaq executive explained the dynamics of this change: "Under the old business model we would have decided what we wanted to build for the next eight weeks, in essence guessing about what the customers wanted. By building, shipping, and storing [computers] in a distribution center we not only increased our costs, but we also created an artificial constraint by tying up critical parts in machines that did not meet customer needs. Secondly, if we built and stored them at a time when component costs were falling, it would be impossible to quickly capture the reductions and pass them on to the customer. . . . You're not pleasing the customer because you're stocking out on things and you may be asking your customers to pay more during a period of declining component prices."

With the BTO system, Compaq does not build an order until it is received, keeping inventory components in parts rather than in completed computers. The result is higher predictability for production and lower finished goods inventory. Cost savings from more efficient inventory man-agement and a more predictable delivery mechanism are passed along to customers. To accomplish this, Compaq is drastically changing both the number and nature of supplier relationships. Synergistic relationships replace traditional transactional business methods. Suppliers become involved very early in the development process. Compaq's focus is on reducing the number of suppliers (50 percent in 1998) and keeping only those which have development capability, with some of these on-site. Their inventories will be located at all Compaq's facilities around the world. Involved suppliers are important in the PC business because of the speed and length of the product-development cycle. Compaq is not building anything today that it was building 6 months or a year ago.

The result of Compaq's Optimized Distribution Model? In 1997, the company lowered inventory levels by increasing inventory turnover from 5 to 14 times a year, with a target of 30 stock turns by year-end 1999. Compaq also increased its ability to hit customer commitments by 33 percent and reduced its cycle time. Revenues in 1997 increased 33 percent over 1996 to $24.6 billion, market value climbed 90 percent, and 188 new products were introduced.

Source: John Teresko, "Replacing Inventory with IT," *Industry Week* (May 4, 1998), pp. 38–42.

Goods and services can be produced, priced, and promoted effectively—but until they are moved through a distribution system from their source to the final customer, no sales will occur. Poierier and Reiter have stressed the importance of efficient distribution channels to the point of saying that there will soon be a time when every customer purchase will be tracked immediately by all the key players in the distribution network. This means that when a customer buys a box of cereal, pertinent data will be provided simultaneously to every member in the distribution channel—to the farming system that harvests the crops, to the breakfast cereal manufacturer, as well as to the grocery store where the cereal was bought.[2]

DISTRIBUTION CHANNELS: AN OVERVIEW

Channel of distribution
Sets of interdependent organizations that are involved in making a good or service available for consumption.

A distribution system, or **channel of distribution,** can be described as "sets of interdependent organizations involved in the process of making a product or service available for consumption."[3] The importance of the distribution function in marketing is apparent when one considers the magnitude of goods and services that are transported and sold at millions of locations throughout the world. The economic impact of distribution is shown in Tables 10.1 and 10.2 for wholesaling and retailing activities in the United States. Other marketing, manufacturing, and physical distribution functions also contribute to the total economic effect of the distributive process.

Many experts believe that the distribution decision is the most important marketing decision a company can make. The design of an organization's distribution system is a key factor in creating customer value and in differentiating one company's offering from that of another. For example, CarMax, a power retailer in the automotive industry, offers its customers a wide assortment of brands and models from its car lots and over the Internet.

The field of distribution is made up of two distinct branches: channels of distribution and physical distribution.[4] *Channels of distribution* consist of a network of intermediaries that manages a flow of goods and services from the producer to the

TABLE 10.1
....
Impact of Wholesaling on the U.S. Economy (1992)

	Sales ($1,000)	*Establishments*	*Employment*
Wholesale trade, total	**3,238,520,447**	**495,457**	**5,791,264**
Durable goods, total	1,593,873,892	313,464	3,349,064
Motor vehicles and motor vehicle parts and supplies	394,104,350	47,274	488,602
Professional and commercial equipment and supplies	262,974,455	46,792	685,092
Machinery, equipment, and supplies	230,003,975	73,865	689,680
Electrical goods	227,784,486	39,303	435,700
Metals and minerals, except petroleum	118,321,902	11,248	138,042
Lumber and other construction materials	89,764,124	19,546	210,726
Hardware, and plumbing and heating equipment and supplies	76,088,078	24,674	241,043
Furniture and home furnishings	58,926,568	16,457	161,460
Miscellaneous durable goods	135,905,954	34,305	298,719
Nondurable goods, total	1,644,646,555	181,993	2,442,200
Groceries and related products	504,566,789	42,874	811,902
Petroleum and petroleum products	281,585,140	16,061	168,519
Farm-product raw materials	136,869,416	11,551	108,710
Chemicals and allied products	132,471,184	14,193	147,010
Drugs, drug proprietaries, and druggists' sundries	129,306,287	6,069	157,855
Apparel, piece goods, and notions	109,202,949	19,553	196,149
Paper and paper products	106,580,435	19,661	269,038
Beer, wine, and distilled alcoholic beverages	59,487,322	5,259	141,821
Miscellaneous nondurable goods	184,577,033	46,772	441,196

Source: 1992 Economic Census: Census of Wholesale Trade, U.S. Summary, U.S. Census Bureau, Washington, DC, 1993.

TABLE 10.2

· · · · · · · · · · · · · · · ·

Impact of Retailing on the U.S. Economy (1992)

	Sales ($1,000)	Establishments	Employment
Retail trade, total	**1,894,880,209**	**1,526,215**	**18,407,453**
Automotive dealers	395,147,882	96,373	1,267,533
Food stores	369,198,584	180,568	2,969,317
General merchandise stores	245,329,695	34,606	2,078,530
Eating and drinking places	195,316,992	433,608	6,547,908
Gasoline service stations	134,705,359	105,334	675,080
Apparel and accessory stores	101,714,474	145,490	1,144,587
Building materials and garden supplies stores	98,832,146	69,483	665,747
Furniture and home furnishings stores	93,206,043	110,073	702,164
Drug and proprietary stores	77,487,573	48,142	587,943
Miscellaneous retail stores	183,941,461	302,538	1,768,644

Source: 1992 Economic Census: Census of Retail Trade, U.S. Summary, U.S. Census Bureau, Washington, DC, 1993.

final customer. The success of this network depends on relationships among manufacturers, wholesalers, retailers, sales representatives, and others. As products move from one intermediary to the next, exchange takes place—exchange of physical goods, intangible services, and value-added dimensions. Marketing activities are performed at each stage.

Physical distribution
Movement of goods and services (logistics) with a focus on transporting and warehousing them through the supply chain.

Physical distribution activities include the actual movement of goods and services (i.e., logistics), with a focus on transporting and warehousing them. Together the channels and physical-distribution functions comprise a comprehensive supply chain that starts with the supplier's suppliers, that is, the materials, parts, and other supplies needed to grow, produce, or manufacture a finished product, as shown in Figure 10.1.[5]

The movement of goods and services can be costly and inefficient, threatening customer satisfaction and profitability. Companies that provide convenience or lower prices through creative distribution solutions (e.g., Compaq's ODM system) have a distinct competitive advantage. Both low-cost and differentiation strategies are achieved through efficient and innovative designs of inbound and outbound logistics, starting with suppliers of the first incoming materials to the supply chain. Automotive manufacturers, such as Ford Motor Co., develop strategic partnerships with suppliers to maintain the lowest possible price structure throughout the whole process. Likewise, wholesale and retail outlets should be selected for both efficiency and effectiveness. Efficient operations use assets advantageously to achieve competitive advantage (regardless of pricing strategy to customers). Effective outlets deliver the most customer value and satisfaction.

Relationship to Organizational and Marketing Strategies

· ·

Distribution strategies are concerned with having the right product in the right place at the right time. Marketing strategies are concerned with product-market decisions—which customers to serve and which customer needs to fulfill. The design

FIGURE 10.1
....
Supply Chain

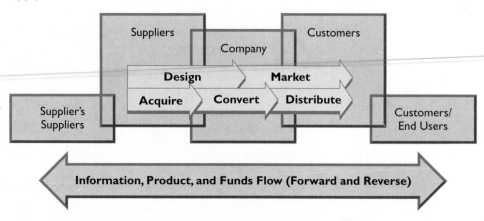

of a distribution channel is a long-term strategic decision that is difficult to change, requiring careful attention to the selection of channel intermediaries and their ability to add customer value and contribute to the marketer's strategic goals. For instance, IBM chooses distributors that reach its customers most effectively and other intermediaries that add value to the distributive process (e.g., FedEx).

The distribution decision interacts synergistically with product, promotion, and pricing decisions to achieve organizational objectives. The customer is at the center of this integrated process, consistent with the marketing concept. Computerization and automation help achieve the marketer's strategic intent through better inventory management and more efficient distribution systems and facilities.

Need for Channel Intermediaries
....

If consumers and organizational customers bought each product directly from its original source, the number of contacts required would be cumbersome and inefficient. Stern and El-Ansary identified four reasons for the emergence and arrangement of distribution-oriented **intermediaries.**[6]

Intermediaries
Retailers, wholesalers, and others responsible for the functions involved in moving goods and services from the producer or manufacturer to the final customer.

1. *Intermediaries arise in the exchange process because they make the process more efficient.* As shown in Figure 10.2, without retailers, each final consumer would have to deal directly with each manufacturer, making the process more complex. This basic form of distribution exists in primitive cultures where households exchange excess production with one another.

2. *Intermediaries arise to overcome the discrepancy between the assortment of goods and services generated by the producer and the assortment demanded by the consumer.* Figure 10.2 shows that the addition of wholesalers minimizes the number of contacts between each manufacturer and retailer. Generally, manufacturers produce large quantities of a few goods, and consumers want a small quantity of a wide variety of goods, creating a need for the following activities:

FIGURE 10.2

....

The Role of Channel Intermediaries

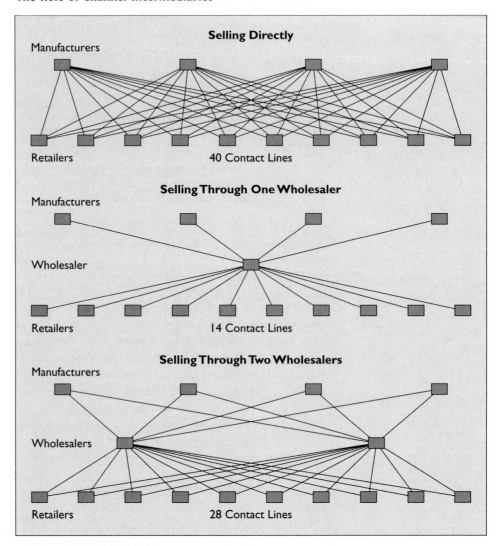

Source: *Marketing Channels*, 3/E by Stern/El-Asary, © 1996. Reprinted by permission of Prentice-Hall, Inc., Upper Saddle River, NJ.

....

- *Sorting out.* For example, grading lumber into broad categories for sale: construction lumber, pattern lumber, and specialty products; then sorting by type, size, closeness, strength, and characteristics that affect the appearance and use of the lumber.

- *Accumulation.* Gathering similar stocks of goods from multiple sources to create one larger homogeneous supply; for example, a pharmaceutical wholesaler accumulates health-related products from numerous manufacturers to provide a complete line of diverse goods to a drug store.

- *Allocation.* Breaking a large homogeneous supply into smaller lots; for example, a tire wholesaler divides carload lots of automobile tires into smaller quantities for small auto repair shops.

- *Assorting.* Building up an assortment of products for resale to the next level of customers; for example, a grocery wholesaler buys many types of products from many producers (e.g., cereal, cleaning supplies, produce, beverages) to provide a complete assortment to a grocery store.

3. *Marketing agencies work together in channel arrangements to routinize transactions.* Each purchase includes ordering, valuing the product, and payment. Some standardized procedures, such as methods of payment, shipping, and communication, are used to overcome the need to bargain in each new situation.

4. *Channels facilitate the search process at all levels.* Manufacturers, wholesalers, and retailers often lack information about customers' wants and needs, and customers often have difficulty finding products to satisfy these needs. Relationships among channel intermediaries make the search process easier. Retailers and wholesalers are organized into industry groups by type of product or business format (e.g., department store, auto parts, electronics). Suppliers tend to be geographically concentrated to decrease delivery time and facilitate comparison shopping. Centralized merchandise marts (e.g., Chicago, Atlanta) bring together retail buyers, manufacturers, and wholesalers. Furniture manufacturers are concentrated in North Carolina, software developers in Silicon Valley, and retail malls offer consumers one-stop shopping.

Functions Performed by Distribution Systems

Critical distributive functions that move suppliers and customers closer together include *exchange, physical supply,* and *facilitating activities.* (See Figure 10.3.) The question is not whether these functions will be performed, but rather who will perform them better than the supplier.

Functions of Exchange.   The exchange function represents the gamut of activities that enter into a transaction: *buying and selling, breaking bulk and creating assortments, negotiating prices and terms of sale,* and *marketing communication.* All channel intermediaries use their expertise to match product assortments to the needs of the next level in the channel. They provide information about products and customers—a two-way communication process.

Functions of Physical Supply.   Physical supply involves *handling, transporting,* and *storing* materials. Raw materials and parts suppliers move products to manufacturers, who deliver them to wholesalers, retailers, consumers, or organizational customers. Each level of distribution takes responsibility for receiving and sending goods to the next level, storing inventories where it is most efficient.

Facilitating Activities.   All channel participants need the assistance of other organizations to complete their tasks. Experts inside or outside a firm may perform facilitating activities. The major facilitating functions include *financing* (credit, loans),

buyers' and suppliers' needs. They also can offer a number of complementary goods to the same geographically concentrated customers.

Merchant Wholesalers.   These independently owned businesses represent the greatest proportion of all wholesalers. They are primarily concerned with purchasing goods from one or more suppliers and selling them to other businesses. They take title to the goods they sell and may take possession. Most are "full service" wholesalers that offer a wide range of sales support and facilitating services to suppliers and customers. According to El-Ansary,[13] the most basic service provided by wholesaler-distributors is to ensure that the right goods are in the right place, at the right time, and at the right price. Services may include repackaging, help in marketing, financing, technical assistance, and other value-added services.

The major strength of merchant wholesalers is their ability to match the needs of business customers and consumers with the output of diverse manufacturers. Producers find it more cost-effective to use merchant wholesalers to get their products to customers than to maintain their own sales branches and sales representatives. The services provided by merchant wholesalers allow manufacturers to concentrate on production, while channel intermediaries assume responsibility for inventory management and its associated risks.[14]

Role of Wholesalers.   A number of wholesalers perform many distribution functions that otherwise would be performed by channel members that precede or follow them. Wholesalers add value to the distribution process and final cost structure in a number of ways. One of their primary roles is to manage inventory at different phases of the supply chain, including warehousing, transporting, taking ownership and title to goods, quick-response ordering, and other activities. Wholesalers also deal in information services and providing market research, accounting, and inventory data forward and backward in the channels.

Wholesaling Strategies.   Strategies pursued by wholesalers can be explained in part by three major theories of market coverage, consistent with the distribution strategies of other channel intermediaries. Intensive, exclusive, or selective market-coverage patterns refer to the placement and number of distributors that will sell a particular good or service. These theories of market coverage also can be applied to the nonprofit sector (e.g., food banks, bloodmobiles, government services). The desired level of coverage can be accomplished by selling through a series of intermediaries (wholesalers, agents, brokers, retailers). At the retail level, coverage includes store and nonstore formats, direct sales, electronic commerce, and other methods of reaching consumers.

Intensive distribution
When marketer uses every available outlet to reach its customers.

Intensive distribution provides the most comprehensive market coverage. The marketer uses every available outlet to reach its customers. For example, drug wholesalers carry broad assortments of pharmaceuticals and other products that they distribute to drugstores and health care facilities. Convenience stores use an intensive distribution strategy to sell frequently purchased, rapidly consumed, low-involvement products, like soda and snacks, through outlets located near consumers.

Exclusive distribution
When only one or a few distributors are allowed to carry one or more product lines from a supplier.

An **exclusive distribution** strategy is selected when only one or a few distributors are permitted to carry one or more product lines from a supplier. Generally, the goods are perceived to be more upscale, expensive, high-involvement purchases. Their quality image is enhanced or maintained by the distributor's image. Wholesalers and retailers may decide to serve an exclusive clientele (although there are legal limits). This strategy is appropriate for specialty goods where the customer is highly involved in the purchase situation or the product category.

Selective distribution
Limits distribution to a few types of intermediaries or retail outlets.

Selective distribution combines the features of intensive and exclusive distribution strategies and is used to limit distribution to a few types of intermediaries or retail outlets. For example, manufacturers and wholesalers may restrict coverage to selected retail stores based on their merchandising strategies or locations. A manufacturer may select only those wholesalers which can represent the company's products favorably to other channel members and final customers.

Trends and Issues in Wholesaling. The major business revolutions described earlier in this book (globalization, increased computerization, advances in technology, and changing management hierarchies) are related to many of the changes and challenges confronting wholesalers. For instance, many buyers and sellers are using shorter distribution channels, cutting out many traditional intermediaries. The need for shorter delivery times and lower costs provides the motivation for shorter channels, facilitated by computerization and automation.

Globalization of business and unstable economic conditions throughout many parts of the world, such as the 1998 Asian and Russian financial crises, create challenges for wholesalers that are engaged in international distribution. Add to this the increasingly intense competition among distributors and potential ethical problems related to the scramble for business. Industry consolidation among both producers and retailers has created larger firms that are capable of managing their own supply chains and distribution functions. Other problems include the high cost of sales calls, the general decline in employee productivity, and management of relationships between producers and wholesalers.

Communication between the wholesaler-distributor, suppliers, and customers is another key issue for merchant wholesalers. For example, they forecast sales demand and provide market information backward in the channel as input for product development and production schedules and provide information about products and services forward in the channel to potential buyers. The valuable services performed by merchant wholesalers make a major contribution to the total U.S. economic output (gross domestic product, or GDP), which was approximately 7.12 percent in 1996.

Retailers

Retailers serve final consumers by being both buyers and sellers of goods and services. As a seller, a retailer must understand the desires and expectations of its target market. As a buyer, a retailer must identify and negotiate with those suppliers that can satisfy the retailer's customers and return a profit to the company. Retailing involves all the activities needed to sell goods and services to final consumers—the end of the supply chain.[15] We are involved with many forms of retailing in our daily lives—from the traditional supermarkets or department stores to Internet commerce and roadside fruit stands.

Distributive functions performed by retailers include the creation of product assortments to satisfy the needs and wants of an identified target market. Retailers break large shipments into smaller sizes and quantities that are suitable for use by

MANAGING CHANGE

Vendor-Managed Inventory and Integrated Supply

 Like consumers who are caught between the needs of their children and parents, wholesalers are the "sandwich generation" of the supply chain, caught between the needs of customers and suppliers in a changing environment. The concept of supply-chain management gives a new twist to the way wholesalers conduct their business, with some implementing a *vendor-managed inventory* (VMI) system. VMI "is the streamlining and integration of the purchasing, receiving, stocking and payables function between wholesalers and key manufacturers."

Many wholesalers have responded to customers' need for cost reductions by assuming more responsibility for inventory management and integrated supply. More wholesalers are extending the concept to a vendor-based VMI because they believe that the greatest potential for cost reduction obtained from vendors lies in process—not product—costs. For decades, businesses have understood and applied product-cost management and cost behavior to the variable costs of production in terms of direct costs of labor, materials, and overhead. Today's managers are paying more attention to nonproduct or process costs through techniques such as activity-based costing and process re-engineering.

A vendor-based VMI removes redundant costs for duplicate efforts in purchasing, selling, invoicing, receiving, and warehousing the products or other functions performed by both the wholesaling firm and its vendors. "The managerial challenge is to streamline the supply chain (reduce duplicate functions) while maintaining flexibility and accuracy for the affected processes."

VMI partners must be chosen carefully, considering the vendor's history of reliability, company policies, and business practices—as well as the wholesaler's readiness and ability to engage in this system. The financial payoff is in cost savings related to the processes of purchasing, stocking, and paying for inventory. However, the cost savings can contribute to the wholesaler's profitability only if the labor costs associated with redundant functions also are reduced. "To put it bluntly, the cost savings for vendor-based VMIs are head-count driven. While this is an unfortunate event for some, it is the use of technology and process re-engineering to reduce labor inputs. In other words, it is increased productivity with your asset base."

Source: Scott Benfield, "Developing a Backdoor Vendor-Managed Inventory," *Supply House Times* 41(3) (May 1998), pp. 78–82.

individuals or households. They provide consumers with useful information to facilitate their purchase decisions, and they develop strategies that make it relatively convenient for consumers to shop. Of increasing importance to consumers, market-focused retailers offer quality products at competitive (or fair) prices. Purchases made by final consumers drive demand backward through the supply chain to originators of goods and services; that is, nothing moves until something is sold.

Retailers can be classified according to form of ownership and control or strategic positioning, as shown in Table 10.3. An understanding of the characteristics of each classification is important for designing suitable retailing strategies.

Classifying Retailers by Ownership and Control. Forms of retail ownership and control range from a small, independent, "mom and pop" operation, such as the corner grocery store in a small town, to a large retail conglomerate made up of mul-

TABLE 10.3
················
Retail Classifications

Ownership and Control	Strategic Positioning
Independent ownership, one-store operation	Margin-turnover classification
	Tangible goods versus services
Chain organization	Type of merchandise carried: general merchandise
Leased department	
Vertical marketing system (VMS)	Type of merchandise carried: food-based retailers
Franchise	
Others	

tiple retail chains with many stores in each chain, like Dayton-Hudson Corp. (Target Stores, Mervyn's, Dayton's, Hudson's, Marshall Field's, Rivertown Trading).

Independent Ownership, One-Store Operation.   This type of retailer is legally described as a sole proprietorship, partnership, or corporation. Many are family-owned small businesses that play a critical role in distributing goods at the retail level, making up a majority of all retail establishments.

Chain.   Chain organizations share common ownership of two or more stores with generally similar merchandise assortments, store appearance, and operating formats. Chain sizes range from an independently owned chain of two stores to very large chains like Wal-Mart Stores, Inc. (largest retailer in the United States and world) and METRO Holding (number two retailer worldwide and leader in Europe). METRO Holding's primary market is Germany, with a global strategy of operating stores throughout Europe, Asia, North Africa, and North America, along with an Internet service provider, to take advantage of the purchasing power in newly industrialized countries.[16]

Leased Department.   Departments in a larger store may be leased to an "outside" company (lessee) with expertise in a particular line of goods (e.g., cosmetics, shoes, or repair services). The lessee owns the merchandise inventory that is available for sale to customers, assumes responsibility for personnel, pays the retailer a percentage of sales generated by the department, and operates the business according to store policies and operating guidelines (e.g., hours of operation, credit policies).

Vertical Marketing System (VMS).   In conventional marketing channels, supply-chain intermediaries operate as independent firms—with no channel member having excessive control over the others. In a vertical marketing system (VMS), any number of producers, wholesalers, and retailers can be coordinated and controlled by the same organization. VMS arrangements may be formal or informal, including single ownership of two or more phases of production and/or distribution, contractual franchise arrangements, or other methods giving one channel member control over others. (VMS channels are discussed later in this chapter.)

Franchise.   A retail franchise is a contractual arrangement between a sponsoring organization (franchisor) and an independent owner (franchisee). Fast-food chains such as McDonald's and Kentucky Fried Chicken (KFC) are prominent franchise systems. Many other types of franchises range from child care centers, cleaning services, lawn care services, and auto parts stores to beauty shops and funeral homes. Worldwide franchising statistics vary, but a 1995 study by Arthur Andersen and the World Franchising Council identified 3000 franchisors and 250,000 franchisees in the United States.[17] In 1996, franchising in the United States accounted for nearly 41 percent of all retail sales, or $800 billion annually, with an estimated 550,000 franchised businesses and 8 million employees.[18] Franchising is growing throughout the world, including Europe, where there were 3691 franchisors and 144,561 franchised units in 1997.[19]

The four major types of franchise systems are manufacturer-sponsored retailer franchise (automobile dealerships), manufacturer-sponsored wholesaler franchise (Pepsi-Cola bottlers and distributors), wholesaler-sponsored retailer franchise (True Value hardware), and service-firm-sponsored retailer franchise (McDonald's restaurants).

Other Forms of Ownership and Control.   Other retail classifications based on ownership include those owned by consumers, government, farmers, and public utilities.

Consumer-Owned Cooperatives.   These cooperatives are formed by final consumers who join forces and pay a fee to operate their own retail outlet. They can obtain lower prices by purchasing in larger quantities, but the process of buying and breaking larger purchases into smaller amounts for each member requires considerable effort. Grocery co-ops are the most prevalent, but some financial co-ops (e.g., credit unions) and public utility co-ops also are in operation to save money for their members.

Government-Owned Retail Establishments.   These are operated primarily to serve the needs of a particular segment of the population. Examples include the base exchanges and commissaries found on or near military installations for the benefit of the U.S. armed forces.

Farmer-Owned Retail Establishments.   The familiar farmers' market can be found in local marketplaces operated by independent farmers and merchants who combine their fruits and vegetables, and sometimes baked goods and handicrafts, to sell directly to consumers. The "store" may be an open area, partially covered, or the back of a pickup truck. The atmosphere is reminiscent of the cracker-barrel general stores of colonial times. Consumers get fresher produce directly from the farm, usually at lower prices, and farmers get instant cash and generally higher margins than those obtained from supermarkets.

Public Utility–Owned Retail Establishments.   These retail organizations sell appliances and other products related to the type of utility they operate. An electrical utility may sell appliances, and telephone companies sell phones and accessories through their own retail outlets.

Classifying Retailers by Strategic Positioning.   Retail organizations also can be classified according to profit margin–inventory turnover ratios, product strategies, and types of merchandise carried (general or food-based).[20]

Margin-Turnover Classification.   Retailers can be classified according to a strategic combination of two dimensions: gross profit margin and inventory turnover ratio. *Gross margin* is equivalent to the average markup percentage (based on retail price) or the difference between the price paid by customers and the cost of the goods paid to suppliers. *Inventory turnover* refers to the number of times during a year that the average amount of inventory on hand is sold.

Tangible Goods versus Service Strategy.   Strategic positioning by retailers may be based on the level of service provided to customers and/or the emphasis on tangible goods versus services in their product assortments. One group of retailers sells services to its customers through separate businesses (e.g., Sears' Allstate Insurance Company). Another strategy is to limit service offerings to those that facilitate the sale of tangible goods (e.g., delivery, bagging groceries). The customer may or may not pay for facilitating services.

Retailers of General Merchandise.   General merchandisers include all nonfood retailers such as department and specialty stores. Other general merchandisers that usually offer a price advantage include full-line discount stores, off-price retailers, retail catalog showrooms, and flea markets and resale shops.

Department Stores.   These retail organizations carry an extensive assortment of noncompeting lines organized into departments. They may be part of national or regional chains, a local independent retailer, or a strategic business unit within a large conglomerate. Criteria established by the U.S. Bureau of the Census for a business to be considered a department store include a minimum of 25 employees and a broad-based merchandise assortment of specified merchandise categories. Department stores typically have higher markups to cover the costs of higher levels of customer service, more elaborate store environments, and other operating expenses.

Specialty Stores.   Specialty stores offer a limited number of lines of goods or services but generally offer customers a wide selection within these specialized lines. Most specialty stores are small or medium-sized establishments or boutiques carrying few lines. Specialty retailers are found in just about every line of goods and services imaginable—and the trend continues to grow. Examples include retailers that concentrate assortments on apparel and accessories, electronics, specialty foods, greeting cards, automotive repair, and so forth.

Full-Line Discount Stores.   These types of discount stores carry a wide assortment of merchandise, differing from department stores by charging lower prices. Other strategic differences related to lower prices include lower profit margins, higher inventory turnover, limited or self-service, no-frills store decor, and less expensive locations. Examples include Wal-Mart Stores, Inc., Kmart Corp., and Target Stores.

Off-Price Retailers.   These may be manufacturer-owned factory outlets (e.g., Hartmarx, Levi Strauss & Co., and Burlington Coat Factory), off-price chains (e.g., T.J. Maxx and Marshalls Inc.), or independent stores that promote national brands at exceptionally low prices. An expanded form of the off-price retailer concept is an off-price mall containing multiple outlets, such as the Belz Outlet Mall or the Sawgrass Mill Mall, both with locations in Florida.

Catalog Showrooms.   These are low-cost, low-overhead warehouse stores where customers make selections from catalogs or floor displays. Both the list price and discounted price for each item are given to emphasize the cost savings. Retailers such as Service Merchandise Co., Inc., carry assortments that consist mainly of housewares, jewelry, watches, electronics, and gifts, plus other items that are popular with their clientele. Typically, orders are placed with a cashier and claimed at a pickup desk.

Flea Markets and Resale Shops.   These are organized and expanded forms of garage sales and yard sales that appear in every community. These retailers have gained popularity in recent years and continue to attract both buyers and sellers. Flea markets, which usually are located in out-of-the way, low-cost locations, rent space to individual vendors for a given period of time. Typical merchandise includes antiques, used household items, tools, and other goods. Resale shops operate more like a traditional retailer, being selective in the items they take to sell and arranging their merchandise in attractive displays. Many resale shops take items on consignment, keeping a percentage of the sales price and giving the remainder to the original owner. People from all economic levels are creating a growth market for retailers like Grow Biz International (operating under franchised names such as Once Upon A Child, Play It Again Sports, and Music Go Round).

Food-Based Retailers.   Food retailers can be classified according to the width and depth of their merchandise assortments, pricing strategy, and level of service provided to customers. The major types of food-based retailers include the conventional supermarket, combination store, superstore, box (limited-assortment) store, warehouse store, convenience store, and hypermarket, as discussed below.

Conventional Supermarkets.   These stores combine low prices and convenient locations, resulting in higher sales volume and inventory turnover. They offer a full line of groceries, meat, and produce and a limited assortment of general merchandise but find it difficult to compete with other food retailers (e.g., Kroger, Winn-Dixie) that offer lower prices, larger selections, or more convenience.

Combination Stores.   These stores are primarily food-based retailers but are combined with a general merchandise store or a drugstore. The two types of stores are operated as one from the perspective of the customer. Examples include Albertson's, Jewel, and Bigg's.

Superstores.   These stores are larger (up to 30,000 square feet or more) and more diverse than conventional supermarkets and generate high sales volumes. Superstores carry many nonfood items (e.g., greeting cards, floral arrangements, housewares), along with specialty food products (e.g., baked goods, deli items, seafood). Kroger Co. and Wal-Mart Stores, Inc., have developed superstore formats that combine supermarket and nonfood merchandise. (The term *superstore* also refers to large power retailers, discussed later in this chapter with retailing trends.)

Box (Limited-Assortment) Stores.   These stores carry a limited line of goods (usually nonperishable), particularly low-priced private labels and generic brands. Customers select merchandise directly from cut cases or shipping cartons and generally bag their own groceries at stores such as Aldi.

Warehouse Stores.   Warehouse stores carry a wider assortment of goods than box stores but focus on a limited number of brands of dry goods with very few perishable items. Warehouse stores such as Costco and Sam's Club are able to buy special deals from their suppliers in order to attract customers with low prices. Merchandise assortments may vary from one day to the next in these no-frills, efficient, low-cost operations that combine the superstore and warehouse store concepts.

Convenience Stores.   Stores such as 7-Eleven follow a location strategy that makes frequently purchased consumer goods available in neighborhoods and other high-traffic areas near their customers. Higher prices are paid for convenient locations and longer operating hours.

Hypermarkets.   These are very large stores, typically ranging from 100,000 to 300,000 square feet in size. They are a combination supermarket and full-line discount general merchandise store with a central checkout, an extension of the French *hypermarché* (e.g., Carrefour). Fred Meyer in the Pacific Northwest illustrates the hypermarket concept. Others, such as Wal-Mart Stores, Inc., have developed this type of store, but with mixed results.

Retailing Strategies.   Two broad theoretical concepts drive retailing strategies: theories of institutional (structural) change and store location. *Theories of structural change* include the retail life cycle concept, wheel of retailing, retail accordion, dialectic process, adaptive behavior, and scrambled merchandising. Retailers who understand these theories can develop proactive and adaptive strategies that enable them to remain profitable in a rapidly changing environment.[21]

The **retail life cycle** is similar to the product life cycle (see Chapter 8) but refers specifically to changes in the structure of retail institutions over time. Like products, retail institutions progress through four identifiable stages of indeterminate length from inception to demise: innovation, accelerated development, maturity, and decline, as illustrated in Figure 10.7a.[22]

The **wheel of retailing theory** describes the evolution of retail institutions as a wheel-like or cyclic progression. It explains the upward spiral of retail innovators who enter the market as low-priced, low-margin, no-frills, low-status operators. Over time, competitive pressures cause the retailer to add more upscale products, more services, and more attractive store surroundings. This results in loss of the original price-conscious consumers, making way for new low-price innovators to enter the market. (See Figure 10.7b.)

The **retail accordion** concept refers to a general-specific-general pattern of expansion and contraction of merchandise lines, although each type of store exists today. The general store that offered broad assortments of unrelated merchandise to early American colonists lost popularity as department stores emerged to fill more specialized needs. Eventually, a broad spectrum of specialty stores evolved to fill these same needs, focusing on a single product line or a few related lines of merchandise. The accordion idea continues as superstores and mass merchants offer one-stop shopping to a diverse customer base. (See Figure 10.7c.)

Retail life cycle
Changes in the structure of retail institutions over time; four stages are innovation, accelerated development, maturity, and decline.

Wheel of retailing theory
Upward spiral of retail innovators that enter the market as low-priced operators but become more upscale over time, making way for new low-priced operators.

Retail accordion
General-specific-general pattern of the expansion and contraction of merchandise lines.

FIGURE 10.7

Theories of Structural Change in Retailing

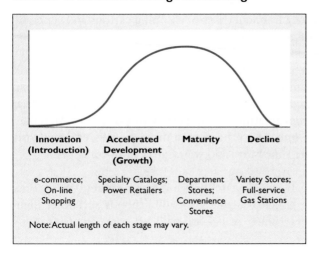

(a) Retail Life Cycle

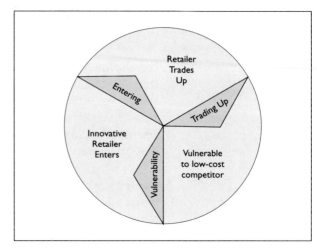
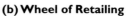

(b) Wheel of Retailing

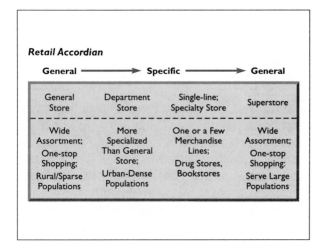

(c) Retail Accordion

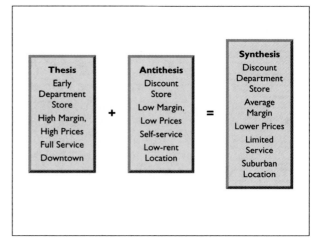

(d) Dialectic Process

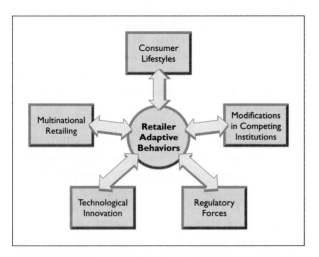

(e) Adaptive Behavior

Dialectic process
Emergence of retail institution in three stages: thesis (original form), antithesis (different form), and synthesis (innovative combination of old and new).

Adaptive behavior theory
Similar to Darwin's theory of natural selection (survival of the fittest).

Scrambled merchandising
Adding unrelated goods and services to a traditional retail assortment to increase sales and profits.

Distinctly different forms of retail institutions emerge as old and new, or substantially different, types of retail institutions adapt to one another. This can be explained as a **dialectic process** with three stages: thesis (original form of retail operation), antithesis (completely different form), and synthesis (innovative combination of old and new), as shown in Figure 10.7d.

The **adaptive behavior theory** of changing retail institutions has its roots in Darwin's theory of natural selection (survival of the fittest). Retailers who anticipate changes in their environments and develop winning competitive strategies will survive and prosper. In an overcrowded retail marketplace, often the only place to gain new business is to take it away from competitors. (See Figure 10.7e.)

Scrambled merchandising refers to the practice of adding unrelated goods and services to a retailer's traditional product assortment to increase sales and profits through quick selling of higher-margin items that often are purchased on impulse. Examples include the addition of sunglasses and snack foods at a gasoline service station and milk and eggs at a drugstore.

Store Location Strategies.   Store location strategies are related closely to manufacturer and wholesaler distribution strategies and to the evolution of retail structures. The complex theories of retail location and site selection are beyond the scope of this chapter. However, location can be viewed from the perspectives of competition and development. Strategic positioning involves not only perceptual comparisons with competitors but also physical placement of retail facilities relative to those of other retailers that compete for the same consumer dollars. For example, fast-food restaurants find it advantageous to locate relatively close to one another. Most discount stores and mass merchandisers operate in free-standing locations with large parking areas, preferably near a large shopping mall in a high-traffic location. Stores that sell shopping goods such as jewelry, furniture, and cars tend to locate near one another to facilitate customers' need to compare merchandise and deals. Malls and strip shopping centers are homes to many specialty retailers and large department stores.

Trends and Issues in Retailing.   The retailing industry is experiencing change in three major areas: store formats and operations, channel relations, and customer characteristics. The trend in *store formats and operations* is toward more nonstore retailing, greater specialization, and more superstores. Many retailers and their customers bypass physical storefronts altogether with direct-response techniques, such as direct marketing (e.g., telemarketing, catalogs, vending machines, and computerized and electronic commerce). Perhaps the most compelling trend is the rapid acceleration of electronic commerce, made possible by advances in technology, communications, and customer databases.

Specialty stores that serve nearly every product category and consumer lifestyle are proliferating. Many are small boutiques that carry everything from sunglasses to souvenirs of your favorite sports team. Others are megaretailers that focus on one product category. Category killers like Toys 'R Us and Home Depot carry large assortments of a particular product line and sell at low prices, making it difficult for department stores and smaller specialty stores to compete with them in that category. Following the "bigger is better" trend, acquisitions and mergers in all retail categories have accelerated retail consolidation for greater domestic and global coverage. At the other end of the spectrum, entrepreneurs continue to develop innovative concepts that change the usual way of doing business, such as grocery shopping over the Internet, fast-food delivery services, and one-product kiosks in malls.

Retailers are under pressure from all sides to cut operating costs by adopting operating methods that are more efficient or lose their competitive advantage. Point-of-sale scanning, computerized order processing, improvements in logistics, and other state-of-the-art applications have become more sophisticated. More demands are placed on suppliers to provide services such as prewrapping delicatessen products or preticketing apparel. At the same time, consumers demand greater value and lower prices, making it necessary to increase profit margins by lowering costs, partially through performing more of the distribution functions in-house.

Trends in *channel relations* focus on heightened competition, building stronger relationships with suppliers and customers, and developing synergies in the supply chain. Many channel relationships have been formalized through acquisitions and mergers that increase consolidation within the industry. Many of these changes are evolving in response to the demands of a changing marketplace.

Shifts are occurring in *customer characteristics.* Customers are better informed and more value conscious. They come from increasingly diverse ethnic and socio-economic backgrounds and have different shopping preferences. They expect more service, more convenience or hassle-free shopping, and lower prices. Increasingly, retail customers expect to be entertained while shopping and are attracted to the ambiance of the store environment.

Other Channel Intermediaries and Facilitators

In addition to wholesalers and retailers, the supply chain includes producers and manufacturers that must determine the most suitable channel strategy for their goods and services and do so in cooperation with other channel members. Physical distribution firms move products from one intermediary to the next until they reach final consumers or organizational customers. They are involved in forecasting market demand, obtaining and processing orders, managing and storing inventory, packing and shipping, and delivering orders to diverse buyers.

CHANNEL SELECTION AND DESIGN

The design of a distribution channel is an important strategic decision because customers must be able to purchase goods and services when and where they find it most satisfying and convenient. Marketing intelligence data can be used to determine customers' buying habits and channel preferences as input for channel design decisions. Channel structure also depends on the firm's resources and objectives. For instance, the opportunity to distribute computer software directly over the Internet may provide a shorter lead time and a better return on assets than distributing through wholesalers or storefronts.

Bucklin[23] explains channel structures in terms of four service level outputs: spatial convenience, lot size, waiting or delivery time, and product variety. *Spatial convenience* refers to the degree of market decentralization or a distribution strategy that is designed to reduce customers' travel time and search costs through convenient locations of intermediaries. As customers place greater value on travel time and search costs, the channel becomes more decentralized and requires more channel intermediaries.

Lot size refers to the number of units that a customer will purchase at any one time. Products that are consumed quickly and replenished frequently require higher levels of service outputs to maintain inventories. When customers can rely on their suppliers to maintain an inventory of wanted items, they can purchase in smaller quantities and hold smaller inventories. The smaller the lot size that is available in a channel, the higher is the service output of that channel, and the higher is the price that can be charged to customers for convenience.

Waiting time or *delivery time* is the time a customer must wait between ordering and receiving goods. Longer waiting times generally mean that the customer will experience greater inconvenience and will need to plan purchases in advance. However, when the customer is willing to wait longer to receive purchases, prices usually are lower.

Product variety refers to the width and depth of assortments. When customers demand a broad assortment of goods, channel members must carry a higher level of inventory. This results in higher channel output and higher distribution costs.

As customers require a higher level of service outputs, the channel expands to include more intermediaries to provide the necessary marketing functions and flows. When channel outputs are higher, customers will pay higher prices for additional service and convenience. Conversely, channel outputs and prices are lower when customers provide more of the marketing functions themselves.

Product variety
Width and depth of retail assortments.

Channel Objectives
. . . .

Inventories will reside in a channel where it is most cost-effective for all channel members to deliver the level of service outputs demanded by customers. Multiple distribution channels may be needed where diverse markets are targeted, each with its own unique demands and objectives. For example, a pharmaceutical manufacturer may distribute painkillers to final users through a variety of wholesalers or agents to drugstore pharmacies, hospitals, doctors' offices, nursing homes, and direct-marketing channels.

Distribution objectives must be consistent with overall marketing and company objectives (e.g., targeted sales levels and profit margins) and product characteristics. Frequently cited objectives include intensity of market coverage; degree of control over inventory and its management; minimization of time or distance; ability to move bulky, customized, or high-cost products; opportunity to provide high levels of customer service; and supplier cooperation. In addition to achieving the company's distribution objectives, channel design must consider company policies and organizational structure (for managing the distribution function). It also must conform to legal and regulatory requirements, such as refraining from unfair restraint of trade and creating conditions for unfair competition.

Channel Length and Number of Intermediaries
. . . .

The number of intermediaries required to achieve the desired intensity of distribution determines channel length. Three channel alternatives related to coverage include intensive, selective, and exclusive distribution. Channels designed for *intensive* distribution include the maximum number of intermediaries and outlets to accomplish the widest coverage possible (e.g., convenience goods). To achieve a *selective* distribution strategy (e.g., shopping goods), a company will choose a limited number of distributors in a more narrowly defined market. An *exclusive* distribution strategy (e.g., specialty goods) is focused on an even narrower market, defined according to geography or type of outlet. When designing the structure of a distribution channel, suppliers must choose among a number of intermediaries that have direct or indirect access to the desired target market. Selected factors that influence the length of distribution channels are listed in Table 10.4.

Selection Criteria for Channel Members

Criteria must be established for selecting each channel intermediary, based on the company's distribution objectives and the number of intermediaries needed to

TABLE 10.4

Factors Influencing Distribution Channel Length

	Factors	Channel Length
Market	1. Number of potential exchanges 2. Expected size of exchange 3. Geographic concentration of market	1. Many = long; few = short 2. Small = long; large = short 3. Concentrated = short; dispersed = long
Marketing mix	1. Unit price 2. Perishability 3. Width of product line 4. Technical, specialized, or customized products 5. Product type 6. Promotion/communication	1. High = short; low = long 2. Perishable = short; nonperishable = long 3. Wide = short; narrow = long 4. Specialized = short; not specialized = long 5. Commodity = long; specialty = short 6. Communication aimed toward consumers = long; aimed toward intermediaries = short
Organization	1. Number of other products or lines 2. Financial resources 3. Level of control desired 4. Management skill	1. Many = short; one/few = long 2. Strong = short; weak = long 3. High level of control = short; low level of control = long 4. Skilled = short; not skilled = long
Intermediary	1. Economy in services required 2. Availability of intermediaries	1. Efficient intermediaries = long; inefficient intermediaries = short 2. Available = long; unavailable = short
Regulatory environment	1. Regulatory restrictions	1. Heavy restrictions = long; light restrictions = short

Source: From Hiam & Schewe, *Portable MBA in Marketing*, NY: John Wiley & Sons, 1992, pp. 336–338. Copyright © 1992 by John Wiley & Sons, Inc. Reprinted by permission of John Wiley & Sons, Inc.

achieve these objectives. Five key factors dominate the criteria for including a channel member in the company's distribution structure: market coverage, costs and other economic criteria, control, flexibility/adaptability, and overall ability to add value.

Market Coverage.   Channel intermediaries should be selected for their ability to achieve the company's distribution objective of reaching the greatest number of potential customers with the fewest transactions. For example, Pepsico Inc. uses bottling companies, distributors, and a vast array of retailers and vending machines to reach soft drink customers. The selection of intermediaries depends on the size of a trade area, number and location of potential customers, and purchasing process pursued for each product line.

Costs and Other Economic Criteria.   The cost of achieving desired market coverage must be consistent with distribution strategy objectives and should not be greater than the benefits to the company and its customers. Shorter channels may not be the least expensive when all channel functions are considered. If, for example, the objective is to open a new market for auto parts in a developing country such as the former East Germany, then the channel design might include a combination of export and import companies, local manufacturers and wholesalers, retailers, and other intermediaries. These companies will share marketing functions and use their individual expertise to gain acceptance from this developing consumer market.

Control.   There is a potential loss of control over a product's sales and distribution when channel intermediaries are used. Wholesalers or distributors that carry lines from a number of manufacturers may neglect one line for others that are more profitable. Of particular concern is the quality of service that will be provided before, during, and after a sale by the intermediary. This is particularly true for high-tech and complex products that may require a specialized salesforce and in-depth product knowledge. More control can be achieved with fewer intermediaries, by performing many distribution functions in-house, and by adherence to established standards.

Flexibility/Adaptability.   Considerable financial and human resources are used to create and maintain long-term channel relationships, which may or may not involve formal contracts. Organizations must be able to respond to changes in the market or company, particularly in industries characterized by rapid change and environmental uncertainty. For example, automotive superstores like AutoNation created problems for traditional car dealerships by amassing large inventories of multiple brands of automobiles and selling cars over the Internet. Some resourceful manufacturers and dealers instituted one-price policies and went on-line to compete with these large retailers. Likewise, computer software developers adapted to market needs by letting customers download software products directly from the Internet.

Overall Ability to Add Value.   Several questions should be answered about an intermediary's ability to add value to the product being marketed or to the distribution process:

1. Can the intermediary perform the necessary distribution tasks that will fulfill our company objectives and customer needs? (Example: Installation and maintenance contracts.)

2. What is the intermediary's ability to add value to perceptions of our product's image in the marketplace? (Example: Distributing jewelry through Tiffany's versus Kmart.)

3. Can the intermediary provide high-quality service outputs within the context of location, quantity, waiting time, and assortment? (Example: A system developed by E-Stamp Corp. allows customers to use the Internet to buy postage. Viable U.S. Postal Service stamps can be printed onto envelopes.)[24]

Evaluation of Channel Efficiency and Effectiveness

Marketers must constantly assess the efficiency and effectiveness of individual channel intermediaries as well as the entire channel. In general, channel members must achieve the goals set out for them in their arrangements with the supplier and must satisfy the criteria established for their selection. Several broad measures are discussed below: market coverage, economic performance, marketing effectiveness, and overall ability to add value.

Market Coverage.   Effective distribution is obtained when the supplier has achieved the desired level of coverage in the designated target market(s). This may include having enough retail intermediaries to reach a substantial number of consumers and enough wholesalers, agents, brokers, or other middlemen to reach desired organizational customers. Other coverage measures include a proactive and well-informed salesforce, product inventories that are available when and where needed by final customers, and sufficient attention given by the intermediary to marketing the supplier's product (i.e., evidence that the intermediary considers it important).

Economic Performance.   Costs of distribution at each channel level and with each intermediary can be determined as a percentage of sales, unit costs, operating profits, contribution margins, marketing program costs, and return on dollars spent for reseller support. Economic measures can be applied to each level of reseller to assess their contribution to strategic channel goals.

Marketing Effectiveness.   Marketing program elements are assessed for their effectiveness in accomplishing sales objectives, with particular emphasis on the communications mix. For instance, personal selling can be evaluated on ability to meet sales objectives. Advertising and other communication efforts can be evaluated on sales and other measures of audience response. Pricing strategies can be reviewed relative to demand elasticity and market characteristics.

Channel members should be evaluated on inventory turnover rate, delivery record, customer service, and other relevant criteria. Studies conducted by KPMG Consulting, Deloitte & Touche, and Consumer Goods Manufacturer agreed that effective supply-chain management relies on efficient inventory management and that optimal inventory levels (minimum levels necessary to support customer

INNOVATE OR EVAPORATE*

Alternative Distribution Channels for Alternative Music

Where do you buy recordings of your favorite artists? Mainstream musicians distribute their sounds through retail outlets such as Tower, Target, or Sam Goody, but what about the newer, harder-to-find alternative sounds? The distribution of music is "a fragmented and faddish business where being seen as alternative—having "street cred"—can be paramount while the definition of "alternative" is constantly shifting. Smaller bands and record labels that perform all genres of music (rock, rap, country, jazz) complain about the difficulty of getting their music "out there." They find that alternative distributors are a favorite option.

Fans of cult bands, local music makers, and new sounds are most likely to buy their recordings in small, independent retail shops. These shops buy from alternative record distributors with grassroots names such as Caroline Distribution and Alternative Distribution Alliance (ADA). These channels gain legitimacy through the support of EMI Capitol Music Group North America, which owns Caroline Distribution, and Time Warner Inc., which has an equity stake in ADA. Alternative distributors keep their identities and their marketing strategies separate from their parent companies, creating a dual distribution system tailored to the needs of customers and suppliers. This allows the larger record labels to work with smaller bands that otherwise would not be worth their while.

Jim Powers, owner of Minty Fresh Inc., a Chicago-based independent record label, says that his company chose ADA as a distributor because "their sales people are into new music and can articulate their passions to the retailer." Rather than sell on the basis of sales figures and product endorsements that might convince a discounter like Target to stock a CD, the key selling point for alternative distributors and independent retailers is the sound of the music itself.

What strategies are available for distributing music? Distributors take the CDs from warehouses and get them into record stores. Most of the powerful major music labels have their own distribution systems, shipping billions of copies of CDs by Madonna, Boyz II Men, and Aerosmith to major retailers. In contrast, alternative distributors deal primarily with independent retailers that will give store space to an innovative new band with a cult following. This channel has lower sales potential but a more profitable customer base of loyal followers and little competition from the larger distributors—making it a lucrative proposition. ADA's 30 sales representatives cover 5800 independent retailers, introducing them to niche bands that their customers will not find anywhere else—a way to "champion certain bands instead of focusing on the more generic big hits." The ADA salesforce, stationed all over the country, can save money and increase sales by introducing more than one band at a time to independent retailers.

The success of alternative music distribution channels depends on personal relationships between distributors and customers and learning what their clientele likes and dislikes. Alternative distributors are "taking the smaller labels and getting them to market, which might not otherwise happen," says a music industry attorney in New York.

*The box title is attributed to James M. Higgins, *Innovate or Evaporate* (Winter Park, FL: New Management Publishing Company, 1995).

Source: Margaret Littman, "No Alternative: Reality Counters Perception in Music Distribution Biz," *Marketing News* 32(16) (August 3, 1998), pp. 1, 13.

service objectives) can improve cash flows and ability to respond to market demands. The KPMG study emphasizes the importance of integration: "Integrating and involving supply chain partners are essential to achieving a competitive advantage in the marketplace."[25]

Overall Ability to Add Value.   Some ways that channel members can add value to the distribution process include the ability to adapt to changing market conditions, to provide market data, and to deliver high-quality customer service. For example, the intermediary must be able to adapt to the entry of a powerful new competitor, or to the problems of a faltering economy, by maintaining customer relationships and providing competitive service. Value also is added through timely and accurate market feedback (e.g., sales trends, customer preferences, competitive actions). Level of commitment to customers can be determined from indicators of high-quality customer service, determined from customer satisfaction surveys, complaints, and level of commitment to training the salesforce and service personnel.

CHANNEL MANAGEMENT

Channel management includes a broad range of issues and responsibilities, following the general marketing management process described in Chapter 3. Four issues are discussed in the following sections: channel power and relationships, vertical marketing systems, legal and ethical concerns, and emerging channel structures in the twenty-first century.

Power and Relationships

Distribution channels rely on a series of relationships among intermediaries. Most channel members are independent organizations with their own objectives and ways of conducting business, but each wants to control its own distribution activities and set standards for its business partners. Ideally, all members in the same channel will operate in an environment of cooperation and mutual trust, but it is more likely that they will have conflicting goals and market orientations. The overriding concern is with control, that is, which member will dominate the distribution channel and set the standards for others in the supply chain.

Channel power
Control and dependence in relationships in the channels of distribution.

   Channel power refers to control and dependence in channel relationships— ". . . the ability of one channel member to get another channel member to do what the latter would not otherwise have done."[26] The member with the most relative power can use any means to influence or control the policies and marketing strategy of another. Bases of power include rewards, coercion, expertness, reference identification, and legitimacy. *Rewards* are economic advantages that accrue if the channel leader's wishes are followed (e.g., assignment of exclusive territories for limiting the number of competing product lines carried). *Coercive power* involves any negative sanction or punishment possible to get other channel members to conform (e.g., late shipments, price increases). *Expert power* is based on a channel follower's perception that the channel leader has special knowledge that will be beneficial. Small retailers may depend on large wholesalers for market information and management assistance. *Referent power* is gained from a superior image or association, based on pride in a present or anticipated relationship (e.g., a car dealer may prefer to open a prestigious Jaguar dealership versus a Kia dealership). *Legitimate power* is based on the belief that the channel leader possesses the right to exert influence on other channel members and to expect compliance (e.g., ownership or contractual agreements, relative size, market position). Note that channel power is relative, and all members have some degree of power, due to their interdependence. The power bases usually work in combination to achieve channel objectives.

Channel conflicts
Vertical and horizontal differences of opinion among channel members.

Vertical and horizontal **channel conflicts** are inevitable in a changing, competitive environment, but conflict must be managed so that previously adversarial suppliers can achieve positive outcomes. Researchers found that a supplier's market-oriented behaviors have a significant effect on all other major channel relationship factors, specifically the market orientation of distributors, the level of trust and commitment, cooperative norms, and satisfaction with financial performance.[27]

Vertical Marketing Systems

Vertical marketing system (VMS)
Organized form of channel control involving any number of intermediaries; integration may be partial or complete.

A **vertical marketing system (VMS)** is an organized form of channel control involving any number of intermediaries (as described earlier within the context of retailing). A channel may be completely or partially integrated. A fully integrated channel has all stages of production and distribution under one ownership or control. It is more common to have partial integration (forward or backward), such as producer-wholesaler, producer-retailer, or wholesaler-retailer. Advantages of a VMS include more cost-effective and profitable distribution alternatives, less interfirm conflict, economies of scale, better bargaining power in negotiations, guaranteed supply, and more opportunity to innovate. The three major forms of VMS are corporate, administered, and contractual.

Corporate backward integration
Retailers own producers or wholesalers that precede them in the channels of distribution.

Corporate forward integration
Manufacturers own their own retail or wholesale outlets or distribution centers.

Administered VMS
Resembles a conventional marketing channel; each member remains independently owned and autonomous but collaborates with others in marketing activities.

Contractual VMS
Independently owned firms at different levels of production and distribution that integrate programs through a formal contract.

Corporate backward integration occurs when retailers own producers or wholesalers that precede them in the channel (e.g., Kroger owns processing facilities). In **corporate forward integration,** manufacturers own their own retail or wholesale outlets or distribution centers (e.g., Radio Shack/Tandy). An **administered VMS** closely resembles a conventional marketing channel, where each member remains independently owned and autonomous but collaborates with the others in marketing activities (e.g., Procter & Gamble Co. and retailers). A **contractual VMS** consists of independently owned firms at different levels of production and distribution that integrate their programs through a formal contract. The three major types of contractual VMS channels are wholesaler-sponsored voluntary chains (e.g., Western Auto), retailer-sponsored cooperative groups (e.g., Ace Hardware), and franchises (e.g., Jiffy Lube, Dunkin' Donuts).[28]

Legal and Ethical Issues

All distribution channel members are subject to the requirements of antitrust and fair dealing legislation in the United States (e.g., Sherman Antitrust Act, Federal Trade Commission Act). They also are subject to international and foreign laws when involved in overseas transactions. Basically, the control that one channel member exerts over another may be considered illegal if it creates a monopoly, restrains trade, or reduces competition (e.g., a large retailer's excessive demands on a small supplier that can be viewed as restraint of trade).

Many ethical issues arise in distribution activities. These are concerned primarily with the buying and selling process and fair treatment of customers and business partners. Unethical marketing activities often focus on how the marketing mix is used to influence customers, suppliers, and others. Areas of particular concern include deceptive advertising, packaging, and labeling; high-pressure sales techniques; product quality and safety; unfair pricing methods; and overcharging. Channel members also are expected to be socially responsible by maintaining a safe environment and contributing to the economic and social well-being of the community.

Emerging Channels: Distribution in the Twenty-First Century

Technology, growth in international markets, and rapid changes in government regulation will drive the major changes in channel relationships in the twenty-first century.[29] In addition, channel design will focus on creating shorter lead times and order-processing cycles and will place more emphasis on service and customer satisfaction. More attention also will be given to increased domestic and global competition and to developing and maintaining strategic alliances.

Technology.   Electronic data-interchange (EDI) capabilities will result in more efficient inventory management and cost reduction by tracking inventory movement throughout the supply chain and by supporting channel alliances. Computerization, electronic commerce, and sophisticated data-interchange technologies will join forces to provide more accurate and timely market data and more effective communication. The potential result of these converging technologies is a more integrated supply chain. Some industrial distribution experts see the integrated supply trend as the eventual end of traditional producer-controlled channels.[30]

The twenty-first century will see more automation in materials handling, warehousing, and physical distribution processes. Bar coding and radio frequency technologies will reach new levels of sophistication in monitoring the movement of everything from freshly picked apples to containerized freight on a ship. Technology has been, and will continue to be, the predecessor of creative destruction (crisis and renewal) described in Chapter 2 and will present major challenges for continuous improvement in distribution if marketers are to remain competitive.

International Markets.   Although overseas markets offer new distribution opportunities, the challenges of international channels are more complex. Primary concerns are the need to minimize delivery lead time and variability and to develop better ways to decrease distribution costs. Companies must gain a better understanding of cultural variations among foreign customers and suppliers and of cross-cultural channel management. Channel members do not need to be directly involved in overseas markets to be affected by international distribution trends. Virtually every channel member has some association with foreign suppliers or customers, global communication technology (e.g., Internet), and foreign competition.

Changing Regulatory Environment.   Deregulation and changing regulations in many industries in the United States and abroad will continue to bring about changes in channel management. In the United States alone, the communications, transportation, and financial industries have undergone significant regulatory changes, generally creating a more competitive and volatile business environment. International regulations such as NAFTA, EC92, and other transnational trade agreements will continue to open new markets and present new distribution challenges. Distributors must have the flexibility to adapt to these changes.

Summary

A channel of distribution is a set of interdependent organizations that combine their efforts to make goods and services available to end-customers. The activities of distribution channels (intermediaries between producers and customers) and physical distribution (logistical movement of goods and services) make a major economic contribution. Channel intermediaries make the exchange process more efficient, match supply and market demand, routinize transactions, and facilitate customers' search processes. Functions performed by distributors include exchange, physical supply, and facilitating activities.

The primary channel intermediaries are wholesalers, retailers, and other merchants or agents. Consumer and organizational channels may be direct or indirect. Direct channels are the shortest and quickest because no intermediaries are involved. Indirect channels use one or more intermediaries, resulting in longer lead times and less control. Multiple channels can be used to reach diverse customer groups. International channels are more complex and costly than domestic channels.

Wholesalers may provide full service, partial service, or no service. The three major types of wholesalers are merchant wholesalers, manufacturers' sales branches and offices, and agent middlemen. Market-coverage strategies may be intensive, exclusive, or selective and can be applied to both the for-profit and nonprofit sectors. Trends and issues in wholesaling include shorter distribution channels, globalization, technological advances, increased competition, industry consolidation, and other factors.

Retailers offer assortments of goods and services to meet the demands of final consumers and can be classified according to form of ownership and control or strategic positioning. Retailers can be classified further in terms of general merchandisers and food merchandisers, as well as location strategies. Three major areas of change in retailing include store formats and operations, channel relations, and customer characteristics.

Channel structure is determined by four service level outputs: spatial convenience, lot size, waiting time, and product variety. Channel length is determined by desired market coverage and types of intermediaries needed. Selection criteria for channel members include market coverage, costs, control, flexibility, and ability to add value to the process. Channel efficiency and effectiveness are evaluated against the same criteria. Channel management focuses on channel power and relationships, vertical marketing systems, legal and ethical concerns, and emerging channel structures for the twenty-first century.

Questions

1. Describe the role and contributions of a distribution system in the U.S. economy and in the world economy. Include an explanation of the difference between distribution channels and physical distribution activities and how each fits into the supply-chain concept.

2. (a) Name all potential intermediaries that might comprise a complex distribution channel, and list the general characteristics of each

intermediary. (b) Describe the general functions performed by channel members.

3. Select a specific industry, such as personal computers, snack foods, or compact disks, and determine at least two different distribution channels that might be pursued by a producer in these industries. Justify each channel alternative selected.

4. For one of the channels selected in Question 3, describe the specific functions that each identified intermediary would perform most effectively.

5. Describe the major types of wholesalers and the services typically performed by each type. Explain the relationship between type of wholesaler and market-coverage strategy. Can a producer use more than one type of wholesaler to distribute the same product to different target markets? Explain.

6. Repeat Question 5, substituting retailer for wholesaler.

7. Assuming that you are a marketing manager for a producer of home-improvement supplies, discuss the criteria that you would use in selecting and evaluating channel members. What factors would be important in determining channel length (number of intermediaries) needed?

8. Discuss the five major issues in channel management, and describe a specific example of how each might have an impact on distribution methods 10 years from now.

Exercises

1. Visit a warehouse or distribution center in your community. Determine the role that this facility plays in the total distribution process for a particular type of merchandise. Evaluate the use of technology.

2. Determine the economic contribution of the various categories of wholesalers and retailers by accessing U.S. Bureau of the Census data on the Internet (Census of Retailing; Census of Wholesaling). Plot the trends in each category

on a graph, and identify any major changes that may be occurring. What are your predictions for the future of each type of intermediary based on census data?

3. Find an example of an international retailer in current business media. Identify the channel(s) of distribution used by this retailer to move goods from producers to customers in another country. Discuss possible problems that might be encountered in this process, including cultural differences, legal and political concerns, and so forth.

Endnotes

1. Charles C. Poireier and Stephen E. Reiter, *Supply Chain Optimization: Building the Strongest Total Business Network* (San Francisco: Berrett-Koehler Publishers, 1996), p. 244.

2. *Ibid.*

3. Louis W. Stern and Adel I. El-Ansary, *Marketing Channels,* 4th ed. (Englewood Cliffs, NJ: Prentice-Hall, 1992), p. 1.

4. Alexander Hiam and Charles D. Schewe, *The Portable MBA in Marketing* (New York: John Wiley & Sons, Inc., 1992), p. 320.

5. For further discussion of the supply-chain model, see Poirier and Reiter, *op. cit.,* Chap. 1.

6. Louis W. Stern and Adel I. El-Ansary, *Marketing Channels* (Englewood Cliffs, NJ: Prentice-Hall, 1988), p. 5; also see Carol H. Anderson, *Retailing: Concepts, Strategy and Information.* (St. Paul, MN: West Publishing, 1993), Chap. 1.

7. *Producer* is used in this discussion as a general term to represent all originators of goods and services, including producers of raw materials, farmers and growers, manufacturers, etc.

8. Anne Marie Chaker, "Makeup Brands Take Note as Day Spas Sell Cosmetics," *Wall Street Journal* (July 8, 1998), pp. B1, B9.

9. Miriam Jordan, "In Rural India, Video Vans Sell Toothpaste and Shampoo," *Wall Street Journal* (January 10, 1996), pp. B1, B5.

10. See Michael R. Czinkota, "Export/Import Marketing: Lessons for Domestic Markets," and John T. Mentzer, "Channel Management 2000," in Jeffrey Heilbrunn (ed.), *AMA Marketing Encyclopedia* (Chicago: American Marketing Association, 1995), pp. 118–119 and 127–132.

11. Yumiko Ono, "Tiffany Glitters, Even in Gloomy Japan," *Wall Street Journal* (July 21, 1998), pp. B1, B18.

12. Adel I. El-Ansary, "Wholesaling: New Ways of Selling, New Forces and Challenges," in Heilbrunn, *op. cit.,* p. 122. (Data obtained from different sources may vary, but they support the size and importance of wholesaling in the distributive process and as a key economic factor.)

13. *Ibid.,* pp. 123–125.

14. For further discussion, see Stern and El-Ansary (1992), *op. cit.*

15. In many cases the supply chain extends the distribution process to product resale and recycling, such as used items sold in resale shops or automobile trade-ins, that result in multiple sales and purchases of the same item.

16. METRO Holding AG, Hoover's Online, August 14, 1998, *http://www.hoovers.com/capsules* and *http://www.hoovers.com/features/industry/retail.*

17. "Worldwide Franchising Statistics: A Study of Worldwide Franchise Associations," Leonard N. Swartz, Worldwide Managing Director, Franchise Services, Arthur Andersen in cooperation with the World Franchising Council (November 1995), Franchising Research WWW site: *http://www.wmin.ac.uk.*

18. Robin Lee Allen, "The NRN 50—The Franchisees: Foodservice's Theory of Evolution: Survival of the Fittest," *Nation's Restaurant News* (January 1998), pp. 12–15ff.

19. European Franchise Survey, European Franchise Federation (August 1997), Franchising Research WWW site: *http://www.wmin.ac.uk.*

20. For further discussion, see Anderson, *op. cit.,* Chap. 4.

21. For further discussion of each of these concepts, see *ibid.,* pp. 128–140.

22. For a complete discussion of the retail life cycle concept, see W. Davidson, A. Bates, and S. Bass, "The Retail Life Cycle," *Harvard Business Review* (November–December 1976), pp. 89–93.

23. Stern and El-Ansary (1988), *op. cit.*; also see Anderson, *op. cit.,* pp. 16–18.

24. Matthew Nelson, "E-Stamp Receives Big Backing for Net-Based Postage Sales," *InfoWorld* (September 29, 1997), p. 68.

25. Anonymous, "SCF Surveys Study Inventory and Integration," *Transportation & Distribution* 39(6) (June 1998), p. SCF15.

26. See Stern and El-Ansary (1988), *op. cit.,* pp. 266–281; and Adel I. El-Ansary and Louis W. Stern, "Power Measurement in the Distribution Channel," *Journal of Marketing Research* 9 (February 1972), pp. 47ff.

27. Judy A. Siguaw, Penny M. Simpson, and Thomas L. Baker, "Effects of Supplier Market Orientation on Distributor Market Orientation and the Channel Relationship: The Distributor Perspective," *Journal of Marketing* 62 (July 1998), pp. 99–111.

28. For further discussion, see Anderson, *op. cit.,* pp. 144–148.

29. See Mentzer, *op. cit.,* pp. 117–121; Anonymous, "Distribution 2000: A View from the Experts," *Industrial Distribution* 1 (January 1998), pp. 48–49; and others.

30. *Ibid.*

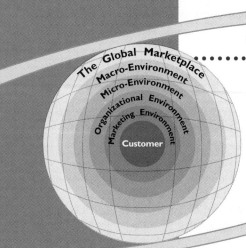

Chapter II

Integrated Marketing Communications Strategy

Integrated Marketing Communications

Pull versus Push IMC Strategies

Financial Aspects of IMC

Streamline Delivers the Goods

Never promise more than you can perform.[1]

Streamline Inc., a Web-based company in Westwood, Massachusetts, is a shopping and delivery service for busy consumers. For a $30 per month fee, each customer receives a "Streamline Box" containing a refrigerator, a freezer, and dry-storage shelves that are stored in the customer's garage. A Streamline field representative with a bar-code scanner then records what the customer keeps in the home refrigerator, freezer, pantry, and medicine chest, resulting in a first draft of the customer's *personal shopping list* (PSL). The PSL is posted on Streamline's Web site so the customer can edit it. As frequently as once a week customers can select from more than 10,000 grocery items or order prepared meals, rent videos, arrange for dry cleaning, and ship UPS packages. After they have done this a few times, customers usually cut their ordering time to 20 or 25 minutes per week.

Founder and CEO Tim DeMello says, "I want to simplify people's lives. That's what I'm passionate about. That's what I believe in." Observers might believe that Streamline is an on-line grocer that competes with similar firms such as NetGrocer, but that would be a wrong conclusion. DeMello insists, "We are not in the grocery business. We are in the lifestyle-solutions business. We are not a product business. We are not a service business. We're a relationship business."

These distinctions are profound. Whereas many Web companies emphasize their cutting-edge technology, Streamline promises customers the cutting edge of service. "We have taken the characteristics of grocery shopping—necessity, frequency, reliability—and leveraged them into a

314

home-based relationship with customers," says DeMello. "That's the asset were creating."

By 2004, DeMello plans to have 8 operating regions, be in the top 12 metropolitan areas, and serve more than 1 million homes to generate more than $5 billion in sales. If this sounds like a "get big fast" strategy, however, DeMello will tell you that you are wrong again. "You have to get your business model absolutely perfect before you do a full-scale launch into the market," says DeMello. "Because if you succeed on the Web, you succeed big. And you can't change a tire on a car that's moving at 80 miles an hour. The way to grow a company is to make it work for one customer. Then you make it work for 10, for 100, and then for 1000." Gina Wilcox, director of strategic relations, says: "We have a laser-like focus on BSFs"—Streamline's target market, the *busy suburban family* (BSF), consists of young and middle-aged couples with high incomes and at least one child. Wilcox notes, "It's easy to get customers. It's harder to get the right customers."

"We collaborate with families that want to run better," says Frank Britt, vice president of marketing. "It's an intimate relationship. Consumers come to depend on us to make their lives simpler and better." One of Streamlines most popular services is called "Don't Run Out." Families identify must-have items and authorize Streamline to replenish each item automatically. "It's extraordinary," says Wilcox. "The consumer makes a purchase decision once, and we fill the order throughout the year. It redefines brand loyalty. It redefines marketing."

Such an intense relationship also redefines strategy. "We've created a two-way channel with our customers," says Tom Jones, CIO and technology wizard. "It's vibrant. It's ongoing. It's reliable. We become part of our customers' lives."

Source: Staff writer, "Streamline Delivers the Goods," *Fast Company* (August 1998), pp. 154–156.

Perhaps Streamline has discovered the ultimate way to success by taking relationship marketing to a new, competitive level. DeMello has analyzed the communications needs of his targeted customers and used an integrated marketing communications mix of advertising, salesforce activity, sales promotion, direct marketing, and publicity to effectively send his message of maximum convenience and superior customer service. He also has structured the remaining marketing-mix elements—product strategy, pricing strategy, and distribution strategy—to be compatible with his overall marketing strategy.

INTEGRATED MARKETING COMMUNICATIONS

Integrated marketing communications (IMC)
Used in marketing to cover all types of marketing activities designed to stimulate demand; sometimes referred to as the *communications mix.*

Designing the integrated marketing communications activities of an organization pushes the manager to the forefront of marketing knowledge. Innovation and creativity make the difference between humdrum marketing and truly outstanding communication of the intended message to target audiences. The term **integrated marketing communications (IMC)** is used in marketing to cover all types of marketing activities designed to stimulate demand. We refer to these various demand-creating activities as the *communications mix.*

The American Productivity & Quality Center (APQC) developed a more concise definition of integrated marketing communications as follows: "IMC is a strategic business process used to plan, develop, execute and evaluate coordinated, measurable, persuasive brand communication programs over time with consumers, customers, prospects and other targeted, relevant external and internal audiences."[2] If we simply substitute the word *marketing* for *brand* in this definition, the concept of IMC broadens to encompass the entire scope of marketing communication activities in both the consumer products market and the business-to-business market.

Communications Theory

Communications theory has important applications in all areas of IMC. Simply stated, *communication* is the transmission of messages. Therefore, the ultimate success of an IMC program rests on its ability to deliver a core message to a target market.

The Communications Flow.   IMC activities involve a forward communications flow. Manufacturers *communicate to* wholesalers, retailers, and ultimate consumers. Resellers *communicate to* their customers. Backward flows of communications also exist and are critical to understanding customers and markets. Communications also can flow horizontally. Retailers exchange ideas among themselves. Consumers are notoriously inclined to spread marketing information. In fact, we even talk about word-of-mouth advertising as if it were a type of communications medium. A 1996 survey of 2006 adults noted that 7 of 10 rated family and friends as the best source of health plan information and that word of mouth was even more important in choosing individual doctors.[3] In almost all communication situations there is a feedback loop that provides information about the effectiveness of the flow of communications.

Elements of Communication.   There are four important elements that help us understand the relation of communications to IMC: the source, the message, the medium, and the receiver.

1. The *source* is the initiator of the message, often a manufacturing or service establishment wanting to transmit some information to customers or resellers.

2. The *message* is the commercial idea being communicated. In advertising, it is the copy; in selling terms, it is the "sales pitch." The message is the substance of what flows from sender to receiver.

3. The *medium* delivers the message. In advertising, the medium may be a television show, a newspaper, a magazine, or any number of other forms. In personal selling, the salesperson is the medium.

4. The *receiver* is the person (or persons) to whom the message is directed. In most cases the receiver is a potential customer. However, a receiver also can be a purchase influencer or a reseller, who then is expected to become a sender to retransmit the message to yet another audience.

FIGURE 11.1
....
The Communication System

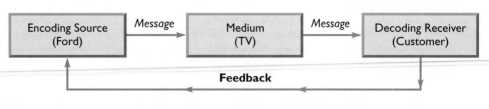

The role of these four communications elements is illustrated in Figure 11.1. The source is an organization, for example, Ford Motor Co. The medium is national network television. The vehicle is "Monday Night Football." The message is an endorsement by a famous quarterback of the company's Taurus automobile. The receiver is a potential customer at home who views the commercial.

Types of Communications. Figure 11.1 is an oversimplification of a highly complex mass communications system, which is illustrated in Figure 11.2.

- *Specific communications.* Specific communications involve the direct transmission of a message from a single source to a single, specific receiver. For example, a salesperson at a Ford dealership in Orlando telephones a customer in the suburbs who owns a Ford Escort purchased several years previously. The salesperson thinks that the customer might be ready for a new car, possibly a Taurus. This specific communication in shown in Figure 11.2a.

- *Selective communications.* Selective communications involve directing messages through a single medium to a limited number of receivers. For example, after talking on the telephone, the salesperson might send a colorful brochure showing the new Taurus to everybody who purchased an Escort 3 years earlier. Figure 11.2b illustrates this communications flow.

- *Mass communications.* Mass communications involve the use of one or more media to reach large numbers of receivers. Figure 11.2c shows such a communications program. Now, instead of the salesperson being the source, the dealer fills this communications role. Three radio stations are selected as media for the commercial message to the entire market. Each radio station reaches some, but not all, of the potential customers. However, every potential buyer is exposed to at least two radio stations.

Distortion and Noise. Not every message reaches its intended receiver, and some arrive hopelessly distorted. *Distortion* is most likely to occur in long communications flows involving several successive media vehicles. Using persons to transmit messages often creates distortion. A manufacturer whose product is purchased and resold first by a wholesaler and then by a retailer has little control over the sales message delivered to the ultimate consumer. This is the reason manufacturers attempt to reach consumers through a controlled IMC campaign.

FIGURE 11.2

. . . .

Three Types of Communication: (a) specific communications, (b) selective communications, (c) mass communication.

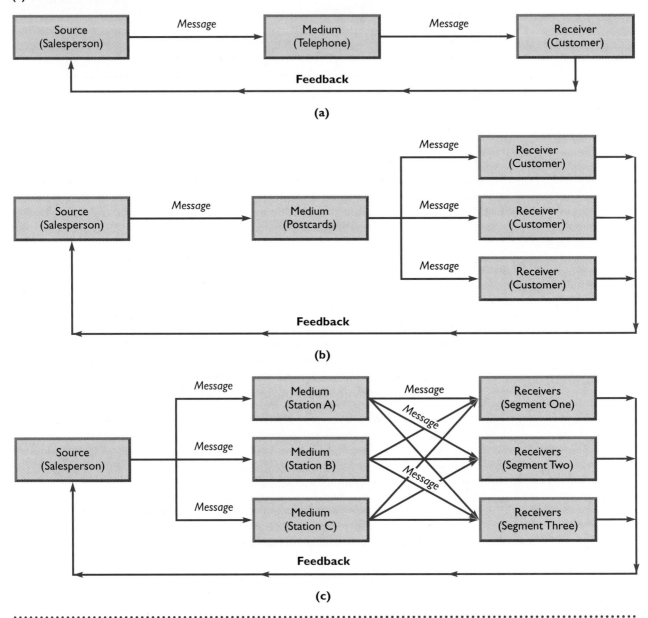

(a)

(b)

(c)

. . . .

Noise, or confusion, is an even more serious problem.[4] It can arise because of faulty transmission, faulty reception, or interference. A small newspaper advertisement crowded in among many others on a cluttered page certainly will be lost. Bad reception and interference are even more likely in broadcast communications. Consumers are not especially interested in advertising and thus do not pay close attention to it. They frequently turn down the volume or switch the radio or television channel whenever a commercial starts. The popularity of the television remote control device stems from the convenience of "zapping" commercials both on the air and when a show is being replayed from a videocassette recorder.[5] However, even if the message comes through, the noise level at the receiving end is very high.

The loudest and most serious noise results from competitive interference. The typical consumer is exposed to many communications flows simultaneously. Often these are directly competitive. Look at a newspaper and note how many directly competing advertising messages it contains. In the same way, how many fast-food or cosmetics commercials do you see in one evening of television watching?

How can a marketer overcome this type of interference? By communicating meaningfully to the right people, at the right time, and with the right message. Effective communication, however, demands conspicuous creativity and requires consistent and persistent efforts. The noise at any one time is too great for marketers to expect immediate results. Over the period of an entire IMC campaign, and certainly in the long run, a well-conceived, continuous, and creative communications program can achieve its objectives.

The Communications Mix

Communications mix
Any communications activity designed to stimulate demand—specifically, advertising, salesforce activity, sales promotion, direct marketing, and publicity/public relations.

Various elements of IMC are combined in the **communications mix.** Specifically, this mix includes advertising, salesforce activity, sales promotion, direct marketing, and publicity/public relations. The term *mix* implies that there are different ways of blending these ingredients as part of an overall IMC program. It also suggests a synergism, in which the total IMC effect is greater than the sum of its parts. In short, the communications mix is an overall creative plan as well as a thoughtfully designed combination of selected ingredients.

Advertising.   *Advertising* is the public communication of messages to select audiences to inform and influence them. Advertising messages are identified with the advertiser and involve payment to the medium employed, whereas public relations/ publicity does not. Advertising is often mass communication. Although some advertising is directed to specific individuals (such as, for example, in the use of direct mail, trade publications, and professional publications), most advertising messages are placed in public media to be seen by large numbers of people.

Salesforce Activity.   Simply stated, *salesforce activity* is any person-to-person or telephone-based activity by a firm's representative that is intended to deliver value to customers. From a management perspective, this involves selecting, training, organizing, deploying, motivating, and supervising a team of field salespersons and establishing account management policies to guide field and internal behaviors. From a salesperson's perspective, this involves all sales process activities associated with personal selling plus related activities required to build relationships and satisfy customers over the long term.

Sales Promotion.   Because *sales promotion* frequently involves reducing prices to distributors or retailers to motivate them to push the sponsor's products, it is easy to forget that non-price-related sales promotional activities are the predominant forms of sales promotion. Sales promotional activities are intended to have an immediate impact on consumer buying behavior.

Direct Marketing.   *Direct marketing* involves a host of activities designed to reach targeted customers without an intermediary organization being involved. For example, database marketing has enabled customized direct-mail programs to become viable methods to reach individual customers with persuasive communications.

Publicity/Public Relations.   *Publicity* is communication of information that is not paid for and does not identify the source of the message. It is sometimes not included as part of the communications mix because it lacks controllability. Publicity can be used for many nonmarketing communications purposes, for example, in connection with a company's dealings with the financial community or in connection with a collective-bargaining situation. To isolate the part of the publicity that is properly part of the communications mix, we use the term *public relations* (PR).[6] For instance, when a company introduces a new product, it may try to have articles about the product appear in magazines and newspapers.

IMC Objectives

In addition to contributing to the overall marketing effort, the major objective of IMC activities is to influence targeted customer groups. IMC does influence sales. In a mail-order business, IMC is the principal means of marketing. But mostly IMC contributes to sales revenue directly by performing two powerful functions: It *conditions,* and it *reinforces.* IMC activities prepare the way for the salesperson by informing customer prospects of the value of the company's products or services. And IMC reinforces sales efforts by reminder reinforcement and after-sales presentations. Postpurchase communication combats negative evaluation. For undecided customers, IMC keeps the flow of information open until the next opportunity for a sale occurs.

The effects of IMC on actual and potential customers have been stated in different terms by several researchers.[7] Their perspective is that potential customers must progress through several states of awareness before they are ready to buy—as illustrated in Figure 11.3. The total population of potential customers can be classified according to these stages. The goal of IMC is to move potential customers toward the state of conviction and actual use. The classification of awareness levels shown in Figure 11.3 is called the **hierarchy of effects model.**

Hierarchy of effects model
The classification of awareness levels that potential customers must progress through before they are ready to buy.

What marketers really want to accomplish with IMC is (1) to create a unified image and (2) to support relationship building with customers and stakeholders. First, the firm must decide specific targets for the IMC campaign (initiators, users, decision makers, influencers, buyers, or gatekeepers). Next, the firm must set communications goals, which Marian Burk Wood suggests fall into five categories:[8]

1. *Build brand equity.* Use IMC to reinforce your brand's value and identity and encourage stronger preference, which should strengthen relationships competitively. In its ads, 3M links Scotchguard's specific benefits such as stain protection with customer value perceptions.

IT'S LEGAL BUT IS IT ETHICAL?

Company Struggles to Get Message Out

Mary Ann Leeper, president, COO, and de facto director of marketing for Female Health Co. (FHC), has only one product. It has been approved by the federal government for consumer use, praised by industry organizations, and is in great demand among those who know it exists. It has been lauded by health advocates, including the World Health Organization (WHO), because it allows women to control their own protection from diseases. A study by Joint United Nations Program on HIV/AIDS (UNAIDS) found the use of this product caused the incidence of sexually transmitted diseases to drop by 35 percent. Leeper's product seems to fill a social need for disease prevention that has global ramifications. In many markets, however, Leeper is not allowed to advertise on television. FHC's product is a female condom brand named Reality.

The makers of Reality are not alone. All makers of birth-control products find it difficult to advertise, even as more sex makes it into mainstream television programming. Two makers of male condoms, both of which are supporting extensive television advertising, declined to comment on how this was accomplished. Spokespeople for both companies said the issue was too contentious.

FHC has had success outside mainstream consumer marketing by developing a program to ed-ucate public health groups, such as Planned Parenthood, university health centers, and state and city health departments on the product's benefits. FHC hopes that by working with these types of organizations, the company can bring Reality to wider acceptance and sales will grow. Then FHC will try again to use traditional media outlets nationwide. In developing countries, where the AIDS epidemic continues to grow, WHO and UNAIDS are helping FHC develop distribution relationships. UNAIDS solicited interest in 180 countries and expected to distribute 8 million Reality condoms during 1997.

As acceptance of the product grows, some experts predict that advertising hurdles will be removed. "It used to be that you couldn't advertise tampons, and they were sold in plain brown wrappers in the store," says Larry Oskin, president of Marketing Solutions Inc. "Now you see ads for Tampax during dinner. Because of the health issues and the AIDS scare, I think it is just a matter of time before you see condom ads all over the national media. It's an issue that is important to the whole community."

Source: Margaret Littman, "A Dose of Reality," *Marketing News* 32(1) (January 5, 1998), p. 2.

2. *Provide information.* Offer details about product uses, availability, buying incentives, or convenience of use. Pall Corp., marketer of fluid filtration and purification products, organized its Web site around industry categories rather than internal divisions. This facilitates client browsing through appropriate industry-related Web pages or using the site's search function to find Pall products and technologies appropriate for solving their problems. Also, clients or contacts can e-mail requests for sales consultations.

3. *Manage demand and sales.* Work to stimulate primary demand (for new or innovative products) or selective demand (perhaps for a mature product) or to

FIGURE 11.3

Hierarchy of Effects Model

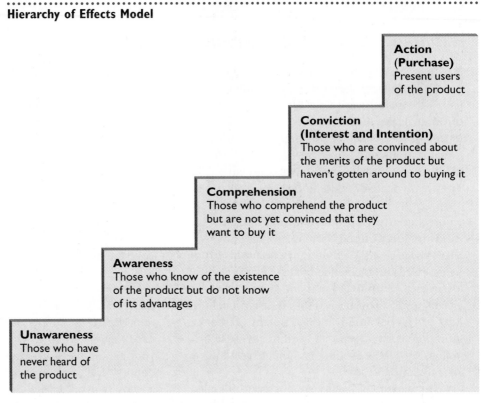

Source: Adapted from Colley, R. H., *Defining Advertising Goals for Measured Advertising Results.* Association of National Advertisers, New York, p. 55. Reprinted by permission.

temporarily dampen demand when the firm is unable to meet demand (or the requested shipping dates). American Express Company used IMC tactics to build selective demand for its corporate card in a highly competitive market affecting customer acquisition, card use, and market share.

4. *Communicate differentiation and enhance positioning.* Convey significant factors of differentiation and positioning relative to competitors' products. For example, United Parcel Service (UPS) stresses the range of guaranteed "urgent delivery" choices such as "same day" and "next day" to differentiate itself from competitors while positioning itself to meet almost any deadline. This is a powerful image for a delivery firm.

5. *Influence attitudes and behavior.* Promote a favorable inclination toward your company and products while encouraging some action, such as recommending your services, contacting your representatives, or completing a purchase order. For instance, A.B. Dick supported the introduction of a new two-color printing press targeted at small printing firms, corporate printing departments, and large commercial printers by using direct mail, public relations, newsletters, and magazine ads to smooth the way for subsequent sales calls. The company em-

phasized the key product benefit—making short-run color printing profitable. Although previously known for its duplicating machines, A.B. Dick's IMC campaign established the company as a maker of full-sized printing presses, and this led to 350 orders totaling more than $20 million.

Wood warns marketers against stretching their IMC strategy and budget over four or five objectives and thus diffusing their IMC effectiveness. It is more effective to concentrate on only one or two IMC goals.

PULL VERSUS PUSH IMC STRATEGIES

Many people think that IMC is directed only toward customers, but important aspects of IMC are directed toward channel intermediaries. Approximately one-third of IMC expenditures is for customer advertising and two-thirds is for sales promotion. The largest portion of these sales promotion expenditures (37 percent of total spending) is for intermediary promotions, whereas the remainder (29 percent of total spending) is for customer advertising. Therefore, approximately 63 percent of total IMC expenditures are aimed at customers and 37 percent at intermediaries.

Customer-targeted IMC consists of **pull-through communications.** The objective of pull-through communications is to build awareness, attraction, and loyalty and reduce search costs, as shown in Figure 11.4. Successful pull-through communications influence customers to seek out certain products or services, thus pulling the product through the channel. Channel intermediaries or resellers must carry these products in order to attract and satisfy target customers.

In contrast, **push-through communications** are directed at channel intermediaries in order to motivate resellers to make a certain product available to customers. Successful push-through communications result in greater availability, fewer stockouts, effective merchandising (shelf space and visual effects), and better marketing efforts by resellers.

Combining both push- and pull-through communications creates the most effective influence on customer response and market share gains.[9] Figure 11.4 outlines the components of push- and pull-through communications.

Pull-Through Communications

Figure 11.4 illustrates the wide range of alternatives in the IMC mix that can be used for effective communications to create customer pull.[10] A good example of the power of communication is the classic case of L&M cigarettes, which had a 17 percent market share prior to the ban on cigarette television advertising. Following the ban, the company decided not to advertise because its people believed that other advertising media were ineffective. L&M is no longer in the market. Without continued reinforcement of the brand and its positioning, L&M faded from customers' minds and from the marketplace.

Customer-directed sales promotions take a variety of formats such as coupons, rebates, sweepstakes, gifts, and rewards. Catalog retailers such as L.L. Bean, Inc., or Eddie Bauer stimulate customer pull every month with mailings to targeted customers. In addition, salesforce activity, direct marketing, and electronic marketing on

Pull-through communications
Customer-targeted IMC activities designed to build awareness, attraction, and loyalty and reduce search costs.

Push-through communications
IMC activities directed at channel intermediaries in order to motivate resellers to make products/services available to customers.

FIGURE 11.4

Push-Pull Communications and Customer Response

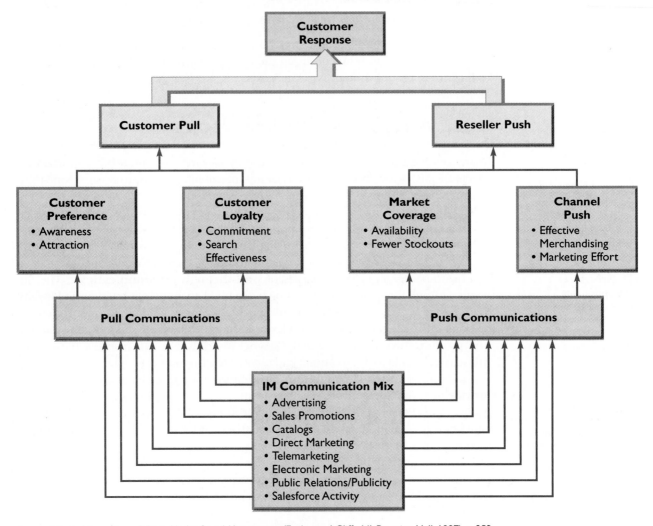

Source: Adapted from Roger J. Best, *Market-Based Management* (Englewood Cliffs, NJ: Prentice-Hall, 1997), p. 253.

Persuasive communications
IMC activities intended to get
target customers to take a
specific action (to purchase
something).

the Internet are forms of IMC that take a customized approach to creating customer pull in the marketplace.

Persuasive communications are intended to get target customers to take a specific action (to purchase something). A firm must be careful in using persuasive communications. If the message is too one-sided in stressing benefits or comparisons with competing products, the message may lose credibility. For example, Paul Wiefels, a marketing consultant, believes that some technology marketers seem too fascinated by their own products. This results in an evangelical zeal that can transform markets, but more often it results in a myopic preoccupation with the trivial and arcane. Consumers are fed product specifications and features instead of useful

INNOVATE OR EVAPORATE*

Video Is Logical for Business-to-Business IMC

Marketers are always looking for innovative ways to send messages and make them stick with targeted audiences. Video can provide the competitive edge to effectively do this. Video tells a story and delivers primary messages consistently and persuasively because it combines sound, print, graphics, and animation, which equates to a powerful impact. Video is relatively easy to produce and offers excellent value for its cost. And video presentations can be modified for different uses through additional editing, changes in audio, or the addition of special effects.

When Sequent Computer Systems of Beaverton, Oregon, wanted to strengthen awareness of its brand name within targeted markets and also wanted to define an image for its product as a high-end, open computing system for *Fortune 500* companies, it decided to use video to launch a customer success program. Sequent's video showed customers discussing why they bought Sequent computers and how they proved successful. The result was increased sales and service revenues.

Boise Cascade Corp. uses video to communicate both inside and outside the company. It sends internal video messages from executives to employees across the company, and it also uses video externally to communicate its environmental preservation practices to profile customers and to promote products. Andrew Drysdale, director of communications at Boise Cascade's environmental and paper division, notes, "In cases where you want to impart more than just factual information, where you want to impart a feeling, a commitment, emotion, sincerity . . . video gives that extra impact."

Video is used internationally by Hewlett-Packard Company's Asia Peripherals (mobile and DeskJet printers) Division's marketing communications program manager, Anton Colton. He says, "Video is efficient for communicating a message both orally and visually, and it's also effective for explaining our positioning and getting our message out." Video communicates a message succinctly and consistently, making it useful for product introductions, product positioning, and building brand equity. It also has the significant advantage of being received when the customer is ready and willing.

*The box title is attributed to James M. Higgins, *Innovate or Evaporate* (Winter Park, FL: New Management Publishing Company, 1995).

Source: Mike Cobb and Dave Sullivan, "Video Is Logical Fit for Business-to-Business," *Marketing News* 31(13) (June 23, 1997), p. 10.

explanations on how the product might fit into their lives or solve problems at work.[11]

Push-Through Communications

Figure 11.4 illustrates that the same wide variety of pull-through communications activities is available for push-through communications efforts. Push-through communications are directed at channel intermediaries and are designed to motivate resellers to become more aggressive in their customer communications and marketing. As shown in Figure 11.4, the objective of push-through communications is to build more effective reseller efforts so that sponsoring firms are able to obtain better market coverage (number of desired distributors) and better merchandising efforts from resellers. This support of resellers' efforts is sometimes called **trade promotions.**

Trade promotions
IMC push-through communications efforts designed to motivate resellers to obtain better market coverage and better merchandising activities.

IMC and Product Life Cycle Stages

There are limits to what communication can accomplish relative to sales levels at different stages of the product's life cycle (PLC). During the introductory stage of the PLC, a firm builds awareness, comprehension, and interest, but market demands may be small, and only limited sales volumes are achievable.

The growth stage of the PLC offers the best opportunity for sales gains using IMC. A firm must invest in IMC during this phase or miss the best opportunity for sales growth because communication results are more likely to have an impact during this period. As markets mature, there are fewer new customers coming into the market, and the effect of IMC on sales diminishes. In declining markets, the firm needs to cut IMC expenditures because they produce little sales response.

FINANCIAL ASPECTS OF IMC

IMC activities can involve huge sums. For example, the cost of a 30-second spot on the Superbowl in 1985 was about $500,000. In 1999, the cost was more than $3 million. In addition, the cost of producing a television commercial is very high. According to one source, a typical commercial in 1998 cost approximately $300,000. Despite these high figures, IMC expenditures in some companies are relatively small when compared with manufacturing and other operational costs. Moreover, this apparent high cost becomes even more modest when the number of consumers reached is considered. For example, if a network television ad is viewed in 20 million homes, the cost of reaching each household is less than 1 cent.

When related to the value of products and services sold, IMC expenditures are not exorbitant. Business-to-business marketing firms, on average, spend less than 1 percent of sales revenue on IMC. Firms marketing consumer goods and services spend in the range of 5 to 10 percent of their sales revenues on IMC—although some companies such as cosmetics firms spend much more.

To measure the effectiveness of IMC, marketers have developed several tools: the customer response index, calculations of communications elasticity, and calculations of communications carryover.

Calculating the Customer Response Index (CRI)

Customer response index (CRI)
A calculation of the changes in customer awareness of ads, comprehension of content, and interest or conviction that measures overall customer response.

Changes in customer awareness of ads, comprehension of content, and interest or conviction as a result of advertising copy are important factors that affect overall customer response. A tool for measuring overall customer response is the **customer response index (CRI),** which can be calculated using this formula:

CRI = % aware × % comprehend × % interest × % intentions × % purchase

Let us assume that the following customer responses occurred after exposure to an ad:

Awareness of the ad was calculated at 63 percent.

Comprehension of the ad was calculated at 54 percent.

Interest in the product was calculated at 77 percent.

Intention to purchase the product was calculated at 68 percent.

Purchase of the product was calculated at 90 percent.

The CRI is calculated this way:

$$CRI = 0.63 \times 0.54 \times 0.77 \times 0.68 \times 0.90$$
$$= 0.16, \text{ or } 16 \text{ percent}$$

Now if the firm and its ad agency believed they could improve "comprehension" from 54 to 67 percent by using a finely tuned communications mix, then the CRI could be improved from 16 to 20 percent:

$$CRI = 0.63 \times 0.67 \times 0.77 \times 0.68 \times 0.90$$
$$= 0.20, \text{ or } 20 \text{ percent}$$

This calculation indicates that improving "comprehension" from 54 to 67 percent should produce an increase in the CRI (and thus a sales increase).

Calculating Communications Elasticity

Communications elasticity
Calculating the change in sales volume per 1 percent change in IMC efforts.

Calculating the change in sales volume per 1 percent change in IMC efforts is a measure of **communications elasticity.** For example, suppose that an increase of 1 percent in communications expenditures produced an estimated 22 percent change in sales volume.[12] Thus a firm with $40 million in sales and a 0.22 communications elasticity could estimate that its sales would increase to $41.67 million with a 20 percent increase in communications, as shown below.

$$Sales = volume \times communications \ elasticity \times price$$
$$= 400,000 \times [1 + (0.22 \times 0.20)] \times \$100$$
$$= \$41.67 \text{ million}$$

Calculating Communications Carryover

Communications carryover
A calculation of the effect of IMC expenditures made in one time period on additional sales responses in subsequent time periods.

IMC expenditures made in one time period produce additional sales response in subsequent time periods. This is termed **communications carryover.** Communications carryover coefficients can range from zero to less than one. The average carryover coefficient is approximately 0.5.[13] Therefore, in the period immediately following a communication, a 0.50 sales effect from the preceding period will carry over, and in the second period, a carryover effect of 0.25 occurs, and so on, until after the period 6, when the carryover sales effect is less than 1 percent. See Figure 11.5 for a graphic representation of this carryover effect.

Budgeting IMC

IMC budgeting decisions constitute one of the most difficult problems in marketing planning. What size budget results in effectiveness? When does the firm reach the level of excess spending? How does a firm ensure that budget constraints relating to operating issues from other functional activities of the firm do not overpower the

1. *Conduct research.* The marketing situation is analyzed looking for marketing opportunities and targets.

2. *Determine objectives.* Short- and long-term IMC objectives are set.

3. *Identify IMC tasks.* The message and media required to achieve the IMC objectives are identified.

4. *Cost the IMC tasks.* The costs involved in the strategy are estimated.

Through the use of computerized systems, the task method approach of IMC budgeting has become less costly and more feasible, resulting in a wider base of use.

Summary

Integrated marketing communications (IMC) are all types of marketing activities designed to stimulate demand. These activities are often called the *communications mix.* Communications theory has important applications in all areas of IMC. Most IMC activities involve a forward communications flow to wholesalers, retailers, and consumers; however, backward flows of communications are critical to understanding customers and markets. Understanding the four elements of communication—the source, the message, the medium, and the receiver—can help us to understand how communications relate to IMC. There are three general types of communications—specific communications, selective communications, and mass communications. Some messages do not reach the intended receiver because of distortion or noise.

Various elements of IMC are combined in the communications mix. The term *mix* implies that there are different ways of blending these elements. Specifically, the mix includes advertising, salesforce activity, sales promotion, direct marketing, and publicity or public relations.

The major objective of IMC activities is to influence targeted customer groups. One way to measure the effectiveness of communications is to measure consumer awareness. One classification model that is used to describe customer awareness is the hierarchy of effects model. The two major goals of IMC are (1) to create a unified image and (2) to support relationship building with customers and stakeholders.

IMC strategies can be classified as pull-through strategies or push-through strategies. The objective of pull-through communications is to build awareness, attraction, and loyalty so that customers will seek out certain products or services. Persuasive communications are part of pull-through communications. Push-through communications, sometimes called *trade promotions,* are directed at channel intermediaries in order to motivate resellers to make the product available to consumers. However, there are limits to what communications can accomplish relative to sales levels depending on the stage of the product life cycle (PLC).

IMC activities can involve huge sums, although relative to the value of the products and services sold, IMC expenditures are usually not exorbitant. To measure the effectiveness of IMC, marketers have developed several tools, such as the customer response index (CRI), calculations of communications elasticity (the change in sales volume related to the change in IMC effort), and calculations of communications carryover (how long the message affects sales response after it is withdrawn).

IMC budgeting decisions are difficult because it is not easy to financially record a direct numerical correlation between IMC activities and sales. Some methods that firms use to budget IMC are the marginal approach, available funds approach, competitive parity approach, percentage of sales approach, fixed sum per unit approach, return on investment approach, and task method approach.

Questions

1. Do you agree that the development of integrated marketing strategy pushed marketing managers to the frontiers of marketing knowledge?

2. Suggest ways in which the concepts of specific, selective, and mass communications might be used by a department store in planning an IMC strategy for lawn and patio furniture.

3. As an executive for a large, multidivision organization, recommend an appropriate integrated marketing communications mix for each of the following products: (a) a medicated soap for dry skin, (b) a facial cosmetic that contains sun-blocking additives and comes in various tones, (c) a hair-coloring system that is temporary (washes out with shampoo in three to five applications), is dispensed in a cream form (easy to apply), will not stain clothes, contains no bleach, and is environmentally friendly, and (d) a hair-removal system that is a cream dispensed from a tube, washes off after 5 minutes (while removing the hair), does not harm the skin, and is safe for facial use.

4. You are in charge of designing an IMC strategy for an instant tea designed to be used in preparing iced tea. However, users have reported using the product to prepare hot tea. You have decided to communicate this alternative product use. You have a $5 million budget. How would you decide how much of this amount to spend on this "hot" new product use?

5. Suggest some reasons why it is important to know exactly how a product is distributed before developing an IMC strategy.

6. A marketing consultant was nearly fired on the spot when he suggested that a firm could decrease its overall marketing expenses by in-creasing its IMC budget. Fortunately, the consultant was able to explain the truth of his position. How would you go about explaining what he meant?

Exercises

1. Identify a firm (either national or local) that within the last 12 months has used a push-through communications strategy effectively. Identify the specific types of IMC activities that the firm used, and explain why you believe this was the correct choice to achieve success.

2. Access the Web site of one of the major agencies or organizations involved in the control of advertising (such as the Federal Trade Commission at *http://www.ftc.gov* or the National Advertising Division of the Better Business Bureau at *http://www.bbb.org*). Determine the agency's current position on ethical and legal issues (such as advertising to children). Do a content analysis of media targeted to this audience, and identify advertisements in electronic and/or print media that demonstrate possible infractions of ethics or regulatory policy. Create new ads that will convey the same message in an ethical and responsible manner.

3. Contact a local new or used automobile dealership that you have identified from perusal of the local newspaper as being a heavy advertiser. Through extensive questioning, identify the specific type of budgeting method the company uses to plan and prepare its IMC activities.

Endnotes

1. Publilium Syrus, "Maxim 528," as quoted in *Bartlett's Book of Business Quotations* (Boston: Little, Brown & Company, 1994), p. 217.

2. Don E. Schultz, "Check Out Your Level of Integration," *Marketing News* (August 18, 1997), p. 10.

3. Robert K. Smoldt, "Turn Word of Mouth into a Marketing Advantage," *The Healthcare Forum Journal* 41(5) (1998), pp. 47–49.

4. For an interesting discussion of clutter in advertising media, see Ralph Andill, "Separating the Message from the White Noise," *Marketing* (April 16, 1998), p. 17.

5. Anonymous, "Zapping," *Marketing* (September 17, 1998), p. 15; Anonymous, "Perimeter Ads Solution to Zapping," *Marketing Week* 20(46) (February 26, 1998), p. 34.

6. Martin L. Bell and Julian W. Vincze, *Managerial Marketing: Strategy and Cases* (New York: Elsevier Science Publishing, 1988), p. 508.

7. Colley's model is found in R. H. Colley, *Defining Advertising Goals for Measured Advertising Results* (New York: Association of National Advertisers, 1961), p. 56.

8. Marian Burk Wood, "Clear IMC Goals Build Strong Relationships," *Marketing News* 31(13) (June 23, 1997), p. 11.

9. For further discussion, see David Reibstein, "Making the Most of Your Marketing Dollars," in *Drive Marketing Excellence* (New York: Institute for International Research, 1994).

10. Gary Lilien, Philip Kotler, and K. Moorthy, *Marketing Models* (Upper Saddle River, NJ: Prentice-Hall, 1992), pp. 329-356.

11. Paul Wiefels, "Change Marketing Tactics as Buyer Attitudes Shift," *Marketing News* 31(12) (June 9, 1997), p. 10.

12. Rajeev Batra, Donald R. Lehmann, Joanne Burke, and Jae Pae, "When Does Advertising Have an Impact? A Study of Tracking Data," *Journal of Advertising Research* 35(10) (September–October 1995), pp. 19-29.

13. Dwight R. Riskey, "How TV Advertising Works: An Industry Response," *Journal of Marketing Research* 34(2) (May 1997), pp. 292-294; and Ron Schults and Martin Block, "Empirical Estimates of Advertising Response Factors," *Journal of Media Planning* (Fall 1986), pp. 17-24.

14. K. S. Palda, *The Measurement of Cumulative Advertising Effect* (Englewood Cliffs, NJ: Prentice-Hall, 1964), p. 80.

15. See *Leading National Advertisers*. This periodical reports the spending by competing brands on measured media: television, radio, magazines, newspapers, and outdoor.

CHAPTER 12

Integrated Marketing Communications Tools

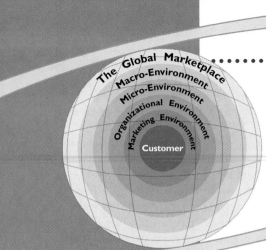

⋯⋯⋯⋯⋯⋯⋯⋯⋯⋯⋯⋯⋯⋯⋯⋯⋯⋯⋯⋯⋯⋯⋯⋯⋯

Managing Salesforce Activity

⋯⋯⋯⋯⋯⋯⋯⋯⋯⋯⋯⋯⋯⋯⋯⋯⋯⋯⋯⋯⋯⋯⋯⋯⋯

Managing the Advertising Program

⋯⋯⋯⋯⋯⋯⋯⋯⋯⋯⋯⋯⋯⋯⋯⋯⋯⋯⋯⋯⋯⋯⋯⋯⋯

Publicity, Direct Marketing, and Sales Promotion

⋯⋯⋯⋯⋯⋯⋯⋯⋯⋯⋯⋯⋯⋯⋯⋯⋯⋯⋯⋯⋯⋯⋯⋯⋯

Justice Department Applies Brakes to Hell-for-Leather Pace of Consolidation in Radio Industry

The successful sales rep of this decade will be a facilitator, not a pitchman, an expert on the customer's total business who coordinates with colleagues to make buying easy and efficient.[1]

As a result of the Telecommunications Act of 1996, which eased restrictions on station ownership, consolidation in the radio industry has been rampant. Over 4000 of the nation's 11,000 radio stations changed hands in the 2 years following passage of the act. Joel Klein, assistant attorney general, intervened in April of 1998 when he objected to a deal that would have added 4 local stations to Chancellor Media's collection of 108. Klein said: "As the radio industry continues to consolidate . . . we will continue to seek relief where radio mergers harm the competition that helped make radio an effective and affordable way to advertise."

Chancellor's funding—and perhaps its inspiration for moving quickly with a consolidation strategy—is purported to have come from Tom Hicks, chairman of Hicks, Muse, Furst & Tate, a Texas leveraged-buyout specialist firm formed in 1989. Since 1995, radio consolidation has turned this former cottage industry into a potential force in the mainstream media business. Infinity Radio, built up by Mel Karmazin but sold to Columbia Broadcast System (CBS) in 1995, was one of the originators of the consolidation trend. But Hicks, Muse, Furst & Tate was not far behind. Today, combined annual revenues of its radio interests are $1.5 billion, virtually equal to those of the radio division of CBS.

When the Justice Department applied the brakes to radio consolidation, Hicks, Muse, Furst & Tate might have viewed this as a tremendous setback. Instead, under Hicks's guidance, Chancellor changed tack and started to add other media assets that could offer inexpensive advertising opportunities: billboards and local television stations. Transformation from a pure radio group into a mixed-media group began in June 1998 when Chancellor paid $610 million in cash to buy 13,000 billboards from Martin Media. Then, in July 1998, Chancellor finalized purchase of Lin Television's dozen local television stations in a reported $1.5 billion agreement. With the Lin Television agreement, Hicks, Muse, Furst & Tate will double its stake in Chancellor to 18 percent. The firm also controls Capstar Broadcasting, another radio group that specializes in stations serving small to midsized markets. And both firms seemed to be following the same radio consolidation strategy to exploit cost efficiencies so as to offer competitive rates to advertisers seeking alternatives to costly television ads.

This building of an integrated media corporation is possible because the Telecommunications Act allows a company to own up to eight stations in a single market and to control up to 35 percent of a market's advertising dollars. However, the Justice Department is proclaiming that ownership boundaries may not be overstepped.

Chancellor has moved into Mexico as well, with a July 1998 purchase of Grupo Radio Centro SA, which is the largest radio broadcaster in Mexico, having 1997 revenues of $82 million amid big advertising by Mexico's newly minted private pension funds.

Sources: Christopher Parkes, "Change of Tack Takes Radio into the U.S. Media Mainstream," *Financial Times* (July 10, 1998), p. 24; and Alejandro Bodip-Memba and Jonathan Friedland, "Chancellor Is Set to Purchase 50% of Radio Centro," *Wall Street Journal* (July 13, 1998), p. B5C.

If the strategy of Hicks, Muse, Furst & Tate in creating an integrated media organization is successful, network radio may indeed become a force in mainstream advertising once again. And if this happens, it will continue a trend of de-emphasizing the importance of the three major television networks to firms seeking to reach mass audiences via their integrated marketing communications activities.

It is becoming increasingly clear that an integrated marketing communications (IMC) approach is critical to developing an effective marketing plan. Although components of the various IMC tasks may be assigned to different parts of a firm, they must be integrated by a single, overall promotion strategy with a common communications purpose. Chapter 11 identified the entire scope of IMC activities, including salesforce activity, advertising, public relations/publicity, direct marketing, and sales promotion. This chapter examines each of these communications tools in greater depth.

MANAGING SALESFORCE ACTIVITY

Management decisions related to salesforce activities are people-related and complicated.[2] Our discussion of the sales process focuses on building customer relationships. A model of this sales process is shown in Figure 12.1. According to this

FIGURE 12.1

The Sales Process

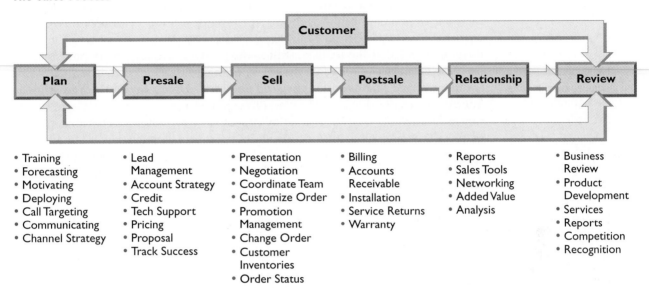

		Presentation	Billing	Reports	Business

* Training
* Forecasting
* Motivating
* Deploying
* Call Targeting
* Communicating
* Channel Strategy

* Lead Management
* Account Strategy
* Credit
* Tech Support
* Pricing
* Proposal
* Track Success

* Presentation
* Negotiation
* Coordinate Team
* Customize Order
* Promotion Management
* Change Order
* Customer Inventories
* Order Status

* Billing
* Accounts Receivable
* Installation
* Service Returns
* Warranty

* Reports
* Sales Tools
* Networking
* Added Value
* Analysis

* Business Review
* Product Development
* Services
* Reports
* Competition
* Recognition

Source: Adapted from Glen S. Peterson, *Higher Impact Sales Force Automation: A Strategic Perspective* (Boca Raton, FL: St. Lucie Press, 1997), pp. 54–65.

model, an organization must determine that its strategic goal is to be customer-focused and ensure that all sales activities are oriented toward this end.

Managing the salesforce involves defining the sales task, investigating the relationship between sales activity and productivity, and determining salesforce structure. It also involves configuring sales territories, determining salesforce size, and addressing human resources issues such as staffing, compensation, direction, and motivation.

Defining the Sales Task

What do salespersons do? Typical salespeople answer by saying, "Too much." One way to determine the sales task for a firm is to consider all the different types of selling and decide which style is best for the firm and its product(s).[3]

Relationship selling
Developing a relationship with the customer to learn about his or her needs, attitudes, and behaviors.

Relationship Selling. Relationship selling involves building customer relationships and cultivating current and future sales opportunities instead of just soliciting immediate business. In relationship selling, the salesperson works closely with prospective customers and the selling company's research and development (R&D) department. In some situations, such as in the capital goods market, it may take several years to complete a sale. The goal is to create a good working relationship with the customer and build the customer's confidence. Through close cooperation, products or services can be developed to meet the customer's particular need. Doing this requires that the salesperson develop a relationship with the customer to learn about his or her needs, attitudes, and behaviors. As Dan Logan notes, this "... is a continuous process based on understanding your target audience . . . ," and building this kind of rapport takes dedication and consistency in approach over time.[4]

Laura Liswood believes that ". . . if customers have [use] one product with you . . . there's a 15 percent likelihood they'll stay loyal to you for 5 years. With two products, that rises to 45 percent; with three, it's up to 80 percent." Over time, the entire buyer-seller relationship tends to shift as the product matures. Sellers can capitalize on these changes to strengthen their relationship with their customers.[5] Cross and Smith introduce a modification they call **database-driven marketing,** which is an interactive, relationship-building kind of marketing centered around a core of customer information. It is "any marketing process in which useful, behavioral, psychographic or demographic information about prospects or customers is stored in the company's database and is used to enhance or prolong the relationship or to stimulate sales."[6] This type of interaction is a form of **relationship marketing** that can be used to foster customer loyalty.

Database-driven marketing
Any marketing process in which useful, behavioral, psychographic, or demographic information about prospects or customers is stored in the company's database and is used to enhance or prolong the relationship or to stimulate sales.

Relationship marketing
An interactive, relationship-building marketing centered around a core of customer information.

Pretransaction Selling versus Posttransaction Servicing.   *Pretransaction selling* is similar in some respects to relationship selling. The objective of pretransaction selling is to evolve a long-standing relationship between the supplier and customer. *Posttransaction servicing* is a different type of selling effort, often assigned to individuals other than those who closed the sale initially. For instance, post-sales servicing of electronic data processing equipment often is assigned to technicians. The objective of post-sales servicing is to keep a customer satisfied.

Cold-Canvas versus Lead Selling.   Almost in direct contrast to relationship selling is cold-canvas selling. Salespersons who call on a "shot in the dark" basis, not knowing whether the prospect needs the product, are *cold-canvas selling*. Cold canvassing, or "prospecting" as it is sometimes called, is rare today in consumer markets. Restrictive local ordinances, the mobility of households, the high proportion of working women, and consumers' unwillingness to buy this way have made it difficult and often ineffective. However, in some industrial and wholesale selling, the cold call is still used, since organizational buyers are sometimes receptive to this approach. Some cold calls are also still used by financial services firms based on pre-qualified lists and by some small businesses who do not seem to acknowledge that this is an inefficient and less effective way to use salespeople.

Lead salespersons only call on prospects known or thought to be interested in buying a company's product or service. Leads can be obtained in many ways. Lists of prospects can be purchased, or respondents to advertising can be contacted. Also, customers suggest names of other prospects. One common prospecting method is the use of an *endless-chain system*. The salesperson attempts to obtain the names of at least two or three new prospects from each person called on. In this way, even if most contacts do not "pan out," there usually is a backlog of prospects to call.

Planned versus Canned Selling.   The day of the unplanned, ad-lib sale is past. All sales presentations are planned to some degree. The extreme in planning is the *canned sales pitch.* Salespeople using this approach follow a script, deviating only to adapt the presentation to special circumstances. Relatively unskilled persons can be effective using canned sales, and the approach works in person or on the telephone.

Experienced salespeople prefer a more flexible approach. However, a sales plan is still used. It may be elaborate or simple, depending on the sales opportunity and the training and inclination of the salesperson. Some salespeople develop very elaborate customer strategies to identify a sales objective and outline how the sales interview will be conducted.

Missionary versus Transaction Selling. *Missionary salespeople* represent manufacturers, calling on customers, resellers, and purchase influencers to stimulate demand and to assist resellers in developing selling programs for the manufacturer's product. Ordinarily, a missionary salesperson does not accept orders. In contrast, the *transaction salesperson* concentrates on booking business. Contrasting these two types of selling situations is sometimes characterized as "order takers versus order getters." Similar in some respects to competitive selling, transaction selling involves making sales in the face of intense competition. These competitive salespeople often are technically trained and are found mostly in industry. Order salespersons are encountered in the marketing of resale items, especially packaged goods distributed through wholesale-retail trade channels.

Creating the Job Description. Sales managers agree that many demands are made on salespeople above and beyond selling, such as completing reports, providing estimates, and sometimes even collecting accounts. Many firms also require salespersons to manage their territory and their customers. These numerous demands often lie at the heart of the problems that arise. The IMC view of salesforce activity stresses the importance of contact with customers but also insists that all activities be planned, directed, and controlled in the same way that all aspects of marketing are managed.

The sales task in a business-to-business environment is noted in Figure 12.2. It is a position description for an account executive and entails many responsibilities apart from selling. Firms differ in the specific nonselling demands they make; however, this position description illustrates the scope and character of many typical requirements.

Investigating the Relationship Between Sales Activity and Productivity

Salesforce automation
The creation of electronic information systems that make sales activities more productive and cost-effective.

Current trends to improve productivity have been driven by the industry trends of re-engineering, downsizing, and rightsizing to achieve lean and effective organizations. One result of these trends is **salesforce automation.** Salesforce automation focuses on productivity and cost reduction in order to deliver value to the customer.[7] Once laptop computers became available in the mid-1980s with two-way communications and the ability to update remote user systems, field salesforce automation became a timely activity because information systems (IS) departments had already automated "back room" processes. Previously, IS had avoided sales and marketing functions because it was viewed as a quagmire of open-ended and constantly shifting needs. Glen S. Petersen notes that one of the earliest success stories was Ciba-Geigy, which reported that a 1 percent increase in salesforce productivity generated a 6.7 percent increase in revenue.[8] Moriarity and Swartz, in a *Harvard Business Review* article, concluded that salesforce automation increased sales by

FIGURE 12.2

....

Position Description for an Account Executive

Account Executive (AE)

I. Job Summary. The Account Executive (AE) is responsible for managing a module of business accounts in the Business Markets Division (BMD). The AE will be on incentive compensation and accountable for protecting the revenue base, generating new revenues by planning and executing moderately complex sales transactions including voice, data, and network systems as well as packaged solutions.

II. Duties and Responsibilities
   A. Responsible for the management of an assigned module (group of accounts) **45%**
      1. Positioning = interface with assigned business customers/key decision makers
      2. Data gathering = compilation of data determining customers' problems
      3. Data analysis = analyzing all data gathered
      4. Designs = conceptual solutions for business problems
      5. Proposals = prepares and presents final communications solutions to customer
      6. Implementation = monitors support team activities, assigns tasks and follows up
      7. Follow-up = ensures implementation is complete as ordered by customer and customer is satisfied with effect of solution on problem

   B. Account planning **25%**
      1. Develops account plans to identify customer needs and proposes solutions
      2. Based on the plan identifies opportunities and assigns priorities and timelines

   C. Development and general administration **30%**
      1. With sales management develops account management and selling skills
      2. Keeps abreast of trends via trade publications and attending seminars
      3. Prepares correspondence and contracts relative to sales activities

III. Major Problems
   A. Develop and maintain state-of-the-art technical knowledge
   B. Establish and position us in accounts not previously penetrated
   C. Demonstrate to customers that we are credible business solutions resource
   D. Sell product line which is more expensive than competition
   E. Acquire necessary support resources from a limited pool

IV. Key Contacts
   A. Support team—technical sales and implementation support
   B. Customer—sell products and services
   C. Industry association—maintain presence and gather intelligence

V. Knowledge and Skill Requirements
   A. Education—bachelor's degree or equivalent experience
   B. Specialist—basic product, customer, and market knowledge
   C. Technical—AE assessment and testing required
   D. Experience—one year in selling environment

VI. Scope
   A. Incumbent reports to sales manager who supervises a group of AEs
   B. Objective to increase module size by 20–22%

Source: Highly adapted from recruiting information sent to Graduate Business School Career Center.

....

10 to 30 percent and resulted in a return on investment in excess of 100 percent.[9] However, what is the strategic initiative for salesforce automation if it can achieve these results? Petersen suggests two: Market success will be determined by (1) delivering superior value to the customer and (2) capturing maximum profit in the delivery of that value.[10]

The question becomes: Where do we begin? Re-engineering and total quality management initiatives advocate a customer focus, but in practice, these techniques are applied more often to processes that are not connected directly to customers. By contrast, the sales process directly relates to customers, and it is necessary to coordinate all the firm's functional activities with sales in order to deliver value to customers. It is this perspective that drives the development of effective automation of field salesforce activities.

Figure 12.3 represents a networked sales automation system where sales reps' laptops are connected with a server via a wide-area network (WAN) or with corporate headquarters via a local-area network (LAN). This automated system can reduce

FIGURE 12.3

Networked Sales Automation System

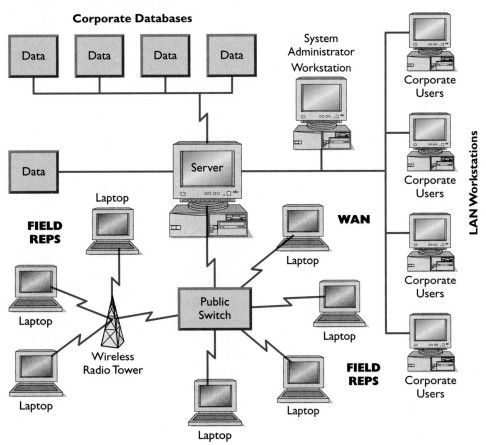

Source: Reprinted by permission from Glen S. Peterson, *High Impact Sales Force Automation: A Strategic Perspective,* St. Lucie Press, Boca Raton, FL, 1997, p. 91. Copyright CRC Press, Boca Raton, Florida.

cycle times because the data are timely, accurate, and readily available; leverage efforts can be organized throughout the company via e-mail (electronic messages); and sales reps can be freed from support functions (such as report writing), thus providing more time, energy, and motivation to interact with customers.

Determining Salesforce Structure

Direct selling
When the firm employs its own salesforce and calls directly on customers.

Indirect selling
When the firm uses the employees of resellers to solicit sales.

The structure of a firm's salesforce corresponds closely with its channel of distribution. There are two selling alternatives: (1) **direct selling,** in which the firm employs its own salesforce and calls directly on customers, and (2) **indirect selling,** in which the firm uses the employees of resellers to solicit sales.

The existence of a sales department indicates a functionally based organization. This is commonly the case when extensive personal contact with customers is required. Even if indirect selling is used, the outside salesforce must be supervised for effectiveness.

The salesforce can be structured several different ways. When a company's product line is extremely broad, the salesforce can be divided according to product lines. This means that separate salesforces are used, even if they call on the same customers. Another way of organizing the salesforce is geographically. A salesperson is viewed as a manager of a territory, responsible for developing business within it. This works well in companies with short or homogeneous product lines and in markets where extreme market segmentation is not encountered. However, if a territory contains several different types of industries, it is often difficult for one individual to be familiar with the special needs of each. This dilemma leads to the assignment of salespeople on a customer-size basis. Large and small customers tend to demand different services. A fourth basis for the assignment of salespeople can be the level or type of customer. For example, different salespeople might call on manufacturing, wholesale, and retail outlets.

It is common to find various combinations of these methods. Any number of combinations is possible. An extremely large company might combine all four types of sales organization: product, territory, size, and customer.

Configuring Sales Territories

Most companies use a geographic basis in assigning the salesforce. Widely dispersed customers and high expenses to reach them make geographic assignments economical. Also, it is easier to provide competitive customer service from a local base. This is done best when the salesperson lives in the territory. Increased morale will occur if territory design results in ease of coverage and relatively equal probability of reaching sales goals.

The question is: Which comes first—design of the salesforce or design of the territories? The two are closely related. A salesforce may be designed to serve specific territories, or territories may be adapted to the size and capabilities of the existing salesforce. Because we already looked at the first approach, we will now focus on the second approach.

Fitting the Sales Territory to the Salesforce.   If a company already has a salesforce, it may develop its territories around these people. A manager determines how many territories the salesforce can handle effectively. Then the total market is divided into this number of geographic areas. Alternatively, the optimal size of territory for a single salesperson is determined. The territories are arranged in order of attractiveness to the firm. Next, people are assigned to territories. The first alternative results in thin coverage of most territories. The second alternative may leave a number of markets uncovered if the existing salesforce is small in number. If the first method assigns too large an area, the result is that fewer than optimal calls will be made on some good customers and less frequent calls will be made on all customers. The second method may cover some markets while it develops others intensively. Volume is sacrificed, and competitors may establish a foothold in the uncovered markets.

Salesforce deployment can affect sales productivity. If improved performance is needed but there is no reason to restructure territories, a redeployment of personnel may do the trick. There also can be some adjustment in coverage at the same time. Changes in the relative importance of various markets do take place. Salespeople do not like to be moved like pawns on a chessboard. Sometimes, however, contentment with an existing situation can cause low productivity. Redeployment may be the solution.[11]

Configuring the Shape of Territories. Designing territories involves two problems. One is the shape of the territory; the other is its size. A territory is only part of an entire market, and the parts must fit together. Within this limitation, however, the territorial parts can be of almost any shape—even a jigsaw configuration is possible. Territories are constructed by combining smaller geographic or political units into larger ones. Rectangles are the easiest to construct, but circular areas are the most economical to serve. The smaller the building blocks, the easier it is to obtain the desired configuration. States are often used, but counties are particularly good because they are the smallest areas for which market data are available.

Figure 12.4 shows how an area might be divided into several geometric territories. In the *rectangular* shape (Figure 12.4a), the market is divided into equal parts by vertical and horizontal lines. The result is artificial and offers no advantages except that the territories are of equal geographic size. The *circular* territory (Figure 12.4b) has this same advantage but also minimizes travel distances if customers are evenly located throughout the territory and the salesperson is located in the center. (Because it is impossible to fill a surface completely by circles, hexagonal territories are shown in the figure.)

Figure 12.4c illustrates two special territorial configurations. The *cloverleaf* design is for a territory with customers clustered in five locations. The salesperson is located at the center and makes trips to the four peripheral markets. The *wedge* design is part of a larger circular territory. The rectangle at the point of the wedge represents a major metropolitan market. Several individuals divide the market, each taking a wedge-shaped territory. This is the most equitable allocation of a market, with the best customers found in the center. No one salesperson gets all the preferred accounts. Each is located at the point of the wedge, concentrating calls in one part of the metropolitan area and making occasional trips to the periphery.

Because customers usually are scattered unevenly, territories with such neat rectangular, circular, cloverleaf, and wedge shapes are rarely possible. Political boundaries and topologic phenomena also make ideal configurations impractical; for

FIGURE 12.4

Shapes of Sales Territories

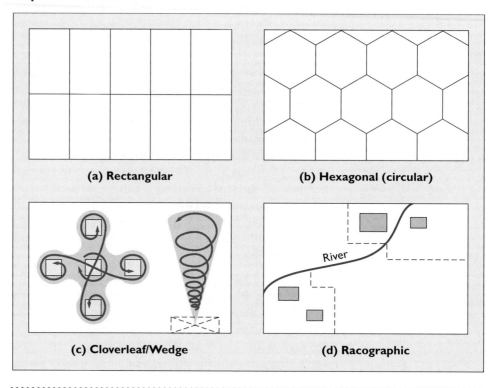

(a) Rectangular

(b) Hexagonal (circular)

(c) Cloverleaf/Wedge

(d) Racographic

example, customers may be concentrated in urban centers that may be historically or accidentally situated. A major river or other travel impediment may cause a deviation from the ideal shape. In practice, designing territories begins with the ideal but ends with compromises to fit each territory to the physical, political, and demographic characteristics of the market. Figure 12.4d illustrates this.

Size of Territories.   The size of a territory depends on several factors. Territories should be about equal—both in revenue potential and in difficulty of servicing. But complete equality is never possible. It is easier to compare performance when territories are approximately equal; in addition, morale is better and bickering over assignments is minimized.

Designing territories that are equal in both potential and workload is problematic because customers are not evenly distributed. There is no solution to the problem. It is solved only by compromise.

Determining Salesforce Size

A firm such as Procter & Gamble Co. has several thousand salespeople. How does the company decide how many salespeople to employ? There are two major approaches to this important question.

Workload Approach. The number of salespeople a firm needs may be calculated by estimating the extent of the selling task and dividing this task by the amount that a single person can handle.[12] For example, a manufacturer of industrial machinery sells to two types of customers: end-users and dealers. In a selected market there are 500 end-users and 100 dealers. Experience indicates that the average salesperson can make approximately 600 sales calls per year. Management wants to determine the number of salespeople necessary to make 12 calls on each of the end-users and 24 calls on each of the dealers during a single year.

To make this determination, management can use a special formula:

$$N = \frac{\sum_{i=1}^{2} F_i C_i}{K}$$

or

$$N = \frac{F_1 C_1 + F_2 C_2}{K}$$

where N = the number of salespeople

F = the call frequency required for a given customer type

C = the number of customers in a type

K = the average number of calls a salesperson can make during a year

Therefore, inserting these figures into the formula, the equation is worked as follows:

$$N = 1/600[12(500)] + [24(100)]$$
$$= 1/600(6000 + 2400)$$
$$= 14$$

Thus, based on the number of customers to be reached and the average of sales calls made per person per year, the firm decided to assign 14 people to this particular sales task.

Marginal Approach. Marginal analysis enables a firm to determine the optimal size of its sales organization. However, practical applications involve making day-to-day decisions about hiring and releasing personnel. Managers know two basic facts about the size of a salesforce: If an additional person is hired, total sales should increase and so will total selling costs. If a salesperson is dismissed, sales will decline and so will expenses. Thus another salesperson should be hired if the extra person will contribute more in gross profit than in cost. In firing or not replacing salespeople, the opposite reasoning applies: If the cost saved exceeds the gross profit sacrificed, the company is better off with a smaller salesforce.

Staffing and Measuring Performance

Managing the salesforce also involves several key human resource issues. This section discusses issues related to staffing and measuring performance.

Recruiting and Evaluating Applicants. Staffing the salesforce starts with understanding the sales tasks to be performed. Good position descriptions are the first step. The second is identifying abilities and characteristics required for the position. These specifications become the criteria for recruiting and evaluating applicants.

The big question is: What abilities and characteristics make a good salesperson? Some combination of intelligence, personality, and experience is desirable—but determining how to measure these elements and what weights to assign to them is less clear.[13] Various testing and rating devices provide management with a useful tool but cannot substitute for the manager's judgment of the fit between applicant and the job to be filled.

Training. Once applicants have been hired, they must be trained. Sales training is a complicated subject and beyond the scope of this discussion. In brief, it involves an orientation to the company and its products and also covers the sales requirements needed for the new position. In many companies, sales training lags behind the need for effective new people.

Measuring Performance. Attempting to distinguish high-performing from low-performing salespeople, Plank and Reid found that what best explained the differences were (in decreasing order of importance) (1) using or processing information, (2) getting information, and (3) giving information.[14] They suggest that today's personal selling position may be conceptualized as the management of personal marketing relationships through effective information management.[15] Instead of focusing on activities, this viewpoint emphasizes a salesperson's mental processes that involve carrying out the position duties effectively. This verifies research by Shapherd and Rentz in 1990 that recognized selling as a complex mental process.[16] However, it is also generally agreed that a customer orientation is the high performer's strongest trait.[17]

Dealing with Turnover. One of the most serious problems in sales management is the high turnover rate of personnel. Salespeople tend to look for opportunities to earn more money, to get a promotion, or to live in a better part of the country. If not actively seeking a new job, they almost always are willing to listen to an attractive offer. Because turnover affects all companies, there are always sales managers trying to find people to fill positions vacated by those who have left or have been discharged. Jones, Kantak, Futrell, and Johnston reviewed the research on salesforce turnover, concluding that many factors enter into the turnover equation.[18] Their research focused on the interaction of leader behavior and work attitudes as a factor in the relationship of job satisfaction and the propensity to leave. In general, leader behavior and job satisfaction appear to be important influences on the decision to leave a company.

Developing a Compensation Plan

Territorial workload is only one factor affecting the payment of salespeople. To attract and hold good people, a compensation plan must meet the requirements of both the employees and the company. Balancing these two requirements is not easy. Salespeople want an adequate income on a regular basis, and they want to be rewarded for their contribution to the firm. For the firm, sales compensation must retain effective people, stimulate them to be productive, and provide control over the sales effort. Several types of compensation programs are available.

Salary Plan. A straight salary is good from the salesperson's point of view because it provides a fixed sum at regular intervals. An expense allowance or reimbursement for expenses is also provided. However, there is no direct and immediate reward for exceptional performance. From the company's viewpoint, straight salary is a fixed cost, so as long as sales are satisfactory, costs are controlled. If sales slip, however, a fixed sales cost can become a problem. In addition, straight salary does not motivate extra effort. However, it does allow the employer to require nonselling activities, which people who are paid commission tend to avoid.

Commission Plan. Under a commission plan, salespeople are paid a fixed or sliding rate based on sales volume or profit contribution. The commission is a reward for doing a job well. It also motivates salespeople to increase productivity. The firm benefits from a performance incentive. And because the commission is calculated on current sales, it pays for itself and is a completely variable cost.

Combination Plan. A combination plan contains both salary and incentive. The salary is high enough to provide the financial security that employees desire. It is also low enough that its fixed-cost aspect does not affect the firm in periods of declining sales. The incentive is paid in the form of a commission—usually on sales greater than a set quota. Thus the salesperson benefits from extra income for better-than-standard performance, and the firm benefits from a partly variable sales expense and some financial incentive to encourage and control marketing effort.

Directing and Motivating the Salesforce

Directing is providing guidance to the salesforce concerning what tasks to perform. Although the compensation plan and territory design should contribute to the desired goal-directed behavior, some form of written and verbal guidance is necessary. However, one of the key aspects of successfully directing the salesforce is motivation.

Motivation can be viewed as the amount of effort a salesperson is willing to expend on each task associated with the job. The process involved in determining motivation and some of the variables that influence the process are shown in Figure 12.5, which is an adaptation of the work of Churchill, Ford, and Walker.[19] The conceptual framework on which Figure 12.5 is based is known as **expectancy theory**, and this theory indicates that the level of effort expended on each task of a salesperson's job will result in a certain level of achievement. It assumes that this performance will be evaluated and rewarded in some way. The salesperson's motivation is determined by three sets of perceptions: (1) **expectancies**—the perceived linkages between expending greater effort on a task and achieving improved performance; (2) **instrumentalities**—the perceived relationship between higher performance and receiving greater rewards; and (3) **valence for rewards**—the perceived desirability of the rewards that might be received.

There are two aspects of expectancy perceptions: magnitude and accuracy. The *magnitude* of a salesperson's expectancy perceptions is the degree to which that person believes expending greater effort will influence job performance—the more a person expects greater effort to produce enhanced results, the higher is his

Motivation
The amount of effort a salesperson is willing to expend on each task associated with the job.

Expectancy theory
The level of effort expended on each task of a salesperson's job that results in a certain level of achievement.

Expectancies
The perceived linkages between expending greater effort on a task and achieving improved performance.

Instrumentalities
The perceived relationship between higher performance and receiving greater rewards.

Valence for rewards
The perceived desirability of the rewards that might be received.

FIGURE 12.5

Factors Influencing a Salesperson's Motivation

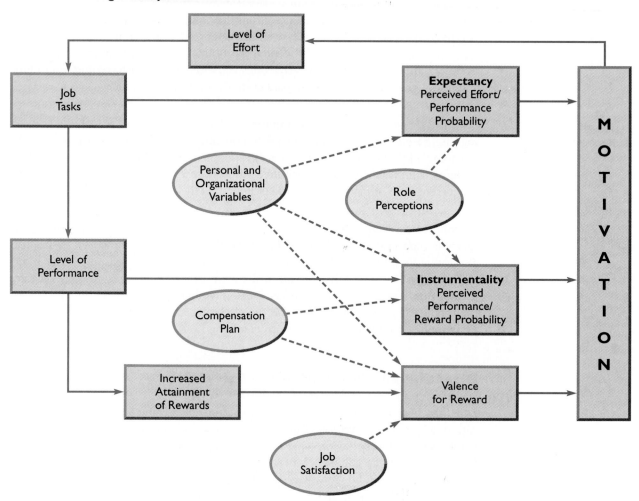

Source: Adapted from Gilbert A. Churchill, Jr., Neil M. Ford, and Orville C. Walker, Jr., *Sales Force Management,* Fourth Edition, Irwin, Homewood, IL, 1993, p. 544. Reprinted with permission of The McGraw-Hill Companies.

or her willingness to devote the efforts necessary. The *accuracy* of expectancy perceptions is how clearly the person understands the relationship between effort expended and results achieved on some performance dimension. If a salesperson's expectancies are inaccurate, he or she spends too much time and energy on activities that have little impact on performance and too little on activities with greater impact. Figure 12.5 indicates that personal and organizational characteristics affect the magnitude and accuracy of expectancy perceptions, as does the individual's perceptions of his or her role in the firm.

Instrumentalities (like expectancies) are a salesperson's perceptions of a probability estimate made about the link between performance and various rewards—an improvement in performance will lead to a specific increased reward such as higher pay or a promotion. If the instrumentality estimate is large, the person believes that there is a high probability that greater performance will increase rewards, and thus he or she will be more willing to expend the effort to achieve better performance. Like expectancies, note that personal and organizational characteristics and the individual's perceptions of his or her role have an impact on instrumentalities. Moreover, the firm's compensation plan influences instrumentality perceptions. The actual link between performance and rewards is determined by the firm's policies and procedures; however, salespersons can have inaccurate perceptions that do affect their actions.

Valence for rewards is a salesperson's perception of the desirability of receiving higher rewards. This leads to the question: Do salespersons consider some rewards of more value than others? The traditional view has been that salespeople value monetary rewards as the highest and most motivating.[20] Several studies support this, but increased pay is not the most desired reward by all salespeople in all companies because this may be influenced by the rewards they are currently receiving. In addition, their satisfaction with current rewards is in turn influenced by their personal characteristics, job satisfaction, and the compensation policy of their firm.

The discussion of factors affecting motivation suggests that salespersons' expectancy estimates and reward valences will likely change as their career progresses. As people age and become experienced, their financial obligations change, their skills and confidence tend to improve, and the rewards they receive—as well as their satisfaction with those rewards—change. All these factors can affect expectancies, reward valences, and in turn motivation.[21]

MANAGING THE ADVERTISING PROGRAM

The second major topic of this chapter is how a firm's integrated marketing communications (IMC) efforts use advertising (mass communications). A key question for marketing managers is how heavily IMC efforts should rely on advertising. Other issues in developing an advertising program involve determining the target customer, the key message, and the medium to be used.

Determining Advertising Opportunities

As mentioned earlier, a critical question for marketing managers is whether a firm should rely heavily on advertising in its IMC efforts. Five key conditions indicate that a favorable opportunity exists.

1. Favorable Trend in Demand.   Effective IMC, especially advertising, is easier when consumer demand is positive. It may be possible to slow the rate of decline of a product or a service when the demand is diminishing, but it is unreasonable to hope that advertising alone can reverse a downward trend.

Advertising can accelerate an increase in demand if the trend is already favorable. For example, most marketers of orange juice for in-home consumption are advertising their reconstituted carton sales rather than frozen concentrated product. This mirrors the trend in actual consumption, since consumers value the convenience of ready-to-drink juice.

MANAGING CHANGE

Ricoh Changes Its Image

Ricoh Corporation, known in the United States for copiers and other office equipment, is trying to change its image. Ricoh has been in semiconductors in the United States since 1981, but this is almost an industry secret. Although Ricoh's semiconductor division generates revenue of between $5 and $6 million per month, its presence has been limited to a sales office in San Jose, California. Mr. Muneo Saimen, vice-president of the semiconductor division, and Mr. Yuko Shige, manager of sales, in a joint interview outlined Ricoh's plans to grow U.S. sales of semiconductors and build more sales offices throughout the United States.

Describing Ricoh's new strategic direction in the United States, Mr. Saimen said: "The first step is to provide standard parts so customers know Ricoh has a semiconductor division." He also cited trade shows as one avenue to gain recognition but said: "For PC EOM customers, we work with IBM and the Taiwan . . . [notebook makers]. We aren't yet working with Dell and Compaq, but we are working on . . . [getting their business]. In Japan . . . Fujitsu and NEC use our (chips) . . . and we provide a global sales network for Asia and Japan and here in the U.S." To that end, Mr. Saimen said, "We plan to open additional sales offices in other parts of the U.S." And Ricoh also plans to more aggressively promote U.S. chip sales through both marketing and advertising channels.

One of the more interesting segments that Ricoh is targeting is the voice-recognition chip market, which is expected to grow dramatically in the future as voice recognition becomes a standard feature on a variety of products such as desktop and in-car PCs and consumer appliances. Mr. Shige provided these details: "We have been working for many years on this technology, but the actual application was not easy to commercialize. We have started the commercial business already, and we found several large applications like cell phones. We also sell to all the cellular companies with our power management ICs already." Industry sources say that Ricoh has a couple of large OEMs interested in its voice-recognition chips, and those companies are currently designing them into systems. Application areas include handheld voice-activated phones, games, and toys.

Ricoh represents an unusual example of a business-to-business manufacturing and marketing firm that will use an integrated marketing communications effort to change its image. The communications efforts by its salesforce, both in sales calls and at trade shows (plus its brochures and other advertising or special promotion activities), will be coordinated and integrated with each other and with other operating functions to align all efforts behind the new strategic direction for semiconductors.

Source: Jim DeTar, "Low-Profile Ricoh Gets Aggressive," *Electronic News* 44(2218) (1998), p.1.

2. Strong Product Differentiation. If a good or service can be clearly differentiated from competitors' offerings, advertising will be effective. Using comparative advertising, a firm contrasts its products' features with a competitor's brand. Probably the most famous comparative advertising approach ever employed was the "Pepsi Challenge." However, this approach is used across all categories of consumer and industrial products.[22] Taco Bell in December 1997 launched a nationwide television campaign with a variation on comparative ads. Taco Bell's traditional competitors are the major fast-food chains of McDonald's, Burger King, Wendy's, and others who have the "hamburger" as the basic item anchoring their menus. In contrast, Taco Bell's menu is based on traditional Mexican food items such as tacos. By using a Chihuahua that eloquently professes his preference for tacos over hamburgers, Taco Bell has differentiated its product and stressed product features all in the same ad.[23]

3. Hidden Attributes. Advertising opportunities are greater when hidden attributes are more important to the consumer than external features that can be identified readily. To take advantage of hidden qualities, such as flavor in foods, purity in drugs, or cleaning power in detergents, consumers often rely on brand identification and advertising claims when making purchase decisions.

4. Emotional Buying Motives. The opportunity to motivate or convince consumers through advertising increases when strong emotional buying motives exist. Emotion is a more powerful tool than argument in advertising.[24] Although at odds with the rational problem solving and logical information processing posed in some consumer buying behavior models, ad people are convinced that emotional appeals are more effective. Constable suggests that an emotional relationship between consumer and product leads to increased use, the opportunity for premium pricing, and a more powerful brand.[25]

5. Adequate Funds. It is the marketing manager's responsibility to determine how elaborate the ad program should be, how much it will cost, and if sufficient funds are available. Unless there are adequate financial resources to support an advertising program of the scope required, an advertising opportunity does not exist.

Whether this and the other four conditions of a good advertising opportunity exist can be determined by a marketing audit and marketing research. In terms of the marketing planning process, a study of the marketing situation should reveal the extent of the required advertising program and whether the firm can afford it.

Identifying the Appropriate Audience(s)

Another key question in developing an IMC program, especially the advertising component, is: With whom should we communicate? All IMC activities are directed at specific target customers. Since most markets are segmented, this means that IMC activities must be directed at the specific market segment(s) the firm is attempting to influence. The need for a feedback loop is evident because the effectiveness of the communication must be evaluated in some fashion.

This does not mean that marketing strategists need only identify a single group of target customers. This is too simplistic for today's highly dynamic, well-informed, and fiercely competitive markets. Many individuals affect the buying process; IMC activities must be planned to reach them all. In addition to customers, purchase influencers must be considered. For example, consumers usually rely heavily on the advice of others in purchasing products such as home interior decorating items or shrubs and flowering trees. Whether these influencers are interior decorators, landscape architects, or relatives and friends, IMC efforts must be designed to reach these individuals. In designing an effective communications mix, it is extremely important to accurately identify those who consume and buy as well as those who influence purchases.

MARKETING IN THE INFORMATION AGE

U.K. Catalog Distributor Changes Customers' Perceptions

Since its founding in 1972, Maplin, Ltd., a catalog distributor, has served the hobbyist market from 48 U.K. retail locations. Each of these locations carried 6000 items such as batteries, tools, computer peripherals, components, and sound and vision and television equipment, while the catalog contained around 22,000 items. Neil Turner, sales and marketing director, said: "Maplin is changing but this is unknown to our customers; some still think they have to buy from the local store. I don't feel we've marketed ourselves properly." To correct this, Maplin is using an IMC program.

Now Maplin is targeting the small-fry trade customer that big distributors ignore. In Neil Turner's words, "…the ones that feel unloved— the 100,000 or so start-ups and applications companies that we have on database." Turner said, "We went to the manufacturers [we carry] and they understood and agreed with us that some customers don't get quality telemarketing support and field sales support." So Maplin added a team of sales and telemarketing personnel.

Since the telesales began in October 1997, sales volumes have gone up fourfold, says David O'Reilly, marketing manager. Customers can use a key-call facility, using a touch-tone pad to order, thus bypassing the need to speak to a person.

Maplin also has targeted the education sector, where electronics is playing an increasingly important role. The company developed a product range that includes videos, books, light-emitting diodes (LEDs), and basic circuit boards, aimed at teachers of electronics, and allied itself with other school catalog suppliers. Every trade customer is issued a CD-ROM that contains information on every product Maplin carries. "Our customers have been crying for it," said Turner. "It contains videos on how to solder, for example, data sheets, picture enlargements and an order form which can be printed off."

Maplin's Internet site has been receiving around 76,000 hits per day, although as yet there is no digital catalog. However, there are plans to develop one. Browsers can find out about product offers and get information on stores, recruitment, and promotions. The final component of Maplin's IMC efforts is a bimonthly booklet, "Communications Direct," that contains information on computer peripherals, network solutions, monitors, and power supplies. It is sent out to IT (information technology) managers and existing customers throughout the United Kingdom.

Source: Staff writer, "Catalogue of Change," *Electronics Times* (May 18, 1998), p. SVIII.

Klein, Inc., Apple Computer, Inc., and Disney World paid $100,000 per month (or more) for attention-getting displays in New York's Times Square or along Sunset Strip in Los Angeles. Even Internet trendsetters such as HotBot and Excite! rely on billboards to be visible in the real world.[33]

Three variations of outdoor media are common. The *30-sheet poster* is the standard billboard form, although a smaller 8-sheet poster is now being made in some urban locations. The message is printed on sheets of paper that are pasted on large wooden or metal frames. *Painted posters*, some of which are rotated every 5 or 6 weeks within a market by relocation of the entire display, are the second billboard type of outdoor medium. The third is the *electronic spectacular,* as is seen in Times Square or Las Vegas. Stunning novel effects are obtained by the use of motion, sound,[34] smoke, and other dramatic devices.[35]

Transportation Media.   Transportation as a medium uses displayed messages inside and outside public transportation vehicles or on the walls of subway stations, airport terminals, and the like. Interior transportation advertising frequently takes the form of placards or *car cards.* Wrigley's chewing gum, for example, has been extensively advertised this way. Exterior or traveling displays appear on the sides of buses, on the backs of taxicabs, and on panels attached to delivery vehicles.

Point of Purchase (POP).   It is extremely difficult to distinguish the use of point-of-purchase (POP) communications from sales promotion. Most firms closely coordinate POP communications with other IMC media use, so the displays involved are considered part of the IMC advertising program. POP materials include advertising attached to the package, window banners, simple or elaborate stages for displaying merchandise, "shelf-talkers," merchandising tags, end-cap displays, floor signs, package stuffers, information booklets, and many others. POP communications reduce the time gap between exposure to a message and opportunity to purchase and therefore stimulates purchases, especially of impulse items.

Miscellaneous Media.   This classification is a catchall for all the other communications media. These include motion-picture advertising, Yellow Pages listings, skywriting, and so on.[36] The category covers most of the other familiar media, but new methods of communicating are constantly being conceived and used experimentally. One recently perfected example of such experimentation is "virtual billboards," which are becoming a reality at sports events and which bring in new sources of revenue for broadcasters and more exposure for advertisers. Unlike stadium billboards of television "burn-ins," which show scores and statistics to viewers, virtual ads appear to be at the stadium but can only be seen by viewers at home. The ads get bigger or smaller as cameras zoom in or out but are blocked—just like real billboards—when the action moves in front of them. For years, movies have used these special effects. Now, employing the same technology that allows missiles to lock onto targets using laser imaging, these effects are being achieved on live television.[37]

Table 12.1 shows the distribution of advertising expenditures by media in selected years. Methods of reporting data have changed over the years. For example, at one time only media costs were included. Currently, the total outlay, including agency commissions, art, and production, is included in the dollar amounts reported by *Advertising Age.* On this basis, the total advertising expenditures by media for 1995 were estimated at $162.9 billion (latest year available, 1997, at $187.5 billion). This compares roughly with about $95 billion in 1985. Over the period of time covered by Table 12.1, radio (principally network), newspapers, magazines, and outdoor advertising all declined in relative importance as television rose from insignificance in 1950 to become the most important medium. However, expenditures on all forms of printed media exceed expenditures on broadcast media.

Dealer Promotion Aspects of IMC Media.   It is important to remember in selecting IMC media that dealer promotion often is required. Dealer promotion falls into two categories. First, promotional efforts may be aimed directly at resellers as a part of the general program to stimulate sales and build a distribution system. This is called *promotion to the trade.* Promoting to the trade is designed to inform resellers about the manufacturer and the product line and normally includes strong

TABLE 12.1

Percentage Distribution of Advertising Expenditures by Media

Medium	1960	1975	1985	1995	1997
Newspapers	31.0	29.8	26.5	36.3	41.7
Magazines					
Consumer	7.6	5.2	10.8	18.8	21.2
Business	5.1	3.3	2.5	3.6	4.1
Farm	.3	.3	.2	.3	.3
Television	13.3	18.8	21.9	37.8	44.5
Radio	5.8	7.1	6.9	11.3	13.5
Direct mail	15.3	14.6	16.4	32.8	36.9
Outdoor	1.7	1.2	1.0	1.1	1.5
Miscellaneous	19.8	19.7	19.2	20.9	20.9

Source: 1960 and 1975 data from Robert J. Coen, "Ad $ Outlook Brightens," *Advertising Age* (September 14, 1981), p. 3; 1985 data from Robert J. Coen, "Ad Spending Falls to Equal Predictions," *Advertising Age* (May 12, 1986), p. 76; 1995 and 1997 figures from McCann Erickson Resource Center, available at *http://www.mccann. com.*

motivational appeals while emphasizing such features as profit margin, merchandise turnover, and selling assistance provided by the manufacturer.

The second category of promotion involving resellers is *advertising through the trade.* When the manufacturer advertises through the trade, the reseller becomes a type of promotion medium. A good example is dealers who *re-advertise* the manufacturer's product under the terms of a cooperative advertising agreement whereby the manufacturer prepares sample advertisements, radio commercials, videotapes, films, etc. for use by resellers. This type of IMC activity extends the manufacturer's communications to ultimate users and develops dealer interest and goodwill.

Evaluating Media Effectiveness: Cost per Thousand, Reach, and Frequency.
Can various media be quantitatively evaluated? Yes! One criterion is cost per reader, or as commonly used, the measure is **cost per thousand (CPM).** We compute CPM as follows:

Cost per thousand (CPM)
The cost of reaching 1000 of a medium's consumers.

$$CPM = \frac{page\ rate \times 1000}{circulation}$$

The cost per thousand for a four-color page in *Sports Illustrated* in 1998 was $58.57. We calculate this by multiplying $188,839 (four-color page cost) by 1000 and dividing that figure by 3,223,810 (circulation). Table 12.2 contains CPM calculations.

Marketing planners may select IMC media with the lowest cost per reader. But CPM calculated costs are seldom the most effective basis for choosing media. Suppose the communication is directed at a special audience—say, for a tennis racquet. The relatively high CPM for *Sports Illustrated* when compared with *Time* or *Newsweek* may not discourage the media planner because of the magazine's superior audience environment.

Probably the most damaging criticism of the CPM criterion is that it is an average and not a marginal value. Assume that the media planner using the CPM data in

TABLE 12.2

....

Advertising Cost per Thousand Selected Magazines

Magazine	Cost	Circulation	CPM
Time	$191,721	4,155,806	$46.13
Newsweek	154,317	3,177,407	48.56
Sports Illustrated	188,839	3,223,810	58.57
Esquire	47,037	674,171	69.77
U.S. News & World Report	112,604	2,224,003	50.63

Source: Compiled from *Ad Age,* June 15, 1998, pp. S1–S28; *Ad Age,* June 29, 1998, p. 22; and *Ad Age,* Special Issue, *The Advertising Century: Money Matters,* "Spending Spree," by Robert J. Cohen, March/April 1999, pp. 126–136.

Table 12.2 selects *Time,* and three ads are planned, not just one. Also assume that only one-fourth of the readers actually are exposed to a given ad. This is called the **reach** of the medium. Now we can estimate the CPM for *new* readers for each ad:

	Cost	Reach	CPM
First insertion	$191,721	1,038,951	$184.53
Second insertion	191,721	779,214	246.04
Third insertion	191,721	584,410	328.06

Reach
The number of customers (readers/listeners/viewers) actually exposed to a given ad.

Making the same assumption about *U.S. News & World Report,* we can calculate the CPM for the new readers as follows:

	Cost	Reach	CPM
First insertion	$112,604	556,000	$202.53
Second insertion	112,604	417,000	270.03
Third insertion	112,604	312,750	360.04

Using these calculations, the media planner would place two insertions in *Time* and one in *U.S. News & World Report* in this order: *Time, U.S. News & World Report, Time*—always selecting the magazine with the lowest incremental CPM. The improvement over three insertions in *Time* is significant:

	Total Cost	Total Reach	CPM
Three insertions in *Time*	$575,163	2,402,575	$239.39
Two insertions in *Time* and one in *U.S. News & World Report*	496,046	2,559,625	208.93

The selection of media on the basis of incremental cost is preferable to their selection on the basis of average cost.

There is another dimension of media selection called **frequency**—the number of times an average reader sees an ad in a given time period. The preceding example

Frequency
The number of times an average customer sees an ad in a given time period.

assumed the sponsor was interested only in new readers. Sponsors usually want both reach and frequency because many believe that repetition is key to customers learning about brand names or product features or special offers. Using again the assumption that one-fourth of a magazine's circulation sees an ad, running an ad twice in *Time* would produce a reach of 1,818,165. Actually, 1,038,951 people would see the ad each time, but on the second insertion, 259,738 (0.25 × 1,038,951) would see it for the second time. With subsequent insertions, the amount of duplication would increase, and frequency would occur. After six insertions, a few readers (about 1100) will have seen the ad six times, others five times, and so on. The average would be 1.8, which is the frequency of the six-times schedule.

Media Models.   Using computers, marketing and operations research specialists combined information regarding markets and media (as well as subjective judgments) to create a variety of marketing and *media models*. (Readers interested in detailed explanations of 18 various marketing models should read Lilien and Rangaswamy, *Marketing Engineering: Computer-Assisted Marketing Analysis and Planning.*)[38] Media models are decision models used to design the media mix. Young and Rubicam, Inc., is credited with the development of the first media model.[39] Within a few years, significant improvements were made in media models. The best known is MEDIAC, developed by Little and Lodish.[40] It searches among alternative advertising schedules to maximize objectives. It does not produce a schedule; it only evaluates alternatives.

Other models have been developed by academics, ad agencies, and media-buying organizations. All make use of the extensive media information available, including cost data from Standard Rate and Data, Inc., and audience information from Arbitron, Simmons Market Research Bureau, and A. C. Nielsen.[41] Some models attempt to determine the value of a schedule; others attempt to maximize reach and frequency. A model such as ADCAD entails very sophisticated measurements of advertising's effect on consumers' attitudes and is a rule-based expert system that allows managers to translate their qualitative perceptions of marketplace behavior into a basis for deciding on advertising design.[42]

However, despite the technological advances in media models, many organizations' media mixes still are created manually, using available market information and applying an understanding of communications objectives.

PUBLICITY, DIRECT MARKETING, AND SALES PROMOTION

In addition to the use of salesforce activities or advertising, three additional components may be used as integral aspects of IMC and the communications mix. Publicity, direct marketing, and sales promotion all must be considered to ascertain their contribution to achieving the objectives established for IMC.

Publicity and Public Relations

Publicity
Any form of nonpaid commercially significant news or editorial comment about ideas, products, or institutions.

The American Marketing Association's official definition of **publicity** is "any form of nonpaid commercially significant news or editorial comment about ideas, products, or institutions."[43] The usual media for publicity are newspapers, magazines, television, and radio. And although not paid for by the firm, it usually supplies most of the information via news releases or other documentation. Because the public generally perceives the media as impartial, information from publicity is viewed more favorably than that from paid advertising, which is viewed as self-serving. Some people may even see publicity as an endorsement of the firm or product or service being discussed. Thus many firms go to considerable time, effort, and expense to ensure that they receive "publicity," that is, mention in the media. However, publicity cannot really be controlled, so what is said and how it is said may result in negative publicity, which can be seriously detrimental to a firm.

Publicity can be a powerful force in a marketing program. Consider, for example, how effective Disney World is in the widespread coverage of its theme park activities in editorial columns and in advertisements of other companies. A spokesperson for the organization once reported that for the opening of the Euro Disney Park it received in publicity the equivalent of over $50 million in media coverage. The reader also will recall that Microsoft Corp. launched Windows 98 with fanfare and intense media coverage, which CEO Bill Gates acknowledged as immensely valuable.

Public relations (PR)
Related to publicity; marketing communications that promote and manage an organization's products and/or image.

Public relations (PR) also can be an effective aspect of communications if creative concepts and tactics are not overemphasized at the expense of being aligned with communications strategy. To achieve this alignment and thus a solutions-orientation for PR, Terry Bader, general manager of Shandwick, a PR agency, suggests that a four-step approach is required. First, PR account representatives need to immerse themselves in the client's industry to understand the competition and the client's marketing goals. Second, after understanding the industry, PR representatives must understand customers' and clients' goals in order to identify issues and opportunities in the situation. Third, PR representatives must develop creative positioning that supports the client's IMC strategy and marketing goals. Fourth, PR representatives must develop tactics compatible with steps 1, 2, and 3.[44]

Direct Marketing

Direct marketing
Interactive system of marketing that uses one or more communications methods to affect a measurable response and/or transaction at any location.

We view **direct marketing** to include all activities that allow a firm to communicate directly with potential customers, who in turn purchase directly from the firm without any intermediaries such as wholesalers or retailers.[45] Catalogs and telephone marketing were the two primary means of direct marketing until 1994, when marketing via the World Wide Web began. Currently, direct marketing is growing in importance and is discussed in depth in Chapter 13.

Sales Promotion

Sales promotion
The use of a variety of short-term communication and incentive methods to stimulate faster and/or greater market response.

Sales promotion is the term used to describe all types of demand stimulation except advertising, publicity, direct marketing, and personal selling. Once a firm's overall communications objectives are established, then specific communications tasks that sales promotion can accomplish within the overall communications mix may be listed. Next, the cost-effectiveness of feasible sales promotion methods are calculated (as explained previously), and a choice is made of those that offer the best results compared with costs.

Sales promotion activities seldom occur alone; they are usually used in conjunction with advertising because the use of both seems to increase their impact. A common ratio of 70:30 is used for consumer goods (70 percent of IMC budget for advertising and 30 percent for sales promotion). Of course, several factors must be considered when using a ratio such as 70:30, including customer behavior and expectations, degree and nature of competition, and stage in the product's life cycle.[46] However, the impact of sales promotion activities is short term, and this factor always must be considered by marketing managers who rely on sales promotion activities to reach their IMC objectives and their marketing strategy objectives.

Available Push Promotions.   The following list contains various push techniques (trade promotions) that are available to IMC planners:

Consumer coupons	Samples of new products
Couponing in retailers' ads	New product introductory events
Premium offers	Prepriced shippers
Money-back offers	Contests
Cents-off promotions	Demonstrations
Tie-in promotions	Fashion shows
Trading stamps	Trade shows
Sweepstakes	

Additional sales promotion activities and devices include the following:

Motion pictures
Videotapes
Catalogs
Celebrity appearances
Display and dispensing equipment
Visual aids for salespeople
Special deals (2 for 1 or temporary price reductions)
Specialty advertising (calendars, pens, T-shirts, etc.)

Evaluating Push Techniques.   In order to illustrate how IMC planners should evaluate customer (consumer and business-to-business) reactions and thus the effectiveness of push techniques, assume that a local dairy offers retailers an extra 25 cents "special deal" above their regular margin of 25 cents per gallon carton. This special deal is intended to stimulate sales of milk. The dairy's sales and distribution costs are 20 cents per gallon carton, and production costs are $1.54. The normal retail selling price to customers is $2.99. In normal (non–trade promotion) months, the dairy generates $1 million in total contribution as calculated below:

$$
\begin{aligned}
\text{Total contribution (current)} &= \text{current volume} \times (\text{retail price} - \text{retail margin} - \\
&\quad\ \text{sales distribution costs} - \text{unit production cost}) \\
&= 1{,}000{,}000 \times (2.99 - 0.25 - 0.20 - 1.54) \\
&= 1{,}000{,}000 \times 1.00 \\
&= 1{,}000{,}000
\end{aligned}
$$

The dairy should be concerned with how much sales would have to increase for a push (trade promotion) to break even or to produce an increase in contribution. The dairy's net of discounts margin drops from $1.00 to 75 cents per gallon. And, as calculated below, sales would have to increase by 33 percent to 1.333 million gallons in order for this special deal to break even.

$$1,000,000 = \text{special deal volume} \times (2.99 - 0.25 - 0.20 - 1.54 - 0.25 \text{ added discount})$$
$$1,000,000 = \text{SD volume} \times 0.75$$
$$\text{SD volume} = 1,000,000 \div 0.75$$
$$\text{SD volume} = 1,333,000$$

Unless the dairy is quite certain that sales volumes will increase by 33 percent or more, to meet or exceed the 1.333 million gallon level, it should not use this special deal push communication.

Summary

This chapter discussed using IMC tools for effective marketing. The first major topic was managing salesforce activity, which is focused on building customer relationships, is people-related, and thus is complicated. It involves defining the sales task, investigating the relationship between sales activity and productivity, and determining salesforce structure. Salesforce managers are also required to configure sales territories, determine salesforce size, and address human resources issues such as staffing, compensation, direction, and motivation.

The second major topic was managing the advertising program. Five conditions determine advertising opportunities: a favorable trend in demand, strong product differentiation, hidden attributes, emotional buying motives, and adequate funds. Once advertising opportunities are identified, IMC managers must identify the appropriate audience to target, develop effective ad content (message), and determine an efficient and effective media mix. Our media mix discussions included dealer promotion aspects; evaluating effectiveness via cost per thousand, reach, and frequency; and media models.

The concluding major topics of the chapter were the three additional components that must be considered for their contribution to achieving the objectives of IMC and the communications mix: publicity, direct marketing, and sales promotion. Publicity is any form of commercially significant news about an organization, idea, or product that is presented in the media but not paid for. Public relations involves communicating information about an organization, product, or idea that is supportive of the firm's mission and marketing goals. Direct marketing includes all activities that allow a firm to communicate directly with potential customers. Finally, sales promotion is any type of activity that stimulates product demand that is not specifically advertising, publicity, public relations, direct marketing, or personal selling.

Questions

1. Assume that you are the IMC manager for BMW and that you have the responsibility for recommending next model year's communications mix. Would you use each of the components (tools) of the communications mix? With what objectives in mind? And in what relative weighting?

2. Suppose that you are the senior vice-president of sales and that your analysis of the size of the salesforce and selling effort deployment indicates that your salesforce is the correct size but that the allocation of selling effort needs adjustment in a number of territories. How would you implement such deployment changes?

3. What is the ideal sales compensation plan, and how does it relate to "motivating" the sales force?

4. Discuss the factors that indicate that advertising should be a major component of your IMC plan.

5. List the various media available to be used by IMC, and detail your reasoning in choosing which is the most effective.

6. Which of the "other components" of IMC (publicity, direct marketing, sales promotion) are essential elements (tools) of IMC?

Exercises

1. Conduct an analysis of shifts in media use among electronic and nonelectronic media over the past decade. Based on this study, determine the effect that the Internet and other emerging technologies have had—and will continue to have—on IMC strategies. Prepare a brief forecast of the direction you believe this industry will take during the first decade of the twenty-first century.

2. Design a personal selling plan for a line of laser printers (or other product of your choice). Include the objectives to be achieved by your plan, the specific IMC tools, and the budgeting method that will be used. Demonstrate specifically how these IMC elements will be integrated with each other—and with the rest of the marketing mix.

3. Design a media mix that would be appropriate for promoting a new restaurant or entertainment venue in your community. Obtain audience profiles and rate cards from the media (or published sources such as the Standard Rate and Data Service), and determine the best combination of media that will achieve your objectives. Determine an appropriate budget, and weigh this against the desired media mix and coverage. Where and how will adjustments be made without sacrificing the media impact if desired expenditures are greater than the budgeted amount?

Endnotes

1. *Fortune Cookies: Management Wit and Wisdom from Fortune Magazine* (New York: Time, Inc., 1993), p. 21.

2. Any number of fine books are available on the subject of sales management, personal selling, and sales promotion. For example, on sales management, see Douglas J. Dalrymple and William I. Cron, *Sales Management: Concepts and Cases,* 4th ed. (New York: John Wiley & Sons, 1992); Thomas R. Wotruba and Edwin K. Simpson, *Sales Management Text and Cases,* 2d ed. (London: PWS-Kent Publishing, 1992); Rolph E. Anderson, Joseph F. Hair, and Alan J. Bush, *Professional Sales Management* (New York: Mc-Graw-Hill, 1988); Richard R. Still, Edward W. Cundiff, and Norman A. P. Govoni, *Sales Management: Decisions, Strategies, and Cases,* 5th ed. (Englewood Cliffs, NJ: Prentice-Hall, 1988); Thomas N. Ingram and Raymond W. LaForge, *Sales Management: Analysis and Decision Making* (New York: Dryden Press, 1989); and Robert R. Hartley, *Sales Management* (Columbus, OH: Merrill Publishing, 1989). On personal selling, see Donald W. Jackson, Jr., William H. Cunningham, and Isabella C. M. Cunningham, *Selling: The Personal Force in Marketing* (New York: John Wiley & Sons, 1988); and Neil M. Ford et al., *Sales Force Performance* (Lexington, MA: Lexington Books, 1984). On salesforce management, see Gilbert A. Churchill, Jr., Neil M. Ford, and Orville C. Walker, Jr., *Sales Force Management,* 4th ed. (Homewood, IL: Irwin, 1993); William J. Stanton, Richard H. Buskirk, and Rosann L. Spiro, *Management of a Sales Force,* 8th ed. (Homewood, IL: Irwin, 1991); and Derek A. Newton, *Sales Force Management: Text and Cases,* 2d ed. (Homewood, IL: Irwin, 1990).

3. Rene Y. Damon, "A Conceptual Scheme and Procedure for Classifying Sales Positions," *Journal of Personal Selling & Sales Management* (Summer 1998), pp. 31–46.

4. Dan Logan, "Integrated Communications Offers Competitive Edge," *Bank Marketing* 26(5) (May 1994), p. 63.

5. Carla B. Furlong, "12 Rules for Customer Retention," *Bank Marketing* 25(1) (January 1993), p. 14.

6. Richard Cross and Janet Smith, "Retailers Move Toward New Customer Relationships," *Direct Marketing Magazine* (December 1994), p. 20.

7. Glen S. Petersen, *High Impact Sales Force Automation: A Strategic Perspective* (Boca Raton, FL: St. Lucie Press, 1997), p. 1.

8. *Ibid.,* pp. 8–9.

9. Roland T. Moriarity and Gordon S. Swartz, "Automation to Boost Sales and Marketing," *Harvard Business Review* (January–February 1989), pp. 100–108.

10. Petersen, *op. cit.,* p. 33.

11. Melissa Campanelli, "Reshuffling the Deck," *Sales and Marketing Management* 146(6) (June 1994), p. 83.

12. For a thorough discussion of the *workload approach,* which is sometimes called the *buildup method,* the reader may reference any current text in salesforce management, such as Churchill, Ford, and Walker, *op. cit.,* pp. 233–237.

13. Shonkar Ganesan, Barton A. Weitz, and George John, "Hiring and Promotion Policies in Sales Force Management: Some Antecedents and Consequences," *Journal of Personal Selling & Sales Management* (Spring 1993), p. 15.

14. Richard E. Plank and David A. Reid, "Difference Between Success, Failure in Selling," *Marketing News* (November 4, 1996), pp. 6–14.

15. *Ibid.*

16. David C. Shapherd and Joseph O. Rentz, "A Method for Investigating the Cognitive Processes and Knowledge Structures of Expert Salespeople," *Journal of Personal Selling & Sales Management* (Fall 1990), pp. 55–70.

17. Ronald E. Michaels and Ralph L. Day, "Measuring Customer Orientation of Salespeople: A Replication with Industrial Buyers," *Journal of Marketing Research* (November 1985), p. 443.

18. Eli Jones, Donna Massey Kantak, Charles M. Futrell, and Mark W. Johnston, "Leader Behavior, Work Attitudes and Turnover of Salespeople: An Integrative Study," *Journal of Personal Selling & Sales Management* (Spring 1996), p. 13.

19. Churchill, Ford, and Walker, *op. cit.,* pp. 540–568.

20. See, for example, Neil M. Ford, Orville C. Walker, Jr., and Gilbert A. Churchill, Jr., "Differences in the Attractiveness of Alternative Rewards Among Industrial Salespeople: Additional Evidence," *Journal of Business Research* (April 1985), pp. 123–138; and Laurence B. Chonko, John F. Tanner, Jr., William A. Weeks, and Melissa R. Schmitt, "Reward Preferences of Salespeople," Research Report No. 91-3, Center for Professional Selling, Baylor University, Waco, Texas, 1991.

21. Refer to material by William L. Cron, Alan J. Dubinsky, and Ronald E. Michaels, "The Influence of Career Stages on Components of Salesperson Motivation," *Journal of Marketing* (January 1988), pp. 78–92; and Churchill, Ford, and Walker, *op. cit.,* p. 547.

22. Stuart Van Auken and Arthur J. Adams, "Attribute Upgrading Through Across-Class, Within-Category Comparison Advertising," *Journal of Advertising Research* (March–April 1998), pp. 6–16.

23. Gregg Cebrzynski, "Taco Bell Ad: Gordita Whips the Whopper," *Nations Restaurant News* (July 20, 1998), p. 3; and Staff writer, The Associated Press, untitled news item, *Marketing News* (August 31, 1998), p. 7.

24. Linda Westphal, "Use Your 'Emotional Mind' When Writing Copy," *Direct Marketing* (July 1998), p. 66.

25. Cathy Constable, "Use Advertising to Help Make Good Times Better," *Marketing News* (February 2, 1998), p. 4.

26. See Jay Klitsch, "Making Your Message Hit Home: Some Basics to Consider When Selecting Media," *Direct Marketing* (June 1998), pp. 32–33; and Robert McKim, "Choosing the Right Media for Your Message," *Target Marketing* (October 1997), pp. 86–91.

27. Brian Steinberg, "Large Radio Concerns Are Expected to Post Robust Second-Quarter Results," *Wall Street Journal* (July 13, 1998), p. B5C.

28. Verne Gay, "TV Stand-Alone 15s Make Inroads at Nets," *Advertising Age* (August 19, 1985), p. 1.

29. Scott Hume, "Doe-Anderson Tries Branding in 10 Seconds," *Adweek* (March 16, 1998), p. 3.

30. Alistair Cristopher, "Blink of an Ad," *Time* (August 3, 1998), p. 51.

31. Brad Edmondson, "In the Driver's Seat," *American Demographics* (March 1998), pp. 46–52.

32. David Pugh, "The Outdoor Industry Comes in from the Cold," *Marketing Week* (March 14, 1997), pp. 16–22.

33. Marc Bunther, "The Great Outdoors," *Fortune* (March 1, 1999), pp. 150–157.

34. Debra Sparks, "Musical Billboards," *Financial World* (February 18, 1997), pp. 48–51.

35. Charles R. Taylor, "A Technology Whose Time Has Come or the Same Old Litter on a Stick? An Analysis of Changeable Message Billboards," *Journal of Public Policy & Marketing* (Spring 1997), pp. 179–186.

36. Paul Nolan, "Beach Blanket Billboards," *Potentials in Marketing* (September 1998), p. 10.

37. Staff writer, The Associated Press, "Virtual Billboards Becoming Reality at Sport Events," *Marketing News* (August 31, 1998), p. 11.

38. For an excellent general explanation of marketing and media computer models, see Gary L. Lilien and Arvind Rangaswamy, *Marketing Engineering: Computer-Assisted Marketing Analysis and Planning* (Reading, MA: Addison-Wesley, 1998).

39. See W. T. Moran, "Practical Media Decisions and the Computer," *Journal of Marketing* (July 1963), p. 26.

40. MEDIAC was presented in John D. C. Little and Leonard M. Lodish, "A Media Planning Calculus," *Operations Research* (January–February 1969), p. 1. For a description of how a commercial bank used this media planning model, see Leonard M. Lodish, *The Advertising Promotion Challenge: Vaguely*

Right or Precisely Wrong (New York: Oxford University Press, 1986).

41. These are the most widely used media audience research services. Arbitron and A. C. Nielsen provide audience and program ratings for broadcast media. Simmons Market Research Bureau provides print media data as well as information on product use. There are other useful secondary research sources for use in media planning, including Standard Rate and Data Service and Leading National Advertisers.

42. Raymond R. Burke, Arvind Rangaswamy, Joshua Eliasberg, and Jerry Wind, "A Knowledge-Based System for Advertising Design," *Marketing Science* 9(3) (Summer 1990), pp. 212–229.

43. *Marketing Definitions* (Chicago: American Marketing Association, 1960).

44. Terry Bader, "PR Responds to New Demand for Solutions," *Marketing News* 32(14) (July 7, 1997), p. 7.

45. Richard P. Bagozzi, José Antonio Rosa, Kirti Sawhney Celly, and Francisco Coronel, *Marketing Management* (Englewood Cliffs, NJ: Prentice-Hall, 1998), p. 406.

46. Del I. Hawkins, Roger J. Best, and Kenneth A. Coney, *Consumer Behavior: Implications for Marketing Strategy*, 4th ed. (Homewood, IL: BPI/Irwin, 1989), pp. 643–654.

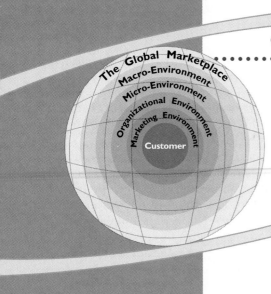

CHAPTER 13

Direct Marketing

Direct Marketing Defined

Factors Leading to the Growth of Direct Marketing

Direct Marketing Tools

Objectives of Direct Marketing

Integrated Direct Marketing Communications

The Direct Marketing Process

Issues in Direct Marketing

Trends in Direct Marketing

"It is as simple as turning on your computer, and right there are all the pockets of your financial life on the screen, from your 401(k) and IRA to your brokerage and bank accounts," says Charles Schwab as he describes his vision of how people will handle their personal finances in a few years. And where does Schwab fit in? "We'll be the consolidator, the integrator. We'll be the utopia."[1]

Cutting Out the Middleman: Direct from Dell to You

The made-to-order marketing model works in Asia as well as in the United States. When Dell Computer Corp. first entered the Asian market, some observers wondered if an impersonal, direct approach would work in a region where business relies heavily on contacts and connections. There was apparently no need to worry. Dell's Asia-Pacific sales reached $863 million in 1997, an 85 percent increase over 1996—despite the regional financial crisis. Asian customers purchase PCs from Dell in much the same way as American buyers. They can make a telephone call to a toll-free operator and detail the specific hardware and software configuration they want. They also may visit Dell's Web site (generating over US$4 million a day in 1998). Within a few minutes, customers will receive a specification through their fax for signature. Operators then send the order to the factory floor, where the models are assembled, tested, and freight-forwarded to the customer within 10 working days. "This way of buying computers may not be quite right for your retired uncle looking for a replacement for his old Remington [typewriter]. But it is ideal for Dell's customers—experienced users, corporate purchasers, and government agencies. And it holds key advantages for Dell." (*Asian Business,* p. 12)

Dell Computer Corp. revolutionized the computer industry by following the principle that customization and direct delivery of computer systems are the best strategy for meeting the needs of business and government customers and final consumers in a rapidly changing global business environment. The business revolves around a direct-selling philosophy that has paid off handsomely for entrepreneurial founder Michael Dell and investors in the company. Fourteen years after Dell was founded in a University of Texas dormitory room, Michael Dell, at 33 years of age, was worth $7 billion; sales had climbed over the previous 3 years from $3.4 billion to $12.3 billion (53 percent compound annual growth); and profits had increased from $140 million to $944 million (89 percent annual growth). This Fortune 500 company is growing twice as fast as any competitor, and it has doubled its worldwide PC market share. Dell Computer Corp. is the world's leading direct marketer of computer systems, is among the largest computer systems manufacturers in the world, and had the top-performing large company stock of the 1990s.

Dell Computer Corp. achieves sustainable competitive advantage through its ability to design and customize products to meet end-user requirements and to provide them with a wide selection of peripheral software. In addition to its strength in direct selling, Dell maintains market leadership as a result of cost containment, channel domination, continuous innovation, and an ability to meet the needs of its customers with short delivery times. Dell holds little or no inventory, and products are assembled as soon as an order is placed. When the product is completed and checked, it is shipped at once. A just-in-time inventory process that is supported by extensive and efficient supplier relationships and elimination of middlemen through a direct distribution channel enable Dell to be a value-added, low-cost, build-to-order marketer of PCs.

To understand Dell's outstanding results, it is important to consider how the company exploits the direct-selling model for custom-made computers. The company's success is due to being able to operate with no finished goods inventory, using the latest high-margin components, using direct channels to customers, and receiving timely direct payment from large business customers or credit-card companies without waiting for payment from resellers.

Source: Chris Lydgate, "Cutting Out the Middleman," *Asian Business* 34(5) (May 1998), pp. 12–13; Andrew E. Serwer, "Michael Dell Rocks," *Fortune* (May 11, 1998), pp. 59–70; Andrew E. Serwer, "Michael Dell Turns the PC World Inside Out," *Fortune* (September 8, 1997), p. 76; Dell Computer Corp. financial reports and company information.

Social and lifestyle changes in consumer markets have escalated the demand for more convenient shopping. Most of today's consumers suffer from a "poverty of time," a result of fast-paced, hectic work lives and lack of time for personal activities. The result is an increase in purchases made from direct-selling, direct-action advertising, and electronic media sources. Likewise, commercial enterprises, government agencies, and nonprofit organizations rely more than ever on direct marketing approaches to buy and sell a vast array of goods and services.

U.S. sales revenues that are attributable to direct marketing activities were estimated at nearly $1.4 trillion in 1998. Direct marketing media expenditures for the same period reached $162.7 billion—representing 57 percent of all advertising expenditures. The number of people employed in direct marketing also increased in 1998 due to this surge in direct marketing activities. More than 24.6 million people were employed in this sector in 1998, with 14.0 million in consumer direct marketing and 10.6 million in business-to-business direct marketing. Growth in direct marketing is expected to continue at a rate greater than that for all U.S. sales and employment. But is direct marketing efficient? You be the judge. Spending 11.9 cents on direct marketing advertising results in $1 of direct marketing sales.[2]

DIRECT MARKETING DEFINED

Direct marketing
Interactive system of marketing that uses one or more communications methods to effect a measurable response and/or transaction at any location.

The Direct Marketing Association defines **direct marketing** as ". . . an interactive system of marketing which uses one or more advertising media to effect a measurable response and/or transaction at any location."[3] This definition includes four key elements:

1. Direct marketing is an interactive two-way communication system between a marketer and a prospective customer.

2. The targeted customer is always given an opportunity to respond.

3. The communication can take place wherever and whenever there is access to communications media.

4. All direct marketing activities can be measured.

The Direct Marketing Association applied a media-based definition of direct marketing for the purposes of its 1998 economic impact study:

> Any direct communication to a customer or business recipient that is designed to generate (1) a response in the form of an order (direct order), (2) a request for further information (lead generation), and/or (3) a visit to a store or other place of business for the purchase of a specific product(s) or service(s) (traffic generation).[4]

See Table 13.1 for sales growth related to each objective.

Direct marketing activities include characteristics of both marketing communication and distribution strategies. The resulting process is an integrated marketing program that focuses the resources of an organization on the needs of an individual buyer.

Integrated Marketing Communications Perspective

Direct marketing represents an increasingly important aspect of the integrated marketing communications mix (see Chapters 11 and 12), as well as the overall marketing mix. However, there are some distinct differences between direct marketing and general advertising. Direct marketing involves selling to individuals one at a time versus selling to broad groups of customers simultaneously, providing all information needed to make a purchase, personalizing communications, providing an immediate response mechanism (i.e., toll-free telephone number, Internet address, or mail response format), and marketing programs that are driven by comprehensive databases.[5] Descriptions of direct marketing strategies include building customer relationships and obtaining direct responses through a variety of marketing communications methods and media.

The typical integrated direct marketing campaign employs multiple direct marketing tools in a sequence of promotional activities. A customer's first exposure to the launching of a new car model may be through newspaper publicity about a local auto show or road test reports in *Motor Trends* magazine. Next, the customer may be exposed to paid advertising in print and broadcast media and is offered an easy response mechanism to obtain additional information (e.g., a toll-free telephone number or World Wide Web address). After this response, the customer may receive direct mail brochures, a video, and/or a telephone call to follow up on the

TABLE 13.1

....

Consumer and Business-to-Business Direct Marketing Sales: By Marketing Objective and as Percent of Total U.S. Sales

	Sales (Billions of Dollars)*			Compound Annual Growth, %	
	1994	1998	2003	1993–1998	1998–2003
Consumer					
Direct marketing sales:	$ 519.60	$ 759.20	$ 1,098.30	7.9	7.7
Direct order	174.00	247.10	349.90	7.3	7.2
Lead generation	247.40	368.70	541.60	8.3	8.0
Traffic generation	99.20	143.40	206.30	7.6	7.5
Total U.S. consumer sales	$4,710.80	$6,118.30	$ 7,808.60	5.4	5.0
DM consumer sales as percent of total U.S. sales	11.0	12.4	14.1	—	—
Business-to-Business					
Direct marketing sales:	$ 380.00	$ 612.20	$ 974.90	10.0	9.8
Direct order	113.70	174.70	269.00	9.0	9.0
Lead generation	237.10	393.10	639.00	10.6	10.2
Traffic generation	28.20	44.40	67.40	9.5	8.7
Total U.S. business-to-business sales	$9,072.70	$12,179.50	$16,057.00	6.1	5.7
DM business-to-business sales as percent of total U.S. sales	4.2	5.0	6.1	—	—

*Sales in current (nominal) dollars, not adjusted for inflation.
Source: Reprinted from *Economic Impact: U.S. Direct Marketing Today 1998* with permission from The Direct Marketing Association, Inc.

inquiry. The next step may be a personal sales encounter, followed by further communication that is designed to elicit a response. Major economic growth categories related to direct marketing are presented in Table 13.2.

Distribution Channel Perspective

....

Traditional distribution strategies have focused on maximizing efficiency in the selection of channels and intermediaries. Now the focus has shifted to maximizing effectiveness and efficiency through channel designs, such as direct marketing, that excel in meeting the distribution needs of consumers and organizations. This is the shortest channel of distribution from the producer to the consumer or organizational buyer, as described in Chapter 10 (i.e., zero-level channel, nonstore retailing). Direct marketers do not require a retail storefront or traditional sales location. Inventory management remains the responsibility of the seller until the buyer takes possession of the product or experiences the service. In a direct distribution system, the sales process may be initiated by either the seller or the customer, and the good or service is delivered directly to the customer.

As the opening scenario indicated, more and more customers are showing a preference for the direct sales model for computer and network products as they seek more speed and customization for their purchases. The traditional channel for

TABLE 13.2
....
Comparison of Major Economic Growth Categories, Highlighting Growth Surge in Direct Marketing

Economic Growth Category	Compound Annual Growth, %	
	1993–1998	*1998–2003*
Direct marketing ad expenditures	7.9	6.4
Total U.S. ad expenditures	7.2	5.7
Direct marketing sales revenue	8.8	8.6
Total U.S. sales revenue	5.4	6.0
Direct marketing employment	5.4	4.8
Total U.S. employment	2.4	1.2

Note: From 1998 to 2003, direct marketing is forecast to become an increasingly efficient advertising medium with steady sales growth and slower growth in ad spending and employment; direct marketing outpaces U.S. economic growth.
Souce: Reprinted from *Economic Impact: U.S. Direct Marketing Today 1998* with permission from The Direct Marketing Association, Inc.

selling expensive, high-tech products has been from manufacturer to distributor to reseller to end-user. Increased direct selling of computers and peripherals by means such as telephone, mail order, and on-line sales ("e-commerce") has eliminated many distributors from the sales process. In late 1998, Compaq Computer Corp. and Hewlett-Packard Co. announced that they would do limited direct selling. Large distributors, such as Ingram Micro, Inc., are feeling the pressure brought on by direct-selling computer manufacturers such as Gateway and Dell but are finding new ways to add value to the direct-selling process.[6]

Consumer markets are heterogeneous and complex and choose different distribution channels for their shopping activities. However, an increasing number of buyers are finding the Internet to be the most efficient and satisfying place to shop. The Internet has brought attention to its value as a distribution channel because of characteristics that are either unique or shared with other marketing channels. These characteristics include the ability to inexpensively store large amounts of information at different virtual locations; the availability of powerful and inexpensive ways to search, organize, and disseminate information; interactivity; the ability to provide rich perceptual experiences; the relatively low entry costs for sellers; and the ability to provide physical distribution for certain products such as computer software.[7]

FACTORS LEADING TO THE GROWTH OF DIRECT MARKETING
....

Direct marketing has experienced phenomenal growth as a result of customers' time constraints, an increase in niche marketing, availability of specialized media, computerized databases, advances in technology and electronic media, and global business expansion. The effects of these factors are interrelated, and they tend to work in combination with one another to achieve direct marketing objectives.

INNOVATE OR EVAPORATE*

E-Commerce and Direct Distribution in the Insurance Industry

"Direct interaction with consumers via the Internet and on-line services will have a dramatic impact on one of the enduring icons of the insurance industry—the insurance salesperson," according to a global study conducted by International Business Machines Corp.'s (IBM's) Global Insurance Industry Division and The Economist Intelligence Unit. Responses from 160 senior management executives from property-casualty and life insurance companies in nine countries indicated that "insurance agents skilled enough to provide expert customer service to affluent customers have the best chance of preserving their jobs against a wave of alternative distribution channels cresting over the next 5 years." Some believe that electronic delivery channels will replace independent agents. Others say, "Consumers will always want to be taken care of. Insurance is not one-size-fits-all. Just because a policy is on the Internet doesn't mean it will give you the best coverage you need. I don't think we'll ever see wholesale delivery of insurance over the Internet." Still others say, "Agents are not ignoring the Internet; they are embracing it." Other channels include competition from banks, financial service companies, and other emerging direct marketers.

This study highlights the differences and the interaction between traditional direct marketing tools and emerging technologies. With advances in electronic channels, the World Wide Web has become important as both a promoter and a distributor of insurance and other services. However, it is not uncommon for innovative insurers to maintain multiple access points to market their policies, including mail, telephone, PC, and personal contact with agents—an integrated marketing communications approach.

*The box title is attributed to James M. Higgins, *Innovate or Evaporate* (Winter Park, FL: New Management Publishing Company, 1995).

Source: Gregory A. Maciag, "Access and Distribution: For Customers Who Want It All," *National Underwriter* 102(10) (March 9, 1998), p. 33; Diane West, "Alternative Outlets Boost Demands on Agents, Study Finds," *National Underwriter* 101(24) (June 16, 1997), pp. 21–22.

Niche marketing
Focus on a small segment of the market that exhibits homogeneous needs and response to marketing offers.

Consumers and organizations alike have found it necessary to maximize the use of their time when making purchases. Thus the opportunity to "buy direct" and eliminate unnecessary middlemen, while keeping prices low, has considerable appeal when compared with a lengthy interaction with a sales representative or fulfillment of a multistaged mail or telephone order. **Niche marketing,** by its very nature, is conducive to direct marketing because of the close relationship between buyers and sellers. Focusing on a small niche of the market enables the marketer to become well informed about the needs of customers in that segment and to use direct marketing as an effective quick-response strategy. However, the niche must be large enough to be profitable, have attractive growth potential, and be free of intense competition.

Direct marketing has enjoyed much success because of the availability of specialized media that can carry promotional messages to a narrowly defined population. These media run the gamut from newspapers to the World Wide Web—all highly targeted to a special audience of readers, listeners, or subscribers.

Another key factor in the growth of direct marketing is the proliferation of computerized databases. This information can be found in internal sources such as company records and customer credit-card accounts and in external sources such as marketing research and commercial data suppliers. Marketing efforts can be targeted to specific customers based on the detailed personal or company information that is available from databases.

Technology is a major force in the growth of direct marketing. In particular, the tendencies of buyers and sellers to complete their transactions directly has evolved as a result of the increased use of computers, advances in worldwide telecommunications capability, and the extensive use of electronic media.

In conjunction with each of the preceding factors, direct marketing continues to experience growth because of the globalization of markets for all types of goods and services. The expansion of U.S. catalogers and mail-order businesses into Europe and other overseas markets, as well as the expansion of foreign mail-order companies into the United States, has accelerated the use of direct marketing channels on a global basis. For example, Avon Products, Inc., sells its beauty products door-to-door in China, Brazil, and Poland. Japanese customers can buy cookware from Williams-Sonoma, Inc., and apparel from L.L. Bean, Inc., Lands' End, Inc., and Hanna Andersson, Inc., through catalogs.[8] U.K. businesses spent more than £7.2 billion on direct marketing in 1997, up from £4.5 billion in 1994. Growth in direct-mail expenditures was "somewhat stratospheric . . . putting a stress on the capacity of the postal services, and on the ability of consumers to absorb it all."[9] Direct marketers also experienced tremendous growth in the use of telemarketing and database marketing, along with commercial radio and customer magazines, with the Internet as the newest medium for direct marketing.

DIRECT MARKETING TOOLS

Direct marketing tools may be personal (direct selling) or nonpersonal (direct-action advertising, electronic media). While both consumer and organizational purchases can be made directly from a manufacturer or distributor, more business-to-business transactions are made through direct channels, primarily to decrease costs and time and to increase profits. This is due in part to the size, complexity, and specialized nature of many organizational purchases, as well as to the need to understand each customer's situation. See Table 13.3 for a summary of direct marketing sales by medium and market.

Direct Selling

Direct selling
Personal direct marketing tools, including direct mail, catalogs, telemarketing, in-home or in-office sales, and vending machines.

Methods of **direct selling** include direct mail, catalogs, telemarketing, in-home or in-office sales, and vending machines. Personal direct selling includes telemarketing and personal contact in the customer's home or office. This method is used frequently for many consumer goods and services, such as cosmetics, jewelry, and household goods. Direct mail and catalogs also are used to promote a variety of products, such as apparel and music or books, in the consumer sector. Organizational customers may purchase a wide range of goods such as auto parts and office supplies through direct mail and catalogs.

TABLE 13.3
·················
Value of U.S. Consumer and Business-to-Business Sales Driven by Direct Marketing, by Medium and Market

Direct Marketing Medium	Sales ($Billions)*			Compound Annual Growth, %	
	1993	1998	2003	1993–1998	1998–2003
Direct mail	$282.6	$429.8	$652.8	8.7	8.7
Consumer	182.4	267.8	390.6	8.0	7.8
Business-to-business	100.2	161.9	262.2	10.1	10.1
Telephone marketing	316.9	482.2	725.5	8.8	8.5
Consumer	146.5	209.5	298.6	7.4	7.3
Business-to-business	170.4	272.7	428.9	9.9	9.5
Newspaper	130.5	192.6	287.7	8.1	8.4
Consumer	87.3	124.6	178.6	7.4	7.5
Business-to-business	43.2	68.0	109.1	9.5	9.9
Magazine	48.8	74.0	109.9	8.7	8.2
Consumer	26.8	39.0	55.4	7.8	7.3
Business-to-business	22.0	35.0	54.5	9.7	9.3
Television	57.8	94.1	146.5	10.2	9.3
Consumer	35.8	56.7	85.4	9.6	8.5
Business-to-business	21.9	37.5	61.1	11.4	10.3
Radio	20.3	34.9	54.0	11.3	9.1
Consumer	11.8	19.9	30.0	11.0	8.6
Business-to-business	8.5	15.0	24.0	12.0	9.9
Other	42.8	64.0	94.7	8.4	8.2
Consumer	28.9	41.7	59.7	7.6	7.4
Business-to-business	13.9	22.3	35.0	9.9	9.4
Total	899.6	1,371.5	2,073.2	8.8	8.6
Consumer	519.6	759.2	1,098.3	7.9	7.7
Business-to-business	380.0	612.2	974.9	10.0	9.8

*Sales in current (nominal) dollars, not adjusted for inflation.
Source: Reprinted from *Economic Impact: U.S. Direct Marketing Today 1998* with permission from The Direct Marketing Association, Inc.

Direct-action advertising
Direct-response advertising in print and broadcast media.

Direct-action advertising refers to direct-response advertising in both print and broadcast media. Direct marketing activities that use the Internet, television, cable, facsimile, video, and other electronic media continue to gain customers as the general population becomes better informed and has easier access to the technology.

Direct Mail. This is the most predominant direct-selling method and includes everything from a simple black-and-white postcard to an impressive multicolor professional package. Catalogs, letters, brochures, pamphlets, flyers, and other printed materials, along with computer disks or CDs, videotapes, and other promotional items, are mailed directly to customers.

Benefits of direct mail include the ability to precisely target selected customers through the use of databases and mailing lists, to tailor the marketing message to the specific needs and characteristics of a prospective customer, to create unique, personalized marketing approaches, and to measure customer response rate. Direct mail can be used at all stages in the buying process, from making prospective customers aware of a purchase problem, to providing information during the search process and evaluation of purchase alternatives, to reinforcing a customer's choice after the sale has been made. T. Rowe Price, a financial services firm, uses direct mail to introduce new mutual funds to its high-net-worth clients. The company sends personalized letters signed by a high-level manager. Although personalized letters take time and effort to create, they are less expensive than producing an advertisement and have helped to double response rate.[10]

On the other hand, the proliferation of direct mail has become a nuisance for many people as they deal with mounds of "junk mail," giving this tool a negative image and a high probability that it will be thrown away. For example, Reader's Digest Association has faced continued weak responses to direct mail promotions because customers are overwhelmed by the commercial clutter that fills their mailboxes.[11]

Catalogs.   Catalogs have become the most popular form of direct mail for many of the same reasons that all areas of direct marketing have experienced phenomenal growth. Two catalogs that spurred the growth of this industry were those of Montgomery Ward & Co., Inc., and Sears, Roebuck and Co. in 1872 and 1886, respectively.

Total catalog sales were approximately $78.6 billion in 1997 and are projected to reach $106.8 billion by 2002. Approximately 60 percent are expected to come from consumers and 40 percent from business customers. Catalog advertising expenditures reached nearly $11 billion in 1998 and are expected to reach $12.5 billion by 2002, with nearly one-half million people employed in this industry. The growth in overall catalog advertising expenditures, sales, and employment is expected to outpace the rate of total U.S. growth in these same categories, but may be somewhat more conservative as the industry enters the twenty-first century.

Catalog marketers can cut distribution costs and reach selected customers, and customers can save precious time and shop at their convenience wherever they may be. Catalogs are used by all types of for-profit and nonprofit organizations to reach their consumer and business markets. Many manufacturers, retailers, and distributors use multiple distribution channels that might include catalogs, retail stores, and personal selling. For example, a customer may make a purchase from J.C. Penney Company, Inc., or Service Merchandise Co., Inc., by ordering from a catalog, ordering by telephone, ordering on-line over the Internet, or visiting a store. Soon more catalogs may also be made available to customers on CDs or videos.[12]

Telemarketing.   Telephone marketing is an efficient direct marketing tool that includes all direct-response advertising communications, generally using Wide Area Telephone Service (WATS) for outbound (OUT WATS) and inbound (IN WATS) operations or conventional, private line, or other telecommunications services. Telephone direct marketing generated sales of $482.2 billion in 1998, and this is estimated to reach $727.5 billion in 2003.[13]

A well-planned telemarketing program uses the latest telecommunications hardware, software, and database technologies, generally as part of an integrated marketing communications program. It focuses on personal interaction and building relationships with customers. Telephone marketing is second only to personal selling as the most intensely personal promotional medium.[14] The advantages of this direct marketing tool include its ability to provide immediate feedback, flexibility, incremental effectiveness when used with other media, methods of building and maintaining customer goodwill, and opportunities to offer higher levels of customer service. In addition, it is a highly productive tool and has a relatively low cost per contact.

Home or Office Personal Selling.   Many direct marketing programs are based on personal selling opportunities where a sales representative takes goods and services to a customer's home or office. The most common form of this type of direct marketing is the party plan followed by such firms as Tupperware and Mary Kay Cosmetics and the door-to-door approach used by Avon Products, Inc. As more women have entered the work force in the United States, many of these direct-selling events have moved from the customer's home to his or her workplace. This is often complemented by the use of a catalog for order placement at a later time when it is convenient for the customer.

Vending Machines.   Vending machines have become more sophisticated over the years and offer a wide array of goods and services. They can dispense tangible goods such as hot and cold foods and beverages and cigarettes. They also can dispense service products such as airline insurance policies. They can be operated with coins or a card, and they can make change for a dollar. Some even "talk" to customers via preprogrammed computer chips.

Direct-Action Advertising

Direct-action advertising can be described in terms of direct response in print media and direct response in broadcast media, as detailed below. The objective of direct response is to motivate the customer to purchase the good or service at the time that it is offered. The offer may include incentives to persuade the customer not to delay the buying decision.

Direct Response: Print Media.   The most frequently used print media for direct-response campaigns are magazines, newspapers, inserts, and supplements. Magazines and newspapers may include all direct-response space advertising, inserts, and other advertising formats. The direct-response program objectives may be to achieve immediate sales, generate leads, or increase store traffic. Specialty magazines have become an increasingly effective medium for direct-response marketing because of their highly targeted audiences. While their distribution may not be wide, their ability to hit the right audience is cost-efficient and effective. Potential customers can read about a good or service and immediately place an order directly by mail, telephone, facsimile, or Internet. The key to success for marketers using print media to elicit direct response is to select the right magazine or newspaper for their target market and to gain exposure to as many target customers as possible. This is not always easy, because general advertisers also are targeting many of the same customers.

Direct Response: Broadcast Media.   In addition to print media, direct-response campaigns also may communicate with customers through broadcast media (television and radio). Television is particularly effective because of its ability to demonstrate products in use and provide a response mechanism such as a toll-free telephone number, a physical location, or a Web site where the customer can place an order. The use of interactive television is expected to increase as the number of computer WebTV systems in households increases (an estimated 40 percent by the end of 1998).[15] A large number of customers will use set-top boxes to access the Web—and the direct marketing opportunities that the combined television and Internet have to offer.

Radio is everywhere—in homes, cars, and offices, at the beach, in the grocery store, and in every other place you can imagine. Customers are tuned in to their radios in large numbers while they work at their home or office, drive their cars, and engage in leisure activities. Although a radio message is usually short and fleeting, it can motivate customer response and support other direct marketing media. Radio commercials provide potential customers with contact information so that they may purchase the item offered from the advertiser or a third party (such as independent distributors). Although radio messages are fleeting, advertisers can select programs that are most listened to by their target market—and therefore achieve higher response rates.

Electronic Media

Electronic media
Television, cable, Internet, facsimile, video, etc.

Technological advances have accelerated the use of **electronic media** in direct marketing. The most commonly used tools are television, cable, and the Internet. Facsimile, video, and other media also are used in many campaigns. An accelerated rate of technological advances in these media has increased their attractiveness to direct marketers.

Television and Cable.   Both television and cable have been important marketing media for many years. However, advances in the interactive capability of these media have increased their usefulness to direct marketers.

Cable offers direct marketers an array of specialized target markets. Audiences of cable channels such as CNN (news), ESPN (sports), MTV (music videos), and the Weather Channel each share common characteristics that make them attractive targets for certain goods and services. Cable channels also include the Home Shopping Network and other shopping networks that sell directly to customers, often using infomercials extensively in addition to direct advertising. In contrast to the cheap image of home shopping in its early days, today's direct marketers include more upscale products and represent major fashion retailers. Television home shopping is expected to increase with the proliferation of specialized channels and their interactive capability. Whether television and cable are used to elicit direct response or to support other advertising and personal selling efforts, these electronic media are a critical element in an integrated communications mix.

The Internet.   Advances in information technology and the digital revolution have made the Internet the marketplace of choice for many buyers and sellers as they engage in e-commerce. Accessibility and interactivity are the key advantages of the Internet as a direct marketing tool. Reliable statistics on Internet traffic and sales are difficult to find because of the newness and rapid growth of this medium. Some indicators of the magnitude of direct marketing opportunities on the Internet can be found in company examples, sales and marketing costs, and buying activity, as shown in Figure 13.1.

Analysts predict that the phenomenal growth of Internet marketing (e-commerce) will continue well into the twenty-first century, fueling the worldwide economy. In 1998, 100 million people throughout the world used the Internet, up from 3 million people in 1994. Experts predict that this number will increase to 1 billion by 2005. Electronic commerce among businesses for commercial transactions has improved productivity significantly in creating, buying, distributing, selling, and servicing goods and services. Business-to-business commerce is estimated to grow to $300 billion by 2002. The digital delivery of goods and services via the Internet is expected to escalate in the distribution of software programs, newspapers, music CDs, airline tickets, securities, consulting services, entertainment, banking and insurance, education, and health care, for example.[16] In developing direct marketing strategies, marketing managers should consider the following:[17]

- Recognize that consumer markets are heterogeneous and complex and that the Internet is but one of many distribution channels in a vast array of conventional retail channels; also consider consumer and organizational purchasing processes.

- Identify unique characteristics of the Internet as a distribution channel, as well as characteristics that are shared with other marketing channels, as a basis for determining differentiation strategies and maintaining competitive advantage.

- Evaluate the substitutability of the Internet for distribution functions that are performed by traditional channel intermediaries.

- Determine the suitability of the Internet versus other channels for marketing a good or service with certain characteristics.

In addition, those companies who are later adopters of direct marketing via the Internet (e.g., Encyclopedia Britannica) must manage the disruption of traditional business models when Internet-based technology is added to the marketing mix. They must ask how the Web will affect customer needs, sales and marketing, production and operations, and company personnel. As one CEO said when asked how the Internet was changing his company, "It totally changes everything. It changes the way we process and manufacture all the way through to how we market, sell and deliver."[18] Federal Express Corp., Holiday Inns, Inc., and other companies with successful Internet marketing programs tend to agree that "the Internet initiative must bring into the fold information systems, marketing, and customer support among other departments; Web sites must be interactive, allowing the user to take control of the experience; and the strategy must be part of the overall marketing program, not its forgotten stepchild."[19]

Facsimile, Video, and Other Media.   A number of other tools are used in direct marketing programs, generally in combination with other media. Facsimile (fax)

Direct Marketing on the Internet: A Business Perspective

- *Ordering and customer service.* Cisco Systems, Dell Computers, and Boeing's spare parts business benefited from putting their ordering and customer service operations on the Internet. Their success indicates that most of this business will involve the Internet within the next 5 years. Boeing expects to use the Internet to automate up to 60 percent of the spare parts orders that it presently receives by phone, fax, and mail by the year 2000. Combined with 50 percent of its orders presently received over the private airline network, Boeing expects that up to 90 percent of its orders will be transmitted electronically.

- *Lower sales and marketing costs.* New customers can be added to a Web business at little or no added cost, thus making traditional sales organizations, distribution channels, and other direct marketing media more efficient. As noted above, Boeing uses the Internet as an efficient sales tool for its spare parts business. The selling points for Boeing's new airline customers is the ability to check availability of parts, obtain price information, order parts, and track orders on the Internet. To illustrate the reduction in marketing costs, Boeing processed about 20 percent more shipments in 1997 over the previous year with the same number of personnel and avoided about 600 customer service calls a day because customers tracked their own orders.

- *Procurement.* General Electric's Lighting Division shifted a primarily manual multi-step system of procurement to a more efficient electronic system using the Internet. GE Lighting experienced significant gains in responsiveness, improved service, and reduced labor and material costs. As of late 1997, eight divisions of General Electronic are using an on-line procurement system.

- *Inventory reduction.* IBM's Personal Systems Group uses the Internet and private networks to reduce inventory levels and to target customer needs more precisely. Each month the marketing department estimates PC sales, and production planning departments determine manufacturing and materials factory capacity throughout the company. Based on companywide demand and supply inputs, production schedules are assigned, and procurement personnel negotiate with suppliers. Quick response is made possible by electronic communication between factories, marketing, and purchasing departments.

- *Lower cycle times (time it takes to build a product).* In 1994, Chrysler, Ford, GM, Johnson Controls, and twelve of their suppliers began working together to improve material flow within their supply chain and shorten production cycles as part of the Manufacturing Assembly Pilot (MAP). The Automotive Network Exchange (ANX), which is expected to be fully implemented by 2000, is a private network that runs over the Internet and links manufacturers and suppliers worldwide to achieve further reductions in product development and manufacturing cycles.

- *More efficient and effective customer service.* Cisco's Internet customer service activities are expected to increase productivity by 200 to 300 percent, saving $125 million in customer service expenses. Dell, UPS, and FedEx also use the Internet successfully for customer service and technical support.

- *New sales opportunities.* Twenty-four-hour access via the Internet makes it relatively easy for companies to attract new customers. Dell Computer found that 80 percent of customers and half the small businesses that purchased from its Web site were first-time Dell customers. One of four said they would not have purchased if they could not do so via the Web site.

- *Ability to achieve economies of scale and analyze past purchases.* Amazon.com, an upstart Internet bookseller, applies cutting-edge technology to analyze past purchases in order to customize recommendations to each buyer. Amazon achieves economies of scale and high productivity ratios by making it easy to search for 3.1 million titles (fifteen times more than any existing bookstore) without the costly overhead of multimillion-dollar buildings and large numbers of personnel. Amazon's 1600 employees each generate an average of $375,000 in annual revenues (compared with Barnes & Nobles' 27,000 employees).

Source: Emerging Digital Economy (1998), U.S. Department of Commerce, *http://www.ecommerce.gov,*
Chap. 3: "Electronic Commerce between Businesses"; Robert D. Hof, Ellen Neugorne, and Heather Green, "Amazon.com: The Wild World of e-commerce," *Business Week* (December 14, 1998), pp. 106–119.

....

transmissions are used to transmit written and graphic communications between two fax machines over telephone lines. American Telephone & Telegraph Co. (AT&T) was among the first to recognize the potential of fax as a direct-response medium, first sending a direct mail piece to business executives whom they urged to respond by fax for further information about AT&T's equipment or services.[20]

Direct marketers often use videocassettes and videodisks in place of print catalogs. Videos have an appeal to marketers of fashion apparel, automobiles, and other goods and services (e.g., insurance, travel destinations) because of their ability to show the good or service in use. They can be used to explain complex details and provide answers to questions frequently asked by buyers.

Kiosks (free-standing sales units) are placed in retail stores and malls and other public locations. Direct purchases may be made either electronically by computer or in person. Customers can use the kiosk to check on the availability of merchandise and to place an order. They can complete financial transactions using banking kiosks and complete a variety of other types of transactions. Direct marketing has an array of media that can be used to elicit a direct response by including a toll-free telephone number, Internet address, or regular telephone number, for example.

OBJECTIVES OF DIRECT MARKETING

Direct customer response
One-on-one customer contact where the customer responds directly to the seller's offer.

The two major objectives of direct marketing are to build relationships with customers and to obtain a **direct customer response.** However, not every direct marketing campaign is intended to invoke an immediate transaction. Some direct marketing techniques may be used in combination with other elements of the communications mix, such as backup for the salesforce, reinforcement of other media advertising, and other purposes.

Build Customer Relationships

Relationship building is an important element of direct marketing. Because sales representatives, distributors, and others are involved in direct contact with customers, they may be perceived as an extension of the product they are selling. This total product concept must be consistent with the needs of a particular target market, and it must be communicated effectively. To accomplish this, sales and marketing efforts focus on building relationships with the most important and profitable customers.

Relationship marketing
Building long-term customer relationships beyond a single transaction.

Relationship marketing may include the development of a continuous relationship with a number of unique market segments (or individuals), multiple products, multiple channels, and differentiated messages. The marketing program is customized to each segment. Customer loyalty programs, such as frequent-flier awards, often are used to develop long-term relationships, and this enhances the success of direct marketing programs.

Direct Response or Transaction

In addition to building relationships, another objective of direct marketing is to elicit a direct, immediate response from customers—that is, a one-time transaction (that may grow into repeat business if a relationship is established). Avon's door-to-door selling techniques, Tupperware's home parties, Amazon.com's on-line Internet book sales, direct mail pieces sent to prospective customers, television shopping networks, and telemarketing are examples of methods used to motivate targeted customers to make an immediate purchase or place an order for a specified time of delivery.

The interactive nature of many of the direct-response techniques often allows the seller to tailor the sales message to the needs of the buyer, increasing the probability of closing a sale quickly. The intended purpose of direct-response advertising through any medium is to stimulate a direct order, generate a qualified lead that can result in a sale, or drive store traffic for advertised products.[21]

INTEGRATED DIRECT MARKETING COMMUNICATIONS

Direct marketing tools must be integrated among themselves to create consistency and synergies in their impact on the target audience. Likewise, direct marketing programs should be integrated with other elements of the marketing mix (product, place, price, and promotion) and communications mix (advertising, personal selling, sales promotion, public relations).

Integration Across Direct Marketing Tools

When direct-selling, direct-action, and electronic media are used in combination, the result is greater than when any one medium is used in isolation. Multiple exposures to the same message are more likely to get customers' attention, help them to remember the message, and move them to act on an offer. For example, a retailer may send a direct mail piece to a charge account customer announcing the arrival of a new catalog in the near future, followed by the catalog itself. Next, the customer may receive a telephone call that highlights a particular product in the catalog (that the retailer's database indicates the customer has an interest in). In addition, the customer may see a magazine advertisement that provides a telephone number or Internet address for additional information or placing an order.

Integration with Other Communications Mix and Marketing-Mix Elements

Direct marketing tools have become increasingly important as elements in the overall communications mix (discussed in Chapters 11 and 12). In turn, the communications mix is but one aspect of the overall marketing mix and must be coordinated with product, pricing, and distribution decisions. Table 13.4 illustrates the direct marketing activities of a number of diverse industries. Retailers, financial institutions, insurance companies, and the others represented in the table generally rely on a combination of the direct marketing tools described in this chapter, such as direct mail, personal selling, electronic media, and so forth.

TABLE 13.4
....
Direct Marketing Industry: Key Growth Areas

Consumer DM Advertising Expenditures (Top 10)	DM Spending 1998 ($billion)	DM Expenditures: Annual Est. Growth Rate (%), 1998–2003
(a) Consumer direct marketing industries		
Nonstore retailers	$8.8	3.1
General merchandise stores	7.0	3.8
Depository institutions (including banking)	4.7	7.4
Transportation equipment (including auto mfg.)	4.4	10.1
Educational services	3.1	7.0
Home furnishings stores	2.9	1.7
Food and kindred products	2.9	3.3
Insurance carriers and agents	2.7	2.6
Real estate	2.7	2.8
Health services	2.4	1.6
Total consumer DM ad expenditures (52% of total)	$41.6	

Consumer DM Sales (Top 10)	DM Sales 1998 ($billion)	DM Sales: Annual Estimated Growth Rate (%), 1998–2003
(a) Consumer direct marketing industries		
Nonstore retailers	$101.3	6.9
Real estate	49.5	3.6
General merchandise stores	45.9	9.8
Automobile dealers and service stations	41.5	9.9
Membership organizations	36.8	7.2
Food and kindred products	35.5	5.9
Health services	32.8	12.8
Insurance carriers and agents	31.4	4.0
Depository institutions (including banking)	29.9	7.3
Personal and repair services	25.8	6.5
Total consumer DM sales (56.7% of total)	430.3	

Business-to-Business DM Ad Expenditures (Top 10)	DM Spending 1998 ($billion)	DM Expenditures: Annual Est. Growth Rate (%), 1998–2003
(b) Business-to-business direct marketing industries		
Business services	$8.6	6.7
Communications	6.9	7.0
Wholesale trade	6.5	10.7
Transportation services	5.2	6.4
Printing and publishing	5.2	6.1
Electrical machinery and equipment	4.0	7.9
Insurance carriers and agent	3.9	10.6
Chemicals and allied products	3.7	5.6
Professional services	3.3	11.3
Industrial machinery and equipment	3.0	10.5
Total business-to-business DM ad expenditures (60.9% of total) 50.3		

TABLE 13.4 (continued)
....
Direct Marketing Industry: Key Growth Areas

Business-to-Business DM Sales (Top 10)	DM Sales 1998 ($billion)	DM Sales: Annual Estimated Growth Rate (%) 1998–2003
(b) Business-to-business direct marketing industries		
Business services	$99.2	11.8
Insurance carriers and agents	42.7	12.2
Real estate	40.7	10.8
Wholesale trade	31.3	7.4
Chemicals and allied products	27.6	7.2
Printing and publishing	27.1	8.6
Industrial machinery and equipment	25.6	9.4
Professional services	23.0	10.7
Food and kindred products	22.8	7.4
Electrical machinery and equipment	20.7	10.0
Total business-to-business DM sales (58.9% of total)	360.6	

Note: These numbers have not been inflation adjusted; they represent current (nominal numbers). Rankings are based on 1998 statistics.
Source: Reprinted from *Economic Impact: U.S. Direct Marketing Today 1998* with permission from The Direct Marketing Association, Inc.

THE DIRECT MARKETING PROCESS
....

Direct marketing process
Development and maintenance of customer databases, interactive marketing systems, and procedures for measuring results.

The **direct marketing process** consists of developing and maintaining customer databases, an interactive marketing system, and a procedure for measuring results. Each element of the direct marketing process is related to the primary decision variables that underlie direct marketing programs: the offer (including the product), creative aspects, media (including lists, if appropriate), timing and sequencing, and customer service provisions.[22]

Direct marketing planning should be coordinated with the organization's strategic planning process and should be consistent with other marketing activities in order to achieve a sustainable competitive advantage. An emphasis on low costs of operation, an offering that is uniquely differentiated from that of competitors, a highly focused (or niche) strategy, or some combination of these approaches can lead to long-term competitive advantage.

Customer Databases
....

Customer database
Computerized record of information such as customers' personal characteristics, buying habits, and past purchase records that is used to develop direct marketing programs.

Those firms with an accurate, up-to-date **customer database** have the potential to dominate a market based on knowledge of their customers' buying habits, motives, lifestyles, and demographics. Within the context of direct marketing, a *database* is a set of records that contains information about customers. Data generally include relevant personal information about individuals or companies and their past buying

MARKETING AND ENTREPRENEURSHIP

High Impact from Low-Tech Direct Marketing

 When buyers enter the annual International Housewares Show in Chicago's 1.3 million-square-foot McCormick Place convention center, they are confronted with more than 60,000 retailers, distributors, and buyers of houseware products from all over the world. More than 2000 exhibitors present an array of eye-catching displays, such as Rubbermaid Incorporated's 10,000-square-foot booth. Then there's Bakertowne Co., Inc., in a 20- by 15-foot booth in the rear of its section, a "small fish in a big pond," said Lou Kahn, the company's vice-president, and there's the 10-by-10-foot booth used to promote Doumar Products' adhesive remover. Both are competing with the industry giants for sales leads and orders.

Being small can be a disadvantage at a large trade show—unless you use smart marketing that allows "firms operating from guppy-size booths to compete with the sharks." The integration of multiple direct marketing tools can make a firm more competitive. For example, Bakertowne Co., Inc., an importer and distributor of houseware and industrial goods, estimates that as much as 15 percent of the contacts made at the show result in new business leads, and many of these leads result in new business deals. Kahn and other smaller exhibitors find success in using

direct marketing techniques before a trade show, such as sending direct mail and scheduling appointments with prospects. Postcard-sized mailers are inexpensive and effective because they can be mailed to prospects before the show and they are easy to read and carry. The cards should tell the prospect about product introductions, giveaways and promotions, and the company's location at the show. Other direct marketing techniques might include attention-getting demonstrations to help generate leads or make a direct sale. Print and broadcast media can be used along with the direct sales approach at the trade show, as well as direct mail pieces, incentives, and so forth. This is particularly cost-effective if you can get coverage (paid ads and/or publicity) for your company and product line on cable stations, in newspapers, or in other media that are likely to be seen or heard by trade show attendees. The trade show itself is a powerful direct marketing medium, but it makes its greatest impact when it is combined with other marketing tools.

Source: Michelle Wirth Fellmann, "Small Booth, Big Show, Big ROI. Really," *Marketing News* 33(3) (February 1, 1999), pp. 1, 16.

behavior, for example. Because databases play a critical role in successful direct marketing, they must be developed and managed carefully.

Role in Integrated Direct Marketing.   Target marketing strategies depend on a high level of detailed consumer or organizational customer knowledge. As a result, databases have gained importance in determining which direct marketing tools to use and how to combine them most effectively. For example, a database may provide historical customer data that tell which customers are most likely to respond to telemarketing versus direct mail and the types of products they are most likely to buy. It also may provide information about the total sales generated by each medium and its cost-effectiveness.

A database serves a number of purposes. It enables a marketer to identify the most profitable customers and obtain more business from them. It can be used to identify and qualify the best prospects and convert them to customers, identify past customers and reactivate them, and identify the company's most profitable products. A database also provides input for marketing managers who are responsible for developing appropriate promotional, pricing, and distribution policies; identifying new markets and ways to enter them; measuring the results of marketing efforts; increasing productivity; and decreasing costs while increasing sales volume.[23]

Developing and Managing a Database.   A database is more than just a customer list, although the two terms are sometimes confused. A database includes not only demographic characteristics but also customers' buying preferences and behavior, media habits, and other useful information. Direct responses from customers include valuable information that can be added to the database over a long period of time. This information can be used to determine buying trends, additional opportunities, or potential problems that may be experienced with a particular customer or market segment.

In addition to company-generated data that are useful for direct marketing, there are a number of customer lists that can be used. The most common types are potential customers with a demonstrated interest in a product and a willingness to buy, potential customers with similar identifiable characteristics but unknown willingness to buy, and customers who have bought from the company previously. Lists may be created and maintained in-house or rented from outside sources, such as list brokers.[24]

Interactive Marketing System

Interactive marketing systems
Technology-based selling systems consisting of computers, software, databases, and telecommunications technology.

Interactive marketing systems have grown from a simple salesperson-customer transaction to technology-based selling systems. Thus computers, software, databases, and telecommunications technologies are combined into one system to enable organizations to sell directly to their customers, particularly those with whom they want to build long-term relationships. Customer relationship management requires a disciplined system that maximizes the value of customer relationships and ensures that individual customer needs are profitably satisfied at the right time, in the right channel, and with the right offer.[25] The components of a hypothetical direct marketing system are illustrated in Figure 13.2. Although direct marketing system designs vary from one situation to another, the basic components generally include an automated, computerized database, efficient telecommunications, an interactive communication system (which includes both inbound and outbound call centers), order-fulfillment facilities and procedures, a well-developed customer service function, and retention and loyalty programs.

Measuring Results

Although direct marketing is an efficient way to serve a chosen target market, it is costly and time-consuming to implement. Therefore, results of a direct marketing program must be monitored to determine whether or not it has been successful—and why. The effectiveness of each tool used in a marketing campaign can be measured individually and collectively to determine the relative contribution that each

FIGURE 13.2

Components of a Direct Marketing System

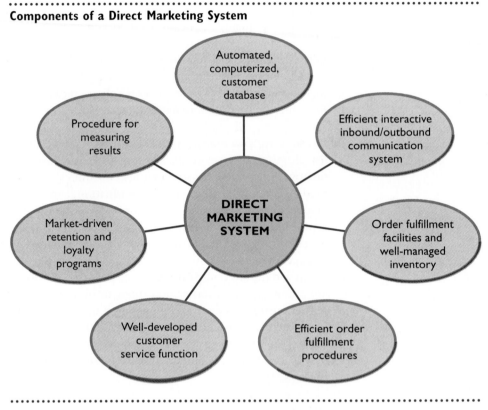

has made to the final result. For example, test marketing can be used to determine customer reactions to any element of the direct marketing approach, such as media and message reactions, attitudes toward the marketer and the product, and so forth. Measures can be used throughout a direct marketing campaign to analyze customer responses and at the end of a campaign to determine whether sales or other objectives were met.

The results of a direct marketing program can be measured in a number of different ways. Sales responses can be measured against campaign objectives to determine if they were achieved. A cost-benefit analysis can be performed to determine the efficiency and effectiveness of resources used. Follow-up research can be conducted with customers to determine their level of satisfaction or problems they may have experienced with the purchase or the transaction.

In business-to-business direct marketing, results may be measured with marketing and sales productivity (MSP) systems.[26] Both large and small companies can expect improvements in productivity and effectiveness if they use MSP information networks as management tools to measure automated routine tasks and gather and interpret data. Some examples include salesperson productivity (e.g., sales calls, order entry and status, tracking leads, managing accounts), direct mail and fulfillment, and telemarketing (e.g., merging, cleaning, and maintaining mailing and calling lists, ranking prospects).

ISSUES IN DIRECT MARKETING

Direct marketing continues to increase in popularity as a marketing communication and distribution method. However, there are issues and concerns that must be faced by both customers and direct marketing organizations. Key factors that affect decisions by both buyers and sellers are discussed briefly, along with selected legal, ethical, and social issues.

Customer-Related Issues

Although many consumers and businesses are responsive to direct marketing efforts, many others are reluctant to make purchases in this way. The factors that motivate or discourage this type of purchase are discussed next.

Factors Motivating Use. A number of key factors contribute to consumers' and organizational buyers' decisions to purchase directly from a supplier. Key factors include a desire for quick and convenient order fulfillment, lower prices due to elimination of middlemen, a proliferation of specialized media targeted to their needs and preferences, availability of interactive media for purchasing in homes and offices, and more technologically savvy buyers.

Factors Discouraging Use. Many of the factors that diminish customers' ability or willingness to purchase directly include lack of comfort with interactive technology, unavailability of direct salespeople in the home or office, preference for hands-on in-store shopping experiences, and privacy or ethical issues (discussed below).

Organization-Related Issues

The major issues involved in the adoption of direct marketing programs by organizations (both for-profit and nonprofit) include use of resources and measures of effectiveness. Others include legal, ethical, and social factors (discussed later).

Resource Utilization. The need to become more efficient by cutting operating costs is a primary motivator for using a direct marketing strategy. Direct marketing efforts can be targeted precisely toward select groups of customers and individuals with a high expectation of success. The absence of a middleman makes it possible to significantly reduce processing time and transactional costs, although direct marketers are responsible for all marketing functions that are performed by other channel members in traditional distribution channels.

Another key issue revolves around the time and effort that must be put into creating and maintaining a direct marketing system. Further, databases are in constant need of updating and need dedicated effort if their benefits are to be maximized. The main question is whether other selling methods might provide a greater return for the time and money invested.

Effectiveness Measures. It is often difficult to measure success in direct marketing because the measures themselves are not satisfactory. A comprehensive approach can be taken by breaking down the direct marketing system into its various components and analyzing the effectiveness of each one. For example, sales results, mail or telephone inquiries, or other responses can be used to measure the effectiveness of each direct marketing medium. Message effectiveness might be assessed with communications measures such as recognition or recall tests or attitude measures. Customer service effectiveness can be measured with customer satisfaction surveys and monitoring of transactions.

Legal, Ethical, and Social Issues

Both buyers and sellers have a number of concerns about the legal, ethical, and social aspects of direct marketing. Two issues are selected for discussion here: invasion of privacy and multilevel marketing (pyramid) schemes.

Invasion of Privacy. One of the greatest drawbacks to consumers who are inclined to purchase directly is the invasion of their privacy. The ability of direct marketers to create databases that contain all types of personal information is a major concern. The problem is exacerbated by the fact that a company may sell its customer database to another organization, often without its customers being aware of this sharing of personal information.

Multilevel Marketing (Pyramid). With the popularity of direct selling, there has been a growth in multilevel marketing businesses, sometimes referred to as *pyramid schemes.* Many multilevel marketers are responsible and deal within the confines of the law and ethical judgment; others may not. The problem lies with the balance between a focus on sales of a product versus the building of a salesforce that returns profits to each level above it (i.e., a pyramid). In this case, the customers are actually the lower levels of the salesforce that feed orders and profits to those above—making it attractive to continue to recruit large numbers of sales representatives who may be required to purchase and carry an inventory of the product.

TRENDS IN DIRECT MARKETING

The future of direct marketing appears to be determined by three related factors: databases, technology, and communication. The importance of automated, computerized, comprehensive databases has been stressed throughout this chapter. As markets become more global and populations become more diverse, databases will continue to provide more efficient and effective ways to identify homogeneous market segments that can be targeted with direct marketing programs. The future of database management is intertwined with the future of technology and the improvements that technology continues to provide, such as the linking of multiple databases for more complete customer information and continuous follow-up throughout an entire sales process.

The communications mix is in a state of change because of shifts in media use by buyers and sellers and general advances in telecommunications capabilities throughout the world. In particular, the Internet is expected to make even more inroads as the chosen medium for many shoppers. The proliferation of cable channels, satellite broadcasting systems, and cellular technology will continue to offer more direct marketing media options. The more that marketers and their customers are linked electronically, the less need there will be for personal contact or in-store transactions. Newspapers and other print media will continue to be challenged by readers and advertisers as to their relevance in the twenty-first century. Many have found success by using multiple distribution channels (e.g., print, Internet) to disseminate news and advertising content. The increased power of Internet service providers and those who control Internet "portals," or access points, are influencing increasing numbers of buyers to read, browse, and shop electronically. At the same time, customers expect a satisfactory level of individual attention and service. It is just that the traditional ways of delivering customer satisfaction are giving way to newer, more efficient, and more effective—and better-informed—ways of doing so.

Summary

Direct marketing is an interactive two-way marketing communication system between a marketer and a prospective customer, who is always given a chance to respond. The communication can take place whenever and wherever there is access to communications media. Direct marketing communication is designed to elicit a direct order response, generate sales leads, or generate customer traffic. Direct marketing represents an increasingly important aspect of the integrated marketing communications mix. Direct marketing also can be viewed from a distribution channel perspective, since it represents the zero-level, or shortest, channel between customers and suppliers.

Phenomenal growth in direct marketing is attributable to customers' time constraints, an increase in niche marketing, availability of specialized media and computerized databases, advances in technology and electronic media, and global business expansion.

Direct marketing tools include direct selling (direct mail, catalogs, telemarketing, home or office personal selling, and vending machines), direct-action advertising (direct response in print or broadcast media), and electronic media (television, cable, Internet, facsimile, video, and other media). Media selection is one of the major decisions that must be made by direct marketers, since each medium has its advantages and disadvantages for the product market that is targeted.

The primary objectives of direct marketing are to build relationships with customers and to obtain a direct customer response. Customer relationships are enhanced by customized marketing programs and well-managed databases.

The direct marketing process consists of developing and maintaining customer databases, an interactive marketing system, and a procedure for measuring results. Direct marketing planning should be coordinated with an organization's strategic planning process and should be consistent with other marketing activities.

Accurate, up-to-date customer databases make it possible for direct marketers to dominate a market based on knowledge of their customers' buying habits, motives, lifestyles, and demographics. Databases are used to determine which customers to target and how to reach them (media, message). They are also used to measure the results of a direct marketing campaign. Direct marketing is part of an interactive marketing system of computers, software, databases, and telecommunications technologies.

Although direct marketing is increasing in popularity as a marketing communication and distribution method, there are a number of issues that should be considered. Direct marketing is appealing to consumers and organizational customers who desire speed, convenience, and lower prices—particularly those who are more technologically savvy. Organizations may find the effort required to create and manage databases to be a negative factor, despite their usefulness. Customers may resist direct marketing efforts because they are uncomfortable with interactive technology, prefer hands-on shopping, or are concerned about privacy issues or multilevel marketing techniques. The future of direct marketing is driven by three related factors: databases, technology, and communication.

Questions

1. Describe the direct marketing strategy pursued by Dell Computer Corp., and analyze the reasons for its success. What future changes, if any, do you believe will be made to this strategy based on current trends? Justify your answer.

2. Based on the Direct Marketing Association's definition of direct marketing, identify and give a current example of each of the four key elements of a direct marketing strategy that were described in the chapter.

3. Explain the relationship between direct marketing and (a) the integrated marketing communications mix and (b) channels of distribution.

4. Identify the factors that have contributed to the phenomenal growth of direct marketing, and discuss your predictions for the future of direct marketing (i.e., media, customers, etc.).

5. Assume that you have been given the responsibility of developing a direct marketing campaign for a new type of insurance policy. Discuss the objectives of your campaign and how you will measure the results.

6. Describe and evaluate the pros and cons of each of the direct marketing tools that can be used for (a) direct selling, (b) direct-action advertising, and (c) electronic media. Give examples to illustrate each tool.

7. Discuss the components of the direct marketing process (databases, interactive marketing system, measurement of results) relative to selling books or other publications to an identified market segment.

8. Evaluate the major issues that confront direct marketers, and discuss how you believe these will impact direct marketing strategies in the twenty-first century.

Exercises

1. Conduct a content analysis of a favorite magazine or newspaper, and evaluate the number of direct marketing communications that appear in that issue. Analyze the following factors: (a) ability to reach and influence the intended target market, (b) appropriateness of the medium and the message, and (c) direct-response mechanism used to attain implied objectives.

2. Identify a direct marketing campaign that appears in multiple types of media. Evaluate each medium used in terms of its ability to create synergy with other media and its impact on the reader/viewer/listener. Provide actual examples, if possible.

3. Contact a direct marketer, and learn the process that was followed for a recent campaign. If possible, obtain examples of campaign materials and critique their effectiveness in achieving direct marketing objectives.

Endnotes

1. Erick Schonfeld, "Schwab Puts It All Online," *Fortune* (December 7, 1998), pp. 94–100.

2. Direct Marketing Association, Inc., *1998 Economic Impact: U.S. Direct Marketing Today,* available at *http://www.the-dma.org/services1/libres-ecoimp.*

3. Mary Lou Roberts and Paul D. Berger, *Direct Marketing Management* (Englewood Cliffs, N.J.: Prentice-Hall, 1989), p. 2.

4. Direct Marketing Association, *op. cit.*

5. Alexander Hiam and Charles D. Schewe, *The Portable MBA in Marketing* (New York: John Wiley & Sons, 1992), p. 373; Roberts and Berger, *op. cit.,* p. 4.

6. Maricris G. Briones, "What Technology Wrought: Distribution Channel in Flux," *Marketing News* 33(3) (February 1, 1999), pp. 1, 15.

7. Robert A. Peterson, Sridhar Balasubramanian, and Bart J. Bronnenberg, "Exploring the Implications of the Internet for Consumer Marketing," *Journal of the Academy of Marketing Science* 25(4) (1997), pp. 329-346.

8. Veronica Byrd and Wendy Zellner, "The Avon Lady of the Amazon," *Business Week* (October 24, 1994), pp. 93-96; Melissa Dowling, "Catching the Wave to Japan: U.S. Mail-Order Companies Penetrate Japanese Market," *Catalog Age* 13(2) (February 1996), p. 55; Gregory A. Patterson, "U.S. Catalogers Test International Waters," *Wall Street Journal* (April 19, 1994), p. B1.

9. Ken Gofton, "Direct Action," *Marketing* (October 8, 1998), pp. 26-27.

10. Dom Del Prete, "Direct Mail Pays Big Dividends for Financial Services Marketers," *Marketing News* 31(20) (September 29, 1997), pp. 1, 8.

11. G. Bruce Knecht, "Reader's Digest Faces Marketing Challenge," *Wall Street Journal* (April 24, 1997), p. B22.

12. Direct Marketing Association, *op. cit.,* Catalog Industry Analysis: Key Growth Areas.

13. *Ibid.,* Value of DM Driven Sales by Medium and Market.

14. For further discussion, see Roberts and Berger, *op. cit.,* Chap. 11.

15. B. G. Yovovich, "Webbed Feat," *Marketing News* 32(2) (January 19, 1998), pp. 1, 18.

16. Internet data in this paragraph are taken from Lynn Margherio, Project Director, U.S. Department of Commerce, *The Emerging Digital Economy*, available at *http://www.ecommerce.gov.* This report includes data from research conducted by Morgan Stanley, Forrester Research, leading financial analysts, and other professional sources.

17. Peterson, Balasubramanian, and Bronnenberg, *op. cit.*

18. Michael Krauss, "The Web and the Company Must Work Together," *Marketing News* 32(19) (September 14, 1998), p. 8.

19. Tom Dellecave, Jr., "The 'Net Effect,'" *Sales & Marketing Technology* (March 1996), pp. 17-21, in John E. Richardson (ed.), *Marketing 97/98, Annual Editions* (Sluice Dock, Guilford, Conn.: Dushkin Publishing Group, 1999), pp. 211-215.

20. Roberts and Berger, *op. cit.*, p. 427.

21. Direct Marketing Association, *op. cit., 1998 Economic Impact: U.S. Direct Marketing Today.*

22. Roberts and Berger, *op. cit.*, pp. 5-8.

23. *Ibid.*, pp. 147-148.

24. *Ibid.*, pp. 95-99.

25. Anonymous, *Customer Relationship Management: Practical Applications*, available at *http://www.recsys.com/Relman5.htm.*

26. V. Kasturi Rangan, Benson P. Shapiro, and Rowland T. Moriarity, Jr., *Business Marketing Strategy: Cases, Concepts, and Applications.* (Chicago, Ill.: Irwin, 1995), pp. 573-582.

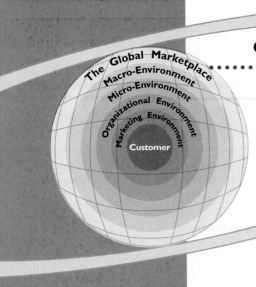

CHAPTER 14

Pricing Strategy

The Role of Price in Strategic Marketing

Product Life Cycle Pricing

Psychological Pricing

Strategic Pricing Models

Pricing Strategy and Break-Even Analysis

Pricing Strategy Decisions: Issues, Problems, and Legal Concerns

Pricing Strategy and IMC

Toyota Camry Pricing

The Camry is Toyota's most popular selling model internationally. When Toyota set the initial price for the 1998 model Camry at a lower price than the 1997 model, it marked the second successive year that a "value" pricing strategy was applied. As one of the major players in the global automobile industry, Toyota realized that competition from other Pacific Rim firms with a lower cost base was becoming more intense. These low-cost competitors were taking aim at the "value" component of the customer's purchasing decision and attempting to add value to their lower-priced models in a manner that would increase their market share.

Toyota's response was to challenge its designers and operations engineers to add product features to the Camry without adding to the costs of production. In fact, since 1995, Toyota has cut $2.5 billion in costs by using fewer parts and stripping waste from production systems. The result was that customers obtained additional product features (benefits) without corresponding increases in prices. Therefore, perceived customer value was enhanced, allowing Toyota to have a competitive advantage in the mind of the customer.

The value decade is upon us. If you can't sell a top-quality product at the world's lowest price, you're going to be out of the game.[1]

Source: Brian Brenner, Larry Armstrong, Kathleen Kerwin, and Keith Naughton, "Toyota's Crusade," *Business Week* (April 7, 1997), pp. 104-114.

Toyota wisely identified that value pricing would allow it to remain competitive in the global auto making industry. The company recognized that customers perceive benefits as having three components: service benefits, brand benefits, and product benefits—and offered its customers increased product benefits. Pricing is certainly one of the most complex and difficult of the strategy-making tasks facing marketing managers.[2] In this chapter we will be discussing the formidable task of formulating pricing strategy for the firm. Prior to this point in the book, it would have been difficult to discuss the multiple issues involved in pricing strategy because marketing managers are required to simultaneously consider the other elements of the marketing mix, which have been discussed in previous chapters. Many of the aspects involved in establishing a pricing strategy depend on managerial decisions made at each of the stages of the marketing planning process.

THE ROLE OF PRICE IN STRATEGIC MARKETING

Price
The monetary amount a buyer pays for a good or service and/or the revenue expectation from a sale.

In order to understand the role of pricing in strategic marketing, we must begin by defining price. Simply stated, **price** is the monetary amount a buyer pays for a good or service. But the real meaning of price is not so simple. Both the buyer and seller have differing views of the meaning of price. An additional complicating factor is *market complexity.* Market complexity is the result of such factors as the proliferation of product/service offerings, the geographic scattering of customers, the segmentation factors operating in most markets, the wide variety of differing conditions affecting market transactions, and the internal pricing conflicts at work in any organization. Market complexity makes setting the right price extremely difficult, yet it is often a key factor in the success of a firm's marketing strategy.[3] Moreover, a firm's pricing strategy must be coordinated with indirect and nonprice competitive strategies. What happens to a firm that promises value at the right price and then does not deliver? "Unless a brand has substance to support its promises, its equity begins to deteriorate," says Marc C. Particelli of Booz, Allen & Hamilton, Inc. An example is Compaq Computer Corp., which in the early 1990s steadfastly maintained premium pricing policy because for years its technologic superiority had justified the policy. However, the increasing "value" of competitive PCs with equivalent quality and technology at lower prices forced Compaq to abandon premium pricing.[4]

Buyer's versus Seller's Point of View

Purchasing power
The money available to spend for the purchase of desired goods or services.

To the ultimate consumer or organizational customer, the price paid for a product represents giving up something of value (money). This is usually viewed as **purchasing power,** because money spent on one purchase cannot be used for some other purchase. For every consumer, this exchange represents a choice process, choosing among alternatives of what to purchase. Perhaps you may recall your own childhood experience when, for the first time, you stood before the candy display at the local convenience store trying to decide what you would buy with the two quarters clutched in your hand. Remember how hard the decision was? Perhaps you can even recall the myriad of conflicting emotions. Regardless of what you finally chose, you may have been reluctant to turn away from the display because buying one item meant that others could not be purchased. As consumers, most of us face these same hard decisions for a lifetime. Even a reseller who buys goods to supply to others views price in this same manner. Paying a price is a choice process of what to buy—and it means giving up something of value.

From the seller's point of view, price can be something quite different. Sellers know that price determines the revenue stream that has a direct impact on profits achieved. Thus, to the selling organization, price is the **revenue expectation** from a sale. Closely related to this revenue expectation viewpoint is the parallel view that price is the **accumulation of costs** incurred in developing, manufacturing, and marketing a product plus some profit margin factor. Financial executives and production personnel most often have this point of view, especially when the firm uses a cost-plus pricing strategy (which will be discussed below). However, marketing personnel must think of price as but one element in the marketing mix and therefore must focus on the total marketing program and how the pricing strategy fits the overall marketing thrust of the organization.

Price is important and cannot be viewed in isolation, especially in highly competitive markets, because it has a direct impact on the other elements of the marketing mix. If a firm's pricing strategy is a significant element of its competitive positioning, and especially if price is a competitive advantage, then price must be viewed as having meaning only in relation to the total marketing program. Therefore, the most appropriate view of price is that it is an integral part of the firm's marketing program, which in turn drives the revenue stream and thus makes profits achievable.

An Example of Pricing Complexity

In many global markets, portable telephones (referred to as "cell phones" or "handi's" in various parts of the globe) are a fast-selling item often desired for their "prestige" value as much as for their communication benefits. When a global Swedish manufacturer such as Ericsson establishes a pricing strategy for an individual marketplace, it is a complex task because of the many marketplace factors that vary from one locale to another. For example, in the U.S. market, Ericsson and all competitors virtually give away the actual cell phone and count on the revenue stream that results from use of the product as their source of income. The telecommunications company that receives the multimonth contract for service must pay a commission or fee to both the manufacturer of the cell phone and to the sales agent who signs up the customer. These long-term service contracts, plus the task of initially programming the cell phone to enable customer use, represent an indirect pricing strategy that must be developed by prior agreement among manufacturer, reseller, and service provider.

Meanwhile, in Australia, Ericsson had to develop a totally different pricing strategy because in this market all cell phones ("handi's") are sold at a price that is independent of the price paid to initially program the product and independent of any long-term service provider contract. Thus Ericsson's cell phone may sell for A$99 to the customer, while the reseller also charges the customer A$49 for initially programming the phone. In addition, the customer must sign a minimum of a 24-month service provider contract that contains minimum monthly fees, as well as an additional fee based on frequency of use. Thus, while the reseller may advertise in Australia that the Ericsson cell phone is priced at only A$99, the real cost to the customer may easily amount to a minimum of A$550 over the 24-

Revenue expectation
The price that determines the revenue stream derived from a sale.

Accumulation of costs
Closely related to revenue expectation, but the parallel view that price is the accumulation of costs involved in developing, manufacturing, and marketing the product plus some profit margin factor.

month period of the service contract required of every purchaser. To the customer, therefore, the total price is A$550, whereas to the reseller the total revenue (price) from the sale may be only A$99, and to the service provider the revenue stream (price) over 24 months will be a minimum of A$451. What is the revenue stream (price) for Ericsson? This depends on the margin available from the sales to the reseller plus whether there are any fees or commissions that accrue from the service contract.

Actual Price

Obviously, many variables affect the actual price a buyer pays. It is virtually impossible for a marketing manager to anticipate and plan for all these different variables. What the marketing manager can do is develop a general approach to pricing strategy or a policy that is consistent with the organizational mission and objectives. Such a pricing approach is flexible and allows for minor changes that will be required to adjust the final buyer's price to the prevailing market conditions. In many firms, this price is called the **base price. Actual price** paid by the consumer then becomes the result of extras added to or discounts deducted from the base price.

We can now state that a firm's pricing strategy consists of three elements:

1. The established base price

2. The relationship between prices of the various items in a product/service line, because such pricing requires that differentials exist between items in a multiple line

3. The specific discount structure used to adjust individual prices to actual market conditions

Pricing Conflicts

Although we have become accustomed to encountering conflicts in developing product strategy, in designing channel strategy, and in creating promotional strategy, we must bluntly note that pricing-strategy disagreements are more heated than in any other area of marketing planning. Perhaps this is so because more executives from a variety of functional areas within a firm are involved in establishing pricing as opposed to other areas of marketing planning. Perhaps it is also so because, as noted earlier, many selling firms use the pricing viewpoint of accumulation of costs. Regardless of the reasons, pricing conflicts arise at the following three levels: within the firm, within the channel system, and between the firm and the business environment (i.e., between the firm and competitors, between the firm and government, and between the firm and customers where ethical considerations may be involved).

Conflicts Within the Firm. There are three types of pricing conflicts that occur within the firm. First, in many firms there is no agreement about the basic function of pricing strategy. Is it to generate sales volume, or is it to produce profits? These two points of view are often incompatible. A second conflict involves individuals within the firm who are concerned with rate of return, payback, or cash flow and who often pressure for high prices because of a concern for high costs

Base price
The general price established to be consistent with the firm's organizational mission and objectives.

Actual price
The result of extras added to or discounts deducted from the base price paid by the consumer.

and diminishing returns on marketing activities.[5] A third conflict involves individuals who are concerned with market share and increasing volume and who tend to pressure for low prices because of the desired long production runs and economies of scale. The second and third types of conflicts can overlap and obviously need to be resolved.

Conflicts Within the Channels. Channel members are both buyers and resellers, and it is these two conflicting roles that may cause disagreement with manufacturers' pricing policies. While acting as buyers, channel members almost always desire to have lower prices. While acting as resellers, however, they often desire to maximize revenue flows, which leads to a desire for high prices. A further conflict relates to resale price maintenance. Although some resellers comply voluntarily with manufacturers' suggested retail prices, other resellers may not because of market conditions.

Conflicts with Competitors. Probably the most obvious, visible, and serious conflicts are conflicts with competitors. In **oligopolistic markets,** this occurs because one firm's prices affect its competitors' sales volumes. In more competitive markets with less product differentiation, pricing strategy may be the key to competitive behavior. However, even in monopolistic markets, competitive pressures may still exist because of potential substitute goods/services or potential competitors.

Oligopolistic markets
Markets where one firm's prices affect its competitors' sales volumes.

Conflicts with Governmental Agencies and Public Policy. A firm's pricing also may result in a conflict with governmental agencies. All pricing strategies must be developed to comply with existing laws and enforcement policies, but what if the result is contrary to the firm's objectives? Pricing that is not legal must be changed, but what about those gray areas that depend on decisions by regulatory agencies or the courts to ascertain legality? In general, a firm will never enjoy a long-term benefit from questionable pricing strategies, and thus such strategies should always be avoided. However, even legal pricing strategies may be viewed as contrary to public policy. Often very visible national or multinational firms who attempt to raise prices find that public opinion will pressure national governments or their agencies to attempt to intervene. One such example is pricing of pharmaceutical products that are viewed as providing a socially desirable benefit. High prices are always subject to public debate and public pressure to ensure that governmental agencies insist on the lowest possible price. In fact, in some countries, the government controls all pricing for pharmaceuticals.

Pricing Strategy as a Competitive Edge

As we move into the twenty-first century, marketing analysts are labeling the 1990s as a decade when pricing became a key competitive weapon. The power of effective pricing strategies to produce results in the marketplace is not equaled by any other component of the marketing mix. Thus pricing must be used with caution because ineffective or improper pricing could effectively destroy an otherwise well-conceived marketing program.[6] There are three essential elements to consider when establishing pricing strategy as a competitive component. The first and most important element is the firm's pricing policy, which defines the kind of pricing strategy to be followed. Regardless of whether the firm is marketing high-, medium-, or low-priced products, it must decide if its specific prices will be above, comparable with, or below competitors' prices. Generally, it is not possible for a firm to have extreme pricing positions. For example, a company would not offer some products or services priced below competitors' while also offering other products priced above competitors'.

The second essential element is the relationship of pricing to other marketing-mix factors. As previously noted, pricing cannot be considered alone; it is a component of the marketing program. Using direct pricing competition may force compliance by competitors, but indirect and non-price-competitive techniques may be more desirable because the competition may not be able to match such activities. The most desirable competitive approach is to include both price and nonprice elements, particularly exceptional customer service or an exceptionally unique offering, in the competitive arsenal.

The third essential element in pricing strategy is the relationship of pricing and the product life cycle. Pricing strategies applicable to each stage in the cycle are significantly different. For example, in the introductory stage, there are two commonly used alternatives to consider: pricing above or below competitive products. The overall span and success of the life cycle are directly dependent on the product's competitive distinctiveness; thus pricing at any stage in the cycle must reflect dynamic customer characteristics and market competitive conditions.

PRODUCT LIFE CYCLE PRICING

Pricing strategy decisions are closely related to the position of the good/service in its life cycle. This section discusses in some detail the pricing strategy that is usually appropriate for each of the stages in the life cycle.

Introductory Stage

The pricing strategy that is appropriate for a new product depends on its degree of distinctiveness (compared with substitutes) and the length of time this distinctiveness is expected to last. If the product has distinctive aspects that are expected to last for more than a few years, then the firm may be able to price at a premium in order to quickly recover development costs and perhaps to maximize shorter-term profits. However, in today's extremely competitive marketplace, it is highly unusual for such a distinctive advantage to last for more than a few months. If the product does not have any distinctive aspects, one should question if the new product should be introduced. However, if it is introduced, it must be priced at or below competing products. This is so because without distinctiveness the product has limited opportunities for success unless it is priced below the competition.

The traditional wisdom is that new products with perishable distinctiveness should be introduced with either a **skimming price** (price above or comparable with the competitive product)[7] or a **penetration price** (price much lower than the competitive product). The choice between skimming and penetration pricing is

Skimming price
A price comparable with or above that of a competitive product.

Penetration price
A price much lower than that of a competitive product.

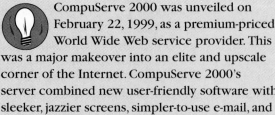

INNOVATE OR EVAPORATE*

CompuServe Pitches Upscale Niche

CompuServe 2000 was unveiled on February 22, 1999, as a premium-priced World Wide Web service provider. This was a major makeover into an elite and upscale corner of the Internet. CompuServe 2000's server combined new user-friendly software with sleeker, jazzier screens, simpler-to-use e-mail, and premium financial and business services. Its aim was to persuade advertisers to stop ignoring CompuServe and pay premium rates for its on-line ads and marketing deals. Since being purchased by America Online (AOL), CompuServe had been in a maintenance mode.

"It's upscale," Myer Berlow, the AOL senior vice-president says of CompuServe. "It's so focused on a different audience that you can get double and triple the mass-market rate for it." Myer suggested that 30 percent of CompuServe's audience had household incomes greater than $100,000, compared with just 21 percent for AOL.

Some media buyers said that despite competition from a host of Web sites that target a similar audience, CompuServe should be able to get some type of premium. But they doubted the premium could be more than 20 to 30 percent above AOL's typical ad rates, which were about $40 for 1000 impressions (hits on the ad).

A pioneer in offering on-line access nearly three decades ago, CompuServe faded from view as the Web experienced dramatic growth. It began to be seen as a backwater for techies and engineers. "Several years ago, everybody knew who CompuServe was," says Jonn Behrman, chief executive of Beyond Interactive, an Ann Arbor,

Michigan, interactive-media buyer. "Now it just doesn't pop up on the radar screen. It's something that failed and lost."

The new pricing and positioning represented a key test of the strategy promoted by AOL's president, Robert Pittman. AOL had 16 million subscribers (compared with 2 million for CompuServe), so Pittman pushed development of a portfolio of other brands of Web server companies to serve niche markets. From 1996 through 1998, AOL made several acquisitions in pursuit of this strategy.

Because in early 1999 CompuServe carried few ads, the first hurdle was to convince advertisers to take a new look at CompuServe 2000. "It's not a service that's top-of-mind," said Mayo Stuntz, Jr., CompuServe's president. "But there is a brand there." CompuServe 2000 subscribers could call up articles from a variety of financial news wires that are not widely marketed to individuals (including Dow Jones Newswires). CompuServe also hosted a variety of finance-oriented discussion groups considered to be a cut above the usual chat room of cyberspace.

Some observers, however, suggested that this may be the cyberspace equivalent of slapping some extra trim on a Chevy and calling it a Cadillac.

*The box title is attributed to James M. Higgins, *Innovate or Evaporate* (Winter Park, FL: New Management Publishing Company, 1995).

Source: Adapted from Thomas E. Weber, "AOL Pitches Upscale Niche in Cyberspace," *Wall Street Journal* (February 22, 1999), pp. B1, B4.

Elasticity of demand
When relatively small changes in price result in large changes in units sold.

based on the expected **elasticity of demand.**[8] Demand is said to be *elastic* when relatively small changes in price result in large changes in units sold. On the other hand, demand is said to be *inelastic* when relatively large changes in price result in small changes in units sold. Thus, if demand is inelastic, a skimming price is appropriate, and if demand is elastic, a penetration price is chosen.

Growth Stage

· · · · · · · · · · · · · · · · · · · ·

Pricing in the growth stage of the life cycle must consider the relationship of the competitors. Because competitors have entered the market, the pricing decision must be based on both maintaining market share and the relationship between pricing and the rest of the marketing mix. Frequently in the growth and early maturity stages, a limited number of firms dominate industry sales. This situation is called an *oligopoly.*

A classic example occurred in the contact lens industry, where Bausch & Lomb, Inc., enjoyed 100 percent of the market for about 3 years after its 1970 innovative introduction. Correctly appraising the situation, Bausch & Lomb used price skimming as its introductory pricing strategy. However, by 1978, when the industry became highly competitive, Bausch & Lomb's market share had dropped to less than 50 percent. In response to this situation, the company announced a significant price reduction (about 25 percent), and its market share recovered to over 60 percent.[9] Generally speaking, when a few firms dominate a market, any major competitor can expect that if it were to raise prices, the competition would not match such a raise, fearing that increased prices would have too dramatic an impact on volumes sold. Conversely, if any major competitor were to reduce prices, the reduction would be quickly matched again, because otherwise the lowest-priced competitor would capture a disproportionately large gain in market share.

The significant factor in such a situation is that no competitor can price unilaterally. Instead, pricing strategy must be developed with special consideration of competitors' pricing tactics and their expected reactions to any price changes initiated. In oligopolistic markets, price stability often occurs because lower prices would cause diminished margins and lost profits for everyone. However, as we saw in the preceding Bausch & Lomb example, the dominant competitor may desire to maintain the largest share of the market in order to maintain lower production costs. Thus decreased margins may be less damaging than lower unit sales volumes. In such situations, a pricing leadership role is often assumed by the competitor with the largest share of the market.

But how should the late-entering competitor price a new product? Even though the innovator firm is in an advantageous position, the late entrant may be able to gain market share. If the new entry has distinctive product features, then pricing at a premium or competitive pricing combined with heavy promotional expenditures may succeed in establishing a position for the late entrant. Conversely, if distinctiveness is lacking, then parity pricing combined with heavy promotional expenditures also may be successful. Papa John's Pizza is an example of a late-entry firm with a product distinctiveness (in this situation, a superior product feature—fresh components versus preprocessed) that wrestled away market share from Pizza Hut by aggressive advertising and other integrated marketing communications (IMC) activities.

Maturity Stage

· · · · · · · · · · · · · · · · · · · ·

When a product's rate of sales growth levels off and begins to decline, the maturity stage has been reached. There are usually a large number of competitors in the market, and product distinctiveness does not exist. Many close-substitute products are available to buyers, and margins have reached low levels. In this situation, no competitor can price very much above or below the prevailing market price. Too low a price may result in a price war that benefits no one, whereas too high a price likely will result in substantial loss of market share. The best examples of this situation can be found in the retailing, fast-food, and airline industries. All are currently highly visible examples.

Pricing in the mature stage also may encounter the entrance of an aggressive price-cutter. These late-entering competitors perceive an opportunity to carve out significant market share by re-establishing prevailing competitive prices at a lower level. The new entrant may introduce a "no frills" version of the product or use modified channel structures, private branding, or some other technique designed to minimize its cost structure, thereby allowing some margin for profits even at the new lower price. Therefore, all competitors in a mature market face constant pressure to lower margins while also often being pressured by rising costs.

Decline Stage
. . . .

Loss leader
A product priced low to attract more buyers.

The decline stage is reached when unit sales volumes have eroded over more than a short term. Frequently, product distinctiveness no longer exists. Some competitors even may face inferior distinctiveness. Marketers of these products often attempt to price just below the market. Sometimes their products may even be priced as a **loss leader** (a product priced low to attract more buyers).[10] However, the continued marketing of such products may be desirable in order to fill out a product line or until a new product is ready to be launched as a replacement. The pricing strategy must be designed to equate with competitors' prices or, if possible, to be just below the market price.

PSYCHOLOGICAL PRICING
. . . .

Psychological price
Price that is supposed to produce sales responses as a result of emotional reactions rather than as a result of objective analysis.

When establishing pricing strategy, the marketer must consider not only objective factors such at the relationship of pricing and the product life cycle but also subjective factors[11] such as psychological pricing. A **psychological price** is one that is supposed to produce sales responses as a result of emotional reactions rather than objective analyses. Although used mostly by retailers, some business-to-business marketers also have used psychological pricing. Three types of price adjustments— odd pricing, prestige pricing, and psychological discounting—are commonly used because of their perceived psychological effects.

Odd Pricing
. . . .

Odd pricing
The practice of establishing resale prices that end in odd numbers.

Odd pricing is the practice of establishing resale prices that end in odd numbers (e.g., $19.97). Visit any retail firm and you will see odd pricing in action. Although all retailers are convinced that odd pricing is effective, there is no commonly recognized body of research that validates this viewpoint. However, although used

IT'S LEGAL BUT IS IT ETHICAL?

Fingerhut's Credit Pricing for Low-Income Customers

Recently, the credit-card industry has focused its direct marketing efforts on the previously ignored low-income consumers. This is a difficult market characterized by very high interest rates, tenacious collectors, and loads of bad debt. Fingerhut Corp. began developing this segment about 50 years ago using catalogs and selling almost entirely on credit. In September 1998, however, a Minnesota state judge ruled that some of Fingerhut sales violate the state's usury law, which limits interest on installment sales to 8 percent. The judge also found that Fingerhut misled customers by advertising a "one-month free trial period" while charging interest, although not requiring a payment during the first month of the installment sale. Fingerhut denied all the charges, claiming that its sales fell under an exception to the usury law known as a "time-price sale" and that it did not make loans that involved interest charges. Instead, Fingerhut offered customers two prices: a cash price or an installment (delayed-payment) price, and customers were free to choose which price they wanted to pay.

Today Fingerhut sells everything from cookware to coveralls, with sales totaling $1.5 billion in 1998 to customers with average household incomes of $27,700. The company also has developed its own list of 30 million names, even though Fingerhut is little known outside its targeted low-income groups. This database includes much of the 40 percent of U.S. households with the lowest incomes—the so-called sub-prime lending targets. For decades, lists like the one developed by Fingerhut had been valuable to lenders for the purpose of not lending to these people. But now the consumer-loan industry, lead by Citigroup, Sears, Roebuck and Co., Bank One Corp., and Household International, Inc., sees them as growth opportunities. Kathy Madison, vice-president of marketing at the Household Finance Corp. unit of Household International, says, "Finding profitable customers continues to be one of the greatest challenges of this business."

But it's a tough market. For example, Fingerhut has about 11 million customers who at one time or another have not paid for their purchases. Generally speaking, Fingerhut uses a high end of the competitive pricing strategy combined with a 24.9 percent interest rate. In September of 1998, Fingerhut was experiencing a delinquency rate of 21.9 percent on its merchandise loans compared with just 6.8 percent at Sears (and Sears views this as too high). As a result, Fingerhut set aside $260 million to cover such losses in 1998. However, on the positive side, Fingerhut's customers respond to card offers five times more frequently than the industry response rate of 1.3 percent, which reduces marketing costs. And almost all of Fingerhut's customers carry a balance and incur finance charges.

Will Lansing, president of Fingerhut, says, "We feel good about what we do." The company offers people spurned by other lenders a way to buy things they could not otherwise afford; high margins are necessary to cover the extra risk. However, as credit has become more widely available and more reasonably priced for lower-income groups, such consumers have found new options and new skepticism.

Source: Joseph B. Cahill, "Credit Companies Find Tough Rival at Bottom of Consumer Market," *Wall Street Journal* (December 29, 1998), pp. A1, A4.

FIGURE 14.1

Market-Based Pricing Model

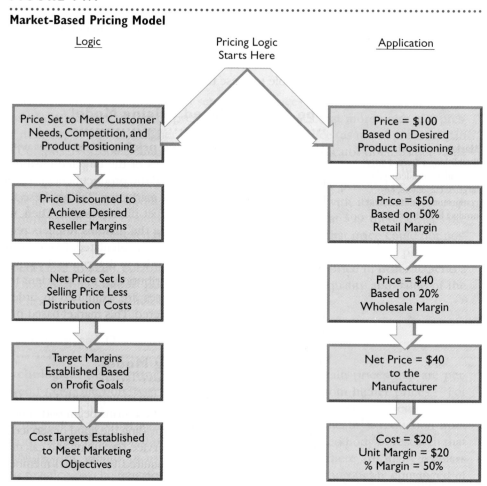

Source: Market-Based Management Strategies by Best, Roger, © 1997. Reprinted by permission of Prentice-Hall, Inc., Upper Saddle River, NJ.

in prices. But because the cost of manufacturing is already established, the resulting sales are at reduced margins and the expected profit levels are never reached. If the pricing process had begun with a market focus (customers, competitors, and product position), the firm would recognize that cost reductions were needed to achieve desired margins and profit levels.

The Value-Based Pricing Model

As illustrated in Figure 14.3, the **value-based pricing** model recognizes that buyers make a comparison between a good's or service's perceived reasonable price (called the **reference product**) and the actual price of the good or service that the con-

Value-based pricing
A pricing strategy that maximizes customers' expected value perceptions.

Reference product
A purchased product for which customers can recall perceptions of price paid and benefits derived.

FIGURE 14.2
....
Cost-Plus Pricing Model

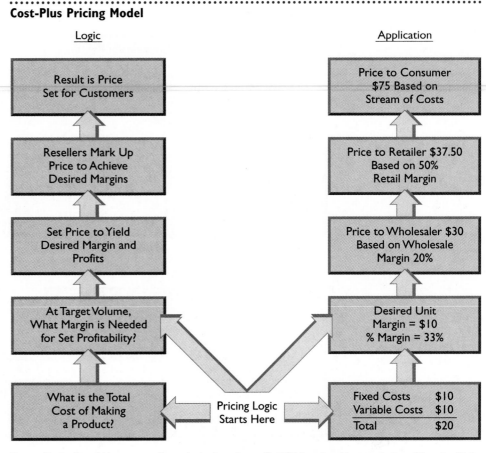

Logic   Application

Result is Price
Set for Customers

Price to Consumer
$75 Based on
Stream of Costs

Resellers Mark Up
Price to Achieve
Desired Margins

Price to Retailer $37.50
Based on 50%
Retail Margin

Set Price to Yield
Desired Margin and
Profits

Price to Wholesaler $30
Based on Wholesale
Margin 20%

At Target Volume,
What Margin is Needed
for Set Profitability?

Desired Unit
Margin = $10
% Margin = 33%

What is the Total
Cost of Making
a Product?

Pricing Logic
Starts Here

Fixed Costs $10
Variable Costs $10
Total $20

Source: Market-Based Management Strategies by Best, Roger, © 1997. Reprinted by permission of Prentice-Hall, Inc., Upper Saddle River, NJ.
....

Focal product
A product being considered for purchase.

Benefits comparison
A customer comparison of perceived benefits from a focal product relative to a reference product.

sumer is considering for purchase (called the **focal product**). The model assumes that a variety of contextual factors are used by potential purchasers in order to determine perceptions about the product or service attributes of both the reference product and the focal product. Some of these contextual factors could be brand recognition or brand equity, organizational image, reseller or retailer reputation, and past experiences.

Based on the consumer's perceptions of the reference product and focal product, he or she performs a **benefits comparison** to establish two additional perceptions. First, the consumer decides on the reasonableness of a price for the reference product; then he or she forms a perception of the quality of the focal product. For example, well-developed organizational images such as those of IBM, Intel, Microsoft, or Xerox, or reseller reputations such as those of Wal-Mart, Kmart, Sears, and Target, or brand equity such as Tide, Kleenex, Frigidaire, and Sunkist all are used by customers as indicators of quality.

FIGURE 14.3

....

Value-Based Pricing Model

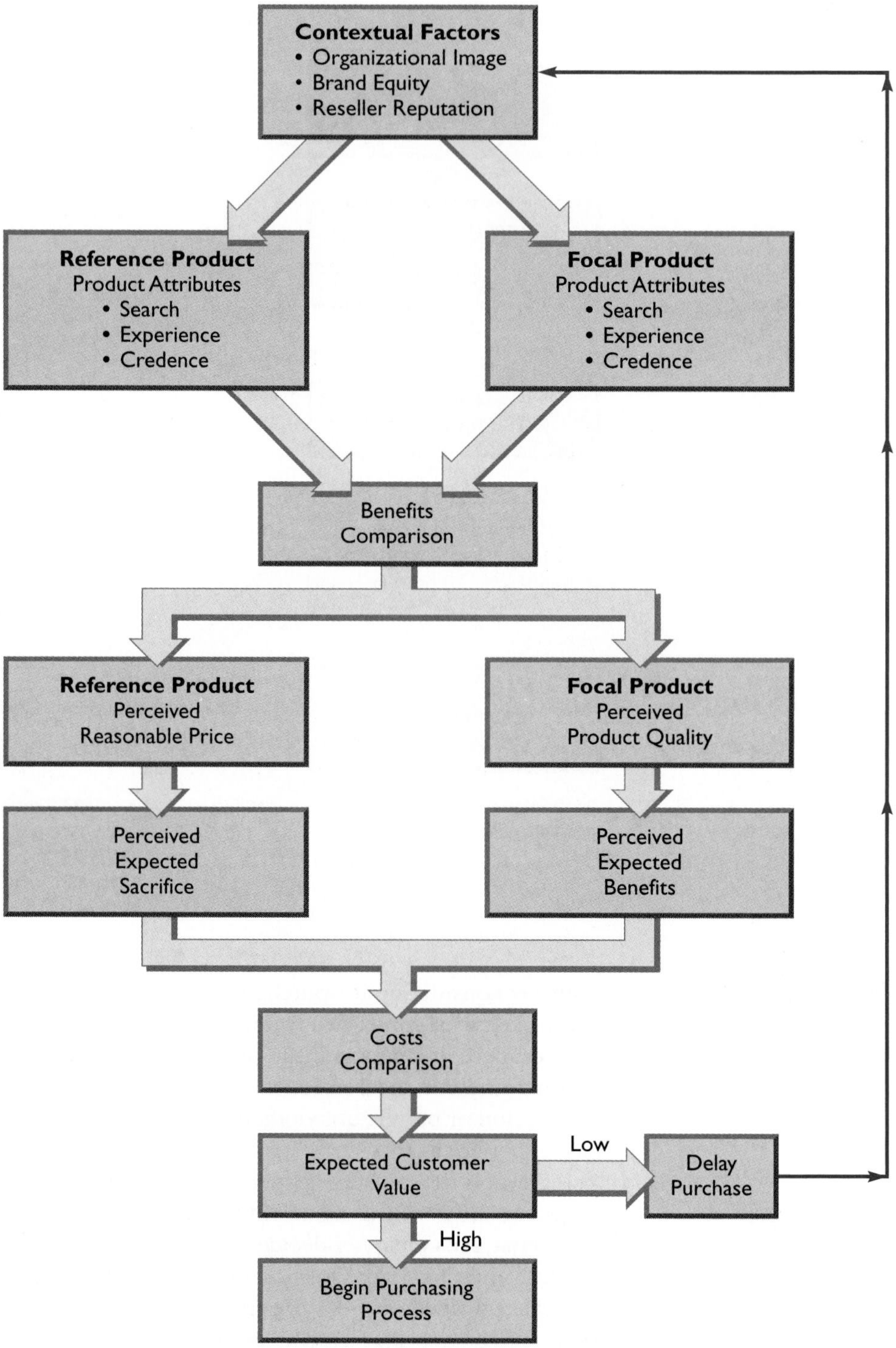

Source: Adapted from Earl Naumann, *Creating Customer Value* (Cincinnati, Ohio: Thomson Executive Press, 1995).

....

The greater the perceived risks involved in the purchase, the more important become the contextual factors that work as extrinsic cues for the customer. In many service purchases, because there is such an intangible component involved, these contextual factors assume an even greater importance. In conjunction with the good or service attributes, contextual factors and stored attitudes based on past experiences combine to create the perceptual basis on which customers rely to establish both their perceived quality of the focal product and their perceived reasonable price for the reference product.

For example, a customer shopping for shoes initially satisfies the contextual factors by visiting a retailer satisfactorily shopped previously and by examining shoes of a nationally advertised brand with a superior reputation. Trying on a pair of shoes, the customer compares (focal product) attributes with attributes of shoes previously purchased (reference product). This is the "benefits comparison" process (noted in the model), such as: Will they be comfortable, stylish, durable, and so forth? Next, the customer recalls perceptions of price and value received from reference products (past purchases), perhaps remembering having paid $80 the last time this brand was purchased and enjoying comfortable, long-lasting, and stylish benefits. These recalled perceptions are compared with similar perceptions now being formed about the focal product (trial shoes). Perhaps the current price is $95, but the design is more appealing and the customer expects equal durability. This involves the customer in both the "costs comparison" process and the "expected customer value" aspects of the model. Although the price is higher, the durability is equal and the stylishness is superior, so the customer's expected value is high and a purchase is made.

The next stage of the process involves the development of a third set of two parallel perceptions as a result of the benefits comparison stage of the process. One of the two parallel perceptions involves the customer establishing a perception of what is the expected sacrifice based on the reference product's perceived reasonable price. The other parallel perception involves using the already developed perceived quality of the focal product as the basis for developing a perception of the expected benefits. Then the customer performs the cost comparison based on the two parallel perceptions—it is a comparison made between the perceived expected sacrifice and the perceived expected benefits. The result of this comparison is the **expected value** that the customer perceives in the purchase situation. If this expected value is high, a purchase usually is initiated. Conversely, if this expected value is low, the purchase is usually declined. The key to understanding this process is realizing that the purchaser is trading off the known benefits of previously used products against the perceived expected value (benefits) of the next purchase.

Expected value
Results from a benefits comparison; must be high for a purchase to occur.

The potential customer's expected value is the result of comparing the expected benefits to expected sacrifice. This sacrifice may include total life cycle costs of use; however, by increasing expected benefits while holding expected sacrifice constant, sellers are able to enhance perceived customer value and thereby increase the probability of a sale (recall the Toyota strategy in the opening scenario). In addition, sellers could decrease the expected sacrifice while holding expected benefits constant, which also results in enhanced customer value. This is the approach used by several retail chains that introduced "everyday low prices" as a competitive pricing strategy in the early 1990s. Whatever methods are used to increase expected customer value, it is imperative to keep clearly in mind that expected customer value is a dynamic concept.[14] As Martyn Straw, an adman at Geer, DuBois, Inc., the agency for Jaguar Ltd., says, "value is the new prestige."[15] What today constitutes a good value may tomorrow or next week or next month become a poor value. If we accept the premise that the greater the expected value, the greater is the willingness to buy, then we must agree with Earl Naumann's observation that sometimes "the sale [price] is just too good to pass up. The consumer may stock up [buy] to 'save money.'"[16]

PRICING STRATEGY AND BREAK-EVEN ANALYSIS

Although break-even analysis is often viewed as an accounting concept, it is also an extremely useful way to evaluate the profit potential and risk associated with a pricing strategy. We will examine from a marketing viewpoint the usefulness of calculating break-even volume and break-even market share.

Break-Even Volume

Break-even
When net profits equal zero.

It is useful to calculate the break-even volume for any planned pricing strategy (and marketing plan). Since **break-even** occurs when net profits are zero, what number of units needs to be sold to break even? For example, if we produce a unit of product whose selling price is $100 with a variable cost per unit of $50, the result is a margin of $50. Ordinary business activity incurs fixed expenses (marketing and direct operating expenses) of $5 million. Calculating the break-even volume would result in an answer of 100,000 units.

$$
\begin{aligned}
\text{Net profits} &= \text{volume (unit price} - \text{unit variable cost)} - \text{marketing expenses} \\
&\quad + \text{operating expenses} \\
0 &= \text{volume (\$100} - \$50) - \$2 \text{ million} + \$3 \text{ million} \\
\text{Volume} &= (\$2 \text{ million} + \$3 \text{ million})/(\$100 - \$50) \\
&= \$5 \text{ million}/\$50 \\
&= 100{,}000 \text{ units}
\end{aligned}
$$

We see from this example that break-even volume is the number of units needed to cover fixed expenses based on a specific margin per unit sold. This break-even calculation can be calculated graphically as indicated in Figure 14.4 but can be computed more directly with the following formula:

$$
\text{Break-even volume} = \frac{\text{fixed expenses}}{\text{margin per unit}}
$$

The lower the break-even volume is relative to the expected sales volumes for a firm and its manufacturing capacity, the greater will be the profit potential and the lower will be the risk of a price strategy that does not achieve the firm's planned-for profit levels.

FIGURE 14.4
....
Break-Even Analysis

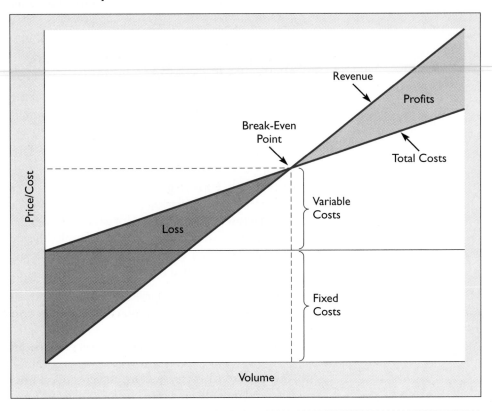

Break-Even Market Share and Risk
....

Determining the break-even volume is normally an unconstrained calculation; therefore, the reasonableness of the volume figure requires additional insight and calculations to afford understanding. In contrast, market-share calculations are constrained and must fall between zero and 100 percent. Thus, if a market analyst calculates a break-even market share, this will provide a better basis from which to judge profit potential and risk. This computation of break-even market share requires the analyst to divide the break-even volume of the firm by the size of the target market, as shown below:

$$\text{Break-even market share} = \frac{\text{break-even volume (in units)}}{\text{market demand (units)}} \times 100$$

If in our example the total market demand for the industry were 1 million units per year, then the break-even market share would be 10 percent when the firm's break-even volume is 100,000 units. If the firm's targeted market share is only 5 percent, then the risk of achieving sales below break-even is small. However, if the targeted market share is 15 percent, then the risk of not achieving break-even sales is much greater, and the pricing strategy may need to be re-examined.

PRICING STRATEGY DECISIONS: ISSUES, PROBLEMS, AND LEGAL CONCERNS

Each step in the pricing process may present management with complex issues and problems that require sophisticated analytical techniques. Some of the major issues involved in establishing an effective pricing strategy and some methods for resolving these issues are discussed next.

Product-Line Pricing

Many manufacturers produce a line of products designed to meet the needs of their various targeted customer groups. For example, the manufacturer of power lawn maintenance equipment may offer the following list of seven major products in its line, with some containing a number of models:

Four staggered-wheel rotary-engine mower models priced from $280 to $480
Four in-line small-wheeled rotary-engine mower models priced from $300 to $500
Three in-line large-rear-wheeled rotary-engine mower models priced from $375 to $550
Four heavy-duty rotary-engine mower models priced from $490 to $600
Three riding mowers priced from $900 to $2200
Four commercial/institutional rotary-engine mowers priced from $1100 to $4000
Three edge-trimmer models priced from $95 to $195

In order to effectively market a line of products for a particular market segment, pricing differentials must be established for each item in the line. These are all differentials from the base price. The size of the differential established often depends on the differences in costs, product features, and forecasted volume expectations, as well as customers' responses. However, the line also may include one or more promotional items that will be sold at less than average total costs in order to attract potential customers. Resellers would be encouraged to trade up customers to better-performing, higher-priced equipment to achieve higher profits (assuming that this is done in a legal and ethical manner).

The theoretical goal in setting product-line prices is to improve the marketability and profitability of the entire line.[17] However, other pricing goals are to be competitive, to satisfy user needs, and also to satisfy resellers' needs—all of which may require flexibility and willingness to compromise. For example, many retailers use a pricing method known as **price lining.** The merchant may set pricing differentials that are applied to all items sold, such as the following prices for six different levels in a line of women's dresses (which vary in terms of design, quality of materials, and construction):

Price lining
When a merchant sets price differentials for each model (or variation) in a line of products.

$49.95 $69.95 $89.95 $119.95 $149.95 $199.95

Price lining simplifies the customer's decision by holding constant one key variable in the final selection of style and brand within a line. The customer knows that all dresses sold at $49.95 will be similar in quality—even though the styles and colors may be different. The customer also knows that the higher-priced dresses will be of higher quality.

Manufacturers also use price lining to meet resellers' needs for price lining and to be profitable at the various price levels. This is an excellent example of market-driven pricing. And although price lining is less common in other areas of marketing, it is this pressure of both consumers and resellers that dictates the pricing alternatives that are open to any manufacturer. This market pressure also reaffirms why a cost-plus pricing process may be dysfunctional.

Structuring Discounts

Establishing a set of discounts to adjust the base price for variations in product offerings, customer expectations, and competitive activity constitutes the pricing structure of a firm.[18] Discounts (and extras) can be designed to apply to almost any pricing situation. A number of typical situations exist, and these are discussed in the following paragraphs.

Trade Discounts. A customary practice that developed over a number of years is the granting of discounts based on a customer's position in the channel of distribution. These discounts are usually referred to as **trade discounts** (or *functional discounts*). The various channel (reseller) positions that are regularly granted discounts include retailer (dealer), jobber (middleman who buys from manufacturers and sells to retailers), and wholesaler (distributor). Discounts granted to resellers for performing their usual tasks as channel members are granted exclusively to all resellers who are categorized as belonging to that specific trade category. For example, if a wholesaler qualifies for a specific discount, then another reseller category such as a retailer will never be granted the discount regardless of how large and important that retailer becomes. Since the various categories of resellers do not theoretically compete with each other, these discounts traditionally have been viewed as not having a restraining effect on competition. Thus they are seen as acceptable from a legal standpoint. Of course, the large-volume and therefore powerful retailer mentioned earlier will negotiate other forms of discounts and concessions from the manufacturer to compensate for not being granted additional trade discount categories.

Quantity Discounts. A common discount granted by many sellers is one based on orders for large volumes. Generally, two types of volume discounts are negotiable: cumulative and noncumulative. **Cumulative discounts** are granted on the total volume of purchases made by a single customer over some designated time period, such as a financial year or a calendar quarter year. The negotiated size of the discount is usually based on past volumes purchased or on expected volumes. **Noncumulative discounts** are based only on the quantity purchased in a specific order.

Important legal requirements must be met when volume discounts are negotiated. The cumulative quantity discount is difficult to defend on the basis of cost savings, and without this factor, it may be in violation of the Robinson-Patman Act,

Trade discounts
Discounts granted to customers based on their position (categorization) within the channel of distribution.

Cumulative discounts
Quantity discounts granted on the total volume of purchases made by a single customer over some designated time period (often a year).

Noncumulative discounts
Granted to a customer based only on the quantity in a specific single order.

if the planned pricing discounts are not available to customers who expect such reductions as a result of IMC activities, again the sale will not be successful. Of course, the availability of the product at the planned locations is also important. All the components of the marketing mix must be coordinated in order for special IMC activities to achieve maximum success.

Summary

Price is the monetary amount a buyer pays for a good or service. However, both the buyer and seller have different views on the meaning of price. Pricing conflicts occur within a firm because of differing views of the role of price, within the channels because of the differing needs of buyers and reseller, and within the environment—including competitors, governmental agencies, and public policy.

Pricing strategy decisions are closely related to the position of the good or service in the product life cycle. In the introduction stage, the appropriate pricing strategy depends on the product's degree of distinctiveness. In the growth stage, the pricing strategy must focus on competitors' pricing tactics. As a product matures, pricing tends to stabilize as a result of the similarity of products in the competitive environment. During the decline stage, pricing tends to be lower to attract more buyers or until a replacement product can be introduced.

A psychological price is one that is supposed to produce sales responses as a result of emotional reactions. Odd pricing is the practice of establishing resale prices ending in odd numbers. Prestige pricing is the practice of setting high prices for products with unique or unusual distinctiveness. Psychological discounting is the practice of using certain prices that are perceived to be markdowns from higher prices.

Pricing strategy became increasingly important through the 1990s as a competitive factor. Three strategic approaches to pricing models are market-based pricing, cost-plus pricing, and value-based pricing. Market-based pricing is based on the needs of the target customer, the features of competitive products, and the specific product benefits the firm is marketing. Cost-plus pricing is based on the desired profit margin plus the costs of making and distributing the product. Value-based pricing is based on the concept that customers' willingness to buy is directly related to their perceptions of expected value.

Break-even analysis also relates to pricing strategy. This accounting concept is an extremely useful way to evaluate the profit potential and risk associated with a particular pricing strategy.

A variety of pricing issues, problems, and legal concerns have an impact on a firm's overall marketing strategy, including various discounting methods such as trade, quantity, promotional, and location discounts. It is important to ensure that all pricing decisions fit into the overall marketing plan, are harmonized with the entire marketing mix, and are integrated and coordinated with IMC activities.

Questions

1. A pricing strategy called *skimming* involves charging a high price to early adopters on the premise that they highly value the product. Later the price is dropped. What are the possible negative aspects of price skimming?

2. When videotapes of movies were first sold to the public, they were priced at about $80, but currently, they are priced as low as $5. If a penetration pricing strategy had been used, what do you think would have happened? Who benefited from the early pricing strategy?

3. What is the role of break-even analysis in pricing strategy?

4. Contrast and compare market-based pricing methods with cost-plus pricing methods. What are some of the criticisms of using cost-plus pricing? Do you agree with these criticisms?

5. Explain value-based pricing methods with special concern about "expected value."

6. What is the relationship between pricing strategy and the other aspects of the marketing strategy?

7. How would you describe the relationship between pricing strategy and IMC activities?

8. Explain the differences between cumulative discounts and noncumulative discounts.

9. Explain the difference between uniform delivered pricing and FOB pricing.

Exercises

1. Visit a local clothing specialty store (for either men's or women's apparel), and without questioning any employee, inspect price tags on the merchandise and decide if the store is using psychological pricing. Then attempt to figure out what price-lining strategy is being used (if any) and what the price break points are. Write down your findings for later reference. Next, ask an employee (or the manager or owner, if possible) what the pricing policy is and if the store uses price lining. Make a comparison of your own independently developed figures with those provided by the store. As a closing item, ask if the store uses psychological pricing of any kind.

2. Choose three local mobile phone service providers to telephone. Ask each for an explanation of the costs of their services. Take notes while talking to each service provider, and also complete your notes after the conversation ends. Now compare your notes and be prepared to share your findings with the class, including which service you believe offers the "best" prices.

3. Visit at least three competing supermarkets and record the shelf prices for the same 10 items at each location (or choose more than 10 items if you like). In your list of items, be certain to include 1 gallon of whole milk, 1 pound of bananas, 1 pound of T-bone (or porterhouse) steak, 1 pound of ground beef (hamburger), 1 pound of butter, one standard-sized can of Niblets brand corn, one 2-liter bottle of regular Coca-Cola, and 1 pound of fresh tomatoes. Compare the prices you find and determine if there is any difference in the pricing strategies being used by the different supermarkets.

Endnotes

1. "Fortune Cookies: Management Wit and Wisdom," *Fortune* magazine, edited by Alan Deutschman (New York: Vintage Books, 1993), p. 28.

2. Useful references on the general topic of pricing are Gerard Tellis, "The Price Elasticity of Selective Demand: A Meta-Analysis of Econometric Models of Sales," *Journal of Marketing Research* (November 1988), pp. 331–341; and Thomas Nagle and Reed Holder, *The Strategy and Tactics of Pricing* (Englewood Cliffs, N.J.: Prentice-Hall, 1995).

3. Michael V. Marn and Robert L. Rosiello, "Managing Price, Gaining Profit," *Harvard Business Review* (September–October 1992), pp. 84–94.

4. Christopher Power, Walecia Konrad, Alice Z. Cuneo, James B. Treece, and bureau reports, "Value Marketing: Quality, Service and Fair Pricing Are the Keys to Selling in the '90s," *Business Week* (November 11, 1991), pp. 132–140.

5. Bob Donath, "Promise 'em Anything, But Give 'em a Price," *Marketing News* (January 18, 1998), p. 5.

6. Thomas Nagle, "Make Pricing a Key Driver of Your Marketing Strategy," *Marketing News* (November 9, 1998), p. 4.

7. For a discussion of price skimming, see David Besanko and Wayne Winston, "Optimal Price Skimming by a Monopolist Facing Rational Consumers," *Management Science* (May 1990), pp. 555–567.

8. For a summary of elasticity studies, see Dominique M. Hanssens, Leonard J. Parsons, and Randall L. Schultz, *Market Response Models: Econometric and Time Series Analysis* (Boston: Kluwer Academic Publishers, 1990), pp. 187–191.

9. See "Bausch & Lomb: Hardball Pricing Helps It to Regain Its Grip on Contact Lenses," *Fortune* (July 16, 1984), p. 78.

10. Vicki Clift, "'Loss Leaders' Not Just for Retailers Anymore," *Marketing News* (February 1, 1999), p. 7.

11. K. N. Rajendran and Gerard J. Tellis, "Contextual and Temporal Components of Reference Price," *Journal of Marketing* (January 1994), pp. 22–34.

12. Christopher Farrell *et al.*, "Stuck! How Companies Cope When They Can't Raise Prices," *Business Week* (November 15, 1993), pp. 146–155.

13. *Ibid.*

14. Alexander Hiam and Charles D. Schewe, *The Portable MBA in Marketing* (New York: John Wiley & Sons, 1992), p. 314.

15. Power et al., *op. cit.*

16. Earl Naumann, *Creating Customer Value* (Cincinnati, Ohio: Thomson Executive Press, 1995), p. 118.

17. See David J. Reibstein and Hubert Gatignon, "Optimal Product Line Pricing: The Influence of Elasticities and Cross-Elasticities," *Journal of Marketing Research* (August 1984), p. 259.

18. Please note that the pricing structure may include extras as well as discounts. An *extra* is a charge added to the base price to compensate the seller for the cost of unusual buyer requirements. For example, if a special packaging or handling process is required, or if prepriced labels are requested, then unless the buyer has significant purchasing power to offset the additional costs, the seller would attempt to add on an extra charge.

19. Legal title to goods priced FOB passes to the purchaser when the merchandise is accepted by the carrier, and the purchaser is liable for all transportation costs incurred.

20. Richard Gibson, "With Egg on Its Face, McDonald's Cuts the 55-Cent Specials to Breakfast Only," *Wall Street Journal* (June 4, 1997), p. B7.

PART FOUR

Managing Marketing Efforts

15. Control and Measurement of Marketing Performance
16. The Marketing-Oriented Organization

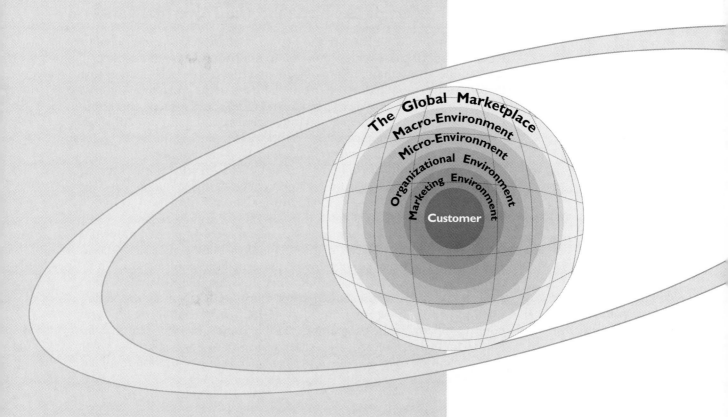

The Global Marketplace
Macro-Environment
Micro-Environment
Organizational Environment
Marketing Environment
Customer

CHAPTER 15

Control and Measurement of Marketing Performance

Controlling Marketing Efforts

Levels of Analysis

Measuring Performance

While some marketers, using old "tried and true" approaches, are facing a crisis, innovative practitioners are meeting the challenge. With a more comprehensive approach to productivity—effective efficiency—marketers using better measurement techniques, more sensible strategies, and more effective systems of monitoring and evaluating productivity will win the day.[1]

Measuring Performance in the Toy Business: Noodle Kidoodle Takes on Barbie® and the Power Rangers®

Despite "Furby® fever" during the 1998 toy-selling season, traditional toy retailers complained about a shortage of hot products on the market. Sales results show that kids are outgrowing the simple mass-market toys that previously dominated the toy market (e.g., dolls and action figures) at much younger ages. Today's kids demand more sophisticated entertainment (e.g., sports equipment, computer games), and many stop buying toys altogether. The impact of this trend was felt during the 1998 holiday selling season, when most toy retailers "make their numbers" for the year. Same-store sales for the 704 domestic outlets of Toys 'R' Us Inc., the largest toy store retailer, dropped 7 percent from the previous year. Sales increased only a modest 2 percent during that same time for Kay-Bee Toys, a subsidiary of Consolidated Stores, Inc.

On the basis of 1998 performance, analysts recommended only one toy stock in the first quarter of 1999: Noodle Kidoodle (ticker:NKID), a chain of 42 stores that specialize in educational toys and software. In comparison with Toys 'R' Us and Kay-Bee Toys, Noodle Kidoodle's same-store holiday sales were up 12 percent. During 1998, Noodle Kidoodle's stock surged 153 percent, from a low of $3\frac{1}{4}$ to $9\frac{1}{2}$, reaching $11\frac{5}{8}$ at one point. Company plans for opening 12 more outlets in 1999 caused analysts to up their predicted stock price from $12 to $14 a share for 1999.[1]

Noodle Kidoodle's excellent performance is due to the following key success factors:

- *Industry and market.* The company operates in the only high-growth segment of the toy industry.
- *Merchandise appeal.* The company's product assortment (educational software, videos, books, science kits, puzzles) appeals both "to kids looking for entertainment beyond GI Joe and Barbie and to anxious yuppie parents desperate to give Junior an intellectual boost in a hypercompetitive society."
- *Location, location, location.* Noodle Kidoodle's stores are mostly located in affluent suburbs in the northeastern, southern, and midwestern United States.
- *Consumer lifestyle.* Noodle Kidoodle's stores appeal to parents and children who want to turn shopping into "quality time."
- *Shopping as entertainment.* The 8000-square-foot stores are more intimate than an impersonal Kmart or Toys 'R' Us and larger than typical specialty shops. Stores are "well lit, carpeted, and brightly decorated." There are story times, clowns, and musicians. As CEO Stanley Greenman says, "We want the trip to Noodle Kidoodle to be fun in and of itself."
- *Service and customer convenience.* Shelves are placed where children can reach them, salespeople are well trained, and gift-wrapping is free.

- *Try-before-you-buy policy.* In addition to frequent product demonstrations, children can play with the toys, run the computer software, and look at videos before deciding what to buy.

Other privately held companies, such as Imaginarium and Store of Knowledge, follow similar concepts, but Noodle Kidoodle is the only publicly traded toy retailer following this format. There is no indication that the major toy retailers will make any radical changes in their product mix to imitate Noodle Kidoodle, where over half the merchandise is not even available at the mass-market stores. The reason is that superstores like Toys 'R' Us are "designed to compete in a high-volume, low-cost, low-service arena" and cannot afford to devote the shelf space and personnel necessary to sell more sophisticated products.

Noodle Kidoodle's 1998 revenues were just under $100 million—a mere "dollhouse next to Toys 'R' Us's $11 billion mansion." At the same time, Toys 'R' Us slipped from number 2 in 1997 to number 10 in 1998 on *Fortune* magazine's list of America's most admired specialty retailers. The winds of change are having an impact on consumer lifestyles, products that are consistent with these lifestyles, and the fortunes of the manufacturers and retailers who are responsible for satisfying the demands of the marketplace.

Sources: Jeremy Kahn, "A Toy-Stock Story for Value Investors," *Fortune* (March 1, 1999), p. 256; and Eryn Brown, "America's Most Admired Companies," *Fortune* (March 1, 1999), p. F3.

As the opening quote indicates, marketing must be both effective and efficient. The importance of marketing and the size of marketing budgets have grown in the face of increasingly higher levels of worldwide competition. Because marketing activities generate revenues, profitability, and visibility, marketing budgets have not been as vulnerable to cost cutting as some other functional areas of a business. In discussing the productivity crisis in today's businesses, Sheth and Sisodia observe that although marketing represents the largest *discretionary* spending area in most companies, it is also an area where many companies would like to devote even more resources. These authors believe that this situation will not persist and see clear indications that CEOs are demanding greater accountability from marketing than ever before.[2]

Throughout this book, the focus has been on marketing operations in a rapidly changing global environment. This chapter addresses the need for accountability in marketing, with a focus on performance and the need for strategic control of marketing efforts at the business-unit level. Assessment of functional level performance was discussed in other chapters in the context of integrated marketing communications (IMC), pricing, marketing intelligence, and other topics.

Excellence in marketing is goal-directed and is driven by the quest for satisfied customers and efficient, effective, and profitable operations. Marketing experts constantly attempt to identify the key success factors that characterize top performers. In general, most of the market leaders emphasize planning and control; use capital, human resources, and technology efficiently and effectively; are market share leaders; and know their markets well. Dynamic, successful marketers obtain synergies from the relationship between performance, excellence, and power. Table 15.1 presents a summary of selected top-performing global firms and most-admired U.S. companies that operate in a variety of industries.

The most innovative and successful marketers prosper because of their ability to manage and use information about their internal operations and external environments. They continuously monitor uncertain and volatile environments that are characterized by intensified competition, industry consolidation, demanding customers, powerful suppliers, and shifting channel power. They develop successful strategies based on an informed analysis of their markets and their own operating results.

On the other hand, a lack of understanding of events in the marketing environment can have a negative impact on profitability and customer satisfaction. Several well-known marketers got "off track" with their strategies and suffered losses in revenues and earnings over the past decade.

Dayton-Hudson Corp. has been recognized as a successful, well-managed retailer for several decades. However, its Mervyn's apparel and softgoods chain experienced difficulties in 1987. Company executives identified the problem as one of execution rather than strategy and were challenged to develop marketing strategies that would get them back on track and keep them there. The company made a major turnaround following the October 1987 stock market crash and a hostile takeover raid by the Dart Group. By 1989, Dayton-Hudson's earnings, operating margins, and stock price had returned to solid growth. The turnaround was accomplished in part by emphasizing Mervyn's merchandising and purchasing rather than its previous focus on growth and opening new stores. Mervyn's also created a quality control team and undertook a multimillion-dollar store remodeling program. As a result, operating margins nearly doubled.

In other actions, Dayton-Hudson equipped its Target stores with electronic scanners to improve customer checkout efficiency and inventory control. This decision increased Target's sales per square foot ($198 compared with Kmart's $148) and operating margin. This type of management response to performance indicators has earned Dayton-Hudson Corp. and its subsidiaries many accolades as one of the top retailers in the United States. The company was ranked fifth among general merchandisers and one hundred and seventh among the largest firms throughout the world in *Fortune*'s 1998 Global 500 ranking, third among general merchandisers in *Fortune*'s 1999 list of America's most admired companies based on its corporate reputation for eight key attributes of success, and fourth among discount and fashion retailers in *Business Week*'s 1998 Industry Rankings of the Standard & Poor's 500.[3]

TABLE 15.1

Top-Performing Global Firms, 1997, and Most-Admired U.S. Companies, 1998

a. The Fortune Global 500: The World's Largest Corporations

Rank	Company	Revenues, $mil	Profits, $mil	Assets, $mil	Stockholders' Equity, $mil	Employees
1	General Motors	178,174.0	6,698.0	228,888.0	17,506.0	608,000
2	Ford Motor	153,627.0	6,920.0	279,097.0	30,734.0	363,892
3	Mitsui	142,688.0	268.7	55,070.5	5,272.1	40,000
4	Mitsubishi	128,922.3	388.1	71,407.8	7,569.4	36,000
5	Royal Dutch/Shell	128,141.7	7,758.2	113,781.4	59,981.8	105,000
6	Itochu	126,631.9	(773.9)	56,307.9	2,956.6	6,675
7	Exxon	122,379.0	8,460.0	96,064.0	43,660.0	80,000
8	Wal-Mart Stores	119,299.0	3,526.0	45,525.0	18,502.0	825,000
9	Marubeni	111,121.2	140.4	55,403.4	3,563.9	64,000
10	Sumitomo	102,395.2	209.8	42,866.1	4,318.6	29,500

b. The Fortune Global 500: Ranked by Performance (Biggest Increase in Revenues)

Rank	Company	% change in revenues from 1996	1997 revenues, $mil
1	Republic Industries	335.7	10,305.6
2	Duke Energy	242.8	16,308.9
3	Morgan Stanley Dean Witter	200.5	27,132.0
4	Bell Atlantic	130.8	30,193.9
5	Boeing	101.9	45,800.0
6	AXA	94.3	76,874.4
7	NGC	84.3	13,378.4
8	SBC Communications	78.8	24,856.0
9	Travelers Group	76.2	37,609.0
10	Credit Suisse	74.5	48,242.1

c. America's Most Admired Companies
(Eight Key Attributes* of Reputation and Overall Return to Shareholders)

Rank	Company	Total Return 1998	Total Return 1993–98
1	General Electric	41.0%	34.2%
2	Coca-Cola	1.3%	26.1%
3	Microsoft	114.6%	68.9%
4	Dell Computer	248.5%	152.9%
5	Berkshire Hathaway	52.2%	33.8%
6	Wal-Mart Stores	107.6%	27.6%
7	Southwest Airlines	338.4%	6.6%
8	Intel	69.0%	50.6%
9	Merck	41.3%	37.0%
10	Walt Disney	(−8.5%)	16.9%

*The eight attributes are innovativeness, quality of management, employee talent, quality of products/services, long-term investment value, financial soundness, social responsibility, and use of corporate assets.

Source: Part (a) and part (b) reprinted from the August 3, 1998 issue of Fortune by special permission; copyright 1998, Time, Inc. Part (c) reprinted from the March 1, 1999 issue of Fortune by special permission; copyright 1999, Time, Inc.

As Dayton-Hudson Corp.'s experience indicates, marketing performance must be controlled and measured throughout all stages of the managerial process. Managers who understand why results were not as planned have taken a major step toward correcting mistakes.

CONTROLLING MARKETING EFFORTS

An evaluation of a firm's marketing performance starts with an understanding of the management process and the role that measurement of results plays in that process. The components of the management process work together to generate target levels of productivity and profitability. Performance measurement is an integral part of the strategic planning process, including control, coordination, and value creation.

The Managerial Process

Management decisions involve basic problems that must be solved, questions that must be asked, and information that is needed to analyze and evaluate operating results. These decisions are driven by a firm's strategic plan and should be evaluated during each stage in the managerial process, which includes (1) analysis related to the problem that is being addressed, (2) planning, (3) execution, and (4) control. The results of this assessment of marketing successes and failures provide feedback for both short- and long-range planning. (See Figure 15.1.) For example, to attain

FIGURE 15.1

The Managerial Process

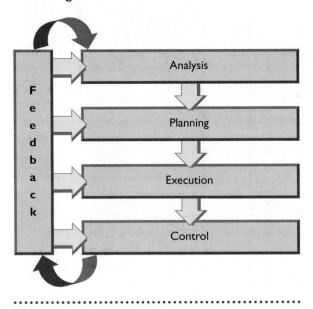

MARKETING IN THE GLOBAL VILLAGE

Turnaround at Volkswagen

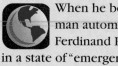 When he became chairman of the German automaker Volkswagen in 1993, Ferdinand Piech declared that VW was in a state of "emergency" and vowed that a shakeup would have the company back on course. Despite losses of $1.35 billion in 1993, VW has come out of its crisis by trimming the workforce, reducing the number of car platforms, and driving down suppliers' prices.

Profits in 1995 nearly tripled to $320 million on sales of about $61 billion, and share price rose 57 percent to $364. Profit margins, however, were lagging due to low productivity (VW was still one of the world's least efficient car makers). Aggressive rivals such as Fiat and Ford undercut VW's prices, causing margins to shrink; European market growth was stalling; and upstarts such as South Korea's Daewoo Corp. invested billions in plants in central Europe. In response to these trends, Piech counted heavily on gaining efficiencies by shrinking VW's wide range of platforms down to four by 1998 while simultaneously keeping their designs highly distinctive. This involved evaluating VW's expensive German workforce, which numbered 101,000 and accounted for a major portion of VW's worldwide payroll and wage costs. Some 30,000 of these workers were considered unnecessary, as were three of the nine top management board members.

By 1999, Piech had turned VW into one of the strongest car companies in the world as a result of a tumultuous turnaround. He introduced a 4-day work week in union-heavy Germany and spent $1 billion to buy the high-class Bentley, Bugatti, and Lamborghini brands. In 1998, VW's profits rose 63 percent over 1993's $1.1 billion loss, to $3.6 billion before taxes, and the company sold over 4.7 million vehicles, putting VW on a par with Toyota as the world's third-largest automobile maker. Profit margins and share price continue to rise, quality has improved more than any other auto maker in the past 5 years according to J. D. Power & Associates, and the new Beetle is bringing buyers into VW dealerships, where they also are attracted to other VW models. Piech's assessment of Volkswagen's performance and the contribution of each functional area were instrumental in determining his strategic direction for the company.

Sources: Janet Guyon, "Getting the Bugs Out at VW," *Fortune* (March 29, 1999), pp. 96–102; and David Woodruff, David Lindorff, and Elisabeth Malkin, "VW Is Back—But for How Long?" *Business Week* (March 4, 1996), pp. 66–67.

corporate financial goals, the necessary funds for inventory investment must be allocated, buyers must be motivated to select the right products, and the performance of marketing personnel and product lines must be evaluated.

Marketing managers must act quickly and decisively to solve problems that occur in daily business operations, which may lead to a shorter-range perspective. However, when the strategic planning process includes an evaluation of operating results, management must address the implications of developments in the markets where they operate. This includes competitive activities, economic trends, and other relevant environmental factors. This type of analysis helps the marketer anticipate future scenarios and encourages a longer-range strategic view.

FIGURE 15.2
....

Marketing Efficiency and Effectiveness

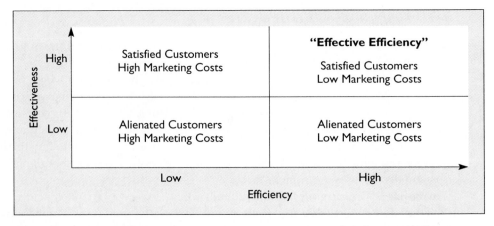

Source: AMA Marketing Encyclopedia (1995), p. 222. Reprinted by permission of the American Marketing Association.

Profitability and Productivity
....

Marketers often find it difficult to measure marketing productivity accurately because marketing expenditures (inputs) cannot easily be related to specific results (outputs) due to their intangibility. Sheth and Sisodia suggest that a definition of marketing productivity should be based on the amount of desirable output obtained for each unit of input, that is, quality as well as quantity.[4] Efficient and effective use of marketing resources should incorporate attention to both customer acquisition and customer retention. (See Figure 15.2.)

A number of approaches to improving marketing productivity are described in Table 15.2. These include the use of better marketing accounting systems, greater use of collaborative strategies, better domain definition, unbundling and rebundling of services, rationalizing the marketing mix, use of information technology, and better monitoring and control of personnel and marketing practices.[5]

The Control Process and Strategic Planning
....

A strategic plan without a plan for control and measurement of marketing performance may be doomed to failure. Therefore, performance evaluation should be considered throughout the entire strategic planning process; that is, who is accountable for achieving the strategic goals, and how should the results be measured?

Control and the Managerial Process.   Control is an important element of the managerial process, as shown in Figure 15.1. There are a number of issues that managers must resolve in order to design and implement an effective control process: identification of key variables to measure or control, performance standards and

TABLE 15.2
....
Approaches to Improving Marketing Productivity

Better marketing accounting
* *Activity-based costing.* Understand where resources are being spent, where customer value is being created, and where money is being made or lost.

Greater use of collaborative strategies
* *Partnering.* Treat your suppliers and customers as partners in lowering systemwide costs and adding value.
* *Relationship marketing.* Be selective about customers, and take a long-term, win-win perspective.
* *Marketing alliances.* Share resources and opportunities with other companies serving the same customers.

Better domain definition
* *Make vs. buy: Insourcing vs. outsourcing.* Focus on your marketing core competencies and let outside experts handle the rest.
* *Getting customers to do more work.* Lower costs and increase customer satisfaction by adding customers to the value chain.

Unbundling and rebundling of services
* Uncover the hidden costs of free service, and create new revenue sources.

Rationalizing the marketing mix
* *Umbrella branding.* Increase return on branding by developing brand names with broad applicability to multiple products and markets.

* *Rationalizing and recycling advertising.* Remove conflicts of interest in agency compensation methods, unbundle advertising creation and placement, and understand advertising life cycles.
* *Reducing product proliferation.* Variety does not always equate to value; reduce customer confusion and marketing costs by matching product lines with distinct market segments.

Use of information technology
* *Data-based marketing.* Target marketing efforts more precisely, but ensure that you are creating additional value for the customer and are acutely sensitive to privacy concerns.
* *Front-line information systems.* Deploy information tools where they have the greatest impact on customer service and satisfaction: at the front line.
* *Marketing and the global information highway.* Prepare now for a radically different, more integrated mode of marketing in the future, predicated on "total customer convenience."

Better monitoring and control
* *Adjusting compensation of marketing personnel.* Compensation drivers must be linked to the need for effective efficiency in all marketing activities.
* *Continuous assessment of marketing practices.* Beware of creeping marketing incrementalism; take a periodic "zero-based" view of marketing practices.

Source: Sheth, Jagdish and Rajendra S. Sisodia, (1995), "Improving Marketing Productivity," in *Marketing Encyclopedia: Issues & Trends Shaping the Future.* Jeffrey Heilbrun, ed., Chicago, IL: American Marketing Association, pp. 223–236. Reprinted by permission of the American Marketing Association.

measures, assessment and reassessment procedures, and provision for corrective action. Each of these issues is described briefly within the context of strategic control at the business-unit level.

* *Key variables to be measured or controlled.* The selection of key variables should relate to a company's mission statement and strategic objectives. The goals to achieve these objectives generally can be categorized as financial (e.g., return on investment, net profit), efficiency (e.g., productivity in terms of use of assets, personnel performance), or effectiveness (e.g., market leadership, competitive

positioning, customer satisfaction). The nature of these variables transcends all functional areas of an organization as they relate to marketing, taking into consideration both internal and external factors.

- *Standards of performance.* Performance expectations are based on a company's strategic goals, the standards that are met or exceeded by leading marketers. Standards may be established on the basis of the company's vision for the future (i.e., its positioning relative to competition or others in the same industry), historical company data and forecasts for future performance, or by benchmarketing against key success factors in the industry. Performance standards are set for the entire company and for subunits that comprise the company. Standards for one organizational level should support the standards of the other levels. Performance standards usually are viewed within the parameters of some time designation, preferably with the ability to compare with previous time periods, industry standards, company goals, and so forth. Many companies today are benchmarking their operations against leading companies within their own industry or in unrelated industries.

- *Performance measures.* Performance generally is controlled by measuring factors such as profitability, sales, market share, shareholder value, employee productivity, and customer satisfaction. Although individual variables are analyzed, managers usually consider a number of standards simultaneously that combine to provide an overall measure of performance. Even though the most common variables that are used to represent an organization's performance are quantitative (e.g., net profit, return on equity), many qualitative measures (e.g., customer satisfaction, attitude change toward the company or its products) are also considered in an overall assessment of performance. For example, a firm might consider the efficiency of its operation based on cost containment and contribution margins and the productivity of its personnel who make goods in the factory, salespeople who call on the company's customers, or the rate of new product introduction into the market.

  Qualitative factors that are more elusive, and hence more subjective, help management gain a better understanding of overall performance. For example, customer satisfaction, product quality (as it is perceived by the customer), and return on investment in advertising can be combined with quantitative factors in measuring performance.

- *Assessment/reassessment.* Data for discrete (one-time) or continuous assessment of marketing performance can be found in the company's financial and accounting reports (financial ratios are discussed later), sales data and salesforce reports (by product, territory, etc.), feedback from customers and employees, and other sources. Assessment can be conducted by individuals within the company or by outside consultants.

- *Correcting identified problems or weaknesses.* Once problem areas have been identified, they should be prioritized for action. Based on an understanding of the problem, management next develops a plan to improve the situation. The most successful plans include input from all stakeholders in the process and its outcomes. A plan for implementation of the corrective measures should be developed, authority and responsibility should be assigned, and actions should be monitored and fine-tuned as needed. At this point it is helpful to continue to seek feedback from all affected parties.

Anaylsis and Strategic Planning: An Ongoing Process.   The early chapters of this book represented a broad view of marketing management and strategic planning. They addressed the general question, "What will we do?" ("What objectives does our company want to achieve?" and "What strategies will we use to reach our objectives?") Subsequent chapters concentrated on narrower functional marketing-mix areas, addressing the more specific question, "How will we do it?" ("How shall we use our marketing mix and operate our business on a day-to-day basis?") That is, "What tactics will we use to carry out strategies?" and "What resources are needed for implementation?"

In this chapter the questions addressed in an assessment of marketing performance are, "Did we do, or are we doing, what we set out to do?" and "Why did we or didn't we do it?" During the execution phase, the question "What is/isn't working so far?" also should be addressed. (See Figure 15.3.)

FIGURE 15.3
....
Analysis and Strategic Planning: An Ongoing Process

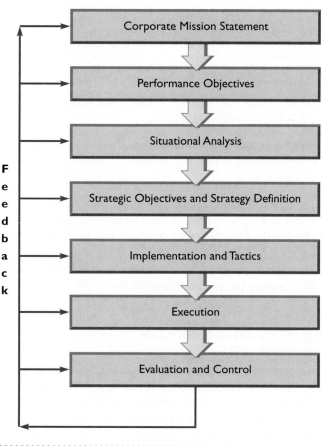

Coordination Across Functions.   As indicated in the discussion of the relationship between the managerial process, control, and strategic planning, marketing cannot be isolated from other areas of an organization. The control process must consider the sources and uses of funds, personnel issues, shared technologies, production schedules, research and development (R&D) expenditures, and other factors as they affect marketing outcomes. Measurement of the efficiency and effectiveness of cross-functional performance provides a method to identify areas that achieve synergy in the ways they work together to achieve a common goal, as well as those areas that need to develop cross-functional synergies.

Economic Value Added (EVA): Value Creation.   The use of capital is a major concern to all organizations. **Economic value added (EVA)** analysis provides a way to evaluate business performance by analyzing profits and the cost and uses of capital, represented by the formula

$$\text{EVA} = \text{net operating profit} - (\text{costs of capital} \times \text{capital employed})$$

> **Economic value added (EVA)**
> Method of evaluating business performance by analyzing profits and the cost and uses of capital.

where net operating profit = operating profit − taxes.[6]

This formula is based on the idea that every firm will employ capital for uses such as plant, inventory, working capital, and other assets, but recognizing that the capital employed has a cost that should be included when valuing business performance. Aaker[7] identified four routes to increasing EVA:

1. Increase profit by reducing costs or increasing revenue without using more capital.

2. Invest in high-return products—the basis for all marketing strategy.

3. Decrease the cost of capital—with a higher ratio of debt to equity or a less risky business portfolio.

4. Use less capital—many firms have improved their performance dramatically by making better use of existing assets and being less capital-intensive in their operations.

Highly regarded companies such as The Coca-Cola Company, American Telephone & Telegraph Co. (AT&T), Quaker Oats Co., Briggs & Stratton Corp., CSX, and many others have experienced huge increases in the value of their companies by employing the principles of EVA. Managers from top-performing companies such as these know the answers to the questions: What is the true cost of capital? How much capital is tied up in our operation?[8]

LEVELS OF ANALYSIS

The performance of an organization can be evaluated at the corporate or strategic, business, and functional or operating levels of the firm. (See Figure 15.4.) Although different factors may be emphasized at different organizational levels, three major concerns generally are addressed: performance versus plan, execution of the plan, and capital expenditures. In each case, the company seeks to determine whether it has made the best use of its resources. Although examples are given of issues to be

FIGURE 15.4

••
Levels of Analysis

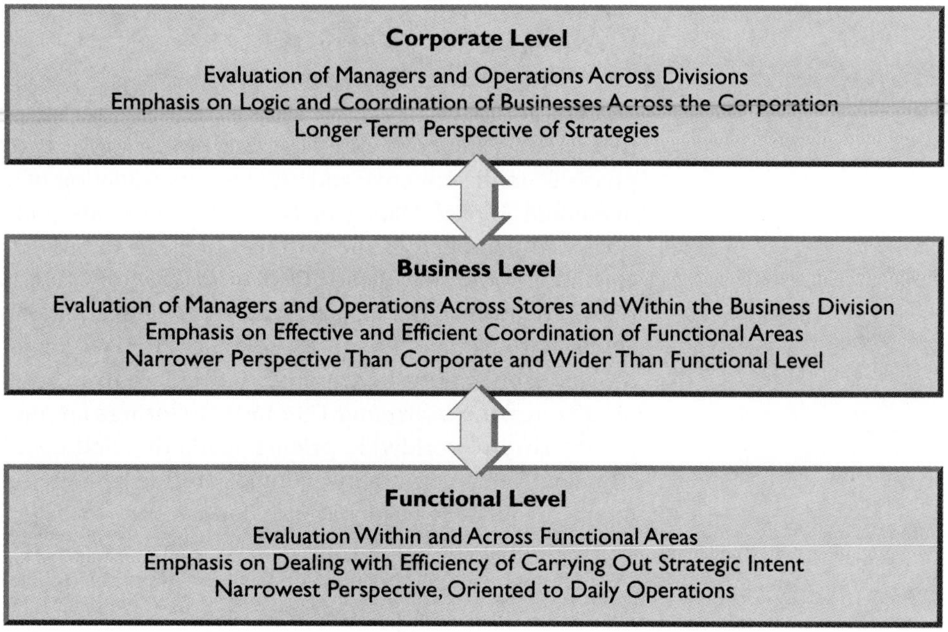

Corporate Level

Evaluation of Managers and Operations Across Divisions
Emphasis on Logic and Coordination of Businesses Across the Corporation
Longer Term Perspective of Strategies

Business Level

Evaluation of Managers and Operations Across Stores and Within the Business Division
Emphasis on Effective and Efficient Coordination of Functional Areas
Narrower Perspective Than Corporate and Wider Than Functional Level

Functional Level

Evaluation Within and Across Functional Areas
Emphasis on Dealing with Efficiency of Carrying Out Strategic Intent
Narrowest Perspective, Oriented to Daily Operations

examined at each organizational level, the emphasis in this section is on analysis of results at the functional level.

At all levels of a company, the question that must be answered is, "How can we better exploit our current internal resources (financial, human, physical, technological, and organizational) to achieve a clear, sustainable competitive advantage?" As Waterman observed in *The Renewal Factor,* opportunity knocks softly and in unpredictable ways.[9] Today's business leaders must face—and manage—constant change, with the goal of prospering from the forces that decimate their competition. Analysis provides critical information for marketers to use in planning, executing, controlling, and revising strategy and to help them to be ready for opportunity when it knocks.

Corporate Level Analysis
••••••••••••••••••••••••••••••••••••••

At the corporate or strategic level, analysis encompasses all business units or all divisions of a multibusiness organization. Large firms may have several different business formats, operate in multiple industries, or represent different stages in the channels of distribution. Managers and operations are evaluated across divisions to determine their contribution to the corporate bottom line, with the objective of balancing all businesses profitably. Emphasis is on the logic and coordination of the businesses that make up the corporation, taking a longer-term perspective of strategies for organizational effectiveness ("what to do"). One important measure of organizational effectiveness focuses on the use of financial resources, with the objective of achieving the highest possible return for each dollar invested by the firm. This would include, for example, capital expenditures such as expansion activities, major equipment purchases, or acquisitions or merger activities.

Business Level Analysis

Analysis at the business level takes a narrower perspective of the environment than that taken at the corporate level but broader than that at the functional level. Emphasis is on the effective and efficient coordination of all functional areas to ensure maximum impact. Managers, business operations, and other factors are evaluated across all units within the business division to answer the basic question of how each unit performed against its planned performance standards. Results provide inputs to determine the most advantageous allocation of money, personnel, and other assets. For example, Procter & Gamble Co. (P&G) launched a plan in 1998 to redesign its operations in response to pressure from large international retailers. Wal-Mart Stores, Inc., Carrefour USA Inc., and others are pushing suppliers such as P&G to standardize worldwide pricing, marketing and distribution. P&G is changing its strategy from a country-by-country setup to a limited number of powerful departments organized on a global scale for category management (e.g., hair care, diapers, soap). Implementation of the plan is expected to take two years and relies heavily on increasing sales and market share in international markets—where many countries are experiencing economic crises.[10]

A firm's operating plan establishes performance standards that can be used for comparison with actual results during and after execution. This is an integral part of the strategic planning and control process. If performance is below expectations, analysis may reveal explanations that are not evident otherwise. Evaluation during the early stages reveals strengths and weaknesses and permits management to make necessary revisions in a timely manner. For example, a lower than desired profit level may be caused by a number of interacting factors, such as higher than average advertising expenses and short-run price cuts taken to achieve a high sales volume. Or changes in the firm's operating environment (such as a labor strike in a key supplier's factory) may make it necessary to re-evaluate the original plan.

At the business level, each functional area can be evaluated to determine its role in the execution of marketing strategies and its contribution to overall financial performance. Business-level analysis also looks outward to the company's operating environment to assess market opportunities and demand for the firm's products and services. (See discussion of environmental factors in Chapter 1.) An evaluation of information about current conditions and the ability to anticipate future events and activities enable a firm to be proactive in influencing environmental forces rather than merely reacting to them.

Functional (Operating) Level Analysis

At the functional, or operating, level, analysis is concerned with the efficiency of carrying out the strategic intent ("how to do it") within and across the functional areas of a business unit. The planning horizon is shorter term as managers concentrate on the details of carrying out the firm's strategy on a day-to-day basis. The overriding goal is to coordinate all departments and functions in order to execute corporate strategy successfully and achieve corporate objectives. Performance at the functional level can "make or break" performance goals at the business level and therefore should be measured and controlled for its contribution to the overall efficiency and effectiveness of the organization.

The Marketing Mix. All relevant aspects of the marketing mix are evaluated to determine how well the plan has been executed: product and pricing strategies, marketing communications mix, distribution, and customer service. A 30-month-long study by the Marketing Metrics Research Project found that only a small minority of U.K. firms thoroughly assess their marketing performance—although most believe that their assessments are adequate.[11] Marketers are always anxious to measure everything else but are less keen on being measured themselves. The results of this research indicate that those who do not understand their brand equity position have little idea how good—or bad—their marketing is. Most marketers compare sales with plan, with an increased focus on shareholder value, but not customer value. The distinction should be made between marketing performance and expenditure effectiveness when measuring marketing results. Marketing expenditure should be viewed as an investment, not a cost, and the resulting asset and its valuation should be measured by the firm's brand equity.

Unsuccessful execution may be due to ineffective product management, unreliable suppliers, or errors in identifying customer wants. Or adjustments may be needed in the communications mix, pricing, or distribution channels. Conversely, factors responsible for successful tactical execution also can be identified and taken advantage of. Next, we will look briefly at the need for performance evaluation within selected functional areas and the combined effect of these functions as they interact to produce operating results at the strategic level.

Product managers determine market needs and forecast market demand. They determine prices and distribution channels and play a key role in developing integrated communications programs. These tasks must be accomplished within the context of company policies, budgets, competitive pressures, and the interaction of these factors with other functional areas of the firm. There are a number of approaches to this type of analysis, but the most efficient method is to use complex statistical computer models that can handle individual and combined effects. Table 15.3 suggests various spreadsheet approaches and decision models that can be used to plan and evaluate marketing decisions.

Sales forecasting models are used to estimate demand and sales. Anticipated sales levels are used to determine production and inventory levels for a specified selling period, the amount of salesforce coverage needed, the most effective communication methods, and optimal distribution channels. During and after execution, analysis of sales and inventory data provides information about the accuracy of forecasts and the possible need to adjust original estimates.

Analysis of pricing strategies is needed to determine market response to the selected price points. What is the price elasticity? Does the range of prices offer customers sufficient alternatives? Are the price points psychologically appropriate? Are the gross margins high enough to achieve the firm's profit objectives and/or low enough to achieve sales objectives? What effect do margins and profit objectives have on prices that can be paid to suppliers? Do new price lines or price points need to be introduced?

Channel members need information to plan inventory assortments, determine basic stock needs, and make projections about customer responses to the goods

TABLE 15.3
· · · · · · · · · · · · · · · ·
Marketing Control and Decision Models

The following software programs are computer-based models that may be invaluable to managers concerned with marketing control and/or other marketing decisions. Many are Excel spreadsheet-based but some are stand-alone models that are either commercially available or available in the public domain.

Excel Spreadsheets	*Non-Excel Models*	*Commercial Non-Excel Models*
ADBUG Advertising budgeting	**ADCAD** Ad copy design	**Expert Choice** Evaluate alternatives
ADVISOR Communications planning	**Cluster Analysis** Market segmentation	**Decision Tree** Evaluate alternatives
ASSESSOR Market pretest	**Conjoint Analysis** Product design	**Geodemographics** Site planning
CALLPLAN Sales call planning	**Multinomial Logit Analysis** Market forecasting	**Neural Net** Market forecasting
Choice-Based Segmentation Market segmentation	**Positioning Analysis** Market forecasting	
GE: Portfolio Product planning		
PIMS Marketing strategy		
Promotional Spending Analysis Effectiveness of promotions		
Sales Resource Allocation Territorial design		
Value-in-Use Pricing Total value pricing		
Visual Response Modeling Define shape of market		
Yield Management Maximize hotel occupancy		
Competitive Bidding Preparation of bid pricing		

Source: G. Lilien/A. Rangaswamy, *Marketing Engineering,* exhibit 1.11, page 25. © 1998 by Gary L. Lilien and Arvind Rangaswamy. Reprinted by permission of Addison Wesley Longman.

and services offered. Projections may be based on knowledge of characteristics of the firm's customers and how they use products and services, and results can be measured against these projections.

The performance of marketing managers is evaluated in several ways: achievement of sales objectives, expense control, and contribution to profit margins. High performance often results in bonuses or profit-sharing plans. Effective use of assets such as inventory can be evaluated from several interrelated perspectives. The productivity of each dollar invested in inventory is analyzed to determine whether an optimal balance between stock and sales (in dollars and units) is being achieved and whether the investment in inventory is producing the desired level of sales and profits. Stock turnover rates, optimal reorder points, and reorder quantities also are evaluated. The marketer who is concentrating on building market share (e.g., low profit margin to high asset turnover ratio) will have a different philosophy than one who is content with maintaining the status quo (e.g., average profit margin to average asset turnover ratio).

Integrated Marketing Communications (IMC).   Ways to measure the effectiveness of integrated marketing communications programs were discussed in Chapters 11 and 12. Analysis includes an evaluation of the promotional mix (advertising, personal selling, sales promotion, publicity, and public relations), as well as services offered by the firm. The marketer's goal is to obtain the highest return possible from each dollar spent on communication with target customers. Analytical models, often using databases, point-of-sale scanner data, or other customer response information, can be used to identify the most cost-effective communications mix to achieve the highest levels of sales and/or profit goals.

Questions to be addressed include: Are the promotional message, media, and timing effective in achieving the marketer's objectives? Is the intended message reaching the target audience, and with the desired results? An evaluation of the effect of salesforce expenditures is necessary, particularly in comparison with high-technology alternatives and an increasing use of self-service methods. Have the sales personnel been trained properly? Are they carrying out the firm's strategic intent and making their sales goals? Is the compensation plan motivating high levels of performance?

Sales promotion efforts are analyzed to determine whether they are being used appropriately and how they are integrated with IMC. How do customers respond to special events, "giveaways," contests, couponing, trade shows, or other sales promotion tools? Are packaging and other visual factors effective "silent" salespeople?

The effectiveness of publicity and public relations efforts should be evaluated to determine whether they have been directed to the right media and individuals. What results have been obtained from these communication channels? Should other options be explored?

Execution of a marketing strategy often involves services that accompany purchases. Are the right services being offered? Do some services contribute to expenses only and not to sales? Should other services be offered to meet the needs of customers and to differentiate the firm's offerings from competitors?

According to Graham,[12] a successful marketing program can be evaluated in eight tangible ways employing a number of measures:

1. It differentiates a company from the competition.

2. It creates a flow of new business leads.

3. It keeps the company in the minds of customers and prospects.

4. It gives the company a strong hold on the marketplace.

5. It communicates a company's expertise and knowledge.

6. It gives the company a long-term orientation.

7. It is customer-oriented.

8. It is a vital force in customer retention.

Other Functional Areas.   The performance of a company's operations, accounting and control, and human resources functions also should be evaluated relative to their impact on performance of the marketing function and the company as a whole. Control of the operations function includes analysis of factors such as maintenance of physical facilities, efficient space utilization, risk management and security, and in many cases performance of technological applications.

The accounting function is concerned with recording, maintaining, and analyzing data that are used to evaluate financial performance and control marketing operations. One popular approach is activity-based accounting, a method for analyzing where money is being spent, where value is being added for customers, and where the business is operating at a profit (or loss). Other tools used by accounting and finance areas include the marketing information system (MIS) and the marketing decision support system (MDSS) described in Chapter 4. The accounting function conducts an ongoing analysis to compare sales, profits, and other performance indicators across functional areas and business units.

Performance evaluation of the human resources function focuses on employee productivity. Employee compensation is a major expense for most companies, making productivity an issue for personnel at every level of an organization. Measures may vary according to individual responsibilities but generally are based on output and results. For example, top-level marketing executives are evaluated and rewarded according to their ability to generate profits for the company, and entry-level employees may be evaluated on the basis of number of customers served, efficiency on a production line, and so forth. Each of these has an impact on overall marketing performance.

Performance Evaluation Across Functions: An Example.   Functional-area decisions are interrelated and must operate within the context of a larger organization, as shown in Figure 15.5. To illustrate, at the operating level of an electronics retail establishment, support for a special sale event featuring television sets will require money, personnel, physical resources, management expertise, and other company assets. Analysis of sales reports, financial statements, and other timely data provides a basis for effective resource allocation among the various departments and functions involved.

When the company's television buyer decides to feature the television sets, managers in other functional areas also must make decisions. Buyers must identify the best suppliers and the best product styles and prices and negotiate favorable terms of sale. Merchandise managers must estimate demand and plan store inventories, perhaps decreasing inventory levels in other areas if the total departmental budget is not increased. Those responsible for designing and delivering an IMC program must decide how to promote and display the televisions—working with other internal departments and outside media sources. Promotion and dates for delivering the television sets must be coordinated. Operations efficiency is concerned with receiving and processing the television deliveries and taking measures to prevent theft. Accounting performance is concerned with recording and analyzing accurate data related to the television inventory and sales from the time the purchase order is placed until the customer pays the final bill for the merchandise. Human re-

FIGURE 15.5
....
Interrelationship of Functional Areas in Marketing Analysis

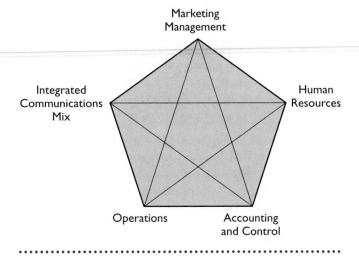

sources effectiveness and efficiency measures relate to employee productivity (sales and other support functions), scheduling, customer service, sales performance, and other factors.[13]

MEASURING PERFORMANCE
....

The process of measuring performance starts with deciding which factors to analyze; that is, what are the key questions? Next, criteria must be established as standards for performance, and key ratios should be calculated for comparison with past performance and industry competitors.

Factors to Analyze
....

Marketing managers are concerned with assessing the results of current efforts, determining why strategies are (or are not) working, identifying environmental changes and their effect on operations, and maximizing opportunities for growth. Control measures are selected in line with the firm's mission and objectives.

The following hierarchy of questions needs to be answered to obtain the type and quality of data needed to evaluate performance at the business-unit level:

1. What is/isn't working? Consider the results of current efforts. This may be the most important question to be answered about the effectiveness of marketing strategies. For example, we might want to know whether lower prices are achieving market-share objectives.

2. Why are strategies working or not working? Take an objective look at the company and its competitors.

3. Have marketing strategies been implemented according to plan? Have all resources (financial, human, physical, etc.) been used efficiently and effectively?

4. What are direct and indirect competitors' current and evolving marketing strategies and tactics? What is their impact on the company's ability to meet its performance objectives?

5. What significant trends and critical events are occurring within the firm's macro- and micro-environment that affect all competitors in the industry? Analyze the effect of these environmental forces on the firm's operations and those of its competitors. Determine whether all firms in the industry are affected in the same way. Develop strategies to control or respond to these forces.

Answers to these questions form a basis for evaluating possible opportunities (or problems), which leads to another level of analysis: Do untapped growth opportunities exist? Are these opportunities in current market segments or in new markets? How much are these opportunities expected to contribute to sales and/or profits? Will the returns justify the investment cost?

Key Performance Criteria

A firm establishes performance criteria consistent with its mission and objectives. Typically, marketing managers are concerned with overall performance in five key areas as they apply to design and implementation of the marketing mix: profitability, activity, productivity, liquidity, and leverage. Each performance measure is described briefly below.[14]

- *Profitability* indicates the marketer's success or failure for a specified time period and is a measure of the portion of each dollar of sales or investment that the marketer can retain in the business.

- *Activity,* or *asset turnover,* is analyzed to determine how effectively the marketer is using resources, such as inventory and equipment, to generate sales revenues.

- Whereas *activity* refers to the effective use of assets, *productivity* refers to the efficient use of assets, such as plant capacity, advertising dollars, or personnel, to generate sales and profits.

- Performance criteria also include *liquidity,* which is the marketer's ability to pay maturing debts in the short term.

- *Leverage* is a measure of the relationship between the total value of assets used to operate the business and the amount actually owned by the investors. This ratio varies according to the marketer's operating philosophy and tolerance for risk.

Key Ratios and Their Implications

A firm's financial and accounting records contain readily available data for evaluating performance. It is important to remember, however, that it is the individual products, people, plans, and procedures that make the numbers in these financial ratios "happen."

Key ratios provide a convenient and easily interpreted method for evaluating marketing results. Examples of frequently used ratios are given next for the five key

FIGURE 15.6

....

Using Key Ratios to Evaluate Marketing Performance

1. Profitability:

Profit on Sales
Rate of Return on Total Assets
Rate of Return on Net Worth
Gross Margin Return on Inventory Investment

2. Activity:

Inventory Turnover
Asset Turnover
Receivables Turnover
Collection Period

3. Productivity:

Space
Personnel
Accounts Payable to Sales

4. Liquidity:

Current Ratio
Quick Ratio
Current Liabilities to Net Worth
Current Liabilities to Inventory

5. Leverage:

Total Assets to Net Worth (Equity)
Debt to Equity (Net Worth)

....

performance areas defined previously: profitability, activity, productivity, liquidity, and leverage. (See Figure 15.6.) Each ratio is calculated and briefly interpreted. Managers also would compare the resulting ratios (1) to industry averages to indicate this marketer's performance relative to competition and (2) to the firm's present and past ratios to determine whether performance is better or worse than in the previous period.

Profitability.   Regardless of the profitability measure that is used, the overriding issue is how to operate effectively (strategic viewpoint) and efficiently (operating plans and tactics). A key problem that arises in measuring profitability is deciding which measure to use. Profit, the amount of money left for the marketer after paying suppliers, employees, landlords, taxes, and all other expenses, is measured relative to other indicators, such as sales, assets, or the owners' equity (net worth). The

FIGURE 15.7

Income Statement and Balance Sheet Example

Income Statement

Net Sales		$140,000
Less Cost of Goods Sold	80,000	
Gross Margin	60,000	
Less Operating Expenses	45,000	
Net Profit (Before Taxes)		15,000

Balance Sheet

Assets

Total Current Assets	$ 70,000	
Long-term Assets	150,000	
Total Assets		220,000

Liabilities and Owners Equity

Total Current Liabilities	40,000	
Long-term Liabilities	120,000	
Total Liabilities		160,000
Owners Equity (Net Worth)	60,000	
Total Liabilities and Owners' Equity		220,000

following indicators of profitability are discussed here: (1) profit on sales, (2) rate of return on total assets, and (3) rate of return on net worth.

A hypothetical income statement and balance sheet are shown in Figure 15.7 to provide data for calculating the ratios below. The resulting ratios are briefly discussed and interpreted.

Profit on sales
Percentage of each dollar of revenue that a firm retains as profit.

The formula for **profit on sales** (net profit margin) is Net profit/net sales.

Calculation: 15,000/140,000 = 10.7 percent

This ratio represents the percentage of each dollar of revenue that the firm retains as profit. In the example, the firm keeps nearly 11 cents of every dollar after paying all operating expenses. Assuming that the industry average is 9 percent, the firm's performance is above the industry average for this type of business. This may be attributed to a higher markup policy or lower operating costs compared with competitors.

Return on assets
Relates profits to the assets required to produce them.

The formula for rate of **return on assets** is Net profit/total assets.

Calculation: 15,000/220,000 = 6.8 percent

This ratio determines the payback on assets used to operate the business by relating profits to the assets required to produce them. For the marketing firm in our example, a total of $1 in assets (e.g., inventory, fixtures, equipment, property, etc.) is required to generate less than 7 cents in profit. In general, the larger this ratio, the better is the marketer's performance. Assuming that the industry average is 10 percent, the firm's return on assets is considerably less than the industry average. This ratio may be due to low sales revenues or to excessive or nonproductive assets.

The formula for rate of **return on net worth** is Net profit/net worth.

Return on net worth
Payback on equity (amount the owners have invested in the business).

Calculation: 15,000/60,000 = 25.0 percent

This ratio represents the payback on equity. The marketer in our example is receiving about 25 cents in profit for each dollar the owners have invested in the business. In general, a larger ratio is related to effective use of the owners' capital. Assuming that industry ratios indicate that return on net worth should be at least 15 percent, the company is performing above the industry average.

Activity.   Ratios used to measure activity, or asset turnover, include (1) inventory turnover, (2) asset turnover, (3) receivables turnover, and (4) collection period.

The formula for **inventory turnover** is Cost of goods sold/average inventory at cost.

Inventory turnover
Number of times the average amount of inventory carried is completely sold out during a selling period.

Calculation: 80,000/32,000 = 2.5 times per year

This ratio represents the number of times that the average amount of inventory carried is completely sold out. In general, a stockturn that is too high or too low relative to the industry should be avoided. While high ratios are desirable, they may indicate inventory levels that are too low or ordering that is too frequent. Low ratios may indicate nonproductive or aging inventory. In our example, we assume that the company has an average investment in inventory of $32,000 at cost. If the industry average is 4 stockturns per year, the company is performing below the industry average, signaling a problem for this marketer. Note that the turnover ratio will be the same, whether sales and inventory are valued at cost or retail (net sales/average inventory at retail).

The formula for **asset turnover** is Net sales/average total assets.

Asset turnover
Measure of marketer's efficiency in using all available assets to generate sales revenues.

Calculation: 140,000/220,000 = 0.64 times

This ratio measures the marketer's efficiency in using all available assets to generate sales revenues. Ideally, the highest possible level of sales should be generated with the lowest possible investment in assets. If industry ratios indicate an average asset turnover of 1.5, then this firm's asset turnover of 0.64 times during a year is significantly lower than the industry average. This performance ratio indicates that the firm may have difficulty generating sales with available assets. If sales are lower than expected, analysis should identify nonproductive, inappropriate, or excessive assets.

The formula for **receivables turnover** is Net sales/average accounts receivable.

Receivables turnover
Amount of credit purchases and length of time that customers take to pay for purchases.

Calculation: 140,000/10,000 = 14 times per year

This ratio relates the amount of credit purchases and length of time that customers take to pay for purchases. When a customer purchases goods with credit rather than cash, inventory dollars are converted to accounts receivable. A high percentage of credit purchases will result in a low receivables turnover ratio and the need to finance operations from sources other than cash sales during the average collection period. In our example, if accounts receivable average $10,000, a receivables turnover ratio of 14 times per year means that credit customers take nearly 4 weeks to pay their accounts (52 weeks/14).

The formula for **collection period** is (Accounts receivable/net sales) $\times$ 365.

Collection period
Average number of days that customers take to pay their accounts.

Calculation: $(10,000/140,000) \times 365 = 26.1$ days

The collection period is the average number of days that customers take to pay their accounts. This ratio, which is closely related to the receivables turnover calculated earlier, should be consistent with the company's credit terms. If the firm's collection period is much longer than average, this may indicate lenient credit policies or the desire to generate revenues from consumer debt. On the other hand, the marketer may need to have stricter policies for credit authorization and collection.

Productivity. Productivity ratios may be calculated relative to space, personnel, customer transactions, and other factors. Performance measures used for illustration below include (1) space, that is, sales per square foot of selling space, (2) personnel, that is, selling payroll as a percent of net sales, and (3) accounts payable to sales.

The formula to determine **space productivity** is Net sales/square foot of selling space.

Space productivity
Amount of sales per square foot of selling space (also may be expressed in linear or cubic feet).

Calculation (based on 1100 square feet): $140,000/1100 = \$127.27$ per square foot

As the final link in the distribution channel for consumer goods, retailers are particularly interested in this ratio. The high cost of retail space has led to a focus on increased productivity in terms of sales per square foot (or linear foot, or cubic foot). This ratio may determine merchandise assortments and their location in a store. In our example, the $127.27 generated for each square foot of selling space would be examined relative to industry averages for the merchandise category or store type that it represents. When sales per square foot are higher than industry averages, the firm is using its space more productively than its competitors, on average. (Profit per square foot is another important productivity ratio. Calculation: Net profit/ square foot of selling space = $15,000/1100 = \$13.64$.)

The formula used to determine **personnel productivity** is Selling expense/ net sales.

Personnel productivity
Percentage of sales dollars used in payment and benefits given to sales and sales support personnel.

Calculation: $12,000/140,000 = 8.57$ percent

Selling expenses may include all forms of payments and benefits given to the salesforce and sales support personnel. The ratio indicates the percentage of each dollar of sales that must be used to pay salaries, wages, commissions, and benefits to employees. Assuming selling expenses of $12,000 and an industry average of 7.5 percent (or 7½ cents of every sales dollar), then the firm's personnel productivity is slightly higher than the industry average, indicating the ability to compete effectively in this area.

The formula used to determine the productivity of **accounts payable to sales** is Accounts payable/net sales.

Accounts payable to sales
Percentage of each sales dollar owed to suppliers.

Calculation: 20,000/140,000 = 14.29 percent

This ratio represents the percentage of each sales dollar that is owed to suppliers. It demonstrates the degree to which sales figures are financed by other businesses. In our example, where accounts payable total $20,000, slightly over 14 cents of each dollar in sales must be used to pay these accounts. If the industry average is 25 percent, for example, the firm's accounts payable to sales ratio indicates that, on average, this marketer owes considerably less to other businesses than its competitors.

Liquidity.   Day-to-day operations are directly affected by the firm's degree of liquidity. Frequently used liquidity ratios are (1) current ratio, (2) quick ratio, (3) current liabilities to net worth, and (4) current liabilities to inventory

Current ratio
Firm's ability to pay short-term debt (includes inventory).

The formula for the **current ratio** is Current assets/current liabilities.

Calculation: 70,000/40,000 = 1.75

The current ratio is a measure of the firm's ability to pay short-term debt. A ratio of 1.0 indicates that current liabilities equal current assets, which means that the firm should be able to meet its short-range obligations. A ratio of less than 1.0 indicates that liabilities exceed assets and that if the current liabilities are called, the firm cannot readily pay them. A ratio greater than 1.0 indicates the extent of the firm's assets beyond current debt. A benchmark ratio is 2:1; therefore, the marketer in our example has a relatively healthy current ratio. In general, a larger ratio is desirable, although it may suggest a very conservative attitude toward buying inventory and other assets on credit.

Quick ratio
Firm's ability to pay short-term debt (excludes inventory).

The formula for the **quick ratio** is (Current assets − inventory)/current liabilities or (Cash + marketable securities + receivables)/current liabilities.

Calculation: (70,000 − 32,000)/40,000 = 0.95

The quick ratio is similar to the current ratio, except that inventory is excluded from the calculation of assets. The rationale for this exclusion is that if assets need to be liquidated quickly to pay debt, they may need to be sold below the desired margin. Therefore, the real value of this asset may be questionable. In general, a benchmark ratio is 1:1, but the higher this ratio, the better is the marketer's position to pay current debt. In this example, the firm would be able to meet nearly all its creditors' demands for immediate payment on short notice.

Current liabilities to net worth
Relates short-term liabilities to owner's actual investment.

The formula for **current liabilities to net worth** is Current liabilities/net worth.

Calculation: 40,000/60,000 = 66.7 percent

This ratio relates short-term liabilities to the owners' actual investment in the business. In our example, for every dollar the owners have invested in the business, they owe nearly 67 cents to their creditors. In general, the higher the ratio, the greater is the financial risk associated with the firm. That is, creditors actually may own more of the business than the stockholders, placing the owners in a precarious position. The liabilities of the firm in our example should be at or above the industry average when compared with net worth.

Current liabilities to inventory
Relates short-term liabilities to retailer's investment in inventory.

The formula for **current liabilities to inventory** is Current liabilities/inventory.

and conclusions from prior analysis. Statistical and mathematical models are useful for objectively describing, estimating, and predicting events and behavior. Qualitative analysis, although more subjective, can provide in-depth explanations of attitudes and behavior. Whether or not the results of analysis are really useful depends on both the quality of data inputs and management's ability to interpret and apply the findings.

At this point it is important to consider the sources and quality of data used in measuring marketing performance. Since the quality of data is directly related to their accuracy and suitability for the type of analysis needed, the data sources must be chosen carefully. As noted previously, data can be obtained from both primary and secondary information sources. These sources may be either internal or external to the company.

Secondary Data Sources.   *External secondary data* are gathered by someone else for another purpose, making it difficult for marketing managers to control their quality or apply them to new situations. Frequently used sources include U.S. government surveys and documents, industry reports, and trade association data. Government data may be obtained from a wide variety of sources, such as the U.S. Census reports of population at the federal, state, and local levels, and publications that report industry trade data, Commerce Department statistics, and many others. Publications such as Dun & Bradstreet and Standard & Poor's, provide useful data for comparing a company's results with those of its competitors. Trade associations generally disseminate trade-related data to industry members, such as the semiconductor or restaurant industry. Performance ratios, based on aggregate industry statistics, provide a benchmark for evaluating a company's performance compared with the industry. Other indicators of industry performance for large and small firms may be available from books, films and periodicals, or special seminars.

Internal secondary data can be used to identify the existing problems and provide information for daily operations. The marketing decision support system (MDSS), described earlier in this book, should contain high-quality, useful data that apply to both internal and external management concerns.

Operating statements, customer billings, purchase orders, employee records, and other company data are generated routinely as a part of day-to-day business operations or for a specific purpose. They are readily available for marketing management decisions. Operating statements contain a record of the company's profits and losses, cost of goods sold, expenditures, and other accounting and financial indicators of good and bad performance. For example, a decrease in profits may be due to an increase in costs, a decrease in sales, or both. Historical data also can be obtained from operating statements to use as inputs in sales forecasts or for projecting future performance goals. Note that although past data can provide a useful basis for evaluating performance, they should not dictate future strategies.

Employee records may include information concerning work schedules, job productivity, training, sales reports, and feedback from customers. These data can be used to identify specific divisions or personnel that represent the best and worst sales performance or highest costs or to make decisions about retention or training programs.

Customer records provide a company with data about its target market (who and where their customers are, what and when they buy, how much they buy, and

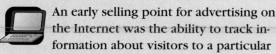

MARKETING IN THE INFORMATION AGE

Measuring Internet Traffic

An early selling point for advertising on the Internet was the ability to track information about visitors to a particular Web site. However, as one author says, "For all the techno-savvy out there, measuring traffic on the Web remains a very inexact science." Different rating companies come up with different results, which makes it difficult to target Internet marketing as precisely as originally expected and to evaluate results with confidence.

SportsLine USA, Inc., and America Online, Inc., spent an unexpected hour discussing conflicting data on the number of people that visit their Web sites when they met in early 1998 to review their marketing deal. Exasperated, both sides agreed to analyze the numbers from different rating companies and return to the issue later. Kenneth Dotson, SportsLine's vice-president for marketing, said, "We weren't getting anywhere—we weren't even looking at the same measurements." Such skirmishes over measuring Internet traffic have become all too common. Despite the Web's reputation as a digital marketplace where advertisers can reach precise target markets and gather volumes of data on their buying habits, the technology for providing these data has not kept up with the promise. Variations in the basic measurement techniques for the most popular Web sites are so numerous that a list of the top 25 sites is instantly disputed. If measurement methods are not reliable, then the resulting discrepancies in the data are frustrating to managers who rely on them to determine how much of their advertising budgets should go to the Web.

By 2002, on-line advertising revenues are expected to reach $9 billion, nine times the $1 billion spent in 1997. Web sites use the number of "hits" (times a page or part of a page are called up) to measure their own popularity. They then try to measure the "unique visitors" to a site so that a person calling up several pages is not measured more than once—but this is still an inexact science that does not provide completely impartial data.

Simply measuring the number of people who visit a particular Web site is not as easy as it appears. Media Metrix, Inc. (founded by market research firm NPD Group, Inc.), pioneer and market leader among rating services, has been challenged by a number of startup firms such as RelevantKnowledge, Inc., NetRatings, Inc., PC Data, Inc., and Nielsen Media Research (known for television research). Competition should ensure higher-quality research, but each firm uses different methods for monitoring use with conflicting results. For example, the top 25 Web site lists in spring 1998 from Media Matrix and RelevantKnowledge shared only 19 names. Both ranked the search engine Yahoo! in the top three but disagreed on the ratings of the other top two slots.

What methods do these firms use to track Internet use? Media Matrix surveys 30,000 people who agree to install software on their PCs to track use. Monthly ratings are calculated on the basis of reach (percentage of visitors to a Web site versus the total number of Web users). RelevantKnowledge surveys 11,000 Internet users by telephone, with plans to expand to an international survey base of 20,000. Its monthly ratings are based on the number of first-time users who visit a site. NetRatings recruits its sample group directly from the Web, with plans to expand to a base of 25,000 people from the 2000 it used at launch. NetRatings' data are presented in a number of ways, including top sites determined by page views (most times a particular page is loaded into a browser) per person. Nielsen's planned database of 10,000 users is selected through random-digit phone calls, and Internet use is tracked on non-PC devices similar to television set-top boxes that are connected to the Internet.

Marketers have become more sophisticated in targeting ads and tracking their efficiency. For example, Grey Interactive Worldwide combines ratings from multiple services to target specific audiences and measure the response. Fragrance Counter, a cosmetics retailer, used ratings data from Media Metrix and RelevantKnowledge to choose sites that were popular with women and then used its own proprietary technology to determine the success of its ads. The company was able to determine the "click rate" (percentage of users who clicked on the ad) and percentage who purchased a product on different sites. Accurate measurement of the success of Web site ads becomes more essential as on-line buying continues to escalate (estimated at $4.8 billion for 1998).

Sources: Heather Green, "The New Ratings Game" and "Tracking Who Surfs Where," *Business Week* (April 27, 1998), pp. 73–74, 78; Heather Green, Gail DeGeorge, and Amy Barrett, "The Virtual Mall Gets Real," *Business Week* (January 26, 1998), pp. 90–91; Paul C. Judge, "Are Tech Buyers Different?" *Business Week* (January 26, 1998), pp. 64–65, 68.

how they pay for their purchases). This information is useful for market analysis, communications strategies, and other marketing decisions throughout all phases of a marketing program. The type of customer information needed for decision making should be determined in advance by management, and an effective system should be developed for data gathering, recording, and analysis.

Problems with the Use of Secondary Data Sources.   Although secondary data are easily obtained and valuable in analyzing marketing situations, managers should be aware of three potential problems associated with the use of secondary sources: (1) units of measurement, (2) class definitions, and (3) publication currency.[15]

1. *Units of measurement.* Although secondary data may be available on the subject being analyzed, they may not be the same as needed for the current situation. For example, the size of a company can be reported in terms of annual sales, profits, or number of employees. If the marketer is interested in comparing sales for one specific product category with its competitors but only has data on total business results, a satisfactory comparison cannot be made. The income of consumers in a particular market may be expressed according to an individual, family, household, or spending unit. A marketer who targets young singles would not find income data meaningful if it were only reported for family units. The unit of measurement must be consistent with the marketer's needs if it is to be useful.

2. *Class definition.* Data may be available in the right units of measurement for the present problem but may not be provided in categories or "class boundaries" that are useful for the marketer's needs. The marketer who wants to compare sales in one trading area of a city with those of competition may have an internal sales database by customers' zip codes, but secondary data may only be available in voting districts or city precincts. Consumer income data for a mar-

ket may be available for single individuals in increments of $15,000 (0 to $14,999, $15,000 to $29,999, etc.), but the marketer's analysis may require increments of $10,000 (0 to $9999, $10,000 to $19,999, etc.). In these cases, the class definition would be inappropriate, and modifications would diminish the precision of the data used in analysis.

3. *Currency of information.* Although most marketing decisions require up-to-date information, there may be several years between data collection and publication or dissemination. This is particularly true for most government census data and other public data that may be published only every 5 or 10 years. Proprietary data may not be available to outside parties for some period of time, if at all. Rapid shifts in markets, movement of competitors in and out of the market, shifting economic indicators, and other changes in the marketer's environment require current data for analysis. In this case, the only alternative may be to collect primary data.

Criteria for Judging the Accuracy of Secondary Data. Criteria for determining the accuracy or precision of data include an assessment of (1) the source used, (2) the purpose of publication, and (3) general evidence of quality.[16]

1. *The source used.* Errors may be found in data-collection methods, analysis, and reporting. Secondary sources often obtain data previously gathered from other sources. For example, *The Statistical Abstract of the United States* is a widely used secondary source of secondary data obtained from other government and trade sources. Copying data from one place to another may result in inaccuracies or misinterpretation, making it advisable to consult and evaluate the primary source where the data were first published. Only the primary source of secondary data can provide general evidence of the quality of the research.

2. *The purpose of publication.* One indication of the accuracy of data is related to the purpose of the publication in which they appear. The data may be of questionable quality if they are published by a source that is selling something, promoting private interests or one side of a controversial issue, or is not identified. Thus it is advisable to determine the motives of the publication's sponsors.

3. *General evidence regarding quality.* The original data source should present the data in context and with fewer errors. Evidence of quality includes the reputation of the research group, the organization's ability to collect the data, appropriateness of the sample, method of data collection and analysis, qualifications and training of personnel who gathered the data, extent of nonresponse and other sources of bias, and presentation, as in the accuracy and organization of results.

Primary Data Sources. Since the analysis of operating results depends mainly on secondary data, a discussion of primary data collection methods is beyond the scope of this chapter. However, there is a relationship between primary data sources and the original design of the marketer's information system. Issues to be addressed within the context of primary data collection include the requirements and format for data concerning sales records, operating costs, capital expenditures, personnel, and other important data. When deciding between secondary and primary data sources, it is important first for a marketing manager to know the specific problems that need to be solved and the questions that need to be answered with the data that are readily available.

Primary data have the advantage of providing timely, in-depth answers to questions that secondary data cannot address satisfactorily. Primary data may be as complex as a comprehensive market research study conducted to determine customer response to changes in a product line or as simple as "want lists" created in response to customer requests. Warranty cards, responses to promotional efforts (such as direct mail, couponing, special offers), and other forms of direct communication with customers also provide valuable primary data.

Grocery retailers obtain volumes of data from store "loyalty" cards that are issued to their customers for check-cashing identification and other purposes. Researchers examined the use of these cards in the United Kingdom in terms of their commercial effectiveness and as a way to measure and evaluate retail grocers' performance.[17] Loyalty cards are part of a strategy aimed at maximizing the potential of the retailers' customer base. The goal is to increase both the number of shopping trips and the amount spent per trip. Loyalty is determined by quantified sales measures and consumer panel data. From these data, retailers can analyze customers' purchases and other store-related behavior for different levels of store loyalty. The results are useful for profiling and targeting selected market segments and for assessing response to marketing efforts.

Good-quality primary data can be obtained from professional research firms and subscription services for a fee and/or on a contractual basis. However, the marketer has the most control over data quality when using primary sources. Primary data can be evaluated against most of the criteria described for judging the accuracy, quality, and usefulness of secondary data.

Summary

· ·

Marketing must be both effective and efficient; therefore, the focus in this chapter is on the need for accountability in marketing operations. The emphasis is on performance and the need for strategic control of marketing efforts at the business-unit level. An evaluation of a firm's marketing performance starts with an understanding of the managerial process and the role that measurement of results plays in that process and the achievement of profitability and productivity targets. Performance measurement is an integral part of the strategic planning process, including control, coordination, and value creation.

The control process includes an identification of the key issues to be measured or controlled, performance standards and measures, assessment and reassessment, and correcting identified problems or weaknesses. The control process should be continuous and coordinated across all functional areas and should consider the economic value added by each business unit.

Performance evaluation occurs at all levels of an organization: corporate, business, and functional (operating). Measurement of marketing perform-ance is concerned primarily with all relevant elements of the marketing mix, with a great deal of attention paid to integrated marketing communi-cations. It is also useful to evaluate the perform-ance of other functional areas (e.g., accounting, human resources, operations) as they impact mar-keting outcomes.

The key questions to be answered in measuring performance are: What is (or is not) working? Why are the strategies working (or not working)? Have marketing strategies been implemented according to plan? Likewise, analysis includes an assessment of competition and the firm's environment. Key performance criteria include measures of prof-itability, activity, productivity, liquidity, and leverage. Ratio analysis of data in each category provides the marketer with information about the firm's posi-tion relative to the industry and its own past per-formance. The strategic profit model (SPM) is an integrated framework that is useful for planning and analyzing marketing strategies. Profitability, as-set turnover, and leverage are the primary ratios used to analyze performance.

The sources and quality of data used to meas-ure performance have a significant impact on the quality of analysis that can be performed. Consid-erable secondary data are available from either in-ternal or external sources, gathered by another party for another purpose. Problems with the use of secondary data are related to units of meas-urement, class definition, and currency of in-formation. Criteria for judging the accuracy of secondary data include the source used, the pur-pose of the publication, and general evidence of quality. Primary data (gathered for the present pur-pose) have the advantage of being timely and pro-viding in-depth answers and quality control.

Questions

1. Describe the managerial process. Explain the relationship between the managerial process and (a) profitability and productivity and (b) strategic planning.

2. Describe the elements of the control process used to measure marketing performance in a typical firm.

3. Discuss the types of operating results that typically are analyzed at the corporate (strategic), business, and functional (operat-ing) levels of a business. Give specific exam-ples, and indicate why you believe each is useful for making and evaluating marketing management decisions.

4. Describe the relationship between an analy-sis of the macro- and micro-environments and an analysis of each of the functional areas at the operating level. Include specific applications for the following:

   a. Product mix (sales forecasting, pricing strategy, buying, inventory control)

   b. Integrated communications mix (all aspects of the promotional mix)

   c. Operations (productivity, risk management)

   d. Accounting and control (MDSS inputs and use)

   e. Human resources (personnel data)

5. A product manager in an electronics manu-facturing firm decides to add a line of new, high-tech, high-priced items to the product line. Although this line generally would com-pete at regular price with comparable brands in the higher-priced home electronics line, the manager plans to enter the market with a penetration pricing strategy to gain volume and market share from competitors. Explain how this decision will impact other func-tional areas of the business and be affected by them.

6. Marketers must answer a series of questions for a comprehensive evaluation of their over-all performance. List these questions, and ex-plain how each is helpful in an analysis of a

company's performance results. Compared with a large company, would it be useful for a small company to seek answers to these same questions in evaluating marketing performance? Defend your answer.

7. Discuss the problems that may be encountered when using secondary sources of information for managerial decisions. What criteria can be used to determine the accuracy of secondary data? If the data are published in a reputable publication, is that a guarantee of their accuracy? Why or why not?

8. When is it appropriate to collect primary data? Give a specific example relative to computer software that is targeted to both final consumers and organizational buyers. Assume that the marketer wants to enter new markets with the company's software. Suggest several sources of external secondary data that may be helpful in making the right decision, as well as potential sources of internal secondary data. Give specific examples of how each source can be used for additional insights.

Exercises

1. Review current business media to determine any changes that have occurred in the business operations or industries of the market leaders described in this book. If any of these companies has experienced significant successes or failures, analyze the reasons for these changes.

2. Describe each of the key performance criteria that were discussed in this chapter. Obtain an annual report or other financial statements from a marketing firm and calculate as many of these ratios as possible with available data. Be sure to include each of the following criteria: profitability, activity, productivity, liquidity, and leverage. Compare the results with published industry ratios (see comparative ratios that can be found in

Dun's Industry Ratios, Robert Morris, *The Almanac of Financial Ratios,* or other sources). Interpret your findings in terms of the success of this company's performance relative to the entire industry.

3. Using the financial statement(s) that provided the basis for analysis in Exercise 2, analyze the results within the context of the strategic profit model, focusing on each of the individual ratios (profitability, asset turnover, leverage) as well as the return on investment (ROI) calculated for the entire model. Suggest some ways that the resulting ROI figure could be increased by management decisions with regard to any or all components of the strategic profit model.

Endnotes

1. Jagdish N. Sheth and Rajendra S. Sisodia, "Improving Marketing Productivity," in Jeffrey Heilbrun (ed.): *Marketing Encyclopedia: Issues and Trends Shaping the Future* (Chicago: American Marketing Association, 1995), p. 218.

2. *Ibid.,* p. 219.

3. Mary J. Pitzer, Michael Oneal, and Tim Smart, "How Three Master Merchants Fell from Grace," *Business Week* (March 16, 1987), pp. 38–40; Eryn Brown, "America's Most Admired Companies," *Fortune* (March 1, 1999), pp. 68ff; Jeremy Kahn, "The Fortune Global 500: The World's Largest Corporations," *Fortune* (August 3, 1998), pp. 130ff; "Business Week's Industry Rankings of the S&P 500," *Business Week* (March 30, 1998), pp. 123ff.

4. Sheth and Sisodia, *op. cit.,* pp. 221–223.

5. *Ibid.,* pp. 223–236.

6. David A. Aaker, *Strategic Market Management,* 5th ed. (New York: John Wiley & Sons, 1998), pp. 119–120.

7. *Ibid.,* p. 120.

8. Shawn Tully, "The Real Key to Creating Wealth," *Fortune* (September 20, 1993), pp. 38–50.

9. Robert H. Waterman, Jr., *The Renewal Factor: How the Best Get and Keep the Competitive Edge* (New York: Bantam Books, 1987).

10. Peter Galuszka, Ellen Neuborne, and Wendy Zellner, "P&G's Hottest New Product: P&G," *Business Week* (October 5, 1998), pp. 92, 96.

11. Tim Ambler, "Why Is Marketing Not Measuring Up?" *Marketing* (September 24, 1998), pp. 24–25.

12. John R. Graham, "Ways to Evaluate Your Marketing Program," *Nation's Restaurant News* (March 23, 1998), pp. 32, 62.

13. For further discussion of cross-functional analysis of operating results, see Carol Anderson, *Retailing: Concepts, Strategy and Information* (Minneapolis/St. Paul: West Publishing Company, 1993), pp. 659–666.

14. This section is adapted from *ibid.,* pp. 666–677.

15. Gilbert A. Churchill, *Marketing Research: Methodological Foundations,* 4th ed. (New York: Dryden Press, 1987).

16. *Ibid.*

17. Judith Passingham, "Grocery Retailing and the Loyalty Card," *Market Research Society* (January 1998), pp. 55–63.

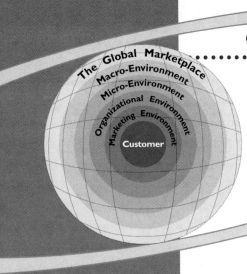

CHAPTER 16

The Marketing-Oriented Organization

The Marketing Organization's Structure

The Evolving Marketing Organization

Integrated Management Systems

Recent Trends in Management Practice

The Virtual Organization

We know how to invest in technology and machinery, but we're at a loss when it comes to investing in human capital.[1]

A Virtual Organization in Operation

Oticon Holdings A/S is a company located in an old factory just north of Copenhagen, Denmark. Operating profit in 1995 was approximately $20 million on total revenues that exceeded $160 million, generated by Oticon's 150-person staff. These figures represent nearly a 10-fold increase from the company's 1990 levels. Oticon recently announced several technologic developments that resulted in the world's first digital hearing aid, and many observers believe that Oticon is developing new products about twice as fast as any competitor. Therefore, if you were to visit Oticon, you would expect to find a bustling organization. However, even though you would find that Oticon has lots of workstations, phones, and computers, no one sits at a desk. You would find no one in the hall or at the water cooler. In fact, hardly anyone is at the factory location. As Lars Kolind, company spokesperson and leader—not necessarily president or CEO—says: "Hearing aids are not the core of what this company is about. It's about something more fundamental. It's about the way people perceive work. There's a paradox here. . . . We're not fast on the surface. But we're fast underneath."

Kolind joined Oticon in 1988 and found it deeply troubled. He cut costs and increased productivity in order to achieve profitable operations but realized that to match competitors, Oticon would have to be totally redesigned. On the first day of 1990, Kolind issued a four-page memorandum specifying that the family-owned company that had a 100-year history was doing away with a formal organization. All employee titles were erased. There would no longer be assigned offices. He wrote that the enemy of the company was itself. Projects became the defining unit of work. Teams, which included technical and human resources, were formed, dissolved, reformed, and disbanded continuously. It also was decreed that there would be no distinction between project leaders and other workers. Kolind wanted an environment where the customer came first and where Oticon's people could grow professionally and personally, so Oticon could become effective, efficient, and action-oriented.

Source: Polly Labarre, "This Organization Is Dis-Organization," *Fastcompany* (June–July 1996), *www.fastcompany.com/03/oticom.html.*

The adoption of a marketing-oriented viewpoint has profoundly affected the way in which many firms organize and operate. The impact is visible at every level, from chief executive to marketing trainee, and is seen to some degree in every facet of a firm's activities. We see it in finance, in research and development (R&D), in manufacturing, and of course, in sales. Peter Drucker, the universally acclaimed guru of management thinkers, has said that the purpose of a business is "to create a customer." He also stated that marketing is "a central dimension of the entire business."[2]

THE MARKETING ORGANIZATION'S STRUCTURE

We could say that a marketing organization is one that views its whole business according to its basic function—pleasing the customer. Concern and responsibility for marketing therefore must permeate all areas of the enterprise, and carrying out the marketing task is the responsibility of the entire company, because satisfying customers is everybody's job.[3] However, at each management level, the marketing tasks are slightly different.[4]

The Role of Top Management

In 1985, a report by Coopers & Lybrand, Inc. indicated that although only 29 percent of the chief executives believed that marketing was the most important management area in 1983, two years later 64 percent held that view. The report stated, "Strategic marketing, marketing strategies, and marketing plans which help corporations hold or develop a competitive advantage have become paramount management challenges and major unresolved business issues."[5] According to the head of one executive search firm, clients are increasingly asking to locate chief executive officer (CEO) candidates with "savvy, marketing skills, and vision." John Bassler noted that "profitability-minded boards of directors want CEOs who can establish a strong customer focus and marketing strategy and to clearly communicate it to all reporting managers throughout the company."[6]

Top managers determine the kind and size of company theirs should be. In the very broadest sense, the CEO must answer this question: "Who is our customer, and how do we satisfy him or her—now and in the future?" By defining the customer, it is possible to make plans to provide specific goods and services designed to satisfy the targeted groups. Top management is able to determine which ventures to support and which to abandon. We refer to these kinds of marketing-oriented decisions as *corporate strategic planning.*

The company's top management also gives specific marketing-oriented direction to those at lower levels in the company so that these people can develop appropriate marketing strategies and tactics to carry out the company's mission. Top management establishes objectives for its various divisions. It also may set policies that will guide operating people in making lower-level decisions. Finally, of course, top management establishes an organization capable of carrying out the company's mission and objectives as well as creating a climate conducive to effective performance. To illustrate how important this kind of leadership can be to a company, consider the situation at Club Med Inc. Club Med Inc. was a company that grew dramatically in its early years as a result of the unique operating formula established at its vacation club locations. However, when faced with the reality of a rapidly changing market during the 1990s, the company recruited for its president's office Phillippe Bourguignon. Bourguignon had been CEO of Euro Disney SCA, where he had turned a loss situation into a profit maker in a little more than 2 years.[7]

The Role of Divisional Management

In decentralized companies, the second tier of management often is called the *divisional level.* The divisional level may be an entire company, such as a subsidiary of a large parent corporation, or in smaller firms, the second level might be a group of similar products managed by a divisional vice-president. Regardless of nomenclature, a hierarchy exists, and this next-lower management level has a specific marketing role.

The division manager is responsible for developing a long-range marketing strategy consistent with the company's mission—one that will achieve the objectives assigned to the division. Marketing is a most important element in a division's overall plan. The marketing strategy is aimed at a particular group of potential customers (usually labeled a *market segment*). It entails decision making in the four critical areas of marketing management: products, distribution, communications, and pricing. Manufacturing plans, financial plans, and work force plans also are needed. But the principal thrust of a division's program is almost always marketing, because the basic purpose of a company—its very reason for existing—is to develop customers and provide customer satisfaction. Obviously, a marketing strategy is not developed until exhaustive research concerning the consumer, the competition, and all the other external influences has been completed.

Strategic business units (SBUs)
Operate more or less independently to reach established goals by manufacturing and supplying a product (or product line) to a distinctive market segment that differs from the market served by the remainder of the firm.

As companies have grown, especially through acquisition or by diversification, it has become useful to define another level of strategic management. Within the division or business group there may exist a number of **strategic business units (SBUs).** These business units are operated more or less like individual businesses, and their managers have considerable authority over the manner in which they seek to achieve their objectives. This is the level of management where specific decisions are made about the products or services to be offered and the markets to be served. If an SBU has more than one product or market, it may organize itself around these products and markets. It may have several products/markets in its portfolio of offerings. These products/markets usually are directed by middle managers known as *product* or *market managers*. Although these managers do not have as far-reaching authority as do division or even SBU managers, they often are responsible for developing strategies for the entire marketing program, including those activities performed outside the marketing department.

The Role of Functional Management

At the operational level, many businesses are organized along functional lines. That is, a division or SBU often is divided into at least three specialized areas: manufacturing, marketing, and finance. These functional departments are managed by persons who develop the detailed programs (or tactics) necessary to carry out the divisional strategy. These action-oriented programs usually are associated with the short run, a period of 1 year or less.

The marketing department is the key functional group in a company's effort to implement a marketing orientation focused on customers. It contributes in two very important ways. First, as a functional department specializing in marketing, it has the responsibility of working out the short-term tactical details of a division's long-range marketing plan. Managers of specialized marketing activities, such as product planning, advertising, and personal selling, develop short-run programs for their areas. The manager of the marketing department makes sure that the various tactical plans are integrated.

The marketing department's second contribution to the company's overall marketing effort is in its role as an intelligence-gathering arm of the firm. Corporate strategic planning and divisional and SBU long-range planning require information about customers, competition, and social, economic, and political developments. Similarly, information about the company's past sales and profits is required. It is often the responsibility of the marketing department to gather this marketing research information from external and internal sources. Very large companies with extensive and sophisticated marketing intelligence needs expand the research function into a complete marketing information and control system, often referred to as a *marketing intelligence system.*

In carrying out these two important responsibilities, the marketing department becomes the key group in a company. However, it does not run the company, nor do marketing managers intrude into the domains of other functional managers, dictating how their jobs should be done. Marketing gives purpose and direction, and a company operates best not when marketing people run it but when all those making business decisions do so from a marketing point of view.

The Flow of Authority

In most organizations, power is concentrated in the hands of the owners or their hired managers. Operationally, power is centered in the office of the CEO. To accomplish the organization's objectives, this power is delegated to subordinates within the organization. The delegation of authority is not without constraints. It must take place within the framework of established policies, job descriptions, job relationships, and cultural norms of the organization.

Line authority
The power to issue instructions and delegate authority to others in the organization.

Line Authority.   One type of delegated authority is line authority. **Line authority** involves the power to issue instructions to other designated persons. A plant manager is authorized to operate a factory and may, in turn, delegate authority for performing specialized manufacturing activities to various foremen or department heads. Foremen, in turn, may delegate some authority to production group leaders. Sales authority is delegated to a general sales manager, who usually delegates authority to regional or district sales managers. The regional sales manager, in turn, delegates authority to individual salespeople. Thus the component positions in a business are linked by the flow of line authority.

Responsibility for performing staff (advisory) activities is often delegated to specialists. Staff executives have no power over other functions. A staff executive, however, often requires the support and cooperation of these people. In place of line authority, the power of persuasion and the influence of skill and knowledge must be exercised. In a way, the staff executive must rely on an authority of ideas instead of an authority of position.

The delegation of authority creates a one-on-one, vertical relationship of superior and subordinate. In larger organizations such as the military, authority must be dispersed throughout the various levels within the system before delegation can take place. The dispersion is accomplished by decentralization.

Decentralization.   Decentralization can be accomplished in several ways. First, the responsibility and authority to implement marketing plans may be assigned geographically to district or local managers. This method is used most commonly in organizing the sales department. It also is used in decentralized retail organizations, such as Sears, Roebuck and Co. and J.C. Penney Company, Inc. Marketing responsibilities also may be assigned functionally. Advertising, sales, marketing research, and physical distribution frequently are headed by individual functional managers. A third way to decentralize the marketing management authority is on the basis of products. Occasionally, product decentralization is carried all the way through the organizational structure. The result is that a company may have parallel organizational arrangements for different product lines. For instance, Procter & Gamble Co. has separate marketing organizations servicing retail food stores. One group represents such food products as cake mixes, another group sells soaps and detergents, and still another sells health and beauty products. The product management system generally is used by firms that offer a wide variety of products or brands to a relatively homogeneous group of customers.

Marketing manager
The person charged with the task of directing a firm's efforts to serve (satisfy) a particular class of customer.

A fourth method of decentralizing marketing authority is through the use of marketing managers.[8] The **marketing manager** is the person charged with the task of directing a company's efforts to serve a particular class of customer. For instance, an industrial products company that sells products both to manufacturers called *original equipment manufacturers* (OEMs) and to distributors for use as replacement parts may use separate marketing managers, one for each class of trade. Fractional-horsepower electric motors provide an example. General Electric Co.

(GE) sells motors to Maytag for installation in home washing machines and dryers. It also sells motors to electrical wholesalers, who in turn sell them to appliance repair companies. GE may very well use two marketing managers, one for OEM customers (such as Maytag) and another for so-called after-market (resale) customers. The marketing manager system generally is used when a firm has a relatively short and standardized line of products used by customers in a number of different applications.

It is possible to combine two or more of these four methods of decentralization into a single complex method. Basic divisions may be made along either product or market lines. Planning, marketing research, and promotional tasks could be assigned to functional departments. A traditional line organization might be used for the sales department. We refer to this type of structure as **matrix management** because these various components have overlapping concerns and must coordinate their activities closely.

Another matrix arrangement is shown in Figure 16.1. The basic approach is functional. The marketing manager directs two product managers and also supervises a corporate staff of marketing specialists. These functional managers assist the

Matrix management
Involves dual lines of authority and reporting responsibilities, which results in overlapping concerns.

FIGURE 16.1

Example of a Matrix Structure

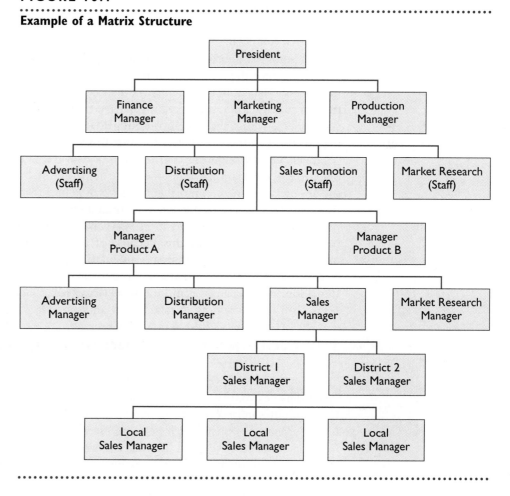

marketing director in developing overall plans and procedures. They also have functional responsibility for the activities of their counterparts who work for the product managers at the next-lower level of the organization. For example, the product *A* advertising manager would consult with the corporate advertising manager on matters of company policy, such as the use of corporate identification marks, advertising agency selection, and obtaining frequency and space discounts in advertising media. The product *A* advertising manager, however, reports to the product manager, not to the corporate advertising manager.

Product manager
A line executive with direct responsibility for the total marketing of a product.

In Figure 16.1, the **product manager** is a line executive with direct responsibility for the total marketing of a product. However, many product managers are considered to be staff. They have no direct authority over anybody else in the organization, but they nonetheless have responsibility for managing their assigned products at a profit. This is where the "authority of ideas" comes into play. Any organizational conflict that may arise because of a lack of direct authority ultimately must be resolved by the line executives involved. However, if the product manager is doing the job well, such crises are not likely to occur often. This remains one of the most serious drawbacks of the product manager form of organization, though.

The Flow of Information

The other important flow that traditionally linked the components of an organization is that of information. In the past, much of this flow was related directly to the flow of authority and to the staff's responsibility for preparing instructions and reports. However, the overall information flows within an organization move more freely and in far more complex ways than do those required by the basic organization. As noted earlier, staff executives have no line authority over other functional components within the system, but they do exchange information with them, carrying out assigned responsibilities through this exchange of ideas.

It is largely through this transfer of information that a business system becomes operative. Organizational relationships can be defined and communicated, but in the absence of dynamic information flows, it is impossible for the system to be active. Only by reacting to information about a change in its environment can a company adapt to external threats to its survival or respond to opportunities on which to base its expansion programs. Because of the functional importance of the information flow and the fact that serious management problems are encountered in connection with it, considerable attention has been paid to the management of information. In no area is this more critical than in marketing management.

THE EVOLVING MARKETING ORGANIZATION

The past 50 years have seen many changes in marketing organization. Contemporary forms bear only a slight resemblance to those that existed prior to World War II. Despite the improvements, problems continue to exist.[9] Because the marketing function changes constantly, it is by no means certain that the best organizational form has yet been developed. The discussion of marketing organization that follows assumes this point of view. The dynamic character of a marketing organization is stressed.

MARKETING IN THE INFORMATION AGE

Who Owns Ideas?

Employees of many major firms are required to sign a document promising (1) not to reveal company secrets and (2) that their ideas, intellectual property, and so forth belong to their employer. But many of today's activities require swapping proprietary information with outsiders, and perhaps the real ownership of ideas is not either corporate or personal but something becoming known as a *community of practice*. The Institute for Research on Learning (IRL), a spin-off of Xerox Corp.'s Palo Alto Research Center, has a mission to study how people learn that is considered basic research for the information age.

The fundamental finding of IRL's work is that learning is social and happens in groups. This is a finding with immense implications for managers because not all groups learn. You cannot randomly assemble a group of people and expect them to learn. Instead, IRL suggests that groups that learn—*communities of practice*—have special characteristics. To begin with, they emerge on their own because they are drawn together by social and professional pressures. Members collaborate, use each other as sounding boards, and learn from each other.

Brook Manville, director of knowledge management at McKinsey & Co., defines a community of practice as "a group of people who are informally bound to one another by exposure to a common class of problem." Like professional societies, however, communities of practice are responsible only to themselves. There is no boss, and no one owns them. A person joins and stays because there is something to learn and contribute in a social group setting, so output belongs to the group. Unlike affinity groups and clubs that are about fellowship or the "grapevine" and other networks that support work but are not the focus of work, communities of practice have a distinct place in the informal work organization. Although not a box on the organization chart, they have a social charter, an agenda, a deadline, accountability, and a membership list. But communities of practice are so obvious that we do not usually notice them.

Since organizational learning depends on these often not very visible groups, should they be managed? A study by Purser of Loyola University in Chicago and Pasmore and Tenkasi of Case Western Reserve in Cleveland indicates that communities of practice are almost immune to conventional management. Since learning in communities of practice seems to depend on informal exchanges, attempts to manage may kill them. However, if you cannot manage communities of practice, you can at least help them. How? By recognizing that they are important and by facilitating their informal exchanges. For example, let them build their own intranet, use conferencing facilities, and even put some of their get-togethers on the organization's expense accounts.

At National Semiconductor Corp., communities of practice have been officially recognized and given certain roles, for example, reviewing microchip designs or adding cross-functional perspectives to business-unit projects. Says Skip Hovsmith, director of National Semiconductor's mobile-computing research, "We're decentralized, but we had to share and collaborate, pressured by the convergence of markets and shorter product lifetimes. Communities of practice are the bridge."

Source: Thomas A. Stewart and Victoria Brown, "The Invisible Key to Success," *Fortune* (August 5, 1996), pp. 173–178.

FIGURE 16.2
....
Marketing Organization Circa 1946

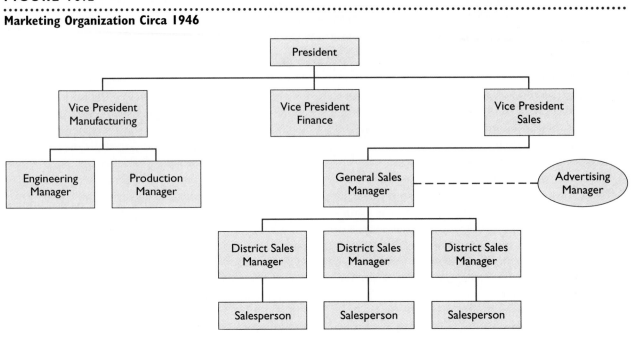

The Marketing Organization Circa 1946
....

Figure 16.2 presents an organizational chart of a typical firm engaged in marketing in the immediate post–World War II period. It is generally similar to the structures that prevailed for many years prior to that date.

Three traditional organizational components—manufacturing, finance, and sales—dominate the structure. Two important and distinct entities exist within the manufacturing area: the engineering department, which is responsible for the design and development of products, and the production department, which is responsible for manufacturing the firm's products. Line authority within the sales division was delegated by the general sales manager to district sales managers. These individuals, in turn, assigned sales authority to individual salespersons in the various territories. One staff marketing position is shown: an advertising manager reporting to the general sales manager. The advertising manager had no authority over others in the organization but was limited to preparing advertising plans and serving as a point of contact with an advertising agency. (The reader should not be surprised to know that this form of organization still exists.)

In the decade following the end of World War II, a number of important developments occurred. First, most companies experienced rapid, and sometimes disruptive, growth. Doubling in size was quite normal, and tenfold increases in the level of business were common. Many firms in this period diversified rapidly, driven partly by profit possibilities and partly to hedge against the uncertainty of single-line manufacture and marketing. Important technologic developments occurred, along with changes in manufacturing methods that were largely the result of automation. There also were changes in the way in which customers used the products and raw materials they purchased, as well as dramatic changes in the level of sophistication in customers' purchasing practices. Another aspect of technologic change was the R&D explosion. The pent-up technology that broke through in the postwar period made many prewar products obsolete. This increased level of R&D resulted in the rapid obsolescence of even some of the newer products, and the life expectancies of all products were cut substantially.

The favorable economic conditions that prevailed in the postwar period made it possible for many new businesses to get started. Their entry, together with diversification moves by established firms, resulted in increased competition of three distinct types. First, there were new firms selling products similar to those already on the market, and because of technologic improvements, these firms were able to sell their products at lower prices. Second, there was the competition of new products from established companies. Finally, there was the dramatic impact of new product competition from entirely new businesses.

Changing technology, new products, and increased competition demanded tremendous capital outlay, and costs mushroomed. Growth, diversification, adaptation of technologic breakthroughs, massive R&D, and increased competitive pressure forced postwar firms into a period that some writers called *profitless prosperity.* Insistence on profit control, increased skill in selling, and greater attention to productivity became focal points of management's attention. (These same factors re-emerged as key concerns in the 1990s.)

The Marketing Organization Circa 1960

Figure 16.3 presents a hypothetical organization that adapted to the economic and technologic developments between 1946 and 1960. The principal changes in structure occurred in the manufacturing area. Growth and diversification forced the enlargement, and in some cases the decentralization, of manufacturing. The products blocks (*A, B,* and *C*) could represent either product or geographic separation in manufacturing (probably both). Some of the decentralization also was the result of companies searching for lower-cost manufacturing locations. Within the engineering division, activities began to be specialized. Design and methods engineering were required to support the manufacturing operation, and a separate engineering activity was dedicated to product R&D. Although R&D groups and departments had existed previously, they became more common in this period. Some specialization also occurred in finance. Corporate financial planning, occasionally headed by a company economist, became a separate department within the financial division. Routine financial work such as accounting and budgeting was handled in another department.

Changes in the sales area were quite modest. In a few firms, a second specialist arose—the marketing research manager. Marketing research as a field was over 50 years old, but it had infrequently been awarded organizational status. Strangely enough, in some of the early organizational arrangements, the marketing research manager actually reported to the company's financial officer, not to the sales manager.

The changes made between 1946 and 1960 did not adequately solve the economic and technologic problems that had developed. Indeed, some of the organizational developments actually aggravated already existing situations. Among the

FIGURE 16.3

Marketing Organization Circa 1960

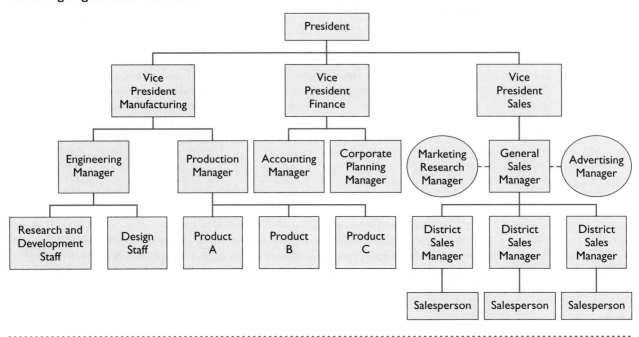

principal difficulties encountered in the mid-1950s was the entrenched product and manufacturing orientation in most firms. The changes that had taken place in manufacturing—decentralization, specialization of production, and the emergence of strong R&D groups—often led to a product-oriented company philosophy. The question usually was, "Can we make it?"—not, "Is there a market for it?"

A second major problem was a lack of coordination among sales, engineering, and manufacturing departments. Although engineering and production often reported to a common superior, there was little attempt to coordinate their activities more than was necessary to accommodate the manufacturing needs of the company. Coordination with sales occurred seldom, if ever.

Following a brief post–Korean War slump in the economy, prosperity generally prevailed, and most companies continued to grow. Unfortunately, profit margins became tighter and tighter. In part, this was the result of continuously rising costs. More important, however, was the decline in the number of profitable business opportunities. The cream apparently had been skimmed. Early on, capital had been poured into those projects that offered the best return. Only less profitable or marginal projects remained. It was in this condition that many companies entered the 1960s.

The Marketing Organization Circa 1980

The dynamic changes in competitive activities, customer expectations and demands in the period between 1960 and 1980, and the problems created by them led to some further important changes in the philosophy and structure of business. The

FIGURE 16.4

··

Marketing Organization Circa 1980

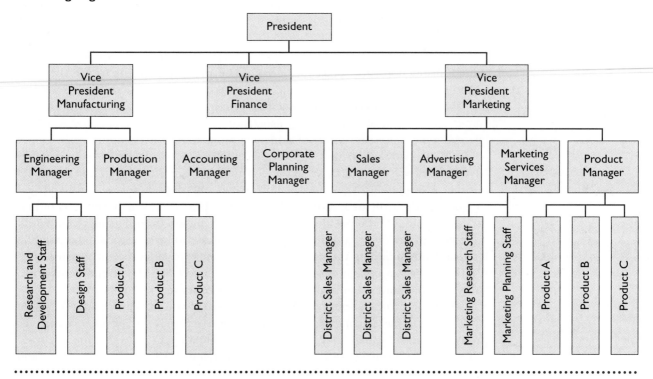

philosophical change involved the adoption of the marketing orientation concept, which focused efforts on the customer rather than on production capability. It demanded the integration of all marketing activities within the overall marketing effort and the integration of marketing with nonmarketing activities within the firm. Finally, it emphasized the importance of profit goals rather than sales goals. The organizational impact of the marketing concept is shown in very simple form in Figure 16.4.

The organizational changes in the period were almost entirely within the old sales department. The name changed. The term *sales* was replaced by *marketing*. However, it was not simply a change in terminology, for a new top-level management post was created. It was a line management position, and its incumbent was charged with the responsibility of carrying out all the marketing activities within the firm and of coordinating such activities with other company functions. This top marketing post carried different names in different companies. Whether titled vice-president of marketing, director of marketing, or simply marketing manager, the post reflected the ascendancy of the marketing concept to a visible position in the organizational structure.

Important developments took place within the new marketing department. The older marketing activities—sales, advertising, and marketing research—now reported to a common supervisor, the top marketing executive. A new marketing staff position was developed to coordinate various aspects of marketing, to work out detailed marketing programs for particular products or markets, and to provide liaison with other parts of the company. As we have already noted, the marketing manager was charged with coordinating all company efforts on behalf of a selected group of customers. The product manager, or brand manager, as the new marketing position commonly was called, was responsible for coordinating all company efforts on behalf of assigned products.

We will use the terms *brand manager* and *product manager* synonymously, although distinctions are sometimes drawn. The most common is to use the term *brand manager* exclusively in connection with consumer packaged-goods marketing. The term *product manager* seems to be used rather generally in both consumer and industrial marketing organizations. Often the product manager was charged with the responsibility of achieving programmed levels of profits.[10]

By 1970, many companies had adopted the product manager system. As might have been expected, companies in the consumer products field were the first to do so. Some industrial firms followed. Unfortunately, the product manager system failed to work satisfactorily in a number of companies. Uncertainty as to the type of person who should fill the position, failure to define the job carefully, and the inherent difficulties of achieving coordination in organizations long accustomed to operating independently hindered the development of a viable product manager system. Personnel turnover was high, results were slow to materialize, disappointments grew, and some companies returned to traditional organizational methods.[11]

Other companies attempted to find ways to make the product manager system work. For example, as a means of injecting more strategic thinking and concern for profitability into its marketing organization, Ocean Spray Cranberries, Inc., changed its organization from a traditional brand manager system to one that gave profit and strategy responsibilities to division business managers. In general, internal training, careful guidance and supervision by top management, and a great deal of patience have enabled a large number of companies to make the system work satisfactorily. The shakedown seems to have occurred, and it appears that the general form of organization shown in Figure 16.4 was followed by most companies in the 1980s.

Marketing Organizations in the 1990s

It is always difficult to recognize organizational trends in their early stages, and it is almost impossible to generalize about marketing organizations in the year 2000 and beyond. Companies continually experiment, and it is only after some passage of time that clear indications of new developments can be seen. However, some developments in recent years suggest several new directions. The considerable need for a constant flow of ideas for new products or other ventures has led some management leaders to separate the acquisition and expansion operations from the rest of the business. Often called *new-venture departments,* such units usually are not profit centers. Operating divisions therefore are not burdened with the specific costs of searching for and developing new products. Also, the search for new products or other ventures is not hindered by concern for or vested interests in established products.

The 3M Company is probably the best known of the companies that "disorganize" for new products. The Mac Group at Apple Computer Corp. functioned in almost complete isolation from the rest of the business as it developed Macintosh Office.

Another variant in the marketing-oriented organization appears to have developed in a number of large industrial companies. Ironically, it represents a return to an organizational form from which the organizational structures of the 1970s evolved. Known as the *strategic business unit,* it constitutes a "business within a business." We have already noted its role in the contemporary management hierarchy. In its earliest forms it was simply thought of as a return to a general management structure in which functional departments reported to the same executive, who in turn was held responsible for the profitable operation of the unit. The initial reason for the return to this basic structural form was to localize responsibility for performance and to achieve better coordination among manufacturing, marketing, and finance. However, it became evident at about the same time that much greater strategic flexibility could be achieved within the general management organizational scheme. Rather than trying to achieve corporate objectives by driving a monster organization in a single strategic direction, it made much more sense to let a number of separate entities within the business develop their own strategic plans within the framework of overall company policy. The concept of the strategic business unit evolved.

In one large firm in this evolutionary period, the Monsanto Company, product managers in one of the divisions (which would be called an SBU) were assigned the task of developing the total business plan for the unit. The plan, of course, was the general manager's plan, but the fact that it was prepared by a marketing person was significant. The importance of marketing was not diminished in this process. In fact, it was enhanced, because the business plan was a marketing plan. However, it was also a general business plan, embracing all the other functions. Thus marketing assumed its most logical role, not of running the business but of leading it in directions where its capabilities could best be used in serving its customers.

The SBU became the basis for a fundamental change in the way in which many (large) companies developed overall company strategy. Instead of simply being turned loose to maximize their respective positions, the business units were carefully managed as instruments of corporate strategy.

An important concept in architecture as well as management is that form follows function. This concept is directly applicable to marketing management. Organization should be the servant of strategy, not the reverse. As the marketing task changes, new organizational forms will unquestionably evolve to respond to the new assignment.

As we have seen, organizational changes have characterized the development of marketing. They will continue. Just as consumer affairs departments developed to deal with the challenge of consumerism, and new product departments were created to expedite the development of new offerings, so we can expect to see modifications occur in the present organizational arrangements in marketing. No organizational structure should be cast in concrete. To permit organization to dictate strategy would be absurd. At the same time, a company cannot be constantly changing its structure, nor should its managers ever fall into the trap of thinking that organizational change can be substituted for strategy. Form should follow function, and the best organizational arrangement is the one that permits a company to implement the most effective marketing plans it can devise. Conformance to this principle has brought the marketing organization to the state in which we find it today. It will surely dictate the organizational forms to be employed in the future.

INTEGRATED MANAGEMENT SYSTEMS

During the 1980s, a number of methods to improve organizational performance were embraced by firms eager to improve effectiveness and efficiency. These methods included systematized problem solving, various quality control methods, just-in-time inventory control, and continuous process improvement.[12] All these techniques helped to improve productivity, to develop innovative products, to reduce costs, to improve time to market, to improve quality, and to increase customer satisfaction and shareholder value. However, despite these results, many organizations in the last half of the 1990s were still experiencing an increasingly competitive environment while facing slow growth, declining market share, low return on assets, declining shareholder value, sagging morale, or some combination of these elements.

In order to counteract these negatives, some firms are turning to a variety of new solutions such as rapid-response initiatives and strategic alignment that basically seek to achieve customer satisfaction in a dynamic marketplace. However, some organizational writers[13] are suggesting that all these concepts are components to an overarching system called the **integrated management system (IMS).** The rationale is that during the 1980s the major challenge facing most organizations related to the need to significantly enhance the quality of both product and service offerings as well as the quality of internal operations. During the early 1990s, the challenge for managers shifted to re-engineering and restructuring in order to continuously transform and renew strategies, operations, work culture, people management and development, product development, customer service, mission, and values—all before the competition did so. Often the stakes were continued survival, because organizations that did not or could not continually reinvent themselves eventually would fall behind the competition. Xerox Corp., American Telephone & Telegraph Co. (AT&T), and more recently Kodak Co. and International Business Machines Corp. (IBM) are examples of firms that were market leaders but did not keep pace with industry changes. However, IBM and Hewlett-Packard Co. are current examples of firms that have renewed themselves successfully. How is it that some firms seem to be able to constantly renew while others seem less able to accomplish renewal?

Self-assessment and an integrated management system (IMS), when combined with the will and resources to do so, seem to be the key ingredients necessary to manage change on the targeted, leveraged, and accelerated basis necessary for organizational renewal. IMS is a closed-loop management system where all elements are interdependent (thus the need for bidirectional arrows in Figure 16.5). In the following paragraphs we will discuss how the typical IMS functions.

Integrated management system (IMS)
Involves re-engineering and restructuring in order to continuously transform and renew strategies, operations, work cultures, people management and development, product development, customer service, mission, and values to ensure continued survival in a highly competitive business environment.

Key Elements of the Integrated Management System

The integrated management system (IMS) involves several key elements: attention to customer needs; strong vision, mission, and values; careful strategic planning, business assessment, and business planning; the development of strategic objectives; a determination of critical performance measures and performance drivers; process improvement; and a final management review of the results.

FIGURE 16.5
· ·

The Integrated Management System

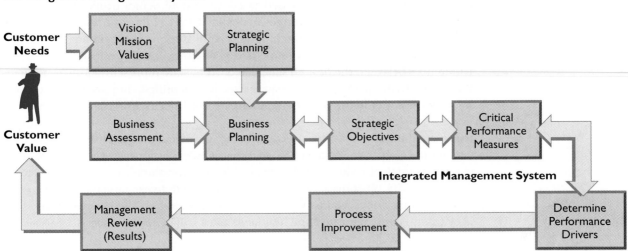

Source: Adapted from Ken Breen, Jerry Pecora, and Tome McCabe, "A New Dimension: Integrated Management Systems," *Quality Digest* (August 1997), pp. 36–41.

· ·

Customer Needs. Most organizations today proclaim that they are customer-focused and that success is determined by how well the organization gives customers what they want (satisfies customers). However, there is often a big gap between what is professed and what is delivered. Management needs to determine how well the organization surveys customer needs, improves customer value, measures customer satisfaction, resolves disputes, manages customer databases, manages customer relationships, retains customers, and integrates these activities into every aspect of daily operations.

Vision, Mission, and Values. *Vision* is the firm's perception of where the organization is going (strategic direction), and it is derived from the desire to profitably satisfy customer needs. The vision is translated into a *mission*—what to do, for whom, and why. In combination, the vision and mission direct the organization (employees) toward achieving a set of uniform objectives. The core *values* of the organization provide a common framework for decision making and taking action to achieve the strategic objectives.

Strategic Planning. Based on vision and mission, *strategic planning* produces measurable goals and objectives that are converted into business strategies, structures, systems, policies, and plans to ensure that everyone is working to achieve the strategic objectives. It determines where the firm is now, where it is going, and how it will get there.

Business Assessment. The organization should conduct a *business assessment* (determining where the firm is today) at least once yearly that corresponds with the

IMS model. Thus each element of the model will have a category of survey questions, for example, customer needs/values or critical performance measures, and each item on the survey is expressed as a desired state. Senior managers rate the organization on each element using a five-point Likert scale from strongly agree to strongly disagree, and each element is viewed in three ways: approach or method, deployment (extent to which the method is deployed), and results (performance). Differences between the desired state and current state represent performance gaps that need attention. Once performance gaps are identified, they are prioritized and then used as input to the business planning process. The output is the business plan.

Business Planning.   In *business planning,* management establishes financial targets for the organization as well as goals and objectives for the various function areas, for example, product development objectives or market expansion objectives or productivity objectives. *Objectives* are quantified 1-year targets, whereas *goals* are 5-year milestones against which progress is measured. The business plan states how resources are allocated and how objectives will be reached.

Strategic Objectives.   The *strategic objectives*—what the organization must achieve—are the basis for the business plan and are monitored continuously throughout the year. The business plan usually attempts to meet all stakeholder needs.

Critical Performance Measures.   In order to use IMS effectively, management must define the *critical performance measures* that drive the organization. Typical examples of critical performance measures are return on assets, return of equity, yield, defect rate, on-time deliveries, process efficiency, employee productivity, supplier effectiveness, sales plan versus actual, and customer satisfaction index.

Critical Performance Drivers.   Once the critical performance measures are established, management must determine which performance factors have the greatest impact on achieving objectives. For example, if improving the frequency of sales contacts and reducing the time between order placement and order delivery will increase customer satisfaction, then these become *drivers* or top business priorities.

Process Improvement.   The next step is to identify the processes that have the most impact on each performance driver. To achieve quantum performance gains on performance driver processes quickly, rapid-response teams are appointed and trained on a just-in-time basis. The rapid-response teams take action only on those processes deemed to be critically important to achieving strategic goals.

Management Review.   IMS is an iterative method, whereby early stages in the method may need to be repeated if later stages indicate the need to revisit previous stages to ensure effectiveness. Nonetheless, to complete the model, management must review IMS as a complete entity. Management must review all predictive measures and results, assess progress of all key improvement initiatives, make certain all targets are achieved, analyze gaps in performance, and take necessary corrective action. This review should be at each organizational level and at frequent intervals. The actual interval depends on the recent history of the firm in meeting its strategic objectives. If the firm has been unsuccessful recently, a crisis mode of operation exists.

The IMS Organization

Exactly what form of organization will be necessary to use IMS effectively has not yet become clear. Some firms have used self-directed work teams, whereas others have opted for temporary special task forces or rapid-response teams. Part of the answer may lie in determining whether the performance drivers involve only processes that are internal to the organization or also involve processes that have components that are external and thus involve suppliers or customers or other stakeholders. As time passes and more firms gain experience with IMS, the most effective modifications to organizational structure will become clear.

RECENT TRENDS IN MANAGEMENT PRACTICE

In order to determine the most effective modifications to organizational structure that will be necessary for future effectiveness, one also must consider several recent trends in management practice. These trends are discussed in the following paragraphs.

Total Quality Management

Total quality management (TQM)
Involves a customer focus, strategic planning and leadership, continuous improvement of all business systems and processes, and empowerment and teamwork in order to pursue quality as a basis for satisfying customers.

During the 1980s, many organizations embraced the concepts involved in using **total quality management (TQM)**. Although it is impossible to cover TQM thoroughly with a brief explanation, it is possible to examine the basic attributes of TQM, which are (1) customer focus, (2) strategic planning and leadership, (3) continuous improvement, and (4) teamwork and empowerment.

In order to maximize the potential benefits of TQM concepts, the organization must take the customer into consideration. The basic tenet of effective marketing is satisfying customers, and today's customers demand quality goods and services. As noted by Dean and Evans, "Today most managers agree that the main reason to pursue quality is to satisfy customers."[14] The American National Standards Institute (ANSI) and the American Society for Quality Control (ASQC) define *quality* as "the totality of features and characteristics of a product or service that bears on its ability to satisfy given needs." However, many organizations and customers now define quality as goods and/or services that meet or exceed customer expectations, and they believe that quality is a requirement for successful global competition. Thus TQM has become a standard requirement for effective marketing and for creating competitive advantage. So what are the basic attributes of TQM?

Customer Focus.   Since the customer is the judge of quality, TQM must be concerned with all product attributes that provide value in the eyes of the customer and that lead to customer satisfaction and loyalty. A number of factors have an impact on value and satisfaction during purchase and use or consumption of goods and services. These factors include the relationship between the organization and customers. This relationship is based on trust and confidence in the offered goods and services and leads to customer loyalty.

However, the organization that differentiates itself by offering features that enhance the good/service thereby meets or exceeds customer expectations. By exceeding customer expectations, a firm establishes a competitive edge. In this manner, TQM becomes a basic and key element of business strategy used for both customer retention and gaining market share. To be effective, TQM demands constant awareness of emerging customer and market requirements, plus ongoing measurement of those factors that drive customer satisfaction.

Strategic Planning and Leadership.   Market leadership based on TQM requires a long-term viewpoint, commitment of resources, and implementation of TQM concepts as key components to organization strategy. Planning, organizing, and executing TQM activities require a major commitment from all members of an organization. Strategies, plans, and budgets all need to reflect these long-term commitments to customers, employees, stockholders, and suppliers (some of the most important stakeholders). Such aspects as employee training and development, supplier development, and development of technology become key elements of this commitment and need regular review and assessment of progress toward established goals.

Leadership is the most important aspect of this commitment. Top-level managers must publicize internally their belief in TQM, and they must take part in the creation of strategies, systems, and activities designed not only to satisfy customers but also to exceed their expectations. Top managers must be role models for the whole organization. They must exhibit direct guidance of the activities and decisions of all portions of the organization and encourage participation and creativity by all employees. In addition, they must reinforce the corporate TQM values and commitment necessary to achieve satisfied customers even when costs and time schedules conflict with quality—otherwise the employees will view TQM as just another passing fad or latest management technique of the month. Over the long run, organizations cannot sustain TQM without strong ongoing top management leadership.

Continuous Improvement.   In order to achieve the highest level of quality and competitiveness, it is necessary for any organization to have a well-developed and well-executed continuous improvement system. Continuous improvement systems are likely to include at least several of the following approaches:

- Reducing errors, defects, and waste in operating activities, systems, and procedures

- Improving productivity and effectiveness in using resources

- Improving cycle-time performance and responsiveness to customers

- Improving customer value through new and improved products and services

Continuous improvement systems are necessary if the organization is to achieve quality, be efficient, and be responsive to customers, all of which will result in marketplace advantages. Implementing continuous improvement requires a basis (preferably quantitative) for assessing progress. This quantitative basis also becomes an information base for future improvement cycles. Customer satisfaction, the quality of products, and the effectiveness of internal processes all must be measured in order to meet organizational goals. These measurements must be based on reliable information, data, and analysis. The factors necessary for assessment and improvement include customer demographics and other facts, market surveys, competitor analysis, supplier capabilities and history, employee-related data, operating systems

MANAGING CHANGE

Companies Are Creating Programs to Help Employees Learn Leadership

 A common viewpoint is that business needs better leadership but that understanding how to teach leadership is still primitive. Because markets evolve, the definition of leadership mutates quickly. Today's standard of leadership—influencing human behavior in an environment of uncertainty—is extremely difficult to teach. Professor Ronald Heifetz, of Harvard's Kennedy School of Government, suggests that today's leaders focus on helping people find their own way through "adaptive challenges," which are problems without apparent solutions.

Some companies noted for producing effective leaders, Hewlett-Packard Co., Fuji Photo Film Co., Ltd., Xerox Corp. of Japan, General Electric Co., McKinsey and Company, Inc., and Pepsico, Inc., have been building quantifiable processes that bring discipline to leadership development. Attempting to develop leadership involves the "soft" side of management, yet today's competitive business environment tends to attract and promote people with "hard" management skills. However, as Roger Enrico, vice chairman of Pepsico, says, "The soft stuff is always harder than the hard stuff. Human interactions are a lot tougher to manage than numbers and P&Ls. So the trick is to make the soft stuff hard, to operationalize it."

Contemporary leadership involves aligning people toward common goals and empowering them to take the actions needed to reach them. This means leaders must be worthy of respect. Relinquishing the old command-and-control approach to leadership that General Electric Co. chief Welch, Pepsico CEO Wayne Calloway, and other leaders are doing requires voluntary compliance (and agreement). An example of this is

Jean Kvasnica at Hewlett-Packard Co., who heads a multifunctional sales team serving a major customer (hundreds of millions in purchases) but has few traditional aspects of authority. No one on the team reports to her, and she does not formally evaluate their performance or give them raises.

How does Jean motivate? She says, "They have to believe I know what I'm doing and won't waste their time." One of the team members, Javier Castelblanco, says, "Jean has vision and intense commitment to the successful outcome of a project, but the idea that makes it successful could come from anyone. She's not selfish about it."

All these companies routinely fire people who do not meet their standards. Pepsico's Calloway says, "Occasionally it's very important to have a public hanging." But once future stars are identified, these firms invest heavily in formal training and education—GE spends $500 million annually. However, as Steve Kerr, director of GE's Crotonville School explains, "I wish I could tell you that courses are the key, but they are not." Pepsico's Calloway says, "Among the elements of teaching leadership, 80 percent is experience. Our first line of offense is just to put them in the job."

Calloway and others believe that diversity of experience is a key factor in learning leadership. AlliedSignal's CEO Lawrence A. Bossidy agrees, but adds that the most fascinating assignment in the world may not teach you much unless your boss gives you a long leash.

Source: Sherman Stratford and Ani Hadjaian, "How Tomorrow's Leaders Are Learning Their Stuff," *Fortune* (November 11, 1995), pp. 90–105.

records, product and service performance records, and historical cost and financial records. Analysis of these factors is based on statistical reasoning and forms the basis for continuous improvement.

One approach that many organizations use as a basis to begin continuous improvement is to measure the costs of poor quality (or nonconformance); in this manner they identify improvement opportunities. The cost of poor quality includes items such as costs of scrap and wastage, costs of inspection, costs of rework (in all internal systems, not just production), costs of warranty claims, and costs of customer returns. With experience, most firms can isolate key success factors that are major elements in need of concentrated efforts directed at continuous improvement.

Teamwork and Empowerment.   In order to achieve organizational quality goals, teamwork must function at all levels. Dean and Evans have suggested that teamwork should be viewed in three distinct dimensions: horizontal, vertical, and interorganizational.[15] *Horizontal teamwork* more commonly takes the form of **cross-functional work teams,** in which team membership is drawn from a cross section of work groups and traditional functional departmental boundaries. Cross-functional work teams bring together persons with a variety of viewpoints and work experiences to foster cooperation in solving problems that transcend multiple departments within the organization.

Vertical teamwork involves cooperation between all organization levels of the firm. Team membership includes representatives drawn from top management, supervisory personnel, and shop-floor employees. As with cross-functional teams, one of the major advantages of vertical teamwork is the wealth of work experience and viewpoints that are focused in a cooperative environment designed to enhance the problem-solving capabilities of the team.

For teamwork to be effective, employees must be empowered to participate in making decisions that affect the organization and especially their work area. The individual who best knows the job is the person performing it. Developing and implementing new and improved systems will be most effective when implementation is initiated through employee involvement teams. Organizations should encourage teamwork and risk taking by removing the fear of failure, sharing success stories throughout the organization, implementing suggestion systems that react quickly, providing employee feedback, rewarding employees for implemented suggestions, and providing the necessary technical and financial support required to develop suggestions.

In many firms, empowering employees requires a profound shift in management philosophy. Employees at various levels within the organization will require training in teamwork skills in order to achieve effectiveness. However, participation in teamwork by everyone in the organization, as well as suppliers and customers, often will lead to creativity and innovation and thereby increase customer satisfaction and market share.

Re-engineering/Process Redesign.   A discussion of TQM would be incomplete without at least a brief reference to re-engineering. **Re-engineering** (also known as *process redesign*) is a type of continuous improvement, but it is continuous improvement with the potential for dramatic improvement in quality, speed of work cycle, and reduced costs because it involves fundamentally changing the processes

Cross-functional work team
Involves membership drawn from a cross section of work groups and traditional functional departments within a firm (and sometimes from external suppliers or customers).

Vertical teamwork
Involves cooperation between all organizational levels of a firm.

Re-engineering
Involves fundamentally changing work processes with the potential for dramatic improvement in quality, speed of work cycle, and reduced costs. Also known as *process redesign*.

by which the work gets done. When the implementation of incremental changes to operations usually associated with continuous improvement systems proves to be insufficient in enabling an organization to achieve its goals or objectives, then re-engineering is called for. For example, if a 5 percent improvement in speed of work, costs, and quality is insufficient because the leading competitor is already ahead by 50 percent in these factors, then process redesign is necessary.

Process is what connects customer expectations to the goods or services they receive. Process is what ensures or fails to ensure that goods/services meet or exceed customer expectations. Redesigning processes to reduce waste is the basis of re-engineering. If a process is not driven by customer expectation but is instead driven by cost accounting or a functional specialization, it may be ripe for redesign. The general principles of redesign include reducing handoffs, eliminating steps, performing steps in parallel instead of in sequence, and involving key people early. The results of re-engineering are often startling, and frequently those involved wonder why it was not done this way in the past. But the key aspect of redesign driven by customer expectations is the fact that it leads to increased customer satisfaction and competitive advantage.

Managing Change

Modern organizations confront a turbulent environment that requires rapid, flexible responses to changing conditions. Today, "doing business as usual" is ineffective.[16] Moreover, globalization of business necessitates effective and speedy communications and coordination across multiple time zones and far-flung geographic locations. Time constraints dictate reduction in reaction time as well as necessitating effective business processes such as just-in-time inventory, orders, scheduling, payments, manufacturing, distribution, and so on. Change has become the norm and unpredictable or unforeseen situations the basic reality for many firms.[17]

As a result, organizational theory indicates that in order to achieve sustainability, firms must change or adapt. Such adaptations range from specific responses to complete overhaul of strategic direction.[18] Previously we discussed the evolution of the marketing organization, but here we will re-emphasize that recent major changes in the corporate focus center on how the organization interacts with its environment. Management theories emerged that considered sources of organizational dependence on the business environment to include people, resources, markets, or information and how they could be controlled and influenced.[19] In order to develop mechanisms to support adaptation to change, both intracompany and intercompany coordination is needed. Information technology frequently is regarded as an integral component of these shifts in organizational design.[20] Electronic integration (EI) enabled the formation of new organizations that transcended traditional boundaries, and information technology was a critical force in this transformation of competition, firm structures, and firm boundaries.[21] Such agile, market-driven companies shuffle resources to meet customer needs[22] by implementing strategic alliances and interorganizational collaborations and partnerships.[23]

Guiding the development of new entrepreneurial units or deciding how to reformulate traditional organizational structures is a very difficult task. One new model that is being developed includes a network of corporate units, independent organizations, and entrepreneurs. These new model organizations are lean, flexible, adaptive, and responsive to both customer needs and market requirements. Key features include an understanding of customer needs and product selections that offer value to customers.[24] The term coined to describe such an organization is *dynamic network,* which is a controlled interlinkage of only those work groups required for the creation and marketing of a particular product or service (bundle of benefits) at a particular point in time. Such a highly flexible organizational arrangement can readily adapt to changes in technologies, markets, and demand levels by adding or subtracting work groups to the network.

Members of these work groups do what is called *collaborative work*. Collaborative work often involves increased levels of cooperation and coordination, both within and between organizations. Communications networks and information technology are the tools that make collaborative work possible, and telecommuting (or homework) makes work groups more productive.[25] With modern technology and group software, a work group can function almost like a single entity, even if its members are geographically widely dispersed.[26]

THE VIRTUAL ORGANIZATION[27]

As mentioned previously, information technology is the fundamental supporting tool required to perform the critical activities of modern businesses in a highly competitive environment. Information technology enables organizations to make effective and efficient changes in the way work is performed[28] and offers real potential for changing the way people work.[29] Some companies are forming international collaborative alliances to develop a sustainable competitive advantage.[30] Teams, committees, or work groups are fundamental to these organizations, and thus group behavior becomes a key concern. Some of these electronically linked groups behave like real social groups, even though they share no physical space, their members are invisible, and their interactions are asynchronous.[31] Information technology allows organizations to create more flexible structures designed to maximize the experience and expertise of their employees and to make it available wherever needed. This has led to the **virtual organization.**

Virtual organization
A collaborative network of employees, linked by integrated computer and information technologies, who draw on vital resources as needed and are not constrained by physical locations or by complex contractual arrangements.

Virtual organizations began 15 to 20 years ago as people envisioned the possibility of using technology for work at home.[32] Some now believe that it has become an economic necessity for corporate executives and a research area for business theorists.[33] The virtual organization takes the flexible specialization concept a step further than the dynamic network organization, because it is not constrained by either physical locations or by complex contractual arrangements.[34] Corporations are evolving into virtual enterprises using integrated computer and communications technologies to link all their employees together. Such collaborative networks are not defined by the usual physical walls around a specific space at a designated location. Instead, collaborative networks draw on vital resources as needed, regardless of where they are located physically and regardless of who owns them.[35] This does not mean that such organizations do not occupy a physical space—they do, but physical space need no longer be a fixed site.[36] Slow to modify, traditionally defined, and sharply delineated companies are evolving into virtual organizations with

Virtual office
The operational domain of any firm whose work force includes a significant number of remote workers.

Virtual product
New products or services demanded by customers, which change continuously to satisfy customer needs, wants, and desires.

structures and systems that are loose and fuzzy in order that they may assume whatever form is needed to respond to a rapidly changing marketplace.[37] Advocates for Remote Employment and the Virtual Office (AREVO) define the **virtual office** as the operational domain of any business or organization whose work force includes a significant proportion of remote workers.[38]

Virtual organizations are emerging because customers are demanding new goods and services: the **virtual product.** Virtual goods or services include 1-hour prescription eyeglasses, 1-hour development of photographs, overnight delivery, digital cameras, and a growing number of other instant-gratification goods or services. For an entity or object to be *virtual* used to mean that it possessed powers or capabilities of another entity or object. Now the term means that previously well-defined structures begin to lose their edges, seemingly permanent things start to change continuously, and goods and services adapt to match our desires. Virtual products can be made available at any time, in any place, and in any variety; but they can only be offered because of the latest innovation in information processing, organizational dynamics, and marketing and manufacturing systems. Virtual products deliver instant customer gratification in a cost-effective value-added way, can be produced in diverse locations and offered in a great number of models or formats, and ideally are produced instantaneously, customized to the customer's request. Only the virtual organization can deliver these virtual goods and services.[39]

Virtual organizations are reliant on cyberspace (the medium in which electronic communications flow and software operates) and initially will exist only across conventional organizational structures. Barnatt has identified four different versions of the virtual organization:[40]

1. *Telecommuting.* With telecommuting, or working at home, employees use a remote terminal to access their office system.

2. *Hot-desk environment.* In a hot-desk environment, individual desks are abandoned. Employees arriving at work are allocated a desk for the day from which they can access their electronic mail and computer network files.

3. *Hoteling.* Hoteling acknowledges the fact that many workers have no need of a permanent desk at their parent company. Instead, they spend much of their working lives with clients, using client facilities much like a hotel.

4. *Virtual teams.* By working in virtual teams, people collaborate closely but may be physically located in a variety of locations.

The growth of the virtual organization is fueled by three factors:[41]

1. Rapid evolution of electronic technologies, which facilitate digital, wireless transfer of video, audio, and test information

2. Rapid spread of computer networks

3. Growth of telecommuting, which will enable companies to provide faster response to customers, reduce facility expenses, and assist workers to meet their child-care and elder-care responsibilities

In the past, managers were restricted in their choice of organizational form and often used information technology as a tool for downsizing and restructuring.[42]

Currently, because computer systems have assumed many of the communications, coordination, and control functions within organizations, managers have the option to choose technology-driven control systems that can support the flexibility and responsiveness of a decentralized organization, as well as the integration and control of a centralized organization. Technology can be used to shape the organization into more flexible and dynamic structures.[43]

Summary

Although satisfying customers must be the concern and responsibility of everyone in the marketing organization, the tasks of top managers, divisional managers, and functional managers are different. Different organizational structures affect the flow of authority, the flow of information, and other linkages within the organization.

Over the past decades, the marketing organization has evolved from one dominated by manufacturing, finance, and sales to one whose focus is on the customer and coordinating marketing activities. Most recently, marketing organizations have added new venture departments to meet the need for new ideas and new business ventures.

The integrated management system (IMS) is one that has been proposed as a method to improve organizational performance. IMS is a closed-loop management system that, when implemented correctly, enables organizations to concentrate their efforts on satisfying their customers' needs in a value-added manner. Key elements of the IMS include customer needs; the organization's vision, mission, and values; strategic planning; business assessment; business planning; strategic objectives; critical performance measures; critical performance drivers; process improvement; and management review.

Total quality management and continuous process improvement have had a significant impact on management practice and organizational design over the past 20 years. Marketers also need to manage change from a global perspective and a look at future trends in organizational functional design.

The virtual organization and virtual products may be what the future holds for effective and efficient marketing organizations in the twenty-first century.

Questions

1. Describe in your own words the three tiers of responsibility that occur for marketing managers in marketing-oriented organizations.

2. Contrast and compare how the flow of authority versus the flow of information affects the linkages within organizations and how they in turn affect organizational structure.

3. With reference to the appropriate exhibits within the chapter, describe how the marketing organization within firms evolved from the 1960s to the 1980s.

4. What do you believe are the major advantages for a firm that uses IMS to improve organizational performance?

5. Describe what you believe the impact of TQM has been on marketing management.

6. How has the impact of continuous process improvement on marketing management differed as compared with your answer to Question 5?

7. What are the advantages to a firm of a virtual organization form of functional design?

Exercises

1. Using the resources of the local Chamber of Commerce, establish which local company employs the largest number of people (Note: Omit governmental agencies, universities, and colleges.) Locate this firm's latest five annual reports, and analyze them to see if there has been any reported major reorganization of the firm. Also telephone the firm and contact the human resources manager to ask how the organization of the firm has changed over the last 5 years. If there is no reported reorganization, or if the HR manager says the firm has not changed over the last 5 years, ask the question: "Why do you think there has not been the need to change the organization in the last 5 years given the dramatic advances in information technology and information management?"

2. Contact a large local hospital or similar health care facility, again speak with the manager of human resources, and ask how the organization, compensation, and evaluation of the nursing staff has changed recently (this can be within the last 10 years). Be particularly careful to ask about changes in the layers of management.

3. Contact the manager of your local bank, and ask how the organization of the bank has changed recently. Ask if these changes have resulted from governmental regulations, from consolidation within the banking industry, or from competitive and market factors.

Endnotes

1. Peter Senge, *The Fifth Discipline: The Art and Practice of the Learning Organization* (New York: Currency/Doubleday, 1990), p. 15.

2. Peter Drucker, *Management: Tasks, Responsibilities, Practices* (New York: Harper & Row, 1974), p. 61.

3. Frederick E. Webster, Jr., "The Changing Role of Marketing in the Corporation," *Journal of Marketing* 56 (October 1992), pp. 1–17.

4. *Ibid.*

5. "Strategic Marketing Priority of Chief Execs," *Marketing News* (January 13, 1986), p. 1.

6. John Bassler, "Companies Want CEOs with Strong Marketing Vision," *Marketing News* 23 (May 1986), p. 17.

7. Cecile Daurat "Paradise Regained?" *Forbes* (March 22, 1999), pp. 102–104.

8. M. Hanan, "Reorganize Your Company Around Its Markets," *Harvard Business Review* (November–December 1974), p. 63.

9. John P. Workman, Jr., Christian Hombur, and Kjell Gruner, "Marketing Organization: An Integrative Framework of Dimensions and Determinants," *Journal of Marketing* (July 1998), pp. 21–41.

10. The position of the product (brand) manager, its challenges, and its problems have received considerable attention in the literature. See, for example, V. P. Buell, "The Changing Role of the Product Manager in Consumer Goods Companies," *Journal of Marketing* (July 1975), p. 3; G. R. Gremmil and D. L. Wileman, "The Product Manager as an Influence Agent," *Journal of Marketing* (January 1973) p. 26; and Steven Lysonski, "A Boundary Theory Investigation of the Product Managers' Role," *Journal of Marketing* (Winter 1985), p. 26.

11. See, for example, "The Brand Manager: No Longer King," *Business Week* (June 9, 1973), p. 58; and Robert S. Wollowitz, "Product Management Lagging," *Advertising Age* (January 14, 1985), p. 14.

12. *Ibid.*

13. Ken Breen, Jerry Pecora, and Tome McCabe, "A New Dimension: Integrated Management Systems," *Quality Digest* (August 1997), pp. 36–41.

14. James W. Dean, Jr. and James R. Evans, *Total Quality: Management, Organization, and Strategy* (Minneapolis, Minn.: West Publishing Company, 1994), p. 12.

15. *Ibid.*, pp. 17–19.

16. P. Keen, *Shaping the Future: Business Design Through Information Technology* (Boston: Harvard Business School Press, 1991).

17. Robert F. Hurley and Tomas M. Hult: "Innovation, Market Orientation, and Organizational Learning: An Integration and Empirical Examination," *Journal of Marketing* (July 1998), pp. 42–54.

18. P. D. Jennings and P. A. Zandbergen, "Ecologically Sustainable Organizations: An Institutional Approach," *Academy of Management Review* 20 (1995), pp. 1015–1052.

19. H. J. Leavitt and H. Bahrami, *Managerial Psychology: Managing Behavior in Organizations,* 5th ed. (Chicago: University of Chicago Press, 1996).

20. G. DeSanctis and B. M. Jackson, "Coordination of Information Technology Management: Team-Based Structures and Computer-Based Communication Systems," *Journal of Management Information Systems* 10(4) (1994), pp. 85–110.

21. A. Kambil and J. E. Short, "Electronic Integration and Business Network Redesign: A Roles-Linkage Perspective," *Journal of Management Information Systems* 10(4) (1994), pp. 59–83.

22. R. E. Miles and C. C. Snow, "Causes of Failure in Network Organizations," *California Management Review* 241(5) (1992), pp. 53–72.

23. N. F. Piercy and D. W. Cravens, "The Network Paradigm and the Marketing Organization: Developing a New Management Agenda," *European Journal of Marketing* (1995), pp. 7–34.

24. D. W. Cravens, S. H. Shipp, and K. S. Cravens, "Reforming the Traditional Organization: The Mandate for Developing Networks," *Business Horizons* 37(4) (1994), pp. 19–28.

25. B. W. Stuck, "Collaboration: Working Together Apart," *Business Communications Review (Networking Supplement)* (February 1995), pp. 9–11ff.

26. S. A. Bly, S. R. Harrison, and S. Irwin, "Media Spaces: Bringing People Together in a Video, Audio, and Computing Environment," *Communications at the ACM* 36(1) (1993), pp. 28–47.

27. Much of this section is adapted from Susan E. Yager, "Everything's Coming Up Virtual," *Crossroads,* ACM's first electronic publication, 1997. Reprinted by permission of the author.

28. E. Turban, E. McLean, and J. Wetherbe, *Information Technology for Management* (New York: John Wiley & Sons, 1996).

29. S. Daniels, "The Disorganized Organization," *Work Study* 44(2) (1995), pp. 20–21.

30. A. J. Bailetti and J. R. Callahan, "The Coordination Structure of International Collaborative Technology Arrangements," *R&D Management* 23(2) (1993), pp. 129–146.

31. T. Finholt and L. S. Sproull, "Electronic Groups at Work," *Organization Science* 1(1) (1990), pp. 41–64.

32. H. C. Lucas, Jr. and J. Baroudi, "The Role of Information Technology in Organization Design," *Journal of Management Information Systems* 10(4) (1994), pp. 9–23.

33. B. Caldwell and J. Gambon, "The Virtual Office Gets Real," 1997, available at *http://techweb.cmp.com/iw/563/63mtoff.htm.*

34. C. Barnatt, "Office Space, Cyberspace and Virtual Organization," *Journal of General Management* 20(4) (1995), pp. 78–91.

35. S. E. Bleecker, "The Virtual Organization," *Futurist* 28(2) (1994), pp. 9–14.

36. T. L. Dixon, "Virtual Organizations: Success Stories," 1995, available at *http://mansci1.uwaterloo.ca/~msci604/summaries/virt_org.html.*

37. N. Duratta, "Communicating for Real Results in the Virtual Organization," *Communications World* 12(9) (1995), pp. 15–19.

38. Advocates for Remote Employment and the Virtual Office (AREVO), 1996, *http://www.globaldialog.com/~morse/arevo/.*

39. W. H. Davidow and M. S. Malone, *The Virtual Corporation: Structuring and Revitalizing the Corporation for the 21st Century* (New York: Harper Business Press, 1992).

40. C. Barnatt, *op. cit.*

41. R. Barner, "The New Millennium Workplace: Seven Changes That Will Challenge Managers—and Workers," *Futurist* 30(2) (1996), pp. 14–18.

42. L. M. Applegate, J. I. Cash, Jr., and D. Q. Mills, "Information Technology and Tomorrow's Manager," *Harvard Business Review* 66(6) (1988), pp. 128–136.

43. S. E. Yager, "Everything's Coming Up Virtual," 1997, available at *www.acm.org/crossroads/xrds4-1/organ.html.*

Index

Accessory equipment, 222
Accountability, 416. *See also* Performance
    and relating to customers, 156
Account executive (AE), job description
    for, 338
Accounting
    activity-based costing and, 421
    performance analysis and, 430
Accounting firms, 82, 254
Accounts payable to sales ratio,
    436–437
Accumulation of costs, 390
Activity, ratios for, 435–436
Activity-based costing, 421
Actual price, 391
Adaptability, channel intermediaries and,
    305
Adaptation, strategic planning and, 82–83
Adaptive behavior, in retailing, 300
Adaptive behavior theory, 301
ADCAD, 356
Adidas, 74
Administered VMS, 309
Adoption process
    of product, 234, **262**
    for services, 262–263
Adoption theory, 234–236
Advertising, 319. *See also* Advertising me-
    dia; Direct marketing
    audience(s) for, 349
    direct-action, 370
    opportunities for, 347–349
    of organizational goods, 223
    rationalizing and recycling, 421
    through the trade, 354
Advertising media, 194–195, 350–356
Advertising program, management of,
    347–356
Advocates for Remote Employment and
    the Virtual Office (AREVO),
    471
After-market (resale) customers, 453
Age
    buying behavior and, 147
    market segmentation and, 196, 197
Age-cohort groups, subculture compar-
    isons across, 140–141
Agent middlemen, 291–292
Agricultural goods, 222
Airline industry, 60–61. *See also* specific
    airlines
    situational factors and, 199–200
Alcoholic beverage producers, 194
Alliances. *See* Strategic alliances
Allied Signal, 49
Alternative Distribution Alliance (ADA),
    307
Amazon.com, 375
American Airlines, 45, 109
American Express, 74, 232
American Marketing Association
    Code of Ethics of, 84, 85–86
    publicity defined by, 356
American Productivity & Quality Center
    (APQC), 316

America Online (AOL), 267, 394, 441
    services marketing and, 247–248
Ameritech, 49
Analysis. *See also* Performance
    levels of, 424–431
    and strategic planning, 423
Ancillary services, 254, 264–265
Andersen Consulting, 267–268
Antecedent states, 154
Antismoking movement, 125–126
Antitrust legislation, 309
Apple Computer Corp., 460
Application, positioning by, 212
Approvers, and buying center, 174
Arbitron, 356
Art of War (Sun Tzu), 63
Asia
    market growth in, 187
    wholesaling and, 293
Assessment, continuous, 421, 422
Asset turnover, 432, 433, **435**
Assurance, and service quality, 268
AT&T (American Telephone & Telegraph
    Co.), 36, 80, 376
AT&T Global Information Systems, 138
AT&T Universal, 24
Athletic shoe industry, 72
Attitudes, 152
Attributes
    advertising and, 349
    evaluating services and, 261
Au Bon Pain, 275
Audience(s)
    for advertising, 349
    information about, 356
Audit, marketing, 107, 121–124
Augmented product, 220
Authority, flow of, 451–454
Automation, 310
    salesforce, 337–340
Automobile industry. *See also* Japan; spe-
    cific auto makers
    channels of distribution for, 289
    Internet marketing by, 375
    megamergers in, 39
    plight of, 34–35
    trucks, vans, and sport utility vehicle
        sales, 70
    value-added marketing in, 22–23
    world-class buyers and sellers in,
        161–162
Automotive Network Exchange (ANX),
    375
AutoNation, 305
Available funds approach, 328
Avon Products, Inc., 369, 372
Awards, for customer contact personnel,
    275–276
Awareness of product, 234

Baby Bell subsidiaries, 36
Baby-boomers, 41, 149
Backer Spielvogel Bates Worldwide, 206
Backward integration, corporate, 309
Bader, Terry, 357

Bakertowne Co., Inc., 380
Balance sheet, 434
Banana Republic, 74
BancOne, 21, 138
Bank of America, 45
Bannikov, Viktor, 68
Barnatt, C., 471
Barnes & Noble, 175
Barriers, to reaching customers, 194–195
Base price, 391
Basic level, of relating to customers, 156
Bassler, John, 449
Bauer, Eddie, 323
Bausch & Lomb, Inc., 395
Baxter International, 21
Bean, L.L., 323
Behavioral market descriptors, 199–200,
    203–204
Behrman, Jonn, 394
Beliefs, 152
Belz Outlet Mall, 297
Benchmark, 268
    of competition, 138
    in global market, 37
    for services, 268–269
Benefit market segmentation, 200–201,
    204–205, 260
    positioning by, 212–213
Benefits comparison, 401
Berlow, Myer, 394
Berry, Leonard L., 269, 275
Better Business Bureaus (BBBs), 398
Beyond Interactive, 394
Bias issues, and marketing intelligence,
    116–118
Bicycle industry, 40
Big Three auto makers, 35, 38. *See also*
    Automobile industry
Billboards, 351–352
Biometrics, 47
Birth stage, of natural ecocycle, 32
Blockbuster, 52
Bloomingdale's Inc., 264
Blueprinting, 270, 271
Boeing, 375
Boise Cascade Corp., 325
Bossidy, Lawrence A., 467
Bourguignon, Phillippe, 450
Boutiques, 301
Bowerman, Bill, 33
Box (limited-assortment) stores, 298–299
Brand, 230, 239–242, **240**
    multiple names of, 240
Brand equity, 239, **240**–242, 320
Brand images, 148
Brand loyalty, 242
    in service purchasing, 262
Brand manager, 460
Break-even analysis, 404–406
British Airways, 21
Britt, Frank, 315
Broadcast media, direct-response advertis-
    ing and, 372–373
Budgeting, for IMC, 327–330
Build-to-order (BTO) concept, 279–280

Bunn, Michele D., 176
Burnett, Stephen C., 232–233
Business buying behavior. *See* Organizational buying behavior
Business level, marketing performance analysis at, 426
Business markets, 163–167
Business mission, 65–66
Business organizations, buying by, 171
Business purchasing. *See also* Organizational buying behavior
  extended taxonomy of buying decisions and, 176, 177
  home-office workers and, 165
  by state and local governments, 166–167
  types of purchase decisions and, 175–176
Business revolutions
  globalization as, 36–39
  technologies and, 38, 43–46
Business strategy, 62
Business-to-business buying
  decisions for, 176–181
  process of, 169–172
Business-to-business direct marketing
  growth areas in, 378–379
  sales of, 366
Business-to-business markets, bases for segmenting, 201–205
Business-to-business sales, value of direct marketing-driven, 370
Buyers, 9. *See also* Organizational buying behavior
  and buying center, 175
  price and, 389–390
  value-oriented, 43
Buyer-seller relationships, 155–156
  in business purchasing, 182
  long-term, 156
Buying. *See also* Business-to-business buying; Consumer buying process
  organizational, 22
Buying behavior, 21–22. *See also* Business purchasing; Consumer(s); Organizational buying behavior
  business markets and, 161–163
  changes in markets and, 21–22
  family/household, 145–146
  personal influences on, 146–149
  psychological influences on, 149–152
  social and cultural influences on, 137–146
Buying center, 173, **174**–175
Buying decisions, AOL and, 248
Buying motives, emotional, 349
Buying power, trends in, 42
Buying unit. *See* Customer(s)

Cable television, direct marketing via, 373
Cadbury's, 55
Calloway, Wayne, 467
Canned selling, 336–337
Cannibalization, 225
Capital expenditures, SPM analysis of, 439
Capital goods, 223
Capitalism, in central Europe, 186
Car cards, 353
CarMax, 253–254, 281

Caroline Distribution, 307
Castelblanco, Javier, 467
Catalogs, 369, 371
  distributors of, 352
  IMC and retailers, 323
  showrooms for, 298
Caterpillar, Mitsubishi and, 101
CBS, 333
Central Europe, market segments in, 186–187
Cereal producers, 52
Chain stores, 295
Chancellor Media, 333–334
Change, 29–57
  managing, 54–56, 469–470
  and marketing decisions, 50–56
  opportunities and, 53–54
  strategic planning and, 78–84
Channel conflicts, 309
Channel of distribution, 281–286
  for consumer goods, 286–287
  direct distribution and, 366, 368
  direct marketing and, 366–367
  efficiency and effectiveness of, 306–308
  emerging, 310–311
  information superhighway as, 47
  intermediaries in, 283–285, 303–304
  international, 289–291
  legal and ethical issues of, 309–310
  management of, 308–311
  members of, 291–302
  multiple, 289
  objectives of, 303
  organizational and marketing strategies and, 282–283
  for organizational goods, 223, 286–287
  pricing conflicts within, 392
  retailers in, 293–302
  selection and design of, 302–308
  structures and marketing systems, 286–291
  vendor-managed inventory and integrated supply and, 294
  wholesalers in, 291–293
Channel power, 308–309
Channel relations, trends in, 302
Charismatic leadership. *See* Visionary and charismatic leadership phase
Chief executive officer (CEO), role of, 449–450
China, market size in, 194
Chinese Economic Area (CEA), 187
Choice Ride, 218–219
Choice stage, of consumer buying process, 135
Chrysler Corporation, 22, 48, 50, 52
  Daimler-Benz and, 39
Cigarettes, 125–126, 208
  ban on television advertising, 323
Circuit City, 253
Cisco Systems, 375
Claritas Inc., 206
Class. *See* Social class
Classification, of goods, 220–224
Clausewitz, Carl von, 63
Cloverleaf sales territory configuration, 341
Club marketing programs, 156
Club Med Inc., 450
Coca-Cola, 48

Code of Ethics, of American Marketing Association, 84, 85–86
Cold-canvas selling, 336
Colgate-Palmolive India Ltd., 289–290
Collaborative strategies, 421, 470
Collection period ratio, **436**
Collins & Aikman (C&A), 23
Colton, Anton, 325
Columbia Healthcare system, 52
Combination compensation plan, 345
Combination stores, 298
Commercial organizations
  in business markets, 163–164
  buying by, 171
Commission plan, 345
Communication methods, media and, 350–356
Communications
  persuasive, 324–325
  pull-through, 323–325
  push-through, 323, 324, 325–326
  technologies, 44
  theory, 316–319
Communications carryover, 327, 328
Communications elasticity, 327
Communications mix, 316, **319**–320
Community of practice, 455
Compaq Computer Company, 74, 82, 279–280, 367
Comparative advertising, 348–349
Compensation
  of customer contact personnel, 275–276
  of marketing personnel, 421
  of salesforce, 344–345
Competitive advantage, sustainable, 63, 76–78
Competitive analysis, 106
Competitive edge, pricing strategy as, 392–393
Competitive parity approach, to IMC budgeting, **329**
Competitive positioning, 212, 256
Competitive strategy, 62
Competitors and competition, 70–72
  in airline industry, 61
  AOL and, 248
  benchmarking of, 138
  and business-to-business purchases, 178
  comparative advertising and, 348–349
  direct and indirect, 6, 106
  global, 3–4
  marketing intelligence and, 94–95
  opportunity through, 53
  pricing conflicts with, 392
Complaints, handling of, 269
Complementors, 79
Complexity, and strategic planning, 81–82
Complex services, 266
CompuServe, 248, 256, 394, 398
Computer-aided design (CAD), 23
Computer control and decision models, 428
Computerization, 37
Computerized databases, 369
Computers
  expansion of applications, 3
  growth of networks, 38
  printers, 2

rate of change and, 179
service provided by companies, 256
virtual organization and, 471
Confusion/environmental uncertainty
    phase, of marketing organization
    ecocycle, 35
Conservation/constraints phase, of mar-
    keting organization ecocycle,
    34
Conservation stage, of natural ecocycle,
    32
Consideration set, 135
Consistency, of product mix, 225
Consolidation, in radio industry, 333–334
Constraints. *See* Conservation/constraints
    phase
Consumer(s). *See also* Buying behavior;
    Customer(s)
    age-cohort groups of, 140–141
    group influences on, 143–146
    information superhighway and, 47
    products and, 152–153
    situational influences on, 153–154
    strategic planning and, 127
Consumer adoption process, 234
Consumer behavior, 126. *See also* Con-
    sumer buying behavior
Consumer buying behavior, 125–127
    and consumer buying process,
        127–138
    individual influences on, 146–152
    organizational buying behavior and,
        167–169
    products and, 152–153
    relationship marketing and, 155–158
    situations and, 153–154
    social and cultural influences on,
        137–146
Consumer buying process, 127–137
Consumer direct marketing
    growth areas in, 378
    sales of, 366
Consumer goods, 220–221
Consumer lifestyles, 200, 206–208
Consumer-loan industry, 397
Consumer marketing channels, 286–287
Consumer markets, bases for segmenting,
    196–201
Consumer-owned cooperatives, 296
Consumer publications, 53
Consumer sales, value of direct
    marketing-driven, 370
Consumer satisfaction policies, 231–232
Consumer socialization, 137
Contact lens industry, 395
Continuous improvement, and TQM,
    466–468
Contractual VMS, 309
Control
    channel intermediaries and, 305
    over marketing efforts, 418–424
    in problem solving, 100–102
    of strategic planning, 76
    of strategy implementation, 255
Convenience, consumer needs and, 364
Convenience goods, 220, 221
Convenience stores, 299
Cooper-Martin, Elizabeth, 208
Coopers & Lybrand, Inc., 449
Coordination, across functions, 424

Core competencies, 47
    change and, 53
Core services, 253, 254, 264
Corning Inc., 25
Corporate backward integration, 309
Corporate culture, change and, 53
Corporate forward integration, 309
Corporate level
    decision making and, 96
    marketing performance analysis at,
        425–426
    planning and, 64
Corporate mission statement, 255
Corporate strategic planning, 450
Corporations, world's largest, 417
Cosmetics industry
    distribution channels in, 289
    service in, 254
Cost(s)
    accumulation of, 390
    channel intermediaries and, 305
    packaging and, 230
    of providing services, 266
    as strategy, 77
Cost per thousand (CPM), 354
    media expenditures and, 354–356
Cost-plus pricing model, 399–400, 401
CPS. *See* Creative problem solving (CPS)
Creative destruction, 36
    as natural ecocycle stage, 32
Creative innovation, 36
**Creative problem solving (CPS),
    97–**102
Creativity. *See* Renewal/creativity/innova-
    tion and choice/values identifica-
    tion phase
Credence properties, of services, **261**
Credit-card industry, 397
Credit records, database for, 110
CRI. *See* Customer response index (CRI)
Crisis/critical event phase, of marketing
    organization ecocycle, 34–35
Critical performance, 464
Cross-functional teams, 15, 35
    platform teams, 48
Cross-functional work team, 468
Cross-shoppers, 264
Cult bands, 307
Cultural issues, 8
Culture, 137. *See also* Social class; Sub-
    culture
    buying behavior and, 137–146
    and consumer buying process, 131
    international marketing and, 310
Cumulative discounts, 407
Current liabilities to inventory ratio,
    437–438
Current liabilities to net worth ratio,
    437
Current ratio, 437
Customer(s). *See also* Consumer(s)
    attracting and keeping, 257
    in business markets, 163–167
    business revolutions and, 38
    characteristics of, 302
    cost of losing, 274
    direct marketing and, 376–377, 383
    external relationships with, 52
    long-term relationships with, 139
    in marketing environment, 5–6

    marketing process and, 22
    multiculture base in U.S., 39
    push-pull communications and, 324
    recovering sales and, 257
    responsiveness in chosen segment, 195
    retention of, 272–273
    strategic planning and, 69–72, 84–87
    targeting segments of, 138, 264
    understanding of, 138–139
Customer base, composition of, 69–72
Customer-contact personnel, FIS and,
    110–111
Customer-cost-price relationship, in ser-
    vices, 265
Customer database, 379–381
Customer involvement, 260–261
Customer markets, 6
Customer-oriented marketing organiza-
    tion, 95
Customer-oriented strategies, 20, 21
**Customer response index (CRI),
    326–**327
Customer satisfaction, 20–24, 85, 86,
    257
    AOL and, 248
    customer-oriented strategies and, 20–24
    measurement of, 137
Customer service, 250. *See also* Service(s)
    benefits of, 256–259
    blueprinting of, 270, 271
    companies with outstanding, 268
    complaint handling and, 269
    satisfaction and quality in, 257
    via Internet, 375
Customer value, 126
    and positioning, 210–211
    and target marketing, 189
Customization, 11, 364
Cycles. *See also* Product life cycle (PLC)
    marketing ecocycle, 31–36
    natural ecocycle, 32–33
Czechoslovakia, 186–187

Daimler-Benz (Daimler-Chrysler), 29–30,
    39, 239. *See also* Chrysler
    Corporation
Dart Group, 416
Data
    method for collecting, 103–104
    primary, 103 , 443–444
    secondary, 103, 440–443
Database, 53, 108–112, **111**
    customer, 379–381
    design and creation of, 111–112
    direct marketing and, 369
    external data and information type, 110
    internal data and information type, 110
    management of, 112
    MDSS, 109
    MIS, 108, 109
    privacy issues and, 117–118
    types and uses of, 109–111
Data-based marketing, 421
Database-driven marketing, 336
Database marketing, 13, 369. *See also* Re-
    lationship marketing
Data sources, for performance measure-
    ment, 439–444
Dayton-Hudson Corp., 191, 416
Debt, age and, 147

Debt to equity ratio, **438**
Decentralization, 452–454
Deciders, and buying center, 174
Decision(s). *See* Marketing decisions
Decision making. *See* Marketing decisions; Strategic planning
Decision-making levels of firm, 95–96
Decision models, 109, 356
Decision support system. *See* Marketing decision support system (MDSS)
Decline stage (product life cycle), 232, 235
  pricing in, 396
Decoding, 317
Defense industry, 52
Delivery, and service, 252–253, 262, 270–276
Delivery time, 303
Dell, Michael, 364
Dell Computer Corp., 363–364, 367, 375
Demand
  advertising and, 347–348
  derived, 167
  elasticity of, 394
  forecast of, 113
  for organizational goods, 222–223
Demand management, as IMC objective, 320–321
DeMello, Tim, 314–315
Demographics
  changes in U.S., 40
  market descriptors and, 196
  of marketplace, 7
  services segmentation by, 259
Department stores, 297
Depth, of product line, 225–228
Deregulation, 310–311
  of airline industry, 60, 61
Derived demand, 161, **167**
Design
  of database, 111–112
  of packaging, 229
  of services, 263–267
Developing countries, as market, 194
DHL International, 187
Dialectic process, 300, **301**
Dick, A. B., 322
Differentiation, 77. *See also* Product differentiation
  conveying, 322
  positioning and, 209
Diffusion process, 234
Direct-action advertising, 370, 372–373
Direct competitors, 106
Direct costs, for services, 266
Direct customer response, 376
Direct distribution, 368
Direct mail, 351, 370–371
Direct marketing, 320, **357,** 363–386, **365**
Direct Marketing Association, 365
Direct marketing process, 379–382
Direct-response advertising, 372–373
Direct selling, 340, 363–364, **369**–370
Discount, 407–409
Discounting, psychological, 398
Discount operations, 13
  full-line stores, 297
Disney World, publicity for, 357
Distortion, in communication, 317

Distribution
  physical, 282
  reaching market segment and, 194–195
Distribution channels. *See* Channel of distribution; Place
Distribution networks, in central Europe, 187
Distribution of income. *See* Income distribution
Distribution strategies, 13, 279–313
Distribution systems, functions of, 285–286
Diversity, marketing intelligence and, 94–95
Divisional management, role of, 450–451
Division level, planning and, 64
Do-it-yourself (D-I-Y) market, 42
Door-to-door sales, 372
Dotson, Kenneth, 441
Dropout stage, of product life cycle, 232
Drysdale, Andrew, 325

Early adopters, 234
Early majority adopters, 236
Eaton, Robert, 22
EC92, 311
Ecocycle, marketing, 31–36
E-commerce, 367, 368, 374
Economic conditions, and business-to-business purchases, 178–179, 179–180
Economic performance, of effective distribution, 306
Economic status, buying behavior and, 147
Economic value added (EVA), 424
Economies of scale, at supermalls, 87
Economy
  information age, 37
  retailing and, 282
  services and, 249–250
  wholesaling and, 281
EDI. *See* Electronic data-interchange (EDI)
Educational software, 44–45
Effectiveness of marketing, 107, 420. *See also* Performance
Efficiency of marketing, 420. *See also* Performance
e-Generation, 199
El-Ansary, Adel I., 283, 292
Elasticity of demand, 394
Electronic data-interchange (EDI), 310
Electronic games, 44
Electronic integration (EI), 469
Electronic media, 373–376
Electronics, virtual organization and, 471
Emerging markets, 194
Emerging technologies, 37
EMI Capitol Music Group North America, 307
Emotion, buying, advertising, and, 349
Empathy, and service quality, 268
Employees. *See also* Compensation; Personnel issues; Salesforce
  as internal customers, 272
  internal marketing and, 23–24
  leadership training for, 467
Empowerment
  in customer service, 275
  TQM and, 468

Encoding, 317
Endless-chain system, 336
Enrico, Roger, 467
Entertainment industry, 44, 52
Entrepreneurial phase, of marketing organization ecocycle, 33–34
Entrepreneurship
  female, 18
  managing change and, 469–470
  retailing and, 302
Environment, 5–9. *See also* Ecocycle
  external macro-, 7–9, 68
  external micro-, 6–7, 69
  imbalance of force in, 80
  internal, 6
  legal, 8
  and market segmentation, 191
  packaging and, 228–229
  physical, 7–8
  political, 8
  technology and external, 44–45
  technology and internal, 45
Environmental analysis
  in creative problem solving, 98
  external, 68–73
Environmental scanning and forecasting, 72–73
Environmental uncertainty. *See* Confusion/environmental uncertainty phase
Environment-oriented cultural values, 139
Ericsson phones, 390–391
E-Stamp Corp., 306
Ethical issues
  AOL and, 248
  in direct marketing, 384
  of distribution channels, 309–310
  and marketing intelligence, 116
  market segmentation and, 208
  social responsibility and, 83–84
Ethnicity
  market segmentation and, 196
  in U.S. population, 40, 198
Europe, direct marketing to, 369
European Common Market, 37
European Union, Swatchmobile in, 239
EVA. *See* Economic value added (EVA)
Evaluation
  postpurchase consumer, 135–137
  of product, 234
  of strategic planning, 76
  of strategy, 255
Evoked set, 135
Excel spreadsheet-based control and decision models, 428
Exchange
  distribution systems and, 285
  services and, 261
Exchange relationships, 9
Excite, Inc., 48
Exclusive distribution, 292–293
Execution, of strategy, 76, 255
Expectancies, 345, 346
Expectancy theory, 345
Expected value, 403
Expenditures, on media, 353
Experience properties, of services, **261**
External buyers, organizing purchasing and, 162–163

External data and information type, of database, 110
External environment
   analysis of, 68–73
   and business-to-business buying, 176–180
   and market segmentation, 191
   technology and, 44–45
External macro-environment, 7–9
External marketing intelligence, for database, 111–112
External micro-environment, 6–7
External opportunities and threats, information on, 105–106
External relationships, 51–53
External search, 131, 133
Extractive products, 222

Facilitating
   distribution systems and, 285–286, 302
   sales rep and, 333
Facsimile marketing, 374–376
Fair Credit Reporting Act, 117
Fair dealing legislation, 309
Family
   and consumer buying process, 131
   services for, 254
Family/household life cycle, and buying behavior, 145–146
Family of orientation, 144
Family of procreation, 144
Farmer-owned retail establishments, 296
Federal Communications Commission (FCC), 116
Federal government. *See also* Regulation
   purchasing by, 166–167
Federal Trade Commission (FTC), 116, 117, 398, 408
Federal Trade Commission Act, 309
FedEx, 60, 179
Female condom, advertising of, 321
Female Health Co. (FHC), 321
Financial considerations
   and business-to-business purchases, 179–180
   in consumer buying process, 130
   in IMC, 326–330
Financial resources, 106
   for information gathering, 114
   strategic planning and, 73
Fingerhut, 397
Firms
   pricing conflicts within, 391–392
   top-performing global, 417
FIS. *See* Front-line information system (FIS)
Five-factor model of profitability, 71–72, 79
   six forces adaptation of, 79, 80
Fixed sum per unit approach, 329
Flea markets, 298
Flexibility
   channel intermediaries and, 305
   strategic planning and, 82–83
Flexible structures, 49
FOB pricing. *See* Free-on-board (FOB) pricing
Focal product, 401
Focus strategy, 77, 78
Follett Corp., high-tech operation of, 83

Food-based retailers, 298–299
Ford, Henry, 67
Ford Motor Co., 21, 39, 67–68, 189, 190, 282, 317
Forecast, 113
   environmental, 72–73
Foreign governments, purchasing by, 167
Foreign markets, 186–187
For-profit buying, 172
Fortune Global 500, corporation rankings and, 416, 417
Forward integration, corporate, 309
Four Ps, 38
Franchise operation, 295–296
   types of, 296
Frederick Brewing Co., 229
Fred Meyer stores, 299
Free-on-board (FOB) pricing, 408
Freight equalization, 409
Frequency, 355–356
Frequent flier programs, 156
Front-line information system (FIS), 110–111, 421
Front-line workers, 275
FTC. *See* Federal Trade Commission (FTC)
Fuji, 78
Full-line discount stores, 297
Functional area
   decisions and, 95, 96, 430–431
   strategies for competing in product market, 63
Functional discounts, 407
Functional (operating) level
   marketing performance analysis at, 426–431
   planning and, 64
Functional management, 451
Funds, advertising and, 349
Futrell, Charles M., 344

Games, electronic, 44
Gap, Inc., 74, 242
Gatekeepers, and buying center, 175
Gates, Bill, 35, 357
Gateway, 367
GDP. *See* Gross domestic product (GDP)
General Agreement on Tariffs and Trade (GATT), 37
General Electric Co. (GE), 14, 35, 49, 232, 452–453
   Internet marketing via, 375
   lighting Division of, 168
General Foods Corporation, 240
General merchandise, retailers of, 297–298
General Motors, 22, 54, 231, 232
   Ford and, 67
   Saturn and, 53
Generation X, 43, 147, 202
Generation Y, 43, 147
Geographic changes, in United States, 41, 42
Geographic market descriptors, 198–199, 201–203
Geographic sales territory configuration, 340
Geographic segmentation, in services, 259
Geographic zones, pricing in, 409
Germany, auto industry and, 38
Global information highway, 421

Globalization, 3, 20, **36**–39
   market segmentation and, 205–206
   and trends in U.S. market, 39–43
   wholesaling, distribution, and, 293
Global marketing, 239
   countries as segments of, 186–187
   marketing intelligence and, 105
GLOBAL SCAN system, 206–208
Global superhighway, in marketing, 14, 15
Goal(s), 464
Goal-directed marketing, 416
Goods. *See also* Distribution; Product
   classification of, 220–224
   vs. services, 250–253
Government organizations, purchasing by, 166–167, 171
Government-owned retail establishments, 296
Greenman, Stanley, 415
Grey Interactive Worldwide, 442
Grocery industry, 52
Gross, Bill, 44
Gross domestic product (GDP), 52, 194
Groups, influences on buyers, 143–146
Grove, Andrew, 81
Growth stage (product life cycle), 232, 235, 395

Hackman, Richard, 20
Harley-Davidson, Inc., 91–92
Harrell, Stephen G., 233
Healthcare
   industry, 52
   providers, 43
Heifetz, Ronald, 467
Heileman Brewing Co., 208
Hemp-based products, 229
Hemp-tech, 229
Herres, Robert, 258
Hershey, 55
Hewlett-Packard Co., 2–3, 20, 54, 325, 367
Hicks, Muse, Furst & Tate, 333–334
Hicks, Tom, 333
Hidden attributes, advertising and, 349
Hierarchies
   management, 37, 38, 47–50
   of social class, 142
Hierarchy of effects model, 320, 322
Hierarchy of needs theory, 149, 150
Higgins, James M., 98, 100
Home Depot, 42
Home-office workers, 165
Home Shopping Network, 373
Horizontal teamwork, 468
Hospital chains, 52
Hot-desk environment, 471
Hoteling, 471
Households (U.S.), 40. *See also* Family/household life cycle
Hovsmith, Skip, 455
Human resources, 75, 107
   needs for, 51
   strategic planning and, 73–74
Hungary, as market segment, 186–187
Hurst, David, 31
Hypermarkets, 299

Iacocca, Lee, 34
IBM (International Business Machines), 25, 54, 232, 375

Ideas, ownership of, 455
IMC. *See* Integrated marketing communications (IMC)
Implementation
    of service delivery, 270–276
    of solutions to problems, 100
    of strategic planning, 75
    of strategy, 255
Improvement, 11
IMS. *See* Integrated management system (IMS)
Income distribution, in United States, 41–42
Income statement, 434
Independent ownership, one-store retail operation, 295
Indirect competitors, 106
Indirect costs, for services, 266
Indirect selling, 340
Industrial products, distribution channels for, 288
Inelastic demand, 394
Inept set, 135
Inert set, 135
Infinity Radio, 333
Inflection point. *See* Strategic inflection point
Influencers, and buying center, 174
Information. *See also* Data; Marketing intelligence
    in consumer buying process, 131–133
    on external opportunities and threats, 105–106
    flow of, 454
    as IMC objective, 320
    international marketing research and, 115
    issues in acquisition and use, 113–114
    for marketing decisions, 96–97, 104–107
    organizational resources for, 114–115
    research quality and, 115
    sources of, 107–113
Information age economy, 37, 46–47
Information pyramid, 108
Information superhighway, 37, 46–47
Information systems (IS) departments, 337
Information technologies, 13, 38, 44–45, 421
    direct advertising and, 374
    virtual organization and, 470
Ingram Micro, Inc., 367
In-house expertise, 114
In-house research task, 113
Initiators, and buying center, 174
Innovation, 11, 36, 100–101. *See also* Renewal/creativity/innovation and choice/values identification phase
    adoption process for services, 262–263
    technological, 44–45
Innovators, 234, 237
Inseparability, of service and delivery, **252**–253
Institute for Research on Learning (IRL), 455
Institutions, buying by, 167, 171–172
Instrumentalities, 345, 346
Insurance industry, 43, 258, 368
Intangibility, of services, **252**

Integrated direct marketing communications, 377
    database target marketing strategies in, 380–381
Integrated management system (IMS), 462–465
Integrated marketing communications (IMC), 11, 13, 314–331, **315**
    accountability and, 416
    advertising and, 347–356
    direct marketing and, 365–366
    managing salesforce activity and, 334–347
    media for, 350–356
    performance analysis of, 429
    pricing strategy and, 409–410
    push vs. pull strategies, 323–326
    tools of, 333–360
Integrated media organization, 334
Intel, 79, 82
Intellectual property, 455
Intensive distribution, 292, 303–304
Interactive direct-response techniques, 377
Interactive marketing systems, 365, **381**
Interactive technology, customer service through, 21
Intermediaries, 6–7, **164, 283**–285, 284, 302
Internal environment
    and market segmentation, 191
    technology and, 45
Internal marketing, 6, **23**–24
Internal organizational environment, 6
Internal organizational influences, and business-to-business buying, 180
Internal records, for database, 111
Internal relationships, 51
Internal search, 131, 133
International distribution channels, 289–291
International Housewares Show, 380
International marketing research, 115
International markets, emerging distribution channels and, 310
International organizational analysis, 73–74
International regulations, 311
International scope of marketing, 20
Internet, 3, 44, 47, 186, 374. *See also* World Wide Web
    direct marketing via, 367, 369, 374, 375
    e-Generation and, 199
    electronic shopping on, 48
    measuring traffic of, 441–442
    organizational flexibility and, 82
    privacy issues and, 117–118
Intrawest, 264
Introduction stage (product life cycle), 232, 234, 393
Intuition, in creative problem solving, 97–98
Invasion of privacy. *See* Privacy issues
Inventory
    Compaq's distribution strategy and, 279–280
    information on, 427–428
Inventory records, database for, 110

Inventory turnover ratio, **435**
Investment, in strategic unit, 63
Investment advising, 254
IN WATS, 371
IS. *See* Information systems (IS) departments

Japan
    automobile industry and, 35, 38
    innovation processes in, 100–101
    value creation in, 87
JapanVALS™, 206
Java programming language, 74
Jefferson Project, 76
Jensen, William, 232
Jobbers, 228
Joe Camel, 125
Johnson & Johnson, product safety and, 230
Johnson Controls, 23
Johnston, Mark W., 344
Jones, Eli, 344
Jones, Tom, 315

Kahn, Lou, 380
Kantak, Donna Massey, 344
Karmazin, Mel, 333
Kay-Bee Toys, 414
Kellogg Co., 240
Kentucky Fried Chicken, 296
Kerr, Steve, 467
Kiosks, 376
Klein, Joel, 333
Kmart, 414
Knight, Phil, 33, 35
Knowledge Adventure, 44
Kolind, Lars, 448–449
Kvasnica, Jean, 467

Laggards, 236
LAN. *See* Local-area network (LAN)
L&M cigarettes, 323
Lansing, Will, 397
Late majority adopters, 236
Latin America, market growth in, 187
"Law of the lens," 108, 112
Leadership
    salesforce interaction with, 344
    in services, 256
    and TQM, 466
    training employees for, 467
    visionary and charismatic, 35
Lead selling, 336
Learning, and memory, 151–152
Leased departments, in stores, 295
Leeper, Mary Ann, 321
Legal environment, 8
Legal issues
    in direct marketing, 384
    of distribution channels, 309–310
    marketing decisions at AOL and, 248
    and marketing intelligence, 116
Legislation, antitrust and fair dealing, 309
Lehman Brothers, Inc., 187
Leverage, 432, 433
    ratios for, 438
Leveraged buyouts, in radio industry, 333
Levi Strauss & Co., 191
Levitt, Theodore, 220

Lexington Brewing Co., 229
Liability, product, 230, 231
Life cycle
   buying behavior and stage of, 147
   family/household, 145–146
   product, 44, 232–236
   retail, 299
Life roles, in groups, 144–146
Lifestyle, 40, 43, **148**
   buying behavior and, 147–148
   consumer lifestyle segments, 206–208
Lifestyle system. *See* VALS™ (Values and
      Lifestyle) system
Likert Scale, 464
Lilien, Gary L., 356
Line authority, 452
Line extension, 225
Lin Television, 334
Liquidity, 432, 433
Liswood, Laura, 336
Little, John D. C., 356
Local-area network (LAN), 339
Local governments, purchasing by, 166
Location. *See also* Place
   of stores, 301
Location discounts, 408
Lockheed (Lockheed Martin), 52
Lodish, Leonard M., 356
Logan, Dan, 335–336
Logistics
   in business-to-business market segmen-
      tation, 205
   situations, 52–53
Long-term relationships, 11
   and business purchasing, 182
Long-term strategic planning, 76–78
Loss leader, 396
Lot size, 303
Low-cost strategy, 77
Loyalty programs, 155

Macro-environment, 7–9, 38, **68**
Made-to-order marketing model,
      363–364
Madison, Kathy, 397
Magazines, advertising in, 350–351
Mail-order businesses, 369
Malls, off-price, 297
Management
   of advertising program, 347–356
   change and, 53, 469–470
   of database, 112
   of distribution channels, 308–311
   divisional, 450–451
   functional, 451
   market-driven, 157–158
   process of, 418–419
   review in IMS organization, 464
   of salesforce, 334–347
   service and, 272
   tools for segmentation decisions,
      206–208
   top, 449–450
   trends in, 465–470
Management structure, 47–50
   flattening of, 47–48
   hierarchies and, 37, 38, 47–50
Managers. *See* Management; Marketing
      managers
M&Ms, 55

Manufactured organizational products,
      222
Manufactured-sponsored wholesaler fran-
      chise, 296
Manufacturers, 162, 398
   sales branches and offices, 291
Manufacturer-sponsored retailer franchise,
      296
Manufacturing Assembly Pilot (MAP), 375
Manville, Brook, 455
Manville Corp., product safety and, 230
Maplin, Ltd., 352
Marginal approach, 328, 343
Margin-turnover classification, of retailers,
      297
Markdowns, 398
Market(s), 192. *See also* Globalization; Or-
      ganizational buying behavior
   buying behavior and, 21–22
   customer and, 6, 21–22
   for long term, 24–26
   matching with organization, 94
   measurement and forecasting demand,
      113
   reasons for subdividing, 188–189
   in strategic planning process, 72
Market-based pricing model, 399, 400
Marketbasket analysis, 155
Market complexity, 389
Market coverage, 305, 306
Market demand, 105, 178
Market descriptors
   behavioral and situational, 199–200
   demographic and socioeconomic, 196
   psychological and psychographic,
      200
Market-driven management, 157–158
Marketers, change management by, 54
Marketing, 4. *See also* specific types
   changes in function of, 16–17
   changes in relationship with other
      business functions, 17–18
   changing role of, 2–27
   control and decision models, 428
   controlling efforts of, 418–424
   customer involvement in, 22
   and entrepreneurship, 18, 19
   global, 14, 15, 68, 239
   international scope of, 19
   introduction of term, 459
   in nonprofit organizations, 18–19
   relationship, 181–183
   strategic planning, organizational lev-
      els, and, 64
   as value exchange, 9
Marketing and sales productivity (MSP)
      systems, 382
Marketing audit, 107, 121–124
Marketing concept, 10–11
Marketing decisions
   and creative problem solving, 93–102
   key information for, 104–107
   legal and ethical ramifications of, 248
   strategic vs. tactical, 78
**Marketing decision support system
      (MDSS), 83, 109**
   availability of, 114
   market segmentation and, 206
   performance analysis and, 430
Marketing ecocycle, 31–36

Marketing effectiveness, of effective distri-
      bution, 306–308
*Marketing Engineering: Computer-Assisted
      Marketing Analysis and Planning*
      (Lilien and Rangaswamy), 356
Marketing environment, 5–9
Marketing function (4 Ps), 38
Marketing information
   issues in acquiring, 113–118
   sources for consumer buying process,
      133
Marketing information system (MIS),
      53, **109**
   availability of, 114
   market segmentation and, 206
   performance analysis and, 430
Marketing intelligence
   and creative problem solving, 91–124
   as segmentation tool, 206
Marketing intelligence system, 94–95,
      451
Marketing intermediaries, 6–7
Marketing management, 4–5, 13–20
   and strategic planning, 62–64
Marketing manager, 452
   activities of, 15
   product life cycle implications for,
      233–234
Marketing Metrics Research Project, 427
Marketing mix, 6, 11–13, 75
   customer service and, 259
   direct marketing and, 377
   for organizational goods, 223–224
   performance analysis of, 426–429
   pricing and, 393
   productivity and, 421
   service characteristics and, 251
   technology and, 46
Marketing myopia, 66
**Marketing organization ecocycle,
      33**–36
Marketing-oriented organizations, 448–472
Marketing performance. *See also* Perfor-
      mance
   control and measurement of, 414–445
Marketing program, designing and imple-
      menting, 193
Marketing research, 102–104
   international, 115
   objective of, 51
Marketing strategies
   distribution and, 282–283
   product life cycle and, 233
Market potential, 105
Market segmentation, 41–42, 186–208,
      188. *See also* Target marketing
   basics of, 188–191
   in business-to-business markets,
      201–205
   ethical issues in, 208
   international implications of, 205–206
   multiracial U.S. marketplace and, 198
   positioning strategies and, 208–213
   process of, 191–195
   selection of segments, 195–208
   in services, 259–260
Market segments, 192–193. *See also* Mar-
      ket segmentation
   combining variables to identify, 205
   long-term stability of, 195

Market share, break-even analysis and, 405–406
Market size
    for business and organizational markets, 167
    for market segmentation, 194
Marriott International Inc., 275
Mars Company, 55
Marshall, Janice, 218–219
Martin Marietta, 52
Martin Media, 334
Mary Kay Cosmetics, 372
Maslow, Abraham, 149, 150
Mass communications, 317, 318
Mass customization, 11, 143
Mass marketing, 188
Mass merchandisers, brands and, 242
MasterCard, American Express and, 74
MasterCare auto service centers, 274–275
Matrix management, 453–454
Maturity stage (product life cycle), 232, 235
    pricing in, 395–396
Maytag, 453
McDonald's, 39, 133, 296
McGinnis, Marjorie, 229
McIntyre, John, 2
McKinsey & Co., 194
MDSS. *See* Marketing decision support system (MDSS)
Measurement, 113, 414–445. *See also* Evaluation
Media
    advertising expenditure distribution and, 353
    dealer promotion aspects of, 353–354
    electronic, 373–376
    for IMC, 350–356
    information about, 356
    for publicity, 356–357
MEDIAC, 356
Media Matrix, 441
Media Metrix, Inc., 441, 442
Media models, 356
Medium, 316
Megaretailers, 301
"Me generation," 149
Memory, learning and, 151–152
Mercedes-Benz. *See* Daimler-Benz (Daimler-Chrysler)
Merchandising. *See also* Retailers and retailing; Wholesalers and wholesaling
    scrambled, 301
Merchant wholesalers, 292
Mergers
    in radio industry, 333
    of retailers, 301
Mervyn's, 416
Message, 316
Metal Park, 68
METRO Holding, 295
Mexico, Chancellor Media in, 334
Micro-environment, 6–7, 38, **69**
Micro-marketing, 190–191
Microsoft Corp., 35, 54, 74, 79, 82, 357
Middlemen, 164
    agent, 291–292
    direct marketing and, 363–364
Minty Fresh Inc., 307
MIS. *See* Marketing information system (MIS)

Mission, in IMS, 463
Missionary selling, 337
Mission-driven strategic planning, 65–68
Mission statement, 65, 67, 255
Mitsubishi, Caterpillar and, 101
Mitsukoshi Ltd., 290–291
Modified rebuy, 175–176
Monopoly, 80
Monsanto Company, 461
Montague, David, 40
Montague Corp., 40
Montgomery Ward & Co., Inc., 371
Moral values. *See also* Values (social)
    and marketing intelligence, 116
Morgan, Fred, 230, 231
Moriarty, Roland T., 337
Motion-picture advertising, 353
Motivation
    and buying behavior, 149
    of salesforce, **345**–346
Moving Comfort, Inc., 19
MSP systems. *See* Marketing and sales productivity (MSP) systems
Multicultural base, in United States, 39
Multilevel (pyramid) marketing, 384
Multiple brand names, 240
Multiple segmentation, 189–190
Multiracial marketplace, 198

National Semiconductor Corp., 455
Natural ecocycle, 32–33
Natural systems, organizational ecocycle and, 31–32
Naumann, Earl, 404
Naylor, Mary, 191
NEC Corp., Hewlett Packard and, 2–3
Need
    consumer recognition of, 128–131
    positioning by, 212–213
Needs hierarchy. *See* Hierarchy of needs theory
Negative reference group, 143–144
NetGrocer, 314
NetRatings, 441
Network organization, 25
Network radio, 333–334
Networks
    strategic, 15
    virtual organization and, 471
New American Dream Study, The, 202
New marketing, 11, 156–157, 182–183
New products, 223, 238–239
Newspapers, advertising in, 350
New task purchase, 176
New-venture departments, 460
Niche marketing, 41, **190, 368**
Nielsen, A. C., 356, 441
Nike, 33–34, 35–36, 72
Noise, in communication, 318–319
Noncumulative discounts, 407
Nonprofit buying, 172
Nonprofit sector
    distribution channels and, 288
    marketing in, 9, 19–20
Nonstore retailing, 366
Noodle Kidoodle, 414, 415
Nordstrom department stores, 256
North American Free Trade Agreement (NAFTA), 37–39, 311
Novell, 76

Objectives, 464
    strategic, 75
Occupation, buying behavior and, 147
Ocean Spray Cranberries, Inc., 460
Odd pricing, 396–397
ODM strategy. *See* Optimized Distribution Model (ODM)
OEMs. *See* Original equipment manufacturers (OEMs)
Office of Management and Budget (OMB), 198
Off-price retailers, 297
Oligopolistic markets, 392
Oligopoly, 395
One-to-one marketing, 190–191
On-line interactions. *See also* E-commerce
    of e-Generation, 199
    shopping, 44, 48
On War (Clausewitz), 63
Operating environment, 69
Operating level, planning and, 64
Operating results, SPM analysis of, 439
Operating supplies, 222
Opportunities
    for advertising, 347–349
    information on external, 105–106
Optimized Distribution Model (ODM), 279–280
Optional services, 254
O'Reilly, David, 352
Organization
    for IMS, 465
    marketing-oriented, 448–472
    matching market with, 94
    structure of, 173
Organizational analysis (internal), 73–74
Organizational buying behavior, 22, 161–175. *See also* Business-to-business buying
    consumer buying behavior and, 167–169
Organizational culture
    in entrepreneurial stage, 33
    and service delivery, 270–273
Organizational environment, 6, 38
Organizational goods, 220–224
Organizational level of firm, 95, 96
Organizational marketing channels, 287–288
Organizational resources, 74, 114–115
Organizational services, customer expectations of, 254
Organizational strategies, distribution and, 282–283
Organizational structures
    changes in, 15–16
    redesigned, 3–4
    and service delivery, 270–273
Organization issues, in direct marketing, 383–384
Original equipment manufacturers (OEMs), 164, 452–453
Oskin, Larry, 321
Other-oriented cultural values, 139
Oticon Holdings A/S, 448–449
Outdoor advertising, 351–352
Outsource research task, 113
OUT WATS, 371

Packaging, product strategy and, 228–230
Painted posters, 352
Pall Corp., 321
Papa John's Pizza, 395
Paramount, 52
Parasuraman, A., 269
Parks, Missy, 19
Particelli, Marc C., 389
Partnering, 421
Partnership level, of relating to customers, 156
Partnerships, strategic, 15
Parts or components, 222
Party plan, 372
PC Data, Inc., 441
Peapod, 48
Penetration price, 393–394
Penney, J.C., Company, Inc., 242, 452
Pepsi Cola, 348
Perceived quality, 240–241
Perceived risk, 260–261
Percentage of sales approach, 329
Perception, 150
    buying behavior and, 149–151
Perceptual mapping, and positioning decisions, 210
Performance, 414–445
    benchmarking and, 268–269
    cross-functional analysis of, 430–431
    data sources for, 439–444
    measuring, 422, 431–444
    ratios for evaluating, 432–438
    service as, 272
    staffing and measurement of, 343–344
    top-performing global firms, 417
Performance objectives, 68, 255
Perishability, of services, **253**
Permanent promotional allowances, 408
Personal influences
    and business-to-business buying, 181
    on buying behavior, 146–149
Personality, buying behavior and, 148
Personal selling
    from home or office, 372
    of organizational goods, 223
Personal shopping list (PSL), 314
Personnel issues. *See also* Salesforce
    in service delivery, 273–274
Personnel productivity ratio, **436**
Persuasive communications, 324–325
Petersen, Glen S., 337
Pet products, 70
Pfeiffer, Eckhard, 279
Physical distribution, 282
Physical environment, and natural conditions, 7–8
Physical resources, 75
    strategic planning and, 73
Physical supply, distribution systems and, 285
Physical surroundings, 153, 154
Piech, Ferdinand, 419
Pittman, Robert, 394
Pizza Hut, 395
Place, distribution channel and location as, 11, 12
Plank, Richard E., 344
Planned selling, 336–337

Planning. *See also* Strategic planning
    of service tasks and activities, 269–270
PLC. *See* Product life cycle (PLC)
Point of purchase (POP) advertising, 353
Point-of-sale (POS) system, 109
Poland, 186–187, 194
Polaroid camera, 398
Political issues, 8
    and business-to-business purchases, 180
Polling, of Generation Xers, 202–203
POP advertising. *See* Point of purchase (POP) advertising
Population of U.S.
    multiracial nature of, 198
    by race and age, 197
    shifts of, 40
Position-based work, 48–49
Positioning, 208–213
    vs. differentiation, 209
    perceptual mapping and, 210
    of services, 256
Positive reference group, 143
POS scanner data, database for, 110
Postpurchase evaluation, by consumers, 135–137
Posttransaction services, 231–232, 336
Power, in distribution channels, 308–309
PowerMaster, 208
Powers, Jim, 307
PR. *See* Public relations (PR)
Preemptive move strategy, 77, 78
Prestige pricing, 398
Pretransaction selling, 336
Price, 389
    actual and base, 391
    in marketing mix, 11, 12
    positioning by, 212
Price-cutting, in airline industry, 61
Price lining, 406
Price sensitivity, market segmentation and, 260
Pricing, 388–410
    and break-even analysis, 404–406
    as competitive edge, 392–393
    conflicts in, 391–392
    discount structuring, 407–409
    and IMC, 409–410
    impact on manufacturer, 398
    of organizational goods, 223
    performance analysis and, 427
    product-line, 406–407
    psychological, 396–398
    for services, 265–266
Primary data, 103, 443–444
Primary reference groups, 143
Primary services, 253–254, 264
Print media, direct-response advertising and, 372–373
Privacy issues, 384
    and marketing intelligence, 116, 117
    relationship marketing and, 155
Private labels, 242
PRIZM (Potential Rating Index by Zip Market) system, 206–207
Proactive level, of relating to customers, 156
Problem
    positioning by solutions, 212–213
    recognizing and identifying, 99

Problem solving. *See* Creative problem solving (CPS)
Process improvement, 464
Process machinery or installations, 222
Process redesign, 468
Procter & Gamble Co., 225, 226–227, 230, 232, 342, 452
Product, 219–220
    augmented, 220
    classification of goods and, 220–224
    consumers and, 152–153
    in marketing mix, 11–12
    strategy issues for, 224–232
Product attributes, positioning by, 211–212
Product class, positioning by, 212
Product concept, 10
Product depth, 225–228
Product differentiation, 209
    advertising and, 348–349
Product introduction process, 238
Production concept, 10
Production positioning strategy, 193
Productivity, 432, 433
    improving marketing, 421
    ratios, 436–437
    salesforce deployment and, 341
Product liability, 230, 231
Product life cycle (PLC), 44, 232–236
    IMC and, 326
    implications for marketing managers, 233–234
    pricing in, 393–396
    shortened, 57
    strategies for, 235
    theoretical and real-life concepts, 232–233
Product line, 225
    determining, 224–225
Product-line pricing, 406–407
Product management, 47–48
Product manager, 454, 460
Product market, business strategy and, 62
Product mix, 225, 226–227
Product safety, 230
Product strategy, 218–244
Product tampering, 230
Product user, positioning by, 212
Product variety, 303
Product width, 225–228
Profit, market size and potential for, 194
Profitability, 432
    customer role in, 138
    five-factor model of, 71–72
    ratios for, 433–435
Profitless prosperity, 457
Profit on sales ratio, **434**
Project-based work, 48–49
Project teams, 50
Promotion, 11, 13. *See also* Sales promotion
    packaging and, 229–230
    push, 358
    trade, 326
    to the trade, 353–354
Promotional allowances, 408
PSL. *See* Personal shopping list (PSL)
Psychographic/lifestyle segmentation, in services, 259–260

Psychological and psychographic market descriptors, 200, 204
Psychological discounting, 398
Psychological influences, on buying behavior, 149–152
Psychological price, 396–398
Public and private entities, in micro-environment, 7
Publicity, 320, **356**–357
Public relations (PR), 320, **357**
Public utility-owned retail establishments, 296
Pull-through communications, 323–325
Purchasing (organizational), 161–162. *See also* Buying behavior; Consumer(s)
Purchasing power, 389
Push promotion, 358–359
Push-through communications, 323, 324, 325–326
Pyramid marketing, 384

Quality
    and automobile industry, 22–23
    and business purchasing, 182
    and consumer buying process, 134
    dimensions of service, 268
    identifying gaps in, 270
    at Mars, 55
    positioning by, 212
    product, 224–225
    and relationship marketing, 156
    and service standards, 267–270
Quantity discounts, 407–408
Quick ratio, 437

Race
    market segmentation and, 196, 197
    multiracial U.S. marketplace and, 198
Radio
    advertising on, 351
    consolidation in industry, 333–334
R&D. *See* Research and development (R&D)
Rangaswamy, Arvind, 356
Rate of change, and business-to-business purchases, 178–179
Rate of diffusion, of services, **262**
Rational action, 32, 33
Ratios, for evaluating market performance, 432–438
Raw materials, 222
Reach, 355
Reactive level, of relating to customers, 156
Re-advertising, 354
Reality (female condom), 321
Reassessment, of marketing performance, 422
Rebuys, 175–176
Receivables turnover ratio, **435**–436
Receiver, of message, 316
Recognition, of customer contact personnel, 275–276
Recognition technology, 47
Rectangular sales territory configuration, 341
Reebok, 72

Re-engineering, 258, 339, **468**–469
Reference groups, 143–144
Reference product, 400
Regulation
    environment of, 310
    influences of, 179–180
    marketing intelligence issues and, 116
    of pricing discounts, 407–408
Reid, David A., 344
Relationship marketing, 14–15, 117, **155**–158, **336, 376,** 421
    and business purchasing, 181–183
    buyer-seller relationships and, 155–156
    and new marketing, 156–157, 182–183
    and privacy issues, 155
    technology and, 45–46
    vs. transaction marketing, 24–25
Relationships
    in distribution channels, 308–309
    external, 51–53
    internal, 51
    long-term, 139
Relationship selling, 335–336
RelevantKnowledge, 441, 442
Reliability, of service quality, 268
Renewal/creativity/innovation and choice/values identification phase, of marketing organization ecocycle, 35–36
Renewal process, leadership and, 35
Renewal stage, of natural ecocycle, 33
Rentz, Joseph O., 344
Resale shops, 298
Research, 113–118. *See also* Information; Marketing intelligence; Sources of information
    for decision making, 96–97
    problem solving and, 93
Research and development (R&D), and functional area of firm, 95
Research plan, in marketing research, 103
Research studies, 53
Reseller markets, 171
    product-line pricing and, 406
Reservation system, database for, 110
Resource allocation, in strategic planning, 75
Resources
    financial, 106
    human, 107
    organizational analysis (internal) and, 73–74
    technological, 107
Responsiveness, and service quality, 268
Retail accordion, 299, 300
Retailers and retailing, 164, 293–302
    chains, 253
    decentralization in, 452
    impact on U.S. economy, 282
    nonstore, 366
Retail life cycle, 299, 300
Return on assets ratio, **434**–435
Return on investment (ROI) approach, 259, **329**
Return on net worth ratio, **435**
Returns, services and, 261
Reuter, Edzard, 29
Revenue expectation, 390
Rewards. *See* Compensation
Ricoh Corporation, 348

Ries, Al, 208, 211
Risk
    break-even analysis and, 405–406
    perceived, in service purchasing, 260–261
    pricing and, 403
Ritz-Carlton Hotel Co., 24
R.J. Reynolds Tobacco Co. (RJR), 208
Robbins, A. H., product safety and, 230
Robinson-Patman Act, 407–408
Rocking the Ages (Smith and Clurman), 202
Rockwell International Corp., 14–15
Rogers, Everett, 234
ROI. *See* Return on investment (ROI) approach
Rollout, 236, 239
Rubbermaid Incorporated, 380
Russia, wholesaling and, 293

Sabre system, 109
Safety, product, 230
Saimen, Muneo, 348
Saito, Takashi, 20
Salary plan, 345
Sales. *See also* Selling
    activity vs. productivity, 337–340
    process of, 335
    task of, 335–337
Sales automation system, 339–340
Salesforce. *See also* Sales territories; Staffing
    activity by, 319
    compensation of, 344–345
    directing and motivating, 345–347
    managing, 334–347
    size of, 342–343
    structure of, 340
    turnover in, 344
Salesforce automation, 337–340
Sales forecasting models, 427
Sales management, as IMC objective, 320–321
Salespeople
    job description for, 337
    types of selling and, 336–337
Sales promotion, 319–320, **357**–358
Sales records, database for, 110
Sales revenue, expenditure on IMC, 326
Sales territories, 340–342
Sales training, 344
SAP's, 74
Saturn automobile, 53
Sawgrass Mill Mall, 297
SBU. *See* Strategic business unit (SBU)
Scanning, environmental, 72–73
Scrambled merchandising, 301
Search properties, of services, **261**
Searle, G. D., product safety and, 230
Sears, Roebuck, 54, 231, 242, 257, 371, 452
SEC. *See* Securities and Exchange Commission (SEC)
Secondary data, 103, 440–443
Secondary reference groups, 143
Secure electronic transaction (SET), 44
Securities and Exchange Commission (SEC), 254
Segmentation. *See* Market segmentation; Market segments

Selective attention, **150**–151
Selective communications, 317, 318
Selective distribution, 293
Selective interpretation, 151
Selective retention, 151
Self-concept, 148–149
Self-improvement benefits, 200–201
Self-oriented cultural values, 139
Sellers, 9, 389–390. *See also* Buyer-seller relationships
Selling
  concept of, 10
  direct, 340, 369–370
  indirect, 340
  personal, 372
  relationship, 335–336
  types of, 336–337
Semimanufactured goods, 222
Sequent Computer Systems, 325
Service(s), 247–276. *See also* Distribution; Product; Service marketing
  benchmarking of, 268–269
  competitive positioning of, 256
  customer-cost-price relationship and, 265
  customer service, 256–259
  design of, 263–267
  economic impact of, 249–250
  vs. goods, 250–253
  leadership in, 256
  levels of, 253–254, 267
  marketing-mix implications of, 251
  marketing productivity and, 421
  marketing strategy for, 247–276
  planning tasks and activities for, 269–270
  pricing strategy for, 265–266
  quality standards for, 267–270
  strategic planning and, 255–256
  target customers for, 264
  as value, 255–259
  warranty—post-sales, 231–232
Service delivery and implementation, 252–253, 270–276
Service-firm-sponsored retailer franchise, 296
Service image, 256
Service marketing
  issues in, 259–263
  market segmentation and, 259–260
  trend expectations in, 251
ServiceMaster, 23
Service provider loyalty, 262
Service recovery, 272–273
SET. *See* Secure electronic transaction (SET)
Shandwick (PR agency), 357
Shapherd, David C., 344
Sharp, 78
Sherman Antitrust Act, 309
Sheth, Jagdish N., 415
Shige, Yuko, 348
Shoe industry. *See* Athletic shoe industry
Shopping goods, 220, 221
SIC. *See* Standard Industrial Code (SIC)
Simmons Market Research Bureau, 356
Single-segment marketing strategy, 190–191
Sisodia, Rajendra S., 415
Situational analysis, 255

Situational market descriptors, 199–200, 203–204
Skimming price, 393–394
Skywriting, 353
Smart cards, 21, 155
Smith, Craig N., 208
Smoking, 125–126, 208
Social class, 131, 140–142
Social issues, 8
  in direct marketing, 384
Socialization agents, 137
Social responsibility, ethics and, 83–84
Social surroundings, 153–154
Societal marketing concept, 10–11
Society, buying behavior and, 137–146
Socioeconomic market descriptors, 196
Source, in communication, 316
Sources of information, 107–113
Southwest Airlines, 61, 67, 75, 125, 256
Space productivity ratio, **436**
Spatial convenience, 302
Special promotional allowances, 408
Specialty goods, 220, 221
Specialty stores, 297, 301
Specialty superstores, 13
Specific communications, 317, 318
Spielberg, Steven, 44–45
SPM. *See* Strategic profit model (SPM)
Sports entrepreneurs, women as, 19
SportsLine USA, 441
Sport utility vehicles (SUVs), sales of, 70
Staffing
  and measuring performance, 343–344
  for service performance, 274
Stakeholders, 83
Standard Industrial Code (SIC), 201
Standardization, lack of, in service production, 261
Standard & Poor's 500, 416
Standard Rate and Data, Inc., 356
Staples, 46, 249
Starbucks, 16
Starmann, Richard, 409
Start-up phase, of marketing organization ecocycle, 33–34
State governments, purchasing by, 166
Status, 144–146. *See also* Social class
Stern, Louis W., 283
Store brands, 230, 242
Stores
  locations of, 301
  trends in formats and operations of, 301
Straight rebuy, 175
Strategic 3Cs, 65
Strategic alliances, 26, 52 –53, 421
Strategic business unit (SBU), 64, 450–451, 461
Strategic growth phase, of marketing organization ecocycle, 34
Strategic inflection point, 79–81
Strategic marketing
  price and, 389–393
  vs. tactical marketing, 78
Strategic objectives, 255, 464
Strategic opportunism, 67
Strategic partnerships, 15
  distribution and, 282

Strategic planning, 60–89, 255–256
  consumers and, 127
  control and, 420–424
  in IMS, 463–464
  and TQM, 466
Strategic pricing models, 399–404
Strategic profit model (SPM), 438–439
Strategic readiness, 66–67
Strategic vision, 67
Strategic windows, 66
Strategies, 50–51. *See also* specific strategies
  of Clausewitz, 63
  of Sun Tzu, 63
Strategy, 62–63
Straw, Martyn, 404
Streamline Inc., 314–315
Strengths, organization, 106–107
Structures. *See* Management structure
Stuntz, Mayo, Jr., 394
Subculture, 139–140
Substitutes, and imbalance of environmental forces, 80
Sun Microsystems, 74
Sun Tzu, 63
Supermalls, in Japan, 87
Supermarkets, 298
Superstores, 21, 253, 298
  private labels, store brands, and, 242
  specialty, 13
Suppliers, 6
Supply chain, 283
Supply chain links, 52
Surroundings, consumer buying and, 153–154
Sustainable competitive advantage, 70, 76–78
SUVs. *See* Sport utility vehicles (SUVs)
Swartz, Gordon S., 337
Swatchmobile, 239
Synergy, 77, 78
Systems. *See* Marketing ecocycle

Taco Bell, 348
Tactical marketing, vs. strategic marketing, 78
Tactics, 51, 63–64
  for strategic planning, 75
  for strategy implementation, 255
Takeuchi, Hirotaka, 100–101
Tangible goods vs. service strategy, 297
Tangibles, in service quality, 268
Target market(s) and marketing, 75, 117, 189. *See also* Market segmentation
  customer segments and, 138
  and customer value, 189
  database, 380–381
  selection of, 187
  for services, 264
  strategies for, 189–191
Target stores, 242, 416
Task definitions, 154
Task environment, 69
Task method approach, to IMC budgeting, **329**
Taxonomy of business-to-business buying decisions, 176, 177
Taylor, Elmer D., 233
TBWA Chiat/Day, 202, 203

Teams
  cross-functional, 48
  project, 50
  TQM and, 468
  virtual, 471
Technological resources, 107
  strategic planning and, 74
Technology, 43–46. *See also* Information
      superhighway
  advances in, 3, 8
  and business-to-business purchases,
      178
  and direct marketing, 369
  and distribution channels, 310
  emerging, 37
  information, 421
  in insurance industry, 258
  as segmentation tool, 206
  virtual organization and, 471–472
Telecommunications, 3
Telecommunications Act (1996), 333
Telecommuting, 471
Telemarketing, 369, 371–372
Telephone companies, customer privacy
      and, 117
Television advertising, 351, 373
Temporal perspectives, 154
Tenneco, 49
Test marketing, 236–238
Thermos, 50
30-sheet poster, 352
3Com, 232
3Cs, 65
3M Company, 460–461
Threshold spending level, 329
Thurber, James, 103
Tiffany & Co., 290–291
Time
  for decision making, 97, 114–115
  poverty of, 82
Time Warner Inc., 307
Title Nine Sports, 19
Tobacco industry, 125–126, 194, 208
Torelli, Hans B., 232–233
Total assets to net worth ratio, **438**
Total quality management (TQM),
      465–469
Toy business, 414–415
Toyota Camry, pricing of, 388
Toys 'R' Us, 301, 414–415
TPN. *See* Trading Process Network
      (TPN)
TQM. *See* Total quality management
      (TQM)
Trade, globalization and, 37
Trade agreements, 311
Trade association market data, 53
Trade discounts, 407
Trademark, 240
Trade promotions, 326
Trading Process Network (TPN), 168
Training
  of salesforce, 344
  in service performance, 274–275
Traits, personality, 148
Transaction marketing, vs. relationship
      marketing, 24–25
Transaction selling, 337
Transnational trade agreements, 311

Transportation, technology innovations
      and, 45
Transportation media, 353
Trial of product, 234
Trout, Jack, 208, 211
Trucks, sales of, 70
Tupperware, 372
Turning point. *See* Strategic inflection
      point
TWA, 200
Tylenol, product safety and, 230

Umbrella branding, 421
Uncertain services, 266
Uncertainty, and strategic planning, 81–82
Uniform delivered pricing, 408–409
United Parcel Service (UPS), 60, 177–178,
      322
United Services Automobile Association
      (USAA), 258
United States. *See* specific issues
United States Postal Service (USPS), 183,
      306
Uptown cigarettes, 208
USAA, 51
  new product of, 218–219
Users, and buying center, 174

Valence for rewards, 345–346, 347
VALS™ (Values and Lifestyle) system,
      206–207
Value (economic). *See also* Price (value)
  and consumer buying process, 134
  of distribution channel members, 305,
      308
  EVA and, 424
  service as, 255–259
  and target marketing, 189
Value-added marketing, 22–23
Value-adding process, 16, 305–306
Value-based pricing model, 400–404
Value chain, 87
Value defined in marketplace, 11
Value exchange, marketing as, 9
Value-oriented buyers, 43
Value proposition, 210
Values (social)
  in American society, 125–126
  cultural, 137–139
  of IMS, 463
Variability, of services, **252**
Varney, Christine, 117
Vending machines, 372
Vendor-managed inventory (VMI) system,
      294
Vertical marketing system (VMS), 295,
      309
Vertical teamwork, 468
Viacom, 52
Video, 325, 374–376
Virtual office, 471
Virtual organization, 448–449, **470**–472
Virtual product, 471
Virtual teams, 471
Visa, American Express and, 74
Vision, in IMS, 463
Visionary and charismatic leadership
      phase, of marketing organization
      ecocycle, 35

Vivendi, 205
VMI system. *See* Vendor-managed inven-
      tory (VMI) system
VMS. *See* Vertical marketing system (VMS)
Volkswagen, 211, 419
Volvo Cars, Ford and, 39

Waiting time, 303
Wal-Mart, 80, 199, 242, 264, 295, 299
Walt Disney World, 275
WAN. *See* Wide-area network (WAN)
Warehouse stores, 299
Warranty—post-sales services, 231–232
WATS. *See* Wide Area Telephone Service
      (WATS)
Weaknesses, organization, 106–107
Web. *See* Web sites; World Wide Web
Web companies, Streamline Inc. as,
      314–315
Web shopping, 44
Web sites, 47. *See also* Internet; On-line
      interactions
  electronic shopping and, 48
  measuring traffic of, 441–442
  privacy issues and, 117–118
Webster, Frederick E., Jr., 176, 187, 210
WebTV, 373
Wedge sales territory configuration, 341
Welch, John F. (Jack), 35, 49, 467
Wessel, Ellen, 19
Weyerhaeuser, 21
Wheel of retailing theory, 299, 300
Whirlpool, 232
Whole Foods Market, 190
Wholesalers and wholesaling, **291**–293
  impact on U.S. economy, 281
Wholesaler-sponsored retailer franchise,
      296
Wide-area network (WAN), 339
Wide Area Telephone Service (WATS),
      371
Width, of product line, 225–228
Wilcox, Gina, 315
Wind, Yoram, 176
Women's sports equipment and apparel,
      19
Wood, Marian Burk, 320, 323
Work-at-home trend, 165
Workers. *See* Personnel issues
Workload approach, to salesforce size,
      343
Work teams. *See* Teams
World Franchising Council, 296
World Wide Web, 3. *See also* Internet
  marketing via, 357
  privacy issues and, 117–118
Wrigley's chewing gum, advertising of, 353

Yahoo!, 44, 441
Yankelovich Partners, 202
Yellow Pages listings, 353
Young & Rubicam, Inc., 186, 194, 356
Youth market, 41

Zeithaml, Valarie A., 269
Zen, creative problem solving and, 101
Zero defect, in service provision, 273
Zero-level channel, 366
Zone pricing, 409